Latin American
Civilization

SEVENTH EDITION, REVISED AND UPDATED

LATIN AMERICAN CIVILIZATION

HISTORY AND SOCIETY, 1492 TO THE PRESENT

edited by

BENJAMIN KEEN

Northern Illinois University

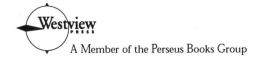

Westview
PRESS

A Member of the Perseus Books Group

Copyright © 2000, 1996, 1991 by Westview Press, A Member of the Perseus Books Group

Published in 2000 in the United States of America by Westview Press, Inc., 5500 Central Avenue, Boulder, Colorado 80301, and in the United Kingdom by Westview Press, 12 Hid's Copse Road, Cumnor Hill, Oxford OX2 9JJ

Find us on the World Wide Web at www.westviewpress.com

Library of Congress Cataloging-in-Publication Data
Latin American civilization : history and society, 1492 to the present / edited by Benjamin
Keen.—7th ed.
     p.   cm.
   Includes bibliographical references.
   ISBN 0-8133-3623-6 (pbk.)
   1. Latin America—Civilization.   2. Spain—Colonies—America—History.   I. Keen,
Benjamin, 1913–
F1408.3.L274   1999
980—dc21   99-049416
                                                                                  CIP

Printed and bound in the United States of America

The paper used in this publication meets the requirements of the American National Standard for Permanence of Paper for Printed Library Materials Z39.48-1984.

10   9   8   7   6   5   4

Contents

PART THREE: COLONIAL BRAZIL

PART FIVE: LATIN AMERICA
IN THE TWENTIETH CENTURY

Preface

Since the appearance of the last edition of this book, what may be called the "permanent" crisis of Latin America has significantly deepened. By mid-1999 the economic storm that began in the Far East in 1997 had spread to Latin America, throwing much of the area into political and social turmoil sometimes verging on chaos. In Ecuador, for example, a general strike with overwhelming popular support forced the president to rescind his neoliberal economic program amid continuing demands for his resignation. Some of the strongest economies of the region—Brazil, Argentina, Chile—were in deep recession, with growing unemployment and desperate efforts, as in the case of Brazil, to bolster their failing currencies with loans from the IMF and other traditional neoliberal remedies. Colombia experienced the worst economic crisis in its history combined with a major political crisis as a thirty-year-old Marxist guerrilla organization, the Armed Revolutionary Forces of Colombia (FARC), moved from victory to victory over the U.S.-supported military and a variety of right-wing paramilitary forces. It now controls almost 50 percent of the national territory. In neighboring Venezuela a military populist, Lieutenant Colonel Hector Chávez, won a stunning electoral victory in December 1998 to become president with an anti-neoliberal program and a promise to end the pervasive corruption and make drastic constitutional changes. Inevitably, the growing economic and political crisis engendered loss of faith in and rejection of such prophets of neoliberalism as President Fernando Cardoso of Brazil and President Carlos Menem of Argentina. There was growing evidence that the Latin American economic crisis formed part of a cyclical world capitalist depression whose basic cause was overproduction. The duration and long-term effects of this depression cannot be foreseen, but it was clearly bad news for Latin America.

Given the prime importance of the economic factor and the great number of political events, of varying importance, I have chosen to summarize developments in those areas by updating the introductions to the twentieth-century chapters. An important addition, filling a long-felt need, is a new chapter, "Latin American Women, Past and Present: The Struggle for Equality and Social Justice." It traces the course of women's struggle from Aztec and Inca times to the present and introduces the reader to some of its heroines, including such little-known figures as Micaela, wife and adviser of rebel Tupac Amaru; Flora Tristan, gifted and enchanting early-nineteenth century Peruvian feminist; and Amanda Labarca, the early-twentieth-century

Chilean feminist and educator. To the chapter entitled "Latin American Roads to Socialism" I have added a penetrating essay, "Neoliberalism and Culture," by Brazilian Dominican Frei Betto, friend of Fidel Castro and winner of Brazil's most prestigious literary award for a book of memoirs, *Baptism of Blood.*

In organization and approach, this reader closely conforms to Benjamin Keen and Keith Haynes, *A History of Latin America* (6th ed., 1999), but it forms a useful companion to other texts in the field.

Benjamin Keen
Santa Fe, New Mexico

PART ONE

INDIAN & HISPANIC ORIGINS

1

ANCIENT AMERICA

L ATIN AMERICAN colonial society, and Spanish American colonial society in particular, was shaped largely by the interaction of Hispanic (Spanish and Portuguese) invaders with the Indian peoples who had inhabited the American continents for many thousands of years. The Indians usually responded to the arrival of European invaders with armed resistance. After the European conquest, the Indians continued to resist with a variety of strategies: revolts, flight, riots, sabotage, and sometimes even the use of their masters' legal codes for purposes of defense and offense. Thanks to this unyielding spirit, and despite immense loss of life and inestimable suffering, the Indian communities in key areas of Latin America survived the storm of conquest and colonial oppression with their cultural identity largely intact. However, the Hispanic-Indian interaction did lead to some acculturation on the part of the Indians. This took the form of a more or less nominal acceptance of Christianity and a more willing acceptance of European tools, work animals, crafts, foods, and other material elements. Resistance to Hispanic rule, however, characterized Indian-Hispanic relations in general and was a major source of tension in colonial life.

Indian culture and the ways in which the Indians responded to the Hispanic invaders were shaped by their own long history on these continents. The Indians arrived from Asia by way of the Bering Strait no less than forty thousand years ago and in the course of time spread over both the American continents and eventually developed a wide range of cultural types, ranging from nomadic groups of hunters and food gatherers to the elaborate empires of the Aztecs and the Inca and the culturally advanced Mayan states. These three civilizations had certain features in common. All three were based on intensive farming that made possible the development of a large sedentary population and considerable division of labor. These civilizations, however, also evolved along distinctive lines. Mayan culture was distinguished by impressive achievements in writing, calendrical science, mathematics, and architecture. The Aztecs were mighty warriors, and a distinctive feature of their religion was large-scale human sacrifice. The Inca were the greatest empire builders of ancient America, and they made a serious and largely successful effort to unify the institutions and language of their extensive empire.

Modern scholars recognize that despite the decapitation and degradation of these states by the Conquest, many of their institutions and much of their culture survived into the nineteenth century and even down to the present. Thus, the history and culture of colonial Latin America (and even modern Latin America) cannot be understood without some knowledge and understanding of the high civilizations of ancient America.

1. AZTEC WARFARE

Warfare was the basis of Aztec existence, and warriors shared with priests the places of greatest honor and influence in Aztec society. An important object of warfare was the procurement of captives to be sacrificed on the altars of the gods whose goodwill brought victory to the Aztec banners. Thus, in the words of George C. Vaillant, "war led to sacrifice and sacrifice led back to war, in ever-widening cycles." Our principal source of information concerning Aztec life and customs is the monumental work of the Spanish friar Bernardino de Sahagún (1499–1590), who carefully recorded a vast store of material obtained from native informants. His great General History of the Things of New Spain *contains the following native account of an Aztec military campaign.*

The ruler was known as the lord of men. His charge was war. Hence, he determined, disposed, and arranged how the war would be made. First he commanded masters of the youths and seasoned warriors to scan the [enemy] city and to study all the roads—where [they were] difficult, where entry could be made through them. This done, the ruler first determined, by means of a painted [plan], how was placed the city which they were to destroy. Then the chief noted all the roads—where [they were] difficult, and in what places entry could be made.

Then he summoned the general and the commanding general, and the brave warriors, and he commanded them how they were to take the road, what places the warriors were to enter, for how many days they would march, and how they would arrange the battle. And he commanded that these would announce war and send forth all the men dexterous in war to be arrayed, and to be supplied with provisions for war and insignia.

Reprinted, by permission, from *The Florentine Codex: General History of the Things in Spain* by Fray Bernardino de Sahagún. Book 8: *Kings and Lords.* Translated by Arthur J. O. Andersen and Charles E. Dibble. Copyright 1954 by the School of American Research, Santa Fe.

The ruler then consulted with all the majordomos. ... He ordered them to take out all their [goods held in] storage, the tributes, costly articles—insignia of gold, and with quetzal feathers, and all the shields of great price.

And when the majordomos had delivered all the costly devices, the ruler then adorned and presented with insignia all the princes who were already able in war, and all the brave warriors, the men [at arms], the seasoned warriors, the fearless warriors, the Otomí, and the noblemen who dwelt in the young men's houses.

And when it had come to pass that the ruler adorned them, when he had done this to the brave warriors, then the ruler ordered all the majordomos to bear their goods, all the costly devices, and all the valuable capes there to battle, that the ruler might offer and endow with favors all the [other] rulers, and the noblemen, and the brave warriors, the men [at arms] who were about to go to war, who were to be extended as if made into a wall of men dexterous with arms. And the ruler forthwith called upon the rulers of Texcoco and Tlacopan and the rulers in all the swamp lands, and notified them to proclaim war in order to destroy a [certain] city. He presented them all with costly capes, and he gave them all insignia of great price. Then he also ordered the common folk to rise to go forth to war. Before them would go marching the brave warriors, the men [at arms], the lord general, and the commanding general.

The lords of the sun, it was said, took charge and directed in war. All the priests, the keepers of the gods, took the lead; they bore their gods upon their backs, and, by the space of one day, marched ahead of all the brave warriors and the seasoned warriors. These also marched one day ahead of all the men of Acolhuacan, who likewise marched one day ahead of all the Tepaneca, who similarly marched one day ahead of the men of Xilotepec; and these also marched one day ahead of all the so-called Quaquata. In like manner the [men of] other cities were disposed. They followed the road slowly and carefully.

And when the warlike lands were reached, the brave warrior generals and commanding generals then showed the others the way and arranged them in order. No one might break ranks or crowd in among the others; they would then and there slay or beat whoever would bring confusion or crowd in among the others. All the warriors were extended there, until the moment that Yacauitztli, [god of] the night, would descend—that darkness would fall. And when they already were to rise against the city to destroy it, first was awaited tensely the moment when fire flared up—when the priests brought [new] fire—and for the blowing of shell trumpets, when the priests blew them.

And when the fire flared up, then as one arose all the warriors. War cries were raised; there was fighting. They shot fiery arrows into the temples.

And when they first took a captive, one fated to die, forthwith they slew him there before the gods; they slashed his breast open with a flint knife.

And when the city had been overcome, thereupon were counted as many captives as there were, and as many Mexicans and Tlatilulcans as had died. Then they apprised the ruler that they had been orphaned for the sake of Uitzilopochtli; that men had been taken captive and been slain. And the ruler then commanded the high judges to go to tell and inform all in the homes of those who had gone to die in war, that there might be weeping in the homes of those who had gone to war to die. And they informed those in the homes of as many as had gone to take captives in war that they received honors there because of their valor. And they were rewarded according to their merits; the ruler accorded favors to all—costly capes, breech clouts, chocolate, food, and devices, and lip rods and ear plugs. Even more did the ruler accord favors to the princes if they had taken captives. He gave them the offices of stewards, and all wealth without price—honor, fame, renown.

And if some had done wrong in battle, they then and there slew them on the battlefield; they beat them, they stoned them.

And if several claimed one captive, and one man said, "He is my captive," and another man also said, "He is my captive": if no man verified it, and also if no one saw how they had taken the captive, the lord of the sun decided between them. If neither had an advantage of the two who claimed the captive, then those who had taken four captives, the masters of the captives, decided that to neither one would the captive belong. He was dedicated to the Uitzcalco [or] they left him to the tribal temple, the house of the devil.

And when the city which they had destroyed was attained, at once was set the tribute, the impost. [To the ruler who had conquered them] they gave that which was there made. And likewise, forthwith a steward was placed in office, who would watch over and levy the tribute.

2. THE HALLS OF MONTEZUMA

The political organization of the Aztec state on the eve of the Spanish Conquest represented a mixture of theocracy and royal absolutism. The barbaric splendor and elaborate ceremonial that marked the household of the great war chief Montezuma are vividly described by an eyewitness, the conquistador *and historian Bernal Díaz del Castillo (1492–1581?).*

The Great Montezuma was about forty years old, of good height and well proportioned, slender, and spare of flesh, not very swarthy, but of the natural

---

Bernal Díaz del Castillo, *The True History of the Conquest of New Spain*, translated and edited by A. P. Maudsley, London, the Hakluyt Society, Cambridge University Press, 1908–1916, 5 vols., II, pp. 60–63.

colour and shade of an Indian. He did not wear his hair long, but so as just to cover his ears, his scanty black beard was well shaped and thin. His face was somewhat long, but cheerful, and he had good eyes and showed in his appearance and manner both tenderness and when necessary, gravity. He was very neat and clean and bathed once every day in the afternoon. He had many women as mistresses, daughters of Chieftains, and he had two great Cacicas as his legitimate wives. He was free from unnatural offences. The clothes that he wore one day, he did not put on again until four days later. He had over two hundred chieftains in his guard, in other rooms close to his own, not that all were meant to converse with him, but only one or another, and when they went to speak to him they were obliged to take off their rich mantles and put on others of little worth, but they had to be clean, and they had to enter barefoot with their eyes lowered to the ground, and not to look up in his face. And they made him three obeisances, and said: "Lord, my Lord, my Great Lord," before they came up to him, and then they made their report and with a few words he dismissed them, and on taking their leave they did not turn their backs, but kept their faces towards him with their eyes to the ground, and they did not turn their backs until they left the room. I noticed another thing, that when other great chiefs came from distant lands about disputes or business, when they reached the apartments of the Great Montezuma, they had to come barefoot and with poor mantles, and they might not enter directly into the Palace, but had to loiter about a little on one side of the Palace door, for to enter hurriedly was considered to be disrespectful.

For each meal, over thirty different dishes were prepared by his cooks according to their ways and usage, and they placed small pottery braziers beneath the dishes so that they should not get cold. They prepared more than three hundred plates of the food that Montezuma was going to eat, and more than a thousand for the guard. When he was going to eat, Montezuma would sometimes go out with his chiefs and stewards, and they would point out to him which dish was best, and of what birds and other things it was composed, and as they advised him, so he would eat, but it was not often that he would go out to see the food, and then merely as a pastime. ...

Let us cease speaking of this and return to the way things were served to him at meal times. It was in this way: if it was cold they made up a large fire of live coals of a firewood made from the bark of trees which did not give off any smoke, and the scent of the bark from which the fire was made was very fragrant, and so that it should not give off more heat than he required, they placed in front of it a sort of screen adorned with figures of idols worked in gold. He was seated on a low stool, soft and richly worked, and the table, which was also low, was made in the same style as the seats, and on it they placed the table cloths of white cloth and some rather long napkins of the same material. Four very beautiful cleanly women brought water for his hands in a sort of deep basin which they call *xicales*, and they held others like plates below to catch the water, and they brought him towels. And two other women brought him tortilla bread, and as soon as he began to eat they placed before him a sort of wooden screen painted over with gold, so that no one should watch him eating. Then the four women stood aside, and four great chieftains who were old men came and stood beside them, and with these Montezuma now and then conversed, and asked them questions and as a great favour he would give to each of these elders a dish of what to him tasted best. They say that these elders were his near relations, and were his counsellors and judges of law suits, and the dishes and food which Montezuma gave them they ate standing up with much reverence and without looking at his face. He was served on Cholula earthenware either red or black. While he was at his meal the men of his guard who were in the rooms near to that of Montezuma, never dreamed of making any noise or speaking aloud. They brought him fruit of all the different kinds that the land produced, but he ate very little of it. From time to time they brought him, in cup-shaped vessels of pure gold, a certain drink made from cacao, and the women served this drink to him with great reverence.

Sometimes at meal-times there were present some very ugly humpbacks, very small of stature and their bodies almost broken in half, who are their jesters, and other Indians, who must have been buffoons, who told him witty sayings, and others who sang and danced, for Montezuma was fond of pleasure and song, and to these he ordered to be given what was left of the food and the jugs of cacao. Then the same four women removed the table cloths, and with much ceremony they brought water for his hands. And Montezuma talked with those four old chieftains about things that interested him, and they took leave of him with the great reverence in which they held him, and he remained to repose.

3. Aztec Industry and Commerce

Division of labor and perfection of craftsmanship among the Aztecs attained perhaps the highest point of development compatible with what was essentially an Upper Stone Age technology. The relatively vast scale on which the general exchange of goods and services was carried on is shown by the activity at the great market at Tenochtitlán, as described below by Cortés in a letter to the emperor Charles V. Trade was not confined to Aztec territory.

The *Letters of Cortés to Charles V*, translated and edited by Francis A. McNutt, New York, 1908, 2 vols., I, pp. 257–259. Reprinted by permission of the publishers, the Arthur H. Clark Company, from Francis A. McNutt's *Fernando Cortés, His Five Letters of Relation to the Emperor Charles V.*

The city has many squares where markets are held, and trading is carried on. There is one square, twice as large as that of Salamanca, all surrounded by arcades, where there are daily more than sixty thousand souls, buying and selling, and where are found all the kinds of merchandise produced in these countries, including food products, jewels of gold and silver, lead, brass, copper, zinc, stone, bones, shells, and feathers. Stones are sold, hewn and unhewn, adobe bricks, wood, both in the rough and manufactured in various ways. There is a street for game, where they sell every sort of bird, such as chickens, partridges, quails, wild ducks, flycatchers, widgeons, turtle-doves, pigeons, reed-birds, parrots, owls, eaglets, owlets, falcons, sparrow-hawks and kestrels, and they sell the skin of some of these birds of prey with their feathers, heads, beaks, and claws. They sell rabbits, hares, and small dogs which they castrate, and raise for the purpose of eating.

There is a street set apart for the sale of herbs, where can be found every sort of root and medical herb which grows in the country. There are houses like apothecary shops, where prepared medicines are sold, as well as liquids, ointments, and plasters. There are places like our barber shops, where they wash and shave their heads. There are houses where they supply food and drink for payment. There are men, such as in Castile are called porters, who carry burdens. There is much wood, charcoal, braziers, made of earthenware, and mats of divers kinds for beds, and others, very thin, used as cushions, and for carpeting halls, and bed-rooms. There are all sorts of vegetables, and especially onions, leeks, garlic, borage, nasturtion, watercresses, sorrel, thistles, and artichokes. There are many kinds of fruits, amongst others cherries, and prunes, like the Spanish ones. They sell bees-honey and wax, and honey made of corn stalks, which is as sweet and syrup-like as that of sugar, also honey of a plant called maguey, which is better than most; from these same plants they make sugar and wine, which they also sell.

They also sell skeins of different kinds of spun cotton, in all colours, so that it seems quite like one of the silk markets of Granada, although it is on a greater scale; also as many different colours for painters as can be found in Spain and of as excellent hues. They sell deer skins with all the hair turned on them, and of different colours; much earthenware, exceedingly good, many sorts of pots, large and small, pitchers, large tiles, an infinite variety of vases, all of very singular clay, and most of them glazed and painted. They sell maize, both in the grain and made into bread, which is very superior in its quality to that of the other islands and mainland; pies of birds, and fish, also much fish, fresh, salted, cooked and raw, eggs of hens, and geese, and other birds in great quantity, and cakes made of eggs.

Finally, besides those things I have mentioned, they sell in the city markets everything else which is found in the whole country and which on account of the profusion and number, do not occur to my memory, and which also I do not tell of, because I do not know their names.

Each kind of merchandise is sold in its respective street; and they do not mix their kinds of merchandise of any species; thus they preserve perfect order. Everything is sold by a kind of measure, and, until now, we have not seen anything sold by weight.

There is in this square a very large building, like a court of justice, where there are always ten or twelve persons, sitting as judges, and delivering their decisions upon all cases which arise in the markets. There are other persons in the same square who go about continually among the people, observing what is sold, and the measures used in selling, and they have been seen to break some which were false. ...

4. THE CONDITION
OF THE AZTEC PEASANTRY

Among the Aztecs, as among many other peoples of ancient Mexico, the basic social unit was a group called the calpulli *(pl.* calpultin)*, which was a territorial as well as a kinship organization. The* calpulli *offered its members a certain collective security and other advantages, but the life of the Aztec free commoners was probably a fairly hard one. Even harder was the lot of serfs* (mayeque) *attached to the private estates of Aztec nobles. The royal chronicler of the Indies, Gonzalo Fernández Oviedo y Valdés (1478–1557), describes the condition of these people and other aspects of the Aztec social order.*

The Indians of New Spain, I have been told by reliable persons who gained their information from Spaniards who fought with Hernando Cortés in the conquest of that land, are the poorest of the many nations that live in the Indies at the present time. In their homes they have no furnishings or clothing other than the poor garments which they wear on their persons, one or two stones for grinding maize, some pots in which to cook the maize, and a sleeping mat. Their meals consist chiefly of vegetables cooked with chili, and bread. They eat little—not that they would not eat more if they could get it, for the soil is very fertile and yields bountiful harvests, but the common people and plebeians suffer under the tyranny of their Indian lords, who tax away the greater part of their produce in a manner that I shall describe. Only the lords and their relatives, and some principal men and merchants, have estates and lands of their own; they sell and gamble with their lands as they please, and they sow and harvest them but pay no tribute. Nor is any tribute

Gonzalo Fernández de Oviedo y Valdés, *Historia general y natural de las Indias*, Asunción, Paraguay, 1944–45, 14 vols., X, pp. 110–114. (Excerpt translated by the editor.)

paid by artisans, such as masons, carpenters, feather workers, or silversmiths, or by singers and kettle-drummers (for every Indian lord has musicians in his household, each according to his station). But such persons render personal service when it is required, and none of them is paid for his labor.

Each Indian lord assigns to the common folk who come from other parts of the country to settle on his land (and to those who are already settled there) specific fields, that each may know the land that he is to sow. And the majority of them have their homes on their land; and between twenty and thirty, or forty and fifty houses have over them an Indian head who is called *tiquitlato*, which in the Castilian tongue means "the finder (or seeker) of tribute." At harvest time this *tiquitlato* inspects the cornfield and observes what each one reaps, and when the reaping is done they show him the harvest, and he counts the ears of corn that each has reaped, and the number of wives and children that each of the vassals in his charge possesses. And with the harvest before him he calculates how many ears of corn each person in that household will require till the next harvest, and these he gives to the Indian head of that house; and he does the same with the other produce, namely kidney beans, which are a kind of small beans, and chili, which is their pepper; and *chia*, which is as fine as mustard seed, and which in warm weather they drink, ground and made into a solution in water and used for medicine, roasted and ground; and cocoa, which is a kind of almond that they use as money, and which they grind, make into a solution, and drink; and cotton, in those places where it is raised, which is in the hot lands and not the cold; and pulque, which is their wine; and all the various products obtained from the maguey plant, from which they obtain food and drink and footwear and clothing. This plant grows in the cold regions, and the leaves resemble those of the cinnamon tree, but are much longer. Of all these and other products they leave the vassal only enough to sustain him for a year. And in addition the vassal must earn enough to pay the tribute of mantles, gold, silver, honey, wax, lime, wood, or whatever products it is customary to pay as tribute in that country. They pay this tribute every forty, sixty, seventy, or ninety days, according to the terms of the agreement. This tribute also the *tiquitlato* receives and carries to his Indian lord.

Ten days before the close of the sixty or hundred days, or whatever is the period appointed for the payment of tribute, they take to the house of the Indian lord the produce brought by the *tiquitlatos;* and if some poor Indian should prove unable to pay his share of tribute, whether for reasons of health or poverty, or lack of work, the *tiquitlato* tells the lord that such-and-such will not pay the proportion of the tribute that had been assigned to him; then the lord tells the *tiquitlato* to take the recalcitrant vassal to a *tianguez* or market, which they hold every five days in all the towns of the land, and there sell him into slavery, applying the proceeds of the sale to the payment of his tribute. ...

All the towns have their own lands, long ago assigned for the provision of the *orchilobos* or *ques* or temples where they kept their idols; and these lands were and are the best of all. And they have this custom: At seeding time all would go forth at the summons of the town council to sow these fields, and to weed them at the proper time, and to cultivate the grain and harvest it and carry it to a house in which lived the pope and the *teupisques, pioches, exputhles* and *piltoutles* (or, as we would say, the bishops, archbishops, and canons and prebendaries, and even choristers, for each major temple had these five classes of officials). And they supported themselves from this harvest, and the Indians also raised chickens for them to eat.

In all the towns Montezuma had his designated lands, which they sowed for him in the same way as the temple lands; and if no garrison was stationed in their towns, they would carry the crops on their backs to the great city of Temestitan [Tenochtitlán]; but in the garrison towns the grain was eaten by Montezuma's soldiers, and if the town did not sow the land, it had to supply the garrison with food, and also give them chickens and all other needful provisions.

5. Mayan Industry, Commerce, and Agriculture

The Spanish bishop Diego de Landa's (1524–1579) Relation of the Things of Yucatán *is our principal source of information on the native way of life in northern Yucatán before and after the Conquest. In the following extract from Landa, mention of the use of foreign trade, money, and credit points to the existence among the ancient Maya of a fairly complex economy, in which exchange played a significant part. The references to cooperative effort in agriculture, hunting, and fishing suggest the importance of the communal element in Mayan life.*

The trades of the Indians were making pottery and carpentering. They earned a great deal by making idols out of clay and wood, with many fasts and observances. There were also surgeons, or, to be more accurate, sorcerers, who cured with herbs and many superstitious rites. And so it was with all the other professions. The occupation to which they had the greatest inclination was trade, carrying salt and cloth and slaves to the lands of Ulua and Tabasco, exchanging all they had for cacao and stone beads, which were their money; and with this they were accustomed to buy slaves, or other beads, because they were fine and good, which their chiefs wore as jewels in their feasts; and they had others made of certain red shells for money, and as jewels to adorn

Reprinted from Alfred M. Tozzer, ed., "Landa's *Relación de las cosas de Yucatán*," Vol. 18, pp. 94–97. Cambridge, Mass.: Harvard University Press, 1941. Reprinted by permission of the author and the Peabody Museum of Archaeology and Ethnology, Harvard University.

their persons; and they carried it in purses of net, which they had, and at their markets they traded in everything which there was in that country. They gave credit, lent and paid courteously and without usury. And the greatest number were the cultivators and men who apply themselves to harvesting the maize and other grains, which they keep in fine underground places and granaries, so as to be able to sell (their crops) at the proper time. Their mules and oxen are the people themselves. For each married man with his wife, they are accustomed to sow a space of four hundred feet, which they call a "hun uinic," measured with a rod of twenty feet, twenty feet wide and twenty feet long.

The Indians have the good habit of helping each other in all their labors. At the time of sowing those who do not have their own people to do their work, join together in groups of twenty, or more or less, and all together they do the work of all of them (each doing) his assigned share, and they do not leave it until everyone's is done. The lands today are common property, and so he who first occupies them becomes the possessor of them. They sow in a great number of places, so that if one part fails, another may supply its place. In cultivating the land they do nothing except collect together the refuse and burn it in order to sow it afterwards. They cultivate the land from the middle of January and up to April, and they sow in the rainy season. They do this by carrying a little bag on their shoulders, and with a pointed stick they made a hole in the ground, and they drop there five or six grains, which they cover over with the same stick. It is a wonder how things grow, when it rains. They also joined together for hunting in companies of fifty more or less, and they roast the flesh of the deer on gridirons, so that it shall not be wasted, and when they reach the town, they make their presents to their lord and distribute the rest as among friends. And they do the same in their fishing.

6. THE MAYAN SOCIAL ORDER

Ancient Mayan society was highly stratified and divided into four classes: nobility, priesthood, commoners, and slaves. A hereditary ruler with civil, religious, and military functions was at the head of the government. The hierarchical order of society was reflected in the pattern of settlement in the Mayan towns: The homes of the nobles, priests, and the wealthy were clustered around the ceremonial center, and the huts of the peasantry lay on the outskirts. For this, as for other aspects of Mayan life, Bishop Landa's Relación *is our chief source.*

After the departure of Kukulcan, the nobles agreed, in order that the government should endure, that the house of the Cocoms should have the chief

Tozzer, "Landa's *Relación*," pp. 26, 62, 85–87. Reprinted by permission of the author and the Peabody Museum.

power; because it was the most ancient or the richest family, or because at this time he who was at the head of it was a man of the greatest worth. This being done, since within the enclosure there were only temples and houses for the lords and the high priest, they ordered that other houses should be constructed outside, where each one of them could keep some servants, and to which the people from their towns could repair, when they came to the city on business. Each one then established in these houses his mayordomo, who bore for his badge of office a short and thick stick, and they called him *caluac*. He kept account with the towns and with those who ruled them; and to them was sent notice of what was needed in the house of their lord, such as birds, maize, honey, salt, fish, game, cloth and other things, and the *caluac* always went to the house of his lord, in order to see what was wanted and provided it immediately, since his house was, as it were, the office of his lord.

It was the custom to seek in the towns for the maimed and blind, and they supplied their needs.

The lords appointed the governors, and if they were acceptable confirmed their sons in the offices, and they charged them with the kind treatment of the poor people, the peace of the town and to occupy themselves in their work of supporting themselves and the lords.

All the lords were careful to respect, visit and to entertain the Cocom, accompanying him, making feasts in his honor and repairing to him with important business, and they lived in peace with each other amusing themselves with their accustomed pastimes of dancing, feasts and hunting. ...

Before the Spaniards had conquered that country, the natives lived together in towns in a very civilized fashion. They kept the land well cleared and free from weeds, and planted very good trees. Their dwelling place was as follows: in the middle of the town were their temples with beautiful plazas, and all around the temples stood the houses of the lords and the priests, and then (those of) the most important people. Then came the houses of the richest and of those who were held in the highest estimation nearest to these, and at the outskirts of the town were the houses of the lower class. And the Wells, if there were but few of them, were near the houses of the lords; and they had their improved lands planted with wine trees and they sowed cotton, pepper and maize, and they lived thus close together for fear of their enemies, who took them captive, and it was owing to the wars of the Spaniards that they scattered in the woods. ...

Beyond the house, all the town did their sowing for the nobles; they also cultivated them (the fields) and harvested what was necessary for him and his household. And when there was hunting or fishing, or when it was time to get their salt, they always gave the lord his share, since these things they always did as a community. If the lord died, although it was the oldest son who succeeded him, the other children were very much respected and assisted and regarded as lords themselves. And they aided the other *principales* inferior to the lord in all these ways, according to whom he was and the favor which he enjoyed with his lord. The priests got their living from their offices and from offerings. The lords governed the town, settling disputes, ordering and settling the affairs of their republics, all of which they did by the hands of leading men, who were very well obeyed and highly esteemed, especially the rich, whom they visited, and they held court in their houses, where they settled their affairs and business usually at night. And if the lords went out of their town, they took with them a great many people, and it was the same way when they went out of their homes.

7. MAYAN RELIGIOUS LIFE

The great object of Mayan religion and worship was, as Landa concisely puts it, "that they [the gods] should give them health, life, and sustenance." The priesthood owed its influence to its assumed intimacy and power of intercession with the divine beings. Human sacrifice, vividly described below, was practiced from a very early period, but it did not assume mass proportions among the Maya until the tenth century and was a result of growing Mexican influence.

The natives of Yucatan were as attentive to the matters of religion as to those of government, and they had a high priest whom they called *Ah Kin Mai* and by another name *Ahau Can Mai*, which means the Priest Mai, or the High-Priest Mai. He was very much respected by the lords and had no *repartimiento* of Indians, but besides the offerings, the lords made him presents and all the priests of the towns brought contributions to him, and his sons or his nearest relatives succeeded him in his office. In him was the key of their learning and it was to these matters that they dedicated themselves mostly; and they gave advice to the lords and replies to their questions. He seldom dealt with matters pertaining to the sacrifices except at the time of the principal feasts or in very important matters of business. They provided priests for the towns when they were needed, examining them in the sciences and ceremonies, and committed to them the duties of their office, and the good example to people and provided them with books and sent them forth. And they employed themselves in the duties of the temples and in teaching their sciences as well as in writing books about them.

They taught the sons of the other priests and the second sons of the lords who brought them for this purpose from their infancy, if they saw that they had an inclination for this profession.

Tozzer, "Landa's *Relación*," pp. 27–28, 108–113, 115–120. Reprinted by permission of the author and the Peabody Museum.

The sciences which they taught were the computation of the years, months and days, the festivals and ceremonies, the administration of the sacraments, the fateful days and seasons, their methods of divination and their prophecies, events and the cures for diseases, and their antiquities and how to read and write with the letters and characters, with which they wrote, and drawings which illustrate the meaning of the writings.

Their books were written on a large sheet doubled in folds, which was enclosed entirely between two boards which they decorated, and they wrote on both sides in columns following the order of the folds. And they made this paper of the roots of a tree and gave it a white gloss upon which it was easy to write. And some of the principal lords learned about these sciences from curiosity and were very highly thought of on this account although they never made use of them publicly. ...

They had a very great number of idols and of temples, which were magnificent in their own fashion. And besides the community temples, the lords, priests and the leading men had also oratories and idols in their houses, where they made their prayers and offerings in private. And they held Cozumel and the well of Chichen Itza in the same veneration as we have for pilgrimages to Jerusalem and Rome, and so they used to go to visit these places and to offer presents there, especially to Cozumel, as we do to holy places; and if they did not go themselves, they always sent their offerings, and those who went there were in the habit of entering the abandoned temples also, as they passed by them, to offer prayers there and to burn copal. They had such a great quantity of idols that even those of their gods were not enough; for there was not an animal or insect of which they did not make a statue, and they made all these in the image of their gods and goddesses. They had some idols of stone, but very few, and others of wood, and carved but of small size but not as many as those of clay. The wooden idols were so much esteemed that they were considered as heirlooms and were (considered) as the most important part of the inherited property. They possessed no idols of metal, since there was no metal there. They knew well that the idols were the works of their hands, dead and without a divine nature; but they held them in reverence on account of what they represented, and because they had made them with so many ceremonies, especially the wooden ones. The greatest idolaters were the priests, *Chilans*, the sorcerers and physicians, *Chacs*, and *Nacoms*. The office of the priest was to discuss and to teach their sciences, to make known their needs and the remedies for them, to preach and to publish the festival days, and to offer sacrifices and to administer their sacraments. The duty of the *Chilans* was to give the replies of the gods to the people, and so much respect was shown to them that they carried them on their shoulders. The sorcerers and physicians performed their cures by bleedings of the parts which gave pain to the sick man; and they cast lots so as to know the future in their own duties and in other things. The *Chacs* were four old men who were always chosen anew for each occasion, to aid the priest in carrying on the festivals well and thoroughly. The *Nacoms* were two officers; the first was perpetual and did not bring much honor with it, since it was he that opened the breasts of the human victims whom they sacrificed. The second was a choice made of a captain for war and for other feasts. His duties lasted three years, and he was held in high honor. ...

Besides the festivals in which they sacrificed persons in accordance with their solemnity, the priest or *Chilan*, on account of some misfortune or necessity, ordered them to sacrifice human beings, and everyone contributed to this, that slaves should be bought, or some in their devotion gave their little children, who were made much of, and feasted up to the day (of the festival), and they were well guarded, so that they should not run away or pollute themselves with any carnal sin. And in the meanwhile they led them from town to town with dancing, while the priests, *Chilans* and other officers fasted. And when the day arrived, they all came together in the court of the temple, and if the victim was to be sacrificed with arrows, they stripped him naked, and anointed his body with a blue color, and put a *coroza* on his head. When they had reached the victim, all, armed with bows and arrows, danced a solemn dance with him around the stake, and while dancing they put him up on it and bound him to it, all of them keeping on dancing and gazing at him. The foul priest in vestments went up and wounded the victim with an arrow in the parts of shame, whether it was a man or woman, and drew blood and came down and anointed the faces of the idols with it. And making a certain sign to the dancers, they began one after another to shoot, as they passed rapidly before him, still dancing, at his heart, which had been marked beforehand with a white mark. And in this way they made his whole chest one point like a hedgehog of arrows. If the heart of the victim was to be taken out, they led him with a great show and company of people of the temple, and having smeared him with blue and put on a *coroza*, they brought him up to the round altar, which was the place of sacrifice, and after the priest and his officials had anointed the stone with a blue color, and by purifying the temple drove out the evil spirit, the *Chacs* seized the poor victim, and placed him very quickly on his back upon that stone, and all four held him by the legs and arms, so that they divided him in the middle. At this came the executioner, the *Nacom*, with a knife of stone, and struck him with great skill and cruelty a blow between the ribs of his left side under the nipple, and he at once plunged his hand in there and seized the heart like a raging tiger and snatched it out alive and, having placed it upon a plate, he gave it to the priest, who went very quickly and anointed the faces of the idols with that fresh blood. Sometimes they made this sacrifice on the stone and high altar of the temple, and then they threw the body, now dead, rolling down the steps. The officials below took it and flayed it whole, taking off all the skin with the exception of the feet and hands, and the priest, all bare, covered himself, stripped naked as he was, with that skin, and the others danced with him. And this was considered as a thing of great solemnity amongst them. The custom was usually to bury in the court of the temple those whom they had sacrificed, or else they ate them, dividing him among those who had arrived (first) and the lords, and the hands, feet and head were reserved for the priest and his officials, and they considered those who were sacrificed as holy. If the victims were slaves captured in war, their master took their bones, to use them as a trophy in their dances as token of victory. Sometimes they threw living victims into the well of Chichen Itza, believing that they would come out on the third day, although they never appeared again.

8. HOW THE INCA FORMED A NATION

The Inca made a systematic attempt to unify the institutions and even the language of their extensive empire; that they had considerable success in the latter is shown by the fact that five-sixths of the Indians of the Andean area still speak Quechua, the official language of the empire. The Inca obtained their results with the aid of an elaborate bureaucracy that brought every inhabitant of the empire under the direct and continuous control of an official appointed by the emperor. An important factor in the success of the Inca plan of unification was the policy of resettlement or colonization, described below by Father Cobo.

The entire empire of the Inca, though so extensive and composed of so many diverse nations, was a single commonwealth, ruled by the same laws, statutes, and customs and observing the same religion, rites, and ceremonies. ...

The first thing that these kings did after conquering a province was to remove six or seven thousand families, more or less, as seemed best to them, taking into account the capacity and temper of the population, and to transfer these families to the quiet, peaceful provinces, assigning them to different towns. In their stead they introduced the same number of people, taken from the places to which the former families had been sent or from such other places as seemed convenient; among these people were many nobles of royal blood. Those who were thus domiciled in new lands were called *mitimaes*— that is, newcomers or strangers, as distinct from the natives. This term applied to the new vassals as well as to the old ones who were sent in their places, since both went from their own to foreign lands; even today we use the word in this sense, calling *mitimaes* all those newcomers who have settled in the provinces of this kingdom. In these transfers of population they saw to

Bernabé Cobo, *Historia del Nuevo Mundo*, Seville, 1890–1893, 4 vols., III, pp. 222–225. (Excerpt translated by the editor.)

it that the migrants, both the newly conquered persons and the others, were moved to lands whose climate and conditions were the same as, or similar to, those which they had left behind and in which they had been reared. ...

The Incas introduced these changes of domicile in order to maintain their rule with greater ease, quiet, and security; for since the city of Cuzco, their capital, where they had their court and residence, was so distant from the provinces most lately acquired, in which there were many barbarous and war-like nations, they considered that there was no other way to keep them in peaceful submission. And since this was the principal purpose of the transfer, they ordered the majority of the *mitimaes* whom they sent to the recently conquered towns to make their homes in the provincial capitals, where they served as garrisons, not for wages or for a limited time but in perpetuity, both they and their descendants. As soldiers they received certain privileges to make them appear of nobler rank, and they were ordered always to obey the slightest commands of their captains and governors. Under this plan, if the natives revolted, the *mitimaes*, being devoted to the governors, soon reduced them to obedience to the Inca; and if the *mitimaes* rioted they were repressed and punished by the natives; thus, through this scheme of domiciling the ma-jority of the people of some province in other parts, the king was made secure against revolts in his dominions, and the social and commercial intercourse among the different provinces was more frequent and the entire land was better supplied with all its needs. The Inca profited further by this transfer of their vassals from one part to another in that throughout the length and breadth of the Empire similarity and conformity prevailed in religion and government. All the nations learned and spoke the language of Cuzco, which thus came to be general throughout Peru; for through this change of domi-cile the newly conquered peoples, removed into the interior of the kingdom, learned all this quickly and without difficulty or coercion, and the old vassals who were resettled in place of the new subjects who were being pacified taught it to the natives. The Inca required everyone to absorb their language, laws, and religion, with all the beliefs about these matters that were estab-lished at Cuzco; they either partly or wholly abolished their former usages and rites and made them receive their own. In order to introduce and estab-lish these things more effectively, in addition to transferring people they would remove the principal idol from a conquered province and set it up in Cuzco with the same attendance and worship that it had formerly had; all this was seen to by persons who had come from that province, just as they had done when they had had the idol in their own country. For this reason Indians from every province of the kingdom were at all times in residence in the capital and court, occupied in guarding and ministering to their own idols. Thus they learned the usages and customs of the court; and when they were replaced by others according to their system of *mitas*, or turns, on their return to their own country they taught their people what they had seen and learned in the court.

9. THE VILLAGE BASIS
OF INCAN SOCIETY

The basic unit of Incan social organization was the ayllu, a kinship group whose members claimed descent from a common ancestor. An Inca village typically consisted of several ayllu. The chronicler Garcilaso de la Vega (1539–1616), son of a Spanish noble and an Incan princess, drew an idyllic picture of Indian village life and of the relations between the Inca and their subjects. His account of a happy peasantry going forth with songs and rejoicing to labor in the service of their king is at serious variance with what is known of the chronic unrest and frequent revolts of conquered tribes against their Incan rulers.

In the matter of working and cultivating the fields they also established good order and harmony. First they worked the fields of the sun, then those of the widows and orphans and of those disabled by old age or illness: all such were regarded as poor people, and therefore the Inca ordered that their lands should be cultivated for them. In each town, or in each ward if the town was large, there were men assigned exclusively to look after the cultivation of the fields of the persons that we would call poor. These deputies were called *llactamayu*, or town councillors. It was their task, at the time of plowing, sowing, and harvesting the fields, to ascend at night towers that were made for this purpose, to blow on a trumpet or shell to attract attention, and loudly announce: "On such-and-such a day the fields of the disabled persons will be cultivated; let each betake himself to his assigned place." The people in each precinct already knew, by means of a list that had been made, to which fields they must go; these were the fields of their relatives or closest neighbors. Each one had to bring his own food, whatever he had in the house, so that the disabled persons would not have to provide for them. For they said that the aged, the sick, and the widows and orphans had trouble enough of their own, without being burdened with the troubles of others. If the disabled persons had no seeds they were provided from the storehouses, of which we shall have more to say hereafter. The fields of the soldiers who were away at war were also worked in common, for when their husbands were absent on army duty the wives were counted as widows. And so they performed this favor for them as for needy people. They took great care in the rearing of the children of those who were killed in the wars, until such time as they were married.

After the fields of the poor had been cultivated, each one tilled his own, and they helped each other in groups, cultivating their fields in turn. Then they tilled the fields of the *curaca*, the chief, and these were the last to be

---

Garcilaso de la Vega, *Comentarios reales de los Incas*, Buenos Aires, 1943, 2 vols., I, pp. 227–229. (Excerpt translated by the editor.)

worked in each town or province. In the time of Huaina Capac, in a town of the Chacapuyas, one Indian town councillor gave precedence to the fields of the *curaca*, a relative of his, before those of a widow. He was hanged for breaking the rule that the Inca had established for the cultivation of the fields, and the gallows was set upon the land of the *curaca*. The Inca decreed that the fields of their vassals should have precedence before their own, for they said that the prosperity of his subjects was the source of good service to the king; that if they were poor and needy they could not serve well in war or in peace.

The last fields to be cultivated were those of the king. They worked them in common; all the Indians went to the fields of the king and the sun, generally with great good cheer and rejoicing, dressed in the vestments and finery that they kept for their principal festivals, adorned with gold and silver ornaments and wearing large feathered headdresses. When they plowed the land (and this was the labor that gave them the greatest pleasure), they sang many songs that they composed in praise of their Inca; thus they converted their work into merrymaking and rejoicing, because it was in the service of their God and of their kings.

10. Two Views of the Incan Empire

The debate on the nature of the Incan state that began soon after its downfall continues to be waged in our own times. Successive generations of historians, consciously or unconsciously influenced by political, social, or sentimental biases, have found in the Incan empire whatever type of governmental system or social order they perhaps wanted to find. Some of the pros and cons of this debate are presented in the following selections, written by men who do not clearly belong to either of the two major schools and who are highly regarded for their honesty and objectivity. The first reading is from the Chronicle of Peru, *written in 1551 by Pedro de Cieza de León (1518–1560), a soldier who had traveled throughout the Andean region studying Indian customs and institutions. The second is from the previously cited work of Father Cobo.*

Since these kings ruled over a land of such great length and vast provinces, and in part so rugged and full of snow-capped mountains and sandy, treeless, arid plains, they had to be very prudent in governing so many nations that differed so greatly in language, law, and religion, in order to maintain them

---

Pedro de Cieza de León, *Del señorio de los Incas, Buenos Aires,* 1943, pp. 34–35. (Excerpt translated by the editor.)

in tranquillity and keep peace and friendship with them. Therefore, although the city of Cuzco was the head of their empire, ... they stationed deputies and governors at various points; these men were the wisest, ablest, and most courageous that could be found, and none was so young but that he was in the last third of his age. And since the natives were loyal to such a governor and none dared to rebel, and he had the *mitimaes* on his side, no one, no matter how powerful, dared to rise against him; and if such a rebellion did take place, the village in which the uprising occurred was punished and the instigators were sent to Cuzco. Hence the kings were so greatly feared that if they traveled through the kingdom and merely permitted one of the hangings on their litters to be lifted so that their vassals might see them, the people raised such a great cry as to cause the birds flying on high to fall and be captured by hand; and so great was their fear that they dared not speak ill of even the shadow that the Inca cast. And this was not all; ... if any of his captains or servants went out to visit some part of the kingdom, the people came out to receive him on the road with many presents, never failing, even if he were alone, to comply in detail with his every order.

So greatly did they fear their princes, in this extensive land, that every village was as well organized and governed as if their lord were present in it to punish those who disobeyed him. This fear arose from the power that these lords enjoyed, and from their justice, for all knew that if they did wrong they would certainly be punished and that neither pleas nor bribes would help them. And the Incas always did good works for their subjects, not permitting them to be wronged or burdened with excessive tribute or outraged in any way. They helped those who lived in barren provinces, where their forefathers had lived in great need, to make them fertile and abundant, providing them with the things they required; and to other provinces where they had insufficient clothing, for lack of sheep, they sent flocks of sheep with great liberality. In fine, it was understood that these lords knew not only how to be served by their subjects and to obtain tribute from them but also how to keep up their lands and how to raise them from their first rude condition to a civilized state and from destitution to comfort. And through these good works and through constantly presenting their principal men with wives and jewels, they gained the extreme good will of all, and were so greatly loved that I recall with my own eyes having seen aged Indians, visiting Cuzco, gaze upon the city with tearful lamentations, as they contemplated the present time and recalled the past, when that city so long housed their natural lords, who knew how to gain their service and friendship in other ways than those used by the Spaniards.

∾   ∾   ∾

The yoke that weighed down the necks of these miserable Indians was so heavy that I doubt if all the men in the world, joining together to invent a species of subjection and tyranny as oppressive as that in which they lived, could improve on what the Incas achieved to keep these Indians in a state of submission.

And anyone who carefully considers the system they maintained in administering and conserving their empire will find that all was directed solely toward this end. I could easily prove this by describing in detail the actions they ordered for oppressing their subjects, but it will suffice to say that these poor people were not allowed to own anything privately without the permission of the Inca or his governors, not even to slaughter a sheep or to have two suits of clothes; nor could they eat what they chose, but they had to observe the wishes of the Inca or his governors; nor could they marry whomever they pleased, and still less could they marry off their daughters at their pleasure; nor (what is worse) were they masters of their own wives and children, for the lords took away the wives of some to give them to others, and they took their children to slay them in the sacrifices.

The *caciques* made the round of their districts several times a year, to make sure that the Indians had no more than was allowed them, for they were not permitted to possess gold or silver or to wear fine clothes. They could not own a flock of more than ten animals without special permission; this privilege the Inca would grant to the *caciques*, but in a specified number, which never exceeded fifty or a hundred heads; and the caciques themselves could not wear fine clothes unless they received them from the Inca as a reward for some distinguished service. Daughters ordinarily were in the power of their parents until the age of ten, and thereafter they were at the disposition of the Inca. All persons, no matter how noble their rank, when entering the presence of the king took off their sandals and placed light burdens on their shoulders as a sign of homage and reverence. In speaking to the Inca they kept their eyes lowered and did not look him in the face, while he maintained a visage of notable gravity and replied with few words, spoken in such a low voice that they could scarcely be heard. Only the great lords, by special privilege, seated themselves before him.

And since the Incas had no other aim in their method of government than to place their vassals daily in a state of greater subjection and servitude, to please them each of their governors and *caciques*, both high and low, applied himself to the attainment of their objective, which was to exhaust the strength of the Indians until they were unable to raise their heads. And since the Incas were very capable men, they were not found wanting in the craft and skill required for the difficult task of taming nations so barbarous and indomitable. The principal method that they used for this purpose was to keep

Bernabé Cobo, *Historia del Nuevo Mundo*, III, pp. 279–281. (Excerpt translated by the editor.)

their subjects poor and continually occupied with excessive labors, so that being oppressed and abased they might lack the fire and spirit to aspire to revolt. To this end they built great fortresses, opened roads, constructed terraces on the hillsides, and compelled them to bring tribute to Cuzco from distances of three and four hundred leagues. With the same aim they introduced many cults and burdened them with many rites and sacrifices, so that when they were free from other labors and services this work alone sufficed to leave them without time to take breath or rest. ...

Moreover, the Incas were much aided in their designs by the great esteem and respect that the Indians felt for them, through which these simple people came to believe that the Incas not only were different from other men in valor and strength but had close kinship, familiarity, and intercourse with the sun and with the *huacas*, basing this erroneous opinion on the testimony of the Incas themselves, who boasted of this relationship, and on the religious claims which the Incas always advanced in making their conquests. And by reason of these things, and because of the diligence with which the Incas propagated the worship of their religion, consuming in its honor so much wealth and so many people that it became the principal occupation of the whole land, the Indians concluded that the gods must be under a great sense of obligation and duty toward the Incas, never failing to favor their designs. They were daily confirmed in this view by the many victories that the Incas won over all kinds of nations, and by the fact that although at the outset they had been so few in number they had placed this whole great empire under their sway. And the esteem that the Indians felt for the Incas was not a little enhanced by the admirable order and harmony that they established in all matters, both in what concerned the good of the commonwealth and in the aggrandizement of the cult of their gods. To this also contributed the nonsense the Incas daily fed their subjects, as a result of which these simple people conceived the Incas to be very close to the gods and endowed with superhuman wisdom, particularly when they saw the beauty and majesty with which the Incas had adorned their court, for which the Indians felt great reverence. ...

Nevertheless, I believe that these measures would not have sufficed to establish so firmly the power of the Incas and the subjection of these peoples if the Incas had not also resorted to severe measures, inflicting deaths and exemplary punishments upon those who attempted to overthrow the existing order. Actually, there were numerous revolts on the part of their subjects, who tried to regain their liberty by this means. ... Many of these terrible chastisements are still fresh in the memories of living men, since their stories have been handed down from father to son. I will cite here two or three of these cases. In a place near Payta an Inca slew five thousand men at one time, and to strike greater fear into his subjects he ordered the hearts of the slain men to be plucked out and placed around the fortress in a circle. In the towns of Otavalo and Caranque, Guaynacapac put to death all the males (except the boys), and for this reason the inhabitants of those towns were long called Guambracuna, which means "lads." ... From which I conclude that it was through strictness and cruelty, more than by any other means, that the Incas succeeded in breaking the spirit of their subjects, in placing them in the strict servitude in which they kept them, and in developing in them the abject submissiveness with which they were obeyed and revered. For theirs was a slavery so rigorous that it is difficult to imagine a worse one, even if we reviewed all the governments of the world of which we have any knowledge.

11. WAR AND CANNIBALISM AMONG THE BRAZILIAN INDIANS

The complex, stratified Aztec, Maya, and Inca societies represent the peaks of Indian cultural development before the coming of the Europeans. A far greater number of Indian groups were organized simply as bands or tribes; some lived by hunting and gathering, and others practiced a shifting slash-and-burn agriculture and supplemented their diets by hunting and fishing. Typical of this tribal level were the Tupi Indians, a linguistic family of tribes inhabiting the eastern seaboard of Brazil. These Indians lived in villages composed of long huts, each sheltering many interrelated families; they cultivated manioc and other food plants, and also hunted and fished. Each hut had its chief and a council of elders and a paramount chief met regularly to discuss the entire tribe's affairs; but chiefs had little power in the egalitarian Tupi societies. A characteristic of the Tupi way of life was constant intertribal warfare for the purpose of capturing prisoners; these captives were later ritually executed and their flesh was cooked and eaten to gain their spiritual strength and perpetuate the tribal feud. André Thevet (1504–1592), a French cosmographer who briefly lived among the Tupinamba of coastal Brazil, describes their mode of warfare and ritual cannibalism.

These savages are much given to warring with their neighbors. ... Having no other way of settling their disputes, they valiantly fight each other. They assemble in groups of six, ten, or even twelve thousand men, with villages pitted against each other. They also fight whenever they meet by chance. ... Before carrying out any great enterprise of peace or war, these savages, especially the older men, assemble to discuss the matter; women and children do not take part in these meetings. In these assemblies they display much gravity and decorum, taking turns speaking and carefully listening to each speaker. A few, because of their distinguished lineage or for some other reason, are permitted to sit on their hammocks.

André Thevet, *Les singularités de la France antarctique*, ed. Paul Gaffarel, Paris, 1878, pp. 184–204. (Excerpt translated by the editor.)

These Indians, like people in other parts of the world, use stratagems to surprise their enemies. ... They stage surprise attacks at night more often than during the day; for this reason they are especially watchful at night, assembling in great numbers to guard against their enemies. As soon as they suspect that their enemies are approaching, they plant innumerable pieces of wood with sharp points (like the traps we use in France) in the earth for a distance of a bowshot around their huts. The points of these sticks protrude from the earth and are very hard to see in the dark. The enemies impale their feet, which are bare like the rest of their bodies, on these sticks; this makes it easy to kill some of the wounded and take the rest prisoners.

These savages consider it a very honorable thing to leave their homes and invade enemy territory, and he who returns home with a number of enemy prisoners is honored like a great king or lord. When the people of one village want to ambush the people of another village they hide like foxes in the nearby woods for a certain period of time, emerging only when they see an opportunity to take their enemies by surprise. Entering the enemy village, they set the huts on fire to force the people to come out with their wives, children, and all their possessions. When these people come out, the two sides attack each other with clubs and wooden swords, and shoot arrows at each other at random; they also bite every part of their enemies' bodies that they can reach, including their perforated lips. Sometimes, in order to intimidate their enemies, they hold up the bones of the men they have killed in war and eaten. In short, they do everything possible to anger their enemies. The prisoners are led away, tied up and trussed like thieves. You cannot imagine the howls and endearments with which warriors are greeted when they return home victorious.

Wives accompany their husbands to war—not to fight, like Amazons—but to carry food and munitions, for warriors sometimes travel as long as five or six months without returning to their villages. When they leave for war they set fire to all their huts and bury their most prized possessions in the earth until they return. The number of wives a man has to serve him varies with his importance. ...

One may wonder why these savages make war against each other since they have more than enough land for their needs, and no rulers or great riches. All I can say is that their wars have little foundation, and that they fight only from a desire for vengeance, like wild animals. They are incapable of reaching any settlement, and justify their continual warfare with the simple statement that the people they fight have been their enemies from time immemorial. As I said above, they assemble in great numbers to march against their enemies, especially if they have recently suffered some injury from them. When they meet they first shoot flights of arrows at each other, then join in hand-to-hand combat, seizing each other by the arms and ears, and dealing each other blows with their fists. ...

So great is their mutual hatred that they sometimes spend an entire day standing the distance of an arquebus shot from each other, hurling threats at their enemies, with such deafening howls and cries that they drown out the sound of thunder, raising their wooden swords and clubs on high, and saying, "We have eaten your relations and we will eat you," and making fearsome faces and other silly threats at each other.

The greatest, cruelest vengeance that these savages can take is to eat their enemies. If they have taken some war prisoners and are not strong enough to carry them away before an attempt is made to rescue them, they will cut off a prisoner's arms and legs and eat them before leaving him, or perhaps each will carry away a piece of his flesh, large or small. But if they can bring their prisoners to their own country, they will eat them just the same. ...

It remains for me to describe how the savages treat these captives. For four or five days they are well treated, after which each captive is given a wife, who may be the captor's daughter, to sleep with him and satisfy his other needs. The captive is given the best food available, and they try to fatten him up like a capon until he is killed. After the prisoner has been well fattened, they kill him, thinking they do him a great honor.

In order that the prisoner may be more easily recognized, they put around his neck a necklace of cotton thread strung with some round fruit or the bones of some fish or animal, resembling rosary beads. If they want to keep him for a space of four or five moons, they attach that number of beads, and remove them one at a time as each moon wanes, killing him when the beads are all gone.

Sometimes, instead of these beads, the savages tie as many little necklaces around the prisoner's neck as he has moons to live. (Note that these savages count only up to five, and mark time only by moons, instead of days, months, or years.) ...

If a child is born of the union between the prisoner and the wife given to him, the savages fatten the child for some time and then eat him or her because the child is the offspring of their enemy.

For the solemn occasion of the execution the savages invite all their friends to come from afar and partake of the prisoner's flesh. On the appointed day the captive, made fast with chains (whose use they have learned from the Christians), lies in his hammock, singing day and night songs like the following, "Our friends the Marakajas are honest men, strong and powerful warriors; they have taken and eaten many of our enemies, and they will eat me the day it pleases them, but I have killed and eaten the relatives and friends of the man who took me prisoner," and much more of the same. One can see from this how little fear they have of death. Once, out of curiosity, I asked some prisoners, strong and handsome men, if they were not anxious about being killed from one day to the next. Laughing and joking, with great coolness and assurance, they replied, "Our friends will avenge us." If someone even suggested the possibility of their being ransomed and freed from the hands of their enemies, they treated it as a great joke.

They treat women and girls taken in war like the men, but give them no husbands. They are not held captive as closely as the men, however, being free to go here and there. But they are made to work in the gardens and to fish for oysters.

I return to the execution. As I noted above, the owner of a prisoner invites all his friends to partake of pieces of the prisoner's flesh, which is served up with great quantities of cahouin, a beverage made of coarse millet and certain roots. All who attend this solemn occasion are adorned with beautiful plumes of different colors, or paint themselves all over. The man who is to deal the fatal blow puts on his best finery and carries a wooden sword richly adorned with various plumes.

As the preparations for his death advance, the prisoner displays ever greater signs of joy. At last he is led, firmly tied with cotton cords, to the public place of execution. He is accompanied by ten or twelve thousand of his enemies. There, after various ceremonies, he is clubbed over the head, as if he were a pig. When he is dead, the wife he has been given makes some slight show of mourning. After his body has been cut into pieces, the savages wash their male children in his blood to teach them to be brave, explaining that when they come of age they must do the same to their enemies. By watching this ceremony the children also learn that the same fate awaits them when they are taken captive. After the body has been dismembered and cooked, it is distributed to all those present, each receiving a piece. The women commonly eat the entrails, while the head is hung up on the end of a pole among the huts as a trophy or symbol of victory. ...

As soon as the execution is over the executioner takes to his bed and remains in his hut without eating or drinking for a space of three days. If he must go somewhere he must be carried, for they foolishly believe that if he walks he will suffer some misfortune or even die. Soon afterwards, using a lancet made from the teeth of an animal called the Cutia, he makes various incisions on his chest and other parts of his body, so that he looks like a mass of slashes.

In response to my questions, several savages informed me that the executioner does this as a token of the honor he derives from having killed his enemy. When I remonstrated with them, pointing out the cruelty of these killings, they rebuffed me, saying that it was shameful for us to pardon our enemies after we had made them prisoners, that it was better to kill them so they would not make war on us a second time. This is the mode of reasoning of these brutish people.

2

THE HISPANIC BACKGROUND

THE INSTITUTIONS, traditions, and values brought to the Americas by Hispanic invaders shaped the future of Latin America more decisively than the culture of the vanquished Indians. Five centuries of struggle against the Moslems had made warfare almost an Hispanic way of life and created a large class of titled fighting men who regarded manual labor and most commerce with contempt. The Reconquest (*Reconquista*), as that struggle is called, was also accompanied by a growing concentration of land in the hands of the Christian nobility and the church. Although serfdom in Castile, in contrast to the situation in Aragón, had virtually ceased to exist by the end of the fifteenth century, the great majority of the peasants were heavily burdened by rents, seigneurial dues, taxes, and tithes. With some regional exceptions, there was little industry. The most lucrative economic activity in Castile—the export of wool to Flanders and Italy—enriched the great nobility who owned vast herds of sheep and extensive pasturages. The Portuguese economy displayed similar weaknesses. The claim of some scholars that a thriving "capitalism" existed in late medieval Spain and Portugal does not bear scrutiny. On the eve of the conquest of the Americas, the economies and societies of both countries presented a predominantly feudal aspect.

A turning point in Iberian peninsular history was the marriage, in 1469, of the heirs apparent to the thrones of Aragón and Castile—Ferdinand and Isabella. The Catholic Sovereigns—the title given to them by the pope in recognition of their crusading zeal—broke the power of the great nobility but allowed this class to retain and even expand its social and economic privileges. The crowning domestic achievement of Ferdinand and Isabella's reign was the surrender of the Moslem city and kingdom of Granada in 1492, after a ten-year siege. More unified politically and religiously than ever before, and avid for the gold and silver that symbolized power and wealth in the age of the commercial revolution, Spain stood ready to launch the great enterprise of the Indies.

1. THE CID CAMPEADOR:
SYMBOL OF SPANISH NATIONALITY

The heroic figure of Ruy Días de Vivar, the Cid Campeador, or Warrior Lord, as he was called by his Moslem soldiers, typifies in Spanish popular tradition the crusading era of Hispanic history. The real Cid, true to the ideals of his times, placed feudal above religious loyalties and ably served the Moslem kings of Saragossa and Valencia against not only Moorish foes but Christian princes. His greatest triumph was the seizure in 1092 of the Moslem city of Valencia in the name of the king of Castile. A thirteenth-century Spanish chronicler describes the aftermath of the victory.

That night the Cid conferred with Alvar Fañez and Pero Bermudez and the other men of his council, and they decided what policy they would adopt with the Moors. On the next day all the Moors of Valencia assembled in the castle, as the Cid had ordered. The Cid seated himself on his dais, with all his nobles around him, and said:

All you good men of the *aliama* of Valencia, you know how well I served and aided the king of Valencia, and how many opportunities I let pass to take this city; now that God has seen fit to make me lord of Valencia, I want it for myself and for those who helped me to take it, subject only to the authority of my lord King Alfonso. You are all in my power, and I could easily take from you everything you have in the world—your persons, your wives, and your children. But I do not want to do this, and I therefore decree that the honorable men among you, who were always loyal to me, shall dwell in Valencia in their homes with their wives. However, each of you may keep only one animal—a mule—and one servant, and you may not own or use weapons unless by my order. All the others I order to leave Valencia and go to live outside the city in the Alcudia, where I once lived. You may keep your mosques in Valencia and outside in the Alcudia, and your *alfaquis* and your own laws; and you shall have your own judges and your sheriff besides those whom I have placed over you. You may keep all your estates, but you shall give me a tithe of all you grow, and I shall have supreme charge of justice and the coinage of money. Now, those who wish to remain with me on these terms may stay; as for the others, they may now leave, taking no possessions, and I shall order that no one harm them.

When the Moors of Valencia heard this they were sad, but the times were such that they had no choice. Within the hour all the Moors, except those that the Cid had ordered to remain, began to leave the town with their wives and children; and as they left the Christians who had dwelt in the Alcudia entered. History relates that so many people left Valencia that their departure required two days. ... This business took a full two months to complete. And thereafter the Cid was called: "My Cid Campeador, Lord of Valencia."

Ramón Menéndez Pidal, *Primera crónica general de España*, Madrid, 1906, 2 vols., I, pp. 591–592. (Excerpt translated by the editor.)

2. THE CATHOLIC SOVEREIGNS

The joint reign of Ferdinand of Aragón and Isabella of Castile was rich in dramatic and important events. They were constructive in their efforts to unify Spain, subdue feudal lawlessness, and activate Spanish industry, but they nevertheless helped to initiate Spain's ultimate decay through their policies of religious intolerance and systematic weakening of the autonomy and political influence of the Spanish towns. This negative aspect of their world was not apparent to the patriotic Jesuit Father Juan de Mariana (1535–1625), whose history of Spain contains a glowing tribute to the Catholic Sovereigns.

Truly it was they who restored justice, previously corrupted and fallen into decay, to its proper place. They made very good laws for governing the towns and settling lawsuits. They defended religion and faith and established public peace, putting an end to discords and tumults, at home as well as abroad. They extended their dominions, not only in Spain but to the farthest parts of the earth. Most laudably, they distributed rich rewards and dignities not on the basis of noble birth or as private favors but according to individual merit, and thus encouraged their subjects to devote their intellects to good work and literature. There is no need to describe the benefits of all this; the results speak for themselves. Truly, where in the world are to be found more learned and saintly priests and bishops, or judges of greater wisdom and rectitude? Before their day one could list very few Spaniards distinguished in science; since their time who can count the Spaniards who have gained fame as scholars?

The king and queen were of average stature and well built; they carried themselves majestically, and their facial expressions were gravely pleasant. The king's naturally fair skin had been tanned in military campaigns; he wore his chestnut hair long and shaved his beard more often than necessary. He had wide eyebrows, a smooth face, a small crimson mouth, narrow teeth, wide shoulders, a straight neck, and a sharp voice; he spoke quickly and thought clearly; his manner was smooth, courteous, and kindly. He was skilled in the art of war, unexcelled in the business of government, and so conscientious that labor seemed to relax him. He was not self-indulgent; he ate simply and dressed soberly. He was a skilful horseman; as a youth he enjoyed playing cards and dice; as he grew older he practiced hawking, and took much pleasure in the flights of herons.

The queen had a pleasant face, blonde hair, and light blue eyes; she used no cosmetics and was exceedingly dignified and modest in appearance. She

---

Juan de Mariana, *Historia de España*, Madrid, 1909, 2 vols., II, p. 239. (Excerpt translated by the editor.)

was devoted to religion and fond of literature; she loved her husband, but her love was mixed with jealousy and suspicion. She knew Latin, an accomplishment that King Ferdinand lacked because he had not received a liberal education; he liked to read histories, however, and to talk with scholars. On the day of his birth, it is said, a certain saintly Carmelite friar of Naples said to King Alfonso, his uncle: "Today in the Kingdom of Aragon is born a child of thy lineage; heaven promises him new empires; great riches, and good fortune; he will be very devout, a lover of the good, and an excellent defender of Christianity." Considering human frailty, it was almost inevitable that among so many virtues there should be certain defects. The avarice that is charged against him can be excused by his lack of money and by the fact that the royal revenues were diverted from their proper use. The severe punishments that also are charged to him were occasioned by the disorder and depravity of the time. Foreign writers have implied that he was a crafty man and one who sometimes broke his word if it was to his advantage. I do not propose to discuss whether this be truth or fiction concocted out of hatred for our nation; I would only point out that malicious men often assign the name of vices to true virtues and, conversely, praise the deceitful vices that resemble virtues; for the rest, the king merely adapted himself to the times and to the language, methods, and strategies that were then in use.

3. THE SPANISH INQUISITION

All of Spain's troubles since the time of Ferdinand and Isabella should not be laid at the door of the Spanish Inquisition, but the operations of the Holy Office unquestionably contributed to the picture of economic decay that Spain presented by the close of the sixteenth century. The blows struck by the Spanish Inquisition at the Conversos (Jewish converts and their descendants, who were frequently charged with heresy) fell on an important segment of Spain's merchant and banking class, the social group that in England and Holland was transforming economic life and preparing the way for the Industrial Revolution. The Santangel mentioned below was condemned by the civil court to burn at the stake, as the findings of the inquisitors required. Ironically, he was a kinsman of that Luis de Santangel, Ferdinand's treasurer, who at the last moment persuaded Isabella to support Columbus's project and who obtained at least half the money needed for the enterprise.

It appears that the accused, the said Luis de Santangel, has openly and very clearly practiced heresy and apostasy from our holy Catholic Faith, perform-

---

Cited in: Manuel Serrano y Sanz, *Orígenes de la dominación española en América*, Madrid, 1918, pp. 114–116. (Excerpt translated by the editor.)

ing and maintaining rites and ceremonies of the old law of Moses, as a true and consummate Jew, especially observing the Sabbath with entire faith and devotion, abstaining on that day from engaging in business, travel, or other lowly tasks, as much and as well as he could, keeping it a holiday with all zeal and devotion, as the Jews do, eating on that day meat and *amin* and many other Jewish foods, both those prepared in his house on Friday for use on Saturday and those brought and sent from the ghetto, getting and lighting clean candles on Friday evening in honor of the Sabbath, as the Jews do, donning a clean shirt and performing other ceremonies such as the Jews on that day are wont to perform. And likewise he zealously observed the holiday of the thin bread, eating ceremonially of the said thin bread, and of no other, this bread being sent to him by Jews, and on such days he would eat from new plates and bowls, keeping and observing the said holiday as best he could. Moreover, he observed the fasts that the Jews call the Great Kippur and Haman, abstaining from food until nightfall and then breaking fast with meat, as the Jews do. Moreover, he did not observe the Christian holidays, or attend mass, or observe the fasts of the Holy Mother Church, but on the contrary he ate meat at Lent; in particular we find that he ate meat stewed in a pan on Good Friday. And that he continually prayed in the Judaic manner, his face turned to the wall, looking toward heaven through a window, bowing and reciting the psalms of David in Spanish, in the Judaic manner; and at the end of each psalm he said not *gloria patri* but instead *Adonai, Adonai*, and he had a psalter in the Spanish language that did not have *gloria patri* or the litany of the saints. And that he had faith and true hope in the said law of Moses, rather than in the evangelical law of our Lord Jesus Christ, defending the said law of Moses as superior to that of Jesus Christ; and that he gave oil for the lamps of the synagogue, and other alms to Jews; and that he had no oratory or other Christian practice. Nor did he kneel at the sounding of the orisons or at the elevation of the Corpus Christi, or cross himself, or say "Jesus." And when riding horseback, if the beast should stumble, in place of saying "Jesus" he used to say *Sadday*, and *Adonai*, as the Jews do; and he abstained from eating the foods forbidden by the law of Moses as much as he could, eating instead the meat of animals slaughtered by Jewish hands, cleansing away the tallow, salting it to draw out the blood before cooking, and removing a certain small round body from the leg. Nor did he eat the flesh of game or birds that had been strangled, but instead he had his chickens and other fowls slaughtered by Jews; and the other game that he purchased he would kill or have killed with a well-sharpened knife, in the Judaic manner.

And as we already had information of the aforementioned matters, the said Luis de Santangel, suspecting this and suspecting that orders had been issued for his seizure, came before us with lying and deceitful words, saying that he, as a good Christian, wished to submit to our justice and confess completely certain errors that he had committed against the faith, and of his own will he bound himself to the punishment of a relapsed heretic if he should not tell the whole truth, and he gave in writing a certain confession in his handwriting, in which he confessed that he had observed certain Judaic ceremonies and fasts, by which it immediately became evident that he had committed perjury and relapsed into heresy, to which charge he had exposed himself of his own will; and after the above-cited confession, with the hope of being released from prison and even of having his goods returned, as we lawfully know, he made other confessions, more extensive than the first, although in none of these did he confess all the heresies that he had committed.

In fine, it appears that the said Luis de Santangel has been and is a negative, obdurate heretic, and that he came to seek reconciliation to the Holy Mother Church with a lying tale, and not in a sincere or contrite spirit, as the case required, and that he is unworthy of forgiveness or of admission to the Holy Mother Church; concerning all of which we have resolved and deliberated with learned men of good conscience, who have seen and examined the said process and the said confessions. And desiring to extirpate and eradicate completely, as by our office we are most strictly bound and held to do, in the name of the Church, all such vile, grave, and wicked errors, so that the name of Jesus Christ may be truly believed, exalted, adored, praised, and served, without any pretence, hypocrisy, or sham, and so that no one may bear the name of a Christian and the air of a lamb who is truly a Jew and has the heart of a wolf; and having before our eyes Our Lord, from whom proceed all just and righteous judgments, we find that we must pronounce and declare, as by these presents we do pronounce and declare, that the said Luis de Santangel has been and is a true heretic and apostate from the faith, negative and obdurate. ... We moreover declare all his goods confiscated for the Treasury and exchequer of the King our lord. ... And since the Holy Mother Church cannot and should not do anything more against the said heretic and apostate, except to withdraw from him its protection and remit him to the secular justice and arm that he may be punished and chastised according to his demerits, therefore, with the customary protestations established in canon law, we remit the said Luis de Santangel, heretic and apostate, to the excellent and virtuous Juan Garcez de Marcella, chief justice of the King our lord in this city, and to its judge and justices, that they may dispose of him as in law and justice they may decree.

4. THE SPANISH CHARACTER

The great movement of the Reconquista—*the Reconquest of Spain from the Moslems—left an enduring stamp on the Spanish character. The soldier of the* Reconquista *was reborn in the* conquistador *of America. Italian historian and diplomat Francesco Guicciardini (1483–1540), who represented Florence in the court of King Ferdinand, left an acid—*

yet often perceptive—account of the Spanish character at the opening of the sixteenth century.

The Spaniards are of melancholy and choleric disposition, darkskinned, small in stature, and haughty by nature. They believe no other nation can compare with them; in speech they brag and puff themselves up all they can. They have little love for foreigners and are very rude to them. They are more inclined to arms, perhaps, than any other Christian nation, and that because they are extremely agile, skillful, and light in movement. In war they have a high regard for honor, and would rather suffer death than dishonor. ...

In their wars they have begun to adopt the Swiss formation, but I question whether this conforms to their nature, for when they form a compact front or wall, in the Swiss manner, they cannot make use of their nimbleness, the quality in which they surpass all others. All Spaniards carry arms, and in the old days they took part not only in foreign wars but in domestic broils, each man siding with one faction or another. For this reason Spain formerly had more cavalrymen, and more skillful ones, than now. In the reign of Queen Isabella peace and order were restored to the kingdom, and that, in my opinion, is why Spain is less of a military power today than at any time in the past.

Spaniards are generally regarded as ingenious and astute people, but they have little taste for the mechanical or liberal arts. Almost all the artisans in the royal court are from France or some other foreign country. Nor do Spaniards devote themselves to commerce, for they think it shameful, and all give themselves the airs of a hidalgo. They would rather eat the meager fare of a soldier, or serve some grandee, suffering a thousand privations and inconveniences, or—before the time of the present king—even take to the roads as a highwayman, than devote themselves to commerce or some other work. True, in certain places they have begun to pay attention to industry, and in some regions they are now producing textiles, clothing, crimson damasks, and gold embroideries. They do this in Valencia, Toledo, and Seville. In general, however, the Spaniards have no liking for industry. Thus the artisans work only when driven by necessity, and then they rest until they have used up their earnings. This is the reason why manual labor is so expensive. It is the same in the countryside, for the peasants will not work hard unless compelled by extreme need. Each one works much less land than he could, and the little land that is farmed is badly cultivated.

There is great poverty in Spain, and I believe this arises less from the quality of the country than from the nature of its people, who lack the inclination

---

Francesco Guicciardini, "Relazione di Spagna," in *Opere*, edited by Vittorio de Caprariis, Milano, 1961, pp. 29–31. (Excerpt translated by the editor.)

to devote themselves to industry and trade. The problem is not that Spaniards leave their country, but that they prefer to export the raw materials that the kingdom yields and buy them back in the form of finished goods; this is the case with wool and silk, which they sell to other nations and then purchase back in the form of woolen and silk cloth. From the resulting poverty arises the misery of the people. Aside from a few grandees of the realm, who live sumptuously, the Spaniards live in very straitened circumstances, and if they have some money to spend, they spend it on clothing and a mule, making a greater show in the street than at home, where they live so meanly and eat so sparingly that it is a marvel to see. Although they can manage with very little, they are not free from greed for gain. Indeed, they are very avaricious, and, since they know no trade, they are given to robbery. Formerly, when there was less rule of law in this kingdom, the whole land swarmed with assassins, a thing favored by the nature of the country, which is very mountainous and sparsely settled. Their astuteness makes them good thieves. There is a popular saying that the Frenchman makes a better lord than a Spaniard, for, although both extort from their subjects, the Frenchman immediately spends what he takes, whereas the Spaniard hoards it. For the rest, the Spaniard, being more clever, surely robs better.

They are not given to letters. One finds little knowledge of Latin among the nobility or among the rest of the population, and that among very few persons. In demonstrations and outward show they are very religious, but not in fact. They are very ceremonious, with many deep bows, great verbal humility, and much use of titles and hand kisses. They assure everyone that he is their *señor*, that they are at his orders; but it is best to keep one's distance with them and give little credit to their words.

Dissimulation is natural to this nation, and one finds masters of this art among all classes. This is the basis of their reputation for astuteness and ingenuity; for the rest, they are not especially faithless or treacherous. In this matter of dissimulation the Andalusians surpass all others, particularly those of the ancient and famous city of Córdoba, home of the Great Captain.[1] From this dissimulation arise their ceremoniousness and their great hypocrisy.

PART TWO

SPAIN IN THE INDIES

3

CONQUEST

THE DISCOVERY of America is linked to a number of great European movements: the decline of feudalism and the rise of the nation-state; the rapid growth of the merchant class and international trade; a series of advances in navigational science and shipbuilding that facilitated European overseas expansion; and a new intellectual climate (the Renaissance) that helped to dispel old geographical dogmas and fired men's curiosity to penetrate the unknown.

More immediately, the discovery of America by Christopher Columbus resulted from the search for an all-water route to the East. That search was promoted by the monarchs of Portugal and Spain in an effort to break the Italian-Arab monopoly of European trade with the East.

From its primary base on Hispaniola the Spanish conquest of the Americas branched out to the other great Antilles (Puerto Rico, Cuba, Jamaica) and simultaneously sent out weak offshoots to the coasts of South and Central America. Slave-hunting and exploring expeditions gradually mapped the coasts of Central America and Mexico and revealed Indian societies far wealthier and more advanced than those found in the West Indies.

The discovery of these societies led to the invasion of Mexico by Hernando Cortés in 1519. The superstitious fears of the Aztec emperor Moctezuma (Montezuma) led him to identify Cortés as the god and priest king Quetzalcoatl, who was believed to have left Mexico long centuries before. These fears enabled Cortés to enter the Indian capital without opposition, but an unprovoked aggression by his lieutenant Pedro de Alvarado precipitated a mortal struggle. Cuauhtémoc, the last Aztec ruler, only surrendered to Cortés in 1521 when Tenochtitlán lay in ruins and its native defenders were dead or starving. From Mexico the stream of conquest flowed south into Guatemala and Honduras; in Nicaragua it joined another current formed by Spaniards coming north from Darien.

The town of Panama, founded in 1519 across the isthmus from Darien, became a base for expeditions seeking golden kingdoms that were rumored to lie southward. After repeated failures, Francisco Pizarro and his companions achieved their aim of reaching and conquering the Incan empire (1532). Before Incan resistance was entirely overcome, however, the conquerors fell out among themselves, and by the time that peace was restored in Peru all the leading conquerors of Peru had come to violent ends.

Contrary to romantic tradition, only a small minority of the *conquistadores* were *hidalgos* (nobles), although many claimed to be such. The majority were plebeians—peasants, artisans, sailors, and soldiers, some with dubious pasts. As the Conquest advanced and consolidated its gains, however, the *conquistadores* were joined by a growing number of clergy, lawyers, royal officials, merchants, and other middle class types. The number of women immigrants was extremely small in the first stages of the Conquest but increased as the sixteenth century wore on.

1. THE MAN COLUMBUS

Christopher Columbus was a figure of transition whose thought and aspirations reflected both the waning Middle Ages and the rising new day of rationalism and capitalism. A major source of information about the Columbian epic is the monumental History of the Indies *of Bartolomé de las Casas (1484–1566), who was with Columbus on Hispaniola in 1500 and whose father and uncle accompanied Columbus on his second voyage. Las Casas describes the appearance and character of the Discoverer.*

As concerns his appearance, he was fairly tall, his face long and giving an impression of authority, his nose aquiline, his eyes blue, his complexion light and tending to bright red; his beard and hair were fair in his youth but very soon turned gray from his labors. He was witty and gay in speech and, as the aforementioned Portuguese history relates, eloquent and boastful in his negotiations. His manner was serious, but not grave; he was affable with strangers and mild and pleasant with members of his household, whom he treated with dignity, and so he easily won the love of those who saw him. In short, he had the appearance of a man of great consequence. He was sober and moderate in eating and drinking, in dress and footwear; he would often say, whether jokingly or angrily: "God take you, don't you agree to that?" or "Why did you do that?" In the matter of Christian doctrine he was a devout Catholic; nearly everything he did or said he began with: "In the name of the Holy Trinity I shall do this" or "this will come to pass," or "may this come to pass." And at the head of everything he wrote he put: "Jesus and Mary, attend us on our way." I have many of these writings in my possession. Sometimes

---

Bartolomé de las Casas, *Historia de las Indias*, Mexico, 1951, 3 vols., I, pp. 29–30. (Excerpt translated by the editor.)

his oath was: "I swear by San Fernando"; when he wanted to affirm the truth of something very important, especially when writing to the King and Queen, he said: "I swear that this is true." He kept the fasts of the Church most faithfully, confessed and took communion very often, said the canonical offices like any churchman or monk, abhorred blasphemy and vain oaths, and was most devoted to Our Lady and the Seraphic Father Saint Francis. He appeared very grateful for benefits received at the divine hand; and it was almost a proverb with him, which he repeated frequently, that God had been especially good to him, as to David. When gold or precious objects were brought to him he would enter his chapel and kneel, asking the bystanders to do the same, saying: "Let us give thanks to the Lord, who made us worthy of discovering such great wealth." He was most zealous in the service of God; he was eager to convert the Indians and to spread the faith of Jesus Christ everywhere, and was especially devoted to the hope that God would make him worthy of helping to win back the Holy Sepulcher. ... He was a man of great spirit and lofty thoughts, naturally inclined—as appears from his life, deeds, writings, and speech—to undertake great and memorable enterprises; patient and long-suffering ... quick to forgive injuries and wishing nothing more than that those who offended him should come to know their error and be reconciled with him. He was most constant and forbearing amid the endless incredible hardships and misfortunes that he had to endure, and always had great faith in the Divine Providence. And as I learned from him, from my own father, who was with him when he returned to settle the island of Hispaniola in 1493, and from other persons who accompanied and served him, he was always most loyal and devoted to the King and Queen.

2. "SAINT AUGUSTINE DOUBTS ... "

Among the numerous legends that surround the Columbus story, perhaps the most popular of all is that which portrays Columbus as seeking to convince his bigoted and dull-witted opponents of the faculty of the University of Salamanca that the earth was round. In reality, the question of the sphericity of the earth never entered the discussions between Columbus and the committee appointed by Queen Isabella to consider his claims. The main issue was the width of the ocean; and on this point the opposition was right. Of pedantry and excessive deference to the authority of the ancients, however, the committee was doubtless guilty, if we may trust Las Casas's lively account of the debate, in which he reveals a warm partisanship for Columbus.

Bartolomé de las Casas, *Historia de las Indias*, I, pp. 157–158. (Excerpt translated by the editor.)

Some said that it was impossible that after so many thousands of years these Indies should be unknown, if there were such places in the world, for surely Ptolemy and the many other astronomers, geographers, and sages that had lived would have known something of them, and would have left some reference to them in writing, since they had written of many other matters; hence, they said, to affirm what Columbus affirmed was to claim to know or divine more than anyone else. Others argued this way: The world is infinitely large, and therefore in many years of navigation it would be impossible to reach the end of Asia, as Christopher Columbus proposed to do by sailing westward. ...

Still others, who vaunted their mathematical learnings, talked about astronomy and geography, saying that only a very small part of this inferior sphere is land, all the rest being entirely covered with water, and therefore it could only be navigated by sailing along the shores or coasts, as the Portuguese did along the coasts of Guinea; the proponents of this view had read precious few books on navigation, and had done even less sailing themselves. They added that whoever sailed directly west, as Christopher Columbus proposed to do, could never return, for supposing that the world was round, and that going westward you went downhill, then once you had left the hemisphere described by Ptolemy, on your return you must go uphill, which ships could not do—truly a subtle and profound reason, and proof that the matter was well understood! Others cited Saint Augustine, who ... denied the existence of antipodes ... and their refrain was: "Saint Augustine doubts." Then someone had to bring up the business of the five zones, of which three, according to many, are totally uninhabitable; this was a commonly held opinion among the ancients, who, after all, did not know very much. Others adduced still other reasons, not worth mentioning here since they came from the kind of people who disagree with everybody—who find any statement illogical, no matter how sound and clear it is, and never lack for reasons to contradict it. ...

And so Christopher Columbus could give little satisfaction to those gentlemen whom the monarchs had convened, and therefore they pronounced his offers and promises impossible and vain and worthy of rejection. Having formed their opinion, they went to the monarchs and stated their views, persuading them that it did not become their royal authority to favor a project that was based on such weak foundations and that must appear vague and unfeasible to any sensible person, even an uneducated one, for if they sponsored it, they would lose the money that they spent on it and would weaken their own standing, with no benefit to anyone. Finally the monarchs sent a reply to Columbus, dismissing him for the time being, though not entirely depriving him of the hope of a return to the subject when their Highnesses should be less occupied with the important business, as they were at that time by the War of Granada.

3. The Discovery of the Pacific

Amerigo Vespucci's theory that the land mass said by Columbus to be part of Asia was really a new continent gained wide though not universal approval in the decade after 1502. If Vespucci was right, then there was another ocean to cross between the New World and Asia. Confirmation of this view was forthcoming in 1513 when Vasco Núñez de Balboa, standing "silent, upon a peak in Darien," looked out upon the waters of the Pacific. The Spanish chronicler Gonzalo Fernández de Oviedo y Valdés, who came to Darien in 1514 in an official capacity, tells the story of Balboa's feat, with some mention of the exploits of his remarkable dog, Leoncico.

For four years the Christians had been in Tierra-Firme; they fought under Captain Vasco Núñez de Balboa, and had made peace with certain *caciques*, in particular with the chieftains of Careta, which lies on the west coast, twenty leagues west of Darien, and of Comogre, and both of them had been baptized. The *cacique* of Careta was called Chima, and they named him Don Fernando, and he had as many as two thousand Indian warriors; the *cacique* of Comogre was a greater lord, and his proper name was Ponquiaco, but they gave him the baptismal name of Don Carlos; he had more than three thousand warriors and ruled over more than ten thousand persons. These *caciques* had grown so peaceful that they sent messengers and canoes; they came and went to and from Darien to see the Christians and communicated with them as with friends. Vasco Núñez, filled with hope by the information that he had secretly obtained from these *caciques*, resolved to set out on Friday, the first day of September, 1513; and he departed from the town of Santa María de la Antigua with eight hundred men in a galleon and nine canoes to search out the secrets of the land, on the pretext of going to seek for mines. On the following Sunday, the fourth day of September, half of this company arrived at Careta in the canoes, and the galleon came later with the rest; there Vasco Núñez disembarked. The *cacique* Don Fernando received him and all his people very well, both those who came in the canoes and those in the galleon. After they had arrived and assembled, Captain Vasco Núñez selected those whom he wished to take with him and left there those who were to guard the galleon and the canoes, and set out for the interior on the sixth day of the month. After a two-day march over a rough, difficult, and mountainous route he approached the vicinity of the *cacique* of Ponca, only to find that he and his people had fled to the hills.

Before proceeding further, I should state that the town that the Christians now call Acla was founded in the abovementioned port of Careta. I also want

Gonzalo Fernández de Oviedo y Valdés, *Historia general y natural de las Indias*, Asunción, Paraguay, 1944–1945, 14 vols., VII, pp. 92–95. (Excerpt translated by the editor.)

to tell of a dog that belonged to Vasco Núñez, called Leoncico, a son of the dog Becerrico of the isle San Juan [Puerto Rico] and no less famous than his father. This dog gained for Vasco Núñez in this and other conquests more than a thousand gold pesos, for he received as large a share in the gold and slaves as a member of the company when the division was made. So, whenever Vasco Núñez went along, the dog was assigned wages and a share like the other captains; and he was so active that he earned his reward better than many sleepy comrades who like to gain at their ease what others reap by their toil and diligence. He was truly a marvelous dog, and could distinguish a peaceable from a wild Indian as well as I or any other who went to these wars. When Indians had been taken and rounded up, if any should escape by day or by night the dog had only to be told: "He's gone, go get him," and he would do it; and he was so keen a pointer that only by a miracle could a runaway Indian escape him. After overtaking him, if the Indian remained still the dog would seize him by the wrist or hand and would bring him back as carefully, without biting or molesting him, as a man could; but if the Indian offered resistance he would tear him to pieces. He was so much feared by the Indians that if ten Christians went with the dog they went in greater safety and accomplished more than twenty without him. I saw this dog, for when Pedrarias arrived in the following year, 1514, he was still alive, and Vasco Núñez lent him for some Indian wars that were made afterwards and gained his shares as was told above. He was a dog of middle size, reddish in color, with a black muzzle, and not elegant in appearance; but he was strong and robust, and had many wounds and scars of wounds that he had received fighting with the Indians. Later on, out of envy, someone gave the dog some poisoned food, and he died. …

On September 13 came the *cacique* of Ponca, reassured by Captain Vasco Núñez, who did him much honor, gave him shirts and hatchets, and made him as comfortable as he could. Since this *cacique* found himself so well treated, he told Vasco Núñez in secret a great deal about the secrets and treasures of the land, which gratified the captain; among other things, he said that a certain number of days' journey from there was another *pechry*, which in their language means "sea"; and he presented Vasco Núñez with some very finely worked pieces of gold. …

On the twentieth of that month, Vasco Núñez set out from the land of this *cacique* with certain guides that Ponca assigned to go with him till they reached the land of the *cacique* Torecha, with whom Ponca was at war; and on the twenty-fourth day of that month they came by night upon the *cacique* Torecha and his people. This was ten leagues beyond the land of Ponca, and was reached by a most difficult route and by crossing rivers in rafts, at great peril to themselves. And there they took some people and some gold and pearls, and Vasco Núñez obtained more extensive information concerning the interior and the other sea, to the South. In Torecha he left some of his people, and set out with about seventy men; on the twenty-fifth of the month, the same day that he had left, he arrived at the village and seat of the *cacique* called Porque, who had absented himself; however, this did not matter to Vasco Núñez, and he went ahead, continuing his search for the other sea. And on Tuesday, the twenty-fifth of September of the year one thousand five hundred and thirteen, at ten o'clock in the morning, Captain Vasco Núñez, leading all the rest in the ascent of a certain bare mountain, saw from its peak the South Sea, before any other of his Christian companions. He joyfully turned to his men, raising his hands and eyes to the skies, praising Jesus Christ and his glorious mother the Virgin, Our Lady; then he sank on his knees and gave thanks to God for the favor that had been granted to him in allowing him to discover that sea and thereby to render such a great service to God and to the Catholic and Most Serene King of Castile, our lord. ... And he ordered them all to kneel and give the same thanks to God for this grace, and to implore Him to let them discover and see the hoped-for great secrets and riches of that sea and coast, for the exaltation and increase of the Christian faith, for the conversion of the Indians of those southern regions, and for the greater glory and prosperity of the royal throne of Castile and its princes, both present and to come.

4. PORTRAIT OF THE CONQUEROR

Historians and biographers do not agree in their estimate of the character and actions of Hernando Cortés. The chronicler Francisco López de Gómara (1511?–1562?), who lived in Cortés's household as his private chaplain for some years, had no doubts concerning the righteousness of either Cortés's actions or the civilizing mission of the Spanish Conquest. His history of the conquest of Mexico, which is actually a biography of Cortés, contains an intimate and not altogether flattering description of his former patron.

Ferdinand Cortés was of good size, broad in shoulders and chest, and of sallow complexion; his beard was light colored, and he wore his hair long. He was very strong, high spirited, and skilled in the use of arms. As a youth he was given to adventurous pranks, but in later years he acquired a mature dignity and thus became a leader in both war and peace. He was mayor of the town of Santiago de Barucoa [in Cuba], which fact the townspeople still regard as their chief title to fame. There he acquired a reputation for the qualities that he later displayed. He was passionately attracted to women, and indulged this proclivity without regard to time or place. It was the same with

Francisco López de Gómara, "Conquista de Méjico," in *Historiadores primitivos de las Indias*, edited by Enrique de Vedia, Madrid, 1852–1853, 2 vols., I, pp. 454–455. (Excerpt translated by the editor.)

games of chance; he played dice exceedingly well and with great enjoyment. Although he drank moderately he was a very hearty eater and kept an abundant table. He bore hunger with great fortitude, as he showed on the march of Higueras and on the sea to which he gave his name. He was very contentious and so was involved in more lawsuits than suited his condition. He spent freely on warfare, on women, on his friends, and to satisfy his whims, but showed himself niggardly in some things; hence some people called him a "wet-weather stream," one that ran high one day and dry the next. He dressed neatly rather than richly, and kept himself scrupulously clean. He took pleasure in keeping a large house and family, with a great display of plate, both for use and for show. He bore himself like a lord, and with such gravity and discretion that it neither caused disgust nor appeared presumptuous. A story has it that as a boy he was told that he was fated to conquer many lands and become a very great lord. He was jealous of the honor of his own house but forward in the homes of others—a common trait of lustful men. He was devout and prayerful, and knew many prayers and psalms by heart; he was very charitable, and on his deathbed especially charged his son with the giving of alms. He usually gave the Church a thousand ducats a year, and sometimes he borrowed money for giving alms, saying that he redeemed his sins with the interest on the money. On his shields and coats of arms he put the motto: *Judicium Domini apprehendit eos, et fortitudo ejus corroboravit brachium meum* [The judgment of the Lord overtook them, and his strength supported my arm[1]]—a text very appropriate to the conquest. Such was Ferdinand Cortés, Conqueror of New Spain.

5. THE MEETING OF CORTÉS AND MONTEZUMA

Few incidents in history have the romantic quality of the meeting between Cortés and Montezuma at the entrance of Tenochtitlán. Two cultures met in the persons of the Indian chieftain and the Spanish conquistador. The remarkable speech of welcome made by Montezuma, as reported by Cortés, supports the view that Montezuma regarded the conqueror as an emissary of the departed Quetzalcoatl, if not Quetzalcoatl himself, about to return to his Mexican realm.

I followed the said causeway for about half a league before I came to the city proper of Temixtitan. I found at the junction of another causeway, which

---

The Letters of Cortés to Charles V, translated and edited by Francis A. McNutt, New York, 1908, 2 vols., I, pp. 232–236.

joins this one from the mainland, another strong fortification, with two towers, surrounded by walls, twelve feet high with castellated tops. This commands the two roads, and has only two gates, by one of which they enter, and from the other they come out. About one thousand of the principal citizens came out to meet me, and speak to me, all richly dressed alike according to their fashion; and when they had come, each one in approaching me, and before speaking, would use a ceremony which is very common amongst them, putting his hand on the ground, and afterward kissing it, so that I was kept waiting almost an hour, until each had performed his ceremony. There is a wooden bridge, ten paces broad, in the very outskirts of the city, across an opening in the causeway, where the water may flow in and out as it rises and falls. This bridge is also for defense, for they remove and replace the long broad wooden beams, of which the bridge is made, whenever they wish; and there are many of these bridges in the city, as Your Highness will see in the account which I shall make of its affairs.

Having passed this bridge, we were received by that lord, Montezuma, with about two hundred chiefs, all barefooted and dressed in a kind of livery, very rich, according to their custom, and some more so than others. They approached in two processions near the walls of the street, which is very broad, and straight, and beautiful, and very uniform from one end to the other, being about two thirds of a league long, and having, on both sides, very large houses, both dwelling places, and mosques. Montezuma came in the middle of the street, with two lords, one on the right side, and the other on the left, one of whom was the same great lord, who, as I said, came in that litter to speak with me, and the other was the brother of Montezuma, lord of that city Iztapalapan, whence I had come that day. All were dressed in the same manner, except that Montezuma was shod, and the other lords were barefooted. Each supported him below his arms, and as we approached each other, I descended from my horse, and was about to embrace him, but the two lords in attendance prevented me, with their hands, that I might not touch him, and they, and he also, made the ceremony of kissing the ground. This done, he ordered his brother who came with him, to remain with me, and take me by the arm, and the other attendant walked a little head of us. After he had spoken to me, all the other lords, who formed the two processions, also saluted me, one after the other, then returned to the procession. When I approached to speak to Montezuma, I took off a collar of pearls and glass diamonds, that I wore, and put it on his neck, and, after we had gone through some of the streets, one of his servants came with two collars, wrapped in a cloth, which were made of coloured shells. These they esteem very much; and from each of the collars hung eight golden shrimps executed with great perfection and a span long. When he received them, he turned towards me, and put them on my neck, and again went on through the streets, as I have already indicated, until we came to a large and handsome house, which he had prepared for our reception. There he took me by the hand, and led me into a spacious room, in front of the court where we had entered, where he made me sit on a very rich platform, which had been ordered to be made for him, and told me to wait there; and then he went away.

After a little while, when all the people of my company were distributed to their quarter, he returned with many valuables of gold and silver work, and five or six thousand pieces of rich cotton stuffs, woven, and embroidered in divers ways. After he had given them to me, he sat down on another platform, which they immediately prepared near the one where I was seated, and being seated he spoke in the following manner:

> We have known for a long time, from the chronicles of our forefathers, that neither I, nor those who inhabit this country, are descendants from the aborigines of it, but from strangers who came to it from very distant parts; and we also hold, that our race was brought to these parts by a lord, whose vassals they all were, and who returned to his native country, and had many descendants, and had built towns where they were living; when, therefore, he wished to take them away with him they would not go, nor still less receive him as their ruler, so he departed. And we have always held that those who descended from him would come to subjugate this country and us, as his vassals; and according to the direction from which you say you come, which is where the sun rises, and from what you tell us of your great lord, or king, who has sent you here, we believe, and hold for certain, that he is our rightful sovereign, especially as you tell us that since many days he has had news of us. Hence you may be sure, that we shall obey you, and hold you as the representative of this great lord of whom you speak, and that in this there will be no lack or deception; and throughout the whole country you may command at your will (I speak of what I possess in my dominions), because you will be obeyed, and recognized, and all we possess is at your disposal.
>
> Since you are in your rightful place, and in your own homes, rejoice and rest, free from all the trouble of the journey, and wars which you have had, for I am well aware of all that has happened to you, between Puntunchan and here, and I know very well, that the people of Cempoal, and Tascaltecal, have told you many evil things respecting me. Do not believe more than you see with your own eyes, especially from those who are my enemies, and were my vassals, yet rebelled against me on your coming (as they say), in order to help you. I know they have told you also that I have houses, with walls of gold, and that the furniture of my halls, and other things of my service, were also of gold, and that I am, or make myself, a god, and many other things. The houses you have seen are of lime and stone and earth. And then he held up his robes, and showing me his body he said to me, "Look at me, and see that I am flesh and bones, the same as you, and everybody, and that I am mortal, and tangible." And touching his arms and body with his hands, "Look how they have lied to you! It is true indeed that I have some things of gold, which have been left to me by my forefathers. All that I possess, you may have whenever you wish."
>
> I shall now go to other houses where I live; but you will be provided here with everything necessary for you and your people, and you shall suffer no annoyance, for you are in your own house and country.

I answered to all he said, certifying that which seemed to be suitable, especially in confirming his belief that it was Your Majesty whom they were expecting. After this, he took his leave, and, when he had gone, we were well provided with chickens, and bread, and fruits, and other necessities, especially such as were required for the service of our quarters. Thus I passed six days well provided with everything necessary, and visited by many of the lords.

6. TWILIGHT OVER TENOCHTITLÁN

For three months the Aztec nation fought for its independence with incredible valor and fortitude. Not until a great part of the city was in ruins, and the streets and canals were choked with corpses, did the gallant Cuauhtémoc, the last Aztec war chief, surrender in the name of his people. An Aztec account of the fall of Tenochtitlán conveys with simple eloquence the pathos of the surrender and the terrible aftermath of the Conquest.

And when night had fallen, then it rained and sprinkled at intervals. Late at night the flame became visible; just so was it seen, just so it emerged as if it came from the heavens. Like a whirlwind it went spinning around and revolving; it was as if embers burst out of it—some very large, some very small, some like sparks. Like a coppery wind it arose, crackling, snapping, and exploding loudly. Then it circled the dike and traveled toward Coyonacazco; then it went into the middle of the lake there to be lost.

None shouted; none spoke aloud.

And on the next day, nothing more happened. All remained quiet, and also our foes [so] remained.

But the Captain [Cortés] was watching from a roof-top at Amaxac—from the roof-top of [the house of] Aztauatzin—under a canopy. It was a many-colored canopy. He looked toward [us] common folk; the Spaniards crowded about him and took counsel among themselves.

And [on our side] were Quauhtemoc and the other noblemen—the vice ruler Tlacotzin, the lords' judge Petlauhtzin, the captain of the armies Motelchiuhtzin; the constable of Mexico; and the lord priest; and also the noblemen of Tlatilulco—the general Coyoueuetzin; the commanding general Temilotzin; the army commander Topantemoctzin; the chief justice Auelitoctzin; the captain of the armies Uitziliuitzin; and the courier Uitzitzin. All of these noblemen were assembled at Tolmayecan; they appeared to consult among themselves how to do that which we were to undertake and how we should yield to [the Spaniards].

Reprinted, by permission, from *The Florentine Codex: General History of the Things in Spain* by Fray Bernardino de Sahagún. Book XII, *The Conquest*, Chs. 39 and 40. Translated by Arthur J. O. Andersen and Charles E. Dibble. Copyright 1953 by the School of American Research, Santa Fe.

Thereafter only two [men] took Quauhtemoc in a boat. The two who took him and went with him were the seasoned warrior Teputzitoloc, and Yaztachimal, Quauhtemoc's page. And the one who poled [the boat] was named Cenyaotl.

And when they carried Quauhtemoc off, then there was weeping among all the common folk. They said: "Now goeth the young lord Quauhtemoc; now he goeth to deliver himself to the gods, the Spaniards!"

And when they had betaken themselves to bring and disembark him thereupon all the Spaniards came to see. They drew him along; the Spaniards took him by the hand. After that they took him up to the roof-top, where they went to stand him before the Captain, the war leader. And when they had proceeded to stand him before [Cortés], they looked at Quauhtemoc, made much of him, and stroked his hair. Then they seated him with [Cortés] and fired the guns. They hit no one with them, but only made them go off above, [so that] they passed over the heads of the common folk. Then [some Mexicans] only fled. With this the war reached its end.

Then there was shouting; they said: "Enough! Let it end! Eat greens!" When they heard this, the common folk thereupon issued forth. On this, they went, even into the lagoon.

And as they departed, leaving by the great road, once more they there slew some, wherefore the Spaniards were wroth that still some again had taken up their obsidian-bladed swords and their shields. Those who dwelt in house clusters went straightway to Amaxac; they went direct to where the ways divide. There the common folk separated. So many went toward Tepeyacac, so many toward Xoxouiltitlan, so many toward Nonoalco. But toward Xolloco and toward Macatzintamal no one went.

And all who lived in boats and [in houses] on poles, and those at Tolmayecan, went into the water. On some, the water reached to the stomach; some, to the chest; and on some it reached to the neck. And some were all submerged, there in the deeps. Little children were carried on the backs [of their elders]; cries of weeping arose. Some went on happy and rejoicing as they traveled crowding on the road. And those who owned boats, all the boatmen, left by night, and even [continued to] leave all day. It was as if they pushed and crowded one another as they set out.

And everywhere the Spaniards were seizing and robbing the people. They sought gold; as nothing did they value the green stone, quetzal feathers and turquoise [which] was everywhere in the bosoms or in the skirts of the women. And as for us men, it was everywhere in [our] breech clouts and in [our] mouths.

And [the Spaniards] seized and set apart the pretty women—those of light bodies, the fair [-skinned] ones. And some women, when they were robbed, covered their face with mud and put on old, mended shirts and rags for their shifts. They put all rags on themselves.

And also some of us men were singled out—those who were strong, grown to manhood, and next the young boys, of whom they would make messengers, who would be their runners, and who were known as their servers. And on some they burned [brand marks] on their cheeks; on some they put paint on their cheeks; on some they put paint on their lips.

And when the shield was laid down, when we gave way, it was the year count Three House and the day count was One Serpent.

7. RENDEZVOUS AT CAJAMARCA

As the conquest of Peru unfolded, it repeated in a number of important ways the sequence of events in Mexico. In one important respect, however, the Peruvian story differs from that of Mexico. If Montezuma's undoing was his passive acceptance of the divinity of the invaders and their inevitable triumph, Atahualpa erred disastrously in his serious underestimation of the massed striking power of the small Spanish forces. Francisco de Jérez (1504–?), secretary to Francisco Pizarro and an active participant in the Conquest, describes the fateful meeting between Spaniards and Inca at Cajamarca.

When the Governor saw that it was near sunset, and that Atabaliba [Atahualpa] did not move from the place to which he had repaired, although troops still kept issuing out of his camp, he sent a Spaniard to ask him to come into the square to see him before it was dark. As soon as the messenger came before Atabaliba, he made an obeisance to him, and made signs that he should come to where the Governor waited. Presently he and his troops began to move, and the Spaniard returned and reported that they were coming, and that the men in front carried arms concealed under their clothes, which were strong tunics of cotton, beneath which were stones and bags and slings; all of which made it appear that they had a treacherous design. Soon the van of the enemy began to enter the open space. First came a squadron of Indians dressed in a livery of different colours, like a chess board. They advanced, removing the straws from the ground, and sweeping the road. Next came three squadrons in different dresses, dancing and singing. Then came a number of men with armour, large metal plates, and crowns of gold and silver. Among them was Atabaliba in a litter lined with plumes of macaws' feathers, of many colours and adorned with plates of gold and silver. Many Indians carried it on their shoulders on high. Next came two other litters and two hammocks, in which were some principal chiefs; and lastly, several squadrons of Indians with crowns of gold and silver.

As soon as the first entered the open space they moved aside and gave space to the others. On reaching the centre of the open space, Atabaliba remained in his litter on high, and the others with him, while his troops did not

Reports on the Discovery of Peru, translated and edited by C. R. Markham, London, the Hakluyt Society, Cambridge University Press, 1872, pp. 52–56.

cease to enter. A captain then came to the front and, ascending the fortress near the open space, where the artillery was posted, raised his lance twice, as for a signal. Seeing this, the Governor asked the Father Friar Vicente if he wished to go and speak to Atabaliba, with an interpreter? He replied that he did wish it, and he advanced, with a cross in one hand and the Bible in the other, and going amongst them: "I am a Priest of God, and I teach Christians the things of God, and in like manner I come to teach you. What I teach is that which God says to us in this Book. Therefore, on the part of God and of the Christians, I beseech you to be their friend, for such is God's will, and it will be for your good. Go and speak to the Governor, who waits for you."

Atabaliba asked for the Book, that he might look at it, and the Priest gave it to him closed. Atabaliba did not know how to open it, and the Priest was extending his arm to do so, when Atabaliba, in great anger, gave him a blow on the arm, not wishing that it should be opened. Then he opened it himself, and, without any astonishment at the letters and paper, as had been shown by other Indians, he threw it away from him five or six paces, and, to the words which the monk had spoken to him through the interpreter, he answered with much scorn, saying: "I know well how you have behaved on the road, how you have treated my Chiefs, and taken the cloth from my storehouses." The monk replied: "The Christians have not done this, but some Indians took the cloth without the knowledge of the Governor, and he ordered it to be restored." Atabaliba said: "I will not leave this place until they bring it all to me." The monk returned with this reply to the Governor. Atabaliba stood up on the top of the litter, addressing his troops and ordering them to be prepared. The monk told the Governor what had passed between him and Atabaliba, and that he had thrown the Scriptures to the ground. Then the Governor put on a jacket of cotton, took his sword and dagger, and, with the Spaniards who were with him, entered amongst the Indians most valiantly; and, with only four men who were able to follow him, he came to the litter where Atabaliba was, and fearlessly seized him by the arm, crying out *Santiago*. Then the guns were fired off, the trumpets were sounded, and the troops, both horse and foot, sallied forth.

On seeing the horses charge, many of the Indians who were in the open space fled, and such was the force with which they ran that they broke down part of the wall surrounding it, and many fell over each other. The horsemen rode them down, killing and wounding, and following in pursuit. The infantry made so good an assault upon those that remained that in a short time most of them were put to the sword. The Governor still held Atabaliba by the arm, not being able to pull him out of the litter because he was raised so high. Then the Spaniards made such a slaughter amongst those who carried the litter they fell to the ground, and, if the Governor had not protected Atabaliba, that proud man would there have paid for all the cruelties he had committed.

The Governor, in protecting Atabaliba, received a slight wound in the hand. During the whole time no Indian raised his arms against a Spaniard. So great was the terror of the Indians at seeing the Governor force his way through them, at hearing the fire of the artillery, and beholding the charging of the horses, a thing never before heard of, that they thought more of flying to save their lives than of fighting. All those who bore the litter of Atabaliba appeared to be principal chiefs. They were all killed, as well as those who were carried in the other litters and hammocks. One of them was the page of Atabaliba, and a great lord, and the others were lords of many vassals, and his Councillors. The chief of Caxamalca was also killed, and others; but, the number being very great, no account was taken of them, for all who came in attendance on Atabaliba were great lords. The Governor went to his lodging, with his prisoner Atabaliba, despoiled of his robes, which the Spaniards had torn off in pulling him out of the litter. It was a very wonderful thing to see so great a lord, who came in such power, taken prisoner in so short a time.

8. How the New Laws Were Received in Peru

A heavy atmosphere of intrigue, broken by recurrent cycles of murderous violence, hung over Peru in the time of the great civil wars. Early in 1544 a new viceroy, Blasco Núñez Vela, arrived in Lima to proclaim the edicts known as the New Laws of the Indies. These laws, the fruit of years of devoted labor on the part of Father Bartolomé de las Casas to save the Indians from destruction, evoked outraged cries and appeals for their suspension from the Spanish landowners in Peru. When these pleas failed, the desperate conquistadores rose in revolt and found a leader in Gonzalo Pizarro, brother of the murdered Francisco Pizarro. The chronicler Gómara describes the reception accorded the New Laws in Peru.

Blasco Núñez entered Trujillo amid great gloom on the part of the Spaniards; he publicly proclaimed the New Laws, regulating the Indian tributes, freeing the Indians, and forbidding their use as carriers against their will and without pay. He took away as many vassals as these laws permitted, and vested them in the crown. The people and the town council petitioned for repeal of these ordinances, except for those which regulated Indian tribute and prohibited the use of Indians as carriers; of these provisions they approved. He did not grant their appeal, but instead set very heavy penalties for those judges who should fail to execute the laws, saying that he brought an express order of the emperor for their enforcement, without hearing or granting any appeal. He told them, however, that they had reason to complain of the ordinances; that they should take their case to the emperor; and

---

Francisco López de Gómara, "Historia de las Indias," in *Historiadores primitivos de las Indias*, I, p. 251. (Excerpt translated by the editor.)

that he would write to the king that he had been badly informed to order those laws.

When the citizens perceived the severity behind his soft words, they began to curse. Some said that they would leave their wives. Actually, some were ready to leave them for any reason, good or bad, since many had married their lady-loves or camp-followers only on account of an order that stripped them of their estates if they did not do so. Others said that it would be much better not to have a wife and children to maintain, if they were to lose the slaves who supported them by their labors in mines, fields, and other pursuits; others demanded payment for the slaves that were being taken from them, since they had bought them from the crown fifth and they bore the royal brand and mark. Still others said that they were ill requited for their labors and services, if in their declining years they were to have no one to serve them; these showed their teeth, decayed from eating toasted corn in the conquest of Peru; others displayed many wounds, bruises, and great lizard bites; the conquerors complained that after wasting their estates and shedding their blood in gaining Peru for the emperor, he was depriving them of the few vassals that he had given them. The soldiers said that they would not go to conquer other lands, since they were denied the hope of holding vassals, but instead would rob right and left all they could; the royal lieutenants and officials complained bitterly of the loss of their allotments of Indians, though they had not maltreated them, and held them not by virtue of their officers but in return for their labors and their services.

The priests and friars also declared that they could not support themselves nor serve their churches if they were deprived of their Indian towns; the one who spoke most shamelessly against the viceroy and even against the king was Fray Pedro Múñoz, of the Mercedarian Order, saying how badly the king rewarded those who had served him so well, and that the New Laws smelled of calculation rather than of saintliness, for the king was taking away the slaves that he had sold without returning the money received for them, and that he was taking away Indian towns from monasteries, churches, hospitals, and the conquistadores who had gained them; and, what was worse, they were laying a double tribute and tax on the Indians whom they took away in this fashion and vested in the crown, and that the Indians themselves were weeping over this. There was bad blood between this friar and the viceroy because the latter had stabbed the friar one evening in Málaga, when the viceroy was *corregidor* there.

9. THE MAN WHO WOULD BE KING

After Gonzalo Pizarro's victory over the viceroy Vela, Pizarro's advisers urged him to proclaim himself king of Peru. But Pizarro hesitated to avow the revolutionary meaning of his actions. The arrival of an envoy of the crown, Pedro de la Gasca, who announced suspensions of the New Laws and offered pardons and rewards to all repentant rebels, caused a trickle of desertions from Pizarro's ranks that in time became a flood. In the end the rebellion collapsed almost without a struggle, and its leaders ended on the gallows or the block. Garcilaso de la Vega describes the execution of Gonzalo Pizarro.

It remains only for me to tell of the pitiful death of Gonzalo Pizarro. He spent all of his last day in confession. ... The ministers of justice, coming and going, sought to hasten the execution of his sentence. One of the gravest of them, angered by the delay, said loudly: "Well! Are they not done with the fellow yet?" All the soldiers who heard him took offense at his disrespect and hurled a thousand oaths and insults at him, but though I remember many of them and knew the man, I will not set them down here nor give his name. He went without saying a word, before it came to blows, something he had reason to fear in view of the indignation and annoyance that the soldiers displayed at his rudeness. A little later Gonzalo Pizarro came out and mounted a saddled mule that was held ready for him. He was covered with a cape; although one author says that his hands were tied, it was not so. They threw one end of a halter over the neck of the mule, in compliance with the law. In his hands he bore an image of Our Lady, to whom he was most devoted. He continually implored her to intercede for his soul. Halfway along he asked for a crucifix. A priest, one of the twelve that accompanied him, gave him one. Gonzalo Pizarro took it and gave the priest the image of Our Lady, kissing with great affection the hem of the dress of the image. With the crucifix in his hands, never taking his eyes from it, he came up to the platform that had been made for his execution. This he ascended, and, standing at one side, he spoke to the people who were watching him. Among them were all the men of Peru, soldiers and citizens, excepting only the grandees who had turned against him—and even some of them were there, disguised and muffled up. He said in a loud voice:

Gentlemen, your worships know well that my brothers and I gained this empire. Many of your worships hold *repartimientos* of Indians that the Marquis, my brother, gave you; many others hold them from me. Moreover, many of your worships owe me money that you borrowed from me; many others have received money from me as free gift. I die so poor that even the clothes I wear belong to the executioner who will cut off my head. I have nothing with which to ensure the good of my soul. Therefore I appeal to those of your worships who owe me money, as well as those who do not, to grant me the alms and charity of having as many masses as possible said for my soul, for I place hopes in God that by the blood and passion of Our Lord Jesus Christ, His Son, and through the alms that your worships grant me, He will have pity of me and will pardon my sins. And may your worships remain with God.

Garcilaso de la Vega, *Historia general del Perú*, Buenos Aires, 1944, 3 vols., II, pp. 276–277. (Excerpt translated by the editor.)

Before he had finished his plea for alms, there arose a general lament, with great moans and sobs and tears, from those who heard his pitiful words. Gonzalo Pizarro kneeled before the crucifix that he bore, and which was placed on a table on the platform. The executioner, who was named Juan Enríquez, came up to place a bandage over his eyes. Gonzalo Pizarro said to him: "I do not need it." And when he saw that Enriquez was raising the sword to cut off his head, he said: "Do your task well, brother Juan." He meant that he should do the job cleanly, and not prolong the agony, as frequently happens. The executioner replied: "I promise it to your Lordship." Saying this, with his left hand he raised his beard, which was long, about eight inches, and round, for it was not the fashion in those days to clip beards. And with one back stroke he cut off his head as easily as if it were a lettuce leaf and held it in his hand, and the body fell slowly to the ground. Such was the end of this good gentleman. The executioner, true to his trade, wanted to despoil him of his clothing, but Diego Centeno, who had come to inter the body safely, forbade him to approach it and promised him a good sum of money for the clothing. And so they bore the body to Cuzco; they buried Pizarro in his clothes, for there was no one to offer him a burial shroud. They buried him in the Convent of Nuestra Señora de las Mercedes, in the same chapel where were buried the two Don Diegos de Almagro, father and son, in order that they might be equal and comrades in all things—in their common conquest of the land, in the common death of all three on the executioner's block, and in the pauper's burial of all three in a common grave, as if they even lacked earth enough to cover each one separately. Fortune made them equal in all things, as if to prevent any one of them from lording it over the others and as if to prevent all three from setting themselves above the Marquis Francisco Pizarro, who was brother of the one and comrade of the other and who was likewise slain and buried in a pauper's grave, as was told above. Thus all four were brothers and comrades in all and for all. Such is the way of the world (as those remarked who viewed these matters dispassionately) with those who serve it most and best, for such was the end of those who won that empire called Peru.

10. ADVICE TO A WOULD-BE CONQUEROR

The conquest of the Americas, like similar enterprises before and after, or like our own gold rushes, attracted a wide variety of people. A common figure in the conquest was the adventurer, who frequently had a military background and not infrequently a past that he preferred to forget. Such, assuredly, were the "fine-feathered birds and great talkers" that Oviedo warns against below. But there were also many young and high-spirited hidalgos, "men of good family who were not reared behind the plow," who sailed in the ships bound for the Indies. In the matter of motives, it is probably safe to assume that of the trinity of motives usually assigned to the Spanish conquistador (God, gold, and glory), the second was uppermost in the minds of most.

Sir captain: Understand me and understand yourself. When you make up a company to go to the Indies, and especially in Seville (for it is there, on the steps of the cathedral, that the soldiers are wont to gather), you should first examine the face of each; having scrutinized the face, you will see part of the evil beneath. But because the outward aspect may deceive you in the choice of a soldier, you should make secret inquiry concerning his habits, his mode of life, his skills, and his nationality; for even in that sacred place[2] there are some who will lie about their countries and even their own names for the sake of going to the Indies. And do not attach much importance to his height and his well-combed beard, but rather try to find out whether he is of good character and family, and a frank and modest man. And if he tells you that he was in the battle of Ravenna, dismiss him, if he is a Spaniard, since he remained alive or was not taken prisoner; and do the same if he speaks of the battle of Pavia; and dismiss him if he tells you that he was in the sack of Genoa or Rome, since he did not get rich; and if he was there, and gambled his wealth away or lost it, do not trust him. Those slashed hose and shoes will not do at all for such lands as the Indies, full of ambushes and thick with trees and hawthorns, where there are so many rivers to swim and so many swamps and bogs to cross.

The dress and the person should conform to your needs; above all do not take a man whose faith is suspect, or one less than twenty-five or more than fifty years old. And do not take such fine-feathered birds and great talkers as those I mentioned above, for in the many years that I have seen them in the Indies, and before that in Europe, I have found that few turn out well. As long as there is gold, or they suspect that they will get it through your hands, they will serve you diligently; but be careful, for the minute that things do not go their way they will either slay you or sell you or forsake you, when they find that you promised them more in Spain than you can produce. ...

And before you begin this examination, examine yourself, and make sure that your aim is to serve God and your king by converting the Indians and treating them well, and by finding a way to lead them to the Republic of Christ. Do not enslave them without cause, or stain your hands with blood without cause or justice, or rob them or remove them from the lands where God created them; he gave them life and humanity not to help you carry out any evil design but in order to save them. ... And do not say that you are going to the Indies to serve the king and to employ your time as a brave man and an *hidalgo* should; for you know that the truth is just the opposite; you are

---

Oviedo y Valdés, *Historia general*, V, pp. 213–218. (Excerpt translated by the editor.)

going solely because you want to have a larger fortune than your father and your neighbors. However, you can do everything you want to do without hurting others or jeopardizing your soul. And do not seek any estate or treasure that might cost you such a price, if in so doing you lose that invaluable treasure by which you were redeemed and God freed you from Hell. ...

Comrade and friend: If you decide to go to the Indies, when you are in Seville ascertain first of all whether the captain with whom you are going is a man who will fulfill what he promises, and learn on the basis of what word or guaranty you are entrusting your life and person to his will—because many of these captains promise what they do not have, know, or understand; and they pay for your person with words that are worth less than feathers; because feathers, though the wind bear them away, at least have some substance and you know their purpose, which is to float in the air aimlessly; but the words of a liar are without substance and, having been said, are invisible and vanish like air. ... Do you not see that he speaks of what is yet to come, and promises what he neither has nor understands? And once you are free of the perils of the sea and the land, which are innumerable, and come to the Indies, if he should succeed, he neither knows nor rewards you; and if you fall ill, he does not heal you; and if you should die, he will not bury you. ... And if he gives you an allotment of Indians, he does not care to ascertain whether you are competent to teach them or whether you yourself have more need of a teacher than of governing others, in order that both your consciences may be at rest. And since these estates are acquired unjustly, God permits them to be lost, and you with them. ...

I observe that for every man who has made his fortune in these parts and has returned to Castile with or without it, an incomparably larger number have lost both their fortunes and their lives. You will say: What should I do? Shall I hold back from going to the Indies, where so many go and return rich—men who were formerly poor and do not measure up to me in ability, merit, or capacity for work? Is it fitting that for lack of courage I should fail to do what so many have done who are older than I and not of such good health and presence? I do not counsel you not to go to the Indies, nor to go there; but I do counsel you, whether you come or not, first to justify yourself with God and to commend yourself to Him. I am aware that it is proper and necessary to seek one's fortune, especially for men of good family who were not reared behind the plow; but let the undertaking be well thought out, and once you have determined upon it, never let greed turn you aside from the loyalty that you owe, and never let necessity give occasion for you to be considered an ingrate or to tarnish your good name; for if you only set your mind to it, in the Indies as elsewhere you can live without offense to your fellowmen.

11. JOURNEY'S END

Of the many bold captains who rode under the banner of Castile to the conquest of the Americas, few lived to enjoy in peace and security the fruits of their valor, their suffer- ings, and their cruelties. "He that killeth with the sword must be killed with the sword," recalled the old conquistador *Oviedo. Certainly there was a kind of poetic justice about the ends met by such notorious and hardened Indian slave-catchers and tormentors as Balboa, Ponce de León, and Pedro de Alvarado. Oviedo presents a partial roll call of the great* adelantados, *or leaders of conquering expeditions, and relates the ends to which they came.*

I do not like the title of *adelantado,* for actually that honor and title is an evil omen in the Indies, and many who bore it have come to a pitiable end. So it was with Don Bartholomew Columbus, the first adelantado in the Indies, brother of the first admiral, who left behind him neither heirs nor any other enduring thing. Look at Ponce de León, adelantado of Florida, slain by the Indians; the adelantado Rodrigo de Bastidas, treacherously slain by the dag- ger blows of his own soldiers; the adelantado Diego Velásquez, who spent in- finite sums on the discovery of New Spain, only to see another enjoy it and himself disappointed. Consider Vasco Núñez de Balboa, adelantado of the South Sea, and its first discoverer, who was beheaded as a traitor, and others with him, although they were all innocent of treason; the adelantado Lucas Vasquez de Ayllón, his Majesty's judge on the Royal Audience that sits here in Santo Domingo, who spent his estate and died in the discovery of a certain province that was given him in the northern regions, and whose body was flung in the sea; Francisco de Garay, adelantado of Panuco, who wasted his substance in arming and going to settle a land he knew nothing of, and who lost everything and finally died, although some say he was poisoned.

Antonio Sedeño spent much money on the conquest of Trinidad and Meta, and in the end was ruined and died disastrously; Diego de Ordaz, somewhat madder than the others, left and lost all he had and sought to settle the River Marañón, and in the end, departing for Spain, died and was cast in the sea; the adelantado Hernando de Soto, governor of the isle of Cuba, after return- ing to Spain loaded with gold, went to settle the mainland [of North America] and died there, leaving no trace or memory of himself. The adelan- tado Simón de Alcazaba was treacherously slain by his soldiers; the adelan- tado Diego de Almagro died a good and Catholic death; and, finally, his com- rade Francisco Pizarro and his brothers, especially Hernando Pizarro, were

---

Oviedo y Valdés, *Historia general,* V, pp. 150–152. (Excerpt translated by the editor.)

slain against all reason and justice by those who were not their judges—but there is another world after this.

The adelantado Francisco Pizarro, later a marquis, was wickedly slain by his enemies and soldiers; the adelantado Pedro de Heredia, governor of Cartagena, is still alive, and no one can tell how he will end; a worse fate than others befell the adelantado Francisco de Orellana, who went to the River Marañón in search of the tribe of the Amazons—or, to put it better, in search of death, although he did not know it—and so met his end at the mouth of the river. ... The adelantado Pedro de Mendoza went to the River Plate and wasted and lost all he had, and sailing for Spain, died and was cast into the sea; the adelantado Pánfilo de Narváez and his followers suffered an even worse fate, for some were eaten by their fellows, and of six hundred men only three escaped, while Narváez drowned in the sea; the adelantado Pedro de Alvarado lived and died violently, for his horse rolled down a steep hill, with him helplessly entangled underneath, and dragged him from cliff to cliff, leaving him in such a state that he died soon after, but not before receiving the Sacraments like a good Catholic. ...

And thus, prudent reader, you may see what sort of title is that of adelantado, that leaves in such conditions those who have held it in the Indies; and it seems to me that after what I have said of the adelantados named above, no man of sound sense will seek to obtain this title in that part of the world.

12. LOPE DE AGUIRRE: AN UNDERDOG OF THE CONQUEST

The principal instrument of Spain's conquest of the New World was the compaña *(warrior band), whose members shared in the profits of an expedition or campaign according to their rank and services. Despite the ostensibly democratic aspect of the campaigns, the captains, large investors, and royal officials dominated the enterprise of conquest and took the lion's share of spoils, land, and Indians for themselves, often leaving the rank-and-file conquistadors seething with discontent. Typical in some respects of the disinherited of the Conquest was the famous Lope de Aguirre, who called himself el* Peregrino, *the Wanderer. In 1581 a mutiny headed by Aguirre resulted in the death of the leader of an expedition sent from Peru in search of a fabled golden kingdom in the Amazonian wilderness. Aguirre now launched an audacious plan to descend the Amazon to the Atlantic, capture Panama, and then cross the Andes for the conquest of Peru and the creation of an independent Peruvian state that would properly reward old conquistadors like himself. Aguirre's wildly improbable plan was doomed to fail, but before his death at the hands of his own men he sent King Philip II a letter that offers a vision of the society created by the Conquest as seen by its underdogs, bitter over their betrayal by the great captains, the viceroys, cunning* letrados *or judges, and their king. Despite its rambling tone, the letter is marked by the originality and power of its style.*

To King Philip, native of Spain and son of Charles the Invincible. From Lope de Aguirre, the least of your vassals, an Old Christian, of middling parents but an hidalgo, native of the Basque country of the kingdom of Spain and citizen of the town of Oñate.

In my youth I crossed the sea to better my fortunes, lance in hand, and to fulfill the obligation of all good men. In twenty-four years I have done you great service in Peru, in the conquest of Indians, in founding towns, and especially in battles and skirmishes waged in your name, always to the best of my ability, without requesting of your officials pay or assistance, as will appear from your royal records.

I firmly believe, most excellent King and Lord, that to me and my comrades you have been cruel and ungrateful; I also believe that you are deceived by those who write you from these distant lands.

I demand, King, that you deal justly with the good vassals that you have in this land, though I and my comrades, ... unable to bear further the cruelties of your judges, viceroys, and governors, have resolved to obey you no longer. Renouncing allegiance to Spain, our native land, we make the cruelest war against you that our forces permit. Believe me, King and Lord, that we do this because we can no longer suffer the great oppression and unjust punishments of your ministers, who in order to benefit their sons and hangers-on have robbed us of our good name, honor, and life. Truly, King, it is a pity, the bad treatment we have received.

I am lame in the right leg from two arquebus wounds I received in the battle of Chuquinga, fighting with Marshal Alonso de Alvarado in response to your call against Francisco Hernández Girón, a rebel against your rule as I and my comrades presently are and will remain until death, for we know now how cruel and faithless you are and give less credit to your promises than to the books of Martin Luther. For we remember how your viceroy the Marquis de Cañete hanged Martín de Robles, a man distinguished in your service; and the brave Tomás Vazquez, conquistador of Peru; and the unhappy Alonso Díaz, who labored more in the discoveries of this kingdom than the scouts of Moses in the desert; and Piedrahita, a good captain who fought many battles in your service. In the battle of Pucara these men brought you victory, and

---

Casto Fulgencio López, *Lope de Aguirre el Peregrino, Primer Caudillo de América*, Barcelona, 1977, pp. 234–240. I am grateful to Professor Thomas Holloway of Cornell University for calling my attention to the peculiar interest of the Aguirre episode and allowing me to use his translation of Aguirre's letter. —B.K.

had they not, Francisco Hernández would now be king of Peru. And do not believe what your judges tell you about the great services they have rendered you, for it is all a myth, unless it is a service to have spent 800,000 pesos from your royal treasury on their vices and misdeeds. Punish them as the wicked men they are.

Look here, King of Spain! Do not be so cruel and ungrateful to your vassals, for while your father and you stayed in Spain, free from care, your vassals have won for you all the kingdoms and lordships that you possess in these parts at the cost of their blood and fortune. Consider, King, that you cannot justly take any wealth from these lands where you risked nothing until you have properly rewarded those who gained them for you with their toil and sweat.

I am certain that very few kings go to hell, because there are so few of you, but even if there were many, none would go to heaven. Even in hell, you would be worse than Lucifer, because you all thirst after human blood. ... For certain, I and my 200 arquebus-bearing ... conquistadors and hidalgos solemnly swear to God that we will not leave a minister of yours alive, for we know what your clemency amounts to. We who live in these parts of the Indies consider ourselves the luckiest men alive, for we observe the Christian faith and commandments of God in full and uncorrupted, maintaining all that is preached by the holy mother church of Rome, and though sinners in life we are ready to suffer martyrdom in defense of God's commandments. ...

So great is the dissolution of the friars in these parts that it would be well for you to make them feel your wrath and punishment, for each acts as high and mighty as if he were a governor. And do not believe what they tell you in Spain, for the tears they shed in your royal presence are in the hope of coming here in order to lord over all. If you want to know what sort of life they lead here, it is to buy and sell, acquire worldly goods, and sell the sacraments of the church for a price. They are enemies of the poor, without charity, ambitious, gluttonous, and arrogant, so that even the humblest friar seeks to command and govern all these lands. Correct these things, King and Lord, for by their bad example they weaken the faith of the natives, and if the dissolution of these friars is not checked, it will be a never-ending source of scandal.

If I and my comrades, for the reasons given above and on account of other things that have happened in the past, have determined to die, you, King, have been the cause thereof because you felt no pity for the toil of your vassals and gave no thought to what you owe them. If you do not look after your vassals and close your eyes to the actions of your judges, your government will surely fail. I do not need to present witnesses; consider only what I tell you. Each of your judges receives an annual salary of 4,000 pesos, and an expense allowance of 8,000 pesos, yet at the end of three years in office each has saved up 60,000 pesos, not to speak of their estates and other possessions.

Withal, if they were content to be served as ordinary mortals, we would be willing to serve them as we do, but for our sins they want us to drop to our knees whenever we meet them and worship them like Nebuchadnezzar. This is intolerable. As one who has suffered and was made lame in your service (and my comrades have grown old and weary in the same), I must warn you not to entrust your royal conscience to those lawyers. It is in your royal interest to keep a sharp eye on them, for they spend all their time planning the marriages of their children, and think of nothing else. The common refrain among them is, "To the left and the right, I claim all in my sight."

The friars here will not bury the poor Indians, and they have the best estates in Peru. The life they lead is truly hard and burdensome, for by way of penance each keeps a dozen young women in his kitchen and as many boys busy with fishing, hunting partridges, and gathering fruit. They must have a share of everything. As a good Christian, I swear, King and Lord, that if you do not correct the evils of this land, you must suffer the divine wrath. I say these things that you may know the truth, though I and my comrades neither expect nor want mercy from you. ...

Ah, what a pity it is that the Emperor, your father, should have conquered proud Germany with the power of Spain and spent so much money from the Indies discovered by us, and that you do not care enough about our old age and weariness to satisfy our hunger for a single day! ...

The captains and other officers whom I lead at present and who promise to die in this enterprise, being men who have suffered great injury, ... pray to God our Lord that you be victorious in your struggle against the French and the Turks and all others who wish to wage war against you in those parts. In these parts, may God grant that we obtain by force of arms the reward that is by right due us, but that you have denied.

A son of your loyal Basque vassals and rebel until death against you for your ingratitude.

Lope de Aguirre, the Wanderer

4

THE EVOLUTION OF
SPAIN'S INDIAN POLICY

DEVISING A WORKABLE labor system for the American colonies was the central problem of Spain's Indian policy. The situation created on the island of Hispaniola by the arrival of Columbus's second expedition has been aptly summed up in the phrase "hell on Hispaniola." Columbus, anxious to prove to the crown the value of his discoveries, compelled the natives to bring in a daily tribute of gold dust. When the Indians revolted they were hunted down, and hundreds were sent to Spain as slaves. Later, yielding to the demand of rebellious settlers for Indian slaves, Columbus distributed the Indians among them in *repartimientos*, or shares, with the grantee enjoying the right to use the forced labor of his Indians. This system, formalized under the administration of Governor Nicolás de Ovando and sanctioned by the crown, became the *encomienda*.

In operation, the *encomienda* in the West Indies became a hideous slavery. The first voices raised against this state of affairs were raised by a company of Dominican friars who arrived on Hispaniola in 1510. Their spokesman was Father Antonio Montesinos, who on Advent Sunday 1511 ascended the church pulpit to threaten the Spaniards with damnation for their offenses against the Indians.

The agitation begun by the Dominicans raised the larger question of the legality of Spain's claim to the Indies. To satisfy the royal conscience, the jurist Doctor Palacios Rubios drew up a document, the *requerimiento*, which was supposed to be read by all conquistadores to the Indians before making war upon them. This document called upon the Indians to acknowledge the supremacy of the church and the pope and the sovereignty of the Spanish monarchs over their lands by virtue of the papal donation of the Indies to Spain in 1493. The Indians were threatened with the disasters of war and enslavement if they refused to acknowledge Spain's hegemony over them.

The famous Bartolomé de las Casas now joined the struggle against the *encomienda* and the doctrines of Palacios Rubios. He won a brilliant but largely illusive victory in the promulgation of the New Laws of 1542. Faced with revolt in Peru and the threat of revolts elsewhere, the Spanish crown offered the colonists a compromise. The laws forbidding enslavement and forced personal service by *encomienda* Indians were reaffirmed, but the right of *encomenderos* to continue collecting fixed amounts of tribute from the natives was confirmed. The crown, however, rejected the demand that the *encomienda* be made hereditary, and the gradual reversion of the *encomiendas* to the crown paved the way for the institution's extinction. But in some regions, such as Paraguay and Chile, the *encomienda* survived almost to the end of the colonial period.

Indian forced labor, once it was legally separated from the *encomienda*, soon appeared in another form. The demand of the colonists for cheap labor was satisfied by legal conscription of Indians, who worked in shifts or relays. But the system was inefficient and could not satisfy the needs of an ever-growing number of Spanish employers for Indian labor. From an early date, therefore, Spanish landowners and other employers resorted to the use of so-called free or contractual labor; however, they often bound the Indians with advances of money and goods, thereby turning them into virtual serfs. In certain industries and areas, however, such as the silver mining area of northern New Spain and the silver mines of Potosí (Peru), more or less free labor came into fairly wide use.

1. THE STRANGE SERMON OF FATHER MONTESINOS

The struggle for justice for the American Indians was begun by a small group of Dominican friars, who were horrified by the sights that they daily saw on the island of Hispaniola. They delegated one of their number, Father Antonio Montesinos, to preach a sermon that would drive home to the Spanish settlers the wickedness of their deeds. Father Antonio's denunciation infuriated the townspeople, who called upon the Dominicans to retract their sentiments in next Sunday's sermon. Otherwise, the townspeople declared, the friars should pack up and get ready to sail for home. In reply, Father Montesinos mounted the pulpit the following Sunday and let loose a second and even more terrible blast against Spanish mistreatment of the Indians. Bartolomé de las Casas describes the opening round in the great controversy over Spain's Indian policy.

Bartolomé de las Casas, *Historia de las Indias*, Mexico, 1951, 3 vols., II, pp. 441–442. (Excerpt translated by the editor.)

Sunday having arrived, and the time for preaching, Father Antonio Montesinos rose in the pulpit, and took for the text of his sermon, which was written down and signed by the other friars, "I am the voice of one crying in the wilderness." Having made his introduction and said something about the Advent season, he began to speak of the sterile desert of the consciences of the Spaniards on this isle, and of the blindness in which they lived, going about in great danger of damnation and utterly heedless of the grave sins in which they lived and died.

Then he returned to his theme, saying, "In order to make your sins known to you I have mounted this pulpit, I who am the voice of Christ crying in the wilderness of this island; and therefore it behooves you to listen to me, not with indifference but with all your heart and senses; for this voice will be the strangest, the harshest and hardest, the most terrifying that you ever heard or expected to hear."

He went on in this vein for a good while, using cutting words that made his hearers' flesh creep and made them feel that they were already experiencing the divine judgment. ... He went on to state the contents of his message.

"This voice," said he, "declares that you are in mortal sin, and live and die therein by reason of the cruelty and tyranny that you practice on these innocent people. Tell me, by what right or justice do you hold these Indians in such cruel and horrible slavery? By what right do you wage such detestable wars on these people who lived mildly and peacefully in their own lands, where you have consumed infinite numbers of them with unheard-of murders and desolations? Why do you so greatly oppress and fatigue them, not giving them enough to eat or caring for them when they fall ill from excessive labors, so that they die or rather are slain by you, so that you may extract and acquire gold every day? And what care do you take that they receive religious instruction and come to know their God and creator, or that they be baptized, hear mass, or observe holidays and Sundays?

"Are they not men? Do they not have rational souls? Are you not bound to love them as you love yourselves? How can you lie in such profound and lethargic slumber? Be sure that in your present state you can no more be saved than the Moors or Turks who do not have and do not want the faith of Jesus Christ."

Thus he delivered the message he had promised, leaving his hearers astounded. Many were stunned, others appeared more callous than before, and a few were somewhat moved; but not one, from what I could later learn, was converted.

When he had concluded his sermon he descended from the pulpit, his head held high, for he was not a man to show fear, of which indeed he was totally free; nor did he care about the displeasure of his listeners, and instead did and said what seemed best according to God. With his companion he went to their straw-thatched house, where, very likely, their entire dinner was cabbage soup, unflavored with olive oil. ... After he had left, the church was so full of murmurs that ... they could hardly complete the celebration of the mass.

2. THE LAUGHTER
OF DOCTOR PALACIOS RUBIOS

The dispute about Indian policy that had begun on the island of Hispaniola and was carried to Spain by the contending parties stimulated discussion of a fundamental question: By what right did Spain claim to rule over the Americas and wage war on their native peoples? The strong tradition of legalism in Spanish life and history as well as the pious professions of the Catholic Sovereigns required that a satisfactory reply be devised to this query. King Ferdinand, who is not particularly remembered by historians for scrupulosity in dealing with his fellow European monarchs, summoned a committee of theologians to deliberate on the matter. The fruit of their discussions was the famous requerimiento, *drawn up by Doctor Palacios Rubios. This document called upon the Indians to acknowledge the supremacy of the church, the pope, and the Spanish kings and to permit the faith to be preached to them. Not until they had rejected these demands, which would be made known to them by interpreters, could war be legally waged on them. The chronicler Gonzalo Fernández de Oviedo y Valdés, who accompanied the expedition of Pedrarias Dávila to the South American mainland in 1514, records in his great history the first use made of the Requirement, and the ironic laughter of Doctor Palacios Rubios as he listened to Oviedo's account of his experience with this curious manifesto.*

After crossing this river we entered a village of some twenty huts; we found it deserted, and the general entered one of the houses, accompanied by all the captains who were there, by the licentiate Espinosa, who was the royal comptroller, factor, and governor, and by his lieutenant Juan de Ayora, and in the presence of all I said to him: "Sir, it seems to me that these Indians do not care to hear the theology of this requirement, nor do you have anyone who can make them understand it. Your worship had better put this paper away until we have caught an Indian and put him in a cage, where he can gradually master its meaning, and the bishop can help to make it clear to him."

And I gave the general the requirement, and he took it, amid the hearty laughter of all who were there. While we were all resting in those huts, waiting for the sun to go down, our sentinels gave the alarm at about two o'clock in the afternoon. And down a very wide and handsome road, bordered with

---

Gonzalo Fernández de Oviedo y Valdés, *Historia general y natural de las Indias*, Asunción, Paraguay, 1944–1945, 14 vols., VII, pp. 131–132. (Excerpt translated by the editor.)

many trees that had been planted for adornment, came more than a thousand Indian bowmen, with much noise and blowing on certain large shells which are called *cobos* and are heard at a great distance. ...

The general quickly left the village to meet the Indians on the road and arrayed his men in battle formation, each line separated from the other by a distance of two hundred paces. He also ordered a bronze cannon of about two hundred pounds to be loaded. Two greyhounds, highly praised by their masters, were to be placed on our wings; we were to fire when he gave the signal; and at that instant the dogs should be loosed and we were all to fall upon the enemy and conduct ourselves like valiant men.

I should have preferred to have that requirement explained to the Indians first, but no effort was made to do so, apparently because it was considered superfluous or inappropriate. And just as our general on this expedition failed to carry out this pious proceeding with the Indians, as he was supposed to do before attacking them, the captains of many later expeditions also neglected the procedure and did even worse things, as will be seen. Later, in 1516, I asked Doctor Palacios Rubios (who had written that proclamation) if the consciences of the Christians were satisfied with that requirement, and he said yes, if it were done as the proclamation required. But I recall that he often laughed when I told him of that campaign and of others that various captains later made. I could laugh much harder at him and his learning (for he was reputed to be a great man, and as such had a seat on the Royal Council of Castile), if he thought that the Indians were going to understand the meaning of that requirement until many years had passed.

3. BARTOLOMÉ DE LAS CASAS:
GOD'S ANGRY MAN

Among the many personalities who intervened in the great controversy about Spain's Indian policy, the figure of Bartolomé de las Casas (1484–1566) has grown most in stature with the passing of the centuries. The world generally knows him best for his flaming tract against Spanish cruelty to the Indians, the Brief Account of the Destruction of the Indies *(1552), a work soon translated into most of the languages of Europe and joyously used by Spain's imperialist rivals to discredit its colonial enterprise. Recent studies in the social history of colonial Latin America tend to confirm las Casas' claims of large preconquest Indian populations and his thesis that a catastrophic population decline occurred as a result of the Conquest. Typical of the tone and contents of the* Brief Account *is its description of the Spanish conquest of Cuba.*

"The Brevissima Relación," in Francis A. McNutt, *Bartholomew de las Casas*, New York, 1909, Appendix I, pp. 328–332. Reprinted by permission of the publishers, G. P. Putnam's Sons.

In the year 1511 the Spaniards passed over to the island of Cuba, which as I said, is as long as from Valladolid to Rome, and where there were great and populous provinces. They began and ended in the above manner, only with incomparably greater cruelty. Here many notable things occurred.

A very high prince and lord, named Hatuey, who had fled with many of his people from Hispaniola to Cuba, to escape the calamity and inhuman operations of the Christians, having received news from some Indians that the Christians were crossing over, assembled many or all of his people, and addressed them thus.

"You already know that it is said the Christians are coming here; and you have experience of how they have treated the lords so and so and those people of Hayti (which is Hispaniola); they come to do the same here. Do you know perhaps why they do it?" The people answered no; except that they were by nature cruel and wicked. "They do it," said he, "not alone for this, but because they have a God whom they greatly adore and love; and to make us adore Him they strive to subjugate us and take our lives." He had near him a basket full of gold and jewels and he said: "Behold here is the God of the Christians, let us perform *Areytos* before Him, if you will (these are dances in concert and singly); and perhaps we shall please Him, and He will command that they do us no harm."

All exclaimed: it is well! it is well! They danced before it, till they were all tired, after which the lord Hatuey said: "Note well that in any event if we preserve the gold, they will finally have to kill us to take it from us: let us throw it into this river." They all agreed to this proposal, and they threw the gold into a great river in that place.

This prince and lord continued retreating before the Christians when they arrived at the island of Cuba, because he knew them, but when he encountered them he defended himself; and at last they took him. And merely because he fled from such iniquitous and cruel people, and defended himself against those who wished to kill and oppress him, with all his people and offspring until death, they burnt him alive.

When he was tied to the stake, a Franciscan monk, a holy man, who was there, spoke as much as he could to him, in the little time that the executioner granted them, about God and some of the teachings of our faith, of which he had never before heard; he told him that if he would believe what was told him, he would go to heaven where there was glory and eternal rest; and if not, that he would go to hell, to suffer perpetual torments and punishment. After thinking a little, Hatuey asked the monk whether the Christians went to heaven; the monk answered that those who were good went there. The prince at once said, without any more thought, that he did not wish to go there, but rather to hell so as not to be where Spaniards were, nor to see such cruel people. This is the renown and honour, that God and our faith have acquired by means of the Christians who have gone to the Indies.

On one occasion they came out ten leagues from a great settlement to meet us, bringing provisions and gifts, and when we met them, they gave us a great quantity of fish and bread and other victuals, with everything they could supply. All of a sudden the devil entered into the bodies of the Christians, and in my presence they put to the sword, without any motive or cause whatsoever, more than three thousand persons, men, women, and children, who were seated before us. Here I beheld such great cruelty as living man has never seen nor thought to see.

Once I sent messengers to all the lords of the province of Havana, assuring them that if they would not absent themselves but come to receive us, no harm should be done them; all the country was terrorized because of the past slaughter, and I did this by the captain's advice. When we arrived in the province, twenty-one princes and lords came to receive us; and at once the captain violated the safe conduct I had given them and took them prisoners. The following day he wished to burn them alive, saying it was better so because those lords would some time or other do us harm. I had the greatest difficulty to deliver them from the flames but finally I saved them.

After all the Indians of this island were reduced to servitude and misfortune like those of Hispaniola, and when they saw they were perishing inevitably, some began to flee to the mountains; others to hang themselves, together with their children, and through the cruelty of one very tyrannical Spaniard whom I knew, more than two hundred Indians hanged themselves. In this way numberless people perished.

There was an officer of the King in this island, to whose share three hundred Indians fell, and by the end of the three months he had, through labour in the mines, caused the death of two hundred and seventy; so that he had only thirty left, which was the tenth part. The authorities afterwards gave him as many again, and again he killed them: and they continued to give, and he to kill, until he came to die, and the devil carried away his soul.

In three or four months, I being present, more than seven thousand children died of hunger, their fathers and mothers having been taken to the mines. Other dreadful things did I see.

Afterwards the Spaniards resolved to go and hunt the Indians who were in the mountains, where they perpetrated marvellous massacres. Thus they ruined and depopulated all this island which we beheld not long ago; and it excites pity, and great anguish to see it deserted, and reduced to a solitude.

4. ALL HUMANKIND IS ONE

What was perhaps las Casas' finest hour came in 1550 when he rose to answer the eminent humanist Juan Ginés de Sepúlveda (1490?–1572?), author of a treatise that sought to prove that wars against the Indians were just. The background of the great debate, held before a junta of theologians summoned by Charles V to decide the matter, was a general reaction in the Spanish court against las Casas' liberal views, as signaled by the partial repeal of the New Laws of 1542. The foundation of las Casas' argument was his eloquent affirmation of the equality of all races, the essential oneness of humankind. The first of the following extracts is from Sepúlveda's treatise on the subject of Indian wars; the second is taken from las Casas' Apologetical History of the Indies.

Now compare these [Spanish] traits of prudence, intelligence, magnanimity, moderation, humanity, and religion with the qualities of these little men in whom you will scarcely find even vestiges of humanity; who not only are devoid of learning but do not even have a written language; who preserve no monuments of their history, aside from some vague and obscure reminiscense of past events, represented by means of certain paintings; and who have no written laws but only barbaric customs and institutions. And if we are to speak of virtues, what moderation or mildness can you expect of men who are given to all kinds of intemperance and wicked lusts, and who eat human flesh?

And do not believe that before the coming of the Christians they lived in that peaceful reign of Saturn that the poets describe; on the contrary, they waged continuous and ferocious war against each other, with such fury that they considered a victory hardly worth while if they did not glut their monstrous hunger with the flesh of their enemies, a ferocity all the more repellent since it was not joined to the invincible valor of the Scythians, who also ate human flesh. For the rest, these Indians are so cowardly that they almost run at the sight of our soldiers, and frequently thousands of them have fled like women before a very few Spaniards, numbering less than a hundred. ...

Could one give more convincing proof of the superiority of some men to others in intelligence, spirit, and valor, and of the fact that such people are slaves by nature? For although some of them display a certain talent for craftsmanship this is not proof of human intelligence, for we know that animals, birds, and spiders do certain work that no human industry can completely imitate. And as regards the mode of life of the inhabitants of New Spain and the province of Mexico, I have already said that they are considered the most civilized of all. They themselves boast of their public institutions, for they have cities constructed in an orderly fashion, and kings, not hereditary but elected by popular vote; and they carry on commerce among themselves in the manner of civilized people.

But see how they deceive themselves, and how much I disagree with their opinion, for in these same institutions I see proof on the contrary of the rudeness, the barbarism, and the inherently slavish nature of these people. For the possession of habitations, of a fairly rational mode of life, and of a kind of commerce is something that natural necessity itself induces, and only

---

Juan Ginés de Sepúlveda, *Tratado sobre las justas causas de la guerra contra los indios*, México, 1941, pp. 105–113. (Excerpt translated by the editor.)

serves to prove that they are not bears or monkeys and are not completely devoid of reason. But on the other hand, they have no private property in their state, and they cannot dispose of or bequeath to their heirs their houses or fields, since they are all in the power of their lords, whom they improperly call kings, at whose pleasure, rather than at their own, they live, attentive to their will and caprice rather than to their own freedom. And the fact that they do all this in a voluntary and spontaneous manner and are not constrained by force of arms is certain proof of the servile and abased spirit of these barbarians. ...

Such, in sum, are the disposition and customs of these little men—barbarous, uncivilized, and inhumane; and we know that they were like this before the coming of the Spaniards. We have not yet spoken of their impious religion and of the wicked sacrifices in which they worshiped the devil as their God, believing that they could offer no better tribute than human hearts. ... How can we doubt that these peoples, so uncivilized, so barbarous, contaminated with so many infidelities and vices, have been justly conquered by such an excellent, pious, and just king as the late Ferdinand the Catholic, and the present Emperor Charles, and by a nation that is most humane and excels in every kind of virtue?

∾   ∾   ∾

From these examples, both ancient and modern, it is clear that no nation exists, no matter how rude and uncivilized, barbarous, gross, savage or almost brutal it may be, that cannot be persuaded into a good way of life and made domestic, mild, and tractable—provided that diligence and skill are employed, and provided that the method that is proper and natural to men is used: namely, love and gentleness and kindness. ...

For all the peoples of the world are men, and the definition of all men, collectively and severally, is one: that they are rational beings. All possess understanding and volition, being formed in the image and likeness of God; all have the five exterior senses and the four interior senses, and are moved by the objects of these; all have the natural capacity or faculties to understand and master the knowledge that they do not have; and this is true not only of those that are inclined toward good but of those that by reason of their depraved customs are bad; all take pleasure in goodness and in happy and pleasant things; and all abhor evil and reject what offends or grieves them. ...

Thus all mankind is one, and all men are alike in what concerns their creation and all natural things, and no one is born enlightened. From this it follows that all of us must be guided and aided at first by those who were born

Bartolomé de las Casas, *Apologética historia de las Indias*, Madrid, 1909, pp. 128–129. (Excerpt translated by the editor.)

before us. And the savage peoples of the earth may be compared to unculti-vated soil that readily brings forth weeds and useless thorns, but has within itself such natural virtue that by labor and cultivation it may be made to yield sound and beneficial fruits.

5. INDIAN FORCED LABOR
IN GUATEMALA

Las Casas died in 1566, at the age of eighty-two, in a convent outside Madrid. Three Spanish kings had listened respectfully to his advice on Indian affairs, had sometimes acted upon that advice, and in their Indian legislation gave pious lip service to the prin-ciples he advocated. But the realities of colonial existence overruled the voice of morality and religion. Legal slavery and personal service under the encomienda *system had largely disappeared by 1600 in New Spain and Peru, but their place had been effectively taken by a system of labor conscription under which all adult male Indians were required to give a certain amount of their time to work in mines, factories, and on farms, ranches, and public works, receiving a small wage for their labor. In New Spain this institution was known as the* repartimiento. *Its operation in this area is described by Thomas Gage (1600?–1656), an observant though highly biased Englishman who spent twelve years as a priest in Guatemala before turning apostate and coming home to write an anti-Spanish book about his experiences.*

The miserable condition of the Indians of that country is such that though the Kings of Spain have never yielded to what some would have, that they should be slaves, yet their lives are as full of bitterness as is the life of a slave. For which I have known myself some of them that have come home from toiling and moiling with Spaniards, after many blows, some wounds, and little or no wages, who have sullenly and stubbornly lain down upon their beds, resolving to die rather than to live any longer a life so slav-ish, and have refused to take either meat or drink or anything else comfort-able and nourishing, which their wives have offered unto them, that so by pining and starving they might consume themselves. Some I have by good persuasions encouraged to life rather than to a voluntary and wilful death; others there have been that would not be persuaded, but in that wilful way have died.

The Spaniards that live about that country (especially the farmers of the Valley of Mixco, Pinola, Petapa, Amatitlan, and those of the Sacatepequez) allege that all their trading and farming is for the good of the common-

Thomas Gage, *The English-American: A New Survey of the West Indies,* edited by A. P. Newton, London, 1946, pp. 230–233.

wealth, and therefore whereas there are not Spaniards enough for so ample and large a country to do all their work, and all are not able to buy slaves and blackamoors, they stand in need of the Indians' help to serve them for their pay and hire; whereupon it hath been considered that a partition of Indian labourers be made every Monday, or Sunday in the afternoon to the Spaniards, according to the farms they occupy, or according to their several employments, calling, and trading with mules, or any other way. So that for such and such a district there is named an officer, who is called *juez repartidor*, who according to a list made of every farm, house, and person, is to give so many Indians by the week. And here is a door opened to the President of Guatemala, and to the judges, to provide well for their menial servants, whom they commonly appoint for this office, which is thus performed by them. They name the town and place of their meeting upon Sunday or Monday, to which themselves and the Spaniards of that district do resort. The Indians of the several towns are to have in a readiness so many labourers as the Court of Guatemala hath appointed to be weekly taken out of such a town, who are conducted by an Indian officer to the town of general meeting; and when they come thither with their tools, their spades, shovels, bills, or axes, with their provision of victuals for a week (which are commonly some dry cakes of maize, puddings of *frijoles*, or French beans, and a little chilli or biting long pepper, or a bit of cold meat for the first day or two) and with beds on their backs (which is only a coarse woolen mantle to wrap about them when they lie on the bare ground) then are they shut up in the town-house, some with blows, some with spurnings, some with boxes on the ear, if presently they go not in.

Now all being gathered together, and the house filled with them, the *juez repartidor*, or officer, calls by the order of the list such and such a Spaniard, and also calls out of the house so many Indians as by the Court are commanded to be given him (some are allowed three, some four, some ten, some fifteen, some twenty, according to their employments) and delivereth unto the Spaniard his Indians, and so to all the rest, till they be all served; who when they receive their Indians, take from them a tool, or their mantles, to secure them that they run not away; and for every Indian delivered unto them, they give unto the *juez repartidor*, or officer, half a real, which is three-pence an Indian for his fees, which mounteth yearly to him to a great deal of money; for some officers make a partition or distribution of four hundred, some of two hundred, some of three hundred Indians every week, and carrieth home with him so many half hundred reals for one, or half a day's work. If complaint be made by any Spaniard that such and such an Indian did run away from him, and served him not the week part, the Indian must be brought, and surely tied to a post by his hands in the marketplace, and there be whipped upon his bare back. But if the poor Indian complain that the Spaniards cozened and cheated him of his shovel, axe, bill, mantle, or wages no justice shall be executed against the cheating Spaniard, neither shall the

Indian be righted, though it is true the order runs equally in favour of both Indian and Spaniard. Thus are the poor Indians sold for threepence apiece for a whole week's slavery, not permitted to go home at nights unto their wives, though their work lie not above a mile from the town where they live; nay some are carried ten or twelve miles from their home, who must not return till Saturday night late, and must that week do whatsoever their master pleaseth to command them. The wages appointed them will scarce find them meat and drink, for they are not allowed a real a day, which is but sixpence, and with that they are to find themselves, but for six days' work and diet they are to have five reals, which is half a crown. This same order is observed in the city of Guatemala, and towns of Spaniards, where to every family that wants the service of an Indian or Indians, though it be but to fetch water and wood on their backs, or to go of errands, is allowed the like from the nearest Indian towns.

6. DEBT PEONAGE IN PERU

The repartimiento, *known in Peru as the* mita, *did not provide Spanish employers with a dependable and continuing supply of labor. As a result, they turned increasingly to the use of free or contractual wage labor. From the first, however, this so-called free labor was associated with debt servitude. An advance of money or goods required an Indian to work for his employer until his debt was paid, often reducing him and his descendants to the condition of virtual slaves or serfs. Debt peonage became extremely widespread in the seventeenth and eighteenth centuries. The Spanish royal officials Jorge Juan and Antonio de Ulloa offer a precise description of how debt peonage, superimposed on* mita *obligations, operated in the Peruvian province of Quito in the first half of the eighteenth century.*

On farming haciendas, an Indian subject to the *mita* earns from fourteen to eighteen pesos a year, the wage varying with the locality or *corregimiento*. In addition, the *hacendado* assigns him a piece of land, about twenty to thirty rods square in size, to grow his food. In return the Indian must work three hundred days in the year, leaving him sixty-five days of rest for Sundays, other church holidays, illness, or some accident that may prevent him from working. The *mayordomo* of the *hacienda* keeps careful record of the days worked by the Indian in order to settle accounts with him at the end of the year.

Jorge Juan and Antonio de Ulloa, *Noticias secretas de América*, Madrid, 1918, 2 vols., I, pp. 290–292.

From his wage the master deducts the eight pesos of royal tribute that the Indian must pay; assuming that the Indian earns eighteen pesos, the most he can earn, he is left with ten pesos. From this amount the master deducts two pesos, two reales to pay for three rods of coarse cloth, costing six reales a rod, from which the Indian makes a cloak to cover his nakedness. He now has seven pesos, six reales with which to feed and dress his wife and children, if he has a family, and to pay the church fees demanded by the parish priest. But this is not all; since he cannot raise on his little plot all the food he needs for his family, he must get from the hacendado each month a half *fanega* of maize, costing six reales, more than double the price if he could buy elsewhere. Six reales, times twelve, come to nine pesos, which is one peso, six reales more than the Indian has left. Thus the unhappy Indian, after working three hundred days of the year for his master and cultivating his little plot in his free time, and receiving only a coarse cloak and six *fanegas* of maize, is in debt one peso and six reales, and must continue to work for his master the following year. . . .

If, to crown his misfortunes, his wife or a child should die, he must somehow find the burial fee demanded by the priest, and so turns to the *hacendado* for another advance. If he is spared the pain of losing a member of his family, the priest demands that he show his gratitude by paying for another church ceremony in honor of the Virgin or some saint, which requires another loan. Thus, at year's end, without money or anything else of value having passed through his hands, the Indian owes his master more than he has earned. The *hacendado* then claims legal control over the Indian and compels him to work for him until the debt is paid. Since it is impossible for the poor Indian to do so, he remains a slave all his life and, contrary to natural law and the law of nations, after his death his sons must continue to work to pay the debt of their father.

5

THE ECONOMY

OF THE SPANISH INDIES

THE ECONOMIC LIFE of the Spanish American colonies reflected both New and Old World influences. Side by side with the subsistence-and-tribute economy of the Indians, there arose a Spanish commercial agriculture producing foodstuffs or raw materials for sale in local or distant markets. To some extent this agriculture served internal markets, as in the mining areas of Mexico and Peru, or intercolonial trade, as in the case of the wine industry of Peru, but its dominant trait, which became more pronounced with the passage of time, was that of production for export to European markets. Spain imposed certain restrictions on colonial agriculture, in the mercantilist spirit of the age, but this legislation was largely ineffective.

Stock-raising was another important economic activity in the colonies. The introduction of domestic animals represented a major Spanish contribution to American economic life, because the ancient Americas, aside from a limited region of the Andes, had no domestic animals for use as food or in transportation. By 1600 the export of hides from Hispaniola to Spain had assumed large proportions, and meat had become so abundant on the island that the flesh of slain wild cattle was generally left to rot. The export of hides also became important during the seventeenth century in the Plate area (modern Argentina and Uruguay).

Mining, as the principal source of royal revenue, received the special attention and protection of the crown. Silver, rather than gold, was the principal product of the American mines. The great mine of Potosí in Upper Peru was discovered in 1545; the rich mines of Zacatecas and Guanajuato in New Spain were opened up in 1548 and 1558 respectively. Silver mining was greatly stimulated in 1556 by the introduction of the patio process for separating silver from the ore with quicksilver. As in other times and places, the mining industry brought prosperity to a few and either failure or small success to the great majority.

The Spaniards found a flourishing handicrafts industry in the advanced culture in Mexico, Central America, and Peru. Throughout the colonial period the majority of the natives continued to supply their own needs for pottery, clothing, and other household requirements. With the coming of the Spaniards new manufacturing industries arose in the towns, stimulated by the high prices of imported Spanish goods. The artisans were organized in guilds (from which Indians were excluded as masters), which included silversmiths, goldbeaters, weavers, and the like.

The period up to 1700 also witnessed a remarkable growth of factory-type establishments (*obrajes*) that produced cheap cotton and woolen goods for popular consumption. A number of towns in New Spain (Puebla, Guadalajara, Cholula, and others) were centers of the textile industry. Other factory-type establishments produced soap, chinaware, leather, and other products. Internal and intercolonial trade, based on regional specialization and particularly on the rise of mining centers that consumed large quantities of agricultural produce and manufacturers, steadily increased in the sixteenth and seventeenth centuries.

1. THE INDIAN AGRICULTURAL HERITAGE

The Indian contributions to colonial and world agriculture were extremely rich and varied. A partial list of these contributions includes such important products as maize, the potato and sweet potato, pineapple, peanut, cultivated strawberry, lima and kidney beans, squash and pumpkin, cacao, rubber, and tobacco. To Europeans of the era of colonization, some of the new American plants appeared to have strange and possibly supernatural qualities. The learned Jesuit José de Acosta (1539?–1600) sought to satisfy Spanish curiosity about the natural productions of the New World in his scientific and historical work, the Natural and Moral History of the Indies *(1590). Among the plants described by Father Acosta are maize, the Indian staff of life; cacao, source of the refreshing chocolate drink first used by the Maya; coca, the magic plant that imparted endurance to the weary frame of the Peruvian Indian; and maguey, the Mexican tree of wonders.*

Turning to plants, I shall speak first of those which are more peculiar to the Indies and afterwards of those which are common both to those lands and to Europe. And because plants were created principally for the maintenance of man, and man sustains himself above all by bread, I should speak first of their bread. ... The Indians have their own words to signify bread, which in

---

José de Acosta, *Historia natural y moral de las Indias*, Mexico, 1940, pp. 265–266, 285–289. (Excerpt translated by the editor.)

Peru is called *tanta* and in other parts is given other names. But the quality and substance of the bread the Indians use is very different from ours, for they have no kind of wheat, barley, millet, panic grass, or any grain such as is used in Europe to make bread. Instead they have other kinds of grains and roots, among which maize, called Indian wheat in Castile and Turkey grain in Italy, holds the first place.

And just as wheat is the grain most commonly used by man in the regions of the Old World, which are Europe, Asia, and Africa, so in the New World the most widely used grain is maize, which is found in almost all the kingdoms of the West Indies; in Peru, New Spain, the New Kingdom of Granada, Guatemala, Chile, and in all the Tierra Firme. In the Windward Isles, which are Cuba, Hispaniola, Jamaica, Puerto Rico, it does not seem to have been used in earlier times; to this day they prefer to use yucca and cassava, of which more later. I do not think that maize is at all inferior to our wheat in strength and nourishment; but it is stouter and hotter and engenders more blood, so that if people who are not accustomed to it eat it in excess they swell up and get the itch.

Maize grows on canes or reeds; each one bears one or two ears, to which the grains are fastened, and though the grains are big they hold a large number of them, and some contain seven hundred grains. The seeds are planted one by one. Maize likes a hot and humid soil. It grows in many parts of the Indies in great abundance; a yield of three hundred *fanegas* from a sowing is not uncommon. There are various kinds of maize, as of wheat; one is large and nourishing; another, called *moroche*, is small and dry. The leaves of the maize and the green cane are a choice fodder for their beasts of burden, and when dry are also used as straw. The grain gives more nourishment to horses than barley, and therefore it is customary in those countries to water their horses before giving them maize to eat, for if they drank after feeding they would swell up and have gripes, as they do when they eat wheat.

Maize is the Indian bread, and they commonly eat it boiled in the grain, hot, when it is called *mote* ... ; sometimes they eat it toasted. There is a large and round maize, like that of the Lucanas, which the Spaniards eat as a delicacy; it has better flavor than toasted chickpeas. There is another and more pleasing way of preparing it, which consists in grinding the maize and making the flour into pancakes, which are put on the fire and later placed on the table and eaten piping hot; in some places they call them *arepas*. ...

Maize is used by the Indians to make not only their bread but also their wine; from it they make beverages which produce drunkenness more quickly than wine made of grapes. They make this maize wine in various ways, calling it *azua* in Peru and more generally throughout the Indies *chicha*. The strongest sort is made like beer, steeping the grains of maize until they begin to break, after which they boil the juice in a certain way, which makes it so strong that a few drinks will produce intoxication. In Peru, where it is called *sora*, its use is forbidden by law because of the terrific drinking it occasions.

But the law is little observed, for they use it anyway, and stay up whole days and nights, dancing and drinking. ...

The cacao tree is most esteemed in Mexico and coca is favored in Peru; both trees are surrounded with considerable superstition. Cacao is a bean smaller and fattier than the almond, and when roasted has not a bad flavor. It is so much esteemed by the Indians, and even by the Spaniards, that it is the object of one of the richest and largest lines of trade of New Spain; since it is a dry fruit, and one that keeps a long time without spoiling, they send whole ships loaded with it from the province of Guatemala. Last year an English corsair burned in the port of Guatulco, in New Spain, more than one hundred thousand *cargas* of cacao. They also use it as money, for five cacao beans will buy one thing, thirty another, and one hundred still another, and no objections are made to its use. They also use it as alms to give to the poor.

The chief use of this cacao is to make a drink that they call chocolate, which they greatly cherish in that country. But those who have not formed a taste for it dislike it, for it has a froth at the top and an effervescence like that formed in wine by dregs, so that one must really have great faith in it to tolerate it. In fine, it is the favorite drink of Indians and Spaniards alike, and they regale visitors to their country with it; the Spanish women of that land are particularly fond of the dark chocolate. They prepare it in various ways: hot, cold, and lukewarm. They usually put spices and much chili in it; they also make a paste of it, and they say that it is good for the chest and the stomach, and also for colds. Be that as it may, those who have not formed a taste for it do not like it.

The tree on which this fruit grows is of middling size and well-made, with a beautiful top; it is so delicate that to protect it from the burning rays of the sun they plant near it another large tree, which serves only to shade it; this is called the mother of the cacao. There are cacao plantations where it is raised as are the vine and the olive in Spain. The province of Guatemala is where they carry on the greatest commerce in this fruit.

The cacao does not grow in Peru; instead they have the coca, which is surrounded with even greater superstition and really seems fabulous. In Potosí alone the commerce in coca amounts to more than 5,000,000 pesos, with a consumption of from 90 to 100,000 hampers, and in the year 1583 it was 100,000. ... This coca that they so greatly cherish is a little green leaf which grows upon shrubs about one *estado* high; it grows in very warm and humid lands and produces this leaf, which they call *trasmitas*, every four months. Being a very delicate plant, it requires a great deal of attention during cultivation and even more after it has been picked. They pack it with great care in long, narrow hampers and load it on the sheep of that country, which carry this merchandise in droves, bearing one, two, and three thousand hampers. It is commonly brought from the Andes, from valleys of insufferable heat, where it rains the greater part of the year, and it costs the Indians much labor and takes many lives, for they must leave their highlands and cold climates in order to cultivate it and carry it away. Hence there have been great disputes among lawyers and wise men about whether the coca plantations should be done away with or no—but there they still are.

The Indians prize it beyond measure, and in the time of the Inca kings plebeians were forbidden to use coca without the permission of the Inca or his governor. Their custom is to hold it in their mouths, chewing and sucking it; they do not swallow it; they say that it gives them great strength and is a great comfort to them. Many serious men say that this is pure superstition and imagination. To tell the truth, I do not think so; I believe that it really does lend strength and endurance to the Indians, for one sees effects that cannot be attributed to imagination, such as their ability to journey two whole days on a handful of coca, eating nothing else, and similar feats. ... All would be well, except that its cultivation and commerce endanger and occupy so many people. ...

The maguey is the tree of wonders, to which the newly-come Spaniards, or *chapetones* (as they call them in the Indies), attribute miracles, saying that it yields water and wine, oil and vinegar, honey, syrup, thread, needles, and a thousand other things. The Indians of New Spain value it greatly, and they commonly have one or several of these trees near their homes to supply their needs. It grows in the fields, and there they cultivate it. Its leaves are wide and thick, with strong, sharp points which they use as fastening pins or sewing needles; they also draw a certain fibre or thread from the leaves.

They cut through the thick trunk when it is tender; there is a large cavity inside, where the sap rises from the roots; it is a liquor which they drink like water, since it is fresh and sweet. When this liquor is boiled it turns into a kind of wine, and if it is left to sour it becomes vinegar. But when boiled for a longer time it becomes like honey, and cooked half as long it turns into a healthful syrup of good flavor, superior in my judgment to syrup made of grapes. Thus they boil different substances from this sap, which they obtain in great quantity, for at a certain season they extract several *azumbres* a day.

2. Spain's Contributions to New World Agriculture

The colonial era saw a notable exchange of agricultural gifts between the Old and the New Worlds. The Spanish crown displayed much solicitude for the agricultural development of the Indies and paid particular attention to the shipping of trees, plants, seeds, and agricultural implements of all kinds. Father Acosta gives an account of the transit of Spanish plants to America and of the rapid rise there of a commercial agriculture producing wine, wheat, sugar, and other products.

Acosta, *Historia natural y moral de las Indias*, pp. 311–315. (Excerpt translated by the editor.)

The Indies have been better repaid in the matter of plants than in any other kind of merchandise; for those few that have been carried from the Indies into Spain do badly there, whereas the many that have come over from Spain prosper in their new homes. I do not know whether to attribute this to the excellence of the plants that go from here or to the bounty of the soil over there. Nearly every good thing grown in Spain is found there; in some regions they do better than in others. They include wheat, barley, garden produce and greens and vegetables of all kinds, such as lettuce, cabbage, radishes, onions, garlic, parsley, turnips, carrots, eggplants, endive, salt-wort, spinach, chickpeas, beans, and lentils—in short, whatever grows well here, for those who have gone to the Indies have been careful to take with them seeds of every description. ...

The trees that have fared best there are the orange, lemon, citron, and others of that sort. In some parts there are already whole forests and groves of orange trees. Marvelling at this, I asked on a certain island who had planted so many orange trees in the fields. To which they replied that it might have happened that some oranges fell to the ground and rotted, whereupon the seeds germinated, and, some being borne by the waters to different parts, gave rise to these dense groves. This seemed a likely reason. I said before that orange trees have generally done well in the Indies, for nowhere have I found a place where oranges were not to be found; this is because everywhere in the Indies the soil is hot and humid, which is what this tree most needs. It does not grow in the highlands; oranges are transported there from the valleys or the coast. The orange preserve which is made in the islands is the best I have ever seen, here or there.

Peaches and apricots also have done well, although the latter have fared better in New Spain. ... Apples and pears are grown, but in moderate yields; plums give sparingly; figs are abundant, chiefly in Peru. Quinces are found everywhere, and in New Spain they are so plentiful that we received fifty choice ones for half a *real*. Pomegranates are found in abundance, but they are all sweet, for the people do not like the sharp variety. The melons are very good in some regions, as in Tierra Firme and Peru. Cherries, both wild and cultivated, have not so far prospered in the Indies. ... In conclusion, I find that hardly any of the finer fruits is lacking in those parts. As for nuts, they have no acorns or chestnuts, nor, as far as I know, have any been grown over there until now. Almonds grow there, but sparingly. Almonds, walnuts, and filberts are shipped there from Spain for the tables of epicures. I have not seen any medlars or services, but those do not matter. ...

By profitable plants I mean those plants which not only yield fruit but bring money to their owners. The most important of these is the vine, which gives wine, vinegar, grapes, raisins, verjuice, and syrup—but the wine is the chief concern. Wine and grapes are not products of the islands or of Tierra Firme; in New Spain there are vines which bear grapes but do not yield wine.

The reason must be that the grapes do not ripen completely because of the rains which come in July and August and hinder their ripening; they are good only for eating. Wine is shipped from Spain and the Canary Islands to all parts of the Indies, except Peru and Chile, where they have vineyards and make very good wine. This industry is expanding continually, not only because of the goodness of the soil, but because they have a better knowledge of winemaking.

The vineyards of Peru are commonly found in warm valleys where they have water channels; they are watered by hand, because rain never falls in the coastal plains, and the rains in the mountains do not come at the proper time. ... The vineyards have increased so far that because of them the tithes of the churches are now five and six times what they were twenty years ago. The valleys most fertile in vines are Victor, near Arequipa; Yca, hard by Lima; and Caracaro, close to Chuquiavo. The wine that is made there is shipped to Potosí and Cuzco and various other parts, and it is sold in great quantities, because since it is produced so abundantly it sells at five or six ducats the jug, or *arroba*, whereas Spanish wine (which always arrives with the fleets) sells for ten and twelve. ... The wine trade is no small affair, but does not exceed the limits of the province.

The silk which is made in New Spain goes to other provinces—to Peru, for example. There was no silk industry before the Spaniards came; the mulberry trees were brought from Spain, and they grow well, especially in the province called Misteca, where they raise silkworms and make good taffetas; they do not yet make damasks, satins, or velvets, however.

The sugar industry is even wider in scope, for the sugar not only is consumed in the Indies but is shipped in quantity to Spain. Sugar cane grows remarkably well in various parts of the Indies. In the islands, in Mexico, in Peru, and elsewhere they have built sugar mills that do a large business. I was told that the Nasca [Peru] sugar mill earned more than thirty thousand pesos a year. The mill at Chicama, near Trujillo [Peru], was also a big enterprise, and those of New Spain are no smaller, for the consumption of sugar and preserves in the Indies is simply fantastic. From the island of Santo Domingo, in the fleet in which I came, they brought eight hundred and ninety-eight chests and boxes of sugar. I happened to see the sugar loaded at the port of Puerto Rico, and it seemed to me that each box must contain eight *arrobas*. The sugar industry is the principal business of those islands—such a taste have men developed for sweets!

Olives and olive trees are also found in the Indies, in Mexico, and in Peru, but up to now they have not set up any mills to make olive oil. Actually, it is not made at all, for they prefer to eat the olives, seasoning them well. They find it unprofitable to make olive oil, and so all their oil comes from Spain.

3. THE POTOSÍ MINE

Spain's proudest possession in the New World was the great silver mine of Potosí in Upper Peru (present-day Bolivia), whose flow of treasure attained gigantic proportions between 1579 and 1635. More than any other colonial resource, the fantastic wealth of Potosí captivated the Spanish imagination. The following selection gives some account of this wealth and of mining practices in the late sixteenth century.

It appears from the royal accounts of the House of Trade of Potosí, and it is affirmed by venerable and trustworthy men, that during the time of the government of the licentiate Polo, which was many years after the discovery of the hill, silver was registered every Saturday to the value of 150 to 200,000 pesos, of which the King's fifth (*quinto*) came to 30 to 40,000 pesos, making a yearly total of about 1,500,000 pesos. According to this calculation, the value of the daily output of the mine was 30,000 pesos, of which the King's share amounted to 6,000 pesos. One more thing should be noted in estimating the wealth of Potosí; namely, that accounts have been kept of only the silver that was marked and taxed. But it is well known in Peru that for a long time the people of that country used the silver called "current," which was neither marked nor taxed. And those who know the mines well conclude that at that time the bulk of the silver mined at Potosí paid no tax, and that this included all the silver in circulation among the Indians, and much of that in use among the Spaniards, as I could observe during my stay in that country. This leads me to believe that a third—if not one half—of the silver production of Potosí was neither registered nor taxed. ... [It should also be noted that] although the mines of Potosí have been dug to a depth of two hundred *estados*, the miners have never encountered water, which is the greatest possible obstacle to profitable operations, whereas the mines of Porco, so rich in silver ore, have been abandoned because of the great quantity of water. For there are two intolerable burdens connected with the search for silver: the labor of digging and breaking the rock, and that of getting out the water—and the first of these is more than enough. In fine, at the present time His Catholic Majesty receives on the average a million pesos a year from his fifth of the silver of Potosí, not counting the considerable revenue he derives from quicksilver and other royal perquisites. ...

The hill of Potosí contains four principal veins: the Rich vein, that of Centeno, the vein called "of Tin," and that of Mendieta. All these veins are in the eastern part of the hill, as if facing the sunrise; there is no vein to the west. These veins run from north to south, or from pole to pole. They measure six feet at their greatest width, and a *palmo* at the narrowest point. From

Acosta, *Historia natural y moral de las Indias*, pp. 238–243. (Excerpt translated by the editor.)

these veins issue others, as smaller branches grow out of the arms of trees. Each vein has different mines that have been claimed and divided among different owners, whose names they usually bear. The largest mine is eighty yards in size, the legal maximum; the smallest is four yards. By now all these mines are very deep. In the Rich vein there are seventy-eight mines; they are as deep as one hundred and eighty and even two hundred *estados* in some places. In the Centeno vein there are twenty-four mines. Such are as much as sixty and even eighty *estados* deep, and the same is true of the other veins and mines of that hill. In order to work the mines at such great depths, tunnels (*socavones*) were devised; these are caves, made at the foot of the mountain, that cross it until they meet the veins. Although the veins run north to south, they descend from the top to the foot of the mountain—a distance calculated at more than 1200 *estados*. And by this calculation, although the mines run so deep it is six times as far again to their root and bottom, which some believe must be extremely rich, being the trunk and source of all the veins. But so far experience has proven the contrary, for the higher the vein the richer it is, and the deeper it runs the poorer the yield. Be that as it may, in order to work the mines with less cost, labor, and risk, they invented the tunnels, by means of which they can easily enter and leave the mines. They are eight feet wide and one *estado* high, and are closed off with doors. With the aid of these tunnels they get out the silver ore without difficulty, paying the owner of the tunnel a fifth of all the metal that is obtained. Nine tunnels have already been made, and others are being dug. A tunnel called "of the Poison" (*del Veneno*), which enters the Rich vein, was twenty-nine years in the making, for it was begun in 1556 (eleven years after the discovery of those mines) and was completed on April 11, 1585. This tunnel crossed the vein at a point thirty-five *estados* from its root or source, and from there to the mouth of the mine was 135 *estados*; such was the depth of that they had to descend to work those mines. This tunnel (called the *Crucero*) is 250 yards in length, and its construction took twenty-nine years; this shows how much effort men will make to get silver from the bowels of the earth. They labor there in perpetual darkness, not knowing day from night; and since the sun never penetrates these places, they are not only always dark but very cold, and the air is very thick and alien to the nature of men. And that is why those who enter there for the first time get seasick, as it were, being seized with nausea and stomach cramps, as I was. The miners always carry candles, and they divide their labor so that some work by day and rest by night and others work at night and rest during the day. The silver ore is generally of a flinty hardness, and they break it up with bars. Then they carry the ore on their backs up ladders made of three cords of twisted cowhide, joined by pieces of wood that serve as rungs, so that one man can climb up and another come down at the same time. These ladders are ten *estados* long, and at the top and bottom of each there is a wooden platform where the men may rest, because there are so many ladders to climb. Each man usually carries on his back a load of two *arrobas* of silver ore tied in a cloth, knapsack fashion; thus they ascend, three at a time. The one who goes first carries a candle tied to his thumb, because, as I mentioned, they receive no light from above; thus, holding with both hands, they climb that great distance, often more than 150 *estados*—a fearful thing, the mere thought of which inspires dread. So great is the love of silver, which men suffer such great pains to obtain.

4. THE COLONIAL FACTORY

The Mexican city of Puebla was a leading industrial center in the colonial period, with numerous workshops (obrajes) *producing cotton, woolen, and silk cloth, hats, chinaware, and glass. The Englishman Thomas Gage, who visited Puebla not many years after the visit described below, observed that "the cloth which is made in it ... is sent far and near, and [is] judged now to be as good as the cloth of Segovia, which is the best that is made in Spain."*

There are in this city large woolen mills in which they weave quantities of fine cloth, serge, and grogram, from which they make handsome profits, this being an important business in this country. ... To keep their mills supplied with labor for the production of cloth and grogram, they maintain individuals who are engaged and hired to ensnare poor innocents; seeing some Indian who is a stranger to the town, with some trickery or pretext, such as hiring him to carry something, like a porter, and paying him cash, they get him into the mill; once inside, they drop the deception, and the poor fellow never again gets outside that prison until he dies and they carry him out for burial. In this way they have gathered in and duped many married Indians with families, who have passed into oblivion here for 20 years, or longer, or their whole lives, without their wives or children knowing anything about them; for even if they want to get out, they cannot, thanks to the great watchfulness with which the doormen guard the exits. These Indians are occupied in carding, spinning, weaving, and the other operations of making cloth and grogram; and thus the owners make their profits by these unjust and unlawful means.

And although the Royal Council of the Indies, with the holy zeal which animates it for the service of God our Lord, of His Majesty, and of the Indians' welfare, has tried to remedy this evil with warrants and ordinances, which it constantly has sent and keeps sending, for the proper administration and the

---

Antonio Vásquez de Espinosa, *Description of the West Indies*, translated by C. U. Clark, Washington: The Smithsonian Institution, 1942, pp. 133–134.

amelioration of this great hardship and enslavement of the Indians, and the Viceroy of New Spain appoints mill inspectors to visit them and remedy such matters, nevertheless, since most of those who set out on such commissions, aim rather at their own enrichment, however much it may weigh upon their consciences, than at the relief of the Indians, and since the mill owners pay them well, they leave the wretched Indians in the same slavery; and even if some of them are fired with holy zeal to remedy such abuses when they visit the mills, the mill owners keep places provided in the mills in which they hide the wretched Indians against their will, so that they do not see or find them, and the poor fellows cannot complain about their wrongs. This is the usual state of affairs in all the mills of this city and jurisdiction, and that of Mexico City; the mill owners and those who have the mills under their supervision, do this without scruple, as if it were not a most serious mortal sin.

5. ON THE SEA-ROAD TO THE INDIES

Throughout the sixteenth century men and goods were carried to the colonies in much the same tiny vessels as those with which Columbus had made his memorable discovery. Danger and hardship attended the long voyage to the Indies from the time a ship left Seville to thread its careful way down the shoal-ridden Guadalquivir to the Mediterranean. Father Tomás de la Torre, one of a number of Dominican friars who accompanied Bishop Bartolomé de las Casas when the Protector of the Indians came to Mexico in 1544, describes the trials of an Atlantic crossing in the days of the galleons.

After boarding our ship we passed the day there, exposed to a burning sun. On the following day (July 10) we hoisted sails with a very feeble wind, because the sailors said that once on the high seas we could navigate with any kind of wind. That day all the other ships got off that difficult and dangerous sandbar at San Lucar. Only ours remained in the middle of the bar and its dangers. They put the blame on the land pilot; but it was really the fault of our sailors, who had ballasted the ship badly, loading all the cargo above deck. That day the fleet moved three leagues out, while we remained on the bar in front of the town, enduring miseries that made a good beginning to our labors and perils.

When the townspeople saw that the ship remained there they thought that something had happened, and the Duke [of Alba] sent a boat to express the regrets of himself and his lady, and to say that if boats were needed to get the

Fray Tomás de la Torre, *Desde Salamanca, España, hasta Ciudad Real, Chiapas, Diario del viaje,* 1544–1545, edited by Frans Blom, Mexico, 1945, pp. 70–73. (Excerpt translated by the editor.)

ship off the bar he would send them. But the crazy sailors, very haughty about all that concerned their business, wanted no help. The captain of the fleet sent a small vessel to let us know that he would wait for us only a day or two. ... The pilot and master of the ship, named Pedro de Ibarra, went to give an account of himself and to complain of the land pilot, who, in accordance with prevailing custom, is supposed to take the ships off the bar. ...

The following day, which was Friday, July 11, we raised sails and with perfectly dry eyes lost sight of our Spain. The wind was good but weak. The sea quickly gave us to understand that it was not meant to be the habitation of men, and we all became so deathly sick that nothing in the world could move us from where we lay. Only the Father Vicar and three others managed to keep their feet, but these three were so ill that they could do nothing for us; the Father Vicar alone served us all, placing basins and bowls before us so that we could bring up our scanty meals, which did us no good at all. There were four or five neophytes in our company, on their way to serve God in the Indies, who usually took care of us, but they also became sick and had to be nursed themselves. We could not swallow a mouthful of food, although we were quite faint, but our thirst was intense.

One could not imagine a dirtier hospital, or one that resounded with more lamentations, than ours. Some men went below deck, where they were cooked alive; others roasted in the sun on deck, where they lay about, trampled upon, humiliated, and indescribably filthy; and although after several days some of them had recovered, they were not well enough to serve those who were still sick. His Lordship the Bishop donated his own hens to the sick, for we had not brought any, and a priest who was going as a schoolteacher to Chiapa helped the Father Vicar. ... We were a pitiful sight indeed, and there was no one to console us, since nearly everyone was in the same condition.

When we left Spain the war with France was at its height, so we departed in great fear of the enemy. On the afternoon of that day those who could raise their heads saw sixteen sails. They feared that they were Frenchmen, and all that night the fleet was much alarmed, although the enemy had greater reason to fear us, because of our superior numbers. But in the morning nothing could be seen, so we decided it was a fleet coming from the Indies. ... In the evening our stomachs quieted down and we did not vomit, but the heat, especially below deck, was intolerable.

Saturday morning we saw a large boat, and, thinking that it was a French spy, a ship went after it. The bark began to escape, when the ship fired a shot, whereupon the bark lowered its sails, was recognized as Spanish, and was permitted to go in peace. The crews of the vessels that heard the shot thought that we had run into Frenchmen and that the ships were firing at each other. When we below deck heard the noise of arms being got ready, we were alarmed and suddenly recovered enough to say a litany; some even confessed themselves. Others made a joke of the whole affair. When we learned it was nothing at all, we returned to our former supine misery. After this there was no more disturbance.

So that those who do not know the sea may understand the suffering one endures there, especially at the beginning of a voyage, I shall describe some things that are well known to anyone who has sailed on it. First, a ship is a secure prison, from which no one may escape, even though he wears neither shackles nor irons; so cruel is this prison that it makes no distinctions among its inmates but makes them all suffer alike. The heat, the stuffiness, and the sense of confinement are sometimes overpowering. The bed is ordinarily the floor. Some bring a few small mattresses; ours were very poor, small, and hard, stuffed with dog hairs; to cover us we had some extremely poor blankets of goat's wool. Add to this the general nausea and poor health; most passengers go about as if out of their minds and in great torment—some longer than others, and a few for the entire voyage. There is very little desire to eat, and sweet things do not go down well; there is an incredible thirst, sharpened by a diet of hardtack and salt beef. The water ration is half an *azumbre* daily; if you want wine you must bring your own. There are infinite numbers of lice, which eat men alive, and you cannot wash clothing because the sea water shrinks it. There is an evil stink, especially below deck, that becomes intolerable throughout the ship when the pump is working—and it is going more or less constantly, depending on how the ship sails. On a good day the pump runs four or five times, to drain the foul-smelling bilge water.

These and other hardships are common on board ship, but we felt them more because they were so foreign to our usual way of living. Furthermore, even when you are enjoying good health there is no place where you can study or withdraw for a little while, and you have to sit all the time, because there is no room to walk about. ... The most disturbing thing of all is to have death constantly staring you in the face; you are separated from it by only the thickness of one board joined to another with pitch.

6. THE GREAT FAIR AT PORTOBELLO

After 1584 the chief port of entry for the legal commerce with South America was the little town of Portobello on the Isthmus of Panama. For a few weeks during the year a brisk trade, strictly supervised by royal officials, was plied in the town square. In the 1730s, when the Portobello fair was visited by two youthful Spanish scientists and naval officers, Jorge Juan (1713–1773), and Antonio de Ulloa (1716–1795), it had long passed its heyday, principally because of the growing influx of foreign interlopers into colonial trade, but it still presented a scene of considerable business activity.

The town of Porto Bello, so thinly inhabited, by reason of its noxious air, the scarcity of provisions, and the soil, becomes, at the time of the galleons, one of the most populous places in all South America. Its situation on the isthmus betwixt the south and north sea, the goodness of its harbour, and its small distance from Panama, have given it the preference for the rendezvous of the joint commerce of Spain and Peru, at its fair.

On advice being received at Carthagena, that the Peru fleet had unloaded at Panama, the galleons make the best of their way to Porto Bello, in order to avoid the distempers which have their source from idleness. The concourse of people, on this occasion, is such, as to raise the rent of lodging to an excessive degree; a middling chamber, with a closet, lets, during the fair, for a thousand crowns, and some large houses for four, five, or six thousand.

The ships are no sooner moored in the harbour, than the first work is, to erect, in the square, a tent made of the ship's sails, for receiving its cargo; at which the proprietors of the goods are present, in order to find their bales, by the marks which distinguish them. These bales are drawn on sledges, to their respective places by the crew of every ship, and the money given them is proportionally divided.

Whilst the seamen and European traders are thus employed, the land is covered with droves of mules from Panama, each drove consisting of above an hundred, loaded with chests of gold and silver, on account of the merchants of Peru. Some unload them at the exchange, others in the middle of the square; yet, amidst the hurry and confusion of such crowds, no theft, loss, or disturbance, is ever known. He who has seen this place during the *tiempo muerto*, or dead time, solitary, poor, and a perpetual silence reigning everywhere; the harbour quite empty, and every place wearing a melancholy aspect; must be filled with astonishment at the sudden change, to see the bustling multitudes, every house crowded, the square and streets encumbered with bales and chests of gold and silver of all kinds; the harbour full of ships and vessels, some bringing by the way of Rio de Chape the goods of Peru, as cacao, quinquina, or Jesuit's bark, Vicuña wool, and bezoar stones; others coming from Carthagena, loaded with provisions; and thus a spot, at all other times detested for its deleterious qualities, becomes the staple of the riches of the old and new world, and the scene of one of the most considerable branches of commerce in the whole earth.

The ships being unloaded, and the merchants of Peru, together with the president of Panama, arrived, the fair comes under deliberation. And for this purpose the deputies of the several parties repair on board the commodore of the galleons, where, in presence of the commodore, and the president of Panama; the former, as patron of the Europeans, and the latter, of the

Jorge Juan and Antonio de Ulloa, *A Voyage to South America*, London, 1772, 2 vols., I, pp. 103–105.

Peruvians; the prices of the several kinds of merchandizes are settled; and all preliminaries being adjusted in three or four meetings, the contracts are signed, and made public, that every one may conform himself to them in the sale of his effects. Thus all fraud is precluded. The purchases and sales, as likewise the exchanges of money, are transacted by brokers, both from Spain and Peru. After this, every one begins to dispose of his goods; the Spanish brokers embarking their chests of money, and those of Peru sending away the goods they have purchased, in vessels called chatas and bongos, up the river Chagre. And thus the fair of Porto Bello ends.

Formerly this fair was limited to no particular time; but as a long stay, in such a sickly place, extremely affected the health of the traders, his Catholic majesty transmitted an order, that the fair should not last above forty days, reckoning from that in which the ships came to an anchor in the harbour; and that, if in this space of time the merchants could not agree in their rates, those of Spain should be allowed to carry their goods up the country to Peru; and accordingly the commodore of the galleons has orders to reimbark them, and return to Carthagena; but otherwise, by virtue of a compact between the merchants of both kingdoms, and ratified by the king, no Spanish trader is to send his goods, on his own account, beyond Porto Bello: and, on the contrary, those of Peru cannot send remittances to Spain, for purchasing goods there.

7. A FOREIGN VIEW OF THE SPANISH COMMERCIAL SYSTEM

By the opening of the eighteenth century it was apparent to thoughtful Spaniards and foreign observers alike that the Spanish commercial policy in the colonies was a dismal failure from the point of view of Spain's general interests. The English publicist John Campbell offered a shrewd analysis of the reasons for this failure.

There is nothing more common than to hear Spain compared to a sieve, which, whatever it receives is never the fuller. How common soever the comparison may be, most certainly it is a very true one; but the means by which all this immense wealth, or at least the far greatest part of it is drawn from the Spaniards, and conveyed to other nations, and in what proportions, is neither so well, nor so generally understood. To account for this shall be our present task. ...

If after the discovery of the New World, as the Spaniards justly enough called it, the government had encouraged trade or manufactures, there is

John Campbell, *The Spanish Empire in America*, London, 1747, pp. 291–299.

great probability that the supreme direction of the affairs of Europe would have fallen into the hands of the Catholic Kings. For, if all the subjects of Spain, without restraint, had traded to these far distant regions, this must have created such a maritime force, as no other nation could have withstood. Or, supposing the trade had been restrained as it is at present, yet, if manufactures had been encouraged, so as that the greatest part of the trade of the West Indies had been driven without having recourse to foreigners, such prodigious sums of money must have rested in Spain, as would have enabled its monarchs to have given law to all their neighbours. But, by neglecting these obvious, and yet certain rules for establishing solid and extensive at least, if not universal dominion, her kings had recourse to those refinements in policy, which, however excellent they may seem in theory, have never yet been found to answer in practice. They were for fixing their commerce by constraint, and for establishing power by the sword; the first, experience has shewn to be impracticable, and the latter, perhaps was the only method whereby they could have missed that end they used it to obtain. In short, by repeated endeavours to secure the wealth of the Indies to Spain absolutely, they scattered it throughout Europe, and by openly grasping at universal monarchy, they alarmed those they might have subdued; so that in process of time, some of those they intended for slaves became their equals and allies, and some their masters.

Yet the princes that took these steps were not either rash and hasty, or voluptuous and profuse, but, on the contrary, were esteemed by all the world the wisest monarchs of their respective times, and, in many things deserved to be so esteemed. They erred, not through want of capacity, or want of application, as their successors did, but for want of considering things in a right light, occasioned purely by their fixing their eyes on that dazzling meteor, universal empire. ...

From what has been said it is evident, that however wise, however penetrating these princes might be, they certainly overshot themselves in their schemes concerning the Western Indies. Instead of looking upon it as an estate, they seemed to think it only a farm, of which they were to make presently the most they could. In doing this, it must be owned, they acted with skill and vigour, for they drew immense sums from thence, which they wasted in Europe to disturb others, and in the end to destroy their own state. Mr. Lewis Roberts, author of the *Map of Commerce*, an excellent book for the time in which it was written, tells us, that it appeared by the records in the custom-house of Seville, that in the space of seventy-four years, computing backwards from the time in which he wrote, the kings of Spain had drawn into that country from America, two hundred and fifty millions of gold, which make about ninety-one millions sterling. He also observes that ... Philip II ... spent more in his reign than all his predecessors in the whole of their respective reigns; though no less than 62 kings had reigned before him. Yet this cunning, this ambitious monarch left his subjects in a manner quite exhausted, and, by establishing a most pernicious system of politics, left the total ruining of his dominions by way of legacy to his successors, a point which with wonderful obstinacy they have pursued ever since.

All who are in any degree acquainted with the history of Europe know, that for a long course of years Spain maintained wars in Flanders, Germany, Italy, and sometimes in Ireland, which created a prodigious expense of treasure and of troops; neither of which from the death of Charles V they were in any condition to spare. As families were reduced by the expense of serving in the army, they were inclined to seek new fortunes in the West Indies: and thus numbers went over thither, not to cultivate the country, or to improve trade, but to strip and plunder those who were there before them. Other great families again concurred with the measures of the crown, in hopes of vice-royalties, and other valuable offices in its conquests: but if ever their schemes were beneficial to their families, which may admit of doubt, certain it is that they contributed more and more to the ruin of the Spanish nation. For, though his Catholic Majesty once possessed Naples, Sicily, Sardinia, Milan, with other territories in Italy, besides all the Low Countries, and some other provinces which are now lost; yet, for want of attending to commerce, and by having no sort of economy, all this turned to his prejudice; and it plainly appeared towards the close of the last century, that with all their boasted sagacity and firmness, the Spaniards had ruined themselves by acquiring too great power, and rendered themselves beggars by misusing their immense riches. With swelling titles and wide dominions, they were despicably weak, and scarce any but copper money was to be seen in a country, which received above twenty millions annually from its plantations.

Before I quit this topic, I must take notice of another thing, which is certainly very extraordinary. This wrong turn in the Spanish policy had a wonderful effect; it made all the enemies of that nation rich, and all its friends poor. Everybody knows that the United Provinces not only made themselves free and independent, but rich and powerful also, by their long war with Spain. Our maritime power was owing to the same cause. If Philip II had not disturbed Queen Elizabeth, our fleet might have been as inconsiderable at the close of her reign as it was at the beginning, when we were pestered with pirates even in the narrow seas. Our plantations abroad were in a great measure owing to expeditions against the Spaniard. Our manufactures at home were the consequence of affording refuge to the king of Spain's protestant subjects. When Queen Elizabeth's successor closed with Spain, he suffered by it, while France, the only country then at war with Spain, was a gainer. I say nothing of Cromwell's breach with Spain, and the advantages he drew from it because the world seems well enough apprized of all I could say on that subject already. ...

By so long a series of mismanagement the Spaniards have brought their affairs into so wretched a situation, that they neither have, nor can have any very great benefit from their vast dominions in America. They are said to be stewards for the rest of Europe; their Galleons bring the silver into Spain, but neither wisdom nor power can keep it there; it runs out as fast as it comes in, nay, and faster; insomuch that the little Canton of Bern is really richer, and has more credit, than the king of Spain, notwithstanding his Indies. At first sight this seems to be strange and incredible; but when we come to examine it, the mystery is by no means impenetrable. The silver and rich commodities which come from the Indies come not for nothing (the king's duties excepted) and very little of the goods or manufactures for which they come, belong to the subjects of the crown of Spain. It is evident, therefore, that the Spanish merchants are but factors, and that the greatest part of the returns from the West Indies belong to those foreigners for whom they negotiate.

6

GOVERNMENT AND CHURCH

IN THE SPANISH INDIES

THE COUNCIL of the Indies, chartered in 1524, stood at the head of the Spanish imperial administration almost to the close of the colonial period. Under the king the council was the supreme legislative, judicial, and executive institution of colonial government. The principal royal agents in the colonies were the viceroys, the captains-general, and the *audiencias*. Viceroys and captains-general had essentially the same functions; these differed only in accordance with the greater importance and size of the territory assigned to the viceroyalty. Each viceroy or captain-general was assisted in the performance of his duties by an *audiencia*, which was the highest court of appeal in its district and also served as the viceroy's council of state.

Provincial administration in the Indies was entrusted to royal officials who governed districts of varying size and importance from their chief towns and who were commonly called *corregidores* or *alcaldes mayores*. The only political institution in the Indies that at all satisfied local aspirations to self-government was the town council, generally known as the *cabildo*. Despite its undemocratic character, inefficiency, and waning prestige and autonomy, the *cabildo* had potential significance. As the only political institution in which the Creoles (American-born Spaniards) were largely represented, it was destined to play an important role in the Creole seizure of power in the coming age of revolution.

The controlling influence of the Catholic church in the social and spiritual life of the colonies was deeply rooted in the Spanish past. Royal control over ecclesiastical affairs, in both Spain and the Indies, was founded on the institution of the *patronato real* (royal patronage). As applied to the colonies, this patronage consisted in the absolute right of the Spanish kings to nominate all church officials, collect ecclesiastical tithes, and found churches and monasteries in the Americas.

Beginning with Columbus's second voyage, one or more clergymen accompanied every expedition that sailed for the Indies. They converted prodigious numbers of natives, and some championed the rights of the Indians against their Spanish oppressors. But many of the later arrivals preferred a life of ease and profit to one of austerity and service. From first to last, the colonies were a scene of strife between regulars and secular clergy about their fields of jurisdiction. The regular clergy were members of the religious orders; the secular clergy made up the ecclesiastical hierarchy from the archbishop to the parish priest. The missionary impulse of the first friars survived longest on the frontier, "the rim of Christendom." The most notable instance of successful missionary effort, at least from an economic point of view, was that of the Jesuit missions in Paraguay.

The Inquisition was established in the Indies by Philip II in 1569. Its independence of other courts, the secrecy of its proceedings, and the dread with which the charge of heresy was regarded made the Inquisition an effective check on "dangerous thoughts," religious, political, or philosophical. Most cases tried by its tribunals, however, concerned not heresy, which was often punished with burning at the stake and confiscation of property, but offenses against morality or minor deviations from orthodox religious conduct, usually punished with much lighter penalties.

1. THE STRUCTURE OF
COLONIAL GOVERNMENT

The shifting pattern of Spain's administration of the Indies in the sixteenth century reflected the steady growth of centralized rule in Spain itself and the application of a trial-and-error method to the problems of colonial government. By the middle of the century the political organization of the Indies had assumed the definitive form that it was to retain, with slight variations, until late in the eighteenth century. The Mexican historian and statesman Lucas Alamán (1792–1853) included an informative sketch of colonial governmental institutions in his classic History of Mexico. *His account, although somewhat abstract and idealized, suggests Alamán's sympathy with the old Spanish regime, but gains much value from his familiarity with the colonial climate of opinion in which he passed his youth and early manhood.*

Among the many kingdoms and lordships that were united in the kings of Spain by inheritance, marriage, and conquest were included the *East and West Indies, islands, and Tierra firme of the Ocean Sea*, the name given to the im-

Lucas Alamán, *Historia de Méjico*, Mexico, 1849–1852, 5 vols., I, pp. 31–34, 40–43. (Excerpt translated by the editor.)

mense possessions that these kings held on the continent of America and adjacent islands, the Philippine Islands, and others in the eastern seas. These vast dominions were ruled by special laws promulgated in various times and circumstances and later brought together in a code called the *Compilation of Laws of the Kingdoms of the Indies*, authorized by King Charles II on May 18, 1680. At the same time the monarch ordered that all the decrees and orders given to the audiencias that did not contravene the compiled laws should continue in force, and that where these laws did not suffice those of Castile, known as the Laws of Toro, should apply.

The discovery and conquest of America coincided with the changes that Charles V made in the fundamental laws of Castile and that his son Philip completed by destroying the *fueros* [privileges] of Aragón. The *cortes* of Castile, Aragón, Valencia, and Catalonia, which formerly had met separately, were transformed and gradually declined in importance until they were reduced to a meeting in Madrid of some representatives or deputies of a few cities of Castile and Aragón, solely for the ceremony of acknowledging and taking the oath of allegiance to the heirs to the throne. All the high functions of government, both legislative and administrative, were vested in the councils, of which there were established in Madrid as many as the monarchy had parts. These councils were in no way dependent upon each other, and had no other relation to each other than that of being under a single monarch. Thus there was the Council of Castile, which was called "royal and supreme" and which the kings had always maintained, though in different forms, to aid them with its advice, and with whose concurrence the dispositions of the monarch had the force of laws, *as if they were proclaimed in the cortes*, a phrase that filled the gap caused by the disappearance of these bodies.

There were also Councils of Aragón, Flanders, and Italy, in addition to those which had jurisdiction over particular departments, such as the Council of the Inquisition, over matters of faith; the Council of the Orders, for the towns that belonged to the military orders of knighthood; and that of the *Mesta*, for the problems arising from the migratory herds of sheep. When, at the beginning of the eighteenth century, the monarchy was reduced in Europe by the War of the Spanish Succession to the Spanish peninsula and adjacent islands, the first three councils were suppressed. Although these councils were endowed with great powers, they derived their authority entirely from that of the monarch, in whose name they performed all their acts and who was the fountainhead and first principle of all power.

Although the Indies were incorporated in the crown of Castile, "from which they could not be alienated totally or in part, under any condition, or in favor of any person," its government was not on that account made at all dependent on the council established for that kingdom; on the contrary, particular care was taken to establish for the colonies a government entirely independent and separate from the Council of Castile. In 1542 was created "the Council of the Indies," to which were assigned the same exemptions and privileges enjoyed by that of Castile; the same power of making laws in consultation with the king; and the same supreme jurisdiction in the East and West Indies and over their natives, even though resident in Castile, subjecting to it the audiencia of the commerce of Seville and expressly forbidding all the councils and tribunals of Spain, except that of the Inquisition, to take cognizance of any question relating to the Indies.

The Council of the Indies, then, was the legislative body in which were framed the laws that governed those vast dominions, it being declared that no law or provision should be obeyed in the colonies that had not passed through the council and had not been communicated by it; it was the supreme court, to which were brought all suits that by reason of the large sums involved could be appealed to this last resort; and, finally, it was the consultative branch of the government in all the weighty matters in which it was judged fitting to hear the Council's opinion. It was also charged with the duty of submitting to the king, through its chamber composed of five councilors, lists of ... candidates from which were filled the vacant bishoprics, canonates, and judgeships of the audiencias. In order to enable it to perform this task more adequately, the viceroys were required to inform the council privately, at stated intervals, concerning residents of the territory under their command who might be worthy of filling these posts. ...

The first governors [in the colonies] were the conquistadores themselves, either under the terms of their capitulations or agreements with the king, as in the case of Pizarro in Peru, or by choice of their soldiers, later confirmed by the crown, as happened with Cortes in New Spain. Later the governmental authority was transferred to the same bodies that were appointed to administer justice, called audiencias. Finally the Emperor Charles V created in Barcelona on November 20, 1542, the two viceroyalties of Mexico and Peru, to which were added in the eighteenth century those of Santa Fe and Buenos Aires, the other provinces remaining under captains-general and presidents, who exercised the same functions as the viceroys and differed from them only in title.

The authority of these high functionaries varied greatly according to the times. In the epoch of the creation of the first viceroyalties it was almost without limits, for the king declared: "In all the cases and affairs that may arise, they may do whatever appears fitting to them, and they can do and dispose just as we would do and dispose ... in the provinces in their charge ... saving only what is expressly forbidden them to do. ..."

In the period we are discussing the power of the viceroys was moderated by prudent compromises, reflected in the participation of other bodies in the different branches of government, although the viceroys retained all the glitter and pomp of their supreme authority. In the arduous and important tasks of public administration ... they were obliged to consult with the *real acuerdo*, the name given to a sitting of the audiencia when it acted as the viceroy's council, although he was not bound to accept the advice of the *oidores* or judges. ... The viceroy was also subject to the *residencia*, which was a judicial review held immediately at the end of his term of office, and to which the judge who was appointed for this purpose summoned all who desired to complain of some offense or injustice.

From the decision of this judge there was no appeal except to the Council of the Indies. But although all these restrictions had a very laudable object— to limit and bring within the scope of the laws an authority that bordered on the royal—distance and the very extent of the authority frequently made these precautions illusory. A viceroy of Mexico ... said in this connection: "If he who comes to govern (this kingdom) does not repeatedly remind himself that the most rigorous *residencia* is that which the viceroy must face when he is judged by the divine majesty, he can be more sovereign than the Grand Turk, for there is no evil action that he may contrive for which he will not find encouragement, nor any tyranny that he may practice which will not be tolerated. ..."

The period of time that a viceroy could remain in office was at first indefinite, and the first two viceroys of New Spain retained their positions for many years. It was later fixed at a period of three years, which was commonly renewed for those who distinguished themselves by their services, or for those who were the objects of the king's favor; finally it was increased to five years. ... The salary also varied, and in Mexico, from the time of the Marquis de Croix in 1766, it was 60,000 pesos a year. ...

The authority exercised by the audiencias in their respective districts may be likened to that enjoyed by the council over all the Indies. These bodies were held in much respect, not only because they possessed great powers, acted as councils to the viceroys with the name of *acuerdo*, and were supreme tribunals from which there was no appeal (save in particular cases, to the Council of the Indies) but also because of their members' reputation for honesty, their discreet conduct and bearing, and even their distinctive attire on public occasions. ... This combination of circumstances made these posts very desirable and their holders objects of envy. Appointments were made according to an established scale, with the judges progressing from less important audiencias to those of higher rank.

In order that these magistrates might be entirely independent and devote themselves to the administration of justice without relations of interest, friendship, or kinship in the place where they exercised their functions, they were strictly forbidden to engage in any kind of commerce or business; to borrow or lend money; to own lands, whether vegetable gardens or estates; to pay visits or attend betrothals and baptisms; to associate with merchants; to receive gifts of any kind; or to attend pleasure or gambling parties. These prohibitions also extended to their wives and children. In order to marry they had to obtain a license from the king, on pain of loss of their positions, and if such a license was granted they were generally transferred to another audiencia. The number of *oidores* varied according to the rank of the audiencia. These tribunals were found not only in the viceregal capitals but wherever else they were necessary.

Such was the general system of government of the kingdoms or large divisions of the Indies.

2. "I HAVE SEEN CORRUPTION BOIL AND BUBBLE..."[1]

Corruption became a structural element of the government of the Indies in the seventeenth century. Colonial officials, high and low, prostituted their trusts in innumerable and ingenious ways. An audacious adventurer who had an intimate knowledge of conditions in the colonies, Gabriel Fernández de Villalobos, marquis of Varinas (1642?–?), showered Charles II with memorials in which he sought to guide the monarch through the bewildering thicket of official misdeeds and warned him that failure to remedy the corruption rampant in colonial government must lead to the loss of the Indies. He was rewarded for his pains by imprisonment in a North African fortress. The following extract from one of his memorials illuminates the technique of a corrupt viceroy.

I shall assume that your Majesty has everywhere excellent ministers, conscientious and learned, and that the Indies are today and have often before been governed by viceroys and *oidores* of notable piety and integrity. ... And certainly some were distinguished by all the virtues; there was one, in particular, of such zeal and integrity that on departing from Mexico City after completing his term of office he received with kindness an Indian who offered him a bouquet of flowers, saying: "This is the first gift I have received in this kingdom." A great viceroy was this, my lord, who died so poor that King Philip II (may he be with God) paid his debts out of the royal treasury. And it may be that these virtues (in addition to the merits of his family) later won for his sons the favor of Philip IV, your Majesty's father.

There were viceroys before and after him who worked in the same righteous spirit. For that reason, in this discourse I shall neither name names nor accuse anyone in particular; I shall speak instead of the evils that I have seen and of the remedies that are necessary. ...

Your Majesty may assume that a high official driven by an immoderate desire to make his fortune will operate in the following manner:

Colección de documentos inéditos ... de las antiguas posesiones españolas de Ultramar, Madrid, 1885–1932, 25 vols., XII, pp. 226–231. (Excerpt translated by the editor.)

First, he will utilize or sell (to put it more precisely), for his own profit and at high prices, every kind of judicial office, *alcaldías mayores*, *corregimientos*, commissions, and *residencias*.

Second, he will also sell the rights to *encomiendas*, licenses, and concessions—authorizations to do various things that are forbidden by the laws and ordinances but that the viceroy may allow.

Third, he will dispose in the same way of all kinds of military positions, such as the titles and commissions of lieutenants, captains, generals, recruiting officers, garrison commanders, constables, and many non-existent posts.

Fourth, he will do the same with all that relates to the public finances, selling drafts on the royal treasury (which is the ruin of your Majesty's estate) and disposing of the offices of revenue collectors, of judges appointed to make various investigations, of officials charged with collecting the royal fifth and making financial settlements, of inspectors of the mines and lands, of *alcaldes* with jurisdiction over water rights, and so forth. ...

Such, my lord, are the articles of faith that your ministers of the Indies observe most diligently.

The minister who does these things, my lord, clearly will be guided not by reason but by his own convenience, and therefore he will surround himself with individuals who will advance his interests; and will encourage these men to commit excesses, while he will always persecute and humiliate the just and virtuous, for these are the only ones he fears.

Such a minister must also seek the good will of superiors as well as inferiors, and share his spoils with them, so that they will write favorably of him to Spain and so that his trickery will be concealed. He must also try to persuade the tribunals to close their eyes to his actions, sometimes through terrorizing them, sometimes by bribing them. ...

Such viceroys and presidents must also go about in fear and distrust of the people, who see what goes on and murmur, complain, denounce it publicly, and compose satires and squibs. ...

All these things together, and each one separately, contribute to the total destruction of the Indies, for every item is a source of political offenses and scandalous crimes that cause infinite miseries.

3. THE *CORREGIDOR*: ENEMY OF THE PEOPLE

The provincial governor—or corregidor, *the title he most commonly bore—occupied a key position in the political hierarchy of the Indies. His supreme authority on the local level, under the viceroy, from whom he usually bought his position, gave him immense power for good or evil. By common consent, he generally employed that power for bad*

ends. The worst abuse of his authority arose in connection with the practice of reparti-
miento or reparto de mercancías, the mandatory purchase of goods for the corregidor
by the Indians of his district. The Marquis of Varinas describes in vivid detail the opera-
tions of the repartimiento.

This corregidor or governor, president or *alcalde mayor*, whose office cost him 10 or 12,000 pesos, must acquire a stock of goods worth 20,000 pesos to sell in his province, in order to make a profit on the money he has expended. ... He sells this merchandise to his poor subjects at six or eight times its true value, and buys up the products of the Indians and Spaniards at four or five times below the current price of the country, using force and threats ... to enrich himself and slake his unnatural thirst for money, as soon as he takes up the tasks of government. ...

The goods that this official receives from the merchants who outfit him, he purchases at steep prices; and he must increase their cost to the Indians accordingly. So the unhappy judge, dragging the chains of his many debts, arrives in his district, which he finds filled with naked Indians and impoverished Spaniards burdened with children and obligations, whose total possessions, if put up at public auction, would not yield 6,000 pesos. Withal, this judge must squeeze out of them more than 30,000 pesos in two years in order to pay his debts, and half as much again if he wishes to make a profit from his office. And if he cannot do this he is beyond salvation (as they say in the Indies), since he is considering only his temporal welfare and forgetting that such a policy may consign him to eternal perdition, as will inevitably ensue if he does not make restitution.

When this judge enters upon his office, his sole concern is to find means of paying off his large debts and to make a profit from his employment; and since time is short, his needs immense, the land exhausted, and his vassals poor, he must use violence and cruelty to attain what equity, moderation, and kindness will not secure.

To this end he must monopolize the products of the land, compelling his miserable vassals to sell all their fruits to him, who, rod in hand, is judge and inspector, merchant, corregidor, and interpreter of his own contract. ...

Let your Majesty's ministers of the Council of the Indies, and your Majesty's confessor, take note that the distribution of goods by the corregidor, made to enable him to buy the products of the district, is never carried out by arrangement with the Indians who have to buy this merchandise. The customary practice is for the Spanish governor to turn the goods over to the Indian *alcaldes* and bosses and to fix prices in collusion with them. ... The Indian bosses never object to the high prices, for they do not have to buy

---

Colección de documentos inéditos, XII, pp. 237–239, 245–246, 249–256. (Excerpt translated by the editor.)

anything; their principal concern is to avoid having to shoulder any part of the burden and to ingratiate themselves with the corregidores, so that they may keep their jobs.

Having agreed on prices and received the goods, the Indian bosses, who are stupid and heartless, count the people living in each town; they make no exception of the widows or of the poor, sick, and aged, but treat all alike, and assign to them by heads the payment they must make for these goods. They take the merchandise, according to the assessment made by the corregidor, to each one's house, place it before him, and tell him the reckoning; he must pay this in the allotted time or else go to rot in prison. As a clear example of the injustice of his distribution, the Indians are often seen wearing scapularies of various colors ... which fell to their lot in the distribution and of which they can make no other use. ...

Your Majesty may imagine from these and similar facts how these Indians fear prison, the threat of which compels the Indian bosses and commoners to submit to their governors; and no wonder, for the Indian prison is a fearful thing. It is a small dark room, without windows or other vent than a very small door. There they must perform their bodily functions, chained by the feet; there are no beds; and as the Indians are brought from other towns, they generally forget to give them any food. They suffer from hunger and thirst and a terrible stench; and since these unhappy beings have been raised in the open country they consider imprisonment worse than death, and therefore many prefer to take their own lives. ...

At the conclusion of one year, the period for which his office is granted (with a second year possible by way of extension), the judge makes another deal with the superior officer who appointed him, and adds another 1 or 2,000 pesos to the original price, unless this sum was included in the original agreement. If he did not do this he would be completely ruined, for in the first year he was occupied with the distribution of his goods ... and he must have the second year to collect payment for his merchandise. ... In any case the judge almost always ends "over-extended" (as they say), with the district owing him for the goods that he distributed—and these debts represent not only the profit that he hoped to make but the sums that he must pay out. On this account the judge resorts to the following expedients, which are all new and greater injustices and injuries to the service of God and of your Majesty:

First, seeing that the end of his term of office and the arrival of a successor are near, the corregidor tries to collect payment from Your Majesty's vassals in four days ... for goods that he had sold on credit for a much longer period.

Second, after his successor has been named he makes a deal with him (if he is the judge of residence), paying him a certain sum; if he is not the judge, he uses this money to have a judge appointed who will absolve him of all guilt.

Third, in any case he will try to obtain a pledge from his successor that he will not permit any inhabitant to lodge any complaints or charges against him in the *residencia*, making it clear to him that whatever befalls the old judge will happen to the new one, since he must of necessity manage his affairs in the same way as his predecessor.

Fourth, since the debt with which he began his term of office—of 10, 12, and 200,000 pesos, with interest added—is so large that his subjects, though exploited with such great severity, simply cannot furnish this sum of money ... , he must choose one of two courses of action. He may remain in the vicinity until he has collected all that is owed him—which is his profit—all the rest having gone to pay his outfitters, his creditors, the official who appointed him, and the judge of residence. In this case Your Majesty's vassals, and the judge who succeeds him, are saddled with a very burdensome and offensive guest who not only obstructs their industry but impoverishes them with his collections. Or he may sell his debts to his successor, taking a partial loss; and since these obligations grow with the passage of time, they come to form an unbearable burden on the Spanish and Indian settlements, so that the people become impoverished and leave their homes, and the district is soon depopulated through these intolerable injuries.

Fifth, the evil ministers often resort to the following expedient: Sometimes, in order to leave no debts outstanding when they quit office, they sell or hire the Indians to owners of workshops to satisfy their debts, using trivial offenses as pretexts. ... At other times they use for pretexts the arrears in the tribute they owe Your Majesty. In other places they commit still greater offenses and violence for the same cause, compelling the Indians to cultivate fields for them, which gives rise to a mass of injuries more numerous than the seeds of grain gathered from the land, for with this pretext fifty Indians are forced to pay the tributes of five hundred. So these Indians must pass their lives in endless labor, lacking food, clothing, or time in which to plant for themselves and their families. They go about continually harassed—men, women, the aged, boys, widows, young girls, and married women, sowing and plowing with their own hands, unaided by oxen or other animals, and threshing the grain with their feet, all without recompense. ...

Sixth, since the first question put in the *residencia* asks the witnesses under oath whether the judge engaged in any business dealings on his own account, it becomes necessary to keep from the judge of residence what everybody else knows. Hence, by one means or another—threats or pleas for mercy, or bad conscience—all are made to swear that the corregidor engaged in no business dealings, either personally or through intermediaries; and this is sworn to by the same persons to whom the judge forcibly sold and distributed the steers, mules, and other merchandise in which he traded during his term of office, and whose grain and other supplies he monopolized. ...

Thus, through such perjury and sins of sacrilege on the part of the persons he suborned, the corregidor obtains an acquittal and quits his office—one which he secured through bribery and fraud, which he entered with usury and oppression, whose duties he performed with violence and injury, and which he left committing sacrilege, bearing false witness before God concerning his actions.

4. "THESE LAWS ARE OBEYED AND NOT ENFORCED"

A striking feature of colonial political life was the frequent nonobservance of Spanish colonial law. Such nonobservance could be legitimated by use of the formula "obedezco pero no cumplo" ("I obey but do not carry out"), employed by a viceroy to set aside unrealistic or unenforceable legislation. Nonobservance of the law was especially frequent in the case of Indian protective legislation, which was systematically flouted. The crown often closed its eyes to such violations, not only because it wished to avoid confrontation with powerful colonial elites but because these laws sometimes collided with the crown's own pressing need for revenue. Hence the contradiction between that protective legislation, so often cited by defenders of Spain's work in America, and the reality of Indian life and labor in the colonies. A Spanish judge of rare integrity, Alonso de Zorita (1511?–1585), who retired to an honorable poverty in 1566 after nineteen years of officeholding in the Indies, calls attention to that contradiction in the following excerpt from his report to the crown.

Who shall tell the sum of the miseries and hardships these poor unfortunate people suffer, without help or succor from any quarter! Who does not turn his face against them, who does not persecute and vex them, who does not rob them and live by their sweat! Since I cannot tell all, but have told enough to make clear the need for a remedy, let me be silent concerning the innumerable crimes that I have personally seen and verified or that I have heard of from trustworthy persons.

The ancient kings and lords never ruled in this way, never took the Indians from their towns, never disrupted their way of life and labor. I cannot believe that Your Majesty or the members of Your Majesty's Council know or have been informed about what is taking place. If they knew of it, they would surely take steps to preserve Your Majesty's miserable vassals and would not allow the Indians to be entirely destroyed in order to gratify the wishes of the Spaniards. If the Indians should die out (and they are dying with terrible rapidity), those realms will very quickly become depopulated, as has already happened in the Antilles, the great province of Venezuela, and the whole

---

Life and Labor in Ancient Mexico: The Brief and Summary Relation of the Lords of New Spain by Alonso de Zorita, translated and edited by Benjamin Keen, New Brunswick, N.J., Rutgers University Press, 1963, pp. 216–218. The notes that appeared in the original publication have been omitted here.

coast of northern South America and other very extensive lands that have become depopulated in our time. The wishes of Your Majesty and his Royal Council are well known and are made very plain in the laws that are issued every day in favor of the poor Indians and for their increase and preservation. But these laws are obeyed and not enforced, wherefore there is no end to the destruction of the Indians, nor does anyone care what Your Majesty decrees. How many decrees, cedulas, and letters were sent by our lord, the Emperor, who is in glory, and how many necessary orders are sent by Your Majesty! How little good have all these orders done! Indeed, the more laws and decrees are sent, the worse is the condition of the Indians by reason of the false and sophistical interpretation that the Spanish officials give these laws, twisting their meaning to suit their own purposes. It seems to me that the saying of a certain philosopher well applies to this case: Where there is a plenty of doctors and medicines, there is a plenty of ill health. Just so, where there are many laws and judges, there is much injustice.

We have a multitude of laws, judges, viceroys, governors, *presidentes*, oidores, corregidores, alcaldes mayores, a million lieutenants, and yet another million alguaciles. But this multitude is not what the Indians need, nor will it relieve their misery. Indeed, the more such men there are, the more enemies do the Indians have. For the more zeal these men display against the Indians, the more influence do they wield; the Spaniards call such men Fathers of their Country, saviors of the state, and proclaim them to be very just and upright. The more ill will such men show against the Indians and friars, the more titles and lying encomiums are heaped upon them. But let an official favor the Indians and the religious (who are bound together, one depending upon the other), and this alone suffices to make him odious and abhorrent to all. For the Spaniards care for one thing alone, and that is their advantage; and they give not a rap whether these poor and miserable Indians live or die, though the whole being and welfare of the country depend upon them.

God has closed the eyes and darkened the minds of these Spaniards, so that they see with their eyes what is happening, yet do not see it, so that they perceive their own destruction, yet do not perceive it, and all because of their callousness and hardheartedness. I have known an oidor to say publicly from his dais, speaking in a loud voice, that if water were lacking to irrigate the Spaniards' farms, they would have to be watered with the blood of Indians. I have heard others say that the Indians, and not the Spaniards, must labor. Let the dogs work and die, said these men, the Indians are numerous and rich. These officials say such things because they have not seen the Indians' sufferings and miseries, because they are content to sit in the cool shade and collect their pay. They also say these things to win the good will and gratitude of the Spaniards, and also because they all have sons-in-law, brothers-in-law, relatives, or close friends among them. These friends and relatives are rich in farms, ranches, and herds; and the officials control a major part of this wealth. That is what blinds them and makes them say what they say and do what they do.

In the old days the Indians had few laws, so few that all knew them by heart, as is told of the Lacedaemonians and the Scythians, and none dared to break those laws. They were well governed, their numbers increased, and they lived happily and peacefully. They were masters of their poor little properties. They did not have to leave their native surroundings to support themselves, but enjoyed the company of their wives, children, and kindred by day and night. They paid their tribute without hardship or undue exertion.

I could say much more on this subject, but to tell it all would weary the reader. Indeed, I think it unnecessary, speaking to a Prince so upright, just, and Christian, to enlarge on what is so notorious and glaring that no man attached to the service of God and Your Majesty will deny it.

5. CITY GOVERNMENT
IN THE SPANISH INDIES

The birth of the colonial city coincided with the passing of the freedom and authority of the communes or towns of Spain. As a result, from the outset the right of the king to appoint municipal officials was accepted without question. Philip II began the practice— which later became general—of selling posts in the town councils to the highest bidders, with the right of resale or bequest of the offices, on condition that a certain part of their value be paid to the crown at each transfer. Gonzalo Gómez de Cervantes, a leading citizen of Mexico, of whose life little is known, criticized the practice and suggested its reform in a memorial addressed to a member of the Council of the Indies, dated 1599.

It is well known and understood that Mexico is the head of all this kingdom and that all the other cities, towns, and places of this New Spain acknowledge it as such. All the more reason, then, that its *regidores* (councilmen) should be outstanding men, of quality, experience, and mature judgment. And the lack of such men has been a cause of many different things, that show a serious weakness. The proof of this is that the majority of the regidores are youths who even twenty years from now will not have enough experience to govern a city; and it is a sorry thing to see those who have not yet left off being children, already made city fathers.

This evil arises from the permission granted by His Majesty for the sale of these offices—whereby they go to those who can pay the most for them, and

---

Gonzalo Gómez de Cervantes, *La vida económica y social de Nueva España al finalizar el siglo XVI*, edited by Alberto Maria Carreño, Mexico, 1944, pp. 93–94. (Excerpt translated by the editor.)

not to those who would render the best honor and service to the common-weal. It is shameful that such youths should be preferred for the posts of regi-dores and other important positions over mature and eminent men who should occupy those offices. Truly, it would redound much more to the service of His Majesty and to the increase of his kingdom, if he gave these council seats to qualified persons, descendants of conquistadores, and others who have served him; they would regard their king and country with greater love, if His Majesty rewarded them for their merits and services, and would be inspired to serve him still more.

It is not seemly that those who yesterday were shopkeepers or tavern keepers, or engaged in other base pursuits, should today hold the best offices in the country while gentlemen and descendants of those who conquered and won the land go about poor, dejected, degraded, and neglected. And it is the city that suffers most from this injustice, because the fixing of market prices, the supervision of weights and measures in the markets, and other very important matters are in a state of great disorder. It would be a very efficacious remedy, if his Majesty were to add a dozen council seats and give them to men of quality, maturity, wisdom, and merit—not by way of sale, but as gifts—and if he were to do the same with the seats that fall vacant. If such a policy were adopted, everything pertaining to his royal estate and the preservation of this realm would be greatly served and advanced.

6. DIALOGUE IN YUCATÁN

Some of the early friars in the Indies were saintly and courageous men who preached not only the gospel of Christ but the message of justice to the Indians. Their point of view is well expressed in a dialogue overheard in a Yucatán village by Father Tomás de la Torre, one of the Dominican friars who accompanied las Casas when the great fighter for Indian rights came to southern Mexico as bishop of Chiapas in 1544.

The sun had already set when we came to a clean looking little church, decorated with branches. We were much pleased and greatly heartened, believing that where the signs appeared we were certain to find charity. After saying a prayer we continued on our way as if spellbound, for we knew nothing of these people and did not know how to talk to them. This was our first

Fray Tomás de la Torre, *Desde Salamanca, España hasta Ciudad Real, Chiapas, Diario del viaje,* 1544–1545, edited by Frans Blom, Mexico, 1945, pp. 150–152. (Excerpt translated by the editor.)

encounter with the Indians, who certainly could do as they pleased with us without fear of resistance; it was we who were afraid of them.

So we came to a village where many Indians were sitting about. When they saw us they rose and gave us seats, which were small stools, no larger than the distance between the extended thumb and forefinger of one hand. ... The father vicar said, "Let us stay here this night, for God has prepared this lodging for us." The Indians, seeing how miserable we were, owing to the cold of the lagoon, made a great bonfire, the first that we had needed since leaving Spain. Then the chief came with half a pumpkin shell filled with water; he washed our feet, and they gave us each two tortillas and a piece of fresh fish and another of sweet potato. We ate and felt much better, and were filled with devotion and wonder to see the charity of these Indians, who the Spaniards claimed were so bestial.

At night came Ximénes, who knew their language, and through him we asked them why they had treated us so kindly. They replied that on the road an Indian had seen us and realized that we were thirsty and had told them so, and for that reason they had sent that pumpkin shell of water and accorded us that hospitality, because they knew that we came from Castile for their good. We took great pleasure in the reply of these barbarians.

That night there arrived a peasant who came with the bishop [Las Casas], Zamora by name, and after we had all lain down to sleep, some on boards and others on small mats that the Indians make of rushes ... , Zamora, the recently-arrived peasant from Castile, and Ximénes, an oldtimer in the country and a conqueror of Yucatan, began to talk, and because their conversation was very diverting I shall set down here what I remember of it.

Said Ximénes to Zamora: "You chose a poor place to stable that beast of yours for the night; the Indians will surely take it and eat it."

Said Zamora: "Let them eat it, by God; we Christians owe them a good deal more than that."

Ximénes: "What the devil do you mean by that?"

Zamora: "I mean that you've robbed them of their property and taken their sons from them and made them slaves in their own land."

Ximénes: "They owe us more than that, for we are Christians."

Zamora: "Christians? A Christian is known by his works."

Ximénes: "We are Christians, and we came to this land to make Christians of them."

Zamora: "I'll bet you came over here because your deviltries made Spain too hot a place for you, or else you would not have left your own country. I swear to God that no one comes to the Indies for any other reason, and myself first of all."

Ximénes: "God alone knows why each man came over; but the main thing is that we conquered this country."

Zamora: "And that is why you expect the Indians to give you their food and property—because you murdered them in their own houses! Good friends you proved to be, indeed!"

Ximénes: "You would not say that if you had shed your blood in the war."

Zamora: "I dare say that even if they had killed you they would not go to Hell, because you made war on them."

Ximénes: "They are dogs, and will not believe in God."

Zamora: "And very good preachers they had in you, for certain."

Ximénes: "Surely, Zamora, you will not go back to Castile."

Zamora: "The devil take me if I carry away a cent that I did not earn with my spade; the Indians owe me nothing."

While this dialogue went on the rest of us kept quiet, lying in the dark, but we could hardly keep from laughing at the humor of Zamora's remarks. On the other hand, we were confounded by the clarity and simplicity of the judgments of this illiterate peasant, who said only what his reason dictated. ...

7. THE SOURCES OF CATHOLIC POWER

By the last decades of the colonial era the discipline of the clergy had become seriously re-laxed, and the unity of the church was rent by unseemly squabbles between monastic and secular clergy and between Creole and peninsular priests. Yet the influence of the church in colonial society, except among a tiny handful of converts to the new materialistic doc-trines of the encyclopedists, remained undiminished. In the following excerpt the Mexican historian Alamán explains the sources of Catholic power.

The immense influence of the Church rested on three foundation stones: respect for religion, remembrance of its great benefactions, and its immense wealth. The people, poorly instructed in the essentials of religion, tended to identify it in large part with ceremonial pomp; they found relief from the te-dium of their lives in the religious functions, which, especially during Holy Week, represented in numerous processions the most venerated mysteries of the redemption. The festivals of the Church, which should have been en-tirely spiritual, were thus transformed into so many profane performances, marked by displays of fireworks, dances, plays, bullfights and cockfights, and even such forbidden diversions as cards and the like, in order to celebrate at great cost the festivals of the patron saints of the towns, into which the Indians poured the greater part of the fruits of their labor. It was this vain pomp, attended by little true piety, that led the viceroy whom I have fre-quently cited [the Duke of Linares] to remark that "in this realm all is out-

---

Alamán, *Historia de Méjico*, I, pp. 64–70. (Extract translated by the editor.)

ward show, and though their lives are steeped in vices, the majority think that by wearing a rosary about their necks and kissing the hand of the priest they are made Catholics, and that the Ten Commandments can be replaced by ceremonies."

The Indians continued to regard the regular clergy with the respect that the first missionaries had justly gained by protecting them against the oppression and violence of the conquistadores and by instructing them not only in religion but in the arts necessary for subsistence. This respect, which grew to be a fanatical veneration, presented no dangers as long as it was accorded to men of admirable virtue, and the government, to which they were very devoted and obedient, found in these exemplary ecclesiastics its firmest support; but it could become highly dangerous if a clergy of debased morals wished to abuse this influence for its own ends. This danger to the government was made still greater by the very precaution that Archbishop Haro had advised to avoid it, for since the high Church positions were intrusted to Europeans, the Americans, who generally enjoyed only the less important posts and benefices, exerted greater influence over the people with whom they were placed in more immediate contact.

The wealth of the clergy consisted not so much in the estates that it possessed, numerous though they were (especially the urban properties in the principal cities like Mexico City, Puebla, and others), as in capital invested in quitrent mortgages on the property of individuals; the traffic in mortgages and the collection of interest made of every chaplaincy and religious brotherhood a sort of bank. The total property of the clergy, both secular and regular, in estates and loans of this kind, certainly was not less than half of the total value of the real estate of the country.

The town council of Mexico City, seeing the multitude of monasteries and nunneries that were being founded, and the large number of persons destined for the ecclesiastical profession, together with the great sums devised to pious foundations, petitioned King Philip IV in 1644 "that no more convents of nuns or monks be established, since the number of the former was excessive, and the number of their woman servants even greater; that limits be placed upon the estates of the convents and that they be forbidden to acquire new holdings, complaining that the greater part of the landed property of the land had come into the hands of the religious by way of donations or purchases, and that if steps were not taken to remedy the situation they would soon be masters of all; that no more religious be sent from Spain, and that the bishops be charged not to ordain any more clerics, since there were already more than six thousand in all the bishoprics without any occupation, ordained on the basis of tenuous chaplaincies; and, finally, that there should be a reform in the excessive number of festivals, which increased idleness and gave rise to other evils." The *cortes* assembled in Madrid at that period petitioned the king to the same effect, and similar reforms were earlier proposed by the Council of Castile, but nothing was done, and things continued in the same state. ...

In addition to the revenues derived from these estates and loans, the secular clergy had the tithes, which in all the bishoprics of New Spain amounted to some 1,800,000 pesos annually, although the government received a part of this sum. ... In the bishopric of Michoacán the tithes were farmed out; this made their collection more rigorous and oppressive, since private interest devised a thousand expedients to burden even the least important products of agriculture with this assessment.

The clergy had a privileged jurisdiction, with special tribunals, and a personal *fuero* which in former times had been very extensive but had greatly diminished with the intervention of the royal judges in criminal cases and with the declaration that the secular courts had jurisdiction in cases involving both principal and interest of the funds of the chaplaincies and pious foundations. The viceroy decided conflicts between ecclesiastical and civil courts, and this prerogative was one of those that gave the greatest luster to his authority.

From the instructions of the Duke of Linares to his successor and from the secret report made by Don Jorge Juan and Don Antonio Ulloa to King Ferdinand VI, it appears that the customs of the clergy had declined at the beginning of the eighteenth century to a point of scandalous corruption, especially among the friars charged with the administration of the curacies or doctrines. In the epoch of which I speak this corruption was particularly notable in the capitals of some bishoprics and in smaller places, but in the capital of the realm the presence of the superior authorities enforced more decorum. Everywhere, it should also be said, there were truly exemplary ecclesiastics, and in this respect certain religious orders stood out. The Jesuits, above all others, were remarkable for the purity of their customs and for their religious zeal, a notable contrast, appearing in the above-cited work by Juan and Ulloa between their comments on the Jesuits and their references to other orders. Their expulsion left a great void, not only in the missions among the barbarians whom they had in charge but in the matter of the instruction and moral training of the people. ... No less commendable were the friars of the order of Saint James, those of the order of Saint Philip, whose oratories had largely replaced those of the Jesuits, and among the hospitaller orders the Bethlehemites, who devoted themselves to primary education and the care of hospitals.

Into these religious orders the rivalry of birth had also penetrated, excepting always the Jesuits, who had no chapters or tumultuous elections and whose prelates were named in Rome by the general of the order, with regard only to the merit and virtue of individuals. Not only did there prevail in some of them the strife between "*gachupines* and creoles," but there were entire communities composed almost exclusively of one or the other element.

7

~

CLASS AND CASTE

IN THE SPANISH COLONIES

THE SOCIAL ORDER that arose in the Spanish colonies on the ruins of the old Indian societies was based, like that of Spain, on feudal principles. All agricultural and mechanical labor was regarded as degrading. The various races and racial mixtures were carefully distinguished, and a trace of Black or Indian blood legally sufficed to deprive an individual of the rights and privileges of white men, including the right to hold public office or enter the professions. In practice, racial lines were not so strictly drawn. For a stipulated sum a wealthy *mestizo* or mulatto could often purchase from the Spanish crown a certificate placing him in the category of whites.

Wealth, not gentle birth or racial purity, was the true distinguishing characteristic of the colonial aristocracy. Legally, the Creoles and peninsular Spaniards were equal. In practice, during most of the colonial period the former suffered from a system of discrimination that denied them employment in the highest church and government posts and in large-scale commerce. In the first half of the eighteenth century their situation improved, and Creoles came to dominate the prestigious *audiencias* of Mexico City and Lima. But in the second half of the century a reaction took place, and high-ranking Creoles were removed from positions in the imperial administration. The cleavage in the colonial upper class grew wider with the passage of time and must be considered a major cause of the Creole Wars of Independence.

The *mestizo* caste had its main origin in a multitude of irregular unions between Spaniards and native women, although mixed marriages were not uncommon, especially in the early period. The mass of mixed bloods were consigned to an inferior social status by their poverty and illegitimate birth. The *mestizo* caste tended to become a lower middle class of artisans, overseers, shopkeepers, and the like.

By contrast with the *mestizo*, no ambiguity marked the position of the Indian in the social scale. Aside from a small and privileged group of hereditary chiefs and their families, the Indians formed a distinct servile class, burdened with many tribute and labor obligations. They lived apart from the whites, in their own communities of pre-Conquest origin, or in towns established by the Spaniards. In many regions they preserved quite intact their ancestral social organization, language, and other culture traits. On numerous occasions they rose against their oppressors in revolts that were generally crushed with great severity.

The virtual disappearance of the native population of the Antilles and the rapid growth of sugar cane cultivation in the islands created an insistent demand on the part of the colonists for Black slave labor. A large Black and mixed population came into being in the regions of plantation culture, notably in the West Indies and on the coasts of Mexico and Venezuela; smaller populations were found in all the large colonial towns, where they were chiefly used as household servants.

Black slavery in the Spanish colonies has been described as patriarchal and humane by comparison with the operations of the system in the English and French colonies, but this judgment, based in considerable part on the Spanish eighteenth-century slave code, has recently been subjected to sharp criticism. Emancipation was legally possible, and occurred with some frequency during the colonial period. Whether slaves or freemen, Blacks occupied the lowest position in the social scale. Unless redeemed by wealth or singular talents, Blacks, mulattoes and other racial mixtures shared this disfavor. Many found employment in the mines, in the mechanical trades, as confidential servants, and in the colonial militia, where they formed separate units under the command of white officers.

1. THE STRUCTURE OF CLASS AND CASTE

The population of the Spanish colonies formed a melting pot of races, white, red, and Black. Their progressive amalgamation was retarded but not halted by a caste system that assigned different social values to the respective races and mixtures. The Spanish officials Jorge Juan and Antonio de Ulloa describe the complicated structure of class and caste of a colonial town—the Caribbean port of Cartagena.

The inhabitants may be divided into different castes or tribes, who derive their origin from a coalition of Whites, Negroes, and Indians. Of each of these we shall treat particularly. The Whites may be divided into two classes,

---

Jorge Juan and Antonio de Ulloa, *Voyage to South America*, London, 1772, 2 vols., I, pp. 29–32.

the Europeans, and Creoles, or Whites born in the country. The former are commonly called *Chapetones*, but are not numerous; most of them either return into Spain after acquiring a competent fortune, or remove up into inland provinces in order to increase it. Those who are settled at Carthagena, carry on the whole trade of that place, and live in opulence; whilst the other inhabitants are indigent, and reduced to have recourse to mean and hard labour for subsistence. The families of the White Creoles compose the landed interest; some of them have large estates, and are highly respected, because their ancestors came into the country invested with honourable posts, bringing their families with them when they settled here. Some of these families, in order to keep up their original dignity, have either married their children to their equals in the country, or sent them as officers on board the galleons; but others have greatly declined. Besides these, there are other Whites, in mean circumstances, who either owe their origin to Indian families, or at least to an intermarriage with them, so that there is some mixture in their blood; but when this is not discoverable by their colour, the conceit of being Whites alleviates the pressure of every other calamity.

Among the other tribes which are derived from an intermarriage of the Whites and the Negroes, the first are the Mulattoes. Next to these the *Tercerones*, produced from a White and a Mulatto, with some approximation to the former, but not so near as to obliterate their origin. After these follow the *Quarterones*, proceeding from a White and a *Terceron*. The last are the *Quinterones*, who owe their origin to a White and *Quarteron*. This is the last gradation, there being no visible difference between them and the Whites, either in colour or features; nay they are often fairer than the Spaniards. The children of a White and *Quinteron* are also called Spaniards, and consider themselves as free from all taint of the Negro race. Every person is so jealous of the order of their tribe or cast, that if, through inadvertence, you call them by a degree lower than what they actually are, they are highly offended, never suffering themselves to be deprived of so valuable a gift of fortune.

Before they attain the class of the *Quinterones*, there are several intervening circumstances which throw them back; for between the Mulatto and the Negro, there is an intermediate race, which they call *Sambos*, owing their origin to a mixture between one of these with an Indian, or among themselves. They are also distinguished according to the class their fathers were of. Betwixt the *Tercerones* and the Mulattoes, the *Quarterones* and the *Tercerones*, etc. are those called *Tente en el Ayre*, suspended in the air, because they neither advance nor recede. Children, whose parents are a *Quarteron* or *Quinteron*, and a Mulatto or *Terceron*, are *Salto atras* retrogrades; because, instead of advancing towards being Whites, they have gone backwards towards the Negro race. The children between a Negro and *Quinteron* are called *Sambos de Negro, de Mulatto, de Terceron*, etc.

These are the most known and common tribes or Castas; there are indeed several others proceeding from their intermarriages; but, being so various, even they themselves cannot easily distinguish them; and these are the only people one sees in the city, the *estancias*, and the villages; for if any Whites, especially women, are met with, it is only accidental, these generally residing in their houses; at least, if they are of any rank or character.

These casts, from the Mulattoes, all affect the Spanish dress, but wear very slight stuffs on account of the heat of the climate. These are the mechanics of the city; the Whites, whether Creoles or *Chapetones*, disdaining such a mean occupation follow nothing below merchandise. But it being impossible for all to succeed, great numbers not being able to procure sufficient credit, they become poor and miserable from their aversion to those trades they follow in Europe, and, instead of the riches which they flattered themselves with possessing in the Indies, they experience the most complicated wretchedness.

The class of Negroes is not the least numerous, and is divided into two parts; the free and the slaves. These [last] are again subdivided into Creoles and *Bozales*, part of which are employed in the cultivation of the *haciendas* or *estancias*. Those in the city are obliged to perform the most laborious services, and pay out of their wages a certain quota to their masters, subsisting themselves on the small remainder. The violence of the heat not permitting them to wear any cloaths, their only covering is a small piece of cotton stuff about their waist; the female slaves go in the same manner. Some of these live at the *estancias*, being married to the slaves who work there; while those in the city sell in the markets all kind of eatables, and cry fruits, sweet-meats, cakes made of the maize, and cassava, and several other things about the streets. Those who have children sucking at their breast, which is the case of the generality, carry them on their shoulders, in order to have their arms at liberty; and when the infants are hungry, they give them the breast either under the arm or over the shoulder, without taking them from their backs. This will perhaps appear incredible; but their breasts, being left to grow without any pressure on them often hang down to their very waist, and are not therefore difficult to turn over their shoulders for the convenience of the infant.

2. THE COLONIAL CITY: MEXICO CITY

Mexico City and Lima were the two great centers of urban civilization in colonial Spanish America. In each an uncrossable chasm separated the world of the white upper class, flaunting its wealth in gay apparel, richly ornamented dwellings, and colorful pageants, from that of the sullen Indian, Black, and mixed-blood proletariat, living in wretched huts amid incredible squalor. The renegade English priest Thomas Gage paints a vivid picture of Mexico City in 1625.

Thomas Gage, *The English-American, a New Survey of the West Indies*, edited by A. P. Newton, London, 1946, pp. 89–92.

At the rebuilding of this city there was a great difference betwixt an inhabitant of Mexico, and a Conqueror; for a Conqueror was a name of honour, and had lands and rents given him and to his posterity by the King of Spain, and the inhabitant or only dweller paid rent for his house. And this hath filled all those parts of America with proud Dons and gentlemen to this day; for every one will call himself a descendant from a Conqueror, though he be as poor as Job; and ask him what is become of his estate and fortune; he will answer that fortune hath taken it away, which shall never take away a Don from him. Nay, a poor cobbler, or carrier that runs about the country far and near getting his living with half-a-dozen mules, if he be called Mendoza, or Guzman, will swear that he descended from those dukes' houses in Spain, and that his grandfather came from thence to conquer, and subdued whole countries to the Crown of Spain, though now fortune have frowned upon him, and covered his rags with a threadbare cloak.

When Mexico was rebuilt, and judges, aldermen, attorneys, townclerks, notaries, scavengers, and serjeants with all other officers necessary for the commonwealth of a city were appointed, the fame of Cortez and majesty of the city was blown abroad into far provinces, by means whereof it was soon replenished with Indians again, and with Spaniards from Spain, who soon conquered above four hundred leagues of land, being all governed by the princely seat of Mexico. But since that first rebuilding, I may say it is now rebuilt the second time by Spaniards, who have consumed most of the Indians; so that now I will not dare to say there are a hundred thousand houses which soon after the Conquest were built up, for most of them were of Indians.

Now the Indians that live there, live in the suburbs of the city, and their situation is called Guadalupe. In the year 1625, when I went to those parts, this suburb was judged to contain five thousand inhabitants; but since most of them have been consumed by the Spaniards' hard usage and the work of the lake. So that now there may not be above two thousand inhabitants of mere Indians, and a thousand of such as they call there mestizoes, who are of a mixed nature of Spaniards and Indians, for many poor Spaniards marry with Indian women, and others that marry them not but hate their husbands, find many tricks to convey away an innocent Uriah to enjoy his Bathsheba. The Spaniards daily cozen them of the small plot of ground where their houses stand, and of three or four houses of Indians built up one good and fair house after the Spanish fashion with gardens and orchards. And so is almost all Mexico new built with very fair and spacious houses with gardens of recreation.

Their buildings are with stone, and brick very strong, but not high, by reason of the many earthquakes, which would endanger their houses if they were above three storeys high. The streets are very broad, in the narrowest of them three coaches may go, and in the broader may go six in the breadth of them, which makes the city seem a great deal bigger than it is. In my time it was thought to be of between thirty and forty thousand inhabitants—Spaniards, who are so proud and rich that half the city was judged to keep coaches, for it was a most credible report that in Mexico in my time there were above fifteen thousand coaches. It is a byword that at Mexico there are four things fair, that is to say, the women, the apparel, the horses, and the streets. But to this I may add the beauty of some of the coaches of the gentry, which do exceed in cost the best of the Court of Madrid and other parts of Christendom; for there they spare no silver, nor gold, nor precious stones, nor cloth of gold, nor the best silks from China to enrich them. And to the gallantry of their horses the pride of some doth add the cost of bridles and shoes of silver.

The streets of Christendom must not compare with those in breadth and cleanness, but especially in the riches of the shops which do adorn them. Above all, the goldsmiths' shops and works are to be admired. The Indians, and the people of China that have been made Christians and every year come thither, have perfected the Spaniards in that trade. The Viceroy that went thither the year 1625 caused a popinjay to be made of silver, gold, and precious stones with the perfect colours of the popinjay's feathers (a bird bigger than a pheasant), with such exquisite art and perfection, to present unto the King of Spain, that it was prized to be worth in riches and workmanship half a million of ducats. There is in the cloister of the Dominicans a lamp hanging in the church with three hundred branches wrought in silver to hold so many candles, besides a hundred little lamps for oil set in it, every one being made with several workmanship so exquisitely that it is valued to be worth four hundred thousand ducats; and with such-like curious works are many streets made more rich and beautiful from the shops of goldsmiths.

To the by-word touching the beauty of the women I must add the liberty they enjoy for gaming, which is such that the day and night is too short for them to end a primera when once it is begun; nay gaming is so common to them that they invite gentlemen to their houses for no other end. To myself it happened that passing along the streets in company with a friar that came with me that year from Spain, a gentlewoman of great birth knowing us to be *chapetons* (so they call the first year those that come from Spain), from her window called unto us, and after two or three slight questions concerning Spain asked us if we would come in and play with her a game at primera.

Both men and women are excessive in their apparel, using more silks than stuffs and cloth. Precious stones and pearls further much their vain ostentation; a hat band and rose made of diamonds in a gentleman's hat is common, and a hat band of pearls is ordinary in a tradesman; nay a blackamoor or tawny young maid and slave will make hard shift but she will be in fashion with her neck chain and bracelets of pearls, and her ear-bobs of some considerable jewels. The attire of this baser sort of people of blackamoors and mulattoes (which are of a mixed nature, of Spaniards and blackamoors) is so light, and their carriage so enticing, that many Spaniards even of the better sort (who are too too prone to venery) disdain their wives for them.

Their clothing is a petticoat of silk or cloth, with many silver or golden laces, with a very broad double ribbon of some light colour with long silver or golden tags hanging down before, the whole length of their petticoat to the ground, and the like behind; their waistcoats made like bodices, with skirts, laced likewise with gold or silver, without sleeves, and a girdle about their body of great price stuck with pearls and knots of gold (if they be any ways well esteemed of), their sleeves are broad and open at the end, of holland or fine China linen, wrought some with coloured silks, some with silk and gold, some with silk and silver, hanging down almost unto the ground; the locks of their heads are covered with some wrought coif, and over it another of network of silk bound with a fair silk, or silver, or golden ribbon which crosseth the upper part of their forehead, and hath commonly worked out in letters some light and foolish love posy; their bare, black, and tawny breasts are covered with bobs hanging from their chains of pearls.

And when they go abroad, they use a white mantle of lawn or cambric rounded with a broad lace, which some put over their heads, the breadth reaching only to their middle behind, that their girdle and ribbons may be seen, and two ends before reaching to the ground almost; others cast their mantles only upon their shoulders, and swaggers-like, cast the one end over the left shoulder that they may the better jog the right arm, and shew their broad sleeve as they walk along; others instead of this mantle use some rich silk petticoat to hang upon their left shoulder, while with their right arm they support the lower part of it, more like roaring boys than honest civil maids. Their shoes are high and of many soles, the outside whereof of the profaner sort are plated with a list of silver, which is fastened with small nails of broad silver heads.

Most of these are or have been slaves, though love have set them loose at liberty to enslave souls to sin and Satan. And there are so many of this kind both men and women grown to a height of pride and vanity, that many times the Spaniards have feared they would rise up and mutiny against them. And for the looseness of their lives, and public scandals committed by them and the better sort of the Spaniards, I have heard them say often who have professed more religion and fear of God, they verily thought God would destroy that city, and give up the country into the power of some other nation. ...

Great alms and liberality towards religious houses in that city commonly are coupled with great and scandalous wickedness. They wallow in the bed of riches and wealth, and make their alms the coverlet to cover their loose and lascivious lives. From hence are the churches so fairly built and adorned. There are not above fifty churches and chapels, cloisters and nunneries, and parish churches in that city; but those that are there are the fairest that ever my eyes beheld, the roofs and beams being in many of them all daubed with gold, and many altars with sundry marble pillars, and others with brazilwood stays standing one above another with tabernacles for several saints richly wrought with golden colours, so that twenty thousand ducats is a common price of many of them. These cause admiration in the common sort of people, and admiration brings on daily adoration in them to those glorious spectacles and images of saints.

It is ordinary for the friars to visit their devoted nuns, and to spend whole days with them, hearing their music, feeding on their sweetmeats, and for this purpose they have many chambers which they call *locutorios*, to talk in, with wooden bars between the nuns and them, and in these chambers are tables for the friars to dine at; and while they dine the nuns recreate them with their voices. Gentlemen and citizens give their daughters to be brought up in these nunneries, where they are taught to make all sorts of conserves and preserves, all sorts of needlework, all sorts of music, which is so exquisite in that city that I dare be bold to say that the people are drawn to their churches more for the delight of the music than for any delight in the service of God. More, they teach these young children to act like players, and to entice the people to their churches make these children to act short dialogues in their choirs, richly attiring them with men's and women's apparel, especially upon Midsummer Day, and the eight days before their Christmas, which is so gallantly performed that many factious strifes and single combats have been, and some were in my time, for defending which of these nunneries most excelled in music and in the training up of children. No delights are wanting in that city abroad in the world, nor in their churches, which should be the house of God, and the soul's, not the sense's delight.

The chief place in the city is the market-place, which though it be not as spacious as in Montezuma his time, yet is at this day very fair and wide, built all with arches on the one side where people may walk dry in time of rain, and there are shops of merchants furnished with all sorts of stuffs and silks, and before them sit women selling all manner of fruits and herbs; over against these shops and arches is the Viceroy his palace, which taketh up almost the whole length of the market with the walls of the house and of the gardens belonging to it. At the end of the Viceroy his palace is the chief prison, which is strong of stone work. Next to this is the beautiful street called *La Plateria*, or Goldsmiths Street, where a man's eyes may behold in less than an hour many millions' worth of gold, silver, pearls, and jewels. The street of St. Austin is rich and comely, where live all that trade in silks; but one of the longest and broadest streets is the street called Tacuba, where almost all the shops are of ironmongers, and of such as deal in brass and steel, which is joining to those arches whereon the water is conveyed into the city, and is so called for that it is the way out of the city to a town called Tacuba; and this street is mentioned far and near, not so much for the length and breadth of it, as for a small commodity of needles which are made there, and for proof are the best of all those parts. For stately buildings the street called *del Aquila*, the Street of the Eagle, exceeds the rest, where live gentlemen, and courtiers, and judges belonging to the Chancery, and is the palace of the Marques del Valle from the line of Ferdinando Cortez; this street is so called from an old idol an eagle of stone which from the Conquest lieth in a corner of that street, and is twice as big as London stone.

The gallants of this city shew themselves daily, some on horseback, and most in coaches, about four of the clock in the afternoon in a pleasant shady field called *la Alameda*, full of trees and walks, somewhat like unto our Moorfields, where do meet as constantly as the merchants upon our exchange about two thousand coaches, full of gallants, ladies, and citizens, to see and to be seen, to court and to be courted, the gentlemen having their train of blackamoor slaves some a dozen, some half a dozen waiting on them, in brave and gallant liveries, heavy with gold and silver lace, with silk stockings on their black legs, and roses on their feet, and swords by their sides; the ladies also carry their train by their coach's side of such jetlike damsels as before have been mentioned for their light apparel, who with their bravery and white mantles over them seem to be, as the Spaniard saith, *mosca en leche*, a fly in milk. But the train of the Viceroy who often goeth to this place is wonderful stately, which some say is as great as the train of his master the King of Spain. At this meeting are carried about many sorts of sweetmeats and papers of comfits to be sold, for to relish a cup of cool water, which is cried about in curious glasses, to cool the blood of those love-hot gallants. But many times these their meetings sweetened with conserves and comfits have sour sauce at the end, for jealousy will not suffer a lady to be courted, no nor sometimes to be spoken to, but puts fury into the violent hand to draw a sword or dagger and to stab or murder whom he was jealous of, and when one sword is drawn thousands are presently drawn, some to right the party wounded or murdered; others to defend the party murdering, whose friends will not permit him to be apprehended, but will guard him with drawn swords until they have conveyed him to the sanctuary of some church, from whence the Viceroy his power is not able to take him for a legal trial.

3. THE *MESTIZO*:
SEED OF TOMORROW

The mestizo *arose from a process of racial fusion that began in the first days of the Spanish Conquest and has continued down to the present. The Spanish jurist Juan de Solórzano Pereira (1575–1655) discusses the status of the* mestizo *in colonial law and opinion.*

Turning now to the persons called mestizos and mulattoes, of whom there are great numbers in the Indies, first let me say that the name mestizo was assigned to the former because they represent a mixture of blood and nationality. ...

Juan de Solórzano Pereira, *Política indiana*, Madrid, 1930, 5 vols., I, pp. 445–448. (Excerpt translated by the editor.)

As for the mulattoes, although for the same reason they belong in the class of mestizos, yet as the offspring of Negro women and white men, or the reverse, which is the most strange and repulsive mixture of all, they bear this specific name which compares them to the species of the mule. ...

If these men were born of legitimate wedlock and had no other vices or defects, they could be regarded as citizens of those provinces and could be admitted to honor and office in them, as is argued by Victoria and Zapata. I am of the opinion that such an intention was the basis of certain royal decrees that permit mestizos to take holy orders and mestizas to become nuns, and admit mestizos to municipal offices and notaryships.

But because they are most often born out of adultery or other illicit unions, since few Spaniards of honorable position will marry Indian or Negro women ... , they bear the taint of illegitimacy and other vices which they take in, as it were, with their milk. And these men, I find by many other decrees, are forbidden to hold any responsible public office, whether it is that of Protector of the Indians, councilman, or notary public, unless they acknowledge this defect at the time of application and receive special dispensation from it; and those who have gained office in any other way are not allowed to keep it.

There are other decrees that forbid them to take holy orders, unless by special dispensation.

I shall content myself for the present with saying that if these mestizos (especially those in the Indies) possess recognized and assured virtue, and sufficient ability and learning, they could be extremely useful in matters relating to the Indians, being, as it were, their countrymen, and knowing their languages and customs. ...

But returning to the question of curacies, although for the reason given above it would be convenient to entrust them to mestizos, great care must be taken with this, for we see that the majority of them come from a vicious and depraved environment, and it is they who do the most harm to the Indians. ... And for this reason many decrees forbid them to visit or live in the Indian towns, and compel them to live in the Spanish towns, or in such towns as may be formed and populated by mestizos and mulattoes. These same decrees order that mestizas married to Spaniards, if charged with adultery, shall be tried and punished like Spanish women.

There are other decrees, of later date, issued in 1600 and 1608, directed to the viceroys of Peru Don Luis de Velasco and the marquis of Montes Claros, saying that the king had learned that the number of mestizos, mulattoes, and *zambahigos* (the children of Negro men and Indian women, or the reverse) was increasing sharply, and ordering them to take appropriate measures that men of such mixtures, vicious in their majority, should not cause injury and disturbances in that kingdom—a thing always to be feared from such people, especially if to the sins that arise from their evil birth are added those that spring from idleness and poor upbringing.

For this reason, although by the ordinances of the viceroy of Peru, Don Francisco de Toledo, they are exempt from paying tribute, by later decrees of the years 1600, 1612, 1619, by the celebrated decrees concerning personal service of 1601 and 1609, and by many others that have been successively promulgated, it is ordered that they pay tribute. And the same decrees command the viceroys to see that the mestizos and mulattoes, like the Indians, are made to labor in the mines and fields. ...

For it does not appear just that this labor [of the mines], which requires such physical strength ... , should be assigned entirely to the wretched Indians, while the mestizos and mulattoes, who are of such evil caste, race, and character, are left to idleness; this contravenes the rule that lewdness should not be more favored than chastity, and that the offspring of legitimate marriage should be more privileged than the illegitimate, as is taught by Saint Thomas and other authorities. ...

From this abuse results the fact that many Indian women desert their Indian husbands and neglect the children that they have by them, seeing them subject to tribute-payments and personal services, and desire, love, and spoil the children that they have out of wedlock by Spaniards or even by Negroes, because they are free and exempt from all burdens—a condition that plainly should not be permitted in any well-governed state.

4. THE INDIAN TOWN

Among the various races and mixtures that composed the population of the Spanish empire in the Americas, the Indians formed a nation apart. Most of them lived in their own self-governing communities in which Spaniards other than the village priest were forbidden to reside. In many regions they maintained intact their ancient clan or tribal organization, language, dress, and customs. Thomas Gage, who spent twelve years as a priest in Guatemala and amassed a tidy fortune from the piety and credulity of his native parishioners, describes the life of the Indian town.

Their ordinary clothing is a pair of linen or woollen drawers broad and open at the knees, without shoes (though in their journeys some will put on leathern sandals to keep the soles of their feet) or stockings, without any doublet, a short coarse shirt, which reacheth a little below their waist, and serves more for a doublet than for a shirt, and for a cloak a woollen or linen mantle (called *aiate*) tied with a knot over one shoulder, hanging down on the other side almost to the ground, with a twelvepenny or two shilling hat, which after

---

Gage, *The English-American*, pp. 234–247.

one good shower of rain like paper falls about their necks and eyes; their bed they carry sometime about them, which is that woollen mantle wherewith they wrap themselves about at night, taking off their shirt and drawers, which they lay under their head for a pillow; some will carry with them a short, slight, and light mat to lie, but those that carry it not with them, if they cannot borrow one of a neighbour, lie as willingly in their mantle upon the bare ground as a gentleman in England upon a soft down-bed, and thus do they soundly sleep, and loudly snort after a day's work, or after a day's journey with a hundred-weight upon their backs.

Those that are of the better sort, and richer, and who are not employed as *tamemez* to carry burdens, or as labourers to work for Spaniards, but keep at home following their own farms, or following their own mules about the country, or following their trades and callings in their shops, or governing the towns, as *alcaldes*, or *alguaziles*, officers of justice, may go a little better apparelled, but after the same manner. For some will have their drawers with a lace at the bottom, or wrought with some coloured silk or crewel, so likewise the mantle about them shall have either a lace, or some work of birds on it; some will wear a cut linen doublet, others shoes, but very few stockings or bands about their necks; and for their beds, the best Indian Governor or the richest, who may be worth four or five thousand ducats, will have little more than the poor *tamemez;* for they lie upon boards, or canes bound together, and raised from the ground, whereon they lay a board and handsome mat, and at their heads for man and wife two little stumps of wood for bolsters, whereon they lay their shirts and mantles and other clothes for pillows, covering themselves with a broader blanket than is their mantle, and thus hardly would Don Bernabé de Guzman the Governor of Petapa lie, and so do all the best of them.

The women's attire is cheap and soon put on; for most of them also go barefoot, the richer and better sort wear shoes, with broad ribbons for shoe strings, and for a petticoat, they tie about their waist a woollen mantle, which in the better sort is wrought with divers colors, but not sewed at all, pleated, or gathered in, but as they tie it with a list about them; they wear no shift next their body, but cover their nakedness with a kind of surplice (which they call *guaipil*) which hangs loose from their shoulders down a little below their waist, with open short sleeves, which cover half their arms; this *guaipil* is curiously wrought, especially in the bosom, with cotton, or feathers. The richer sort of them wear bracelets and bobs about their waists and necks; their hair is gathered up with fillets, without any coif or covering, except it be the better sort. When they go to church or abroad, they put upon their heads a veil of linen, which hangeth almost to the ground, and this is that which costs them most of all their attire, for that commonly it is of Holland or some good linen brought from Spain, or fine linen brought from China, which the better sort wear with a lace about. When they are at home at work they commonly take off their *guaipil*, or surplice, discovering the nakedness of their breasts and body. They lie also in their beds as do their husbands, wrapped up only with a mantle, or with a blanket.

Their houses are but poor thatched cottages, without any upper rooms, but commonly one or two only rooms below, in the one they dress their meat in the middle of it, making a compass for fire, with two or three stones, without any other chimney to convey the smoke away, which spreading itself about the room filleth the thatch and the rafters so with soot that all the room seemeth to be a chimney. The next unto it is not free from smoke and blackness, where sometimes are four or five beds according to the family. The poorer sort have but one room, where they eat, dress their meat, and sleep. Few there are that set any locks upon their doors, for they fear no robbing nor stealing, neither have they in their houses much to lose, earthen pots, and pans, and dishes, and cups to drink their chocolate being the chief commodities in their house. There is scarce any house which hath not also in the yard a stew, wherein they bathe themselves with hot water, which is their chief physic when they feel themselves distempered.

Among themselves they are in every town divided into tribes,[1] which have one chief head, to whom all that belong unto that tribe do resort in any difficult matters, who is bound to aid, protect, defend, counsel, and appear for the rest of his tribe before the officers of justice in any wrong that is like to be done unto them. When any is to be married, the father of the son that is to take a wife out of another tribe goeth unto the head of his tribe to give him warning of his son's marriage with such a maid. Then that head meets with the head of the maid's tribe, and they confer about it. The business commonly is in debate a quarter of a year; all which time the parents of the youth or man are with gifts to buy the maid; they are to be at the charges of all that is spent in eating and drinking when the heads of the two tribes do meet with the rest of the kindred of each side, who sometimes sit in conference a whole day, or most part of a night. After many days and nights thus spent, and a full trial being made of the one and other side's affection, if they chance to disagree about the marriage, then is the tribe and parents of the maid to restore back all that the other side hath spent and given. They give no portions with their daughters, but when they die their goods and lands are equally divided among their sons. If anyone want a house to live in or will repair and thatch his house anew, notice is given to the heads of the tribes, who warn all the town to come to help in the work, and everyone is to bring a bundle of straw, and other materials, so that in one day with the help of many they finish a house, without any charges more than of chocolate, which they minister in great cups as big as will hold above a pint, not putting in any costly materials, as do the Spaniards, but only a little aniseed, and chilli, or Indian pepper; or else they half fill the cup with *atole*, and pour upon it as much chocolate as will fill the cup and colour it.

In their diet the poorer sort are limited many times to a dish of *frijoles*, or Turkey beans, either black or white (which are there in very great abundance, and are kept dry for all the year) boiled with chilli; and if they can have this, they hold themselves well satisfied; with these beans, they make also dumplings, first boiling the bean a little, and then mingling it with a mass of maize, as we do mingle currents in our cakes, and so boil again the *frijoles* with the dumpling of maize mass, and so eat it hot, or keep it cold; but this and all whatsoever else they eat, they either eat it with green biting chilli, or else they dip it in water and salt, wherein is bruised some of that chilli. But if their means will not reach to *frijoles*, their ordinary fare and diet is their *tortillas* (so they call thin round cakes made of the dough and mass of maize) which they eat hot from an earthen pan, whereon they are soon baked with one turning over the fire; and these they eat alone either with chilli and salt, and dipping them in water and salt with a little bruised chilli. When their maize is green and tender, they boil some of those whole stalks or clusters, whereon the maize groweth with the leaf about, and so casting a little salt about it, they eat it. I have often eat of this, and found it as dainty as our young green peas, and very nourishing, but it much increaseth the blood. Also of this green and tender maize they make a furmety, boiling the maize in some of the milk which they have first taken out of it by bruising it. The poorest Indian never wants this diet, and is well satisfied as long as his belly is thoroughly filled.

But the poorest that live in such towns where flesh meat is sold will make a hard shift but that when they come from work on Saturday night they will buy one half real, or a real worth of fresh meat to eat on the Lord's day. Some will buy a good deal at once, and keep it long by dressing it into *tasajos*, which are bundles of flesh, rolled up and tied fast, which they do when, for example's sake, they have from a leg of beef sliced off from the bone all the flesh with the knife, after the length, form, and thinness of a line, or rope. Then they take the flesh and salt it (which being sliced and thinly cut, soon takes salt) and hang it up in their yards like a line from post to post, or from tree to tree, to the wind for a whole week, and then they hang it in the smoke another week, and after roll it up in small bundles, which become as hard as a stone, and so as they need it they wash it, boil it and eat. This is America's powdered beef, which they call *tasajo*. ...

As for drinking, the Indians generally are much given unto it; and drink if they have nothing else of their poor and simple chocolate, without sugar or many compounds, or of *atole*, until their bellies be ready to burst. But if they can get any drink that will make them mad drunk, they will not give it over as long as a drop is left, or a penny remains in their purse to purchase it. Among themselves they use to make such drinks as are in operation far stronger than wine; and these they confection in such great jars as come from Spain, wherein they put some little quantity of water, and fill up the jar with some molasses or juice of the sugar-cane, or some honey for to sweeten it; then for the strengthening of it, they put roots and leaves of tobacco, with other kind of roots which grow there, and they know to be strong in operation, and in some places I have known where they have put in a live toad, and so closed up the jar for a fortnight, or month's space, till all that they have put in him be thoroughly steeped and the toad consumed, and the drink well strengthened, then they open it and call their friends to the drinking of it (which commonly they do in the night time, lest their priest in the town should have notice of them in the day), which they never leave off until they be mad and raging drunk. This drink they call *chicha*, which stinketh most filthily, and certainly is the cause of many Indians' death, especially where they use the toad's poison with it. ...

And thus having spoken of apparel, houses, eating and drinking, it remains that I say somewhat of their civility, and religion of those who lived under the government of the Spaniards. From the Spaniards they have borrowed their civil government, and in all towns they have one, or two, *alcaldes*, with more or less *regidores* (who are as aldermen or jurats amongst us) and some *alguaziles*, more or less, who are as constables, to execute the orders of the alcalde (who is a mayor) with his brethren. In towns of three or four hundred families, or upwards, there are commonly two *alcaldes*, six *regidores*, two *alguaziles mayores*, and six under, or petty, *alguaziles*. And some towns are privileged with an Indian Governor, who is above the *alcaldes* and all the rest of the officers. These are changed every year by new election, and are chosen by the Indians themselves, who take their turns by the tribes or kindreds, whereby they are divided. Their offices begin on New Year's Day, and after that day their election is carried to the city of Guatemala (if in that district it be made) or else to the heads of justice, or Spanish governors of the several provinces, who confirm the new election, and take account of the last year's expenses made by the other officers, who carry with them their townbook of accounts; and therefore for this purpose every town hath a clerk, or scrivener, called *escribano* who commonly continueth many years in his office, by reason of the paucity and unfitness of Indian scriveners who are able to bear such a charge. This clerk hath many fees for his writings and informations, and accounts, as have the Spaniards, though not so much money or bribes, but a small matter, according to the poverty of the Indians. The Governor is also commonly continued many years, being some chief man among the Indians, except for his misdemeanours he be complained of, or the Indians in general do all stomach him.

Thus they being settled in a civil way of government they may execute justice upon all such Indians of their town as do notoriously and scandalously offend. They may imprison, fine, whip, and banish, but hang and quarter they may not; but must remit such cases to the Spanish governor. So likewise if a Spaniard passing by the town, or living in it, do trouble the peace, and misdemean himself, they may lay hold on him, and send him to the next Spanish justice, with a full information of his offences, but fine him, or keep him about one night in prison they may not. This order they have against Spaniards, but they dare not execute it, for a whole town standeth in awe of one Spaniard, and though he never so heinously offend, and be unruly, with oaths, threatenings, and drawing of his sword, he maketh them quake and tremble, and not presume to touch him; for they know if they do they shall have the worst, either by blows, or by some misinformation which he will give against them. ...

Amongst themselves, if any complaint be made against any Indian, they dare not meddle with him until they call all his kindred, and especially the head of that tribe to which he belongeth; who if he and the rest together find him to deserve imprisonment, or whipping, or any other punishment, then the officers of justices, the *alcaldes* or mayors, and their brethren the jurats inflict upon him that punishment which all shall agree upon. But yet after judgment and sentence given, they have another, which is their last appeal, if they please, and that is to their priest and friar, who liveth in their town, by whom they will sometimes be judged, and undergo what punishment he shall think fittest.

8

THE BOURBON REFORMS

AND SPANISH AMERICA

SPAIN MADE A REMARKABLE RECOVERY in the eighteenth century from the state of abject weakness into which it had fallen under the last Hapsburg kings. This revival is associated with the reigns of three princes of the Houses of Bourbon: Philip V (1700–1746), grandson of Louis XIV of France, and his two sons, Ferdinand VI (1746–1759) and Charles III (1759–1788).

The work of national reconstruction reached its peak under Charles III. During his reign Spanish industry, agriculture, and trade made marked gains. Clerical influence suffered a setback as a result of the expulsion of the Jesuits in 1767 and of decrees restricting the authority of the Inquisition. Under the cleansing influence of able and honest ministers, a new spirit of austerity and service began to appear among public officials.

In the field of colonial reform the Bourbons moved slowly and cautiously, as was natural in view of the fact that powerful vested interests were identified with the old order of things. The Casa de Contratación, or House of Trade, was gradually reduced in importance until it finally disappeared in 1790. A similar fate overtook the venerable Council of the Indies, although it was not abolished until 1854. Most of its duties were entrusted to a colonial minister appointed by the king. The Bourbons alternately suspended and tried to rehabilitate the fleet system of sailing, but in the end it was abandoned, the Portobello fleet disappearing in 1740, the Veracruz fleet in 1789. The Portobello and Veracruz fairs vanished contemporaneously. In the same period the trading monopoly of Cádiz was gradually eliminated. The success of the "free trade" policy was reflected in a spectacular increase in the value of Spain's commerce with Spanish America.

The eighteenth century witnessed a steady growth of agricultural, pastoral, and mining production in Spanish America. By contrast with these signs of progress, the once-flourishing colonial handicrafts industry declined, owing to the influx of cheap European wares with which the native products could not compete. Contraband trade, never completely eliminated under the Bourbons, reached vast proportions during the frequent intervals of warfare in which British naval power swept Spanish shipping from the seas.

The most important Bourbon political reform was the transfer to the colonies, between 1782 and 1790, of the intendant system, already introduced in Spain from France. The intendants (provincial governors) were expected to relieve the overburdened viceroys of many of their duties, especially in financial matters, and to develop agriculture, industry, and commerce and generally to promote the welfare of their respective districts. Many of the viceroys and intendants of the reform period were able and progressive men, devoted to the interests of the crown and their subjects. But the same cannot be said of the majority of their subordinates, who, like their predecessors, the *corregidores*, soon became notorious for their oppressive practices. Following the triumph of reaction in Spain after 1788, the familiar evils of administrative corruption, mismanagement, and indifference to the public interest reappeared on a large scale in the colonies as in Spain.

The Creole upper class enjoyed greater opportunities for material and cultural enrichment in the Bourbon era, but the same was not true of Indians, *mestizos*, and other laboring groups. The intolerable conditions of the common people led to major revolutionary outbreaks in Peru, Bolivia, and Colombia (1780–1783) that were sternly suppressed by Spanish arms.

1. THE BOURBON COMMERCIAL REFORMS

The Bourbon reforms in the field of colonial trade represented a supreme effort to recover for Spain a dominant position in the markets of Spanish America. The reform program provided for a stricter enforcement of the laws against contraband; more importantly, it included a series of measures designed to liberalize the commerce between Spain and its colonies while retaining the principle of peninsular trade monopoly. The Bourbon reforms, combined with a rising European demand for Spanish American products, helped to produce a remarkable expansion of colonial trade and prosperity in the last half of the eighteenth century. The Mexican historian Lucas Alamán surveys the beneficial effects of these reforms on the commerce of New Spain.

Commerce with Spain, the only one that was permitted, was restricted until 1778 to the port of Cadiz, where were assembled, under the inspection of the *audiencia* and the House of Trade of Seville, all the goods bound for

---

Lucas Alamán, *Historia de Méjico*, 1849–1852, 5 vols., I, pp. 109–110, 110–113. (Excerpt translated by the editor.)

America. They were carried there in the fleets, which departed each year and whose routes were minutely prescribed by the laws, and in the interval there was no other communication than that of the dispatch boats and the store-ships coming with quicksilver. On the arrival of the fleets a great fair was held at Panama, for all South America, and another in Jalapa for New Spain, whence this town acquired the name of Jalapa of the Fair.

This order of things gave rise to a double monopoly: that enjoyed by the houses of Cadiz and Seville which made up the cargoes and that which was secured at the fairs by the American merchants, who made agreements among themselves whereby particular merchants acquired complete control over certain lines of goods. Since the supply of these goods was not renewed for a long time, it was in their power to raise prices at will, whence arose the high prices of some commodities, especially when maritime war prevented the arrival of the fleets for several years. This condition gave occasion for the arbitrary measures of certain viceroys in fixing retail prices in favor of the consumer, as was done by the second Duke of Albuquerque in 1703.

Commerce with Asia was reduced to a single vessel, known as the "China-ship," which was sent once a year from Manila and, passing in sight of San Blas, arrived at Acapulco, to which came the buyers for the fair that was held there; after the fair it sailed again, carrying the cash proceeds of the sale of the goods that it had brought, the subvention with which the royal treasury of Mexico aided that of Manila, the criminals condemned to serve time in those islands, and those dissipated youths whom their families had consigned to this kind of exile as a disciplinary measure, called "being sent to China." Commerce between New Spain and Peru, Guatemala, and New Granada by way of the Pacific was prohibited for a variety of reasons.

By the ordinance of October 12, 1778, all this system of commerce with Europe was changed. The fleets ceased to come, the last being the one that arrived at Vera Cruz in January of that year, under the command of Don Antonio de Ulloa, so celebrated for his voyage to Peru and his secret report to the king on the state of that kingdom. Commerce thus became free for all Spanish ships sailing from habilitated ports in the peninsula, but it could only be carried on in New Spain through the port of Vera Cruz, and European goods could not be introduced from Havana or any other American place but must be brought directly from Spain.

The results of this change were very important, not only because of the abundance of goods and price reductions that it yielded but also because it ended the monopoly and the vast profits acquired with little labor by the *flotistas*, the name given to the monopolists. These men, finding it impossible to continue their former practices, retired from commerce and invested their capital in agriculture and mining, which they greatly stimulated, especially the latter. Their places were taken by a larger number of individuals, who in order to prosper had to display much activity, and thus instead of a few large capitals there arose many small ones, which, distributed among all the towns, contributed largely to their betterment.

In this same period were lifted the odious restrictions on commerce among the provinces or kingdoms of America; and a royal decree of January 17, 1774, promulgated in the Prado, conceded freedom of trade in the Pacific, though only in the goods and productions of the respective provinces. Later declarations broadened this freedom, removing the restrictions imposed by the aforementioned order in regard to European and Asiatic goods. . . .

The exclusive colonial system of Spain provided great and valuable compensations for the prohibitions that it imposed. If one glances at the balance of trade of Vera Cruz, the only port habilitated in that period for trade with Europe and the West Indies, for the year 1803, one of the last years of peace with England, it will be seen that of the total exports to Spain, worth 12,000,000 pesos, more than a third, or 4,500,000, were in the form of produce, including not only 27,000 *arrobas* of cochineal of a value of 2,200,000 pesos but also 150,000 pounds of indigo, worth 260,000 pesos, and 500,000 *arrobas* of sugar of the value of 1,500,000 pesos, besides 26,600 *quintales* of logwood and 17,000 *quintales* of cotton. Among the exports to various points in America one notes 20,000 *tercios* of flour, 14,700 *varas* of coarse frieze, 1,300 *varas* of baize, 1,760 boxes of soap, and 700 boxes of ordinary Puebla chinaware; all this, with other minor articles, comes to a value of more than 600,000 pesos a year.

The effect of these exports was to give a great value to the sugarcane plantations, while the flour of Puebla, flowing down to Vera Cruz to satisfy not only the needs of that place but also those of Havana, the other islands, and Yucatan, left the provisioning of the markets of Mexico City to the wheatfields of Querétaro and Guanajuato, adding to their value and bringing prosperity to the wheat farmers of those provinces. All this active traffic infused animation and life into our internal commerce. Mexican agriculture today would gladly exchange the sterile freedom to cultivate vines and olives for an exportation of 500,000 *arrobas* of sugar and 20,000 *tercios* of flour.

2. THE REVIVAL OF MINING

The eighteenth century saw a marked revival of the silver mining industry in the Spanish colonies. Peru and Mexico both shared in this advance, but the Mexican mines, whose production had been rising quite consistently since the sixteenth century, forged far ahead of their Peruvian rivals in the Bourbon era. As in the case of agriculture, the increase in production was primarily due not to improved technique but rather to the open-

ing of many new as well as old mines and the growth of the labor force. Although the Bourbon kings and their colonial agents exerted themselves to overcome the backwardness of the mining industry, their efforts were largely frustrated by the traditionalism of the mine owners and by lack of capital to finance necessary changes.

Since the brilliant period of the reign of Charles the 5th, Spanish America has been separated from Europe, with respect to the communication of discoveries useful to society. The imperfect knowledge which was possessed in the 16th century relative to mining and smelting, in Germany, Biscay, and the Belgic provinces, rapidly passed into Mexico and Peru, on the first colonization of these countries; but since that period, to the reign of Charles the third, the American miners have learned hardly anything from the Europeans, but the blowing up with powder those rocks which resist the *pointrole*. This King and his successor have shown a praiseworthy desire of imparting to the colonies all the advantages derived by Europe from the improvement in machinery, the progress of chemical science, and their application to metallurgy. German miners have been sent at the expense of the court to Mexico, Peru, and the kingdom of new Granada; but their knowledge has been of no utility, because the mines of Mexico are considered as the property of the individuals, who direct the operations, without the government being allowed to exercise the smallest influence. ...

After the picture which we have just drawn of the actual state of the mining operations, and of the bad economy which prevails in the administration of the mines of New Spain, we ought not to be astonished at seeing works, which for a long time have been most productive, abandoned whenever they have reached a considerable depth, or whenever the veins have appeared less abundant in metals. We have already observed, that in the famous mine of Valenciana, the annual expenses rose in the space of fifteen years from two millions of francs to four millions and a half. Indeed, if there be much water in this mine, and if it require a number of horse baritels to draw it off, the profit must, to the proprietors, be little or nothing. The greatest part of the defects in the management which I have been pointing out, have been long known to a respectable and enlightened body, the *Tribunal de Minería* of Mexico, to the professors of the school of mines, and even to several of the native miners, who without having ever quitted their country, know the imperfection of the old methods; but we must repeat here, the changes can only take place very slowly among a people who are not fond of innovations, and in a country where the government possesses so little influence on the works which are generally the property of individuals, and not of shareholders. It is

Alexander von Humboldt, *Political Essay on the Kingdom of New Spain*, London, 1822–1823, 4 vols., III, pp. 231–246.

a prejudice to imagine, that the mines of New Spain on account of their wealth, do not require in their management the same intelligence and the same economy which are necessary to the preservation of the mines of Saxony and the Hartz. We must not confound the abundance of ores with their intrinsic value. The most part of the minerals of Mexico being very poor, as we have already proved, and as all those who do not allow themselves to be dazzled by false calculations very well known, an enormous quantity of gangue impregnated with metals must be extracted, in order to produce two millions and a half of marcs of silver. Now it is easy to conceive that in mines of which the different works are badly disposed, and without any communication with one another, the expense of extraction must be increased in an alarming manner, in proportion as the shifts (*pozos*) increasing in depth, and the galleries (*cañones*) become more extended.

The labour of a miner is entirely free throughout the whole kingdom of New Spain; and no Indian or Mestizo can be forced to dedicate themselves to the working of mines. It is absolutely false, though the assertion has been repeated in works of the greatest estimation, that the court of Madrid sends out galley slaves to America, to work in the gold and silver mines. The mines of Siberia have been peopled by Russian malefactors; but in the Spanish colonies this species of punishment has been fortunately unknown for centuries. The Mexican miner is the best paid of all miners; he gains at least from 25 to 30 francs per week of six days, while the wages of labourers who work in the open air, husbandmen for example, are seven livres sixteen sous, on the central table land, and nine livres twelve sous near the coast. The miners, *tenateros* and *faeneros* occupied in transporting the minerals to the place of assemblage (*despachos*) frequently gain more than six francs per day, of six hours. Honesty is by no means so common among the Mexican as among the German or Swedish miners; and they make use of a thousand tricks to steal very rich specimens of ores. As they are almost naked, and are searched on leaving the mine in the most indecent manner, they conceal small morsels of native silver, or red sulphuret and muriate of silver in their hair, under their arm-pits, and in their mouths; and they even lodge in their anus, cylinders of clay which contain the metal. The cylinders are called *longanas*, and they are sometimes found of the length of thirteen centimetres (five inches). It is a most shocking spectacle to see in the large mines of Mexico, hundreds of workmen, among whom there are a great number of very respectable men, all compelled to allow themselves to be searched on leaving the pit or the gallery. A register is kept of the minerals found in the hair, in the mouth, or other parts of the miners' bodies. In the mine of Valenciana at Guanaxuato, the value of these stolen minerals, of which a great part was composed of the *longanas*, amounted between 1774 and 1787, to the sum of 900,000 francs.

3. Colonial Industry in Decline

In the last half of the eighteenth century, colonial manufacturing, after experiencing a long and steady growth, began to decline because of the influx of cheap European wares with which the domestic products could not compete. Industrial decadence was accompanied by a falling-off of internal trade in some areas as Spanish American economic life became increasingly geared to the export of agricultural and pastoral products and the import of European finished goods. Alexander von Humboldt's account of his visits to Mexican manufacturing centers clearly reveals the weakness and backwardness of colonial industry.

The oldest cloth manufactories of Mexico are those of Tezcuco. They were in great part established in 1592 by the viceroy Don Louis de Velasco II, the son of the celebrated constable of Castille, who was second viceroy of New Spain. By degrees, this branch of national industry passed entirely into the hands of the Indians and Mestizos of Querétaro and Puebla. I visited the manufactories of Querétaro in the month of August 1803. They distinguish there the great manufactories, which they call *obrajes*, from the small, which go by the name of *trapiches*. There were 20 *obrajes*, and more than 300 *trapiches* at that time, who altogether wrought up 63,900 *arrobas* of Mexican sheepwool. According to accurate lists, drawn up in 1793, there were at that period at Querétaro, in the *obrajes* alone, 215 looms, and 1500 workmen who manufactured 6,042 pieces, or 226,522 *varas* of cloth (*paños*); 287 pieces, or 39,718 *varas* of ordinary woollens (*xerguatillas*); 207 pieces, or 15,369 *varas* of baize (*bayetas*); and 161 pieces, or 17,960 *varas* of serge (*xergas*). In this manufacture they consumed 46,270 *arrobas* of wool, the price of which only amounted to 161,945 piastres. They reckon in general seven *arrobas* to one piece of *xerguatilla*, and five *arrobas* to one piece of *xerga*. The value of the cloths and woollen stuffs of the *obrajes* and *trapiches* of Querétaro at present amounts to more than 600,000 piastres, or three millions of francs per annum.

On visiting these workshops, a traveller is disagreeably struck, not only with the great imperfection of the technical process in the preparation for dyeing, but in a particular manner also with the unhealthiness of the situation, and the bad treatment to which the workmen are exposed. Free men, Indians, and people of colour, are confounded with criminals distributed by justice among the manufactories, in order to be compelled to work. All appear half naked, covered with rags, meagre, and deformed. Every workshop resembles a dark prison. The doors, which are double, remain constantly

---

Humboldt, *Political Essay on the Kingdom of New Spain*, III, pp. 462–469.

shut, and the workmen are not permitted to quit the house. Those who are married are only allowed to see their families on Sunday. All are unmercifully flogged, if they commit the smallest trespass on the order established in the manufactory.

We have difficulty in conceiving how the proprietors of the *obrajes* can act in this manner with free men, as well as how the Indian workman can submit to the same treatment with the galley slaves. These pretended rights are in reality acquired by stratagem. The manufacturers of Querétaro employ the same trick, which is made use of in several of the cloth manufactories of Quito, and in the plantations, where from a want of slaves, labourers are extremely rare. They choose from among the Indians the most miserable, but such as show an aptitude for the work, and they advance them a small sum of money. The Indian, who loves to get intoxicated, spends it in a few days, and having become the debtor of the master, he is shut up in the workshop, under the pretence of paying off the debt by the work of his hands. They allow him only a real and a half, or 20 sous tournois per day of wages; but in place of paying it in ready money, they take care to supply him with meat, brandy, and clothes, on which the manufacturer gains from fifty to sixty per cent; and in this way the most industrious workman is forever in debt, and the same rights are exercised over him which are believed to be acquired over a purchased slave. I knew many persons in Querétaro, who lamented with me the existence of these enormous abuses. Let us hope that a government friendly to the people, will turn their attention to a species of oppression so contrary to humanity, the laws of the country, and the progress of Mexican industry.

With the exception of a few stuffs of cotton mixed with silk, the manufacture of silks is at present next to nothing in Mexico. In the time of Acosta, towards the conclusion of the sixteenth century, silk worms brought from Europe were cultivated near Panuco, and in la Misteca, and excellent taffeta was there manufactured with Mexican silk.

On my passage through Querétaro, I visited the great manufactory of cegars (*fábrica de puros y cigarros*), in which 3000 people, including 1900 women, are employed. The halls are very neat, but badly aired, very small, and consequently excessively warm. They consume daily in this manufacture 130 reams (*resmas*) of paper, and 2770 pounds of tobacco leaf. In the course of the month of July, 1803, there was manufactured to the amount of 185,288 piastres; viz. 2,654,820 small chests (*caxillas*) of cegars, which sell for 165,926 piastres, and 289,799 chests of *puros* or cegars, which are not enveloped in paper. The expense of manufacture of the month of July alone, amounted to 31,789 piastres. It appears that the royal manufactory of Querétaro annually produces more than 2,200,000 piastres, in *puros* and *cigarros*.

The manufacture of hard soap is a considerable object of commerce at Puebla, Mexico, and Guadalaxara. The first of these towns produces nearly 200,000 *arrobas* per annum; and in the intendancy of Guadalaxara, the quantity manufactured is computed at 1,300,000 *livres tournois*. The abundance of soda which we find almost everywhere at elevations of 2000 or 2500 metres, in the interior table land of Mexico, is highly favourable to this manufacture.

...

The town of Puebla was formerly celebrated for its fine manufactories of delf ware (*loza*) and hats. We have already observed that, till the commencement of the eighteenth century, these two branches of industry enlivened the commerce between Acapulco and Peru. At present there is little or no communication between Puebla and Lima, and the delf manufactories have fallen so much off, on account of the low price of the stone ware and porcelain of Europe imported at Vera Cruz, that of 446 manufactures which were still existing in 1793, there were in 1802 only sixteen remaining of delf ware, and two of glass.

4. POLITICAL REFORM: THE INTENDANT SYSTEM

The intendant reform was made by Charles III in the interests of greater administrative efficiency and increased royal revenues from the colonies. Among their many duties, the intendants were expected to further the economic development of their districts by promoting the cultivation of new crops, the improvement of mining, the building of roads and bridges, and the establishment of consulados (chambers of commerce) and economic societies. The historian Alamán gives a glowing account of the favorable consequences of the establishment of the intendant system in New Spain and of the accomplishments of two model intendants.

The principal source of profit of the *alcaldes mayores* consisted in the traffic they carried on under the pretext of getting the Indians to work, as was recommended by the laws. They assigned them certain tasks and purchased the product at low prices, paying for it in necessary articles of dress and food that were overpriced. Having all authority in their hands, they compelled the Indians to fulfill these contracts with great punctuality, and reaped large profits thereby. This was particularly true in those districts where there was some valuable product, such as cochineal in Oaxaca, which constituted a monopoly for those officers and for the merchants who equipped them with capital and goods. Meanwhile the Indians were cruelly oppressed. A miserable system of administration was this, in which the pecuniary advantage of the governors was rooted in the oppression and misery of the governed! The Duke of Linares, in his vigorous and concise style, characterized it in a few

---

Alamán, *Historia de Méjico*, I, pp. 73–76. (Excerpt translated by the editor.)

words: "Although the jurisdiction of the *alcaldes mayores* is most extensive, I can define it very briefly, for it amounts to this: They are faithless to God from the time they enter upon their employment, by breaking the oath they have taken; they are faithless to their king, because of the *repartimientos* they engage in; and they sin against the common Indians, by tyrannizing over them as they do."

The whole order of things, so unjust and oppressive, ceased with the promulgation of the Ordinance of Intendants, published by Minister [José de] Gálvez on December 4, 1786, and limited at that time to New Spain alone, but later extended, with appropriate modifications, to all Spanish America. In it, under the titles of "the four departments of justice, police, finance, and war," were set forth the most comprehensive rules for the administration of the country in these spheres and for the encouragement of agriculture, industry, and mining. The whole territory of the vice-royalty, including Yucatán and the *provincias internas*, was divided into twelve intendancies, which took the names of their capitals. The corregimiento of Querétaro was retained for civil and judicial matters, but it was made financially dependent on the intendancy of Mexico. To the posts of intendants were appointed men of integrity and intelligence in the performance of their functions. Among those who distinguished themselves by their special merit were the intendants of Guanajuato and Puebla.

Minister Gálvez, at the time when he was in power, sought to place all his relatives in high posts, and their actions justified this preference. Don Matías, his brother, and Don Bernardo, his nephew, succeeded each other as viceroys of Mexico; the latter married in New Orleans, while in command of the expedition that reconquered the Floridas, Doña Felicitas Saint-Maxent, whose two sisters, Doña Victoria and Doña Mariana, married Don Juan Antonio de Riaño and Don Manuel de Flon, respectively. At the time of the creation of the intendancies, the former was assigned that of Valladolid, where he remained only a short time, being transferred immediately to the more important one of Guanajuato; and Flon was placed over that of Puebla.

The strict and honorable Flon reformed great abuses, encouraged all the branches of industry in his province, and notably beautified its capital. Riaño, of equal integrity but of a mild and affable disposition, had served in the royal navy, and to a knowledge of mathematics and astronomy, natural in that profession, united a taste for literature and the fine arts. These interests, and in particular his delight in architecture, he introduced to Guanajuato; through his influence there were erected, not only in the capital but in all the province, magnificent structures, whose building he himself supervised, even instructing the stonecutters in the art of hewing stone. He promoted the study of the Latin classics of the best Spanish writers; it was owing to his influence that the young men of Guanajuato devoted themselves to the study of the Castilian tongue and to its correct pronunciation.

French, the native tongue of his wife, was spoken in their home, and he introduced among the youth of the provincial capital a taste for that language and its literature, together with an elegance of manners unknown in other cities of the province. He was also responsible for the development of interest in drawing and music and for the cultivation of mathematics, physics, and chemistry in the school that had formerly been maintained by the Jesuits. To that end he zealously patronized Don José Antonio Rojas, professor of mathematics in that school and a graduate of the School of Mines. He also established a theater, promoted the cultivation of olives and vines, and diligently fostered the mining industry, the chief wealth of that province, by encouraging the rich citizens of Guanajuato to form companies for the exploitation of old and abandoned mines as well as new ones.

5. THE MORE IT CHANGES ...

Plus ça change, plus c'est la même chose could be fairly applied to Spain's Indian policy. The Ordinance of Intendants, by abolishing the offices of corregidor and alcalde mayor and forbidding their successors, the subdelegates, to engage in the infamous reparto de mercancías, promised to inaugurate a new and better day for the Indian. Despite Alamán's contention (see the previous selection) that the old order of things, "so unjust and oppressive, ceased with the promulgation of the Ordinance of Intendants," other observers came to different conclusions. In Mexico an enlightened prelate, Bishop Manuel Abad Queipo of Michoacán, denounced the entire system of subjection and segregation of the Indians and mixed castes and flatly stated that the natives were worse off than they had been before the intendant reform.

The population of New Spain is composed of some four and a half million inhabitants, who can be divided into three classes: Spaniards, Indians, and castes. The Spaniards number one tenth of the total population but possess almost the entire population or wealth of the kingdom. The other two classes, forming the other nine tenths, can be divided into two parts castes, the other part pure Indians. The Indians and castes are employed in domestic service, agricultural labors, and the ordinary tasks of commerce and industry—that is to say, they are servants and day-laborers for the Spaniards. Consequently there arises between them and the Spaniards that opposition of interests and views that is typical of those who have nothing and those who have everything—between superiors and inferiors. Envy, theft, and unwilling

José María Luis Mora, *Obras sueltas*, Paris, 1837, 2 vols., I, pp. 55–57. (Excerpt translated by the editor.)

service are the traits of the latter; arrogance, exploitation, and harsh treatment, the qualities of the former. These evils are to a certain extent common to all the world. But in America they are immeasurably greater because there are no gradations or intermediate states: all are either rich or wretched, noble or infamous.

In effect, the two classes of Indians and castes are sunk in the greatest abasement and degradation. The color, ignorance, and misery of the Indians place them at an infinite distance from a Spaniard. The ostensible privileges which the laws accord them do them little good and in most respects injure them greatly. Shut up in a narrow space of six hundred *varas*, assigned by law to the Indian towns, they possess no individual property and are obliged to work the communal lands. This cultivation is made all the more hateful by the fact that in recent years it has become increasingly difficult for them to enjoy any of the fruits of their labor. Under the new intendant system they cannot draw on the communal funds [*caja de comunidad*] without special permission from the office of the royal exchequer [*junta superior de la real hacienda*] in Mexico City.

Forbidden by law to commingle with the other castes, they are deprived of the instruction and assistance that they should receive from contact with these and other people. They are isolated by their language, and by a useless, tyrannical form of government. In each town there are found eight or ten old Indians who live in idleness at the expense of their fellows and artfully try to perpetuate their ancient customs, usages, and gross superstitions, ruling them like despots. Incapable, by law, of making a binding contract or of running into debt to the extent of more than five pesos—in a word, of any dealings at all—they cannot learn anything or better their fortune or in any way raise themselves above their wretched condition. Solorzano, Fraso, and other Spanish authors have wondered why the privileges granted them have redounded to their injury; but it is greater cause for wonder that such men as these should have failed to understand that the source of the evil lies in these very privileges. They are an offensive weapon employed by the white class against the Indians, and never serve to defend the latter. This combination of causes makes the Indians indifferent to their future and to all that does not excite the passions of the moment.

The castes are declared infamous by law, as descendants of Negro slaves. They are subject to the payment of tribute, which is punctiliously recorded; as a result, this obligation has become a brand of slavery which neither the passage of time nor the mixture of successive generations can ever obliterate. There are many of these who in their color, physiognomy, and conduct could pass for Spaniards if it were not for this impediment, which reduces them all to the same state. . . .

The Indians as well as the castes are governed directly by magistrates of districts [*justicias territoriales*] whose conduct has measurably contributed to the situation in which they find themselves. The *alcaldes mayores* considered themselves not so much justices as merchants, endowed with the exclusive privilege ... of trading in their province and of extracting from it in a five-year term of office from thirty to two hundred thousand pesos. Their usurious and arbitrary *repartimientos* caused great injuries. But despite this state of affairs two favorable circumstances commonly resulted, one being that they administered justice with impartiality and rectitude in cases in which they were not parties, the other being that they fostered agriculture and industry, in their own interests.

The Spanish government undertook to put an end to these abuses by replacing the *alcaldes mayores* with the subdelegates. But since the latter were not assigned any fixed salary, the remedy proved much worse than the evil. If they adhere to the schedule of fees, among a wretched folk who litigate only against each other, they will inevitably perish of hunger. They must of necessity prostitute their posts, swindle the poor, and traffic in justice. For the same reason it is extremely difficult for the intendants to find suitable individuals to fill these posts. They are sought, therefore, only by bankrupts or by those whose conduct and talents unfit them for success in the other walks of life. Under these conditions, what benefits, what protection, can these ministers of law dispense to the abovementioned two classes? How can they attract their good-will and respect, when extortion and injustice are virtually their livelihood?

6. THE PLAN OF TUPAC AMARU

The general causes of the great revolt of 1780–1781 in Peru are sufficiently clear. More obscure are the precise aims that the rebel leader, Tupac Amaru (José Gabriel Condorcanqui), set for himself. The fiscal, or prosecuting attorney of the viceroyalty of Buenos Aires offers a shrewd and convincing argument in favor of the thesis that the rebel leader aimed at independence.

What is worthy of attention in this affair is not so much the pitiful death of the corregidor Don Antonio de Arriaga, the theft of his fortune, the seizure of the arms that he had in his house, or the outrages committed by the perfidious Tupac-Amaru, as the astuteness, the painstaking care, and the deceptions with which he managed to perform them and to subvert that and other provinces, preparing them to carry out his reprehensible secret designs.

"Visita del fiscal del virreinato de Buenos Aires, enero 15 de 1781," in: Manuel de Odriozola (ed)., *Documentos históricos del Perú*, Lima, 1863, pp. 132–133. (Excerpt translated by the editor.)

It appears that in order to seize the corregidor Arriaga, in his own house, he arranged a banquet for his victim. In order to summon the military chiefs, caciques, and Indians of the province, he compelled the unhappy corregidor to issue or sign orders to that effect. In order to drag him to the gallows in the presence of the multitude with no disturbance, he published a decree, pretending that he acted on His Majesty's orders. On the same pretext, after this horrible deed, he departed for the neighboring province of Quispicanchi, in order to perpetrate similar atrocities on the corregidor and as many Spaniards as he could find, and as soon as he had returned to his town of Tungasuca issued orders to the caciques of neighboring provinces to imitate his example.

And although in the provinces of Azangaro and Carabaya, which belonged to this viceroyalty of Buenos Aires, his wicked designs failed to bear fruit, thanks to the loyalty with which his commissioner Don Diego Chuquiguanca (the cacique and governor of the town of Azangaro) and his sons turned over the dispatches, of which copies are found in the file on this case, the fact is that the province of Quispicachi, since the flight of Don Fernando Cabrera, its present corregidor, is under the sway of the rebel Tupac-Amaru; and he himself asserts in one of the papers written at Chuquiguanca that four more provinces obey his orders. And, knowing as he did the natives' great respect for the orders of the king and their hatred of the corregidores and their European associates, he probably did not find it difficult to incite them to execute the supposed orders of the king.

But the essence of the careful planning and perfidy of the traitor Tupac-Amaru consists in this, that after speaking so often of the royal orders which authorized him to proceed against the corregidores and other Europeans, in his orders, letters, and messages, and in the edicts which he dispatched to Don Diego Chuquiguanca, in order to revolutionize the province and Carabaya, he now says nothing about the orders of the king, and proceeds as the most distinguished Indian of the royal blood and principal line of the Incas to liberate his countrymen from the injuries, injustices, and slavery which the European corregidores had inflicted on them, while the superior courts turned a deaf ear to their complaints. From which it follows that he repeatedly used the name of the king—in a vague way, not specifying our present ruler, Charles III—only to secure the acquiescence of the natives of those provinces in the violence done to Arriaga and to induce them to do the same to other corregidores. And considering these aims partially achieved, he transforms himself from a royal commissioner into a redeemer from injustices and burdens, moved only by pity for his compatriots, preparing the way for them to acclaim him as king, or at least to support their benefactor with arms, until they have raised him to the defunct throne of the tyrannical pagan kings of Peru, which is doubtless the goal of his contrivings.

Actually, he has already succeeded in assembling a large number of Indians, as noted by Colonel Don Pedro la Vallina (who was his prisoner) in a letter contained in the file on this case—and with their aid, it is stated, he defeated and slew some 300 men who came out to halt his advance on Cuzco, and took their weapons to arm the rebels who follow him. He took these first successful steps in his titanic enterprise after certain other things had occurred: the rising that took place in Arequipa as a result of the establishment of a customshouse; the rioting that with less cause broke out in the city of La Paz; the disturbances that occurred in the provinces of Chayanta for the same reason; and the rumors that the natives in other provinces were somewhat restless. When one considers that the rebel Tupac-Amaru, informed of these events, offers the natives freedom, not only from customshouse duties but from sales taxes, tributes, and forced labor in the mines, it must be admitted that he offers them a powerful inducement to follow him, and that there is imminent danger that the party of rebellion will progressively increase unless the most energetic effort is made to slay this insolent rebel, the prime mover of this conspiracy, so that others may be deterred from joining the rebellion and abandoning their loyalty to their legitimate monarch and natural lord, to the detriment of themselves and their commonwealth.

7. A CHARTER OF LIBERTY

Although produced by the same causes, the rising of the Comuneros *in New Granada was a relatively peaceful affair by contrast with the vast upheaval in Peru. Its reformist spirit was reflected in the insurgent slogan:* Viva el rey y muera el mal gobierno! *(Long live the king, and down with the rotten government!) But in view of its organization and its effort to form a common front of all colonial groups with grievances against Spanish authority (excepting only the Black slaves), the revolt of the* comuneros *marked an advance over the chaotic course of events to the south. The popular basis of the* comunero *movement is evident from the terms that the rebel delegates presented to the Spanish commissioners and that the latter signed and later repudiated. A number of important or typical articles follow.*

1. The tax entitled Armada de Barlovento[1] must be abolished so completely that its name shall never again be heard in this kingdom. ...
4. In view of the poverty of this kingdom, stamped paper shall circulate only in sheets of half *real*, for the use of ecclesiastics, religious, Indians, and poor people, and in sheets of two *reales* for the legal titles and lawsuits of persons of some wealth; and no other stamped paper shall circulate. ...
5. The new tax on tobacco shall be completely abolished. ...

Manuel Briceño, *Los comuneros*, Bogotá, 1880, Appendix, pp. 122–132. (Excerpt translated by the editor.)

7. Considering the miserable state of all the Indians, who go about more poorly clothed and fed than hermits, and whose small knowledge, limited faculties, and meager harvests prevent them from paying the high tribute which the *corregidores* exact with such severity, not to mention the stipends assigned to their curates. The total annual tribute of the Indians shall be only four pesos, and that of mulattoes subject to tribute shall be two pesos. The curates shall not collect from the Indians any fee for the administration of holy oils, burials, and weddings, nor shall they compel them to serve as mayordomos at their saints' festivals. The cost of these festivals shall (except when some pious person offers to bear them) be borne by the brotherhood. … Furthermore, those Indians who have been removed from their towns but whose lands have not been sold or transferred shall be returned to their lands of immemorial possession; and all the lands which they at present possess shall be theirs, not only for their use but as their property, which they may use as the owners thereof. …

9. The *alcabala*, henceforth and forever, shall be two per cent of all fruits, goods, cattle, and articles of every kind when sold or exchanged. …

10. Since the cause of the widespread commotions in this kingdom and in that of Lima has been the imprudent conduct of the *visitadores*, who tried to squeeze blood out of stones and destroy us with their despotic rule, until the people of this kingdom, ordinarily so docile and submissive, were made desperate by their growing extortions and could no longer tolerate their tyrannical rule. …, we demand that Don Juan Gutierrez de Piñeres, *visitador* of the royal audiencia, be expelled from this kingdom to Spain, where our Catholic Monarch, reflecting on the results of his arbitrary conduct, shall do with him as he thinks best. And never again must officials be sent us who would treat us so severely and unwisely, for in such a case we shall again join together to repel any oppression that may be directed against us on any pretext whatever.
…

18. All the officers on the present expedition, with the ranks of commander-general, captains-general, territorial captains, lieutenants, ensigns, sergeants, and corporals, shall retain their respective appointments, and shall be obliged to assemble their companies on Sunday afternoon of each week to train them in the use of arms, both offensive and defensive, against the event that an effort be made to break the agreements that we are now making in good faith, and also to aid His Majesty in resisting his enemies. …

21. In filling offices of the first, second, and third classes, natives of America shall be privileged and preferred over Europeans, who daily manifest their antipathy toward us … , for in their ignorance they believe that they are the masters and that all Americans of any kind are their inferiors and servants. And so that this irrational view may disappear, Europeans shall be employed only in case of necessity and according to their ability, good will, and attachment to the Americans, for since we are all subjects of the same king

and lord we should live like brothers, and whoever strives to lord it over others and advance himself against the rule of equality must be removed from among us. ...

32. The order greatly reducing the number of grocery stores has had the result that the stores licensed in each town are owned by the wealthiest or most favored individuals. We therefore ask, as a matter of public benefit, that the right to establish stores be granted to all inhabitants of the kingdom, as was formerly the case, without limitation as to their number.

9
ᔕ

COLONIAL CULTURE
AND THE ENLIGHTENMENT

COLONIAL CULTURE in most of its aspects was a projection of contemporaneous Spanish culture and only faintly reflected native American influences. Colonial culture thus suffered from all the infirmities of its parent but inevitably lacked the breadth and vitality of Spanish literature and art, the product of a much older and more mature civilization.

The church enjoyed a virtual monopoly of colonial education on all levels. Poverty condemned the great majority of the natives and mixed castes to illiteracy. The universities of Lima and Mexico City, both chartered in 1551, were the first permanent institutions of higher learning. Because they were modeled on Spain's University of Salamanca, their organization, curricula, and methods of instruction were medieval.

Within the limits imposed by official censorship and their own backgrounds, colonial scholars, especially those of the sixteenth and early seventeenth centuries, were able to make impressive contributions in the fields of history, anthropology, linguistics, geography, and natural history. The second half of the seventeenth century saw a decline in the quantity and quality of scholarly production. Nevertheless, in this period two remarkable men, Carlos Sigüenza y Góngora, in Mexico, and Pedro de Peralta Barnuevo, in Peru, foreshadowed the eighteenth-century Enlightenment by the universality of their interests and by their concern with the practical uses of science.

Colonial literature, with some notable exceptions, was a pallid reflection of prevailing literary trends in Spain. Among a multitude of poetasters towered a strange and rare genius, one of the greatest poets of the New World, Sor Juana Inés de la Cruz. Sor Juana could not escape the pressures of her environment. Rebuked by the bishop of Puebla for her worldly interests, she ultimately gave up her books and scientific instruments and devoted the remainder of her brief life to religious devotions and charitable works.

Colonial art drew its principal inspiration from Spanish sources, but Indian influence was visible, particularly in sculpture and architecture. As might be expected, religious motifs dominated the sculpture and painting. In architecture the colonies followed Spanish examples, with the severely classical style of the sixteenth century giving way in the seventeenth to the highly ornamented baroque, and in the eighteenth to the even more ornate churrigueresque.

In the eighteenth century Spanish America began to awake from its medieval sleep. A lively contraband in unorthodox ideas accompanied the growing trade between the colonies and non-Spanish lands. Spain, now under the sway of the enlightened Bourbon kings, contributed to the intellectual renovation of the colonies. Spanish or foreign scientific expeditions to Spanish America, authorized and sometimes financed by the crown, stimulated the growth of scientific interests. The expulsion of the Jesuits (1767) removed from the scene the ablest exponents of scholasticism and cleared the way for modest projects of educational reform. But the most significant cultural activity took place outside academic halls—in the economic societies, organized for the promotion of useful knowledge; in private gatherings and coffee houses, where young men ardently discussed the advantages of free trade and the rights of men; and in the colonial press, in which the new secular and critical spirit found articulate expression.

1. THE COLONIAL UNIVERSITY

The colonial university was patterned on similar institutions in Spain and faithfully reproduced their medieval organization, curricula, and methods of instruction. Indifference to practical or scientific studies, slavish respect for the authority of the Bible, Aristotle, the church fathers, and certain medieval schoolmen, and a passion for hairsplitting debate of fine points of theological or metaphysical doctrine were among the features of colonial academic life. In the following selection a Spanish friar describes the University of Lima in the first quarter of the seventeenth century.

The university and Royal Schools are so distinguished that they need envy no other in the world, since they were established by the Emperor Charles V, and later by Philip II, both of glorious memory; they enlarged, ennobled and enriched them, with the same privileges as the University of Salamanca; they endowed the professorial chairs of Prime with 1,000 assay pesos, and those of Vespers with 600, per annum. The Prime chairs are in Theology, Scholastics,

---

Antonio Vásquez de Espinosa, *Description of the West Indies*, translated by C. V. Clark. Washington: The Smithsonian Institution, 1942, pp. 444–446.

Scripture, Law, and Canons; the Vespers, in the Institutes, the Code, the Decretals, three in Philosophy, one in the Indian language for the training of the priests who are to be parish priests or doctrineros; before they are commissioned, they have to be examined and certificated by the Professor of the language.

The Professors are in major part natives of the Indies and especially of this city, where it would appear that the skies, as usually in the Indies, train outstanding and unusual intellects in subtlety and facility, so that in general they are very able and keen witted; this is obvious from the professional positions which they occupy and the pulpits, where remarkable men distinguish themselves in their mastery of science and oratory; but they are unfortunate in living far from the eyes of His Majesty. For after all their labors, since there are so few professorial chairs and so many candidates, and there cannot be many lawyers, after having drudged and done brilliantly, and having spent in attaining the degrees of Licentiate and Doctor, 3,500 pesos, they lose heart, unless they have private means, at seeing themselves unrewarded; so the clerics take benefices and Indian curacies in order to live, and many abandon their books and studies, and never take their degrees.

This University's faculty is important, for it comprises more than 80 Doctors and Masters; the members of the Circuit Court join them, for at the end of the year the fees amount to many ducats. The lecture halls in the schools are excellent, and the chapel very fine, but the most remarkable feature is the amphitheater, where [are held] the public functions and commencements; it is very large and imposing; the display at the granting of whatever degrees are given, is also imposing. They [the faculty] invite the city's nobility as an escort, and meet at the house of the Doctor-to-be in a blare of trumpets, flageolets, and bugles, with a banner which hangs from a window of the house over a canopy on crimson velvet cushions and has the arms of the University and of the graduating Doctor; these are likewise set up in the theater erected in the Cathedral under the royal arms; they remind and notify the invited guests and doctors, who form an escort the evening before; the nobility follow the banner, then the Beadles with their silver maces, then the Masters and Doctors with their insignia, in order of age, closing with the Dean of the faculty and the graduating Doctor; and in this order they repair to the Rector's house, where the members of the Circuit Court await them; with the Rector in their center, they continue in the procession, in order of age. And in this same order the following day they parade till they arrive at the Cathedral, where the theater and the stage have been decorated and provided with seats; Mass is said for them, and at its close after leaving the Cathedral, the newest Doctor of the faculty delivers his burlesque invective, and the Chancellor gives him his degree, just as is done at Salamanca.

2. THE TENTH MUSE

The conditions of colonial life did not favor the development of a rich literature. Isolation from foreign influences, the strict censorship of all reading matter, and the limited audience for writing of every kind made literary creation difficult. Amid "a flock of jangling magpies," as one literary historian describes the Gongorist versifiers of the seventeenth century, appeared an incomparable songbird, known to her admiring contemporaries as "the tenth muse"—Sor Juana Inés de la Cruz (1651–1695). Rebuked by the bishop of Puebla, who wrote under the pseudonym of Sor Filotea, for her interest in secular learning, Sor Juana replied in a letter that is both an important autobiographical document and an eloquent defense of the rights of women to education and intellectual activity.

I was less than three years old when my mother sent an older sister to be taught reading at a school for small children, of the kind called *Amigas*. Moved by sisterly affection and by a mischievous spirit, I followed her; and seeing her receive instruction, I formed such a strong desire to read that I tried to deceive the schoolmistress, telling her that *my mother wanted her to give me lessons.* She did not believe me, since it was incredible; but to humor me she acquiesced. I continued to come and she to teach me, no longer in jest but in earnest; and I learned so quickly that I already knew how to read by the time my mother heard about the lessons from the teacher, who had kept them secret in order to break the pleasant news to her and receive her reward all at once. I had concealed it from my mother for fear that I would be whipped for acting without permission. The lady who taught me still lives—God keep her—and can testify to this.

I remember that at that time, although I had the healthy appetite of most children of that age, I would not eat cheese because I heard that it made one dull-witted, and the desire to learn prevailed more with me than hunger, so powerful in children. Later, at the age of six or seven, when I already knew how to read and write, as well as to sew and do other women's tasks, I heard that in Mexico City there was a university, and schools where the sciences were taught. No sooner had I heard this than I began to badger my mother with pleas that she let me put on men's clothing and go to Mexico City, where I could live with some relatives and attend the university. She would not do it, and quite rightly, too, but I satisfied my desire by reading in a large number of books that belonged to my grandfather, and neither punishments nor rebukes could stop me. Hence when I came to Mexico City men wondered not so much at my intelligence as at my memory and knowledge, at an age when it seemed I would do well to know how to talk.

Sor Juana Inés de la Cruz, *Carta atenagórica, Respuesta a Sor Filotea*, edited by E. Abreu Gómez, Mexico, 1934, pp. 54–58, 66–70. (Excerpt translated by the editor.)

I began to study Latin, in which I had barely twenty lessons; and so intense was my application that although women (especially in the flower of their youth) naturally cherish the adornment of their hair, I would cut it off four or six fingers' length, making it a rule that if I had not mastered a certain subject by the time it grew back, I would cut it off again ... , for it did not seem right to me that a head so empty of knowledge, which is the most desirable adornment of all, should be crowned with hair. I became a nun, for although I knew that the religious state imposed obligations (I speak of incidentals and not of the fundamentals) most repugnant to my temperament, nevertheless, in view of my total disinclination to marriage, it was the most becoming and proper condition that I could choose to ensure my salvation. To achieve this I had to repress my wayward spirit, which wished to live alone, without any obligatory occupation that might interfere with the freedom of my studies or any conventual bustle that might disturb the restful quiet of my books. These desires made me waver in my decision, until, having been told by learned persons that it was temptation, with divine favor I conquered and entered the state which I so unworthily occupy. I thought that I had fled from myself, but—wretched me! I brought myself with me and so brought my greatest enemy, that thirst for learning which Heaven gave me—I know not whether as a favor or chastisement, for repress it as I might with all the exercise that the conventual state offers, it would burst forth like gunpowder; and it was verified in me that *privatio est causa appetitus* [deprivation is the cause of appetite].

I renewed or rather continued (for I never truly ceased) my labors (which were my rest in all the leisure time that my duties left me) of reading and more reading, of studying and more studying, with no other teacher than the books themselves. You will readily comprehend how difficult it is to study from these lifeless letters, denied the living voice and explanation of a teacher, but I joyfully endured all this labor for love of learning. Ah, if it had been for love of God, as was fitting, how worthy it would have been! True, I sought to direct it as much as possible to His service, for my aspiration was to study theology, since it seemed a notable defect to me, as a Catholic, not to know all that can be learned in this life about the Divine Mysteries; and since I was a nun, and not a lay person, it seemed to me an obligation of my state to study literature. ... So I reasoned, and convinced myself—though it could well be that I was only justifying what I already wanted to do. And so, as I have said, I directed the steps of my studying toward the heights of Sacred Theology; it seemed to me that in order to arrive there I should climb the stairway of the human sciences and arts; for how should I understand the language of the Queen of Sciences if I did not know that of her handmaidens?
...

At one time my enemies persuaded a very saintly and guileless prelate, who believed that study was a matter for the Inquisition, to forbid me to study. I obeyed her (for the three months or so that she had power over me) in what concerned my reading, but as for the absolute ban on study, this was not in my power to obey, for although I did not study in books, I studied everything that God created, and all this universal machine served me as a textbook. I saw nothing without reflecting upon it; everything I heard moved me to thought. This was true of the smallest and most material things, for since there is no creature, however lowly, in which one does not recognize the *me fecit Deus* [God made me], so there is no object that will not arouse thought, if one considers it as one should. Thus I looked at and wondered about everything, so that even the people I spoke to, and what they said to me, aroused a thousand speculations in me. How did such a variety of temperaments and intellects come about, since we are all of the same species? What could be the hidden qualities and traits that caused these differences? If I saw a figure I would consider the proportion of its lines and measure it in my mind and reduce it to other figures. Sometimes I would walk about in the front part of a dormitory of ours (a very spacious room); I noticed that although the lines of its two sides were parallel and the ceiling was level, the lines seemed to run toward each other and the ceiling seemed to be lower at a distance than it was close by—from which I inferred that visual lines run straight but not parallel, forming a pyramidal figure. And I speculated whether this could be the reason that caused the ancients to wonder whether the world was a sphere or not. Because although it appeared spherical, this might be an optical illusion, presenting concavities where they perhaps did not exist. ...

This habit is so strong in me that I see nothing without reflecting upon it. I noticed two little girls playing with a top, and I had hardly seen the movement and the object when I began, with my usual madness, to consider the easy motion of the spherical form—and how the impulse, once given, continued independently of its cause, for there was the top dancing at a distance from the girl's hand—the motive cause. Not content with this, I had some flour brought and strewn on the floor, in order to learn whether the top's motion described perfect circles or not; and I discovered that they were only spiral lines that gradually lost their circular character as the impulse diminished. Other children were playing at pins (which is the most infantile game known to children). I began to study the figures they formed, and seeing by chance, that three pins formed a triangle, I set about joining one to the other, remembering that this is said to have been the figure of the mysterious ring of Solomon, in which were depicted some shadowy hints and representations of the most Sacred Trinity, by virtue of which it worked many miracles; it is said that David's harp had the same figure and that for this reason Saul was healed by its sound; the harps we use today have almost the same shape.

But what shall I say, my lady, of the secrets of nature that I have discovered while cooking? I observe that an egg coheres and fries in butter or oil but breaks up in sugar syrup; that to keep sugar fluid it is sufficient to pour on it a little water containing a quince or some other sour fruit; that the yolk and white of an egg are so opposed that each one separately will mix with sugar, but not both together. I shall not weary you with such trifles, which I mention only to give you an adequate notion of my character and which, I am sure, will make you laugh; but, my lady, what can we women know except kitchen philosophy? Lupercio Leonardo aptly said: "It is possible to philosophize while preparing dinner." And I often say, observing these trifles: "If Aristotle had been a cook, he would have written much more." ...

Although I had no need of examples, I have nevertheless been aided by the many that I have read about, in both divine and profane writings. For I have seen a Deborah giving laws, both military and political, and governing a people in which there were so many learned men. I read of that sage Queen of Sheba, so learned that she dared to test with enigmas the wisdom of the wisest of men, and suffered no reproof for it but instead was made the judge of unbelievers. I observe so many illustrious women—some adorned with the gift of prophecy, like Abigail; others, with that of persuasion, like Esther; others with piety, like Rahab; others with perseverance, like Anna, mother of Samuel; and an infinite number of others, endowed with still other kinds of graces and virtues.

If I turn my gaze to the pagans, I first encounter the Sibyls, chosen by God to prophesy the principal mysteries of our faith, in verses so learned and elegant that they arouse our wonder. I see the Greeks adore as goddess of learning a woman like Minerva, daughter of the first Jupiter and teacher of all the wisdom of Athens. I see a Bola Argentaria, who aided her husband Lucan to write the great "Battle of Pharsalia." I see a Zenobia, Queen of Palmyra, as wise as she was brave. An Aretea, the most learned daughter of Aristippus. A Nicostrata, inventor of Latin letters and most learned in Greek. An Aspasia of Miletus, who taught philosophy and rhetoric and was teacher of the philosopher Pericles. A Hypatia, who taught astronomy and studied for a long time in Alexandria. A Leontia, of Greek birth, who wrote against the philosopher Theophrastus and convinced him. A Jucia, a Corinna, a Cornelia, and finally all that multitude of women who won renown under the names of Greeks, Muses, Pythonesses and in the end were nothing more than learned women, regarded and venerated as such by the ancients. Not to mention an infinite number of others of whom the books tell, such as the Egyptian Catherine, who not only read but overcame in debate the wisest sages of Egypt. I see a Gertrude study, write, and teach. And there is no need to wander far afield, for I see a holy mother of my own order, Paula, learned in Hebrew, Greek, and Latin, and most skillful in interpreting the Scriptures—so much so, in fact, that her biographer, the great and saintly Jerome, declared himself unequal to his task. He said, in his usual serious, forceful way: "If all the members of my body were tongues, they would not be enough to proclaim the wisdom and virtue of Paula." He bestowed the same praise on the widow Blesilla and the illustrious virgin Eustoquio, both daughters of the same Paula; for her learning the latter won the name "Prodigy of the World." Fabiola, a Roman lady, was also most learned in the Sacred Scripture, Proba Falconia, a Roman matron, wrote an elegant work in Virgilian measures about the mysteries of our sacred faith. It is well known that our Queen Isabel, wife of Alfonso XII, wrote on astronomy. And ... in our own time there flourishes the great Christina Alexandra, Queen of Sweden, as learned as she is brave and magnanimous, and there are also the excellent Duchess of Abeyro and the Countess of Vallambrosa.

3. COLONIAL JOURNALISM IN ACTION

Colonial newspapers and reviews played a significant part in the development of a critical and reformist spirit and a nascent sense of nationality among the educated Creoles of Spanish America. These periodicals appeared in increasing numbers in the period after 1780. More important than the routine news items they carried were the articles they housed on scientific, economic, and social questions. The Semanario del Nuevo Reino de Granada, *edited between 1808 and 1811 by the distinguished Colombian scientist Francisco José de Caldas (1771–1816), was notable for the high quality of its contents. Caldas himself contributed many of the articles in the* Semanario, *including a brilliant essay on the geography of New Granada, from which the following excerpt is taken.*

Whether we look north or south, whether we examine the most populous or the most deserted places in this colony, everywhere we find the stamp of indolence and ignorance. Our rivers and mountains are unknown to us; we do not know the extent of the country in which we were born; and the study of our geography is still in the cradle. This capital and humiliating truth should shake us out of our lethargy; it should make us more attentive to our interests; it should draw us to every corner of New Granada to measure, examine, and describe it. This truth, engraved in the hearts of all good citizens, will bring them together in order to collect information, donate funds, and recruit men of learning, sparing neither labor nor expense to obtain a detailed reconnaissance map of our provinces. I am not speaking now of an ordinary map; reduced scales and economy must disappear from the minds of our countrymen. Two square inches, at least, should represent a league of terrain. Here should appear the hills, mountains, pastures, forests, lakes, marshes, valleys, rivers, their turns and velocities, straits, cataracts, fisheries, all settlements, all agricultural activities, mines, and quarries—in fine, every-

---

Francisco José de Caldas, *Semanario del Nuevo Reino de Granada*, Bogotá, 1942, 3 vols., I, pp. 51–54. (Excerpt translated by the editor.)

thing above the surface of our land. These features, brought together, will produce a superb map, worthy of New Granada. The statesman, the magistrate, the philosopher, the businessman, will come to look at it to obtain information needed in the performance of their duties; the traveler, the botanist, the mineralogist, the soldier, and the agriculturist will see their concerns depicted in majestic strokes. ... Each province will copy its own section and will guard it religiously. Our youth will be trained in the study of these sections, and in a few years we shall have men capable of conceiving and carrying out great plans. Everywhere we shall hear only of projects; projects of roads, navigation canals, new branches of industry, naturalization of foreign plants; the flame of patriotism will be lighted in every heart; and the ultimate result will be the glory of our monarch and the prosperity of this colony.

If a geographical-economic expedition were formed to survey the whole viceroyalty, composed of an astronomer, a botanist, a mineralogist, a zoologist, and an economist, with two or more draftsmen; if all the provinces contributed toward a fund set up by the wealthy, and especially by the landowners; if the merchants did the same in view of their financial interest in the project; if the Chamber of Commerce [*Consulado*] of Cartagena supported the enterprise as actively as it promotes other projects of the same nature; if the governmental leaders supported it with all their authority—there is no doubt that in a few years we would have the glory of possessing a masterpiece of geographical and political knowledge, and would have laid the foundations of our prosperity.

If this project presents difficulties, there remains no other recourse than to improve our educational system. If instead of teaching our youths trifles ... , we gave them some acquaintance with the elements of astronomy and geography, and taught them the use of some easily-mastered instruments; if practical geometry and geodesy were substituted for certain metaphysical and useless subjects; if on finishing their courses they knew how to measure the earth, make a survey, determine a latitude, use a compass—then we would have reason to hope that these youths, dispersed throughout the provinces, would put into practice the principles they had learned in school, and would make a map of their country. Six months devoted to these interesting studies would qualify a young man to work on the great enterprise of the geography of this colony. I ask the persons responsible for our public education to consider and weigh whether it is more profitable to the State and Church to spend many weeks in sustaining airy systems and all that heap of futile or merely speculative questions than to devote this time to the study of the globe and the land that we inhabit. What do we care about the dwellers on the moon? Would it not be better to learn about the dwellers on the fertile banks of the Magdalena?

The religious orders who have in their charge the missions of the Orinoco, Caqueta, Andaquies, Mocoa, and Maynas should educate the young missionaries in these important subjects. These apostolic men would bring to the barbarians both the light of salvation and that of the useful sciences. Zealous imitators of Fathers Fritz, Coleti, Magnio, and Gumilla, they would leave us precious monuments of their activity and learning. Exact maps, geographical determination, descriptions of plants and animals, and important information about the customs of the savages whom they are going to civilize would be the fruits of these studies. They would serve them as a relief from the tedium and weariness that are inseparable from their lofty ministry.

The rudiments of arithmetic, plane geometry, and trigonometry, of which we possess good compendiums; the use of the graphometer, the gnomon, the quadrant (with some knowledge of how to draw a meridian), and the use of the barometer and the thermometer qualify a young man to assist in the advance of our geographical knowledge.

We have two chairs of mathematics, and that of philosophy offers some instruction in these sciences; thanks to the wise and generous Mutis, we already have an astronomical observatory, where practical experience can be obtained in the use of certain instruments; we have books, and we lack nothing necessary to working for the good of our country. My love for the fatherland dictated these relations. If they are useful to my countrymen, I am already rewarded for the labor they cost me; if not, they will pardon me, taking into account the purity of my intentions.

4. A Colonial Freethinker

The circulation and influence of forbidden books among educated colonials steadily increased in the closing decades of the eighteenth century and the first years of the nineteenth. Encyclopedist influence is strongly evident in the work of the Mexican writer José Joaquín Fernández de Lizardi (1776–1827), whose stormy life spanned the declining years of the colony and the first years of its independence. His masterpiece, El periquillo sarniento (The Itching Parrot), *the first true Spanish-American novel, depicted with harsh realism and biting satire the conditions of Mexican life in the late colonial period. The following episode from* El periquillo sarniento, *laid in Manila, illustrates Lizardi's emphatic dissent from social folly and prejudice of every kind.*

I said before that a virtuous man has few misfortunes to relate. Nevertheless, I witnessed some strange affairs. One of them was as follows: One year, when a number of foreigners had come from the port to the city for reasons of trade, a rich merchant who happened to be a Negro went down a street. He must have been bound on very important business, because he strode

---

José Joaquín Fernández de Lizardi, *El periquillo sarniento*, Mexico, 1897, 2 vols., II(D), pp. 3–7. (Excerpt translated by the editor.)

along very rapidly and distractedly, and in his headlong progress he inadvertently ran into an English officer who was paying court to a rich young creole lady. Such was the shock of the collision that if the girl had not supported him the officer would have fallen to the ground. As it was, his hat fell off and his hair was disheveled.

The officer's pride was greatly wounded, and he immediately ran toward the Negro, drawing his sword. The poor fellow was taken by surprise, and since he carried no arms he probably believed that it was all up with him. The young lady and the officer's companions restrained him, but he raged at the Negro for some time, protesting a thousand times that he would vindicate his injured honor.

So much abuse did he heap on the innocent black that the latter finally said to him in English: "Sir, be quiet; tomorrow I shall be waiting in the park to give you satisfaction with a pistol." The officer accepted, and there the matter rested.

I, who witnessed this incident and knew some English, having learned the hour and place assigned for the duel, took care to be there punctually to see how the affair would end.

At the appointed time both men arrived, each accompanied by a friend who acted as his second. As soon as they met the Negro drew two pistols, presented them to the officer, and said to him: "Sir, I did not intend yesterday to offend you; my running into you was an accident. You heaped abuse on me and even wished to wound or kill me. I had no arms with which to defend myself against you. I knew that a challenge to a duel was the quickest means of quieting you, and now I have come to give you satisfaction with a pistol, as I said I would."

"Very well," said the Englishman, "let's get on. It gives me no satisfaction to fight with a Negro, but at least I shall have the pleasure of killing an insolent rascal. Let's choose our pistols."

"All right," said the Negro, "but you should know that I no more intend to offend you today than I did yesterday. It seems to me that for a man of your position to decide to kill a man for such a trifle is not a matter of honor but a mere caprice. But if the explanation I gave you means nothing, and only killing will do, I don't propose to be guilty of murder or to die without cause, as must happen if your shot or my shot finds its target. So let luck decide who has justice on his side. Here are the pistols; one of them is loaded with two balls and the other is empty. Look them over, give me the one you don't want, and let us take our chances."

The officer was surprised by this proposal. The others said that it was highly irregular—that both must fight with the same weapons; and they offered other arguments that did not convince the Negro, who insisted that the duel must take place on his terms, so that he might have the consolation of knowing that if he killed his opponent it was because Heaven had ordered it or especially favored him—and if he were killed, it would be no fault of his but pure chance, as when a ship is wrecked at sea. He added that since the arrangement favored neither party, since no one knew who would get the loaded pistol, refusal to accept his proposal could only be attributed to cowardice.

No sooner had the ardent young man heard this than he took up the pistols, selected one, and gave the other to the Negro.

The two men turned their backs to each other, walked a short distance, and then turned to face each other. At that moment the officer fired at the Negro—but in vain, for he had chosen the empty pistol.

He stood there as if stunned, believing with the others that he would be the defenceless victim of the Negro's wrath. But the latter, with the greatest generosity, said to the officer: "Sir, we have both come out with whole skins; the duel is over; you had to accept it with the conditions I imposed, and I could wage it on no other terms. I could fire at you if I wished but if I never sought to offend you before, how could I do it now, seeing you disarmed? Let us be friends, if you consider yourself satisfied; but if only my death can appease you, take the loaded pistol and aim it at my breast."

Saying this, he presented the horrible weapon to the officer. The latter, moved by this extraordinary generosity, took the pistol and fired it in the air. Approaching the Negro with outstretched arms, he embraced him, saying with the greatest tenderness:

"Yes, friends we are and friends we shall be eternally; forgive my vanity and madness. I never believed that Negroes were capable of such greatness of soul." "That prejudice still has many followers," said the Negro, warmly embracing the officer.

We who witnessed this incident were eager to strengthen the bonds of this new friendship, and I, who knew them least of all, hastened to introduce myself to them as their friend, and to beg them to take a glass of punch or wine with me at the nearest coffeehouse.

10

∿

SPAIN'S WORK IN AMERICA:

FOR AND AGAINST

FROM THE SIXTEENTH CENTURY to the present, the Spanish record in America has been the subject of intense controversy. In our time the problem has acquired a new relevance because of its connection with the modern struggle of colonial peoples for independence. The West German editor of a 1969 edition of Las Casas's anticolonial tract, the *Very Brief Account of the Destruction of the Indies*, noted this connection when he drew a parallel between the Vietnam War and the Spanish wars of aggression that Las Casas attacked. "The headlines that we hear every morning on the broadcasts," he wrote, "signify that the destruction of the Indies continues. The *Very Brief Account* of 1542 is a backward look into our future."

Las Casas has often been charged with responsibility for the so-called Black Legend of Spanish oppression and cruelty to the Indians. Certainly the *Very Brief Account*, translated into all the major European languages, helped to diffuse more widely the evil reputation that Spain had already acquired in Europe as a result of the Spanish Conquest and the conduct of Spanish soldiery in the Netherlands and elsewhere. But the "legend" had other sources. In 1565 the Italian Girolamo Benzoni published his *History of the New World*, a travel account that contained moving eyewitness descriptions of Spanish cruelty in the Indies, and that was widely read. European critics of Spain's colonial policy even found material for their indictments in the writings of such staunch defenders of Spanish imperialism as the chroniclers López de Gómara and Oviedo.

Various motives inspired foreign attacks on Spain's colonial record in the sixteenth, seventeenth, and eighteenth centuries. Spain's colonial and commercial rivals—above all the English and Dutch merchant capitalists and their governments—used that record as a propaganda weapon in their efforts to wrest from Spain her colonies and colonial markets. But defenders of national independence, religious tolerance, and intellectual freedom—such men as the essayist Montaigne in the sixteenth century and the political philosopher Montesquieu in the eighteenth century—denounced Spanish imperialism not from the viewpoint of a narrow nationalism but in defense of the rights of man. In Spain the memory of Las Casas fell under a deep cloud after 1600. Yet sensitive Spaniards continued to criticize the Spanish Conquest and its aftermath as detrimental not only to the interests of the Indians but of the Spanish people. Typical is the comment of the intellectual reformer Fray Benito Feijóo in the early eighteenth century, "The gold of the Indies keeps us poor, and what is worse, it enriches our enemies. Because we mistreated the Indians, we Spaniards are now the Indians of other Europeans."

The Spanish-American Wars of Independence naturally inspired sharp rhetorical attacks on Spain's work in America. Bolívar, for example, claimed that Las Casas had seen America bathed "with the blood of more than twenty million victims." After independence the Spanish colonial legacy became a major issue in the political struggles of the new states. Liberals condemned Spanish tyranny, obscurantism, and backwardness and insisted on the need to liquidate the colonial heritage; conservatives, who often recalled the old social order with nostalgia, offered at least a partial defense of Spain's colonial rule.

By the last decades of the nineteenth century, however, Latin American historians had begun to modify their interpretations of the colonial era. As economic activity quickened with the growth of European trade and investments, with liberals and conservatives joining in pursuit of material prosperity and political stability, old party lines dissolved, and the liberal anti-Spanish arguments lost much of their raison d'être. After mid-century, moreover, the racist and biological-determinist theories of Spencer, Gobineau, and their disciples increasingly influenced Latin American thought. As a result, historians, whether liberal or conservative, now tended to justify the Spanish Conquest by the workings of a mysterious law of progress, and to shift much of the responsibility for the area's backwardness from Spain to the Indians and mixed bloods, regarded as inherently inferior races.

A revisionist tendency emerged in United States historical studies of colonial Latin America in the same period. The rise of Social Darwinism and America's new status as a colonial power after 1898 disposed U.S. historians to view the Spanish colonial experience with greater sympathy. A major work in this revisionist tradition was Edward G. Bourne, *Spain in America* (1904), which cleverly used the comparative method to put Spanish colonial policies in the best possible light. Bourne's influence permeated Lesley B. Simpson's influential *The Encomienda in New Spain* (1929), a book notable for its vitriolic attack on Las Casas. Beginning in the 1920s, such historians as Arthur Aiton, Irving Leonard, John Tate Lanning, and Lewis Hanke wrote important monographs that corrected errors and exaggerations in the writings of the traditional anti-Spanish school, but sometimes unduly embellished the Spanish colonial record.

In the Hispanic world this twentieth-century revisionism assumed an increasingly tendentious aspect as a result of the rise of acute political and social tensions in that area. In Spain, conservatives responded to a growing threat from the forces of liberalism and radicalism by developing a historical defense of the old order. This defense proclaimed, among other things, the grandeur of Spain's achievement in the New World and denounced Las Casas and other alleged detractors of Spain. A major anti-Lascasian work was Ramón Menéndez Pidal's violent attack on Las Casas, *El Padre Las Casas, su doble personalidad* (1963).

In Latin America, in the same period, conservative circles grew alarmed at the rise of *Indigenismo* and a variety of social revolutionary movements and identified themselves more closely with the Hispanic colonial past. A "White Legend" school of historiography that enjoyed considerable influence in some Latin American countries arose between 1930 and 1950. Its prominent exponents included the Mexican José Vasconcelos, the Argentine Rómulo D. Carbia, the Peruvian Raúl Porras Barrenechea, and the Chilean Francisco Encina.

In recent years a more critical and realistic appraisal of the Spanish colonial process has been developing among historians in the United States, Spain, and Latin America. Factors contributing to this trend include recent studies that confirm the traditional critique of Spanish labor and tribute systems as harshly exploitative, the anticolonialist temper of our time, and a growing awareness of the colonial roots of Latin American underdevelopment and neocolonialism.

1. THE NOBLE SAVAGE
AND THE BLACK LEGEND

In the sixteenth, seventeenth, and eighteenth centuries the so-called Black Legend, the traditional critique of Spanish colonial policy as oppressive and obscurantist, was often joined to the concept of the Noble Savage, of the American Indian regarded as a prime example of unspoiled humanity in the state of nature. The famous novel of Jean-François Marmontel (1723–1799), Les Incas (1777), illustrates this fusion of ideas. The story, pure fiction for the most part, relates the destruction of the Inca Empire; its characters include Las Casas, Pizarro (to whom Marmontel assigns great nobility of character), the "fanatical priest" Valverde, and the Inca Atahualpa. Marmontel, a typical Enlightenment figure, wrote the book to denounce the evils of fanaticism, not a uniquely Spanish wickedness. Indeed, he was careful to begin his preface with the words, "All nations have had their brigands and their fanatics, their times of barbarism, their fits of fury. The finest peoples are those which accuse themselves of their crimes. The

Spaniards have this proud trait, worthy of their character." Typical of the spirit and style of Les Incas *is the following episode, which describes the death of Atahualpa at the hands of the "perfidious priest" Valverde and his accomplices.*

Atahualpa's family slept around him; their eyes were drained of tears, their hearts weary with sobbing. But the prince, filled with gloomy presentiments, could not shut his eyes. He heard the prison doors open. He saw Requelme enter; with him came three men wrapped in long cloaks which covered their faces up to their eyes; there was something frightful about their gaze. A sensation of terror seized Atahualpa; he rose and, overcoming his momentary weakness, stood before them.

"Inca," Requelme said to him, "let us leave this place; there is no need to awake these women and their children. Let the innocents rest in peace. Listen to us. You have been judged and condemned; you must burn at the stake according to the severe letter of the law. But you can save yourself from the flames; and this holy man will explain to you how it may be done."

The prince listened and grew pale. "I know," he said, "that the Council has judged me; but surely you must send me to the Spanish Court, reserving to your king a right that belongs to him alone." "Believe me," continued Requelme, "precious moments are passing; listen to this wise and virtuous man, who pities your misfortunes."

Valverde then spoke. "Do you not wish," he asked the Inca, "to adore the God of the Christians?" "Certainly," replied the unhappy prince, "if this God, as we are informed, is a beneficent God, a powerful and just God, if Nature is his handiwork and the sun itself one of his benefactions, then I adore him together with Nature. What ingrate or madman could reject His love?" "And do you desire to be taught," continued the perfidious priest, "the holy truths that He has revealed to us, to know His cult, and to follow His law?" "I ardently desire it," replied the Inca, "I have already said so. I long to open my eyes to the light, to be instructed, and I shall believe." "God be thanked," exclaimed Valverde, "he is as well disposed as I could hope. Down on your knees, then, and implore this God of goodness and mercy; receive from Him the healthful water that makes His children be born again." The Inca, with humble and meek spirit, knelt and received the holy water of baptism. "The Heavens are open," said Valverde, "and moments are precious." He immediately made a sign to his two henchmen, and the fatal rope stifled the last sighs of the Inca.

Jean-François Marmontel, *Les Incas, ou la destruction de l'Empire du Perou*, Paris, 1777, 2 vols., II, pp. 347–350. (Excerpt translated by the editor.)

The pitiful cries of his children and their mothers spread the news of his death at daybreak. Some Spaniards shuddered at the news; but the multitude applauded the audacity of the assassins, and thought it was enough that they had spared the lives of the wives and children of the unhappy prince, henceforth abandoned to the pity of the Indians.

Pizarro, indignant but discouraged, weary of struggling against crime, after heaping curses on these unspeakable assassins and their fanatical partisans, withdrew to the City of Kings [Lima], whose construction had begun. Licentiousness, robbery, furious rapacity, murder, and pillage raged unchecked; everywhere on the continent the Indian peoples fled, only to fall into the snares or under the swords of the Spaniards.

From the shores of Mexico arrived Alvarado, the friend of Cortés, that scourge of the two Americas. Rival of the new conquerors, he came to hurl himself upon their prey, to glut himself with gold and blood. The whole extent of that immense Empire was devastated. An innumerable multitude of Indians were slaughtered; almost all the rest, led away in chains to perish in the depths of mines, envied the fate of those who had been massacred.

2. THE FATAL LEGACY

In the decades after independence, Latin American leaders debated which road their countries should take to reach the goals of economic progress and political stability. Liberals looked to the United States, England, and France as models of dynamic advance; conservatives proposed to remain in the safe, familiar way of their fathers and retain those features of the colonial regime not incompatible with the new republican order: the supremacy of the Catholic Church, clerical control of education, a hierarchical society with special privileges for the clergy and military, and the like. In 1844 two ardent liberals startled the staid aristocratic society of Santiago with their contributions to the debate. Francisco Bilbao (1823–1865) threw a bombshell with his famous essay on "The Nature of Chilean Society," in which he declared, "Slavery, degradation: that is the past. ... Our past is Spain. Spain is the Middle Ages. The Middle Ages are composed, body and soul, of Catholicism and feudalism." Bilbao was tried and condemned for blasphemy, sedition, and immorality; he lost his university chair, and his book was officially burned by the public hangman. José Victorino Lastarria (1817–1888), more moderate and scholarly, caused a lesser stir with his address, "Investigations on the Social Influence of the Conquest and the Colonial System of the Spaniards in Chile." Despite an occasional factual error—such as the statement that Spain forbade the printing and sale of books of every kind in America—it remains an effective summary of the liberal case against the Spanish colonial regime.

It is well known that the Spaniards who conquered America drenched its soil in blood, not in order to colonize it but to acquire the precious metals it yielded so abundantly. Torrents of adventurers flowed over the New World; they were obsessed by the hope of gaining immense wealth at little cost, and to this end they directed all their activity, sparing no means or violence in order to achieve it. At last reality dispelled their illusions, and the conquistadors, convinced by their own experience that the fertility of the American mines was not as great as they had hoped, gradually abandoned their daring speculations and began to devote themselves to agricultural and commercial enterprises. But this new direction of their ambitions did not yield the benefits that might have been expected, given the potential wealth of the American soil, for they had neither the inclination nor the intelligence to exploit this new source of riches; and their government, for its part, with its absurd economic system, stopped up the very sources of economic progress.

When Spain established her colonies in America, she transplanted thither all the vices of her absurd system of government, vices that multiplied infinitely through causes that had their origin in the system itself. ...

A single leading idea dominated all the decisions of the Spanish Court and its agents in the colonies: this was the idea of maintaining America forever in a blind dependence on Spain, in order to exploit it exclusively, at the cost of the very existence and development of the colonies, and to extract from its possession all possible advantages. From this point of view, the metropolis had a system, a spirit that gave unity to its decisions and sanctified all means necessary to achieve those ends, no matter how unjust and unworthy they might be. For Spain the New World was a very rich mine that should be exploited and whose fruits should be consumed, no matter what devastation the process produced or what effects it might have on future productivity.

To this end Spain subjected the natives to the grossest, most humiliating servitude, declaring them slaves in certain cases and masking their slavery in others with a pretended, ironic respect for their liberty, even as it subjected them to the *mita*, the *repartimiento*, and other oppressive burdens. The tax laws were precisely calculated to benefit the royal treasury and to extract from the colonies all the wealth possible, even at the expense of the very elements of production. Commerce was monopolized for the benefit of Spain, manufacturing and agriculture were surrounded with a thousand restrictions and burdened with so many taxes that there clearly emerged the intention of impeding their future development. ... Communication and commerce with foreign powers were forbidden so strictly that not only was it made a crime to

José Victorino Lastarria, "Investigaciones sobre la influencia social de la Conquista i del sistema colonial de los españoles en Chile," in *Obras completas*, Santiago de Chile, 1909, Vol. VII, pp. 45–69. (Excerpt translated by the editor.)

maintain such relations but a pretended sovereignty of the seas was invoked, as in a royal cedula (1692) that ordered governors "to treat as an enemy ship every foreign ship sailing in American waters without license from this government, even if the vessel belongs to an allied nation."

For the rest, the laws and orders dictated to prevent the intellectual development of the Americans testify to the perverse intention of maintaining them in the most brutal and degrading ignorance, to make them perpetually bow their necks to the yoke of their *natural sovereign* and of all the governors who derived from him all their authority. It was forbidden under severe penalties to sell and print in America books of any kind, even books of devotion; and to introduce books a license was necessary from the Council of the Indies or some other authority anxious to prevent the light of intelligence from penetrating the New World. The few universities and colleges, established and regulated by law, were entirely designed to keep true knowledge from men; to use the happy expression of one American, they were "a monument of imbecility." Entirely subject to the rule of monks, intellectual and moral education was frustrated with the utmost diligence; care was taken to turn out only clergymen or, at most, lawyers and physicians, but all were taught false doctrines. They became accustomed to juggle metaphysical subtleties and the most extravagant theories, and according to the formulas of their useless science they were made to adopt a grotesque and high-sounding style. Thus the Spanish government managed by means of its laws and orders to lead the minds of Americans astray and direct them into anti-social studies that subjected their minds to a perfect slavery and were designed to blind their reason so that they should see "in the king of Spain their absolute lord, who knew no superior or restraint on his power on the face of the earth, whose power derived from God Himself, a king whose person was sacred and in whose presence all should tremble."

In making this rapid survey of the colonial legislation with the aim of investigating its social influence, I must, however, prove my impartiality by noting that the tedium caused by perusal of this monstrous compilation is sometimes relieved by the reading of some provisions that prove the merciful sentiments of their authors. But only "merciful sentiments," mind you, for one does not discover in those provisions, any more than in the rest, that common sense, that foresight, that result from philosophic analysis of the facts—qualities that are salient traits of the wise legislator. In effect, we note various laws designed to regulate the service of the natives in the mines, *encomiendas*, and *repartimientos* to which they were subject, and others that assessed their tributes so that they should not prove too burdensome. There are special laws designed to protect the liberty of the Chilean Indians and grant them more privileges and exemptions than were enjoyed by the Indians of other colonies, doubtless with the aim of attracting the Chilean Indians and ending their wars by means of these mild and protective measures. Undoubtedly these are the laws that have fascinated the defenders of the colonial legislation, who have assumed their good faith and deduced from them arguments to prove the wisdom of Spain and to eulogize the protection that she dispensed to her colonies. But if we recall what was said above concerning the spirit of that code and the system of the metropolis, what were those laws, at most, but the expression of an isolated goodwill, or perhaps a cover with which a corrupt and reactionary Court wished to mask its true intentions and opinions vis-à-vis the unhappy natives of the New World? Be that as it may, those protective laws were a mute and ineffective exception, a dead letter, since their execution, interpretation, and even the right to modify them were in the hands of the colonial governors. ...

This was the dominant thought, the aspirations, the concentrated essence, of the civilization of the sixteenth-century Spaniard: his king and his interest, God, and the glory of war. ...

That civilization, then, was the element that conditioned all the exploits of that remarkable people; it was the origin of all its aberrations and determined the direction of its inclinations; it gave form to its customs. I believe, therefore, that when we examine the civil and political laws that moulded our society, we must consider them the logical result of that civilization and always keep in mind that the foundations of our social structure were laid by fanatical, warlike Spain; that the basis of the administrative system of our colony was the omnipotence of Charles V; and that our religion had for its base the terrorism of the Inquisition.

3. IN DEFENSE OF SPAIN

Conservative ideologists of the post-Independence period, who had lived under Spanish rule and sometimes participated in its overthrow, rarely offered an unqualified defense of the colonial regime. More often, conceding its errors and abuses, they countered the liberal attack by stressing its benefits: the long Pax Hispanica, *the relative mildness of Spanish rule, and the like. A review of Lastarria's "Investigations" by Andrés Bello (1781–1865), the distinguished Venezuelan scholar and educator who as rector of the National University of Chile gave Lastarria the opportunity to make his address, illustrates the thought of an enlightened conservative on the subject. Observe how Bello, conceding the cruelties of the Conquest, diminishes Spanish guilt by shifting responsibility for such acts to a flawed human nature, to a universal law by which the strong oppress the weak in all times and places. This line of defense has often been employed by apologists for Spanish imperialism and imperialism in general.*

Chapter I treats the Conquest and the prolonged struggle between the Chilean colonists and the indomitable Araucanian Indians, and is written with the rapid energy that the material demands. It would have been difficult, in such an outline sketch, for the author to give a more complete idea of those bitter hostilities that fathers passed on to sons generation after generation, and that even now only slumber under the appearance of a peace that is but a truce. Aside from one or another phrase that smacks more of exalted oratory than the moderate language of the historian, I do not find much reason to criticize as intemperate or passionate the account of the cruelty of the conquistadors in this chapter. The historian is obligated to tell things as they happened, and we should not palliate them for fear of dishonoring the memory of the founders of Chile. Injustice, atrocities, perfidy in war, are not uniquely Spanish traits; they are common to all races of all times. If war between fraternal Christian nations in our own cultured, civilized times still assumes a character of savage, soulless cruelty, why should we marvel at murderous battles and the harsh results of victory in war between peoples for whom each other's customs, religion, aspect, or color were entirely alien and repugnant?

The vassals of Isabella, Charles I, and Philip II were the premier nation of Europe; their knightly spirit, the splendor of the Spanish Court, Spain's magnificent and proud nobility, the skill of its captains, the ability of its ambassadors and ministers, the bravery of its soldiers, their daring enterprises, momentous discoveries, and conquests, made Spain a target of detractors because it was an object of envy. The memoirs of that age present horrible scenes to our eyes. The Spaniards abused their power, oppressed, committed outrages, not impudently as Señor Lastarria claims—for one need not be impudent to do what everyone else does in the measure of his power—but with the same regard for humanity, the same respect for the rights of men, that powerful states have always displayed in their dealings with the weak, dealings of which our own moral and civilized time presents too many examples.

If we compare the practice, as opposed to theory, of international law in modern times with that of the Middle Ages and antiquity, beneath insubstantial differences of form and method we find a basic similarity. ... Among the great masses of men that we call nations the savage state in which brute force rules has not ended. Men pay a superficial homage to justice by reference to the commonplaces of security, dignity, protection of national interests, and other equally vague clichés—premises from which a modicum of skill can derive all imaginable consequences. The horrors of war have been partly mitigated, not from greater respect for humanity but because material interests

---

Andrés Bello, review of Lastarria's "Investigaciones," in *Obras completas*, Caracas, 1957, Vol. XIX, pp. 161–166. (Excerpt translated by the editor.)

are better calculated, and as a result of the very perfection to which the art of destruction has been brought. It would be madness to enslave the conquered when there is greater profit in making them tributaries and forced suppliers of the conqueror's industry. The pillagers of old have been transformed into merchants, but merchants whose counters display the motto: *Vae victis* (woe to the vanquished). Colonization no longer brings death to the native inhabitants: why kill them, when it is enough to drive them from forest to forest, from prairie to prairie? In the long run deprivation and famine will achieve the work of destruction without noisy scandal. ...

I do not accuse any nation, but rather human nature. The weak invoke justice, but let them grow strong, and they will prove as unjust as their oppressors.

The picture that Señor Lastarria paints of the vices and abuses of Spain's colonial system he generally supports with documents of irrefutable authenticity and veracity: laws, ordinances, histories, the *Memorias Secretas* of Jorge Juan and Antonio de Ulloa. But profuse shadows appear in the picture; there is something about it that detracts from the impartiality required of the advocate, an impartiality not incompatible with the energetic tone of reproof with which the historian, advocate of the rights of man and interpreter of moral sentiments, should pronounce judgment on corrupting institutions.

To the dominant idea of perpetuating the tutelage of her colonies, Spain sacrificed not only the interests of her colonies but her own; in order to keep them dependent and submissive she made herself poor and weak. While American treasure inundated the world, the Spanish treasury grew empty and her industry remained in swaddling clothes. Colonies served to stimulate the growth of population and the arts in other countries; for Spain they were a cause of depopulation and backwardness. Spain displayed no industrial life or wealth, save in a few emporia that served as intermediaries in the trade between the two hemispheres, emporia in which the accumulated wealth of monopoly flaunted itself amid the general misery.

But we must be just: Spain's was not a *ferocious* tyranny. It chained the arts, clipped the wings of thought, stopped up the very sources of agricultural fertility, but its policy was one of obstacles and restraints, not of blood and torture. The penal laws were laxly administered. In punishing sedition it was not extraordinarily severe; it was as severe as despotism has always been, but no more, at least as concerns its treatment of the Spanish race and until the time of the Revolution that brought freedom to the Spanish dominions.

The prototype of Spanish despotism in America was that of the Roman emperors. There was the same ineffective benignity on the part of the supreme authority, the same pretorian arbitrariness, the same divinization of the Throne, the same indifference to industry, the same ignorance of the great principles that vivify and make fecund human associations, the same judicial organization, the same fiscal privileges. But to compensate for these negative qualities there were others of a different character. That civilizing mission which moves, like the sun, from east to west, and of which Rome was the most powerful agency in the antique world, Spain performed in a more distant, vaster world. No doubt the elements of this civilization were destined to amalgamate with others that should improve it, just as Roman civilization was modified and improved in Europe by foreign influences. Perhaps I deceive myself, but it seems to me that none of the nations that emerged from the ruins of the Empire preserved a more pronounced stamp of the Roman genius: the very language of Spain preserves better than any other the character of that spoken by the masters of the world. Even in material things Spain's colonial administration displayed a touch of the imperial Roman style. To the Spanish government America owes all that is grand and splendid in its public buildings. Let us confess it with feelings of shame: We have hardly been able to maintain the structures erected under the viceroys and captains-general. Remember, too, that Crown revenues were liberally spent for their construction, and that Spain did not impose the taxes and forced labors with which Rome burdened her imperial subjects for the building of roads, aqueducts, amphitheaters, hot baths, and bridges.

4. A REVISIONIST LANDMARK: BOURNE'S *SPAIN IN AMERICA*

Side by side with "Black Legend" attitudes, kindlier attitudes toward the Conquest and Spanish colonial rule appeared in U.S. historical writings of the nineteenth century. William H. Prescott, for example, displayed a definite pro-Spanish bias in his monumental Conquest of Mexico. *Albert Gallatin, Hubert H. Bancroft, and Adolph Bandelier were other North American historians and social scientists who displayed some partiality for the Spanish colonial regime in this period. In the period 1898–1929 professional historians elaborated and synthesized the pro-Spanish elements in the writings of these men. The rise of this revisionist school coincided with the rise of an American empire in the Caribbean and the Pacific, and the new imperialist climate of opinion and America's new status as a colonial power undoubtedly disposed the revisionist historians to view the Spanish colonial experience with greater sympathy. A climactic work of this school was Edward Gaylord Bourne's* Spain in America *(1904). Its clear, simple style made it very readable; its professionalism, reasonableness, and apparent determination to maintain a just balance inspired confidence. Yet on close inspection Bourne's portrayal of Spain's Indian policy appears tendentious and idealized. Observe that he does not list exploitation of Indian labor in his enumeration of "the distinctive feature of the Spanish Indian policy." Note, too, that he relies heavily on the Laws of the Indies for his description of the conditions of Indian life (although elsewhere Bourne showed that he was aware of the frequent divorce between colonial law and practice).*

The Indian legislation of the Spanish kings is an impressive monument of benevolent intentions which need not fear comparison with the contemporary legislation of any European country affecting the status of the working-classes.

The details of the history of the Spanish Indian policy are too voluminous for presentation in this survey of the population of Spanish America; yet they form an important and instructive chapter in the history of the contact of the "higher" and "lower" races, of which unfortunately only the tragic prologue has been made generally familiar through the wide diffusion of Las Casas' tracts on the Indian question. His *Breuissima Relacion de la Destruycion de las Indias*, a voluminous plea prepared to present to Charles V in 1540, was first published twelve years later. Translations into all the principal languages of Europe followed, and its pictures of terrible inhumanity, its impassioned denunciations of the conquerors, and its indictment of the colonial officials became the stock material of generations of historical writers.

It is forgotten that his book was the product of a fierce agitation, or that it was written before the Spaniards had been fifty years in the New World, where their empire lasted three hundred years. Two centuries of philanthropic legislation has been thrown into the background by the flaming words which first gave it impulse. Las Casas was the Lloyd Garrison of Indian rights; but it is as one-sided to depict the Spanish Indian policy primarily from his pages as it would be to write a history of the American Negro question exclusively from the files of the *Liberator*; or, after a century of American rule in the Philippines, to judge it solely from the anti-imperialistic tracts of the last few years. That the benevolent legislation of the distant mothercountry was not, and probably could not be, wholly enforced will not seem strange to those familiar with our experience with federal legislation on the Negro question; but that a lofty ideal was raised and maintained is as true of the Indian laws of Spain as of the Fifteenth Amendment.

All that can be attempted here is an outline sketch of the typical features of Indian society as reorganized by the conquest. The distinctive features of the Spanish Indian policy were the reduction of the Indians to village life, their conversion to the Christian religion, the suppression of their vices and heathen practices, and a training to industry and sobriety so that they should support themselves and contribute to meet the expenses of that colonial establishment. A portion of their labor was to belong either to their encomenderos or to the crown. On the other hand, they were to be protected from the struggle for existence in competition with the heterogeneous elements of a colonial population.

Edward G. Bourne, *Spain in America, 1450–1580*, New York, 1904, pp. 256–262.

In pursuance of these aims the Indians were to live in villages under their own magistrates. Each village, according to its size, had one or two alcaldes and from one to four regidores, who were annually elected by the residents in the presence of the cura, or pastor. These offices were not purchasable, as was the case in the Spanish towns. Each village must contain a church with a mission priest, the expense to be borne by the encomendero out of his tributes. No Indian could live outside his village, nor could any Spaniard, Negro, mestizo, or mulatto live in an Indian village; Spaniards could not tarry over one night, except merchants, who might stay two nights.

In these villages the Indian social life, their marriages, and the like were to be regulated in accordance with Christian principles; schools for teaching Spanish were to be opened; no wine could be sold there, and precautions were to be exercised that the native pulque should not be adulterated or fortified with spirits. Indians could not purchase or bear arms nor ride on horseback. In their religious relations they were exempt from the jurisdiction of the Inquisition. The caciques who had been the chiefs of the Indians before their conversion or reduction might retain that office, and it was recognized as hereditary. They exercised minor jurisdiction, but could not try capital offences. In case they were reported to be oppressive the Spanish officials were to look into their conduct.

The question of Indian tribute and labor was carefully regulated. All male Indians between eighteen and fifty were liable for an annual payment, which was payable in kind either to the crown or to the encomendero, as the case might be; but sometimes it could be commuted into money. The tribute was assessed by officials for the purpose, and protectors of the Indians were appointed to look after their interests. The amount of the tribute in money value was in the later period two or three pesos.

Slavery was absolutely prohibited; the caciques could not hold Indian slaves. In granting encomiendas the descendants of the conquerors, discoverers, and first settlers were to be preferred. Encomenderos could not be absentee landlords. They must provide for the religious instruction of the Indians and protect their rights. If negligent they were liable to forfeit their tributes. In the case of the larger encomiendas the tributes in excess of two thousand pesos were to be available for pensions of deserving persons. Encomenderos must not live in their Indians' villages, nor build houses there, nor allow their slaves to go thither, nor maintain stock-farms in the neighborhood of a village. They must marry within three years after receiving a holding, and could not leave their province without a license, or go to Spain except for some extraordinary emergency.

Many regulations safeguarding the good treatment of the Indians illustrate evils which needed correction. For example, no Spaniard of whatever station could be carried in a litter by Indians. The older form of draughting Indians for labor had been prolific in abuses and was later abolished. Indians could be assigned by the proper officials to work for wages, and the same was done with idle Spaniards, mestizos, and Negroes; but it was forbidden that the Indians should be carried off against their will or kept overtime. If they demanded excessive wages the rate was to be settled by the officials. The absence of beasts of burden in New Spain, before they were introduced by the Spaniards, had necessitated all freight being carried by Indian porters; but the Indians were no longer to be compelled to carry burdens. Nor were Indian laborers to be apportioned to work in vineyards or olive groves, factories or sugar mills. If, however, boys wished to work in a factory to learn the art of weaving it was permitted.

The required service of Indians in the mines was called the "mita." In Peru not more than one seventh part of the Indians could be assigned on the "mita" at once; nor could an Indian be draughted again until all his fellow villagers had completed their turn. In New Spain the "mita" drew only four from each hundred. For this as for all other services they received wages. They were not to be sent to poor mines, or employed in draining them of water.

One of the fullest pictures that we have of the conditions of Indian life in the middle of the colonial era is that of the English friar Thomas Gage, who was for several years stationed in Indian towns in Guatemala, and also served as a teacher of Latin in Chiapa and as lecturer on divinity in the University of Guatemala. After his return he became a Protestant, and his subsequent views in some respects colored his narrative. His incidental notices of Indian conditions impress the reader as indicating on the whole a status superior in its economic possibilities to that of the European peasantry of that day. His chapter devoted to a particular description of Indian life is darkly colored, but not more so than the average conventional picture of peasant life in France on the eve of the Revolution. Gage tells us that the apportionment of Indians as laborers was the occasion of much oppression, and that the wages were inadequate, being only about ten cents a day. Yet it does not appear that the system in Mexico was more oppressive than the French corvée.

5. A REPLY TO BOURNE

Bourne's Spain in America *gave a strong impetus to the reaction in the United States against what is now called the "Black Legend." A further stimulus to the revisionist movement was given by Lesley B. Simpson's* The Encomienda in New Spain *(1929), whose realistic, pragmatic stance went hand in hand with certain procolonialist premises, such as the premise that force or violence was necessary for the spread of civilization. Between 1920 and 1960 U.S. scholars published numerous monographs that served to rehabilitate Spain's colonial policies by demonstrating the industry and honesty of some colonial administrators, the relative laxity of Spanish controls over colonial culture, the high level of some colonial thought, and the "freedom of speech" that allegedly existed in sixteenth-century Spain and Spanish America. In recent years, however, other scholars have begun to view Spain's colonial record with more critical eyes. This reassessment reflects the social consciousness and anticolonialism of our times, concern with the welfare of the masses rather than elites, and understanding of the harmful effects of colonial survivals in Latin American life. By contrast with the traditional critique of Spanish colonialism, it draws its data from economic and social history rather than political history and is based on a sophisticated grasp of the complex mechanism of Spanish colonial rule. Stanley and Barbara Stein describe the "brutal exploitation of American masses."*

The face of Iberian colonialism, of conquest, pacification, and evangelization may be seen in the basic administrative unit of Central Mexico and highland Peru of 1700, the *corregimiento*. There would be found the corregidor de indios or alcalde mayor, a literate Spaniard of generally limited legal training who had obtained appointment by purchase, family connection, or patronage. Since there was no regular promotional system at this bureaucratic level and salaries were low, the corregidor assumed his isolated post to maximize his one- to five-year tenure to accumulate a fortune. Moreover, the corregidor or alcalde mayor had undoubtedly borrowed from merchants at Madrid, Sevilla, Mexico, or Lima to cover outlays on bribes, on the tax of one half the first year's salary (*media anata*), and on clothing, household goods, and travel. On arrival at his post, the corregidor was already integrated into an administrative, financial, and mercantile system whose infrastructure consisted of the Amerindian vassal, half-serf and half-peasant, and whose superstructure might be represented by an affluent ex-viceroy ensconced in his Madrid townhouse with dozens of retainers.

In the Central Andes the corregidor's major responsibility as district chief was to exact from caciques in Amerindian towns the annual quota of draftees for silver and mercury mines—in particular the dreaded mita de Potosí. Enforcement of the labor draft offered corregidores ample opportunity to accept bribes from Indians seeking to escape mine service or from estate owners and sweatshop entrepreneurs seeking extra hands. Yet the most efficient way for such a corregidor to amass a fortune was via the unsanctioned but hallowed practice of forcing Amerinds to accept goods—wanted or unwanted, from mules to mercury—whose quantities and prices he prescribed. The colonial district chief or corregidor handled goods sent by merchants in the viceregal capital, more than likely connected with Sevilla exporters who had originally financed the corregidor's purchase of office. In essence this was an important facet of the system of trade and navigation between Spain and the Indies.

Stanley J. Stein and Barbara H. Stein, *The Colonial Heritage of Latin America: Essays on Economic Independence in Perspective*, copyright © 1970 by Oxford University Press, Inc., pp. 77–81. Reprinted by permission.

To the corregidor, miner, and merchant must be added another representative of the colonial establishment, the parish priest in the *corregimiento de indios*. Because he acquired his position in the devious manner of secular placement, his obligations were often taken lightly. The curate had his commercial "rights" too: "gifts" of food and clothing, religious fees, unremunerated household service. This, of course, is not a comprehensive catalogue of the instruments of bureaucratic extortion in Indian America around 1700: it is only to suggest the secular roots of Amerindian fear of the European and the criollo and their mestizo, mulatto, or cacique assistants.

These intimations of brutal exploitation of Amerindian masses may seem unduly exaggerated. They have not been presented to indict a people but a system. Obviously, only a minority of Iberians profited from the overseas possessions while the mass of Iberians remained oblivious or powerlessly aware of colonial oppression. Nor is it intended to overlook the fact that sensitive Spaniards and Portuguese often denounced exploitation and inhumanity perpetrated by their fellow Europeans in the American colonies. If the condition of the lowest stratum of society in Spanish colonial America was generally wretched, some will insist that the existence of west European peasants, craftsmen, and miners in the sixteenth and seventeenth centuries was equally wretched. This proposition in general is valid, and the difficulties inherent in calculating relative deprivation make criticism difficult unless one probes a bit further.

Were west Europeans forced into mines and kept there in the seventeenth century without surfacing from Monday to Saturday? Was there in operation in western Europe an annual labor draft which forced unwilling laborers to move hundreds of miles to pitheads along with their families, supplies, and pack animals? To change the scene, were there west European occupations in which employers could calculate with frightening accuracy that a worker's life would be no longer than five to ten years in their employment—which the Brazilian planters calculated for Negro slaves on sugar plantations in the first half of the seventeenth century? Or, not to exhaust comparisons but to show their possibilities, could a high west European official have returned from a post after four years of service with an income surplus of between 1 and 1.5 million silver pesos? For example, the Duque de Albuquerque in 1715 paid the Madrid government 700,000 silver pesos to avoid charges of gross malfeasance in office. If the answer to these questions is no, then the historian no matter how insensitive his skin must conclude that west Europeans from the Iberian peninsula utilized the right of conquest to exploit the subordinate peoples of America for personal profit beyond possibilities existing in the metropolis. Colonialism and uplift have always been antithetical.

A civil service invariably mirrors the matrix, metropolitan or colonial, in which it operates. By the end of the seventeenth century, the Spanish and Spanish colonial civil service reflected societies they were designed to administer. The rigidity of Spanish society, the inability or unwillingness to reshape the economy, the stagnation of Spain gave the elite and their wide circle of dependents by birth, marriage, or service few opportunities for employment other than in state service in the metropolis and especially in the colonies. To the colonies flowed a succession of viceroys chosen from the upper nobility and given wide discretion for enrichment. There they administered submissive colonial peoples in conjunction with the colonial audiencias. Beneath viceroys and audiencias came large numbers of Spanish placemen who had purchased preferment, indebted themselves to Spanish moneylenders, and who then proceeded to enrich themselves as corregidores or alcaldes mayores or their lieutenants in isolated Amerindian communities.

Thus by about 1700 the characteristic features of the colonial policy were already well established. Public office at all levels was seen as a legitimate instrument to further private interest over public weal. A monarchy extorting a share of a viceroy's spoils of office symbolized, indeed legitimized, venality, encouraged corruption and showed itself demonstrably incapable of controlling malfeasance in office. It is an ironic commentary on the effects of colonial rule that the very term "cacique"—originally applied to Amerinds who served the colonial elite to exploit the Amerindian masses—was to become in Spain the term for a local boss. Furthermore, the local colonial government of town officials, corregidores, and priests emerged as the core of political power that fused the interests of local elite of wealth, power, and prestige. It was expected that the colonial civil service armed with broad discretionary powers would work closely with local interests to enforce the *status quo* by manipulating the colonial law code. To the elite, law became a norm honored in the breach. To the unprivileged, law was arbitrary and alien, therefore without moral force.

PART THREE

COLONIAL
BRAZIL

11

❧

THE FORMATION
OF COLONIAL BRAZIL

PEDRO ALVARES CABRAL, a Portuguese captain sent to follow up Vasco da Gama's great voyage to India, accidentally discovered Brazil in 1500 and claimed it for his country. Trade and conquest in the Far East claimed Portugal's chief attention at this time, but Portugal did not completely neglect its new possession. Brazilwood, source of a valued red dye, was the first staple of the colony, but sugar soon established its economic leadership. Raids on Indian villages and, after 1550, the importation of Black slaves provided labor for the plantations and sugar mills.

The second half of the seventeenth century saw a crisis in the Brazilian sugar industry, which was faced with severe competition from newly risen Dutch, English, and French sugar colonies in the West Indies. As the first economic cycle of colonial Brazil drew to a close, a second opened with the discovery of gold and diamonds in the regions of Minas Gerais, Goiás, and Mato Grosso, lying west and south of Baía and Pernambuco. But the gold and diamonds were found in limited quantities, and production declined sharply after 1760.

As the interior provinces of Minas Gerais and Goiás sank into decay, the northeast enjoyed a revival based on the increasing European demand for sugar, cotton, and other semitropical products. Between 1750 and 1800 Brazilian cotton production made large strides but as rapidly declined in the face of competition from the more efficient cotton growers of the United States. The beginnings of the coffee industry, future giant of the Brazilian economy, also date from the late colonial period.

Until the decree of January 28, 1808, which opened the ports of Brazil to the trade of all nations, the commerce of the colony was restricted to Portuguese nationals and ships. A significant exception was made in the case of Great Britain, Portugal's protector and ally. By the Treaty of 1654, British merchants were permitted to trade between Portuguese and Brazilian ports.

English ships frequently neglected the formality of touching at Lisbon and plied a direct contraband commerce with the colony. The 1808 decree of free trade only confirmed Great Britain's actual domination of Brazilian commerce.

1. THE PORTUGUESE COLONIZER

Unlike the Spanish conquistadores, who roamed through jungles and mountains in search of golden kingdoms, their Portuguese counterparts were content to remain on the fertile coast of northeast Brazil, where they established a plantation economy producing sugar for the world market. Yet the Portuguese colonizer could deal hard blows when necessity required, as shown by the story of Duarte Coelho, who undertook to settle the captaincy of Pernambuco. Gabriel Soares de Souza, a planter of Baía who wrote one of the earliest and most valuable accounts of colonial Brazil, tells of Duarte's exploits.

The town of Olinda is the capital of the captaincy of Pernambuco, which was settled by Duarte Coelho, a gentleman of whose courage and chivalry I shall not speak here in detail, for the books that deal with India are full of his deeds. After Duarte Coelho returned from India to Portugal to seek a reward for his services, he sought and obtained from His Highness the grant of a captaincy on this coast; this grant began at the mouth of the São Francisco River in the northwest and ran fifty leagues up the coast toward the captaincy of Tamaracá, ending at the Igaruçu River. ... Since this brave captain was always disposed to perform great feats, he determined to come in person to settle and conquer this his captaincy. He arrived there with a fleet of ships that he had armed at his own cost, in which he brought his wife and children and many of their kinsmen, and other settlers. With this fleet he made port at the place called Pernambuco, which in the native language means "hidden sea," because of a rock nearby that is hidden in the sea. Arriving at this port, Duarte Coelho disembarked and fortified himself as well as he could on a high point free of any dominating peaks, where the town is today. There he built a strong tower, which still stands in the town square, and for many years he waged war against the natives and the French who fought at their side. Frequently he was besieged and badly wounded, with the loss of many of his people, but he courageously persisted in his aim, and not only defended himself bravely but attacked his enemies so effectively that they abandoned the neighboring lands. Later his son, of the same name, continued to wage war on them, harassing and capturing these people, called Cayté, until they had abandoned the whole coast and more than fifty leagues in the interior. In

---

Gabriel Soares de Souza, *Tratado descriptivo do Brazil em 1587*, São Paulo, 1938, pp. 27–29. (Excerpt translated by the editor.)

these labors Duarte spent many thousands of *cruzados* that he had acquired in India, and this money was really well spent, for today his son Jorge de Albuquerque Coelho enjoys an income of ten thousand *cruzados*, which he obtains from the retithe, from his tithe of the fishing catch, and from the quit rent paid him by the sugarmills (fifty of these have been established in Pernambuco, and they produce so much sugar that the tithes on it yield nineteen thousand *cruzados* a year).

This town of Olinda must have about seven hundred householders, but there are many more within the limits of the town, since from twenty to thirty people live on each of these plantations, aside from the many who live on farms. Hence if it were necessary to assemble these people with arms, they could place in the field more than three thousand fighting men, together with the inhabitants of the town of Cosmos, which must have four hundred mounted men. These people could bring from their estates four or five thousand Negro slaves and many Italians. This captaincy is so prosperous that there are more than a hundred men in it who have an income of from one to five thousand *cruzados*, and some have incomes of eight to ten thousand *cruzados*. From this land many men have returned rich to Portugal who came here poor, and every year this captaincy sends forty to fifty ships loaded with sugar and brazilwood; this wood is so profitable to His Majesty that he has lately farmed out the concession for a period of ten years at twenty thousand *cruzados* a year. It seems to me that such a powerful captaincy, which yields this kingdom such a great store of provisions, should be better fortified, and should not be exposed for a corsair to sack and destroy—which could be prevented with little expense and less labor.

2. THE SLAVE-HUNTERS

The expanding plantation economy of the Brazilian northeast required a steady supply of cheap labor. The Portuguese met the problem with raids on Indian villages, returning with trains of captives who were sold to plantation owners. The men of São Paulo, lacking the sugar and brazilwood on which the prosperity of the northeast was based, turned to slave-hunting as a lucrative occupation. The prospect of finding gold in the interior made their expeditions doubly attractive. As the coastal Indians were exterminated or fled before the invaders, the bandeirantes, the "men of the banner," pushed ever deeper south and west, expanding the frontiers of Brazil in the process. Almost the only voices raised against their predatory activities were those of the Jesuit missionaries. One of them, believed to be the famous Father Joseph de Anchieta (1534–1597), describes the devastation wrought by the slave-hunters.

Cartas, informaçoes, fragmentos históricos e sermões do Padre Joseph de Anchieta, S. J. (1554–1594). Rio de Janeiro, 1933, pp. 377–378. (Excerpt translated by the editor.)

The number of Indians that have been destroyed in this captaincy of Baía in the past twenty years passes belief; who would think that so many people could be destroyed in so short a time? In the fourteen churches maintained by the Fathers they had brought together 40,000 souls, by count, and even more, counting those who came after—yet today it is doubtful whether the three churches that remain have 3,500 souls together. Six years ago an honored citizen of this city, a man of good conscience and a city official at the time, said that in the two preceding years 20,000 souls, by count, had been brought from the back country of Arabó and that all of them went to the Portuguese plantations. These 20,000, added to the 40,000 of the churches, come to 60,000. Now for the past six years the Portuguese have been bringing Indians for their plantations, one bringing 2,000, another 3,000, some more, others less; in six years this must come to 80,000 souls or more. Now look at the sugar-mills and plantations of Baía, and you will find them full of Guinea Negroes but very few natives; if you ask what happened to all those people, they will tell you that they died.

In this way God has severely punished the Portuguese for the many offenses that they committed and still commit against these Indians, for they go into the interior and deceive these people, inviting them to go to the coast, where, they say, they would live in their villages as they did in their lands, and the Portuguese would be their neighbors. The Indians, believing this, go with them, and for fear they will change their minds the Portuguese destroy their gardens. On arrival at the coast they divide the Indians among themselves, some taking the women, others their husbands, and still others the children, and they sell them. Other Portuguese go into the interior and entice the Indians by saying that they will take them to the churches of the Fathers; and by this means they seduce them from their lands, for it is common knowledge in the backlands that only the Indians in the churches where the Fathers reside enjoy liberty and all the rest are captives. Matters reached such a point that a certain Portuguese, going into the back country in search of Indians, shaved his head like a priest, saying that he was a Father seeking Indians for the churches. This happened at a time when Father Gaspar Lourenço was bound for the interior, and he found these people on the road. When they heard that the Father was going into the backlands they said: "How can that be, when he who brings us says that he is a Father, and that is why we go with him?" And the Portuguese with the shaven head hid himself, not wanting the priest to see him.

The Portuguese travel 250 and 300 leagues to find the Indians, for the nearest ones are by now a great distance away, and since the land is now depopulated most of them die on the road from hunger. There have been Portuguese who seized on the road certain Indians who were enemies of the ones they were bringing, killed them, and gave their flesh to the captives to eat. And when all these people arrive at the coast, seeing that the Portuguese do not keep the promises they made in the interior but separate them from each other, some flee into the forests, never to emerge again, and others die from grief and chagrin that they, who had been free men, should be made slaves.

3. AIMORÉ: WORD OF TERROR

The Brazilian Indian did not accept the loss of land and liberty without a struggle. Indian resistance to white aggression was handicapped by the fatal propensity of the tribes to war against each other, a situation that the Portuguese utilized for their own advantage. Forced to retreat into the interior by the superior arms and organization of the whites, the natives often returned to make destructive forays on isolated Portuguese communities. As late as the first part of the nineteenth century stretches of the Brazilian shore were made uninhabitable by the raids of Indians who lurked in the forests and mountains back of the coast. One tribe that never sought or granted a truce to the whites was the Aimorés. The chronicler Soares de Souza describes their mode of life and warfare.

It seems proper at this point to state what kind of people are those called Aimorés, who have done so much damage to this captaincy of Ilheos, as I have said. The coast of this captaincy used to be inhabited by the Tupiniquins, who abandoned it from fear of these brutes and went to live in the back country; at the present time there are only two very small Tupiniquin villages, situated near the sugar mills of Henrique Luiz.

These Aimorés are descended from other people that they call Tapuias, from whom departed in olden times certain families that went to live in very rugged mountains, fleeing from a defeat inflicted on them by their enemies; and there they lived many years without seeing any other people; and their descendants gradually lost their language, and developed a new one that is not understood by any other nation in the whole country of Brazil. These Aimorés are so savage that the other barbarians consider them worse than barbarians. Some of these were taken alive in Porto Seguro and in Ilheos, and they would not eat, preferring to die like savages.

This people first came to the sea at the River Caravellas, hard by Porto Seguro, and roamed this countryside and the beaches as far as the River Camamú; from there they began to launch attacks near Tinharé, descending to the shore only when they came to make an attack. This people is of the same color as the others, but they are larger and of more robust build. They have no beards or any other hair except on their heads, because they pluck

---

Soares de Souza, *Tratado descriptivo do Brazil*, pp. 56–60. (Excerpt translated by the editor.)

out the hairs on the other parts of their bodies. They fight with very large bows and arrows, and are such excellent bowmen that they never miss a shot; they are marvelously light on their feet, and great runners.

These barbarians do not live in villages or houses like other people, and so far no one has come across their dwellings in the woods; they go from one place to another through the woods and fields; they sleep on the ground on leaves; and if it rains they go up to the foot of a tree and squat there, covering themselves with leaves; no other furnishings have ever been found among them. These savages do not have gardens or raise any food; they live on wild fruit and the game they kill, which they eat raw or poorly roasted, when they have a fire. Both men and women cut their hair short, shearing it with certain canes of which they gather a great number; their speech is rough, projected from their throats with much force; like Basque, it is impossible to write down.

These barbarians live by robbing everyone they encounter, and one never sees more than twenty or thirty bowmen at one time. They never fight any-one face to face, but always employ treachery, for they attack in the fields and roads which they travel, waiting in ambush for other Indians and all other sorts of persons, each hidden behind a tree and never missing a shot. They use up all their arrows, and if the people turn on them they all flee in differ-ent directions, but if they see that their pursuers have dropped their guard they stop and find a place to hide until their pursuers have passed, when they shoot them in the back with their arrows at will. They do not know how to swim, and any river that cannot be forded presents an adequate defense against them; but in order to find a crossing they will go many miles along the river in search of one.

These savages eat human flesh for sustenance—unlike the other Indians, who only eat it for the sake of revenge and in memory of their ancient ha-treds. The captaincies of Porto Seguro and Ilheos have been destroyed and almost depopulated by fear of these barbarians, and the sugar mills have stopped working because all the slaves and the other people have been killed by them. The people on most of the plantations and those who have escaped from them have become so afraid of them that if they merely hear the word "Aimorés" they leave their plantations in search of refuge, the white men among them. In the twenty-five years that this plague has afflicted these two captaincies, they have killed more than 300 Portuguese and 3,000 slaves.

The inhabitants of Baía used to send letters to the people of Ilheos, and men traveled this road along the shore without danger. But when the Aimorés realized this they decided to come to these beaches to wait for the people who passed there, and there they killed many Portuguese and many more slaves. These bandits are such fleet runners that no one could escape them on foot, except those who take refuge in the sea; they dare not enter the ocean, but wait for them to come on shore until nightfall, when they retire. For this reason the road is forbidden, and no one travels it except at great risk of his life. If some means is not found to destroy these savages they will destroy the plantations of Baía, through which they roam at will. Since they are such intractable enemies of all mankind, it was not possible to learn more about their mode of life and customs.

4. THE RISE AND FALL OF VILLA RICA

By the last decade of the seventeenth century the sugar cycle of the northeast had about run its course. It was at this time of acute depression that the discovery of gold in Minas Gerais (1690) gave a new stimulus to Brazil's economic life, led to the first effective settlement of the interior, and shifted the center of economic and political activity from north to south. The story of the rise and fall of the gold mining center of Villa Rica is told by John Mawe (1764–1829), who visited it at the opening of the nineteenth century.

The history of an establishment which, twenty years after its foundation, was reputed the richest place on the globe, was an object of considerable interest to me, and I made many inquiries respecting it from some of the best informed men on the spot. It appears that the first discovery of this once rich mountain was effected by the enterprising spirit of the Paulistas, who, of all the colonists in Brazil, retained the largest share of that ardent and indefatigable zeal for discovery which characterized the Lusitanians of former days. They penetrated from their capital into these regions, braving every hardship, and encountering every difficulty which a savage country, infested by still more savage inhabitants, opposed to them. They cut their way through impervious woods, carrying their provisions with them, and occasionally cultivating small patches of land to afford them food to retreat to, in case of necessity, as well as to keep up a communication with their city, St. Paul's. Every inch of ground was disputed by the barbarous Indians, here called Bootocoodies, who were constantly either attacking them openly or lying in ambush, and but too frequently succeeded in surprising some of them, or their negroes, whom they immediately sacrificed to their horrible appetite for human flesh. They believed the negroes to be the great monkeys of the wood. The bones of the unfortunate sufferers were frequently found exposed, shocking testimonies of the barbarity of their murderers, whom the Paulistas, roused to revenge, invariably shot, wherever they met them. These examples of vengeance answered their desired end; the Indians, terrified as well by the noise as by the fatal effect of the fire-arms, fled with precipitation, believing that the white men commanded lightning and thunder.

John Mawe, *Travels in the Interior of Brazil*, London, 1815, pp. 171–177.

It does not appear that in exploring this territory they received any assistance whatever from the aborigines; they followed the course of rivers, occasionally finding gold, of which they skimmed the surface, and continued to proceed until they arrived at the mountain which is our present subject. Its riches arrested their course; they immediately erected temporary houses and began their operations. The principal men of the party that first settled here, were Antonio Dias, Bartholomew Rocinho, Antonio de Ferrera (filho), and Garcia Ruis. It appears that they took the most direct way to the place, for the roads they then opened are the same which are still used. The fame of their success soon reached the city of St. Paul's; fresh adventurers arrived in great numbers, bringing with them all the negroes they had means to purchase. Other adventurers went from St. Paul's to Rio de Janeiro to procure more negroes, their own city being drained; and thus the news of the lately discovered gold mountain being made known in the Brazilian capital, men of all descriptions went in crowds to this land of promise by the way of St. Paul's, which was the only route then known. The first settlers might have prevented the exposure of their good fortune, had they been able to moderate their joy, and consented to act in concert; but as gold was in such great abundance, every individual appropriated a lot of ground, and thus became a capitalist. Each strove which should make the most of his treasure in the shortest time, and thus there was a continual demand for more negroes, more iron, etc. and, in the general eagerness to obtain them, the secret which all were interested in keeping was disclosed. The Paulistas, independent in spirit, and proud of their wealth, were desirous of giving laws to the newcomers; but the latter determining to oppose this measure, formed themselves into a party under the guidance of Manuel Nuñez Viana, an adventurer of some consequence, who strenuously asserted their claim to equal rights and advantages. Disputes arose on both sides, and were at length aggravated into hostilities, which proved unfavourable to the Paulistas, the great part of whom fled to a considerable station of their own, and there awaited reinforcements. Viana and his followers, without loss of time, went in pursuit of their foes, whom they found on a plain near the site of St. João del Rey. The two parties met on the borders of a river, and a sanguinary battle took place, which ended in the defeat of the Paulistas, who afterwards made the best terms they could. The slain were buried on the margin of the river, which, from that circumstance took the name of Rio dos Mortos.

The Paulistas, bent on revenge, but weakened by defeat, appealed to the sovereign, King Pedro, denouncing Viana and his followers as rebels who were attempting to take the district to themselves, and set up an independent government. The King's ministers, apprized of the state of affairs, and learning by report the immense riches of the country, immediately sent a chief, with a competent body of troops, to take advantage of the strife between the two parties; which, in a country tenable by a few men on account of its numerous strongholds, was a most fortunate circumstance. The name of this chief was Albuquerque; a man of enterprize and perseverance, in all respects qualified for the service on which he was sent. His appearance at first occasioned much confusion and discontent among both parties; and though he was not openly opposed, yet he was in continual alarm. The Paulistas now saw that the riches which they in conjunction with their rivals might have retained, were about to be seized by a third party which would reduce them both to subordination. Disturbances prevailed for some time, but reinforcements continually arriving from Government, tranquillity was at length perfectly established; and in the year 1711 a regular town began to be formed; a government-house, a mint, and a depot for arms were built. A code of laws was enacted for the regulation of the mines; all gold-dust found was ordered to be delivered to officers appointed for that purpose; a fifth in weight was taken for the King, and the remaining four parts were purified, melted into ingots at the expence of Government, then assayed, marked according to their value, and delivered to the owners, with a certificate to render them current. For the greater convenience of trade, gold dust was likewise permitted to circulate for small payments. Notwithstanding these strict regulations, a considerable quantity of the precious metal in its original state found its way to Rio de Janeiro, Bahai, and other ports, clandestinely, without paying the royal fifth, until Government, apprized of this illicit traffic, established registers in various parts for the examination of all passengers, and stationed soldiers to patrol the roads. By these means, gold in immense quantities was seized and confiscated; the persons on whom any was found forfeited all their property, and, unless they had friends of great influence, were sent as convicts to Africa for life. The greatest disgrace was attached to the name of smuggler; and such was the rigour of the law against offenders of this description, that every person quitting the district was obliged to take a certificate stating whither he was going, and what he carried with him. This regulation is still in force, and is rigorously observed.

Villa Rica soon enjoyed a considerable trade with Rio de Janeiro; the returns were negroes, iron, woollens, salt, provisions of various kinds, and wine, all which at that time bore amazingly high profits.

About the year 1713, when Dr. Bras de Silvia was appointed governor, the quantity of gold produced was so considerable that the royal fifth amounted to half a million sterling annually. The mountain became pierced like a honeycomb, as the miners worked every soft part they could find, and penetrated as far as they could, conveying the *cascalhão* which they dug out to a convenient place for washing. In rainy weather the torrents of water running down the sides of the mountain, carried away much earthy matter containing delicate particles of gold, which settled in the ground near its base. When the waters abated, this rich deposit gave employment to numbers of the poorer sort of people, who took it away and washed it at their convenience.

Antonio Dias, the person already mentioned as one of the leaders of the Paulistas, who discovered the place, having become extremely rich, built a fine church, and dying soon after, bequeathed to it considerable funds. It still bears his name. Five or six others were begun and soon finished, as neither wood nor stone was wanting, and the inhabitants were all ready to contribute a share of their property, and to employ their negroes in furtherance of these pious works. A law highly creditable to the wisdom of the Portuguese government was now enacted, to prohibit friars from entering the territory of the mines. What treasures were thus saved to the state, and what a number of persons were thus continued in useful labour, who would else have become burthensome to the community!

The town now underwent many improvements; its streets were more regularly built, and some parts of the side of the mountain were levelled to afford more convenient room for the construction of houses, and the laying out of gardens. Reservoirs were formed, from which water was distributed by means of conduits to all parts, and public fountains were erected in the most convenient and central situations. The mint and smelting houses were enlarged, and rendered more commodious for the transaction of business. About this period the inhabitants amounted to twelve thousand or upwards; those who possessed mines were either the first settlers or their descendants, and as the best part of the district was occupied, the new adventurers who continued to arrive from time to time were obliged to enter into the service of the existing owners until they had learned their methods of working, after which they generally went in search of fresh mines, proceeding along the water-courses and ravines, where they sometimes discovered new sources of wealth. Between the years 1730 and 1750 the mines were in the height of their prosperity; the King's fifth during some years of that period is said to have amounted to at least a million sterling annually.

The mines which produced this immense wealth at length became gradually less abundant; and, as the precious metal disappeared, numbers of the miners retired, some to the mother-country, loaded with riches, which tempted fresh adventurers, and many to Rio de Janeiro and other sea-ports, where they employed their large capitals in commerce.

Villa Rica at the present day scarcely retains a shadow of its former splendour. Its inhabitants, with the exception of the shopkeepers, are void of employment; they totally neglect the fine country around them, which, by proper cultivation, would amply compensate for the loss of the wealth which their ancestors drew from its bosom. Their education, their habits, their hereditary prejudices, alike unfit them for active life; perpetually indulging in visionary prospects of sudden wealth, they fancy themselves exempted from that universal law of nature which ordains that man shall live by the sweat of his brow. In contemplating the fortunes accumulated by their predecessors, they overlook the industry and perseverance which obtained them, and entirely lose sight of the change of circumstances which renders those qualities now doubly necessary. The successors of men who rise to opulence from small beginnings seldom follow the example set before them, even when trained to it; how then should a Creolian, reared in idleness and ignorance, feel any thing of the benefits of industry! His negroes constitute his principal property, and them he manages so ill, that the profits of their labour hardly defray the expences of their maintenance: in the regular course of nature they become old and unable to work, yet he continues in the same listless and slothful way, or sinks into a state of absolute inactivity, not knowing what to do from morning to night. This deplorable degeneracy is almost the universal characteristic of the descendants of the original settlers; every trade is occupied either by mulattoes or negroes, both of which classes seem superior in intellect to their masters, because they make a better use of it.

12

GOVERNMENT AND CHURCH IN COLONIAL BRAZIL

THE PORTUGUESE CROWN first governed Brazil through donatories or lords—proprietors who were given almost complete authority in their territories in return for assuming the responsibilities of colonization. In 1549, convinced that the system had failed to achieve its ends, the king issued a decree limiting the powers of the donatories and creating a central government for all of Brazil. The first captain general of the colony was Thomé de Souza, and Baía was selected as his capital. Governors appointed by the king, and subordinate to the captain-general, gradually replaced the donatories as the political and military leaders of the captaincies.

During the period of the Spanish Captivity (1580–1640), Spain established a *Conselho da India* for the administration of the Portuguese colonies. After Portugal regained her independence, this body continued to have charge of Brazilian affairs. As the colony expanded, new captaincies or provinces were created. In 1763 the captain-general of Rio de Janeiro replaced his colleague at Baía as head of the colonial administration in Brazil, with the title of viceroy. In practice, however, his authority over the other governors was negligible.

Official inefficiency and corruption seem to have been as common in colonial Brazil as in the Spanish Indies. During the reform administration of the Marquis de Pombal (1756–1777) the situation improved but apparently without lasting effects.

The Brazilian church lacked the immense wealth and influence of its counterpart in the Spanish Indies. By comparison with the Spanish monarchs, the Portuguese kings seemed almost niggardly in their dealings with the church. But the control over its affairs was equally absolute.

In Brazil, as in the Spanish colonies, the Jesuits carried on intensive missionary work among the Indians. The priests aimed at the settlement of their Indian converts in villages completely isolated from the whites. Their efforts in this direction led to many conflicts with the Portuguese landowners, who wanted to enslave the Indians for work on their plantations. The clash of interests was most severe in São Paulo, whose halfbreed slave hunters bitterly resented Jesuit interference with their operations.

Like their colleagues in the Spanish colonies, the Brazilian clergy—always excepting the Jesuits and some other orders—were often criticized for their worldly lives and indifference to their charges. Yet such educational and humanitarian establishments as existed were almost exclusively provided by the clergy, and from their ranks came most of the few distinguished names in Brazilian colonial science, learning, and literature.

1. THE ADMINISTRATION OF COLONIAL BRAZIL

The government of Portuguese Brazil broadly resembled that of the Spanish Indies in its spirit, its structure, and its vices. Henry Koster, an astute observer of Brazilian life in the early nineteenth century, describes the political and financial administration of the important province of Pernambuco.

The captaincies-general, or provinces of the first rank, in Brazil, of which Pernambuco is one, are governed by captains-general, or governors, who are appointed for three years. At the end of this period, the same person is continued or not, at the option of the supreme government. They are, in fact, absolute in power: but before the person who has been nominated to one of these places can exercise any of its functions, he is under the necessity of presenting his credentials to the *Senado da Câmara*, the chamber or municipality of the principal town. This is formed of persons of respectability in the place. The governor has the supreme and sole command of the military force. The civil and criminal causes are discussed before, and determined by, the *Ouvidor* and *Juiz de Fora*, the two chief judicial officers, whose duties are somewhat similar: but the former is the superior in rank. They are appointed for three years, and the term may be renewed. It is in these departments of the government that the opportunities of amassing large fortunes are most numerous; and certain it is, that some individuals take advantage of them in a manner which renders justice but a name. The governor can determine in a criminal cause without appeal; but if he pleases, he refers it to the competent judge. The *Procurador da Coroa*, attorney-general, is an officer of considerable weight. The *Intendente da Marinha*, port admiral, is likewise consulted on matters of first importance; as are also the *Escrivão da Fazenda Real*, chief of

---

Henry Koster, *Travels in Brazil*, London, 1816, 2 vols., I, pp. 46–50.

the treasury, and the *Juiz da Alfândega*, comptroller of the customs. These seven officers form the *Junta*, or council, which occasionally meets to arrange and decide upon the affairs of the captaincy to which they belong.

The ecclesiastical government is scarcely connected with that above mentioned; and is administered by a bishop and a dean and chapter with his vicar-general etc. The governor cannot even appoint a chaplain to the island of Fernando de Noronha, one of the dependencies of Pernambuco; but acquaints the bishop that a priest is wanted, who then nominates one for the place.

The number of civil and military officers is enormous; inspectors innumerable—colonels without end, devoid of any objects to inspect—without any regiments to command; judges to manage each trifling department of which the duties might all be done by two or three persons. Thus salaries are augmented; the people are oppressed; but the state is not benefitted.

Taxes are laid where they fall heavy upon the lower classes: and none are levied where they could well be borne. A tenth is raised in kind upon cattle, poultry, and agriculture, and even upon salt; this in former times appertained, as in other Christian countries, to the clergy.[1] All the taxes are farmed to the highest bidders, and this among the rest. They are parcelled out in extensive districts, and are contracted for at a reasonable rate; but the contractors again dispose of their shares in small portions: these are again retailed to other persons: and as a profit is obtained by each transfer the people must be oppressed, that these men may satisfy those above them and enrich themselves. The system is in itself bad, but is rendered still heavier by this division of the spoil. ...

Now, although the expenses of the provincial governments are great, and absorb a very considerable proportion of the receipts, owing to the number of officers employed in every department, still the salaries of each are, in most instances, much too small to afford a comfortable subsistence. Consequently peculation, bribery, and other crimes of the same description, are to be looked for: and they become so frequent as to escape all punishment or even notice; though there are some men whose character is without reproach. The governor of Pernambuco receives a salary of 4,000,000 *reis*, or about 1000 £ *per annum*. Can this be supposed to be sufficient for a man in his responsible situation, even in a country in which articles of food are cheap? His honour, however, is unimpeached; not one instance did I ever hear mentioned of improper conduct in him. But the temptation and the opportunities of amassing money are very great, and few are the persons who can resist them.

2. LOCAL GOVERNMENT:
THE *CAPITÃO-MÔR*

Away from the few large towns, local government in colonial Brazil in effect meant government by the great landowners, or fazendeiros. *In the* câmaras, *or municipal coun-*

cils, the power of these rural magnates was sometimes checked by representatives of the crown or of urban interests, but on their vast estates they were absolute lords. To their personal influence the great planters often joined the authority of office, for the royal governors invariably appointed the capitães-môres, *or district militia officers, from among them. Armed with unlimited power to command, arrest, and punish, the* capitão-môr *(captain-major) became a popular symbol of despotism and oppression. The following selection from Koster's book illustrates his comment that "the whole aspect of the government of Brazil is military."*

I became acquainted and somewhat intimate with the *Capitão-môr* of a neighbouring district, from frequently meeting him, in my evening visits to a Brazilian family. He was about to make the circuit of his district, in the course of a few weeks, and invited one of my friends and myself to accompany him in this review or visit to his officers, to which we readily agreed. It was arranged that he should make us acquainted in due time with the day which he might appoint for setting out, that we might meet him at his sugar-plantation, from whence we were to proceed with him and his suite further into the country.

The *Capitães-môres*, captains-major, are officers of considerable power. They have civil as well as military duties to perform, and ought to be appointed from among the planters of most wealth and individual weight in the several *Termos*, boundaries or districts. But the interest of family or of relations about the Court, have occasioned deviations from this rule; and persons very unfit for these situations, have been sometimes nominated to them. The whole aspect of the government in Brazil is military. All men between the ages of sixteen and sixty, must be enrolled either as soldiers of the line, as militiamen, or as belonging to the body of *Ordenanças*. Of the regular soldiers, I have already spoken in another place. Of the second class, each township has a regiment, of which the individuals, with the exception of the major and adjutant, and in some cases the colonel, do not receive any pay. But they are considered as embodied men; and as such are called out upon some few occasions, in the course of the year, to assemble in uniform, and otherwise accoutred. The expense which must be incurred in this respect, of necessity, precludes the possibility of many persons becoming members of this class, even if the government were desirous of increasing the number of militia regiments. The soldiers of these are subject to their captains, to the colonel, and to the governor of the province. The colonels are either rich planters, or the major or lieutenant-colonel of a regiment of the line is thus promoted to the command of one of these; in this case, and in this case only, he receives pay. I am inclined to think, that he ought to possess some property in the district, and that any deviation from this rule is an abuse; but I am not certain that the law so ordains. The majors and the adjutants are likewise occasion-

Koster, *Travels in Brazil*, I, pp. 252–255.

ally promoted from the line; but whether they are regularly military men or planters, they receive pay; as their trouble, in distributing orders, and in other arrangements connected with the regiment, is considerable.

The third class, that of the *Ordenanças*, consisting of by far the largest portion of the white persons, and of free mulatto men of all shades, have for their immediate chiefs, the *Capitães-môres*, who serve without pay: and all the persons who are connected with the *Ordenanças*, are obliged likewise to afford their services gratuitously. Each district contains one *Capitão-mór*, who is invariably a person possessing property in the part of the country to which he is appointed. He is assisted by a major, captains, and *alferes*, who are lieutenants or ensigns, and by sergeants and corporals. The duties of the *Capitão-mór* are to see that every individual under his command has in his possession some species of arms; either a firelock, a sword, or a pike. He distributes the governor's orders through his district; and can oblige any of his men to take these orders to the nearest captain, who sends another peasant forward to the next captain, who sends another peasant forward to the next captain, and so forth; all which is done without any pay. A *Capitão-mór* can also imprison for twenty-four hours, and send under arrest for trial a person who is accused of having committed any crime, to the civil magistrate of the town to which his district is immediately attached. Now, the abuses of this office of *Capitão-mór* are very many; and the lower orders of free persons are much oppressed by these great men, and by their subalterns, down to the corporals. The peasants are often sent upon errands which have no relation to public business; for leagues and leagues these poor fellows are made to travel, for the purpose of carrying some private letter of the chief, of his captains, or of his lieutenants, without any remuneration. Indeed, many of these men in place, seldom think of employing their slaves on these occasions, or of paying the free persons so employed. This I have witnessed times out of number; and have heard the peasants in all parts of the country complain: it is a most heavy grievance. Nothing so much vexes a peasant as the consciousness of losing his time and trouble in a service which is not required by his sovereign. Persons are sometimes confined in the stocks for days together, on some trifling plea; and are at last released without being sent to the civil magistrate, or even admitted to a hearing. However, I am happy to say, that I am acquainted with some men, whose conduct is widely different from what I have above stated; but the power given to an individual is too great, and the probability of being called to an account for its abuse too remote, to insure the exercise of it in a proper manner.

The free mulattos and free negroes, whose names are upon the rolls, either of the militia regiments which are commanded by white officers, or by those of their own class and colour, are not, properly speaking, subject to the *Capitães-môres*. These officers, and the colonels of militia, are appointed by the supreme government: and the subaltern officers are nominated by the governor of each province.

3. THE JESUIT INDIAN POLICY

The Jesuits early established their leadership in the work of Indian conversion and in the religious and educational life of Brazil in general. They aimed at the settlement of their Indian converts in aldeas, *or villages, where they would live completely segregated from the white colonists, under the tutelage of the priests. The Jesuit Indian program led to many clashes with the Portuguese planters, who wanted to enslave the natives for work on their estates. The planters charged that the Indians in the Jesuit villages "were true slaves, who labored as such not only in the* colegios *but on the so-called Indian lands, which in the end became the estates and sugar mills of the Jesuit Fathers." Replying to these and other accusations, Father Joseph de Anchieta explained the Jesuit Indian policy.*

Every day, in the morning the Fathers teach the Indians doctrine and say mass for those who want to hear it before going to their fields; after that the children stay in school, where they learn reading and writing, counting, and other good customs pertaining to the Christian life; in the afternoon they conduct another class especially for those who are receiving the sacred sacraments. Daily the Fathers visit the sick with certain Indians assigned for this purpose, and if they have some special needs they attend to them, and always administer to them the necessary sacraments. All this they do purely for love of God and for no other interest or profit, for the Fathers get their food from the *colegio*, and they live with the Indians solely because of love of their souls, which have such great need of them. The Fathers make no use of them on plantations, for if the *colegio* needs them for certain tasks, and they come to help, they work for wages, ... and not through force but of their own free will, because they need clothing or implements. For although it is their natural tendency to go about naked, all those who have been raised in the Jesuit schools now wear clothes and are ashamed to go about naked. It is not true, as some say, that the Fathers are the lords of the villages.

When the Portuguese come to the villages in search of Indian labor, the Fathers help them all they can, summoning one of the Indian headmen to take the Portuguese to the houses of the natives to show them the goods they have brought, and those who wish to go they permit to leave without impediment. If the Fathers object at times, it is because the Indians have not finished their farm work, and they have to do this for the sake of their wives and children. In other cases, the Indians are not getting along with their wives, and once they leave for the homes of the Portuguese they never return; such Indians the Father also restrains from going, so that they may continue living with their wives. ...

Cartas, informaçoes, fragmentos históricos e sermões do Padre Joseph de Anchieta, S.J. (1554–1594), Rio de Janeiro, 1933, pp. 381–382. (Excerpt translated by the editor.)

The Indians are punished for their offenses by their own magistrates, appointed by the Portuguese governors; the only chastisement consists in being put in the stocks for a day or two, as the magistrate considers best; they use no chains or other imprisonment. If some Indian who went to work for the Portuguese returns before completing his time, the Father compels him to return to work out his time, and if the Indian cannot go for some good reason the Father arranges matters to the satisfaction of his employer.

The Fathers always encourage the Indians to cultivate their fields and to raise more provisions than they need, so that in case of necessity they might aid the Portuguese by way of barter; in fact, many Portuguese obtain their food from the villages. Thus one could say that the Fathers are truly the fathers of the Indians, both of their souls and of their bodies.

13

⌒

MASTERS AND SLAVES

RACE MIXTURE played a decisive role in the formation of the Brazilian people. The scarcity of white women in the colony, the freedom of the Portuguese from puritanical attitudes, and the despotic power of the great planters over their Indian and Black slave women all gave impetus to miscegenation. Color lines were drawn, but less sharply than in the Spanish Indies, and in colonial Brazil the possession of wealth more easily expunged the "taint" of Black skin.

Slavery played as important a role in the social organization of colonial Brazil as did race mixture in its ethnic make-up. The social consequences of the system were entirely negative. Slavery corrupted both master and slave, fostered harmful attitudes with respect to the dignity of labor, and retarded the economic development of Brazil. The virtual monopolization of labor by slaves sharply limited the number of socially acceptable occupations in which whites or free mixed bloods could engage. This gave rise to a large class of vagrants, beggars, "poor whites," and other degraded or disorderly elements who would not or could not compete with slaves in agriculture and industry.

The nucleus of Brazilian social as well as economic organization was the large estate; this centered about the Big House and constituted a patriarchal community that included the owner and his family, his chaplain and overseers, his slaves, and his *agregados*, or retainers—freemen of low social status who received the landowner's protection and assistance in return for a variety of services. In the sugar-growing northeast the great planters became a distinct aristocratic class, possessed of family traditions and pride in their name and blood.

By contrast with the decisive importance of the *fazenda*, or large estate, most of the colonial towns were mere appendages of the countryside, dominated politically and socially by the rural magnates. But in a few large cities, such as Baía and Rio de Janeiro, other social groups that disputed or shared power with the great landowners existed: high officials of the colonial administration; dignitaries of the Church; wealthy professional men, especially lawyers, and the large merchants, almost exclusively peninsulars, who monopolized the export-import trade and financed the industry of the planters.

1. THE WORLD OF THE SUGAR PLANTATION

The Jesuit priest João Antonio Andreoni (1650–1715), who came to Brazil in 1667 and spent the rest of his life there, wrote a valuable account of the agricultural and mineral resources of the colony. The following excerpts from Andreoni's book illustrate Gilberto Freyre's point that "the Big House completed by the slave shed represents an entire economic, social, and political system."

If the plantation owner must display his capacity in one thing more than another, it is in the proper choice of persons to administer his estate. ...

The first choice that he must make with care, on the basis of secret information concerning the conduct and knowledge of the person in question, is that of a chaplain to whom he must entrust the teaching of all that pertains to the Christian way of life. For the principal obligation of the planter is to teach, or have taught, his family and slaves. This should be done not by some slave born in Brazil, or by some overseer who at best can only teach them their prayers and the laws of God and the Church by word of mouth, but by one who can explain to them what they should believe and what they must do, and how they must do it, and how they are to ask God for what they need. And for this reason, if he must pay the chaplain a little more than is customary, the planter should understand that he could not put the money to better use. ...

The chaplain should live outside the planter's house; this is best for both, because he is a priest and not a servant, a familiar of God and not of men. He should not have any woman slave in his house, unless she be of advanced years, nor should he trade in anything, either human or divine, for all this is opposed to his clerical state and is prohibited by various Papal orders.

It is customary to pay a chaplain, when he is free to say masses during weekdays, forty or fifty thousand *reis* a year, and with what he gains from the saying of masses during the week he can earn a respectable salary—and well earned too, if he does all the things described above. If he is expected to teach the children of the plantation owner, he should receive a just additional compensation. ...

André João Antonil (João Antonio Andreoni), *Cultura e opulencia do Brazil por suas drogas e minas*, edited by Affonso de E. Taunay, São Paulo, 1923, pp. 77–83, 91–102. (Excerpts translated by the editor.)

On the day that the cane is brought to be ground, if the plantation owner does not invite the Vicar, the chaplain blesses the mill and asks God to grant a good yield and to guard those who work in it from all misfortune. When the mill stops grinding at the end of the harvest, he sees to it that all give thanks to God in the chapel. ...

The arms of the plantation owner, on which he relies for the good governance of his people and estate, are his overseers. But if each should aspire to be the head, it would be a monstrous government and would truly resemble the dog Cerberus, to whom the poets fancifully ascribe three heads. I do not say that the overseers should not possess authority, but I say that this authority must be well ordered and subordinate, not absolute, so that the lesser are inferior to the greater, and all to the master whom they serve.

It is fitting that the slaves should understand that the chief overseer has power to command and reprove them, and to punish them when necessary, but they should also know that they have recourse to the master and that they will be heard as justice requires. Nor must the other overseers suppose that their powers are unlimited, especially in what concerns punishment and seizure. The plantation owner, therefore, must make very clear the authority given to each, and especially to the chief overseer; and if they exceed their authority he should check them with the punishment that their excesses deserve—but not before the slaves, lest another time they rise against the overseer, and so that he may not bear the shame of being reproved before them and hence not dare to govern them. It will suffice if the master let a third party make known to the injured slave, and to some of the oldest slaves on the estate, that the master was much displeased with the overseer for the wrong that he had committed, and that if he did not amend his ways he would be immediately dismissed.

The overseers must on no account be permitted to kick slaves—in particular to kick pregnant slave women in the belly—or to strike slaves with a stick, because blows struck in anger are not calculated, and they may inflict a mortal head wound on some valuable slave that cost a great deal of money. What they may do is to scold them and strike them a few times on the back with a liana whip, to teach them a lesson. To seize fugitive slaves and any who fight and slash each other and get drunk, so that the master may have them punished as they deserve, is to show a diligence worthy of praise. But to tie up a slave girl and lash her with a liana whip until the blood runs, or to place her in the stocks or in chains for months at a time (while the master is in the city) simply because she will not go to bed with him, or to do the same to a slave who gave the master a faithful account of the overseer's disloyalty, violence, and cruelty, and to invent pretended offenses to justify the punishment—this may not be tolerated on any account, for it would be to have a ravening wolf rather than a well-disposed and Christian overseer.

It is the obligation of the chief overseer of the plantation to govern the people, and to assign them to their tasks at the proper time. It is his duty to learn from the master who should be notified to cut their cane, and to send them word promptly. He should have the boats and carts ready to go for the cane and should prepare the forms and fuel. He should apprise the master of everything that is needed to equip the sugar-mill before the start of grinding, and when the season is over he should put everything away in its place. He must see that each performs his task, and if some disaster occurs he should hasten to the scene to give what help he can. ...

The slaves are the hands and feet of the plantation owner, for without them you cannot make, preserve, and increase a fortune, or operate a plantation in Brazil. And the kind of service they give depends on how they are treated. It is necessary, therefore, to buy a certain number of slaves each year and assign them to the canefields, the manioc fields, the sawmills, and the boats. And because they are usually of different nations, and some more primitive than others, and differ greatly in physical qualities, the assignments should be made with great care. Those who come to Brazil are the Ardas, Minas, Congos, others from S. Thomé, Angola, Cape Verde, and some from Mozambique, who come in the India ships. The Ardas and Minas are robust. Those who come from Cape Verde and S. Thomé are weaker. The slaves from Angola, raised in Loanda, are more capable of acquiring mechanical skills than those who come from the other regions that I have named. Among the Congos there are also some who are quite industrious, and good not only for work in the canefields but for mechanical tasks and housework.

Some arrive in Brazil very barbarous and dullwitted, and continue so throughout their lives. Others in a few years become clever and skillful, not only in learning Christian doctrine but in mastering trades, and they can be used to handle a boat, carry messages, and perform any other routine task. ... It is not well to remove a slave against his will from the plantation where he has been raised since childhood, for he may pine away and die. Those slaves who were born in Brazil, or were raised from infancy in the homes of whites, form an affection for their masters and give a good account of themselves; one of these who bears his captivity well is worth four slaves brought from Africa.

The mulattoes are even more apt for every task; but many of them, taking advantage of the favor of their masters, are haughty and vicious and swagger about, always ready for a brawl. Yet they and the mulatto women commonly have it best of all in Brazil, because the white blood in their veins (sometimes that of their own masters) works such sorcery that some owners will tolerate and pardon anything they do; not only do they not reprove them, but it seems that all the caresses fall to their share. It is hard to say whether the masters or the mistresses are more at fault in this respect, for there are some of both sexes who permit themselves to be ruled by mulattoes, and not those of the best sort, either, thus verifying the proverb that says that Brazil is the Hell of the Negroes, the Purgatory of the Whites, and the Paradise of the mulattoes—but let some distrust or feeling of jealousy change love into hatred, and it comes forth armed with every kind of cruelty and severity. It is well to make use of their capabilities, if they will make good use of them (as some do, to be sure), but they should not be treated with such intimacy that they lose respect, and from slaves turn into masters. To free mulatto women of loose habits is surely an iniquitous thing, because the money with which they purchase their freedom rarely comes out of any other mines than their own bodies, and is gained with repeated sins; and after they are freed they continue to be the ruination of many.

Some masters are opposed to the marriage of male and female slaves, and they not only are indifferent to their living in concubinage but consent and actually encourage them to live in that state, saying; "You, so-and-so, will in due time marry so-and-so"; and after that they permit them to live together as if they were already man and wife. It is said that the reason why masters do not marry such couples off is because they fear that if they tire of the match they may kill each other with poison or witchcraft, for among them there are notable masters of this craft. Others, after marrying off their slaves, keep them apart for years as if they were unwed, and this they cannot do in good conscience. Others are so negligent in what concerns the salvation of the slaves that they keep them for a long time in the canefields or at the sugar mill without baptism. Furthermore, of those who have been baptized, many do not know who is their Creator, what they should believe, what law they should observe, how to commend themselves to God, why Christians go to Church, why they adore the Church, what to say to the Father when they kneel before him and when they speak into his ear, whether they have souls and if these souls die, and where they go when they leave the body. ...

In what concerns food, clothing, and rest from labor, clearly these things should not be denied them, for in all fairness the master should give a servitor sufficient food, medicine for his sicknesses, and clothing so that he may be decently covered and not go about half-naked in the streets; he should also regulate their labor so that it is not beyond their strength and endurance. In Brazil they say that the slaves must have the three P's, namely, a stick, bread, and a piece of cloth (*páo, pão, e panno*). And though they make a bad beginning, commencing with the stick, which stands for punishment, yet would to God that the bread and clothing were as abundant as the punishment! For it is frequently inflicted for some offense not wholly proved, or else invented, and with instruments of great severity (even if the crimes were proved), such instruments as are not used on brute beasts. To be sure, some masters take more account of a horse than of a halfdozen slaves, for the horse is cared for, and has a groom to find him hay, and wipe his sweat away, and a saddle, and a gilded bridle. ...

Some masters have the custom of giving their slaves one day a week to plant for themselves, sometimes sending the overseer along to see that they do not neglect their work; this helps to keep them from suffering hunger or from daily milling about the house of the master to beg him for a ration of flour. But to deny them both flour and a day for planting, and to expect them to work in the fields by day, from sunrise to sundown, and in the sugar mill by night, with little rest from labor—how shall such a master escape punishment before the Tribunal of God? If to deny alms to one who needs it is to deny it to Christ our Lord, as the Good Book says, what must it be to deny food and clothing to one's slaves? And how shall that master justify his conduct, who gives woolens and silks and other fineries to her who works his perdition and then denies four or five yards of cotton, and a few more of woolen cloth, to the slave who dissolves in sweat to serve him, and barely has time to hunt for a root and a crab-fish for his meal? And if on top of this the punishment is frequent and excessive, the slaves will either run away into the woods or commit suicide, as is their custom, by holding their breath or hanging themselves—or they will try to take the lives of those who do them such great evil, resorting, if necessary, to diabolical arts, or they will clamor so loudly to the Lord that he will hear them and do to their masters what he did to the Egyptians when they vexed the Jews with extraordinary labor, sending terrible plagues against their estates and sons, as we read in the Sacred Scripture. ...

Not to punish their excesses would be a serious fault, but these offenses should first be verified, so that innocent people may not suffer. The accused should be given a hearing, and if the charges are proved the culprits should be chastised with a moderate lashing, or by placing them in chains or in the stocks for a short period. But to punish them overhastily, with a vengeful spirit, with one's own hand, with terrible instruments, and perhaps to burn them with fire or heated sealing wax, or to brand the poor fellows in the face—why, this is intolerable in barbarians, to say nothing of Christian Catholics. ... And if, having erred by reason of their frailty, they themselves come to beg the master's pardon, or find sponsors (*padrinhos*) to accompany them, in such cases it is customary in Brazil to pardon them. And it is well for them to know that this will obtain them forgiveness, for otherwise they may one day flee to some fugitive slave settlement (*mucambo*) in the forest, and if they are captured they may kill themselves before the master can lash them, or some kinsman will take it upon himself to avenge them by the use of witchcraft or poison. Completely to deny them their festivities, which are their only consolation in their captivity, is to condemn them to sadness and melancholy, to apathy and sickliness. Therefore masters should not object if they crown their kings and sing and dance decently for a few hours on certain days of the year, or if they amuse themselves in proper ways of an afternoon, after having celebrated in the morning the holiday of Our Lady of the Rosary, of Saint Benedict, and of the patron-saint of the plantation chapel.
...

Since the management of a sugar plantation requires so many large outlays, as described above, it is plain that the owner must carefully watch the expenses of his household. ...

It is a poor thing to have the reputation of being a miser, but it is no credit to bear the name of a prodigal. He who decides to assume the burdens of a plantation must either retire from the city, shunning its diversions, or maintain two houses—which is notably deleterious to the one from which he is absent and also doubly expensive. To keep one's sons on the plantation is to create country bumpkins who can only talk of dogs, horses, and cattle. To leave them in the city is to permit them to fall into vicious habits and contract shameful diseases that are not easily cured. To avoid both extremes, the best course is to place them in the household of some responsible and honorable relative or friend, where they will have no opportunity to make a false step— a friend who will faithfully keep the parent informed of their good or bad conduct and of their improvement or neglect of their studies. The lad's mother should not be permitted to send him money or to send secret orders for that purpose to the father's correspondent or cashier; nor must it be forgotten that money requested for the purchase of books can also be used for gambling. The father should therefore instruct his attorney or agent not to give the boy anything without his order. For these young fellows can be very ingenious in their pleas for money, and can devise all manner of plausible reasons and pretexts, especially when they are supposed to be engaged in some course of studies. They are perfectly willing to spend three years of pleasant life at the expense of their father or uncle, who is in his sugarcane fields and has no idea of what goes on in town. So when a father boasts that he has an Aristotle in the Academy, it may be that he really has an Asinius or an Apricius in the city. But if the father decides to keep his children at home, content to let them learn to read, write, and count, together with some knowledge of events or history, to enable them to converse in company, he should not fail to watch over them, especially when they reach a certain age. For the broad countryside is also a place of much freedom, and can breed thistles and thorns. And if one constructs a fence for cattle and horses to keep them from leaving the pasture, why should one not keep children within bounds, both inside and outside the house, if experience proves that it is necessary? ...The good example of the father, however, is the best lesson in conduct; and the surest means of achieving peace of mind is to marry off the girls, and the boys as well, at the proper time. If they are content to marry within their station, they will find houses where they can make good matches and receive their rewards.

2. THE FREE POPULATION

Freemen and slaves formed the two great legal categories into which the Brazilian colonial population was divided. However, not all freemen belonged to the master class. Perhaps the most hopeful feature of Brazilian colonial life was the gradual blurring of the color line through race mixture—a circumstance that gave free mulattoes and other mixed bloods a greater social mobility than was possible in any other slave society of modern times.

In the Portuguese South American dominions, circumstances have directed that there should be no division of castes, and a very few of those degrading and most galling distinctions which have been made by all other nations in the management of their colonies. That this was not intended by the mother country, but was rather submitted to from necessity, is to be discovered in some few regulations, which plainly show that if Portugal could have preserved the superiority of the whites, she would, as well as her neighbors, have established laws for that purpose. The rulers of Portugal wished to colonize to an unlimited extent: but their country did not contain a population sufficiently numerous for their magnificent plans. Emigrants left their own country to settle in the New World, who were literally adventurers; for they had not any settled plans of life, and they were without families. Persons of established habits, who had the wish to follow any of the ordinary means of gaining a livelihood, found employment at home; neither could Portugal spare them, nor did they wish to leave their native soil. There was no superabundance of population: and therefore every man might find occupation at home, if he had steadiness to look for it. There was no division in political or religious opinion. There was no necessity of emigration, save that which was urged by crimes. Thus the generality of the men who embarked in the expeditions which were fitted out for Brazil, were unaccompanied by females: and therefore, naturally, on their arrival in that country, they married, or irregularly connected themselves with Indian women, and subsequently with those of Africa. It is true that orphan girls were sent out by the government of Portugal: but these were necessarily few in number. In the course of another generation, the colonists married the women of mixed castes, owing to the impossibility of obtaining those of their own colour: and the frequency of the custom, and the silence of the laws upon the subject, removed all idea of degradation, in thus connecting themselves. Still the European notions of superiority were not entirely laid aside: and these caused the passing of some regulations, by which white persons were to enjoy certain privileges. Thus, although the form of trial for all castes is the same, in certain places only, can capital punishment be inflicted upon the favoured race. The people of colour are not eligible to some of the chief offices of government: nor can they become members of the priesthood.

From the mildness of the laws, however, the mixed castes have gained ground considerably. The regulations which exist against them are evaded, or rather they have become obsolete. Perhaps the heroic conduct of Camarão

---

Henry Koster, *Travels in Brazil*, London, 1816, 2 vols., II, pp. 167–187.

and Henrique Dias, the Indian and negro chieftains, in the famous and most interesting contest, between the Pernambucans and the Dutch, and the honours subsequently granted by the crown of Portugal to both of them, may have led to the exaltation of the general character of the much-injured varieties of the human species of which they were members. Familiarity between the chieftains of the several corps must be the consequence of their embarkation in the same cause, when the war is one of skirmishes, of ambuscades, of continual alarm, of assistance constantly afforded to each other; a patriotic war, against a foreign invader, in which difference of religion exists, and each party mortally hates the other. On these occasions all men are equal; or he only is superior whose strength and whose activity surpasses that of others. The amalgamation of castes which is caused by this consciousness of equality could not have had a fairer field for its full accomplishment, than the war to which I have alluded: and the friendships which were formed under these circumstances would not easily be broken off. Although the parties who had been so united might have been in their situations in life very far removed from each other, still the participation of equal danger must render dear the companions in peril, and make the feelings, which had been roused on these occasions, of long duration; they would continue to act, long after the cessation of the series of occurrences which had called them forth.

The free population of Brazil at the present time consists of Europeans; Brazilians, that is, white persons born in Brazil; mulattos, that is, the mixed caste between the whites and blacks, and all the varieties into which it can branch; mamalucos, that is, the mixed castes between the whites and Indians, and all its varieties; Indians in a domesticated state, who are called generally Tapuyas; negroes born in Brazil, and manumitted Afri-cans; lastly, mestizos, that is, the mixed caste between the Indians and negroes. Of slaves, I shall speak by and by more at large; these are Africans, creole negroes, mulattos, and mestizos. The maxim of the Civil law, *partus sequitur ventrem*, is in force here as well as in the colonies of other nations.

These several mixtures of the human race have their shades of difference of character as well as of colour. First we must treat of the whites. The Europeans who are not in office, or who are not military men, are, generally speaking, adventurers who have arrived in that country with little or no capital. These men commence their career in low situations of life, but by parsimony and continual exertion directed to one end, that of amassing money, they often attain their object, and pass the evening of their lives in opulence. These habits fail not, oftentimes, to give a bias to their dispositions, which is unallied to generosity and liberality. They look down upon the Brazilians, or rather they wish to consider themselves superior to them; and until lately the government took no pains to remove the jealousy which existed between the two descriptions of white persons; and even now, not so much attention is paid to the subject as its great importance seems to require.[1]

The Brazilian white man of large property, who draws his descent from the first Donatory of a province, or whose family has for some generations enjoyed distinction, entertains a high opinion of his own importance, which may sometimes appear ridiculous; but which much oftener leads him to acts of generosity—to the adoption of liberal ideas—to honourable conduct. If he has been well educated and has had the good fortune to have been instructed by a priest whose ideas are enlightened, who gives a proper latitude for difference of opinion, who tolerates as he is tolerated, then the character of a young Brazilian exhibits much to admire. Surrounded by numerous relatives, and by his immediate dependents living in a vast and half-civilized country, he is endued with much independence of language and behaviour, which are softened by the subordination which has been imbibed during his course of education. That this is general, I pretend not to say. Few persons are instructed in a proper manner; and again, few are those who profit by the education which they have received; but more numerous are the individuals who now undergo necessary tuition, for powerful motives have arisen to urge the attainment of knowledge.

I have heard it often observed, and I cannot help saying, that I think some truth is to be attached to the remark, in the country of which I am now treating, that women are usually less lenient to their slaves than men: but this doubtless proceeds from the ignorant state in which they are brought up. They scarcely receive any education; and have not the advantages of obtaining instruction from communication with persons who are unconnected with their own way of life; of imbibing new ideas from general conversation. They are born, bred, and continue surrounded by slaves without receiving any check, with high notions of superiority, without any thought that what they do is wrong. Bring these women forward, educate them, treat them as rational, as equal beings, and they will be in no respect inferior to their countrymen. The fault is not with the sex, but in the state of the human being. As soon as a child begins to crawl, a slave of about its own age, and of the same sex, is given to it as a playfellow, or rather as a plaything. They grow up together: and the slave is made the stock upon which the young owner gives vent to passion. The slave is sent upon all errands, and receives the blame of all unfortunate accidents;—in fact, the white child is thus encouraged to be overbearing, owing to the false fondness of its parents. Upon the boys the effect is less visible in after-life, because the world curbs and checks them: but the girls do not stir from home, and therefore have no opportunities of wearing off these pernicious habits. It is only surprising that so many excellent women should be found among them, and by no means strange that the disposition of some of them should be injured by this unfortunate direction of their infant years.

As vegetation rapidly advances in such climates, so the animal sooner arrives at maturity than in those of less genial warmth; and here again education is rendered doubly necessary to lead the mind to new ideas, to curb the passions, to give a sense of honour, and to instil feelings of that species of pride which is so necessary to a becoming line of conduct. The state of society, the climate, and the celibacy of the numerous priesthood, cause the number of illegitimate children to be very great. But here the *roda dos engeitados*, and a custom which shews the natural goodness of the people, prevent the frequent occurrence of infanticide, or rather render it almost unknown. An infant is frequently during the night laid at the door of a rich person; and on being discovered in the morning is taken in, and is almost invariably allowed to remain: it is brought up with the children of the house (if its colour is not too dark to admit of this), certainly as a dependent, but not as a servant. However, a considerable tinge of colour will not prevent it from being reared with the white children. These *engeitados*, or rejected ones, as individuals who are so circumstanced are called, are frequently to be met with: and I heard of few exceptions to the general kindness with which they are treated. Public feeling is much against the refusing to accept and rear an *engeitado*. The owner of a house, who is in easy circumstances, and yet sends the infant from his own door to the public institution which is provided for its reception, is generally spoken of in terms of indignation. Sometimes a poor man will find one of these presents at his door: and he will generally place it at the landholder's threshold on the following night. This is accounted excusable and even meritorious; for at the Great House the child has nearly a certainty of being well taken care of.

I have observed that, generally speaking, Europeans are less indulgent to their slaves than Brazilians. The former feed them well: but they require from the poor wretches more labour than they can perform, whilst the latter allow the affairs of their estates to continue in the way in which they have been accustomed to be directed. This difference between the two descriptions of the owners is easily accounted for. The European has probably purchased part of his slaves on credit; and has, during the whole course of his life, made the accumulation of riches his chief object. The Brazilian inherits his estate: and as nothing urges him to the necessity of obtaining large profits, he continues the course that has been pointed out to him by the former possessors. His habits of quietude and indolence have led him to be easy and indifferent: and although he may not provide for the maintenance of his slaves with so much care as the European, still they find more time to seek for food themselves. That avaricious spirit which deliberately works a man or a brute animal until it is unfit for farther service, without any regard to the well-being of the creature, which is thus treated as a mere machine, as if it was formed of wood or iron, is, however, seldom to be met with in those parts of the country which I visited. Instances of cruelty occur (as has been, and will yet be seen), but these proceed from individual depravity, and not from systematic, coldblooded, calculating indifference to the means by which a desired end is to be compassed.

Notwithstanding the relationship of the mulattos on one side to the black race, they consider themselves superior to the mamalucos. They lean to the whites; and from the light in which the Indians are held, pride themselves upon being totally unconnected with them. Still the mulattos are conscious of their connection with men who are in a state of slavery, and that many persons, even of their own colour, are under these degraded circumstances. They have therefore always a feeling of inferiority in the company of white men, if these white men are wealthy and powerful. This inferiority of rank is not so much felt by white persons in the lower walks of life: and these are more easily led to become familiar with individuals of their own colour who are in wealthy circumstances. Still the inferiority which the mulatto feels, is more that which is produced by poverty than that which his colour has caused; for he will be equally respectful to a person of his own cast, who may happen to be rich.[2] The degraded state of the people of colour in the British colonies is most lamentable. In Brazil, even the trifling regulations which exist against them, remain unattended to. A mulatto enters into holy orders, or is appointed a magistrate, his papers stating him to be a white man, but his appearance plainly denoting the contrary. In conversing on one occasion with a man of colour who was in my service, I asked if a certain *Capitão-môr* was not a mulatto man: he answered, "he was, but is not now." I begged him to explain, when he added, "Can a *Capitão-môr* be a mulatto man?" I was intimately acquainted with a priest, whose complexion and hair plainly denoted from whence he drew his origin. I liked him much. He was a well-educated and intelligent man. Besides this individual instance, I met with several others of the same description.

The regiments of militia, which are called mulatto regiments, are so named from all the officers and men being of mixed castes; nor can white persons be admitted into them. The principal officers are men of property: and the colonel, like the commander of any other regiment, is only amenable to the governor of the province. In the white militia regiments, the officers ought to be by law white men. But in practice they are rather reputed white men, for very little pains are taken to prove that there is no mixture of blood. Great numbers of the soldiers belonging to the regiments which are officered by white men, are mulattos, and other persons of colour. The regiments of the line, likewise (as I have elsewhere said) admit into the ranks all persons excepting negroes and Indians. But the officers of these must prove nobility of birth. However, as certain degrees of nobility have been conferred upon persons in whose families there is much mixture of blood, this proof cannot be regarded as being required against the mulatto or mamaluco part of the population. Thus an European adventurer could not obtain a commission in these regiments, whilst a Brazilian, whose family has distinguished itself in the province in former times, will prove his eligibility without regard to the blood which runs in his veins. He is noble, let that flow from whence it may.[3]

The late colonel of the mulatto regiment of Recife, by name Nogueira, went to Lisbon, and returned to Pernambuco with the Order of Christ, which the Queen had conferred upon him. A chief person of one of the provinces is the son of a white man and a woman of colour. He has received an excellent education; is of generous disposition; and entertains most liberal views upon all subjects. He has been made a colonel, and a degree of nobility has been conferred upon him; likewise the Regent is sponsor to one of his children. Many other instances might be mentioned. Thus has Portugal, of late years from policy, continued that system into which she was led by her peculiar circumstances in former times. Some of the wealthy planters of Pernambuco, and of the rich inhabitants of Recife, are men of colour. The major part of the best mechanics are also of mixed blood.

It is said that mulattos make bad masters: and this holds good oftentimes with persons of this description, who have been in a state of slavery, and become possessed of slaves of their own, or are employed as managers upon estates. The change of situation would lead to the same consequences in any race of human beings; and cannot be accounted peculiar to the mixed castes. I have seen mulattos of free birth, as kind, as lenient, and as forbearing to their slaves and other dependents, as any white man.

Marriages between white men and women of colour are by no means rare; though they are sufficiently so to cause the circumstance to be mentioned when speaking of an individual who has connected himself in this manner. But this is not said with the intent of lowering him in the estimation of others. Indeed the remark is only made if the person is a planter of any importance, and the woman is decidedly of dark colour; for even a considerable tinge will pass for white. If the white man belongs to the lower orders, the woman is not accounted as being unequal to him in rank, unless she is nearly black. The European adventurers often marry in this manner, which generally occurs when the woman has a dower. The rich mulatto families are often glad to dispose of their daughters to these men, although the person who has been fixed upon may be in indifferent circumstances; for the colour of the children of their daughters is bettered; and from the well-known prudence and regularity of this set of men, a large fortune may be hoped for even from very small beginnings. Whilst I was at Jaguaribe, I was in the frequent habit of seeing a handsome young man, who was a native of the island of St. Michael's. This person happened to be with me on one occasion when the commandant from the Sertão was staying at my house. The commandant asked him if he could read and write: and being answered in the negative, said, "then you will not do": and turning to me added, "I have a commission from a friend of mine to take with me back to the Sertão a good-looking young Portuguese of regular habits, who can read and write, for the purpose of marrying him to his daughter." Such commissions (*encommendas*) are not unusual.

Still the Brazilians of high birth and large property do not like to intermarry with persons whose mixture of blood is *very* apparent: and hence arise peculiar circumstances. A man of this description becomes attached to a woman of colour; connects himself with her; and takes her to his home, where she is in a short time visited even by married women. She governs his household affairs: acts and considers herself as his wife; and frequently after the birth of several children, when they are neither of them young, he marries her. In connections of this nature, the parties are more truly attached than in marriage between persons who belong to two families of the first rank; for the latter are entered into from convenience rather than from affection. Indeed the parties, on some occasions, do not see each other until a few days before the ceremony takes place. It often occurs, that inclination, necessity, or convenience induces or obliges a man to separate from the person with whom he is connected. In this case, he gives her a portion; and she marries a man of her own rank, who regards her rather as a widow than as one whose conduct has been incorrect. Instances of infidelity in these women are rare. They become attached to the men with whom they cohabit: and they direct the affairs of the houses over which they are placed with the same zeal that they would display if they had the right of command over them. It is greatly to the credit of the people of that country, that so much fidelity should be shewn on one side; and that this should so frequently as it is, be rewarded by the other party, in the advancement of those who have behaved thus faithfully, to a respectable and acknowledged situation in society. It should be recollected too that the merit of moral feelings must be judged of by the standard of the country, and not by our own institutions. I have only spoken above of what occurs among the planters; for in large towns, man is pretty much the same everywhere.

The mamalucos are more frequently to be seen in the Sertão than upon the coast. They are handsomer than the mulattos: and the women of this cast particularly surpass in beauty all others of the country. They have the brown tint of mulattos: but their features are less blunt, and their hair is not curled. I do not think that the men can be said to possess more courage than the mulattos. But whether from the knowledge which they have of being of free birth on both sides, or from residing in the interior of the country where the government is more loose, they appear to have more independence of character, and to pay less deference to a white man than the mulattos. When women relate any deed of danger that has been surmounted or undertaken, they generally state that the chief actor in it was a large mamaluco, *mamalucão*; as if they thought this description of men to be superior to all others. Mamalucos may enter into the mulatto regiments; and are pressed into the regiments of the line as being men of colour, without any regard to the sources from which their blood proceeds.

Of the domesticated Indians I have already elsewhere given what accounts I could collect, and what I had opportunities of observing. The wild Indians are only now to be met with at a great distance from the coast of Pernambuco: and although they are very near to Maranhão, and are dreaded neighbors, I had no means of seeing any of them.

I now proceed to mention that numerous and valuable race of men, the creole negroes; a tree of African growth, which has thus been transplanted, cultivated, and much improved by its removal to the New World. The creole negroes stand alone and unconnected with every other race of men: and this circumstance alone would be sufficient, and indeed contributes much to the effect of uniting them to each other. The mulattos, and all other persons of mixed blood, wish to lean towards the whites, if they can possibly lay any claim to relationship. Even the mestizo tries to pass for a mulatto, and to persuade himself and others, that his veins contain some portion of white blood, although that with which they are filled proceeds from Indian and negro sources. Those only who have no pretensions to a mixture of blood, call themselves negroes, which renders the individuals who do pass under this denomination, much attached to each other, from the impossibility of being mistaken for members of any other cast. They are of handsome persons, brave and hardy, obedient to the whites, and willing to please. But they are easily affronted: and the least allusion to their colour being made by a person of lighter tint, enrages them to a great degree; though they will sometimes say, "a negro I am, but always upright." They are again distinct from their brethren in slavery, owing to their superior situation as free men.

3. THE SOCIAL CONSEQUENCES
OF SLAVERY

A forerunner of the Brazilian abolitionists of a later day, Luiz dos Santos Vilhena, regius professor of Greek in Baía from 1787 to 1798, boldly assailed the system of slave labor on which the sugar culture of his province was based. Slavery, and not an enervating tropical climate, he affirmed, was responsible for the dissolute manners and idleness of the Portuguese living in Brazil. The following excerpt from his book on Brazil, written in the form of letters to a Portuguese friend, illustrates the vigor and forthrightness of his attack.

The Negro women and a majority of the mulatto women as well, for whom honor is a delusion, a word signifying nothing, are commonly the first to corrupt their master's sons, giving them their first lessons in sexual license, in which from childhood on they are engulfed; and from this presently arises a veritable troop of little mulattoes whose influence on family life is most

---

Luiz dos Santos Vilhena, *Recopilação de noticias soteropolitanas e brasilicas*, edited by Braz do Amaral, Baía, 1921–1922, 2 vols., I, pp. 138–142. (Excerpt translated by the editor.)

pernicious. But it often happens that those who are called the old masters, to distinguish them from their sons, are the very ones who set a bad example for their families through their conduct with their female slaves, giving pain to their wives and perhaps causing their death. Frequently their black favorites contrive to put the legitimate children out of the way, to avoid any difficulties in the event of the master's death.

There are other men who never marry, simply because they cannot get out of the clutches of the harpies in whose power they have been since childhood. There are ecclesiastics, and not a few, who from old and evil habit, forgetting their character and station, live a disorderly life with mulatto and Negro women, by whom they have sons who inherit their property; in this and other ways many of the most valuable properties of Brazil pass into the hands of haughty, arrogant vagabond mulattoes, to the great detriment of the State. This is a matter well deserving of His Majesty's attention, for if these sugar mills and great plantations are not prevented from falling into the hands of these mulattoes, who ordinarily are profligate and set little store by these splendid properties, having come by them so easily, in due time they will all fall into their hands and be ruined, as has happened to the greater part of those that came into the possession of such owners.

You must also know that the passion for having Negroes and mulattoes in the house is so strong here that only death removes them from the household in which they were born; there are many families that have sixty, seventy, and more superfluous persons within their doors. I speak of the city, for in the country this would not be remarkable. All this black brood, whether mulattoes or Negroes, are treated with the greatest indulgence, and that is why they are all vagabonds, insolent, bold, and ungrateful. ...

The Negroes are harmful in still another way to the State of Brazil. For since all the servile labors and mechanical arts are in their charge, few are the mulattoes, and fewer still the white men, who will deign to perform such tasks. ...

It has been observed that he who comes here as servant to some public official continues to be a good servant until he realizes that the work he does for his master is performed in other households by Negroes and mulattoes, whereupon he begins to plead with his master to find him some public employment not open to Negroes. Some masters yield to their entreaties, finding themselves so badgered and badly served that they are driven to distraction. But if they delay in finding them jobs, their servants leave them, preferring to be vagabonds and go about dying from hunger, or to become soldiers and sometimes bandits, to working for an honored master who pays them well and supports and cherishes them—and this only to avoid having to do what Negroes do in other households.

The same occurs with the serving women who accompany the ladies that come to Brazil. The same prejudice induces them to take to the streets; they prefer suffering all the resulting miseries to living in a home where they are honored and sheltered.

The girls of this country are of such disposition that the daughter of the poorest, most abject individual, the most neglected little mulatto wench, would rather go to the scaffold than serve a Duchess, if one were to be found in this country; that is the reason for the great number of ruined and disgraced women in this city.

The whites born in this land must either be soldiers, merchants, notaries, clerks, court officials, judges, or Treasury officials or else hold some other public occupation that is barred to Negroes, such as surgeon, apothecary, pilot, shipmaster or sea-captain, warehouse clerk (*caxeiro do trapiche*), and so forth. A few others are employed as sculptors, goldsmiths, and the like.

Many used to attend the school established by His Majesty in this city, a school that once boasted of excellent students who prepared for the Church and other learned professions. But when their fathers saw that the school was the fixed target at which the recruiting officers and soldiers aimed their shots, and that their sons were being snatched away for garrison duty, against which their immunities, privileges, and exemptions availed them nothing, they became convinced that the State had no further need of ecclesiastics or members of other learned professions ... , and decided that they would not sacrifice their sons by exposing them to the enmity of autocratic and thoughtless soldiers. ...

Is it not obvious that the inactivity of the whites is the reason for the laziness of the blacks? Why should a man not dig the ground in Brazil who in Portugal lived solely by his hoe? Why should one not labor here who in Portugal knew nothing more than to put one hand to the plough handle and another to the goad?

Why should a man go about here with his body upright who came here bent with labor?

Why should he who knows only obedience want only to command? Why should he who was always a plebeian strut about with the air of a noble?

How plentifully would these blessed lands produce, dear friend, if they were cultivated by other hands than those of savage Negroes, who do no more than scratch their surface!

What great profits they would yield if cultivated by sensible and intelligent men, and if sound views of political economy changed the prevailing system!

No land could boast of greater opulence and plenty than Baía if it were ruled wisely, and if henceforth admittance were denied to slaves, the causes of its backwardness and poverty.

PART FOUR

LATIN AMERICA IN THE NINETEENTH CENTURY

14

THE LIBERATION
OF LATIN AMERICA

MANY FACTORS combined to cause the Latin American Wars of Independence. The discontent of the Creole class with Spanish restrictions on its economic and political activity, the influence of French and English liberal doctrines, the powerful example of the American and French Revolutions, and foreign interest in the liquidation of the Spanish empire in the Americas—all played a part in producing the great upheaval.

The immediate cause of the Spanish American revolutions was the occupation of Spain by French troops in 1808. Napoleon's intervention provoked an uprising of the Spanish people, headed by *juntas*, or local governing committees. Creole leaders in the colonies soon took advantage of Spain's distresses. Professing loyalty to "the beloved Ferdinand VII," a prisoner in France, they forced the removal of allegedly unreliable Spanish officials and formed governing *juntas* to rule in the name of the captive king. Their claims of loyalty did not convince the Spanish authorities, and fighting soon broke out between patriots and loyalists.

Simón Bolívar led the struggle for independence in northern South America, and José de San Martín directed the military efforts of the patriots to the south. In 1822 the enigmatic San Martín resigned command of his army, leaving to Bolívar the task of completing the conquest of Peru, the last Spanish stronghold in the New World. The battle of Ayacucho, won by Sucre, virtually ended the war. Brazil achieved a relatively peaceful separation from Portugal in 1822, under the leadership of Prince Pedro and his adviser José Bonifacio de Andrada.

The Mexican Revolution, initiated in 1810 by the Creole priest Miguel Hidalgo, was continued after his death by another liberal curate, José María Morelos. These men attempted to combine the Creole ideal of independence with a program of social reform in behalf of the Indian and mixed-blood masses. The radicalism of Hidalgo and Morelos alienated many Creole con-

215

servatives, who joined the royalist forces to suppress the revolt. Later, fearing the loss of their privileges as a result of the liberal revolution of 1820 in Spain, the same conservative coalition schemed to bring about a separation from Spain. They found an agent in the ambitious Creole officer Agustín de Iturbide. His Plan of Iguala offered a compromise solution temporarily acceptable to liberals and conservatives, to Creoles and many Spaniards. Slight loyalist opposition was swiftly overcome, and in September 1822, a national congress proclaimed the independence of the Mexican empire.

1. THE CLEAVAGE WITHIN

By the close of the colonial period the Creoles and peninsular Spaniards had become two mutually hostile castes, differing in their occupations and ideas. The Spaniards justified their privileged status by reference to the alleged indolence and incapacity of the natives. The Creoles vented their spleen by describing the Europeans as mean and grasping parvenus. The pro-Spanish historian Lucas Alamán offers many revealing details of the cleavage within the colonial upper class in his classic History of Mexico.

The number of peninsular Spaniards who resided in New Spain in 1808 was in the neighborhood of 70,000. They occupied nearly all the principal posts in the administration, the Church, the judiciary, and the army; commerce was almost exclusively in their hands; and they possessed large fortunes, consisting of cash, which they employed in various lines of business and in all kinds of farms and properties. Those who were not officeholders had generally left their country at a very early age, belonged to poor but honest families, especially those who came from the Basque provinces and the mountains of Santander, and were for the most part of good character. Since they aimed to make their fortune, they were ready to gain it by every kind of productive labor; neither great distances, perils, nor unhealthy climates frightened them. Some came to serve in the house of some relative or friend of the family; others were befriended by their countrymen. All began as clerks, subject to a severe discipline, and from the first learned to regard work and thrift as the only road to wealth. There was some relaxation of manners in Mexico City and Vera Cruz, but in all the cities of the interior, no matter how rich or populous, the clerks in each house were bound to a very narrow and almost monastic system of order and regularity. This Spartan type of ed-

Lucas Alamán, *Historia de Méjico*, Mexico, 1849–1852, 5 vols., I, pp. 8–14. (Excerpt translated by the editor.)

ucation made of the Spaniards living in America a species of men not to be found in Spain herself, and one which America will never see again.

As their fortunes improved or their merits won recognition, they were often given a daughter of the house in marriage, particularly if they were relatives—or they might set up their own establishments; but all married creole girls, for very few of the women there had come from Spain, and these were generally the wives of officeholders. With financial success and kinship to the respectable families of the town came respect, municipal office, and influence, which sometimes degenerated into absolute dominance. Once established in this manner, the Spaniards never thought of returning to their country, and they considered that their only proper concerns were the furthering of their business affairs, the advancement of their communities, and the comfort and dignity of their families. Thus every wealthy Spaniard came to represent a fortune formed for the benefit of the country, a prosperous family rooted in Mexican soil, or, if he left no family, a source of pious and beneficial foundations designed to shelter orphans and succor the needy and disabled—foundations of which Mexico City presents so many examples. These fortunes were formed through the arduous labors of the field, the long practice of commerce, or the more risky enterprise of the mines. Although these occupations did not usually permit rapid enrichment, the economy practiced by these families, who lived frugally, without luxurious furniture or clothing, helped them to attain this goal. Thus all the towns, even the less important ones, included a number of families of modest fortunes, whose parsimony did not prevent the display of liberality on occasions of public calamity or when the needs of the state required it. ...

The creoles rarely preserved these economical habits or pursued the professions that had enriched their fathers. The latter, amid the comforts that their wealth afforded, likewise failed to subject their sons to the severe discipline in which they themselves had been formed. Wishing to give their sons a more brilliant education, suitable to their place in society, they gave them a training that led to the Church or to the practice of law, or left them in a state of idleness and liberty that was deleterious to their character. Some sent their sons to the seminary of Vergara, in the province of Guipuzcoa in Spain, after the institution had won renown as a school providing general instruction, and if this practice had become general it not only would have contributed greatly to the diffusion of useful knowledge in America but would have aided in formation of more durable bonds between Spanish America and the mother country. From the other and pernicious kind of rearing resulted this state of affairs: The European clerks, married to the master's daughters, carried on his business and became the principal support of the family, increasing their wives' inheritances, whereas the creole sons wasted their substance and in a few years were ruined—at which time they looked about for some trifling desk job that would barely keep them alive in preference to an active and laborious life that would assure them an independent existence.[1] The classical education that some of them had received, and the aristocratic manner that they affected in their days of idleness and plenty, made them scornful of the Europeans, who seemed to them mean and covetous because they were economical and active; they regarded these men as inferiors because they engaged in trades and occupations which they considered unworthy of the station to which their own fathers had raised them. Whether it was the effect of this vicious training or the influence of a climate that conduced to laxity and effeminacy, the creoles were generally indolent and negligent; of sharp wits, rarely tempered by judgment and reflection; quick to undertake an enterprise but heedless of the means necessary to carry it out; giving themselves with ardor to the present, but giving no thought to the future; prodigal in times of good fortune and resigned and long-suffering in adversity. The effect of these unfortunate propensities was the brief duration of their wealth; the assiduous efforts of the Europeans to form fortunes and pass them on to their children may be compared to the bottomless barrel of the Danaïdes, which no amount of water could fill. It resulted from this that the Spanish race in America, in order to remain prosperous and opulent, required a continuous accretion of European Spaniards who came to form new families, while those established by their predecessors fell into oblivion and indigence.

Although the laws did not establish any difference between these two classes of Spaniards, or indeed with respect to the mestizos born to either class by Indian mothers, a distinction came to exist between them in fact. With it arose a declared rivalry that, although subdued for a long time, might be feared to break out with the most serious consequences when the occasion should offer. As has been said, the Europeans held nearly all the high offices,[2] as much because Spanish policy required it as because they had greater opportunity to request and obtain them, being near the fountainhead of all favors. The rare occasions on which creoles secured such high posts occurred through fortunate coincidences or when they went to the Spanish capital to solicit them. Although they held all the inferior posts, which were much more numerous, this only stimulated their ambition to occupy the higher posts as well. Although in the first two centuries after the Conquest the Church offered Americans greater opportunities for advancement, and during that period many obtained[3] bishoprics, canonships, pulpits, and lucrative benefices, their opportunities in this sphere had gradually been curtailed. ... The Europeans also dominated the cloisters, and in order to avoid the frequent disturbances caused by the rivalry of birth some religious orders had provided for an alternation of offices, electing European prelates in one election and Americans in the next; but as a result of a distinction introduced between the Europeans who had come from Spain with the garb and those who assumed it in America, the former were favored with another term, resulting in two elections of Europeans to one of creoles. If to this preference in administrative and ecclesiastical offices, which was the principal cause of the rivalry between the two classes, are added the fact that ... the Europeans possessed great riches (which, though the just reward of labor and industry, excited the envy of the Americans ...); the fact that the wealth and power of the peninsulars sometimes gained them more favor with the fair sex, enabling them to form more advantageous unions; and the fact that all these conditions combined had given them a decided predominance over the creoles—it is not difficult to explain the jealousy and rivalry that steadily grew between them, resulting in a mortal enmity and hatred.

2. THE FORGING OF A REBEL

In his valuable, brief autobiography, Manuel Belgrano (1770–1821), one of the fathers of Argentine independence, describes the influences and events that transformed a young Creole of wealth and high social position into an ardent revolutionary. The French Revolution, disillusionment with Bourbon liberalism, the English invasions, and finally the events of 1808 in Spain all played their part in this process.

The place of my birth was Buenos Aires; my parents were Don Domingo Belgrano y Peri, known as Pérez, a native of Onella in Spain, and Doña María Josefa González Casero, a native of Buenos Aires. My father was a merchant, and since he lived in the days of monopoly he acquired sufficient wealth to live comfortably and to give his children the best education to be had in those days.

I studied my first letters, Latin grammar, philosophy, and a smattering of theology in Buenos Aires. My father then sent me to Spain to study law, and I began my preparation at Salamanca; I was graduated at Valladolid, continued my training at Madrid, and was admitted to the bar at Valladolid. ...

Since I was in Spain in 1789, and the French Revolution was then causing a change in ideas, especially among the men of letters with whom I associated, the ideals of liberty, equality, security, and property took a firm hold on me, and I saw only tyrants in those who would restrain a man, wherever he might be, from enjoying the rights with which God and Nature had endowed him. ...

When I completed my studies in 1793 political economy enjoyed great popularity in Spain; I believe this was why I was appointed secretary of the *consulado* of Buenos Aires, established when Gardoqui was minister. The official of the department in charge of these matters even asked me to suggest some other well-informed persons who could be appointed to similar bodies to be established in the principal American ports.

Ricardo Levene, ed., *Los sucesos de mayo contados por sus actores*, Buenos Aires, 1928, pp. 60–71. (Excerpt translated by the editor.)

When I learned that these *consulados* were to be so many Economic Societies that would discuss the state of agriculture, industry, and commerce in their sessions, my imagination pictured a vast field of activity, for I was ignorant of Spanish colonial policy. I had heard some muffled murmuring among the Americans, but I attributed this to their failure to gain their ends, never to evil designs of the Spaniards that had been systematically pursued since the Conquest.

On receiving my appointment I was infatuated with the brilliant prospects for America. I had visions of myself writing memorials concerning the provinces so that the authorities might be informed and provide for their well-being. It may be that an enlightened minister like Gardoqui, who had resided in the United States, had the best of intentions in all this. ...

I finally departed from Spain for Buenos Aires; I cannot sufficiently express the surprise I felt when I met the men named by the king to the council which was to deal with agriculture, industry, and commerce and work for the happiness of the provinces composing the vice-royalty of Buenos Aires. All were Spanish merchants. With the exception of one or two they knew nothing but their monopolistic business, namely, to buy at four dollars and sell for eight. ...

My spirits fell, and I began to understand that the colonies could expect nothing from men who placed their private interests above those of the community. But since my position gave me an opportunity to write and speak about some useful topics, I decided at least to plant a few seeds that some day might bear fruit. ...

I wrote various memorials about the establishment of schools. The scarcity of pilots and the direct interest of the merchants in the project presented favorable circumstances for the establishment of a school of mathematics, which I obtained on condition of getting the approval of the Court. This, however, was never secured; in fact, the government was not satisfied until the school had been abolished, because although the peninsulars recognized the justice and utility of such establishments, they were opposed to them because of a mistaken view of how the colonies might best be retained.

The same happened to a drawing school which I managed to establish without spending even half a real for the teacher. The fact is that neither these nor other proposals to the government for the development of agriculture, industry, and commerce, the three important concerns of the *consulado*, won its official approval; the sole concern of the Court was with the revenue that it derived from each of these branches. They said that all the proposed establishments were luxuries, and that Buenos Aires was not yet in a condition to support them.

I promoted various other useful and necessary projects, which had more or less the same fate, but it will be the business of the future historian of the consulado to give an account of them; I shall simply say that from the beginning of 1794 to July, 1806, I passed my time in futile efforts to serve my country. They all foundered on the rock of the opposition of the government of Buenos Aires, or that of Madrid, or that of the merchants who composed the *consulado*, for whom there was no other reason, justice, utility, or necessity than their commercial interest. Anything that came into conflict with that interest encountered a veto, and there was nothing to be done about it.

It is well known how General Beresford entered Buenos Aires with about four hundred men in 1806. At that time I had been a captain in the militia for ten years, more from whim than from any attachment to the military art. My first experience of war came at that time. The Marqués de Sobremonte, then viceroy of the provinces of La Plata, sent for me several days before Beresford's disastrous entrance and requested me to form a company of cavalry from among the young men engaged in commerce. He said that he would give me veteran officers to train them; I sought them but could not find any, because of the great hostility felt for the militia in Buenos Aires.

...

The general alarm was sounded. Moved by honor, I flew to the fortress, the point of assembly; I found there neither order nor harmony in anything, as must happen with groups of men who know nothing of discipline and are completely insubordinate. The companies were formed there, and I was attached to one of them. I was ashamed that I had not the slightest notion of military science and had to rely entirely on the orders of a veteran officer—who also joined voluntarily, for he was given no assignment.

This was the first company, which marched to occupy the *Casa de las Filipinas*. Meanwhile the others argued with the viceroy himself that they were obliged only to defend the city and not to go out into the country; consequently they would agree only to defend the heights. The result was that the enemy, meeting with no opposition from veteran troops or disciplined militia, forced all the passes with the greatest ease. There was some stupid firing on the part of my company and some others in an effort to stop the invaders, but all in vain, and when the order came to retreat and we were falling back I heard someone say: "They did well to order us to retreat, for we were not made for this sort of thing."

I must confess that I grew angry, and that I never regretted more deeply my ignorance of even the rudiments of military science. My distress grew when I saw the entrance of the enemy troops, and realized how few of them there were for a town of the size of Buenos Aires. I could not get the idea out of my head, and I almost went out of my mind, it was so painful to me to see my country under an alien yoke, and above all in such a degraded state that it could be conquered by the daring enterprise of the brave and honorable Beresford, whose valor I shall always admire.

[A resistance movement under the leadership of Santiago Liniers drives the British out of Buenos Aires. A second English invasion, commanded by General John Whitelocke, is defeated, and the entire British force is compelled to surrender. B.K.]

General Liniers ordered the quartermaster-general to receive the paroles of the officer prisoners; for this reason Brigadier-General Crawford, together with his aides and other high officers, came to his house. My slight knowledge of French, and perhaps certain civilities that I showed him, caused General Crawford to prefer to converse with me, and we entered upon a discussion that helped to pass the time—although he never lost sight of his aim of gaining knowledge of the country and, in particular, of its opinion of the Spanish Government.

So, having convinced himself that I had no French sympathies or connections, he divulged to me his ideas about our independence, perhaps in the hope of forming new links with this country, since the hope of conquest had failed. I described our condition to him, and made it plain that we wanted our old master or none at all; that we were far from possessing the means required for the achievement of independence; that even if it were won under the protection of England, she would abandon us in return for some advantage in Europe, and then we would fall under the Spanish sword; that every nation sought its own interest and did not care about the misfortunes of others. He agreed with me, and when I had shown how we lacked the means for winning independence, he put off its attainment for a century.

How fallible are the calculations of men! One year passed, and behold, without any effort on our part to become independent, God Himself gave us our opportunity as a result of the events of 1808 in Spain and Bayonne. Then it was that the ideals of liberty and independence came to life in America, and the Americans began to speak frankly of their rights.

3. MAN OF DESTINY

There is no more controversial figure in Latin American history than Simón Bolívar (1783–1830). To his admirers or worshippers he is the Liberator of a continent; to his critics he is the proverbial "man on horseback," an ambitious schemer who sacrificed San Martín to his passion for power and glory. Louis Peru de Lacroix, a French member of Bolívar's staff, wrote the following description of the Liberator in a diary that he kept during their stay at Bucaramanga in 1828.

The General-in-Chief, Simón José Antonio Bolívar, will be forty-five years old on July 24 of this year, but he appears older, and many judge him to be fifty. He is slim and of medium height; his arms, thighs, and legs are lean. He has a long head, wide between the temples, and a sharply pointed chin. A

Monseñor Nicolás E. Navarro, ed., *Diario de Bucaramanga, estudio crítico*, Caracas, 1935, pp. 327, 329–331. (Excerpt translated by the editor.)

large, round, prominent forehead is furrowed with wrinkles that are very noticeable when his face is in repose, or in moments of bad humor and anger. His hair is crisp, bristly, quite abundant, and partly gray. His eyes have lost the brightness of youth but preserve the luster of genius. They are deep-set, neither small nor large; the eyebrows are thick, separated, slightly arched, and are grayer than the hair on his head. The nose is aquiline and well formed. He has prominent cheekbones, with hollows beneath. His mouth is rather large, and the lower lip protrudes; he has white teeth and an agreeable smile. ... His tanned complexion darkens when he is in a bad humor, and his whole appearance changes; the wrinkles on his forehead and temples stand out much more prominently; the eyes become smaller and narrower; the lower lip protrudes considerably, and the mouth turns ugly. In fine, one sees a completely different countenance: a frowning face that reveals sorrows, sad reflections, and sombre ideas. But when he is happy all this disappears; his face lights up, his mouth smiles, and the spirit of the Liberator shines over his countenance. His Excellency is clean-shaven at present. ...

The Liberator has energy; he is capable of making a firm decision and sticking to it. His ideas are never commonplace—always large, lofty, and original. His manners are affable, having the tone of Europeans of high society. He displays a republican simplicity and modesty, but he has the pride of a noble and elevated soul, the dignity of his rank, and the *amour-propre* that comes from consciousness of worth and leads men to great actions. Glory is his ambition, and his glory consists in having liberated ten million persons and founded three republics. He has an enterprising spirit, combined with great activity, quickness of speech, an infinite fertility in ideas, and the constancy necessary for the realization of his projects. He is superior to misfortunes and reverses; his philosophy consoles him and his intelligence finds ways of righting what has gone wrong. ...

He loves a discussion, and dominates it through his superior intelligence; but he sometimes appears too dogmatic, and is not always tolerant enough with those who contradict him. He scorns servile flattery and base adulators. He is sensitive to criticism of his actions; calumny against him cuts him to the quick, for none is more touchy about his reputation than the Liberator. ...

His heart is better than his head. His bad temper never lasts; when it appears, it takes possession of his head, never of his heart, and as soon as the latter recovers its dominance it immediately makes amends for the harm that the former may have done. ...

The great mental and bodily activity of the Liberator keeps him in a state of constant moral and physical agitation. One who observes him at certain moments might think he is seeing a madman. During the walks that we take with him he sometimes likes to walk very rapidly, trying to tire his companions out; at other times he begins to run and leap, to leave the others behind; then he waits for them to catch up and tells them they do not know how to run. He does the same when horseback riding. But he acts this way only when among his own people, and he would not run or leap if he thought that some stranger was looking on. When bad weather prevents walking or riding, the Liberator rocks himself swiftly back and forth in his hammock or strides through the corridors of his house, sometimes singing, at other times reciting verses or talking with those who walk beside him. When conversing with one of his own people, he changes the subject as often as he does his position; at such times one would say that he has not a bit of system or stability in him. How different the Liberator seems at a private party, at some formal gathering, and among his confidential friends and aides-de-camp! With the latter he seems their equal, the gayest and sometimes the maddest of them all. At a private party, among strangers and people less well known to him, he shows his superiority to all others by his easy and agreeable ways and good taste, his lively and ingenious conversation, and his amiability. At a more formal gathering, his unaffected dignity and polished manners cause him to be regarded as the most gentlemanly, learned, and amiable man present. ...

In all the actions of the Liberator, and in his conversation, as I have already noted, one observes an extreme quickness. His questions are short and concise; he likes to be answered in the same way, and when someone wanders away from the question he impatiently says that that is not what he asked; he has no liking for a diffuse answer. He sustains his opinions with force and logic, and generally with tenacity. When he has occasion to contradict some assertion, he says: "No, sir, it is not so, but thus. ..." Speaking of persons whom he dislikes or scorns, he often uses this expression: "That (or those) c***." He is very observant, noting even the least trifles; he dislikes the poorly educated, the bold, the windbag, the indiscreet, and the discourteous. Since nothing escapes him, he takes pleasure in criticizing such people, always making a little commentary on their defects. ...

I have already said that the Liberator can assume an air of dignity when among persons who do not enjoy his full confidence or with whom he is not on terms of familiarity; but he throws it off among his own people. In church he carries himself with much propriety and respect, and does not permit his companions to deviate from this rule. One day, noticing that his physician, Dr. Moore, sat with his legs crossed, he had an aide-de-camp tell him that it was improper to cross one's legs in church, and that he should observe how *he* sat. One thing that His Excellency does not know, when at Mass, is when to kneel, stand up, and sit down. He never crosses himself. Sometimes he talks to the person beside him, but only a little, and very softly.

The ideas of the Liberator are like his imagination: full of fire, original, and new. They lend considerable sparkle to his conversation, and make it extremely varied. When His Excellency praises, defends, or approves something, it is always with a little exaggeration. The same is true when he criticizes, condemns, or disapproves of something. In his conversation he frequently quotes, but his citations are always well chosen and pertinent. Voltaire is his favorite author, and he has memorized many passages from his works, both prose and poetry. He knows all the good French writers and evaluates them competently. He has some general knowledge of Italian and English literature and is very well versed in that of Spain.

The Liberator takes great pleasure in telling of his first years, his voyages, and his campaigns, and of his relations and old friends. His character and spirit dispose him more to criticize than to eulogize, but his criticisms or eulogies are never baseless; he could be charged only with an occasional slight exaggeration. I have never heard his Excellency utter a calumny. He is a lover of truth, heroism, and honor and of the public interest and morality. He detests and scorns all that is opposed to these lofty and noble sentiments.

4. THE GREAT CAMPAIGN

A turning point in the struggle for independence in northern South America came in 1819 when Bolívar crossed the Colombian Andes with his army and attacked the Spanish forces in New Granada from a completely unexpected direction. Victory on the field of Boyacá crowned one of the most daring and brilliantly executed military campaigns in history. In the following selection Daniel F. O'Leary (1800–1854), Bolívar's English aide-de-camp and biographer, describes the epic campaign of 1819.

While Bolívar assembled his army in Tame, the royalist forces in New Granada, perfectly equipped and under the command of the ablest officers of the expeditionary army, were quartered in the following manner: Four thousand men garrisoned the northern frontier, separating the provinces of Cundinamarca and Tunja from the plains of Casanare; three thousand well disciplined and well paid men, Spaniards and Americans, guarded the city of Santa Fe and other towns of the interior and the littoral. The cavalry mounted excellent horses; the artillery was well operated and lacked nothing. Add to these resources, which alone were probably enough to defend the country, the natural obstacles presented by the terrain, and Bolívar's project must seem a fantasy. But he counted less on the material force of his army than on the resources of his own genius and on the iron will that made his name so dreaded by the enemies of his country.

From Tame to Pore, the capital of Casanare, the road was inundated. "The territory through which the army had to make its first marches was a small sea, rather than solid land," says Santander in his account of this campaign. On July 27 they encountered obstacles of another kind.

Daniel F. O'Leary, *Bolívar y la emancipación de Sur-América*, Madrid, 1915, 2 vols., I, pp. 664–682. (Excerpt translated by the editor.)

The gigantic Andes, which are considered uncrossable at this season, imposed a seemingly insuperable barrier to the march of the army. For four days the troops battled against the difficulties of these rugged roads—if precipices can be called roads.

The plainsmen regarded these stupendous heights with astonishment and terror, and marveled at the existence of a land so different from their own. As they ascended, each new elevation increased their surprise, for what they had taken for the last peak was only the beginning of other and still loftier mountains, from whose crests they could discern ranges whose summits appeared to lose themselves in the eternal clouds of the firmament. Men who on their plains were accustomed to cross torrential rivers, tame savage horses, and conquer in bodily combat the wild bull, the tiger, and the crocodile were frightened by the forbidding aspect of these strange surroundings. Losing hope of overcoming such stupendous difficulties, their horses already dead from fatigue, they decided that only madmen could persevere in the enterprise, in a climate whose temperature numbed their senses and froze their bodies. As a result, many of them deserted.

The mules carrying the munitions and arms fell under the weight of their burdens; few horses survived the five days of marching; and the fallen animals of the forward division obstructed the road and increased the difficulties of the rear guard. It rained incessantly day and night, and the cold grew worse as they ascended. The cold water, to which the troops were not accustomed, caused diarrhea among them. It seemed as if sorcery had conjured up this accumulation of mishaps in order to destroy the hopes of Bolívar. He alone remained firm among reverses the least of which would have discouraged a weaker spirit. He inspired the troops with his presence and example, speaking to them of the glory that awaited them, and of the abundance that reigned in the country that they were going to liberate. The soldiers listened to him with pleasure and redoubled their efforts.

On the 27th the vanguard dispersed a royalist force of 300 men, advantageously posted in front of Paya, a town in the cordillera. This strong position could bar the passage of an army; the royalist detachment was more than sufficient to defend it against 6,000 men; but the timidity of the Spanish commander saved the army and opened to Bolívar the road to New Granada. ...

After some days of rest, the army resumed its march on July 2. The royalist detachment which had been beaten at Paya retired to Labranza Grande, which was reached by a road that was considered the only passable one at that season of the year. There was another, across the *páramo* of Pisba, but it was so rough that it was hardly used even in the summer. The Spaniards considered it unusable and therefore neglected its defense; Bolívar selected it for precisely that reason. The passage of Casanare through plains covered with water, and that of the portion of the Andes which lay behind us, though rugged and steep was in every way preferable to the road which the army was to take.

At many points immense fallen rocks and trees, and slides caused by the constant rains that made walking dangerous and uncertain, completely obstructed its advance. The soldiers, who had received rations of meat and *arracacha* for four days, threw them away and kept only their rifles, for the climb presented enough difficulties without any burdens. The few surviving horses perished during this day.

As darkness fell the army reached the foot of the *páramo* of Pisba, where it passed a frightful night. It was impossible to have a fire, because there were no dwellings in the vicinity and a steady drizzle, accompanied by hail and a freezing wind, quenched the bonfires made in the open as quickly as they were lighted.

Since the troops were nearly naked, and the majority were natives of the burning plains of Venezuela, it is easier to conceive than to describe their cruel sufferings. The following day they reached the *páramo* itself, a dismal and inhospitable desert, devoid of all vegetation because of its height. On that day the effect of the piercingly cold air was fatal to many soldiers; many fell suddenly ill while on the march and expired in a few minutes. Flogging was used, with success in some cases, to revive frozen soldiers; a colonel of cavalry was saved in this way.

During this day's march my attention was called to a group of soldiers who had stopped near where I had seated myself, overcome with fatigue. Seeing anxiety written on their faces, I asked one of them what was wrong; he replied that the wife of a soldier of the Rifles Battalion was in labor. The next morning I saw the same woman, her babe in her arms, and apparently in the best of health, marching in the rear guard of the battalion. After the birth she had walked for two leagues along one of the worst roads in that rough terrain.

One hundred men would have sufficed to destroy the patriot army while crossing the *páramo*. On the march it was impossible to keep the soldiers together because even the officers could barely stand the hardships of the road, much less attend to the troops. That night was more terrible than the preceding ones, and although the encampment was more sheltered and the rain less frequent, many soldiers died from the effects of their sufferings and privations. As the parties of ten or twenty men descended together from the *páramo*, the President [Bolívar] congratulated them on the approaching conclusion of the campaign, telling them that they had already conquered the greatest obstacles of the march.

On the 6th the division of Anzoátegui reached Socha, the first town in the province of Tunja; the vanguard had arrived there on the preceding day. The soldiers, seeing behind them the crests of the mountains, covered with clouds and mists, spontaneously vowed to conquer or die rather than retreat through those mountains, for they feared them more than the most formidable enemy. In Socha the army received a cordial welcome from the inhabitants of that place and its vicinity. Bread, tobacco, and *chicha*, a beverage made from corn and cane-juice syrup, rewarded the troops for their sufferings and inspired greater hopes for the future. But as the hardships of the soldier diminished, the cares of the general increased. ...

Great was the royalist surprise to learn that they had unwelcome guests in the shape of an enemy army; it seemed incredible that Bolívar should have begun operations and overcome such great obstacles at a time of the year when few dared to undertake even the shortest journeys. ...

Meanwhile the enemy remained in his positions, giving no sign that he wished to accept combat on the plain. After vain efforts to commit him to an action, Bolívar ordered a flank movement in an effort to encircle his right wing. At dawn on the 25th of July, anniversary of the patron saint of Spain and the birthday of Bolívar, the army began to cross the Sogamoso River, which runs through the plains of Bonza.

At midday, as the army defiled through the swamp of Vargas, the enemy appeared on the heights in front.

Since nine in the morning Barreiro had observed the movement of the patriots and had speedily acted to counter it. Both armies immediately got ready for battle. The republicans were forced to occupy an unfavorable position, which Bolívar sought to improve by sending Santander with his division to the heights that dominated the left wing of the Army of Liberation, whose right wing was protected by a swamp.

Barreiro began the action by sending the first battalion *del Rey* against the left wing of the patriot army, to be followed by an attack on its shoulder. Seeing that this corps had seized the heights, where Santander offered very feeble resistance, Barreiro struck at the center of the line with such force that the Rifles and Barcelona battalions broke and gave way.

At that moment all seemed lost, but Bolívar flew to reunite the shattered corps, ordering Colonel Rook and his British Legion to dislodge the enemy from the heights that he had occupied. The fearless Englishman carried out his assignment with brilliant success.

Now the royalist general, fiery and tireless, made a second furious attack on the front of the patriot army. But he gained only a temporary advantage, for Bolívar, making judicious use of his small reserve, decided the fate of the battle with a magnificent cavalry charge.

One word or the efforts of a single individual have sometimes succeeded in calming an insurrection or gaining a triumph. At that critical moment, when everything seemed to favor the Spaniards, who already counted on the complete destruction of the patriot army, and when all—except Bolívar—despaired of victory, Rondón appeared with his squadron of *llaneros*. Bolívar shouted words of encouragement and cried to their leader: "Colonel, save the fatherland!" Rondón followed by his brave soldiers, immediately hurled himself upon the advancing enemy squadrons and threw them back, with a heavy loss of life. The infantry imitated Rondón's feat, and the royalists could not withstand the impetus of the combined attack.

The night put an end to the bloody battle, whose outcome seemed doubtful at certain moments. Twice that day the Army of Liberation believed that all was lost.

Barreiro's communiqué pays tribute to the valor of our troops. "Desperation," he says, "inspired them with an unheard-of valor. Their infantry and cavalry left the gullies into which they had been hurled, and rushed with fury up the heights which they had lost. Our infantry could not resist them." ...

The bravery of Rondón and the calm bravery of the few British troops contributed substantially to victory, or rather to saving the liberating army of New Granada from destruction. In the general order published the next day, Bolivar acknowledged the merits of these brave foreigners by conferring on them the "Cross of Liberators," a distinction which they well deserved. ...

Bolívar's activity and energy appeared to redouble even as his difficulties increased. He never showed himself more worthy of his reputation than after the battle of Vargas. General Páez had not lived up to his agreement to invade New Granada by way of Cúcuta, because he either could not or would not leave the plains of the Apure, so there was no longer any reason to hope for aid from that quarter. The army could rely only on the talents of Bolívar and the expedients that his genius might suggest. Actually, these were enough, as the course of events was to show. ...

After the expected munitions and the convalescents from the hospital had arrived, and after the army had been augmented by numbers of patriotic volunteers, on August 3 the army began its advance on the enemy. Barreiro was forced to evacuate the town of Paipa, and as the patriots approached he withdrew his advance guards to the heights dominating the road to Tunja.

At nightfall the patriots crossed the Sogamoso River and encamped within half a league from the royalists. [The following day Bolívar recrossed the river, apparently returning to his former position at Bonza; but at nightfall he gave a counterorder, crossed the river once more, and, leaving the enemy behind, began a rapid march on Tunja by way of Toca. Ed.] At eleven in the morning he occupied the city and took as prisoners the few soldiers of the garrison, for the governor of Tunja had left that same morning for Barreiro's headquarters with the third *Numancia* battalion and an artillery brigade. The patriot army was received in Tunja with the same joyful demonstrations that had greeted it everywhere.

Bolívar's daring movement terrified the Spaniards and decided the fate of the campaign. The enemy learned of the movement only the next morning, when Barreiro set out for Tunja by the principal road. During the night he turned slightly to the right, and the next morning he entered Motavita, a village a short distance from the city.

A cavalry detachment which had followed his movements, stabbing at his rear guard, caused him a good deal of trouble during the night, and took all his stragglers as prisoners.

On the 7th, Barreiro continued his march, and as soon as Bolívar, by a personal reconnaisance, had assured himself of its direction, he ordered the army to march toward the same point, with the intention of cutting the enemy off from Santa Fe.

At two in the afternoon the first royalists reached the bridge of Boyacá. They were passing over it when the patriot vanguard attacked their rear; simultaneously Santander's division appeared on the heights which dominated the position where Barreiro had drawn up his army.

The battle began with skirmishes between scouts. Meanwhile a column of royalist chasseurs crossed the bridge under the command of Colonel Jiménez and drew up in battle formation. But Barreiro, finding himself unable to do the same with the bulk of his army, ordered it to withdraw about three quarters of a mile from the bridge, and thereby gave the patriots time to cut him off from Santa Fe.

Bolívar immediately ordered Santander to force the bridge, and Anzoátegui simultaneously to attack the right wing and the center of the royalist position. The combat now became general; the Spanish infantry fought very bravely for some time, until Anzoátegui and his lancers enveloped their right wing and took the artillery on which the Rifles battalion had made a frontal attack; the fleeing cavalry was cut down, and when the infantry saw this they surrendered. A bayonet charge decided the day. Jiménez, who defended the bridge and was holding Santander's division in check, fell back when he saw Barreiro's plight, and the rout became general.

Sixteen hundred men laid down their arms. Barreiro, his second-in-command, Jiménez, and the majority of the chiefs and officers were taken prisoner. Artillery, munitions, arms, banners, money, and baggage fell into the hands of the victor. Bolívar personally pursued the fugitives as far as Venta Quemada, where he spent that night.

On the following morning an act of just retribution took place. Vinoni, the traitor, who had played a leading part in the uprising at and surrender of the castle of Puerto Cabello to the Spaniards, was recognized by Bolívar among the prisoners taken during the pursuit; he was immediately hanged.

5. THE ARMY OF THE ANDES

For Argentines the figure of José de San Martín has the same heroic and legendary quality that Bolívar possesses for the peoples of northern South America. Modest and reserved, San Martín was something of an enigma to his contemporaries, and we lack a description as revealing of the man as Peru de Lacroix's sketch of Bolívar. From the military point of view, San Martín's chief claim to greatness is his masterful campaign of the Andes, prelude to the decisive attack on Peru. To this day the standard biography of San Martín is the classic life by Bartolomé Mitre (1821–1906), distinguished Argen-

tine soldier, historian and statesman. Mitre describes San Martín's painstaking prepara-
tions for the passage of the Andes.

San Martín tried to convince the enemy that he planned to invade Chile in the south, whereas he actually intended to strike in the center. This was a fixed major objective of his "war of nerves," and that is why he deceived friend and enemy alike with misleading communications and incomplete confidences, guarding his secret until the last moment. In order to confirm Marcó, the Spanish governor of Chile, in his mistaken views, he devised a new stratagem, which, like all his ruses, bore the stamp of novelty and of a brain fertile in expedients.

Since 1814, San Martín, as governor of Cuyo, had cultivated friendly relations with the Pehuenche Indians, then masters of the eastern slopes of the cordillera south of Mendoza, in order to ensure the safe transit of his secret Chilean agents through the passes they dominated, and to have them on his side in case of an enemy invasion. At the time he assembled his army in the encampment of Plumerillo he decided to renew these relations, with the double object of deceiving the enemy with respect to his true plans, and of giving greater security and importance to the secondary operations which he planned to carry out by way of the southern passes. For this purpose he invited them to a general parley in the Fort of San Carlos, above the boundary line of the Diamond River, with the ostensible object of seeking permission to pass through their lands. He sent ahead trains of mules loaded with hundreds of barrels of wine and skins filled with *aguardiente;* with sweets, bright-colored cloths, and glass beads for the women; and, for the men, horse gear, foodstuffs of all kinds, and all the old clothes that the province could supply, in order to dazzle the allies. On the appointed day the Pehuenches approached the fort with barbaric pomp, blowing their horns, flourishing their long plumed lances, and followed by their women. The warriors were naked from the waist up and wore their long hair untied; all were in fighting trim. Each tribe was preceded by a guard of mounted grenadiers, whose correctly martial appearance contrasted with the savage appearance of the Indians. On approaching the esplanade of the fort, the women went to one side, and the men whirled their lances about by way of greeting. There followed a picturesque sham fight in Pehuenche style, with the warriors riding at full speed around the walls of the redoubt, from whose walls a gun fired a salvo every five minutes, to which the braves responded by striking themselves on the mouth and whooping with joy.

The solemn meeting that followed was held on the parade ground of the fort. San Martín asked permission to pass through the lands of the Pehu-

Bartolomé Mitre, *Historia de San Martín y de la emancipación sudaméricana,* Buenos Aires, 1944, 2 vols., I, pp. 319–334. (Excerpt translated by the editor.)

enches in order to attack the Spaniards through the Planchón and Portillo passes. The Spaniards, he told them, were foreigners, enemies of the American Indian, whose fields and herds, women and children, they sought to steal. The Colo-colo of the tribes was a white-haired ancient called Necuñan. After consulting the assembly and obtaining their opinions with suitable gravity, he told the general that with the exception of three caciques, with whom they could deal later, all accepted his proposals, and they sealed the treaty of alliance by embracing San Martín, one after another. In proof of their friendship they immediately placed their arms in the keeping of the Christians and gave themselves up to an orgy that lasted for eight consecutive days. On the sixth day the general returned to his headquarters to await the result of these negotiations, whose object he kept secret from even his most intimate confidants.

The creole diplomat had foreseen that the Indians, with their natural perfidy—or the dissident *caciques*, at any rate—would report his pretended project to Marcó, as actually happened. But just in case they should not do so, he hastened to communicate it to the Spanish leader directly by means of one of his characteristic ruses, in which he was aided by a coincidence that he had also foreseen. During the reorganization of his army he had cut the supposed communications of the Spaniards of Cuyo with Marcó, and the latter, ignorant of everything that was taking place east of the Andes, sent emissaries to obtain information from the individuals whom he believed to be his official correspondents. Such was San Martín's vigilance that for two years not a single royalist spy had been able to penetrate into Cuyo without being captured in the cordillera by patriot guards who had been warned by secret agents in Chile. The last letters of the Spanish governor met the same fate. With these letters in his possession, San Martin summoned the supposed correspondents to his presence—among them was Castillo de Albo,—showed them the incriminating letters, and with pretended anger (it is said that he even threatened them with a pistol that he had on his desk) forced them to write and sign replies that he dictated. In these replies he announced that "about the 15th of October" a squadron was preparing to leave Buenos Aires for an unknown destination. It was "composed of a frigate, three corvettes, two brigantines, and two transports, all under the command of the Englishman Teler [Taylor]." "San Martín," they added, "has held a general parley with the Pehuenche Indians. The Indians have agreed to everything; we shall see how they carry out their pledges; caution and more caution; for lack of it our people have suffered imprisonment and spoliations. Everything is known here." In another he said that a French engineer had left Mendoza in order to construct a bridge over the Diamond River. San Martín's letters, sent by an emissary who played the role of a double spy, were delivered to Marcó, who believed everything in them, lost his head entirely, and turned the whole province upside down to guard against a double invasion. At the same time

San Martín informed the government of Buenos Aires that the purpose of the parley was to get the Indians "to assist the passage of the army with livestock and horses at the stipulated prices," while to his confidant, Guido, he wrote: "I concluded with all success my great parley with the Indians of the south; they not only will aid the army with livestock but are committed to take an active part against the enemy." As can be seen, San Martín was a well of large and small mysteries, with the naked truth hidden at the bottom.

Marcó, disheartened by the alarming news from his supposed correspondents in Cuyo, and by the simultaneous rising of the guerrillas of Manuel Rodríguez, who extended their excursions between the Maule and the Maipo and made armed assaults on villages in the very vicinity of the capital, dictated a series of senseless and contradictory measures that revealed the confusion in his mind and the fear in his heart. He ordered the ports to be fortified and attempted to convert some of them into islands with the object of preventing a disembarkation; at the same time he equipped a squadron to act against the imaginary fleet of Buenos Aires. He commanded that entrenchments should be thrown up in the pass of Uspallata, that the southern provinces of the kingdom should be mapped and that the entrances to the Maule and Planchón passes should be surveyed; but before these tasks had been completed he ordered strengthening of the guards at all the passes of the cordillera, from north to south. First he concentrated his troops and then he dispersed most of them again, moving them about in empty space. Finding no inspiration in himself, after jerking about like a puppet manipulated by San Martín, he finished by reproducing the man's very gestures, like a monkey; in imitation of the patriot general he held a parley with the Araucanian Indians, but failed to devise a rational plan of defense.

The objective of the astute Argentine leader was fulfilled: the captain-general of Chile sought to defend all its land and sea frontiers simultaneously; consequently he dispersed his army and thus became weak everywhere, never suspecting the point of the true attack. To crown his confusion, the spies he sent to obtain accurate information either did not return or served San Martín by bringing back false reports that led him to commit new errors. Some of his advisers urged him to take the offensive; others, that he persevere in his absurd waiting plan; and only one of them, his secretary, Dr. Judas Tadeo Reyes, the least knowledgeable in warfare, suggested the plan he should have followed: concentrate the 50,000 veteran troops in the capital, disperse the militia troops about the country, and await the invasion in that posture. However, by this time Marcó was so distraught that good and bad counsels were equally useless. He himself graphically depicted his deplorable morale at this time (February 4, 1817): "My plans are reduced to continual movements and variations according to developments and news of the enemy, whose astute chief at Mendoza, kept informed of my situation by his innumerable lines of communication and the disloyal spies who surround me, seeks to surprise me."

But it was not only the threat of impending invasion that made Marcó uneasy. His resources were scanty, and as a result of the stupid system of taxation established by Osorio and continued and intensified by himself, the very sources of further contributions were exhausted. In order to defray the public expenses he levied a tax on exports of grain and flour and imports of wine and sugar; simultaneously he decreed a forced loan of 400,000 pesos to be collected from individuals with an annual income of 1,000 pesos, not excluding civil and military officers, and payable in cash. The sole result of these measures was the spread of demoralization and discontent, which fanned the sparks of insurrection lighted by the agents of San Martín, who announced his immediate arrival at the head of a powerful liberating army. ...

The situation was quite different in the encampment at Mendoza: here there was a methodical activity, an automatic obedience coupled with an enthusiasm born of understanding. A superior will, that knew what it wanted and what it was doing, directed all, inspiring the soldiers with the feeling that victory was certain. In Mendoza it was known what Marcó did, thought, or was going to do, whereas Marcó did not even know what he wanted to do. Everyone worked, each performing the task assigned to him, and they all trusted in their general. Pack mules and war horses were assembled; thousands of horseshoes were forged for the animals; packsaddles were made for the beasts of burden; fodder and provisions were stored; and herds of cattle were rounded up for the passage of the cordillera. Leaders, officers, and soldiers devoted themselves to their respective duties and positions. The arsenal turned out hundreds of thousands of cartridges. The forges blazed day and night, repairing arms and casting projectiles. The indefatigable Father Luis Beltran supervised the construction of new machines by means of which, as he put it, the cannon would fly over the tops of the mountains like condors. The ingenious friar had invented, or rather adapted, a kind of narrow carriage (called *zorra*) of rude but solid construction which, mounted on four low wheels and drawn by oxen or mules, replaced the mounts of the cannon; the guns themselves would be carried on the backs of mules along the narrow, tortuous paths of the cordillera until they reached the plain on the other side. As a precaution, long slings were made in which the carriages and cannon would be hoisted over rough places between mules, as if in litters, one after the other; sleds of hide were also prepared in which heavy objects might be hauled up by hand or by a portable winch when the gradients were too steep for the mules.

Meanwhile the general-in-chief, silent and reserved, planned for everyone, inspected everything, and provided for all contingencies in the most minute detail, from food and equipment for men and beasts to the complicated machines of war, even seeing the cutting edge of his soldiers' sabres.

The army needed a healthful and nourishing food that would restore the soldiers' strength and would be suited to the frigid temperatures through which they must pass. San Martín found this in a popular dish called *char-*

quican, composed of beef dried in the sun, roasted, ground to powder, mixed with fat and chili pepper, and well pounded. A soldier could carry enough of this in his knapsack to last him eight days. Mixed with hot water and roasted maize meal it made a nutritious and appetizing porridge. ... After providing for his soldiers' stomachs, San Martín took thought for their feet—the vehicles of victory. In order to obtain footwear without burdening the treasury, he asked the *cabildo* of Mendoza to collect and send to the camp the scraps of cowhide discarded every day by the slaughterhouses of the city. From these pieces he had the soldiers make *tamangos*, a kind of closed sandal often used by the Negroes. ... He carried economy to extreme lengths in order to show, in his own words, that great enterprises can be accomplished with small means. An order of the day, made public to the sound of drums, asked the people to bring to special depots old woolen rags that could be used to line the *tamangos*, because, San Martín declared, "the health of the soldiers is a powerful machine that if well directed can bring victory; and our first concern is to protect their feet." The horns of slaughtered cattle were used to make canteens, necessary in crossing the waterless stretches of the cordillera. Another decree ordered all the cloth remnants in the stores and tailor shops of the city to be collected, and San Martín distributed them to the soldiers to make into straps for their knapsacks.

The sabres of the mounted grenadiers had lost their sharpness; San Martín had them given a razor-like edge and placed them in the hands of his soldiers, saying they were for cutting off Spanish heads. It was not enough to sharpen swords; arms had to be trained to use them; and martial instruments were needed to nerve the soldiers and to take the place of the officer's voice in battle. San Martín chose the trumpet, an instrument rarely used by American cavalry at that time. The army had only three trumpets. San Martin had some made out of tin, but they were mute. In his application to the government San Martín wrote: "The trumpet is as necessary for the cavalry as is the drum for the infantry. ..."

The general gave the matter of horseshoes his closest attention. Before making a decision he held conferences with veterinarians, blacksmiths, and muleteers; after carefully listening to them, he adopted a model of a horseshoe which he sent to the government telling the officer who carried it to guard it as if it were made of gold and to present it to the Minister of War. ...The army needed thirty thousand horseshoes with a double set of nails. In two months they were forged by artisans who toiled day and night in the shops of the arms factory in Buenos Aires and in the forges of Mendoza.

How was the army to cross the deep ravines and torrents that lay before it? How were the heavy materials of war to ascend and descend the steep slopes of the mountains? And finally, how were the carriages and their loads to be rescued from the depths into which they might fall? These were problems that had to be solved. For river passages a rope bridge of a given weight and length (60 *varas*) was devised, and the piece of cable which was to be shown to the government as a model was entrusted to an officer with the same solemnity as the horseshoe. "It is impossible to transport the artillery and other heavy objects over the narrow defiles and slopes of the cordillera, or to rescue material fallen from the path," wrote San Martín, "without the aid of two anchors and four cables, of a weight that can be transported on mule-back." With this apparatus, moved by a winch, the difficulties of the passage were overcome. ...

Amid this official correspondence concerning the movement of men, materials, and money, an exchange of letters of mixed character took place between the two protagonists of our story: General San Martín and Pueyrredón, Director of the United Provinces of La Plata. Passionately devoted to the same cause, they aided and comforted each other, until they and their mission became one. ...

"You don't ask for much," the Director would write San Martín, "and I feel bad because I don't have the money to get these things for you; but I shall do my best, and by the beginning of October I shall have gotten together thirty thousand pesos for the use of the army." But hardly had Pueyrredón assumed direction of the government and began to make good his promises when there broke out in Córdoba a confused anarchical revolt that threatened to throw the entire Republic into chaos. ...

When the brief uprising of Córdoba had been crushed, the general of the Andes renewed his insistent urging, as has been shown from the official correspondence. The Director provided everything, and when he had satisfied all demands he took up his pen and wrote with humorous desperation and comradely forthrightness: "I am sending official letters of thanks to Mendoza and the other cities of Cuyo. I am sending the officers' commissions. I am sending the uniforms you asked for and many more shirts. I am sending 400 saddles. I am sending off today by post two trumpets—all I could find. In January I shall send 1387 *arrobas* of dried beef. I am sending the 200 spare sabres that you asked for. I am sending 200 tents or pavilions; that's all there are. I am sending the world, the flesh, and the devil! I don't know how I shall get out of the scrape I'm in to pay for all this, unless I declare bankruptcy, cancel my accounts with everyone, and clear out to join you, so that you can give me some of the dried beef I'm sending you. Damn it, don't ask me for anything else, unless you want to hear that they found me in the morning dangling from a beam in the Fort! ..."

When everything was ready the general of the expedition asked for instructions concerning his military and political courses of action. The government, inspired by the same lofty aims as the general, drew up instructions infused with a broad, generous, and resolute spirit, in harmony with San Martín's continental plan; and formulated, in words which deeds were to make good, the liberation policy of the Argentine Revolution in respect to the other peoples of South America, on the basis of independence and liberty for each one of them. "The consolidation of American independence" (said Article I) "and the glory of the United Provinces of South America are the only motives of this campaign. The general will make this clear in his proclamations; he will spread it through his agents in every town, and will propagate it by every possible means. The army must be impressed with these principles. Care must be taken that not a word is said of pillage, oppression, conquest, or retaining possession of the liberated country. ..."

With these instructions in his portfolio, all decisions made, and the army poised at the eastern entrances to the Andes, San Martín, one foot already in the stirrup, wrote (January 24, 1817) his last letter to his most intimate confidant: "This afternoon I set out to join the army. God grant me success in this great enterprise."

6. THE VISION OF BOLÍVAR

Bolívar's most grandiose political conception was a league of friendship and mutual assistance uniting all the Latin American states, under the leadership and protection of Great Britain. To achieve this project, Bolívar invited these and other nations to a congress, which was held in Panama in 1826. In the end this assembly proved an almost total failure. On the eve of the meeting Bolívar wrote down a statement of the advantages to be gained from the proposed confederacy. This document suggests that fear of the Holy Alliance, on the one hand, and of Black and Indian insurrections, on the other, partly influenced Bolívar's decision to summon the Congress of Panama.

The Congress of Panama will bring together all the representatives of America and a diplomat-agent of His Britannic Majesty's government. This Congress seems destined to form a league more extensive, more remarkable, and more powerful than any that has ever existed on the face of the earth. Should Great Britain agree to join it as a constituent member, the Holy Alliance will be less powerful than this confederation. Mankind will a thousand times bless this league for promoting its general welfare, and America, as well as Great Britain, will reap from it untold benefits. A code of public law to regulate the international conduct of political bodies will be one of its products.

1. The New World would consist of independent nations, bound together by a common set of laws which would govern their foreign relations and afford them a right to survival through a general and permanent congress.

2. The existence of these new states would receive fresh guarantees.

3. In deference to England, Spain would make peace, and the Holy Alliance would grant recognition to these infant nations.

Vicenta Lecuna, compiler, and Harold A. Bierck, ed., *The Selected Writings of Bolívar*, New York: Colonial Press, 1951, 2 vols., II, pp. 561–562. Reprinted by kind permission of the Banco de Venezuela.

4. Domestic control would be preserved untouched among the states and within each of them.

5. No one of them would be weaker than another, nor would any be stronger.

6. A perfect balance would be established by this truly new order of things.

7. The power of all would come to the aid of any one state which might suffer at the hands of a foreign enemy or from internal anarchic factions.

8. Differences of origin and color would lose their influence and power.

9. America would have nothing more to fear from that tremendous monster who has devoured the island of Santo Domingo, nor would she have cause to fear the numerical preponderance of the aborigines.

10. In short, a social reform would be achieved under the blessed auspices of freedom and peace, but the fulcrum controlling the beam of the scales must necessarily rest in the hands of England.

Great Britain would, of course, derive considerable advantage from this arrangement.

1. Her influence in Europe would progressively increase, and her decisions would be like those of destiny itself.

2. America would serve her as an opulent domain of commerce.

3. America would become the center of England's relations with Asia and Europe.

4. British subjects in America would be considered the equals of American citizens.

5. The relations between England and America would in time become those between equals.

6. British characteristics and customs would be adopted by the Americans as standards for their future way of life.

7. In the course of the centuries, there might, perhaps, come to exist one single nation throughout the world—a federal nation.

These ideas are in the minds of many Americans in positions of importance who impatiently await the inauguration of this project at the Congress of Panama, which may afford the occasion to consummate the union of the new states and the British Empire. ...

7. HIDALGO: TORCHBEARER
OF THE MEXICAN REVOLUTION

Miguel Hidalgo (1753–1811), the scholarly white-haired priest of the town of Dolores and onetime rector of the college of San Nicolás Valladolid, hardly seemed fitted by background and disposition to head a revolution. It was Hidalgo, nevertheless, who overcame the waverings of his associates when their conspiracy was discovered and who trans-

formed what had been planned as an upper-class Creole revolt into a rising of the masses. Alamán, historian and bitter enemy of the revolution—who knew Hidalgo in the peaceful years before the great upheaval—describes the curate of Dolores.

Don Miguel Hidalgo, being neither austere in his morals nor very orthodox in his opinions, did not concern himself with the spiritual administration of his parish, which he had turned over, together with half the income of his curacy, to a priest named Don Francisco Iglesias. Knowing French—a rather rare accomplishment at the period, especially among churchmen—he formed a taste for technical and scientific books and zealously promoted various agricultural and industrial projects in his parish. He considerably furthered viticulture, and today that whole region produces abundant harvests of grapes; he also encouraged the planting of mulberry trees for the raising of silkworms. In Dolores eighty-four trees planted by him are still standing, in the spot called "the mulberry trees of Hidalgo," as well as the channels that he had dug for irrigating the entire plantation. He established a brickyard and a factory for the manufacture of porcelain, constructed troughs for tanning hides, and promoted a variety of other enterprises.

All this, plus the fact that he was not only generous but lavish in money matters, had won him the high regard of his parishioners—especially the Indians, whose languages he had mastered. It also gained him the esteem of all who took a sincere interest in the advancement of the country, men like Abad y Queipo, the bishop-elect of Michoacán, and Riaño, the intendant of Guanajuato. It seems, however, that he had little basic knowledge of the industries which he fostered, and even less of that systematic spirit which one must have to make substantial progress with them. Once, being asked by Bishop Abad y Queipo what method he used for picking and distributing the leaves to the silkworms according to their age, and for separating the dry leaves and keeping the silkworms clean—concerning which the books on the subject give such elaborate instructions—he replied that he followed no particular order, that he threw down the leaves as they came from the tree and let the silkworms eat as they wished. "The revolution," exclaimed the bishop, who told me this anecdote, "was like his raising of silkworms, and the results were what might be expected!" Nevertheless, he had made much progress, and obtained enough silk to have some garments made for himself and for his stepmother. He also promoted the raising of bees, and brought many swarms of bees to the hacienda of Jaripeo when he bought that estate.

He was very fond of music, and not only had it taught to the Indians of his parish, where he formed an orchestra, but borrowed the orchestra of the provincial battalion of Guanajuato for the frequent parties that he gave in his

Alamán, *Historia de Méjico*, I, pp. 352–354. (Excerpt translated by the editor.)

home. Since his residence was a short distance from Guanajuato, he often visited the capital and stayed there for long periods of time. This gave me an opportunity to see him and to know him. He was fairly tall and stoop-shoul-dered, of dark complexion and quick green eyes; his head bent a little over his chest and was covered by sparse gray hair, for he was more than sixty years old.[4] He was vigorous, though neither swift nor active in his movements; short of speech in ordinary conversation but animated in academic style when the argument grew warm. He was careless in dress, wearing only such garb as small town curates commonly wore in those days.

8. THE REFORMS OF HIDALGO

Hidalgo and Morelos attempted to combine the Creole ideal of independence with a pro-gram of social justice for the oppressed classes of the Mexican population. The following decrees of Hidalgo, issued after his capture of Guadalajara, help to explain why many conservative Creoles fought on the Spanish side against the patriots.

Don Miguel Hidalgo y Costilla, generalissimo of America, etc. By these presents I order the judges and justices of the district of this capital to pro-ceed immediately to the collection of the rents due to this day by the lessees of the lands belonging to the Indian communities, the said rents to be en-tered in the national treasury. The lands shall be turned over to the Indians for their cultivation, and they may not be rented out in the future, for it is my wish that only the Indians in their respective towns shall have the use of them. Given in my headquarters of Guadalajara, December 5, 1810. ...

Don Miguel Hidalgo y Costilla, generalissimo of America, etc. From the moment that the courageous American nation took up arms to throw off the heavy yoke that oppressed it for three centuries, one of its principal aims has been to extinguish the multitude of taxes that kept it in poverty. Since the critical state of our affairs does not permit the framing of adequate provisions in this respect, because of the need of the kingdom for money to defray the costs of the war, for the present I propose to remedy the most urgent abuses by means of the following declarations. First: All slaveowners shall set their slaves free within ten days, on pain of death for violation of this article. Second: The payment of tribute by all the castes that used to pay it shall henceforth cease, and no other taxes shall be collected from the Indians. Third: In all judicial business, documents, deeds, and actions, only ordinary paper shall be used, and the use of sealed paper is abolished.

Alamán, *Historia de Méjico*, II, pp. 25–26. (Excerpt translated by the editor.)

9. THE PLAN OF IGUALA

By a notable irony, the work begun by Hidalgo and Morelos was consummated by a Creole officer, Agustín de Iturbide (1783–1824), who for nine years had fought the insurgents with great effectiveness. Behind Iturbide were conservative churchmen, army officers, and officials, who preferred separation from Spain to submission to the liberal Constitution of 1812, imposed on Ferdinand VII by his revolted army. Lorenzo de Zavala (1788–1836), a brilliant Mexican statesman, publicist, and historian, describes the origin and triumph of the Plan of Iguala.

The year 1820 was born among stormy portents. The gathering of troops on the island of León for dispatch to South America aroused no special interest, for experience had shown the futility of such expeditions. But the news of the first moves made by the army in the palm grove of the port of Santa María, under the orders of the Count of La Bisbal, the reestablishment of the constitution of 1812, caused excitement in Mexico and inspired consternation in Viceroy Apodaca. He perceived that the seeming tranquillity of Mexico was an illusion, for the times were out of joint; he feared to lose in a moment the fruit of his labors and, above all, the glory he had acquired by bringing peace to Mexico—the result of a combination of circumstances that could produce only a momentary effect. The viceroy issued circulars announcing that the rumors being spread about the temper of the troops in Spain were false: *Never was the royal government more solidly established, or military discipline better; never did the king have greater proof of the love of his people and of his armies.* This was said in the government press, the only newspaper permitted to appear; the bishops and priests preached the same thing; but the only result of these measures was to increase alarm and to awaken hopes that were never extinguished. The very concern of the government, and its effort to discredit the news of this movement, only gave them greater currency. Commerce, that reliable index of developments and infallible barometer of political conditions, revealed more through its precautionary measures than any statements the government agents could make to conceal the situation from the public. The efforts of the unfortunate Lacy, in Cataluña, and of the martyred Porlier, in Galicia, were so many proofs that Spain had but temporarily accepted the yoke of an arbitrary power. ... I shall now try to describe briefly and as exactly as possible the state of Mexican public opinion in these circumstances.

The upper clergy and the privileged classes, who saw the revolutionary principles of 1812 rising again to threaten their revenues and their benefices,

---

Lorenzo de Zavala, *Ensayo histórico de los revoluciones de México*, Mexico, 1918, 2 vols., I, pp. 69–79. (Excerpt translated by the editor.)

united as if by instinct to oppose an insuperable barrier, as they thought, to the reestablishment of the Spanish constitution, which had so greatly weakened their influence. The first news of the cry of Riego in the town of Las Cabezas, on January 1, 1820, were received with terror by all those who lived on the credulity and ignorance of the people. Apodaca, a fanatical supporter of the royal power and of the abuses of superstition, formed the project of offering Ferdinand VII an asylum in Mexico against the enterprises of the constitutionalists, assuring him of a throne in a land to which the new doctrines would have no access. What a flattering prospect for the canons and aristocratic classes this was—to make Mexico the center of their power and to form a court that would dispense jobs and honors! The Mexican counts and marquises already saw themselves made grandees of the *first class*, raised to eminent titles and vying with the ancient Spanish nobility in pride, in wealth, and in ignorance! The project tended inevitably toward independence; to be sure, the Mexicans would have been glad to be independent, but it is very doubtful that they would have acquiesced to absolute power. Constitutional monarchy had become fashionable; the Mexicans would have wanted to keep in step with their peninsular fathers; the desire for a republic was not the plan of Apodaca and his advisers. In seeking to revive Napoleon's ancient project to transfer the royal family to Mexico, they only envisioned raising a throne for despotism and placing the immense barrier of the Atlantic between liberal ideas and the new monarchy. As if the example of the United States were not enough to excite new strivings on the part of the people! As if the progress made by the doctrines of anti-legitimacy and the sovereignty of the people among the Mexicans could be destroyed by this step! Futile efforts of a dying power, that only deceived itself with these illusions!

The rapidity with which the new revolution, headed by Riego, Quiroga, and other celebrated leaders, spread throughout Spain burst in a moment the bubble of Viceroy Apodaca. But from his plan there emerged another, in which the viceroy certainly had no part, no matter what may be said by some people who only judge by appearances and do not examine the background and causes of events. Frustrated in their first project, the clergy and the self-styled nobles decided that the moment had arrived to form a plan of independence which would assure a monarchy for Mexico and would summon a prince of the ruling house of Spain to occupy the throne. The idea was not new; the Count of Aranda had proposed it to Charles III fifty years before. It seemed to reconcile the interests of the different parties, it established independence, it made the monarchy secure, it gave guarantees to the Spaniards, and the people received a form of government best suited to their new needs and to their customs and habits. Amid these circumstances the elections of deputies for the Spanish *cortés* took place, and all those named for this mission agreed to present proposals to the assembly that harmonized with this solution. Amid this chaos of opinion and of parties, the viceroy was much perplexed. In April, 1820, arrived a royal order that required everyone to swear loyalty to the constitution. It was obeyed without resistance; the press began to speak freely once again; the dungeons opened to release prisoners held for political opinions; the Inquisition and the tribunal of public security disappeared; liberal ideas had triumphed in both worlds. New enterprises were set on foot—great projects that began under good auspices—and a man was needed, a man who would be valiant, active, energetic, enterprising. Where could he be found?

Popular revolutions present anomalies whose origin or causes are unknowable. Men who have followed one party, who have fought for certain principles, who have suffered for their loyalty to certain views or persons, suddenly change and adopt a completely different line of conduct. Who would ever have thought that the Mexican officer who had shed the blood of so many of his compatriots to maintain his country in slavery was destined to place himself at the head of a great movement that would destroy forever the Spanish power? What would have been thought of a man's sanity if in 1817 he had said that Iturbide would occupy the place of Morelos or would replace Mina? Yet the astonished Mexicans and Spaniards saw this happen.

Don Agustín de Iturbide, colonel of a battalion of provincial troops and a native of Valladolid de Michoacán, was endowed with brilliant qualities, and among his leading traits were uncommon bravery and vigor. To a handsome figure he united the strength and energy necessary to endure the great exertions of campaigning, and ten continuous years of this activity had fortified his natural qualities. He was haughty and domineering, and it was observed that to stay in favor with the authorities he had to remain at a distance from those who were in a position to give him orders. Every time that he came to Mexico City or other places where there were superiors, he gave indications of his impatience. ... It is said that he was involved in a plan hatched at Valladolid in 1809 for the achievement of independence but withdrew because he was not placed in command, though his rank at the time did not qualify him for leadership. Be that as it may, there is no doubt that Iturbide had a superior spirit, and that his ambition was supported by that noble resolution that scorns dangers and does not retreat before obstacles of every kind. He had faced danger and difficulty in combat; he had learned the power of Spanish weapons; he had taken the measure of the chiefs of both parties— and one must confess that he did not err in his calculations when he set himself above all of them. He was conscious of his superiority, and so did not hesitate to place himself at the head of the national party, if he could only inspire the same confidence in his compatriots. He discussed his project with men whose talents would be useful to him in the political direction of affairs, and henceforth he threw himself heart and soul into forming a *plan* that would offer guarantees to citizens and monarchists and at the same time would remove all cause for fear on the part of the Spaniards.

Anyone who examines the famous Plan of Iguala (so called because it was made public in that town for the first time), bearing in mind the circumstances of the Mexican nation at the time, will agree that it was a masterpiece of politics and wisdom. All the Mexicans desired *independence*, and this was the first basis of that document. The killings of Spaniards that had taken place, in reprisal for those that the Spaniards had committed during the past nine years, required a preventive, so to speak, to put an end to such atrocious acts, which could not fail to arouse hostility among the 50,000 Spaniards who still resided in the country. It was necessary to make plain the intentions of the new chief in this respect. Accordingly, he seized upon the word *union* as expressing the solidarity that should exist between creoles and Spaniards, regarded as citizens with the same rights. Finally, since the Catholic religion is the faith professed by all Mexicans, and since the clergy has a considerable influence in the country, the preservation of this church was also stated to be a fundamental basis, under the word *religion*. These three principles, *independence*, *union*, and *religion*, gave Iturbide's army its name of "the Army of the Three Guarantees." The representative monarchical system was established, and various articles stated the elementary principles of this form of government and the individual rights guaranteed to the people. Finally, the Spaniards were given freedom to leave the country with all their property. The expeditionary forces were offered the privilege of returning to Spain at the expense of the public treasury; those who chose to stay would be treated like Mexican soldiers. As can be seen, the plan reconciled all interests, and, raising New Spain to the rank of an independent nation, as was generally desired, with its immense benefits it silenced for the time being the particular aspirations of those who wanted the *republic* on the one hand and the *absolute monarchy* on the other. All the sons of the country united around the principle of *nationality*, putting aside for the moment their different ideals. We shall soon see the sprouting of these germs of ideas, as yet enveloped in mists or suppressed by the great matter of the common cause.

Don Agustín de Iturbide made all these preparations in the greatest secrecy, and to conceal his projects more effectively he entered or pretended to enter the church of San Felipe Neri to take part in religious exercises. There, it is said, was framed the document I mentioned. This display of piety, and the prudence and reserve with which he managed the affair, inspired the viceroy, who also was devout, to entrust him with the command of a small division assigned to pursue Don Vicente Guerrero, whose forces had increased considerably after the arrival of the news of the Spanish revolution. At the end of the year 1820 Colonel Iturbide set out from Mexico City, charged with the destruction of Guerrero but actually intending to join him at the first opportunity to work with him for the achievement of national independence. A few days after his departure from the capital, Iturbide drew near to Guerrero's camp. The latter had routed Colonel Berdejo, also sent out in his pursuit, in a minor clash, and this provided Iturbide with an opportunity to send Guerrero a letter inviting the patriot leader to abandon the enterprise that had cost the country so much futile bloodshed: "Now that the King of

Spain has offered liberal institutions and confirmed the social guarantees of the people, taking an oath to support the Constitution of 1812, the Mexicans will enjoy a just equality, and we shall be treated like free men." He added: "The victories that you have recently gained over the government forces should not inspire you with confidence in future triumphs, for you know that the fortunes of war are mutable, and that the government possesses great resources."

This letter was written very artfully, for at the same time that it suggested a desire to enter into agreements and relations with the insurgents it aroused no suspicion in the viceroy, who interpreted it as reflecting the same policy that had been so useful to him in pacifying the country. Presumably the persons employed by Iturbide to deliver these letters carried private instructions explaining his intentions. General Guerrero replied, with the energy that he always showed in defending the cause of independence and liberty, that he was resolved "to continue defending the national honor, until victory or death"; that he was "not to be deceived by the flattering promise of liberty given by the Spanish constitutionalists, who in the matter of independence [hold] the same views as the most diehard royalists; that the Spanish constitution [offers] no guarantees to the Americans." He reminded Iturbide of the exclusion of the castes in the Cadiz constitution; of the diminution of the American representatives; and, finally, of the indifference of the viceroys to these liberal laws. He concluded by exhorting Iturbide to join the national party, and invited him to take command of the national armies, of which Guerrero himself was then the leader. The vigorous tone of this letter, the sound observations that it contained, the convincing logic of its judgments, produced an astounding effect upon the Mexicans. Iturbide needed no persuasion; we have seen him depart from Mexico City with the intent of proclaiming the independence of the country, and the only matter left unsettled was the precise method of beginning the work, with himself as the leader of the daring enterprise.

He received this letter in January, 1821, and replied to General Guerrero, in a few lines, that he wished to "confer with [him] about the means of working together for the welfare of the kingdom" and hoped that he (Guerrero) "would be fully satisfied concerning his intentions." An agreement was reached for an interview between the two men.[5] General Guerrero himself supplied me with details of what took place at this meeting. The conference was held in a town in the State of Mexico. ... The two chiefs approached each other with some mutual distrust, although that of Guerrero was plainly the more justified. Iturbide had waged a cruel and bloody war on the independents since 1810. The Spanish leaders themselves hardly equaled this unnatural American in cruelty; and to see him transformed as if by magic into a defender of the cause that he had combated, would naturally arouse suspicions in men like the Mexican insurgents, who had often been the victims of their own credulity and of repeated betrayals. Nevertheless, Iturbide, though sanguinary, inspired confidence by the conscientiousness with which he proceeded in all matters. He was not believed capable of an act of treachery that would stain his reputation for valor and noble conduct. For himself, he had very little to fear from General Guerrero, a man distinguished from the beginning for his humanity and for his loyalty to the cause he was defending. The troops of both leaders were within cannonshot of each other; Iturbide and Guerrero met and embraced. Iturbide was the first to speak: "I cannot express the satisfaction I feel at meeting a patriot who has supported the noble cause of independence and who alone has survived so many disasters, keeping alive the sacred flame of liberty. Receive this just homage to your valor and to your virtues." Guerrero, who also was deeply moved, replied: "Sir, I congratulate my country, which on this day recovers a son whose valor and ability have caused her such grievous injury." Both leaders seemed to feel the strain of this memorable event; both shed tears of strong emotion. After Iturbide had revealed his plans and ideas to Señor Guerrero, that leader summoned his troops and officers, and Iturbide did the same. When both armies had been joined, Guerrero addressed himself to his soldiers, saying: "Soldiers: The Mexican who appears before you is Don Agustín de Iturbide, whose sword wrought such grave injury for nine years to the cause we are defending. Today he swears to defend the national interests; and I, who have led you in combat, and whose loyalty to the cause of independence you cannot doubt, am the first to acknowledge Señor Iturbide as the chief of the national armies. Long live independence! Long live liberty!" From that moment everyone acknowledged the new leader as general-in-chief, and he now dispatched to the viceroy a declaration of his views and of the step he had taken. Iturbide sent General Guerrero to seize a convoy of Manila merchants bound for the port of Acapulco with 750,000 pesos; he himself set out for the town of Iguala, forty leagues to the south of Mexico City, where he published the plan which I have outlined. The Spanish troops began to leave Iturbide's division, but the old patriot detachments began to reassemble everywhere to come to his aid.

All Mexico was set in motion by the declaration of Iguala. Apodaca immediately ordered General Liñán to march with a large division against the new leader, to strangle in its cradle this movement of threatening aspect. But this was not the tumultuous cry of Dolores of 1810; the viceroy was not dealing with a disorderly mob of Indians armed with sickles, stones, and slings and sending up the confused cry "Death to the *gachupines*, long live Our Lady of Guadalupe!" He faced a chief of proven bravery, who, supported by the national will and followed by trained leaders, spoke in the name of the people and demanded rights with which they were well acquainted. ... While this chief was making extraordinary progress in the provinces, the capital was in the greatest confusion. The Spaniards residing in Mexico City attributed the successes of Iturbide to the ineptitude of Apodaca, who a short time before, according to them, had been the peacemaker, the tutelar angel, of New Spain; now this same man suddenly turned into an imbecile incapable of governing. They stripped him of his command, replacing him with the Brigadier Francisco Novella. This fact alone suffices to give an idea of the state of confusion in which the last defenders of the Spanish government found themselves. Reduced to the support of the expeditionary forces, the dying colonial regime immediately revealed the poverty of its resources. ... Of the 14,000 soldiers sent to defend the imaginary rights of the Spanish government, only 6,000, at the most, remained—and what could they do against the Mexican army, which numbered at least 50,000 men? Arms, discipline—everything was equal except morale, which naturally was very poor among troops suddenly transported to a strange land, two thousand leagues away from their country. ... Was it surprising that they surrendered, in view of the situation? Thus, between the end of February, when Iturbide proclaimed his plan of Iguala, and September 27, when he made his triumphant entry into Mexico City, only six months and some days elapsed, with no other memorable actions than the sieges of Durango, Querétaro, Cordóba, and the capital. It was at this time that General Antonio López de Santa-Anna, then lieutenant-colonel, began to distinguish himself.

10. A LETTER TO DOM PEDRO

Brazil made a swift and relatively bloodless transition to independence. The immediate causes of separation were the efforts of a jealous Portuguese cortes to revoke the liberties and concessions won by Brazil since 1808 and to force the departure of the prince regent, Dom Pedro, from Brazil. Messages of support from juntas throughout the country, such as the following from the junta of São Paulo, encouraged the prince to defy the Lisbon government and to issue his famous "fico" (I remain).

We had already written to Your Royal Highness, before we received the extraordinary gazette of the 11th instant, by the last courier: and we had hardly fixed our eyes on the first decree of the Cortes concerning the organization of the governments of the provinces of Brazil, when a noble indignation fired our hearts: because we saw impressed on it a system of anarchy and slavery. But the second, in conformity to which Your Royal Highness is to go back to Portugal, in order to travel *incognito* only through Spain, France, and England, inspired us with horror.

They aim at no less than disuniting us, weakening us, and in short, leaving us like miserable orphans, tearing from the bosom of the great family of

---

Maria Graham, *Journal of a Voyage to Brazil, and Residence There, During Part of the Years 1821, 1822, and 1823*, London, 1824, pp. 174–177.

Brazil the only common father who remained to us, after they had deprived Brazil of the beneficent founder of the kingdom, Your Royal Highness's august sire. They deceive themselves; we trust in God, who is the avenger of injustice; He will give us courage, and wisdom.

If, by the 21st article of the basis of the constitution, which we approve and swear to because it is founded on universal and public right, the deputies of Portugal were bound to agree that the constitution made at Lisbon could then be obligatory on the Portuguese resident in that kingdom; and, that, as for those in the other three parts of the world, it should only be binding when their legitimate representatives should have declared such to be their will: How dare those deputies of Portugal, without waiting for those of Brazil, legislate concerning the most sacred interest of each province, and of the entire kingdom? How dare they split it into detached portions, each isolated, and without leaving a common centre of strength and union? How dare they rob Your Royal Highness of the lieutenancy, granted by Your Royal Highness's august father, the King? How dare they deprive Brazil of the privy council, the board of conscience, the court of exchequer, the board of commerce, the court of requests, and so many other recent establishments, which promised such future advantage? Where now shall the wretched people resort in behalf of their civil and judicial interests? Must they now again, after being for twelve years accustomed to judgment at hand, go and suffer, like petty colonists, the delays and chicanery of the tribunals of Lisbon, across two thousand leagues of ocean, where the sighs of the oppressed lose all life and all hope? Who would credit it, after so many bland, but deceitful expressions of reciprocal equality and future happiness!

In the session of the 6th of August last, the deputy of the Cortes, Pereira do Carmo, said (and he spoke the truth) that the constitution was the social compact, in which were expressed and declared the conditions on which a nation might wish to constitute itself a body politic: and that the end of that constitution is the general good of each individual who is to enter into that social compact. How then dares a mere fraction of the great Portuguese nation, without waiting for the conclusion of this solemn national compact, attack the general good of the principal part of the same, and such is the vast and rich kingdom of Brazil; dividing it into miserable fragments, and, in a word, attempting to tear from its bosom the representative of the executive power, and to annihilate by a stroke of the pen, all the tribunals and establishments necessary to its existence and future prosperity? This unheard-of despotism, this horrible political perjury, was certainly not merited by the good and generous Brazil. But the enemies of order in the Cortes of Lisbon deceive themselves if they imagine that they can thus, by vain words and hollow professions, delude the good sense of the worthy Portuguese of both worlds.

Your Royal Highness will observe that, if the kingdom of Ireland, which makes part of the United Kingdom of Great Britain, besides that it is infinitely small compared to the vast kingdom of Brazil, and is separated from England but by a narrow arm of the sea, which is passed in a few hours, yet possesses a governor-general or viceroy, who represents the executive power of the King of the United Kingdom, how can it enter the head of anyone who is not either profoundly ignorant, or rashly inconsiderate, to pretend, that the vast kingdom of Brazil, should remain without a centre of activity, and without a representative of the executive power; and equally without a power to direct our troops, so as that they may operate with celerity and effect, to defend the state against any unforeseen attack of external enemies, or against internal disorders and factions, which might threaten public safety, or the reciprocal union of the province!

We therefore entreat Your Royal Highness with the greatest fervour, tenderness, and respect to delay your return to Europe, where they wish to make you travel as a pupil surrounded by tutors and spies: We entreat you to confide boldly in the love and fidelity of your Brazilians, and especially of your Paulistas, who are all ready to shed the last drop of their blood, and to sacrifice their fortunes, rather than lose the adored Prince in whom they have placed their well-founded hopes of national happiness and honour. Let Your Royal Highness wait at least for the deputies named by this province, and for the magistracy of this capital, who will as soon as possible present to Your Highness our ardent desires and firm resolutions; and deign to receive them, and to listen to them, with the affection and attention, which your Paulistas deserve from you.

May God preserve your Royal Highness's august person many years.

15

↬

DICTATORS AND REVOLUTIONS

AFTER WINNING its independence Spanish America began a long uphill struggle to achieve stable, democratic government. The new states lacked a strong middle class, experience in self-government, and the other advantages with which the United States began its independent career. The result was an age of violence, of alternate dictatorship and revolution. Its symbol was the *caudillo*, or "strong man," whose power was always based on force, no matter what the constitutional form.

Whatever their methods, the *caudillos* generally displayed some regard for republican ideology and institutions. Political parties, usually called Conservative and Liberal, were active in most of the new states. Conservatism drew its main support from the landed aristocracy, the church, and the military; liberalism attracted the merchants, provincial landowners, and professional men of the towns. Regional conflicts often cut across the lines of social cleavage, complicating the political picture.

As a rule the Conservatives regarded with sympathy the social arrangements of the colonial era and favored a highly centralized government; the Liberals, inspired by the success of the United States, advocated a federal form of government, guarantees of individual rights, lay control of education, and an end to special privileges for the clergy and the military. Neither party displayed much interest in the problems of the landless, debt-ridden peasantry who formed the majority of almost every nation.

After the middle of the nineteenth century a growing trade with Europe helped to stabilize political conditions in Latin America. The new economic order demanded peace and continuity in government. Old party lines dissolved as Conservatives adopted the "positivist" dogma of science and progress, while Liberals abandoned their concern with constitutional methods and civil liberties in favor of an interest in material prosperity. A new type of "progressive" *caudillo*—Díaz in Mexico, Núñez in Colombia, Guzmán Blanco in Venezuela—symbolized the politics of acquisition. The cycle of dictatorship and revolution continued in many lands, but the revolutions became less frequent and less devastating.

As the century drew to a close, in a number of countries dissatisfied middle-class and laboring groups combined to form parties, called Radical or Democratic, that challenged the traditional domination of political affairs by the landed aristocracy. But the significance of this movement, like that of the small socialist groups that arose in Argentina and Chile in the 1890s, still lay in the future.

1. THE AGE OF VIOLENCE

"There is no good faith in America," wrote Bolívar in 1829, "nor among the nations of America. Treaties are scraps of paper; constitutions, printed matter; elections, battles; freedom, anarchy; and life, a torment." Many Spanish American observers echoed Bolívar's cry of despair during the chaotic half-century that followed independence. A fiery Chilean liberal, Francisco Bilbao (1823–1865), subjected republican government in Latin America to a penetrating critique in his essay America in Danger, *written in 1862.*

The conquest of power is the supreme goal. This leads to the immoral doctrine that "the end justifies the means. ..." But since there are constitutional provisions that guarantee everyone his rights, and I cannot violate them, I invoke the system of "preserving the form."

If the Constitution declares: "Thought is free," I add: "within the limits established by law"—and since the law referred to is not the constitutional provision but one that was issued afterwards, I inscribe in it the exceptions of Figaro. "Thought is free," but there can be no discussion of dogma or exposition of systems that attack morality. And who is to judge? A commission or jury named in the last analysis by the authorities. And we have the colonial "censorship" reestablished under the guise of the freest institution of all, the jury. Sublime victory of duplicity! "But the form has been preserved."

The electoral power is the only power exercised by the "sovereign people," and it exercises this power not to make the laws but to select the persons who will make them. Very well. The majority vote, then is the expression ... of the popular will.

That is the basis of republican power, and that is why free and legitimate elections establish the legitimacy of power.

Francisco Bilbao, *La América en peligro*, Santiago de Chile, 1941, pp. 34–40. (Excerpt translated by the editor.)

The election is free, it is said; but what if I control the election returns? What if I, the established power, name the inspector of the election returns, if the law permits one to vote twenty times a day in the same election? What if I dominate the elections and frighten my opponents away with impunity?

What happens then? Why, the government is perpetuated in office, and the popular will is flouted and swindled.

But "the form has been preserved," and long live free elections!

"The domicile is inviolable," but I violate it, adding: "save in the cases determined by law." And the "cases" are determined in the last analysis by the party in power.

"The death penalty in political cases is abolished," but I shoot prisoners because I consider that these are not "political cases"; and since I am the infallible authority I declare that these political prisoners are bandits, and "the form has been preserved."

The Executive can be accused before the Chamber of Deputies and is subject to impeachment for one year after leaving office.

But that Chamber has been selected by me, and functions for one year after my departure. The persons who must judge me are my employees, my *protégés*, my creatures, my accomplices. Will they condemn me? No. Nor will they dare to accuse me. I am vindicated, and the "form" has saved me. Montt smiles over the bodies of his eight thousand victims.[1]

"The press is free." But I name the jury, and, backed by the authority of that free institution, I can accuse, harass, persecute; I can silence free speech. Then there reigns, absolute and sovereign, the opinion of one party. I spread the shroud of infamy over the corpse of the vanquished and cry: "The press is free!"

All liberal publicists, it can be said, accept the doctrine of "the separation of powers," as indispensable for the safety of the Republic.

But if the Executive has the power to name the judges; if the Executive participates in the framing of the laws; if the Executive can use the electoral law to name the members of Congress, what remains, in the last analysis, of the famous separation of powers?

"The guarantees established by this constitution cannot be suspended." But if I have the power to declare a province or the Republic in a state of siege, authorized to do so, as in Chile, by a "Council of State" appointed by the President, what security can a citizen have?

This miserable Machiavellianism has "preserved the forms" at the cost of plunging Chile into bloodshed and reaction for a space of thirty years.

There is discussion, the press is free; citizens come together, for they have the right of assembly; an enlightened public opinion almost unanimously clamors for reforms; preparations are made for elections that will bring to power representatives of the reform movement; and then the Executive Power declares the province or the Republic in a state of siege, and the suspended guarantees soar over the abyss of "legal" dictatorship and constitutional despotism!

And then? Either resignation or despair, or civil war, etc., etc. Then revolution raises its terrible banner, and blood flows in battles and on scaffolds. Respect for law and authority is lost, and only force holds sway, proclaiming its triumph to be that of liberty and justice. ...

We have seen that our republican constitutions bear in themselves the germ of "legal despotism," a monstrous association of words that well describes the prostitution of the law. And since despotism, being "legal," is vindicated, the result is that the sentiment of justice is erased from the consciences of men.

Its place is taken by sophistry, duplicity, and intrigue, used to win power at all cost, for power legitimizes everything. ...

Experience proves that in the legal combat of the parties the party in power always gains the victory. Experience shows that the party that conducts itself loyally is swindled and routed. What can be the result of this state of affairs? That justice is forgotten, and success becomes justice. To win, then, is the supreme desideratum.

Then the debased conscience alters even the countenances of men, and their words, in the expression of Talleyrand, serve only "to mask their thought."

Then chaos emerges. Words change their meaning, the tongues of men become as twisted as serpents, their speech grows pompous and hollow, the language of the press is like the tinsel thrown on a grave to adorn "a feast of worms," and the prostitution of the word crowns the evolution of the lie.

The conservative calls himself a progressive.

The liberal protests that he is a loyal Catholic.

The Catholic swears by liberty.

The democrat invokes dictatorship, like the rebels in the United States, and defends slavery.

The reactionary asserts that he wants reform.

The educated man proclaims the doctrine that "all is for the best in the best of all possible worlds."

The "civilized man" demands the extermination of the Indians or of the gauchos.[2]

The "man of principles" demands that principles yield to the principle of the public good. There is proclaimed, not the sovereignty of justice, presiding over the sovereignty of the people, but the sovereignty of "the end"—which legitimizes every "means."

The absolutist proclaims himself the savior of society.

And if it governs with *coups d'état*, states of siege, or permanent or transitory dictatorships, while the constitutional guarantees are flouted, mocked, or suppressed, the party in power will tell you: civilization has triumphed

over barbarism, authority over anarchy, virtue over crime, truth over the lie.
...

We have behind us a half century of independence from Spain. How many years of true liberty have any of the new nations enjoyed?

That is difficult to say; it is easier to reckon the years of anarchy and despotism that they have endured.

Shall Paraguay be the "model" with its forty years of dictatorship?

Or shall it be the Argentine Republic, with its provincial and national dictatorships, culminating in the twenty-year tyranny of Rosas?

And who knows what is to come?

Shall it be Chile, beginning with the dictatorship of O'Higgins and continuing with an intermittent dictatorship of thirty consecutive years?

Shall it be Bolivia, with its terrifying succession of sanguinary dictatorships?

Shall it be Peru, which has had more dictators than legal presidents?

Shall it be Ecuador, with its twenty years of the dictatorship of Flores?

Shall it be New Granada? And there one almost finds the exception, but Obando, the liberal legal president, was "overthrown for being a dictator."

Shall it be Venezuela, with its twenty years of Monagas?

Shall it be the little republics of Central America, and even Mexico? But this will suffice.

And these dictatorships have proclaimed all the principles.

The *pelucones*,[3] the conservatives, the reds, the liberals, the democrats, the Unitarians, the Federalists, all have embraced dictatorship. With the best of intentions the parties genially proclaim: "dictatorship in order to do good."

That is to say: despotism in order to secure liberty.

Terrible and logical contradiction!

2. FACUNDO: BARBARIAN *CAUDILLO*

The caudillo *appeared in many guises. A common type in the first period after independence was the barbarian chieftain, whose rule represented dictatorship in its crudest, most lawless form. A specimen of this breed was Juan Facundo Quiroga, master under Juan Manuel Rosas of the Argentine province of San Juan and the terrible hero of a memorable book by Domingo Faustine Sarmiento (1811–1888).*

D. F. Sarmiento, *Life in the Argentine Republic in the Days of the Tyrants: Or Civilization and Barbarism*, translated by Mrs. Horace Mann, New York, 1868, pp. 76–90.

Facundo, as he was long called in the interior, or General Don Facundo Quiroga, as he afterwards became, when society had received him into its bosom and victory had crowned him with laurels, was a stoutly built man of low stature, whose short neck and broad shoulders supported a well-shaped head, covered with a profusion of black and closely curling hair. His somewhat oval face was half buried in this mass of hair and an equally thick black, curly beard, rising to his cheek-bones, which by their prominence evinced a firm and tenacious will. His black and fiery eyes, shadowed by thick eyebrows, occasioned an involuntary sense of terror in those on whom they chanced to fall, for Facundo's glance was never direct, whether from habit or intention. With the design of making himself always formidable, he always kept his head bent down, to look at one from under his eyebrows, like the Ali Pacha of Monovoisin. The image of Quiroga is recalled to me by the Cain represented by the famous Ravel troupe, setting aside the artistic and statuesque attitudes, which do not correspond to his. To conclude, his features were regular, and the pale olive of his complexion harmonized well with the dense shadows which surrounded it.

The formation of his head showed, not withstanding this shaggy covering, the peculiar organization of a man born to rule. ... Such natures develop according to the society in which they originate, and are either noble leaders who hold the highest place in history, ever forwarding the progress of civilization, or the cruel and vicious tyrants who become the scourges of their race and time.

Facundo Quiroga was the son of an inhabitant of San Juan, who had settled in the Llanos of Lo Rioja, and there had acquired a fortune in pastoral pursuits. In 1779, Facundo was sent to his father's native province to receive the limited education, consisting only of the arts of reading and writing, which he could acquire in its schools. After a man has come to employ the hundred trumpets of fame with the noise of his deeds, curiosity or the spirit of investigation is carried to such an extent as to scent out the insignificant history of the child, in order to connect it with the biography of the hero: and it is not seldom that the rudiments of the traits characteristic of the historical personage are met amid fables invented by flattery. ...

Many anecdotes are now in circulation relating to Facundo, many of which reveal his true nature. In the house where he lodged, he could never be induced to take his seat at the family table; in school he was haughty, reserved, and unsocial; he never joined the other boys except to head their rebellious proceedings or to beat them. The master, tired of contending with so untamable a disposition, on one occasion provided himself with a new and stiff strap, and said to the frightened boys, as he showed it to them, "This is to be made supple upon Facundo." Facundo, then eleven years old, heard this threat, and the next day he tested its value. Without having learned his lesson, he asked the headmaster to hear it himself, because, as he said, the assistant was unfriendly to him. The master complied with the request. Facundo made one mistake, then two, three, and four; upon which the master used his strap upon him. Facundo, who had calculated everything, down to the weakness of the chair in which the master was seated, gave him a buffet, upset him on his back, and, taking to the street in the confusion created by this scene, hid himself among some wild vines where they could not get him out for three days. Was not such a boy the embryo chieftain who would afterwards defy society at large? ...

Facundo reappears later in Buenos Aires, where he was enrolled in 1810 as a recruit in the regiment of Arribeños, which was commanded by General Ocampo, a native of his own province, and afterwards president of Charcas. The glorious career of arms opened before him with the first rays of the sun of May; and doubtless, endowed with such capacity as his, and with his destructive and sanguinary instincts, Facundo, could he have been disciplined to submit to civil authority and ennobled in the sublimity of the object of the strife, might some day have returned from Peru, Chile, or Bolivia, as a General of the Argentine Republic, like so many other brave gauchos who began their careers in the humble position of a private soldier. But Quiroga's rebellious spirit could not endure the yoke of discipline, the order of the barrack, or the delay of promotion. He felt his destiny to be to rule, to rise at a single leap, to create for himself, without assistance, and in spite of a hostile and civilized society, a career of his own, combining bravery and crime, government and disorganization. He was subsequently recruited into the army of the Andes, and enrolled in the Mounted Grenadiers. A lieutenant named Garcia took him for an assistant, and very soon desertion left a vacant place in those glorious files. Quiroga, like Rosas, like all the vipers that have thriven under the shade of their country's laurels, made himself notorious in after-life by his hatred for the soldiers of Independence, among whom both the men above named made horrible slaughter.

Facundo, after deserting from Buenos Aires, set out for the interior with three comrades. A squad of soldiery overtook him; he faced the pursuers and engaged in a real battle with them, which remained undecided for awhile, until, after having killed four or five men, he was at liberty to continue his journey, constantly cutting his way through detachments of troops which here and there opposed his progress, until he arrived at San Luis. He was, at a later day, to traverse the same route with a handful of men to disperse armies instead of detachments, and proceed to the famous citadel of Tucumán to blot out the last remains of Republicanism and civil order.

Facundo now reappears in the Llanos, at his father's house. At this period occurred an event which is well attested. Yet one of the writers whose manuscripts I am using, replies to an inquiry about the matter, "that to the extent of his knowledge Quiroga never attempted forcibly to deprive his parents of money," and I could wish to adopt this statement, irreconcilable as it is with unvarying tradition and general consent. The contrary is shocking to relate. It is said that on his father's refusal to give him a sum of money which he had demanded, he watched for the time when both parents were taking an afternoon nap to fasten the door of the room they occupied, and to set fire to the straw roof, which was the usual covering of the building of the Llanos![4]

But what is certain in the matter is that his father once requested the governor of La Rioja to arrest him in order to check his excesses, and that Facundo, before taking flight from the Llanos, went to the city of La Rioja, where that official was to be found at the time, and coming upon him by surprise, gave him a blow, saying as he did so, "You have sent, sir, to have me arrested. There, have me arrested now!" On which he mounted his horse and set off for the open country at a gallop. At the end of a year he again showed himself at his father's house, threw himself at the feet of the old man whom he had used so ill, and succeeded amid the sobs of both, and the son's assurances of his reform in reply to the father's recriminations, in reestablishing peace, although on a very uncertain basis.

But no change occurred in his character and disorderly habits; races, gambling parties, and expeditions into the country were the occasions of new acts of violence, stabbings, and assaults on his part, until he at length made himself intolerable to all, and rendered his own position very unsafe. Then a great thought which he announced without shame got hold of his mind. The deserter from the Arribeños regiment, the mounted grenadier who refused to make himself immortal at Chacabuco or Maipú, determined to join the montonera of Ramírez, the off shoot from that led by Artigas, whose renown for crime and hatred for the cities on which it was making war, had reached the Llanos, and held the provincial government in dread. Facundo set forth to join those buccaneers of the pampa. But perhaps the knowledge of his character, and of the importance of the aid which he would give to the destroyers, alarmed his fellow provincials, for they informed the authorities of San Luis, through which he was to pass, of his infernal design. Dupuis, then (1818) governor, arrested him, and for some time he remained unnoticed among the criminals confined in the prison. This prison of San Luis, however, was to be the first step in his ascent to the elevation which he subsequently attained. San Martín had sent to San Luis a great number of Spanish officers of all ranks from among the prisoners taken in Chile. Irritated by their humiliations and sufferings or thinking it possible that the Spanish forces might be assembled again this party of prisoners rose one day and opened the doors of the cells of the common criminals, to obtain their aid in a general escape. Facundo was one of these criminals, and as soon as he found himself free from prison, he seized an iron bar of his fetters, split the skull of the very Spaniard who had released him, and passing through the group of insurgents, left a wide path strewn with the dead. Some say that the weapon he employed was a bayonet, and that only three men were killed by it. Quiroga, however, always talked of the iron bar of the fetters, and of fourteen dead men. This may be one of the fictions with which the poetic imagination of the people adorns the types of brute force they so much admire; perhaps the tale of the iron bar is an Argentine version of the jaw-bone of Samson, the Hebrew Hercules. But Facundo looked upon it as a crown of glory, in accordance with his idea of excellence, and whether by bar or bayonet, he succeeded, aided by other soldiers and prisoners whom his example encouraged, in suppressing the insurrection and reconciling society to himself by this act of bravery, and placing himself under his country's protection. Thus his name spread everywhere, ennobled and cleansed, though with blood, from the stains which had tarnished it.

Facundo returned to La Rioja covered with glory, his country's creditor: and with testimonials of his conduct, to show in the Llanos, among gauchos, the new titles which justified the terror his name began to inspire; for there is something imposing, something which subjugates and controls others in the man who is rewarded for the assassination of fourteen men at one time. ...

Something still remains to be noticed of the previous character and temper of this pillar of the Confederation. An illiterate man, one of Quiroga's companions in childhood and youth, who has supplied me with many of the above facts, sends me the following curious statements in a manuscript describing Quiroga's early years: "His public career was not preceded by the practice of theft; he never committed robbery even in his most pressing necessities. He was not only fond of fighting, but would pay for an opportunity, or for a chance to insult the most renowned champion in any company. He had a great aversion to respectable men. He never drank. He was very reserved from his youth, and desired to inspire others with awe as well as with fear, for which purpose he gave his confidants to understand that he had the gift of prophecy, in short a soothsayer. He treated all connected with him as slaves. He never went to confession, prayed, or heard mass; I saw him once at mass after he became a general. He said of himself that he believed in nothing." The frankness with which these words are written prove their truth. ...

Facundo is a type of primitive barbarism. He recognized no form of subjection. His rage was that of a wild beast. The locks of his crisp black hair, which fell in meshes over his brow and eyes, resembled the snakes of Medusa's head. Anger made his voice hoarse, and turned his glances into dragons. In a fit of passion he kicked out the brains of a man with whom he had quarreled at play. He tore off both the ears of a woman he had lived with, and had promised to marry, upon her asking him for thirty dollars for the celebration of the wedding; and laid open his son Juan's head with an axe, because he could not make him hold his tongue. He violently beat a beautiful young lady at Tucumán, whom he failed either to seduce or to subdue, and exhibited in all his actions a low and brutal yet not a stupid nature, or one wholly without lofty aims. Incapable of commanding noble admiration, he delighted in exciting fear; and this pleasure was exclusive and dominant with him to the arranging [of] all his actions so as to produce terror in those around him, whether it was society in general, the victim on his way to execution, or his own wife and children. Wanting ability to manage the machinery of civil government, he substituted terror for patriotism and self sacrifice. Destitute of learning, he surrounded himself with mysteries, and pretended to a foreknowledge of events which gave him prestige and reputation among the commonalty, supporting his claims by an air of impenetrability, by natural sagacity, an uncommon power of observation, and the advantage he derived from vulgar credulity.

The repertory of anecdotes relating to Quiroga, and with which the popular memory is replete, is inexhaustible; his sayings, his expedients, bear the stamp of an originality which gives them a certain Eastern aspect, a certain tint of Solomonic wisdom in the conception of the vulgar. Indeed, how does Solomon's advice for discovering the true mother of the disputed child differ from Facundo's method of detecting a thief in the following instances:

An article had been stolen from a band, and all endeavors to discover the thief had proved fruitless. Quiroga drew up the troop and gave orders for the cutting of as many small wands of equal length as there were soldiers; then, having had these wands distributed one to each man, he said in a confident voice, "The man whose wand will be longer than the others tomorrow morning is the thief." Next day the troop was again paraded, and Quiroga proceeded to inspect the wands. There was one whose wand was, not longer but shorter than the others. "Wretch!" cried Facundo, in a voice which overpowered the man with dismay, "it is thou!" And so it was; the culprit's confusion was proof of the fact. The expedient was a simple one; the credulous gaucho, fearing that his wand would really grow, had cut off a piece of it. But to avail one's self of such means, a man must be superior in intellect to those about him, and must at least have some knowledge of human nature.

Some portions of a soldier's accoutrements having been stolen and all inquiries having failed to detect the thief, Quiroga had the troops paraded and marched past him as he stood with crossed arms and a fixed, piercing, and terrible gaze. He had previously said, "I know the man," with an air of assurance not to be questioned. The review began, many men had passed, and Quiroga still remained motionless, like the statue of Jupiter Tonans or the God of the Last Judgment. All at once he descended upon one man, and said in a curt and dry voice, "Where is the saddle?" "Yonder, sir," replied the other, pointing to a thicket. "Ho! four fusileers!" cried Quiroga. What revelation was this? that of terror and guilt made to a man of sagacity.

On another occasion, when a gaucho was answering to charges of theft which had been brought against him, Facundo interrupted him with the words, "This rogue has begun to lie. Ho, there! a hundred lashes!" When the criminal had been taken away, Quiroga said to someone present, "Look you, my master, when a gaucho moves his foot while talking, it is a sign he is telling lies." The lashes extorted from the gaucho the confession that he had stolen a yoke of oxen.

At another time he was in need of a man of resolution and boldness to whom he could intrust a dangerous mission. When a man was brought to him for this purpose, Quiroga was writing; he raised his head after the man's presence had been repeatedly announced, looked at him and returned to his writing with the remark, "Pooh! that is a wretched creature. I want a brave man and a venturesome one!" It turned out to be true that the fellow was actually good for nothing.

Hundreds of such stories of Facundo's life, which show the man of superior ability, served effectually to give him a mysterious fame among the vulgar, who even attribute superior powers to him.

3. REFORM BY REVOLUTION

Mexico and Argentina were the main battlefields of the struggle between liberalism and conservatism in nineteenth-century Latin America. The movement to which Mexican historians give the name La Reforma, *led by men of such intellectual and moral stature as Benito Juárez and Melchor Ocampo, represented an ambitious effort to transform backward Mexico into a progressive middle-class state. The movement's climactic moment was the adoption of the Constitution of 1857, which ushered in the War of the Reform, which was swiftly followed by the French Intervention. Justo Sierra (1848–1912), brilliant Mexican historian and educator, records the movement of events between the establishment of Santa Anna's last dictatorship and the outbreak of the War of the Reform.*

Juárez, retired to private life by the triumph of the ill-omened Plan of Jalisco, expected from the moment of Santa Anna's coup a policy of persecution and repression of all liberals. He was not surprised, therefore, by his arrest in May 1853, in Etla, nor by his confinement to Jalapa, nor by his violent abduction from a friend's house in Puebla by the wrathful hand of the famous Pepe Santa Anna (who considered it an honor to play the part of a bravo in the service of his father, and who lived the life of a sultan in the sacred city of clericalism), nor by his imprisonment for some days in the horrible dungeons of San Juan de Ulúa, nor by his exile. …

In the middle of 1853 Juárez was in New Orleans. There he found a group of outstanding men who awaited with unshakable faith the end of Santa Anna's tyranny, and who thought constantly about the means of securing the triumph of reform ideas in Mexico. All respected Juárez; his reputation as a governor of unwavering integrity had preceded him in that beehive of ideas and noble ambitions. But the salient personality was that of Ocampo, man of thought and action, agriculturist, naturalist, economist, a public man from

Justo Sierra, *Obras completas*, vol. 12, *Juárez, su obra y su tiempo*, Mexico, 1948, pp. 87–113. (Excerpt translated by the editor.)

love for the public good, with no other ambition than that of doing something for his country. To comprehend the moral grandeur of this disciple of Rousseau and student of Proudhon it is necessary to take into account his absolute disinterest. There is no longer any mystery about the irregular but exalted origin of Señor Ocampo; the mistress of the Hacienda of Pateo bequeathed to him her property ... and the fortune thus acquired he employed for the good of others, improving labor conditions in the regions over which his influence extended and converting his estates into experimental stations for the acclimation of useful plants, for trials of new cultures, and for the production of exquisite botanical specimens. Into this as in all else Ocampo put all the warmth of his passionate soul. A friend of his told me that on one occasion, in the garden of the little station of La Tejería on the railroad from Veracruz to Mexico City, then just begun (this was in 1859), he found the illustrious reformer kneeling with tearful emotion before some splendid Yucatan lilies in bloom. ...

The influence, the ascendancy of Ocampo over the New Orleans group was immense; it was evident in the case of Juárez—nor could it be otherwise. Both men had firm liberal convictions; both had been governors, one in Oaxaca and the other in Michoacán; both had advocated peace and condemned revolutions, joining in support of an honest Federalism and the honorable and moderate administrations of Herrera and Arista; both had bitterly denounced the unprincipled and equivocal revolt of Jalisco. But while Juárez as governor had made concessions to the Church in an obvious effort to placate it, Ocampo had thrown down the gauntlet to the clergy in the matter of parochial obventions. In New Orleans the aspect of things changed; there, assisted by Mata and Ponciano Arriaga, they hammered out the party program on the basis of which the Constitution of '57 would soon be formed. Complete emancipation of the civil power—and not only complete but definitive; to wit: radical destruction of the power of the Church in all that did not concern its strictly spiritual influence, by suppressing the *fueros* and religious communities, and nationalizing church property. The North American scene fortified and confirmed the libertarian ideas of the exiles; they saw clearly the close relation between liberty and prosperity. On one occasion Juárez and Mata walked together along the levee of New Orleans. The future president was astounded by the immense commercial activity he saw taking place in the course of a single hour at that point on the banks of the Mississippi. "The explanation of all this," said Mata, "is a single freedom—that of internal trade; abolish our *alcabalas*, and our prosperity would be as great as theirs." These were the lessons that the Anglo-Saxon world taught the exiles. They helped to keep their convictions firm; all their hatred for the tutelage of the clergy had as its complement a devotion to freedom of conscience, incompatible with the authority of the Church. Hence their lively desire, not only to renew in a future constitution the great charter of individual liberties which the ecclesiastical domination nullified, but to find a way of making them effective by making all administrative action subject to judicial review (*Juicio de Amparo*). ...

The tyranny of Santa Anna had succeeded in unifying the once formless Liberal Party, which worked as a solid phalanx to overthrow the despot; and one could say that the time arrived when all conspired against him—even the bureaucrats, even the soldiers. Sensible conservatives, convinced that Santa Anna's dictatorship was not a government nor an institution, but a vice, viewed without grief, though not without misgivings, the fall of the despot. Their hope was Comonfort—and the man who was the chief, the soul of the revolution of Ayutla was truly capable of inspiring hope. ...

The Revolution of Ayutla, converted into the War of the Reform and then into a struggle with an exotic monarchy based on foreign aid, constitutes the Great Mexican Revolution of our period of independence. It was the work of our national Jacobins, a great and good work. But it began slowly, thanks to the tenacious hopes of Comonfort, who believed that he could avoid war. To aid him in this effort, while keeping alive the promises of the revolution, was the work of Juárez, named by President Álvarez Secretary of Justice and Ecclesiastical Affairs in his coalition cabinet. ...

Juárez rendered a great service to the ideals of the *puros*[5] by acceding to the request of General Álvarez and remaining in the ministry when Ocampo left. Without him the reform measures would have been indefinitely postponed, until the time—for which Comonfort yearned—when all would agree to them. Comonfort's apprehensions were well founded, to be sure; he feared that the clergy would convert a political conflict into a religious question, and that the civil strife would be transformed into a religious war. Truly a calamity that would completely ruin the country! Juárez, no writer of books replete with projects of vengeance and social catastrophe, but a responsible lawgiver, well understood that to convince Comonfort of the convenience of a great reform measure, albeit attenuated, was better and more feasible than to draft a complete code of transcendent reforms that would have died still-born without the aid of Comonfort's victorious sword. Juárez thus rendered a major service to the liberal cause.

This happened after General Álvarez, named provisional president by the junta assembled in Cuernavaca, lost hope that the Congress would assemble in Dolores and decided to come to Mexico City, establishing himself with his ministry in the capital of the Republic. Juárez and Comonfort were the two representative figures of that government.

The Juárez Law organized the administration of justice and set in it the foundation stone of the Reform. Excitement ran high; the conservative newspapers raised the cry of alarm against every effort at innovation; the liberal newspapers with equal insistence demanded a program of struggle, not of peace (no one thought of peace except Comonfort, the Minister of War). General Álvarez thought only of retirement; he urged that Comonfort, his inevitable and necessary successor as provisional president of the Republic, should not be embarrassed by a reform law proclaimed even before the meeting of the Constituent Assembly. In November, 1855, appeared the Juárez Law; Article 42 suppressed the special tribunals (there still were many—of commerce, the treasury, etc.) and exempted from this suppression the ecclesiastical and military tribunals. But they were only to continue temporarily. The first (until the passage of a law that should definitively regulate the ecclesiastical privileges) would have jurisdiction only over common offenses of members of the clergy. Civil affairs were to be under the exclusive control of the common courts. Moreover, ecclesiastics were given the right to reject trial by ecclesiastical courts of a penal character. With respect to the military, something very similar was provided; jurisdiction over civil affairs was also taken away from the military courts, and it was retained only for purely military or mixed offenses, and only if the responsible parties were soldiers.

A true daughter of the Revolution of Ayutla, the Juárez Law was a revolutionary law; given by an authority which had the revolution for its sole source of power, it declared that as a general (federal) law the states could neither modify nor change it. The uproar was great but had been anticipated; Comonfort made common cause with his cabinet; and the protests of the bishop who sought to have the point referred to the judgment of the Pope and the Supreme Court (which objected to an organic court law framed without consulting its opinion) did not deter Juárez from putting the law into immediate effect. In a short time it had assumed the character of a *res adjudicata*, as the jurists say, and so it has been down to our time, because the conquests of the Reform had this peculiarity: once established in law they have been converted into enduring facts; they have been enlarged, but never altered or revoked. ...

The clergy and the army felt the blow of the formidable adversary that rose before them and prepared for combat. Their protests and complaints were the agitated whirlpool that shows on the surface; below was the danger, the permanent conspiracy, the conspiracy that united in intimate contact soldiers and churchmen, that now expanded until it became international, now convulsively contracted to center about the curacies of the mountains, the larger towns, from which sparks constantly flew up, presaging the imminent conflagration. Could the immense popularity of Comonfort quench the fire? Many believed it—but not the bishops, not the heads of Santa Anna's favorite corps, not honest but hopelessly deluded conservatives like Haro and Tamáriz, not the young officers swollen with ambition and bravado like Osollo and Miramón, not Father Miranda.

In December, 1855, General Álvarez resigned and named Comonfort as his substitute; that is why he was called the substitute president. The great doctrine of conciliation was to be put fully into practice. Ocampo had insisted that it would fail; but if it succeeded, revolution would be replaced by a normal evolution, and peace, blessed peace, would be a fact. ... Yet war raised its threatening visage everywhere: a rising in Guanajuato, where Doblado, an individual of many expedients and few scruples, had raised the banner of Comonfort with no plausible motive, was crushed by a piece of paper—a very sensible, worthy, and biting letter from Juan Álvarez—and Doblado bowed his head; the mountains of Querétaro burned with religion and *fueros;* the indefatigable Mejía was on the war path; Uraga sought to take advantage of the discontent of the "old army" with the Juárez Law; Jalisco and the whole North were restless, and bands of outlaws roamed the country in search of spoil. In the Bajío the situation was returning to normal. In Puebla, on the other hand, there broke out a blaze which had to be isolated and smothered before it could spread to the entire country.

The Bishop of Puebla (Don Pelagio Antonio de Labastida y Dávalos, future Archbishop of Mexico) had acquired by his merits, fine intelligence, and social graces, an immense prestige in Puebla society. From the highest to the lowest, that society lived in the Church and by the Church; the aristocratic families were all petrified, embalmed in devotion and mysticism about this canon, that curate, such-and-such a friar, and at the foot of one or another image of Christ or of Our Lady. Life there consisted of pious exercises, of saints' festivals, of processions, of novenas. As for mortal sin, a microbe which pullulated at the bottom of the most angelic beatitudes, it did not show on the transparent surface of that life, as clear as water; high-powered microscopes had not yet come into use. And the populace, vicious and dirty, but much less so than the rabble of the capital, only lived by what it obtained from the convents, by the crumbs of the Church, by the protection and charity of the priests.

And that is why all that concerned the Church touched them to the quick, reached the innermost recesses of their beings, of their interests, of their loves and hates. And with slight shades of difference it was the same everywhere in the Republic, with the exception of some coastal towns, where the salty sea air diluted somewhat the influence of the clergy. The bishops, like Señor Labastida, publicly affirmed that they did not mix in political affairs, that they reproved armed revolts, and that they counseled obedience to the government as long as its dispositions were not in conflict with the Catholic conscience; and what they affirmed they doubtless believed and practiced. This was least of all true, however, of the Bishop of Puebla, who shortly after the events that unfolded in his diocese in the year 1856 showed very plainly what an ardent politician he was. ...

Given the national character, however, even if the bishops had not prompted or desired the revolt it inevitably followed from their protests. These protests affirmed that the Church was suffering grave offenses, unjust attacks that were causing irreparable injury to national Catholicism; the Juárez Law ... they proclaimed to be a rude assault on the most obvious rights of the Church. But how could the clergy resist the attack except by defending themselves, and what better defense than to overthrow the government? All this was clear, and the Catholic populace proceeded with more logic than its prelates, though with less understanding of the situation.

Taking advantage of the feverish atmosphere of Puebla, large groups of the permanent army—on whose support Comonfort, clinging tenaciously to his illusions, still counted—false to their commitments, to their honor, to their oaths, seized the city, which all the spokesmen for military and clerical reaction had made their headquarters. The president determined to atone for his naiveté by striking a hard blow, during the very days when the Constituent Assembly was gathering. The campaign, very prudently and energetically directed, once again placed in bold relief the distinguished soldierly traits of the leader of the Revolution of Ayutla: a desire to spare his soldiers' blood, respect for the advice of experts in the technical aspects of war, and a serene bravery that gave him a kind of heroic aura. The soldiers of the national guard adored him.

Once master of Puebla, where the populace, ever ready to cheer the victor, gave him a friendly reception, the President returned to Mexico City in a better position to sustain two great struggles—one against the clergy, ordering the confiscation of the property of the bishopric of Puebla, and the second against the permanent army, humiliating, degrading, and irritating the officer class. Bishop Labastida, who resisted the orders of the government, was exiled; it was a sound political measure. Clearly, in a city like Puebla the funds of the Church, with or without the wishes of its head, only served to foment conspiracies; it was necessary to deprive the fire of oil, and to give the proof of energy for which the Liberal Party loudly clamored by putting a hand on the most rebellious of the prelates. Away to Europe to conspire went the bishop; he conspired furiously, incessantly, from that moment. Thereby he revealed what lay at the bottom of his heart; Comonfort had not been mistaken.

The degradation of the officers, on the other hand, produced contrary effects. These men thought of nothing but revenge, of settling scores, and they thought about it with pleasure. The future General Sostenes Rocha, who at the time was a petty officer in the Sappers and who was one of the officers stripped of their ranks and confined to towns south of Puebla, relates in his colorful memoirs (as yet unpublished) the ruses to which all these culprits, who naturally regarded themselves as heroes, resorted in order to keep alive. ... One by one they succeeded in escaping from their confinements, drawn to the counter-revolutionary center in Mexico City or called to military posts in certain states (as happened with Rocha), and it is clear that the stages of their flight were from convent to convent, and from curacy to curacy. It would have been better for the country and for Comonfort to have shot three or four of the principal officers and to have imprisoned the rest for two or three years; such energy would have spared the country a great deal of suffering. The writer of these lines cannot forget that as a student, representing the School of Law, he went to plead with President Juárez to spare the life of a great impenitent revolutionary, captured almost *in flagrante delicto* while assaulting a treasure-train under government convoy. The prisoner had a name intimately linked to a glorious date. "It is well," replied Señor Juárez to my petition, "I had already decided to pardon him. But do not forget, and let your friends know, that by pardoning a man of this kind, who thinks that politics signifies disorders and barrack-room revolts, I am sentencing to death many hundreds of innocent people." Perhaps these words could be applied to the perennial clemency of Comonfort. ...

The Juárez Law was the lighted fuse, and its first result the explosion of Puebla, a tremendous rising with its train of sanguinary combats, a costly and difficult campaign, the military degradation of the old army, the confiscation of Church property in that priestly city, and the exile of Bishop Labastida. Comonfort gave constant proofs of his private religiosity, as if to match the professions of obedience made by the clergy each time it questioned the right of the government to subject all social classes to its jurisdiction. ... The attitude taken by the Church, its decision to struggle for its privileges by appealing to religious sentiments (exciting them not against the government but in favor of the Church) gave the sessions of Congress a certain solemn and religious tone. When one heard Zarco, Mata, and Arriaga speak of the fundamental conformity between the Constitution and the Gospel, when they discussed religious tolerance, the Constituent Assembly resembled an assembly of Puritans on the eve of the great English religious wars. All this raised to the highest pitch the political fever of the country. And the press with its immense clamor echoed the tribune and the pulpit; the time of Religious Wars appeared to be drawing near for Mexico. Comonfort meditated—that is to say, he vacillated. Later he sent an agent to Rome in search of reconciliation and an agreement; as might be expected, the Pope would not receive him. Pius IX, a great heart filled with all the fire of apostolic zeal, a warrior and martyr by nature but of small intelligence when compared with his successor, dismissed the Mexican minister from the pontifical throne with the same wrathful and tremulous hand that hurled anathema against the Reform. Very logical, perhaps, but infinitely imprudent and improvident. Heads grew heated in Mexico on receipt of this news, and when an undecided person had made up his mind, he was no longer a simple friend of the civil power but a resolute enemy of the Church. To this attitude of the Pontiff must be ascribed the anti-Catholic tone of the reform press and the iconoclastic and "War-to-the-friar" character of the Three Years' War. ...

Comonfort, no Mirabeau, Napoleon, or Cromwell, yielded here and yielded there, and believed that he was advancing in zigzag fashion; in reality he was zigzagging into the abyss. With the sword of Damocles over the head of the press (the Lafragua Law), he was stern toward the conservative journals and excessively timid with the revolutionary ones. ... He attached the property of the bishopric of Puebla and exiled the bishop; this show of energy frightened the high clergy, but some months later its effect was nullified

by the suspension of the process of seizure. ... The suppression of the
Company of Jesus caused a profound uproar, intensified by the feverish excitement with which the people followed the discussions of the Constituent
Congress. ... When the Bishop of Puebla, awaiting in Havana the possible
revocation of his exile, learned of the suppression of the Company, he understood that the fight had just begun, and departed for Rome.

Arriving in Spain, he found even greater cause for despair. The Lerdo Law
had been promulgated in June (1856). With a severe preamble that summa-
rized the economic reasons justifying the law, and which could be reduced to
the necessity of putting in circulation an almost unproductive mass of wealth,
the minister of the treasury set forth in articles as clear as his character and
intellect the conditions under which disentail should take place. The law left
in the hands of the actual possessors the estates or urban properties belonging to civil (philanthropic, public educational) or ecclesiastical corporations.
Calculating the value of the property by the rent or lease at 6 percent, the resulting sum should constitute a mortgage on the disentailed estate, which was
to pay 6 percent interest to the corporation. This species of mortgage could
on no condition result in a return of the estate to the corporation, but under
certain conditions enumerated in the law it could be put up at auction. ...

During the days that Congress discussed the article of the draft constitution that related not to freedom of worship but to religious toleration, the
capital, and before long the whole Republic, lived in an atmosphere saturated
with the electric tension that presages combat. All upper-class Mexico, the
governing classes *en masse*, arose as one man and presented to the Congress
eloquent memorials pleading that it vote down the Satanic article. This work
of the devil, claimed to be a source of evils compared with which the Deluge
was child's play, declared: "There shall not be promulgated any law or order
that prohibits or impedes the exercise of any religious cult; but since the
Roman, Catholic, Apostolic Faith has been the exclusive religion of the
Mexican people, the Congress of the Union shall seek to protect it by means
of just and prudent laws, providing they do not injure the interests of the
people or the rights of national sovereignty." The authors of the project
could be criticized for not having dared to carry their thinking to its logical
conclusion by proclaiming complete freedom of worship, without any privileged religion, as a consequence of the separation of Church and State.
However, the tremendously excited state of public opinion probably intimi-
dated them—not personally, to be sure, for Arriaga, Mata, Zarco had the
courage of their convictions, but as a commission of the fundamental code
they believed that only their project had any chance of success. They were
mistaken; it was badly beaten in the breach, and under the formidable pressure of the government and popular opinion (the bourgeoisie and the illiterate class), the article disappeared from the draft. ...

The constitution was voted; the great promise of Ayutla, in the words of
the members, was fulfilled. Trembling with horror, the society that lived in

the shadow of the belfry saw the ancient Gómez Farías, the founder of the reform government, take an oath of loyalty to the new law on bended knees, his
hand on the Bible; then the whole country was summoned to take the same
oath. The Church, with some hesitation (some bishops and ecclesiastical dignitaries swore loyalty), because it understood that upon its attitude depended
peace or war, loosened the folds of its long mantle and chose war, like the
Roman senator in Carthage. The nation, placed under a kind of interdict,
displayed nervousness, almost epilepsy. Some refused to swear; others re-
tracted their oaths; all who swore fell under the ban of excommunication.
The crisis was at the very base of society; in the family; in the home; in the
terrible anguish of the public official wavering between his religious duty and
the prospect of misery; in the sobs, the appeals, the reproaches of mothers
and wives; in the homes of the liberals themselves. ...

Comonfort, terribly moved by this social crisis, daily confronted by the
mute and tearful pleading of his mother, was content at the time he took the
oath to ask for immediate reform of the constitution: a really senseless action.
His indecision was immense. One idea had taken hold of his brain: *it was impossible to govern with the constitution*. The Executive, he believed, was made so
impotent in the face of the action of a unitary Congress and the right of intervention—which could be incessant—of the judicial power, that only an
uninterrupted succession of extraordinary powers could enable the President
to govern; and these powers, painful experience told him, were usually denied, so that authority might remain in revolutionary hands.

Yet special powers were indispensable. The whole interior of the country
was up in arms. Puebla witnessed a new revolt, a new siege, a new victory of the
government, a new waste of blood and money that exhausted the resources of
the treasury at a time when the foreign horizons darkened. The question of the
Spanish claims became increasingly urgent and alarming. ... In fine, the foreign intervention that Paredes had asked for, that Santa Anna had demanded,
was in the air of the Mexican Gulf. Money and more money was needed to
conjure away the storm. Where was it to come from? The proceeds of the tax
on disentails were negligible or nil; the clergy had stopped with its interdict a
movement that might have saved both it and the government of Comonfort.

[Under these conditions elections are held for the first congress and president under the Constitution of 1857, and for the members of the Supreme
Court, whose president was also to be Vice President. Comonfort is elected
President; Juárez becomes his Vice President. Comonfort's requests for special powers and a revision of the Constitution are rejected by the Liberal majority in the Congress. In November, 1857, General Félix Zuloaga, an instrument of conservative military and clerical groups, "pronounces" for a
Comonfort dictatorship, dismisses Congress, and arrests Juárez.—B.K.]

The Plan of Tacubaya repealed the Constitution of 1857 as unsuited to the
usages and manners of the country, placed dictatorial powers in the hands of

Comonfort, and referred to a future constituent assembly whose decisions were to be reviewed by the people (*ad referendum*). Comonfort adhered to the Plan two days later. Never did a more modest Caesar, or one with less confidence in himself and his future, pronounce "the die is cast"; he pronounced it almost inaudibly. This man, who was no longer at peace with himself, was to bring peace to the Republic!

Zuloaga was a conservative four-square; if he had joined the Liberal ranks it was from personal loyalty to Comonfort and nothing more. Now, brought to the fore, he was surrounded by counter-revolutionaries who hemmed him in, brought pressure upon him. What did they want? The Constitution no longer existed. There was talk of a grouping or coalition of certain states of the interior, of forces that came and went, of Parodi, of Degollado, of Arteago, of Doblado. True, the Archbishop had declared for the Plan of Tacubaya, and the priest Valdovinos had blessed it. The Church had joyfully "pronounced" in its favor! But this was not enough; the Council of Conservatives, *moderados*, and *puros* formed by Comonfort no longer gave satisfaction. He must go on to destroy the coalition, and above all and before all else he must repeal the Juárez Law; and above all and right away he must repeal the Lerdo Law, the law of disentail; he must return everything to the Church—but quickly, quickly!

The unhappy Comonfort said: "But this law has created new interests, new rights, new positions, and all under my pledge, my signature, my protection!" "What would you do if you were in my position?" the President asked the conservative leader José M. Cuevas. "Repeal the Lerdo Law and put myself in the hands of the conservatives," replied the lawyer. "And if you were in my place, with my background, my ideas, would you do it?" the anxious Comonfort asked. "Not I," replied the reactionary gentleman. "Thanks," Comonfort concluded, "I shall never do it." The next day Zuloaga's brigade "Re-pronounced," disavowing Comonfort as President. And Comonfort, gathering the few forces left to him, declared the Constitution of 1857 re-established. It was a tragic retraction. Twenty days later, standing on the stern of an American ship as it steamed out of Veracruz, he watched the Mexican coasts recede in the distance, and his political dreams merged with the clouds, with the shadows. ...

On the day of Zuloaga's second "pronouncement" (January 11, 1858), Juárez was released by order of Comonfort. The two old friends probably did not speak to each other. Juárez could not recognize Comonfort as President, despite his repentance. Comonfort had accused, judged, and sentenced himself. Juárez, president of the Supreme Court, replaced him, according to the Constitution. It was Comonfort's last service to the liberal cause, though not to his country, for which he died obscurely six years later. The effort to achieve reform by way of persuasion and clemency had failed. The tremendous Three Years' War had begun.

4. ROADS TO THE FUTURE

Another important struggle between Spanish American liberalism and conservatism took place in Argentina between 1830 and 1852. Against the tyranny of Juan Manuel Rosas, representing the narrow interests and views of the great cattlemen of the province of Buenos Aires, the cultured youth of the capital rose in romantic but ineffective revolt. In 1852 Rosas fell, buried under the weight of the many enmities, domestic and foreign, that his policies had aroused. On the eve of the convention of 1853, summoned to draft a new constitution for Argentina, a book by Juan Bautista Alberdi (1810–1884) appeared, entitled Bases and Points of Departure for the Political Organization of the Argentine Republic, *which strongly influenced the work of the delegates. The following selections from this book illustrate the optimistic, "civilizing," and pragmatic temper of Argentine liberalism in the age of Alberdi, Mitre, and Sarmiento.*

Our youth should be trained for industrial life, and therefore should be educated in the arts and sciences that would prepare them for industry. The South American type of man should be one formed for the conquest of the great and oppressive enemies of our progress: the desert, material backwardness; the brutal and primitive nature of this continent.

We should therefore endeavor to draw our youth away from the cities of the interior, where the old order with its habits of idleness, conceit, and dissipation prevails, and to attract them to the coastal towns so that they may obtain inspiration from Europe, which extends to our shores, and from the spirit of modern life.

The coastal towns, by their very nature, are better schools than our pretentious universities. ...

Industry is the grand means of promoting morality. By furnishing men with the means of getting a living you keep them from crime, which is generally the fruit of misery and idleness. You will find it useless to fill the minds of youths with abstract notions about religion if you leave them idle and poor. Unless they take monastic vows they will be corrupt and fanatical at the same time. England and the United States have arrived at religious morality by way of industry; Spain has failed to acquire industry and liberty by means of religion alone. Spain has never been guilty of irreligion, but that did not save her from poverty, corruption, and despotism. ...

The railroad offers the means of righting the topsy-turvy order that Spain

---

Juan Bautista Alberdi, *Bases y puntos de partida para la organización política de la República Argentina*, Buenos Aires, 1951, pp. 62–63, 85–88, 90–92, 240–242. (Excerpts translated by the editor.)

established on this continent. She placed the heads of our states where the feet should be. For her ends of isolation and monopoly this was a wise system; for our aims of commercial expansion and freedom it is disastrous. We must bring our capitals to the coast, or rather bring the coast into the interior of the continent. The railroad and the electric telegraph, the conquerors of space, work this wonder better than all the potentates on earth. The railroad changes, reforms, and solves the most difficult problems without decrees or mob violence.

It will forge the unity of the Argentine Republic better than all our congresses. The congresses may declare it "one and indivisible," but without the railroad to connect its most remote regions it will always remain divided and divisible, despite all the legislative decrees.

Without the railroad you will not have political unity in lands where distance nullifies the action of the central government. Do you want the government, the legislators, the courts of the coastal capital to legislate and judge concerning the affairs of the provinces of San Juan and Mendoza, for example? Bring the coast to those regions with the railroad, or vice versa; place those widely separated points within three days' travel of each other, at least. But to have the metropolis or capital a twenty days' journey away is little better than having it in Spain, as it was under the old system, which we overthrew for presenting precisely this absurdity. Political unity, then, should begin with territorial unity, and only the railroad can make a single region of two regions separated by five hundred leagues.

Nor can you bring the interior of our lands within reach of Europe's immigrants, who today are regenerating our coasts, except with the powerful aid of the railroads. They are or will be to the life of our interior territories what the great arteries are to the inferior extremities of the human body: sources of life. ...

The means for securing railroads abound in these lands. Negotiate loans abroad, pledge your national revenues and properties for enterprises that will make them prosper and multiply. It would be childish to hope that ordinary revenues may suffice for such large expenditures; invert that order, begin with expenditures, and you will have revenues. If we had waited until we had sufficient revenues to bear the cost of the War of Independence against Spain, we would still be colonists. With loans we obtained cannons, guns, ships, and soldiers, and we won our independence. What we did to emerge from slavery, we should do to emerge from backwardness, which is the same as slavery; there is no greater title to glory than civilization.

But you will not obtain loans if you do not have national credit—that is, a credit based on the united securities and obligations of all the towns of the state. With the credits of town councils and provinces you will not secure railroads or anything notable. Form a national body, consolidate the securities of your present and future revenues and wealth, and you will find lenders who will make available millions for your local and general needs; for if you lack money today, you will have the means of becoming opulent tomorrow. Dispersed and divided, expect nothing but poverty and scorn. ...

The great rivers, those "moving roads," as Pascal called them, are yet another means of introducing the civilizing action of Europe into the interior of our continent by means of her immigrants. But rivers that are not navigated do not, for practical purposes, exist. To place them under the exclusive domination of our poor banners is to close them to navigation. If they are to achieve the destiny assigned to them by God of populating the interior of the continent, we must place them under the law of the sea—that is, open them to an absolute freedom of navigation. ...

Let the light of the world penetrate every corner of our republics. By what right do we maintain our most beautiful regions in perpetual brutality? Let us grant to European civilization what our ancient masters denied. In order to exercise their monopoly, the essence of their system, they gave only one port to the Argentine Republic; and we have preserved the exclusivism of the colonial system in the name of patriotism. No more exclusion or closure, whatever be the pretext that is invoked. No more exclusivism in the name of the Fatherland. ...

What name will you give a land with 200,000 leagues of territory and a population of 800,000? A desert. What name will you give the constitution of that country? The constitution is a desert. Very well, the Argentine Republic is that country—and whatever its constitution, for many years it will be nothing more than the constitution of a desert.

But what constitution best fits a desert? One that will help to make it disappear: one that will enable it in the shortest possible time to cease being a desert and become a populated country. This, then, should and must be the political aim of the Argentine constitution and in general of all South American constitutions. The constitutions of unpopulated countries can have no other serious and rational end, at present and for many years to come, than to give the solitary and abandoned countryside the population it requires, as a fundamental condition for its development and progress.

Independent America is called upon to complete the work begun and left unfinished by the Spain of 1450. The colonization, the settlement of this world, new to this day despite the three hundred years that have passed since its discovery, must be completed by the sovereign and independent American states. The work is the same; only its authors are different. At that time Spain settled our lands; today we settle them ourselves. All our constitutions must be aimed at this great end. We need constitutions, we need a policy of creation, of settlement, of conquest of the solitude and the desert. ...

The end of constitutional policy and government in America, then, is essentially economic. In America, to govern is to populate.

5. A MEXICAN RADICAL:
PONCIANO ARRIAGA

Nineteenth-century conservatives and liberals gave little or no attention in their programs to the land problem—the growing concentration of landownership, with all its negative economic, social, and political consequences. In Mexico, however, where the problem of land monopoly had become increasingly acute, and where a social revolutionary tradition existed since the time of Hidalgo, left-wing liberals raised the land question in the Constitutional Convention of 1856–1857. The chief spokesman for this small band of Mexican radicals was Ponciano Arriaga. In a speech remarkable for the modernity of its socioeconomic ideas, Arriaga pungently described the effects of the land monopoly but offered a relatively moderate solution: The state should seize and auction off uncultivated estates more than fifteen square leagues in extent. Arriaga's prophetic insistence that the agrarian reform must sooner or later prevail was to be verified by the events of the Mexican Revolution of 1910.

One of the most deeply rooted evils of our country—an evil that merits the close attention of legislators when they frame our fundamental law—is the monstrous division of landed property.

While a few individuals possess immense areas of uncultivated land that could support millions of people, the great majority of Mexicans languish in a terrible poverty and are denied property, homes, and work.

Such a people cannot be free, democratic, much less happy, no matter how many constitutions and laws proclaim abstract rights and beautiful but impracticable theories—impracticable by reason of an absurd economic system.

There are Mexican landowners who occupy (if one can give that name to a purely imaginary act) an extent of land greater than the area of some of our sovereign states, greater even than that of one or several European states.

In this vast area, much of which lies idle, deserted, abandoned, awaiting the arms and labor of men, live four or five million Mexicans who know no other industry than agriculture, yet are without land or the means to work it, and who cannot emigrate in the hope of bettering their fortunes. They must either vegetate in idleness, turn to banditry, or accept the yoke of a landed monopolist who subjects them to intolerable conditions of life.

How can one reasonably expect these unhappy beings to escape from their condition of abject serfs through legal channels, or hope that the magic power of a written law will transform them into free citizens who know and defend the dignity and importance of their rights?

Francisco Zarco, *Historia del congreso estraordinario constituyente de 1856 y 1857*, Mexico, 1857, 2 vols., I, pp. 546–555. (Excerpt translated by the editor.)

We proclaim ideas and forget realities; we launch on discussions of rights and turn away from stubborn facts. The constitution should be the law of the *land*, but we do not regulate or even examine the state of the *land*. ...

How can a hungry, naked, miserable people practice popular government? How can we proclaim the equal rights of men and leave the majority of the nation in conditions worse than those of helots or pariahs? How can we condemn slavery in words, while the lot of most of our fellow citizens is more grievous than that of the black slaves of Cuba or the United States? When will we begin to concern ourselves with the fate of the proletarians, the men we call Indians, the laborers and peons of the countryside, who drag the heavy chains of serfdom established not by Spanish laws—which were so often flouted and infringed—but by the arbitrary mandarins of the colonial regime? Would it not be more logical and honest to deny our four million poor Mexicans all share in political life and public offices, all electoral rights, and declare them to be things, not persons, establishing a system of government in which an aristocracy of wealth, or at most of talent, would form the basis of our institutions?

For one of two things is inevitable: either our political system will continue to be dominated for a long time to come by a *de facto* aristocracy—no matter what our fundamental laws may say—and the lords of the land, the privileged caste that monopolizes the soil and profits by the sweat of its serfs, will wield all power and influence in our civil and political life; or we will achieve a reform, shatter the trammels and bonds of feudal servitude, bring down all monopolies and despotisms, end all abuses, and allow the fruitful element of democratic equality, the powerful element of democratic sovereignty—to which alone authority rightfully belongs—to penetrate the heart and veins of our political institutions. The nation wills it, the people demand it; the struggle has begun, and sooner or later that just authority will recover its sway. The great word "reform" has been pronounced, and it is vain to erect dikes to contain those torrents of truth and light. ...

Is it necessary, in an assembly of deputies of the people, in a congress of representatives of that poor, enslaved people, to prove the unjust organization of landed property in the Republic, and the infinite evils that flow from it? ... In the realm of a purely ideal and theoretical politics, statesmen discuss the organization of chambers, the division of powers, the assignment of jurisdictions and attributes, the demarcation of sovereignties, and the like. Meanwhile other, more powerful men laugh at all that, for they know they are the masters of society, the true power is in their hands, they exercise the real sovereignty. With reason the people think that constitutions die and are born, governments succeed each other, law codes pile up and grow ever more intricate, "pronouncements" and "plans" come and go, but after all those changes and upheavals, after so much disorder and so many sacrifices, no good or profit comes to the masses who shed their blood in the civil wars, who swell the ranks of the armies, who fill the jails and do forced labor on the public works, who, in fine, suffer all the misfortunes of society and enjoy none of its benefits. ...

With some honorable exceptions, the rich landowners of Mexico (who rarely know their own lands, palm by palm), or the administrators or major-domos who represent them, resemble the feudal lords of the Middle Ages. On his seignorial land, with more or less formalities, the landowner makes and executes laws, administers justice and exercises civil power, imposes taxes and fines, has his own jails and irons, metes out punishments and tortures, monopolizes commerce, and forbids the conduct without his permission of any business but that of the estate. The judges or officials who exercise on the hacienda the powers attached to public authority are usually the master's servants or tenants, his retainers, incapable of enforcing any law but the will of the master.

An astounding variety of devices are employed to exploit the peons or tenants, to turn a profit from their sweat and labor. They are compelled to work without pay even on days traditionally set aside for rest. They must accept rotten seeds or sick animals whose cost is charged to their miserable wages. They must pay enormous parish fees that bear no relation to the scale of fees that the owner or majordomo has arranged beforehand with the parish priest. They must make all their purchases on the hacienda, using tokens or paper money that do not circulate elsewhere. At certain seasons of the year they are assigned articles of poor quality, whose price is set by the owner or major-domo, constituting a debt which they can never repay. They are forbidden to use pastures and woods, firewood and water, or even the wild fruit of the fields, save with the express permission of the master. In fine, they are subject to a completely unlimited and irresponsible power.

6. A DIFFERENT MODEL OF ECONOMIC DEVELOPMENT: BALMACEDA'S PROGRAM FOR CHILE

The formula for Argentine development advocated by Alberdi (see selection 4 in this chapter), with its stress on opening the country to European capital, commerce, and immigrants, may be described as the classic nineteenth-century developmental model and was accepted by most Latin American countries. That model, which flourished from about 1870 to 1914, came to be based on the exchange of a few staples, foodstuffs and raw materials for European and North American finished goods. Such exchange brought greater political stability and some prosperity to the area, but in the long run it created serious problems of dependency (neocolonialism) and underdevelopment. This model was not, however, the only possible or inevitable model for the area. In Paraguay, between 1811 and 1866, a state-directed program of autonomous economic development turned Paraguay into one of the most progressive and prosperous states in South America. This progress was destroyed by the terrible Paraguayan War of 1865–1870, which pitted Paraguay against Argentina and Brazil. In Chile, in the 1880s, President José Manuel Balmaceda offered a nationalistic program for a many-sided economic development that included the promotion of native industry and the Chileanization of the British-dominated nitrate industry. His program provoked a revolt by conservative forces, supported by British interests, that led to Balmaceda's defeat and suicide in 1891. The following excerpts from his speeches suggest the main thrust of his program.

On the Need to Develop National Industry

Economic developments of the last few years prove that, while maintaining a just balance between expenditures and income, we can and should undertake productive national works that will nourish, more especially, our public education and our national industry.

And since I speak of our national industry, I must add that it is weak and uncertain because of lack of confidence on the part of capital and because of our general resistance to opening up and utilizing its beneficial currents.

If, following the example of Washington and the great republic of the North, we preferred to consume our national production, even if it is not as finished and perfect as the foreign production; if the farmer, the miner, and the manufacturer constructed their tools and machines whenever possible in our country's workshops; if we broadened and made more varied the production of our raw materials, processing and transforming them into objects useful for life or personal comfort; if we ennobled industrial labor, increasing wages in proportion to the greater skill of our working class; if the state, while maintaining a balance between revenues and expenditures, devoted a portion of its resources to the protection of national industry, nourishing and supporting it during its first trials; if the state, with its resources and legislation, and all of us together, collectively and singly, applied ourselves to producing more and better and consuming what we produce, then a more vigorous sap would circulate through the industrial organism of the Republic, and increased wealth and well-being would give us the possession of that supreme good of an industrious and honorable people: the capacity to live and clothe ourselves by our own unaided efforts.

On the Concentration of
Chile's Nitrate Wealth in Foreign Hands

The extraction and processing of nitrate must be left to the free competition of the industry itself. But the question of the privately owned and govern-

Fernando Silva Vargas, ed., *El pensamiento de Balmaceda*, Santiago de Chile, Editora Nacional Gabriola Mistral, 1974, pp. 67–68, 84–88. (Excerpts translated by the editor.)

ment-owned nitrate properties is a matter for serious meditation and study. The private properties are almost all foreign owned, and effectively concentrated in the hands of individuals of a single [British] nationality. It would be preferable that these properties belonged to Chileans as well; but if our national capital is indolent or fearful, we must not be surprised if foreign capital fills, with foresight and intelligence, the void in the progress of this region [Tarapaca] left by the neglect of our compatriots. ...

The importance of nitrate in agriculture and industry and the growing tempo of its production counsel the legislator and the statesman not to delay the solution of the problem, and to resolve it by effectively protecting the interests of our nationals. It is true that this must not be done in such a way as to effectively stifle free competition and production of nitrate in Tarapaca, but neither should we allow that vast and rich area to become a mere foreign enclave. We cannot ignore the very real and serious fact that the peculiar nature of the industry, the manner in which the nitrate properties came into being, the absorption of small properties by foreign capital, and even the temper of the races that dispute the dominion of that vast and fertile region, demand a special legislation, based on the nature of things and the special needs of our economic and industrial existence. This question has such profound consequences for the future that upon its solution will in large part depend the development of our private wealth, today removed from that fecund center of labor and general prosperity.

16

~

BRAZIL: FROM EMPIRE

TO REPUBLIC

INDEPENDENT BRAZIL made a relatively easy and rapid transition to a stable political order. To the troubled reign of Dom Pedro I (1822–1831) and the stormy years of the Regency (1831–1840) succeeded the long and serene reign of Dom Pedro II (1840–1889). Brazil's ruling class of great landowners deliberately sacrificed "liberty with anarchy for order and security," in the words of Professor Manchester, and vested the young emperor, called to rule at the age of fifteen, with virtually absolute power. The generally upward movement of Brazilian economic life and the tact, wisdom, and firmness of the emperor contributed to the success with which the system functioned for half a century.

Only one serious foreign crisis—the exhausting Paraguayan War (1865–1870)—marred Dom Pedro's reign. Economic and social change dominated the period. As the sugar-growing northeast and its patriarchal slave society declined because of competition from foreign sugars, coffee-raising São Paulo, which was gradually shifting to the use of free immigrant labor, gained in prosperity and importance. The rise (after 1850) of banks, corporations, stock exchanges, and other institutions of capitalism further weakened the position of the old-style plantation aristocracy.

The new business and landowning groups, employing free labor, grew increasingly impatient with the highly centralized imperial régime and the dominant influence of slave-owning *fazendeiros* within it. Rising antislavery agitation was accompanied by a slower growth of republican propaganda. Popular pressure for emancipation became irresistible. In 1888 the Brazilian Parliament, with the approval of the emperor's daughter, passed a law abolishing slavery. One year later, weakened by the defection of a large portion of the rural aristocracy, by quarrels with the church, and by discontent on the part of the army, the empire was overthrown, Dom Pedro departed into exile, and the victorious rebels proclaimed Brazil a federative republic.

1. DOM PEDRO II:
A POLITICAL PORTRAIT

Historians and biographers of Dom Pedro II (1825–1891) have written sufficiently concerning his amiable, democratic traits, his patronage of arts and letters, and his scholarly tastes and accomplishments. But Dom Pedro's best claim to fame is the skill with which he guided the Brazilian ship of state for almost half a century. Joaquim Nabuco (1849–1910), famous Brazilian abolitionist, diplomat, and historian, paid tribute to the emperor's political wisdom in his monumental biography of his own statesman-father, first published in 1897.

The commanding figure of the Second Empire was that of the Emperor himself. To be sure, he did not govern directly and by himself; he respected the Constitution and the forms of the parliamentary system. But since he determined the fate of every party and every statesman, making or unmaking ministries at will, the sum of power was effectively his. Cabinets had short and precarious lives, holding office only as long as it pleased the Emperor. Under these conditions there was but one way to govern, and that was in agreement with him. To oppose his plans, his policies, was to invite dismissal. One or another minister might be ready to quit the government and the office on whose duties he had just entered, but cabinets clung to life, and the party imposed obedience to the royal will from love of offices, of patronage. So the ministers passively assented to the role that the Emperor assigned to them. The senate, the council of state, lived by his favor and grace. No leader wished to be "incompatible." He alone represented tradition and continuity in government. Since cabinets were short-lived and he was permanent, only he could formulate policies that required time to mature. He alone could wait, temporize, continue, postpone, sowing in order to reap in due season. Whenever he needed to display his own unquestioned authority he shunted the most important statesmen away from the throne. Olinda, perhaps because he had been a kind of rival to the Crown in 1840, only returned to the government in 1848—to be quickly dismissed—when the Emperor already governed alone, and after Olinda had skillfully served his apprenticeship and no longer put his old political pupil in the shade. Bernardo Pereira de Vascon-

Joaquim Nabuco, *Um estadista do imperio: Nabuco de Araujo, sua vida, suas opiniões, sua Epoca,* São Paulo, 1936, 2 vols., II, pp. 374–385. (Excerpt translated by the editor.)

cellos, who had opposed the proclamation of the Emperor's majority, died in 1850 without ever having been made minister. Honorio Hermeto Carneiro Leão, also ... an opponent of the declaration of Dom Pedro's majority—another independent, a great vassal who bent the knee to no man—was called in 1843 and dismissed in February, 1844. Having these examples before them, younger men learned that without the Emperor's confidence and approval they were nothing. ...

On one point he had strong feelings and was very sensitive: He must not be suspected of having favorites. After completing his political apprenticeship he dispensed with the counsels of Aureliano Coutinho and reduced him to the position of a statesman just as dependent, just as ignorant of the high mysteries of state, as the others. He did not want towering personalities at his side and in his counsels, men who might employ his prestige to govern as if they had power of their own over the nation. He never conceded to any statesman that position of unquestioned leadership that Queen Victoria had to recognize—after parliamentary self government had been perfected in her reign—in Gladstone and Disraeli, for example, as independent leaders of the respective parties, possessing a mutual right to return to head the government. No one but he knew what the next day would bring. He set the course of administration, now steering in one direction, now in another; and only he knew the true course of the ship of state. So it was with the slave question; in 1865 or 1866, when Olinda headed the cabinet, the Emperor made his decision. Olinda opposed him, but Dom Pedro won Nabuco, Saraiva, Paula Souza to his side; in the Conservative camp he had the support of Pimenta Bueno. The Paraguayan War crossed his path, and he yielded, putting off the project. Later, with a more amenable president of the council, Zacharias, he pushed the work in the council of state, entrusting to both parties the framing of the future law. Zacharias, however, fell out with Caxias. The war was a primary interest, Caxias was necessary to its success; Zacharias was sacrificed, and with him the Liberal Party. The Conservative Party came to power with a government headed by Itaborahy. The Emperor now put the slave question aside as secondary, in his opinion, to the war; but as soon as the war had ended, the infallible clock of the Palace of São Christovão struck the hour of emancipation. ...

The work of government was carried on in this fashion; what are the Emperor's wishes, what does the emperor not wish? The statesman who would not adjust to these conditions condemned himself to complete failure. For this reason the advocates of a new idea accomplished nothing until they had awakened the interest of the Emperor and gained his sympathy. Once that was attained, all parties and governments followed the Emperor's lead like an avalanche. So it was with everything, especially in the great question of his reign, slavery; the pronouncements of Rio-Branco in 1871, of Dantas in 1884, of Cotegipe in 1885, only came after Dom Pedro had been won over to their point of view. In 1888 Cotegipe took advantage of the absence of the

Emperor to carry out immediate abolition, but if the Emperor had been in the country he also would have been summoned to solve the problem, though in another way.

His power, however, was a spontaneous, natural phenomenon, the result of our social and political condition. If that power had no check it was not because of the Emperor, but because it was impossible to have free elections with a people like the Brazilian, and because free elections would only have made the electorate more attached to the government, whatever it might be—that is, to the power that had the right to make appointments. That is why his power was indestructible. In effect, there was only one means—short of a republican revolution—of compelling him to surrender his personal power: to confront the omnipotent Crown with independent chambers. But that was just the impossibility; that was the great illusion of the propagandists for direct elections, and afterward of the statesmen who expected direct elections to bring about a regeneration of the representative system. That was the dream of the Liberals of 1868, of Paulino de Souza's Conservatives, and of the Baron of Cotegipe. When, after long resisting the project, the Emperor, who in the end always let himself be conquered—but professing to be only conquered and not convinced—yielded, and Saraiva obtained his direct elections, what were the consequences? That as a result of the first experiment in honest elections anarchy and corruption prevailed everywhere; that the parliament came to reflect the general sickness of the localities—the thirst for jobs and influence, the dependence on the government. ...

The Emperor always exercised his power: (1) within the limits of the Constitution; (2) in accord with the fictions and usages of the English parliamentry system as adapted by our own parties; and (3) yielding always to public sentiment and opinion. "The honor of my reign can only consist in complying with the Constitution which I swore to obey." The distinguishing feature of his government was the sacrament of form; from the day on which his majority was proclaimed to that of his abdication he never abandoned his role of constitutional monarch. Then, too, the progress of affairs in his reign was not his work; he was only the clock, the regulator, that marked the time or gave the rhythm. In matters of politics, to be sure, the minister never proposed and the chambers never approved any measure that he had not sanctioned; it was he who sounded both sides of the channel that was being navigated. But the origin of his inspirations was to be found elsewhere. If everything that was deliberate and personal in his reign reflected the Emperor's directing will and consciousness, the march of events always proceeded ahead of the wishes of the imperial mover or moderator. Every day, everywhere, his individual action was annulled by the action of social forces over whose agents, reactions, and collisions he had no control. ...

The Emperor inspired and directed, but he did not govern. He might check on every nomination, every decree, every word of his ministers, but the reponsibility for their actions was theirs. He rarely intervened in the political and administrative machinery—the parties with their adherents and official hierarchies, their personnel and transactions. He did not even wish to know about the internal life of the parties, nor did he establish direct and personal relations with them, but only with the leaders who one day would be presidents of the council. We have seen how he proceeded with the latter: he always reserved the right to dismiss them when he chose; that right he always possessed. All ministries had their elements of disintegration. He could impede or facilitate the process of dissolution, as he pleased; there was always an anxious opposition party at his orders, awaiting a summons; within the ministerial camp itself there were rivalries to be used; and he always had at hand the instrument of dissolution. Throughout his reign, from 1840 to 1889, all the statesmen who served under him were conscious that their mandates were not final, their positions uncertain and dependent. ... But even if their mandates were precarious, even if they entered upon their duties knowing that the first serious disagreement with the monarch must lead to their dismissal, nevertheless the Emperor scrupulously respected the sphere of ministerial action. Nor could the ministers complain of the observations made by the Emperor in the council, for in his role of devil's advocate he elucidated questions, clarified his nominations, deduced precedents, compared the reports brought to him from all quarters ... , lending to each administration the prestige of his high position and the assistance of his vast experience. At the same time he left to the ministers the political patronage, the distribution of jobs among their partisans, and the administration of affairs, including the realization of the ideas they had advocated while in the opposition. In many branches he hardly intervened at all—in the fields of justice and finance, for example.

That is why the most eminent men of the period were proud to hold those positions and competed for them, despite their uncertain tenure and the qualified nature of their mandates. It was from their number, from a small circle in parliament, that the Emperor always made his choices. He was, in fact, free only to alternate the parties, to pass from one group to the group in opposition, on the same conditions, choosing from what was always a league of chieftains the name that best pleased him at that juncture. Thus they were not royal ministers, creatures of the Palace; they were parliamentary ministers, like those of France in the reign of Louis Philippe, not like those of England in the reign of Queen Victoria. The Emperor could dismiss them, as the electorate dismisses them in the United Kingdom, but aside from this difference—that there was no electoral power capable of sustaining its representatives in the case of an appeal to the country—the ministerial mandate was the same. Yet to aspire to hold office, under existing conditions, was both honorable and legitimate. The Emperor was not to blame for the absence of free elections; the parties were infinitely more responsible for this condition than he, who had almost nothing to do with the abuses that corrupted the elections. The monarch did not degrade his ministers; he respected them, treated them with dignity. As a governor he sought only one glory for himself: to make Brazil a model of liberty among the nations. The truth about his reign is summed up in the epigram attributed to Ferreira Vianna: "The Emperor passed fifty years in maintaining the pretense that he ruled over a free people"—that is, in upholding Brazil's reputation before the world, concealing the general indifference of its citizenry toward public affairs, toward their rights and liberties; in practicing and cherishing the cult of the Constitution as the political divinity of the Empire.

If the Constitution was Brazil's Palladium, Parliament was its Forum; it was for seventy years the center of the political life of the country, the scene of struggles for power and liberty. It was not a great historical theater, to be sure, but Brazilians of the old colonial stocks—whatever the feelings of the new nationalities that may in time replace them—will always regard its ruins with veneration. Nothing would have been impossible there for a true political genius, endowed with real ambition and capable of making his ideals come true; unhappily, we never had a statesman who united to genius the qualities of ambition, independence, and will power. Had one existed, he would have found no obstacle in Dom Pedro II. *He* was not responsible for the degeneration of the political spirit of the chambers, in which once had risen men like Villela Barbosa, Vasconcellos, Alves Branco, and Paula Souza. It is absurd, when one observes that the majority of these men evolved from Conservatives into Liberals, in some cases, and from Liberals into Conservatives, in others, to suppose that it was the Emperor who determined these regular movements of opinion from one to another social pole. He was not the source of that skepticism, or indifference, or political lukewarmness, that replaced the ancient fervor, seriousness, and persistence of the epoch of solid and austere character.

...

As with parliament, so with the council of state. A grand political conception was this council of state, one that even England might envy us, heard in all the great questions, guardian of the political traditions of the Empire, in which the opposition was called to collaborate in the wise government of the country, where the opposition had to reveal its plans, its alternatives, its mode of attacking the great problems whose solution fell to the lot of the ministry. This admirable product of the Brazilian genius, which complemented the other and equally admirable device of the Moderative Power, taken from Benjamin Constant, united about the Emperor the finest political talents of both sides, with all their accumulated experience, whenever it was necessary to confer about some serious public issue. It made the opposition, up to a certain point, a participant in the government of the country, the superintendent of its interests, the depository of the secrets of state.

That was the system of the Empire from 1840 to 1889. Political life went on in the chambers, in the press, in the provinces, as in England—but the parties did not display moderation, would not resign themselves to free elections; and as a result the last word belonged, willynilly, to the power that named the ministers, and not to the chambers from which they came. But the difference was hardly apparent, because the Emperor did not upset situations abruptly or capriciously, being always guided by public opinion or necessity. The fact is that this dual mechanism, monarchical-parliamentary, in which the monarch, as well as parliament, was a director, instead of being a kind of automaton moved by the chambers, ensured the tranquility and security of the country for four generations. Had the Emperor not had supreme direction, had he not been the independent arbiter of the parties, had he been limited to signing the decrees presented to him, had he been helpless to change the situation except through the effect of elections, his reign would very likely have been nothing more than a continuation of the regency or an anticipation of the Republic, and the imperial power, slave and instrument of the oligarchy, would have disappeared in a few years in the whirlpool of factions. Men intellectually superior to the Emperor, governing in his name, statesmen of greater capacity than his own, dispensing with his intervention and accustoming the country to regard the throne as vacant, would only have unleashed the forces of anarchy against themselves—while he, by the sagacious and moderate exercise of his role of constitutional emperor, kept his authority intact for half a century, whereas his father, the founder of the Empire, had only managed to stay in power for nine years, and the three regencies for four, two, and three years. ... In all likelihood the author of this nineteenth-century miracle of the South American politics would have died in the palace of São Christovão and today would be resting in the burial ground of the Ajuda, were it not for the illness that began to weaken his mind in 1887, making him—who wished to appear a sort of philosopher-king, such as José Bonifacio de Andrada dreamed that Dom Pedro I might be, a crowned Benjamin Franklin—timid, almost vexed, to be ruling in America in European fashion.

There was much that was noble about this imperial policy, a policy of always pushing down the road that seemed straight to him, scorning the resistance that must be overcome, heedless of the resentments that might one day cut off his retreat. It was a decided and resolute policy that sought to prevent the formation of *maires du palais*, of personalities that might put him in the shade; that sought to extinguish the old revolutionary foci of the First Empire and of the Regency, military and political; that worked to extirpate feudalism, defiant of justice, superior to the law, an asylum for outlaws; that struck down with one blow the powerful slave traffic; that later carried the Five Years' War to the last stronghold of López in the Aquidaban; that attempted to achieve the gradual extinction of slavery in his realm; that sought to subject the Church to the temporal power. But the inner and profound characteristic of the royal policy was its indifference to the interests of the throne. ...

At bottom, Dom Pedro II had the same attitude toward the throne as Dom Pedro I. Neither would maintain himself in power by bloodshed; they would be emperors only as long as the country wanted them, only as long as *everyone* wanted them; they would not haggle with the people. The one willingly made the sacrifice of May 13, 1822, when he implicitly renounced for love of Brazil the crown of Portugal and its Empire; the other did not regret years of self-abnegation and sacrifice for his country. Deposed, he went into exile, burdened with debts which were nothing compared with the charities that he had provided out of his civil list. And he paid these debts, in what was perhaps the only case of its kind in the history of monarchy, by selling the furniture and jewels of his palace at public auction, leaving to the State his library, his only wealth (except his property in Petropolis), without even disputing ownership of the properties of São Christovão.

The Emperor's persistent policy of indifference toward consequences was thus a policy of tacit renunciation. It was not the policy of a sovereign convinced that the monarchy was necessary to the country and determined to regard it as his primary political interest. If they dismissed him, the fault would not be his; an honorable settlement of this kind would do for him. In one of his notes the Emperor wrote: "If the mistaken conduct of the monarchical parties should give victory to the republicans, what will that prove? The monarch will not on that account cease to be an honest and disinterested man—disinterested in all that does not touch the welfare of his country, which for him cannot exist outside the Constitution."

This voluntary dependence of his on the good will of the country was so strong that, deposed from the throne, he did not once affirm his right to rule by virtue of any of the old pacts—that of the Independence, of the Constitution, of April 7, of his majority, and much less by virtue of his traditional Portuguese right.

His was a policy entirely independent of circumstances, indifferent to the personal consequences of his actions. It did not lean on any class, corporation, or party; it presumed the general good will; it rested on the spirit of progress, on trust in his rectitude, on the movement imparted to society by new reforms, on confidence in the general good sense, on disinterested support that would frustrate the intrigues of private interests and assure the unimpeded progress of the nation. ... If the result should prove the contrary, the royal stoic would resign his throne without a murmur, regretting only for love of Brazil—perhaps his only passion—that he must die in a foreign land, and leaving for posterity to say: *Victrix causa diis placuit, sed victa Catoni.*[1]

2. BLACK SLAVERY UNDER THE EMPIRE

Under the empire, as in colonial times, Black slavery formed the massive base of virtually all of Brazil's significant economic activity. The condition and prospects of the Black people in Brazil aroused the lively interest of foreign visitors. Two North American travelers present a summary view of the situation.

The subject of slavery in Brazil is one of great interest and hopefulness. The Brazilian Constitution recognizes, neither directly nor indirectly, color as a basis of civil rights; hence, once free, the black man or the mulatto, if he possess energy and talent, can rise to a social position from which his race in North America is debarred. Until 1850, when the slave-trade was effectually put down, it was considered cheaper, on the country-plantations, to use up a slave in five or seven years and purchase another, than to take care of him. This I had, in the interior, from intelligent native Brazilians, and my own observation has confirmed it. But, since the inhuman traffic with Africa has ceased, the price of slaves has been enhanced, and the selfish motives for taking greater care of them have been increased. Those in the city are treated better than those on the plantations: they seem more cheerful, more full of fun, and have greater opportunities for freeing themselves. But still there must be great cruelty in some cases, for suicides among slaves—which are almost unknown in our Southern States—are of very frequent occurrence in the cities of Brazil. Can this, however, be attributed to cruelty? The Negro of the United States is the descendant of those who have, in various ways, acquired a knowledge of the hopes and fears, the rewards and punishments, which the Scriptures hold out to the good and threaten to the evil; to avoid the crime of suicide is as strongly inculcated as to avoid that of murder. The North American Negro has, by this very circumstance, a higher moral intelligence than his brother fresh from the wild freedom and heathenism of Africa; hence the latter, goaded by cruelty, or his high spirit refusing to bow to the white man, takes that fearful leap which lands him in the invisible world.

In Brazil everything is in favor of freedom; and such are the facilities for the slave to emancipate himself, and, when emancipated, if he possess the proper qualifications, to ascend to higher eminences than those of a mere free black, that *fuit* will be written against slavery in this Empire before another half-century rolls around. Some of the most intelligent men that I met with in Brazil—men educated at Paris and Coimbra—were of African descent, whose ancestors were slaves. Thus, if a man have freedom, money, and merit, no matter how black may be his skin, no place in society is refused

---

D. P. Kidder and J. C. Fletcher, *Brazil and the Brazilians*, Philadelphia, 1857, pp. 132–138.

him. It is surprising also to observe the ambition and the advancement of some of these men with Negro blood in their veins. The National Library furnishes not only quiet rooms, large tables, and plenty of books to the seekers after knowledge, but pens and paper are supplied to such as desire these aids to their studies. Some of the closest students thus occupied are mulattoes. The largest and most successful printing establishment in Rio—that of Sr. F. Paulo Brito—is owned and directed by a mulatto. In the colleges, the medical, law, and theological schools, there is no distinction of color. It must, however, be admitted that there is a certain—though by no means strong— prejudice existing all over the land in favor of men of pure white descent.

By the Brazilian law, a slave can go before a magistrate, have his price fixed, and can purchase himself; and I was informed that a man of mental endowments, even if he had been a slave, would be debarred from no official station, however high, unless it might be that of Imperial Senator.

The appearance of Brazilian slaves is very different from that of their class in our own country. Of course, the house-servants in the large cities are decently clad, as a general rule; but even these are almost always barefooted. This is a sort of badge of slavery. On the tables of fares for ferry-boats, you find one price for persons wearing shoes (*calçadas*), and a lower one for the *descalças*, or without shoes. In the houses of many of the wealthy Fluminenses you make your way through a crowd of little woolly-heads, mostly guiltless of clothing, who are allowed the run of the house and the amusement of seeing visitors. In families that have some tincture of European manners, these unsightly little bipeds are kept in the background. A friend of mine used frequently to dine in the house of a good old general of high rank, around whose table gambolled two little jetty blacks, who hung about their "pai" [father] (as they called him) until they received their portions from his hands, and that, too, before he commenced his own dinner. Whenever the lady of the house drove out, these pets were put into the carriage, and were as much offended at being neglected as any spoiled only son. They were the children of the lady's nurse, to whom she had given freedom. Indeed, a faithful nurse is generally rewarded by manumission.

The appearance of the black male population who live in the open air is anything but appetizing. Their apology for dress is of the coarsest and dirtiest description. Hundreds of them loiter about the streets with large round wicker baskets ready to carry any parcel that you desire conveyed. So cheaply and readily is this help obtained, that a white servant seldom thinks of carrying home a package, however small, and would feel quite insulted if you refused him a *preto de ganho* to relieve him of a roll of calico or a watermelon. These blacks are sent out by their masters, and are required to bring home a certain sum daily. They are allowed a portion of their gains to buy their food, and at night sleep on a mat or board in the lower purlieus of the house. You frequently see horrible cases of elephantiasis and other diseases, which are doubtless engendered or increased by the little care bestowed upon them.

3. THE ANTISLAVERY IMPULSE

Black slavery was the great domestic issue of Dom Pedro's reign, and after 1880 the abo-
litionist movement assumed the character of a popular crusade. In Joaquim Nabuco, son
of a distinguished liberal statesman of the empire, Brazilian abolitionism found a leader
of towering intellectual and moral stature. His eloquent indictment of slavery, O
Abolicionismo *(1883), made a profound impression in Brazilian intellectual circles. In*
one chapter of this book, Nabuco examines the social and political consequences of slavery
in Brazil.

History knows no example of free government founded on slavery. The
governments of antiquity were not based on the same principles of individual
liberty as modern states; they represented a very different social order. Since
the French Revolution there has been only one notable case of democracy
combined with slavery—the United States; but the southern states of the
Union never were free governments. American liberty, taking the Union as
whole, actually only dates from Lincoln's Proclamation freeing the millions
of slaves in the South. Far from being free, the states south of the Potomac
were societies organized on the basis of the violation of all human rights.
American statesmen like Henry Clay or Calhoun, who compromised or identified themselves with slavery, did not properly calculate the force of the antagonism that was later to prove so formidable. The ensuing course of
events—the rebellion in which the North saved the South from committing
suicide through the formation of a separate slave power, and the manner in
which the rebellion was crushed—proves that in the United States slavery did
not affect the social constitution as a whole, as is the case with us. The superior part of the organism remained intact, and even strong enough to bend
the hitherto dominant section of the country to its will, despite all its complicity with that section.

Among us there is no dividing line. There is no section of the country that
differs from another. Contact is synonymous with contagion. The whole cir-
culatory system, from the great arteries to the capillaries, serves as a channel
for the same impurities. The whole body—blood, constituent elements, res-
piration, force and activity, muscles and nerves, intelligence and will, not only
the character but the temperament, and above all the energy—is affected by
the same cause. ...

In the southern states of the American Union a social color line was
drawn. The slaves and their descendants did not form part of society. Race
mixture took place on a very small scale. Slavery devastated the soil, ob-

Joaquim Nabuco, *O Abolicionismo*, São Paulo, 1938, pp. 167–195. (Excerpt translated by the
editor.)

structed industrial growth, prepared the way for economic bankruptcy, impeded immigration—produced, in fine, all the results of that kind that we know in Brazil; but American society was not formed from units created in that process. ...

In Brazil just the opposite occurred. Brazilian slavery, though based on the difference between the two races, never developed a prejudice against dark skin, and was infinitely more sagacious in that respect. The contacts between the races, from the first colonization by the donatories until today, have produced a mixed population; and the slave who receives his certificate of freedom simultaneously acquires the rights of citizenship. Thus there are no perpetual social castes among us; there is not even a fixed division into classes. The slave, as such, practically does not exist for society, for he may not even have been registered by his master, who in any case can alter the registration at will. For the rest, registration in itself means nothing, since the government does not send inspectors to the fazendas, nor are the masters obliged to account for their slaves to the authorities. This being, who enjoys no more right of protection by society than any other piece of personal property, on the day after he has gained his freedom becomes a citizen like any other, with full political rights. Furthermore, in the very shadow of his own captivity he can buy slaves, perhaps—who knows?—some child of his old master. This proves the confusion of classes and individuals, and the unlimited extent of social crossings between slaves and free men, which make the majority of Brazilian citizens political mixed-bloods, so to speak, in whom two opposed natures struggle: that of the master by birth and that of the domesticated slave.

Our slavery extended its privileges to all without distinction: white man and black, *ingenuos* and freedmen, slaves, foreigners and natives, rich and poor; and in this way it acquired a redoubled capacity for absorption and an elasticity incomparably greater than it would have had if there were a racial monopoly of the institution, as in the South of the United States. In 1845, the year of the Aberdeen Bill,[2] Macaulay said in the House of Commons: "I think it not improbable that the black population of Brazil will be free and happy within eighty or a hundred years. I do not see a reasonable prospect of a like change in the United States." He appears to have been as correct in his insight into the relative happiness of the Negro race in the two countries as he was wrong in his belief that the United States would lag behind us in the emancipation of its slaves. What deceived the great English orator in this case was his assumption that the color line was a social and political force in favor of slavery. On the contrary, its chief strength consists in banishing race prejudice and opening the institution to all classes. But for this very reason the greatest possible ethnic chaos prevailed among us, and the confusion that reigns in the regions where the process of national unity is working itself out with all those heterogenous elements reminds one of the proud disorder of the incandescent stars.

Athens, Rome, and Virginia were, to draw an analogy from chemistry, simple mixtures in which the different elements retained their individual properties; Brazil, on the other hand, is a compound in which slavery represents the causal affinity. The problem that awaits solution is how to make a citizen of this compound of master and slave. The problem of the American South was very different, because there the two species did not mix. Among us slavery did not exert its influence exclusively below the Roman line of *libertas*; it also exerted it within and above the sphere of *civitas*; it leveled all the classes, except the slaves, who always live in the social depths; but it leveled them by degrading them. Hence the difficulty, in analyzing its influence, of discovering some feature in the temperament of the people, or in the aspect of the country, or even in the social heights most distant from the slave huts, which should not be included in the national synthesis of slavery. Consider our different social classes. They all present symptoms of retarded or impeded development, or what is worse, of artificial, premature growth. ...

An important class whose development is impeded by slavery comprises the cultivators who are not landowners and the dwellers in the countryside and the hinterlands in general. We have already seen the unhappy state of this class, which constitutes nearly our entire population. Since they lack all independence and are dependent on another man's whims, the words of the Lord's Prayer, "Give us this day our daily bread," have for the members of this class a concrete and real significance. Their plight is not that of workers, who, dismissed from one factory, can find work in another establishment, or of day laborers who can go to the labor market to offer their services, or of families which can emigrate; they constitute a class without means or resource—taught to consider work a servile occupation, having no market for its products, and far removed from a region of wage labor (if there is such an *El Dorado* in our country)—a class that consequently must resign itself to living and raising its children in dependency and misery.

This is the picture which a compassionate sugarmill owner presented of a section—the most fortunate section—of this class at the Agricultural Congress held in Recife in 1878:

> The cultivator who is not a sugarmill owner leads a precarious life; his labor is not remunerated; his personal dignity is not respected; he is at the mercy of the sugarmill owner on whose land he lives. There is not even a written contract to bind the interested parties; everything is based on the absolute will of the sugarmill owner. In exchange for a dwelling, often of the most wretched kind, and for permission to cultivate a patch of manioc, invariably situated in the most unproductive land—in return for this the sharecropper divides equally with the sugarmill owner the sugar obtained from his crop. The owner also gets all the syrup and rum derived from the sugarcane; all the refuse—an excellent fuel for the manufacture of sugar; and all the sugarcane leaves, which provide a succulent food for his cattle. Thus the landowner receives the lion's share—all the more unjustly when it is remembered that the sharecropper bears all the expense of

planting, cultivation, cutting, and preparation of the cane, and of its transport to the sugarmill.

And this is a favored class, that of the sharecroppers, below which there are others who have nothing of their own, tenants who have nothing to sell the landowner and who lead a nomadic existence, having no obligations to society and denied all protection by the State.

Consider now the other classes whose development is retarded by slavery—the working and industrial classes, and the commercial classes in general.

Slavery does not permit the existence of a true working class, nor is it compatible with the wage system and the personal dignity of the artisan. The artisan himself, in order to escape the stigma with which slavery brands its workers, attempts to widen the gulf that separates him from the slave, and becomes imbued with a sense of superiority that is based in one who himself emerged from the servile class or whose parents were slaves. For the rest, there can be no strong, respected, and intelligent working class where the employers of labor are accustomed to order slaves about. As a result, the workers do not have slightest political influence in Brazil.

Slavery and industry are mutually exclusive terms, like slavery and colonization. The spirit of the former, spreading through a country, kills every one of the human faculties from which industry springs—initiative, inventiveness, individual energy, and every one of the elements that industry requires—the formation of capital, an abundance of labor, technical education of the workers, confidence in the future. Agriculture is the only Brazilian industry that has flourished in native hands. Commerce has prospered only in the hands of foreigners. ... The advent of industry has been singularly retarded in our country, and it is barely making its entrance now.

Brazilian large-scale commerce does not possess the capital available to foreign commerce, in either the export or the import trade; and retail trade, at least as concerns its prosperous sector, with its own life, is practically a foreign monopoly. At various times in our history this has provoked popular demonstrations, proclaiming that retail commerce must become Brazilian, but this cry was characteristic of the spirit of exclusivism and hatred of competition, no matter how legitimate, in which slavery reared our people. More than once it was accompanied by uprisings similar in character but actuated by religious fanaticism. Those who supported the program of closure of Brazilian ports, and of annulling all the progress made since 1808, were unaware that if we took retail commerce away from foreigners it would not pass into native hands but would simply create a permanent shortage of goods—because it is slavery, not nationality, that prevents any significant development of Brazilian retail trade.

In relation to commerce, slavery proceeds in this fashion: It shuts off to trade, whether from distrust or from a spirit of routine, all of the interior except the provincial capitals. Aside from the towns of Santos and Campinas in

São Paulo, Petropolis and Campos in Rio de Janeiro, Pelotas in Rio Grande do Sul, and a few other cities, outside the capitals you will not find a business establishment that is more than a little shop selling articles necessary for life, and these are generally crudely made or adulterated. Just as you will find nothing that betokens intellectual progress—neither bookstores nor newspapers—so will you find no trace of commerce except in the ancient rudimentary form of the store-bazaar. Consequently, aside from the articles that are ordered directly from the capital, all commercial transactions take the form of barter, whose history is the history of our whole interior. Barter, in fact, is the "pioneer" of our commerce, and represents the limits within which slavery is compatible with local exchange.

Yet commerce is the fountainhead of slavery, and its banker. A generation ago it supplied plantation agriculture with African slaves; many rural properties fell into the hands of slave traders; and the fortunes made in the traffic (for which counterfeit money sometimes had a great affinity), when not converted into town and country houses, were employed in assisting agriculture by way of loans at usurious rates. At present the bond between commerce and slavery is not so dishonorable for the former, but their mutual dependence continues to be the same. The princes of commerce are slave owners; coffee always reigns on the exchanges of Rio and Santos; and commerce, in the absence of industry and free labor, can function only as an agent of slavery, buying whatever it offers and selling whatever it needs. That is why in Brazil commerce does not develop or open new perspectives for the country; it is an inactive force, without stimuli, and conscious that it is merely an extension of slavery, or rather the mechanism by which human flesh is converted into gold and circulates, within and outside the country, in the form of letters of exchange. Slavery distrusts commerce, as it distrusts any agency of progress, whether it is a businessman's office, a railroad station, or a primary school; yet slavery needs commerce—and so the latter tries to live with it on the best possible terms. But so long as slavery endures, commerce must always be the servant of a class, and not an independent national agent; it cannot thrive under a régime that will not permit it to enter into direct relations with consumers, and will not allow the population of the interior to rise into that category.

Of the classes whose growth slavery artificially stimulates, none is more numerous than that of government employees. The close relation between slavery and the mania for officeholding is as indisputable as the relation between slavery and the superstition of the All-Providing State. ... Take at random any twenty or thirty Brazilians in any place where our most cultured society is to be found; all were, or are, or will be government employees—if not they, then their sons.

Officeholding is ... the asylum of the descendants of formerly rich and noble families that have squandered the fortunes made from slavery, of which it can be said, as a rule, as of fortunes made by gambling, that they neither last nor bring happiness. But officeholding is also our political olive tree, that shelters all those young men of brains and ambition but no money who form the great majority of our talented people. Draw up a list of distinguished Brazilian statesmen who solved their personal problem of poverty by marrying wealth (which meant, in the great majority of cases, becoming humble clients of the slaveowners); make up another list of those who solved that problem by acquiring government jobs; in those two lists you will find the names of virtually all our outstanding politicians. But what this means is that the national horizons are closed in all directions—that fields that might offer a livelihood to men of other than commercial talents, such as literature, science, journalism, and teaching, are severely restricted, while others that might attract men of business ability are so many closed doors, thanks to lack of credit, to the narrow scope of commerce, to the rudimentary structure of our economic life. ...

But can we have this consolation, that having degraded the various professions and reduced the nation to a proletariat, slavery at least succeeded in making the landowners a superior class, prosperous, educated, patriotic, worthy of representing the country intellectually and morally?

As concerns wealth, we have already seen that slavery ruined a generation of farmers whose place was taken by slave labor. From 1853 to 1857, when the obligations formed during the period of the slave traffic should have been in the process of liquidation, the mortgage debt of the city and province of Rio de Janeiro rose to sixty-seven thousand *contos*. The present generation has been no more fortunate. A large part of its profits was converted into human flesh, at a high price, and if an epidemic were to devastate the coffee plantations today, the amount of capital that the agriculture of the whole Empire could raise for new plantings would horrify those who believe it to be in a flourishing state. On top of this, for the past fifteen years there has been talk of nothing but "aid to agriculture." In 1868 appeared a little work by Sr. Quintino Bocayuva, *The Crisis of Agriculture*, in which that notable journalist wrote: "Agriculture can only be revived by the simultaneous application of two types of aid that cannot be longer delayed: the establishment of agricultural credit and the procurement of labor." The first measure was to be "a vast emission" based on the landed property of the Empire, which would thus be converted into ready money; the second should be Chinese colonization.

For fifteen years we have heard on all sides the cry that agriculture is in *crisis*, in need of aid, in agony, facing imminent bankruptcy. The government is daily denounced for not making loans and increasing the imposts in order to enable the fazendeiros to buy still more slaves. A law of November 6, 1875, authorized the government to give its guarantee to the foreign bank—no other could make its notes circulate in Europe—which would lend money to the planters at a rate lower than that of the domestic money market. In order to have sugar centrals and improve their product, the landowners must have the nation build them at its expense. The same favor has been asked for coffee. On top of sugar centrals and money at low interest rates, the great planters demand railroad freight rates set to their liking, official expositions of coffee, Asiatic immigration, exemption from any direct tax, and an employment law that would make the German, English, or Italian colonist a white slave. Even the native population must be subjected to a new agricultural recruitment in order to satisfy certain Chambers of Commerce; and, above all, the rate of exchange, by an economic fallacy, must be kept as low as possible so that coffee, which is paid for in gold, may be worth more in paper money. ...

As concerns its social functions, a landed aristocracy can serve its country in different ways: by working to improve the condition of the surrounding population of the countryside in which its estates are situated; by taking the direction of the progress of the nation into its own hands; by cultivating or protecting art and literature; by serving in the army and the navy or distinguishing itself in a variety of careers; by becoming the embodiment of all that is good in the national character, of the superior qualities of the people—of all that merits being preserved as tradition. We have already seen what our landed aristocracy achieved in each of these respects, when we noted what the slave system over which it presides has done to the land and the people, to the masters and the slaves. Since the class for whose profit it was created and exists is not an aristocracy of money, birth, intelligence, patriotism, or race, what is the permanent role in Brazil of a heterogeneous aristocracy that cannot even maintain its identity for two generations?

When we turn from the different classes to social institutions, we see that slavery has either turned them to its own interests, when of compromising tendency, or created a vacuum about them, when hostile, or hampered their formation, when incompatible with the slavery system.

Among the institutions that have identified themselves with slavery from the start, becoming instruments of its pretensions, is the Church. Under the system of domestic slavery, Christianity became mixed with fetishism, just as the two races mixed with each other. Through the influence of the wet nurse and the house slaves on the training of the children, the mumbo-jumbo terrors of the converted fetishist exert ... the most depressing influence on the minds of the young. The faith, the religious system that results from this fusion of African traditions with the antisocial ideal of the fanatical missionary is a jumble of contradictions that only a total lack of principle can seek to reconcile. What is true of religion is true of the Church.

Our bishops, vicars, and confessors do not find the sale of human beings repugnant; the Bulls that condemn it have become obsolete. Two of our prelates were sentenced to imprisonment at hard labor for declaring war on Freemasonry; none, however, was willing to incur the displeasure of the slavocracy. ...

Take another social force that slavery has appropriated in the same way—patriotism. The slavocracy has always exerted itself to identify Brazil with slavery. Whoever attacks it immediately falls under suspicion of connivance with foreigners, of hostility toward the institutions of his own country. Antonio Carlos de Andrada was accused by the slave power of being un-Brazilian. To attack monarchy in a monarchical country, to attack Catholicism in a Catholic country, is perfectly proper, but to attack slavery is national treason and felony. ...

But as with all the moral forces that it subjugated, slavery degraded patriotism even as it bent it to its will. The Paraguayan War offers the best illustration of what it did to the patriotism of the slaveowning class, to the patriotism of the masters. Very few of them left their slaves to serve their country; many freed a few blacks in order to win titles of nobility. It was among the humblest strata of our population, descendants of slaves for the most part—the very people that slavery condemns to dependence and misery—among the illiterate proletarians whose political emancipation slavery indefinitely postponed—that one felt beating the heart of a new *patria*. It was they who produced the soldiers of the Volunteer Battalions. With slavery, said José Bonifacio de Andrada in 1825, "Brazil will never form, as she must form, a spirited army and a flourishing navy"—because with slavery there can be no true patriotism, but only a patriotism of caste or race; that is, a sentiment that should unite all the members of society is used to divide them. ...

Among the forces of progress and change around which slavery has created a vacuum as hostile to its interests, the press is notable—and not only the newspaper but the book, and everything that concerns education. To the credit of our journalism, the press has been the great weapon of struggle against slavery, the instrument for the propagation of new ideas; efforts to found a "black organ" have always collapsed. Whether insinuated timidly or affirmed with energy, the dominant sentiment in all our journalism, from North to South, is emancipation. But in order to create a vacuum around the newspaper and the book, and around all that could foster abolitionist sentiment, slavery has instinctively repelled the school and public education, maintaining the country in ignorance and darkness—the milieu in which it can prosper. The slave hut and the school are poles that repel each other.

The state of public education under a slave system interested in universal ignorance is well illustrated by the following excerpt from a notable report by Sr. Ruy Barbosa, reporter for the Commission on Public Instruction of the Chamber of Deputies:

"The truth—and your Commission wants to be very explicit on this point, displease whom it may—is that our public instruction is as backward as is possible in a country that regards itself as free and civilized; that decadence and not progress prevails; that we are a people of illiterates, and that the rate of illiteracy is declining at an intolerably slow rate if it is declining at all; that our academic instruction is infinitely below the scientific level of the age; that our youth leave the secondary schools more and more poorly prepared for advanced study; and that popular education, in the capital as in the provinces, is merely a desideratum. ...

Among the forces whose emergence slavery has impeded is public opinion, the consciousness of a common destiny. Under slavery there cannot exist that powerful force called public opinion, that simultaneously balances and offers a point of support to the individuals who represent the most advanced thought of the country. Just as slavery is incompatible with spontaneous immigration, so will it prevent the influx of new ideas. Itself incapable of invention, it will have nothing to do with progress. ...

And because we lack this force of social change, Brazilian politics are the sad and degrading struggle for spoils that we behold; no man in public life means anything, for none has the support of the country. The president of the council lives at the mercy of the Crown, from which he derives his power; even the appearance of power is his only when he is regarded as the Emperor's lieutenant and is believed to have in his pocket the decree of dissolution—that is, the right to elect a chamber made up of his own henchmen. Below him are the ministers, who live by the favor of the president of the council; farther down still, on the third plane, are found the deputies, at the mercy of the ministers. The representative system, then, is a graft of parliamentary forms on a patriarchal government, and senators and deputies only take their roles seriously in this parody of democracy because of the personal advantages they derive therefrom. Suppress the subsidies, force them to stop using their positions for personal and family ends, and no one who had anything else to do would waste his time in such *skimaxai*, such shadow boxing, to borrow a comparison from Cicero.

Ministers without support from public opinion, who when dismissed fall into the limbo of forgotten things; presidents of the council who spend their days and nights seeking to fathom the esoteric thinking the Emperor; a Chamber of Deputies conscious of its nullity and wanting only to be left alone; a Senate reduced to being a *prytaneum*; political parties that are nothing more than employment agencies and mutual benefit societies for their members. All these ostensible evidences of a free government are preserved by national pride like the consular dignity in the Roman Empire, but what we really have is a government of primitive simplicity in which responsibilities are infinitely divided while power is concentrated in the hands of one man. He is the chief of State. When some leader seems to have effective authority and power, individual prestige, it is because at that particular moment he happens to be standing in the light cast by the throne. Let him take one step to the right or left away from that sphere of light, and he vanishes for ever into the darkness. ...

There is only one autonomous, irresponsible power among us; only that power is sure of the morrow; it alone represents a permanent national tradition. The ministers are nothing more than secondary and sometimes grotesque incarnations of that superior entity. Casting his eyes about him, the Emperor finds not a single will, individual or collective, that limits his own. In that sense he is as absolute as the Czar or the Sultan, although he is at the center of a modern government provided with all the superior organs, such as parliament, which neither Russia nor Turkey possesses; parliamentary supremacy, which Germany does not have; freedom of the press, which very few countries have. What this means is that instead of being called an absolute ruler the Emperor should rather be called the permanent prime minister of Brazil. He does not appear before the chambers; he allows great latitude, especially in matters of finance and legislation, to the cabinet; but not for a single day does he lose sight of the march of affairs or fail to be the arbiter among his ministers.

This so-called *personal government* has been explained by the absurd theory that the Emperor corrupted an entire people; that he demoralized our politicians by means of supreme temptations after the manner of Satan; that he stole the virtue of parties which never had ideas or principles, save as a field of exploitation. The truth is that this government is the direct result of the practice of slavery in our country. A people accustomed to slavery does not prize liberty or learn to practice self-government. Hence the general abdication of civic functions, the distaste for the obscure and anonymous exercise of personal responsibility, without which no people can be free, since a free people is only an aggregate of free individuals. These are the causes that have resulted in the supremacy of the only permanent and perpetual element—the monarchy.

PART FIVE

LATIN
AMERICA
IN THE
TWENTIETH
CENTURY

17

⤳

THE MEXICAN REVOLUTION

THE MEXICAN REVOLUTION of 1910 developed into the first major effort in Latin American history to uproot the system of great estates and peonage, to curb foreign control over the national resources, and to raise the living standards of the masses. The famous Constitution of 1917 spelled out this social content of the revolution.

The revolution's first leader, the martyred Francisco Madero, emphasized narrow political rather than social objectives. But popular pressure forced his successor, Venustiano Carranza, to accept a personally uncongenial program of reform. Even after the return of peace in 1920, reform proceeded slowly and uncertainly. By 1928 many revolutionary leaders, grown wealthy and corrupt, had abandoned their reformist ideals.

Popular discontent with the rule of "millionaire Socialists" produced an upsurge of change in the administration of President Lázaro Cárdenas (1934–1940). Cárdenas distributed land to the villages, strengthened labor, and weakened foreign economic influence by the expropriation of the oil industry. His moderate successors virtually abandoned land reform but promoted irrigation and electrification projects that chiefly benefited large private farms and supported industry, which made notable progress. The shift to the right reached its climax in the presidency of Gustavo Díaz Ordaz (1964–1970). Discontent mounted among peasants and urban workers, whose real income shrank under chronic inflation and whose organizations had become docile instruments of a ruling party (the Partido Revolucionario Institucional—PRI) that governed with an increasingly heavy hand. Savage suppression by the army and police of a peaceful student protest in the capital in October 1968, with hundreds of students and bystanders killed or wounded and other hundreds imprisoned, dismayed the country.

President Jose López Portillo (1976–1982), took office amid growing optimism about Mexico's economic future, an optimism that resulted from the discovery of vast new oil and gas deposits on Mexico's east coast. But the resulting oil boom, accompanied by a large expansion of production in capital-intensive industries and agribusiness operations, did not create many jobs and further deformed Mexico's economic structure as labor and acreage were diverted from staple food production. Meanwhile Mexico's foreign debt grew at an alarming rate. The bubble burst in 1981 when a growing world oil glut caused oil prices to fall sharply. The country sank into recession, a major devaluation of the peso occurred, capital was withdrawn from the country, and fears grew of an imminent default on Mexico's foreign debt of some $85 billion. López Portillo turned to the U.S. government and bankers for aid. The resulting rescue operation tied financial aid to austerity measures that hit Mexico's poor the hardest. López Portillo's successor in the presidency, Miguel de la Madrid (1982–1988), continued and intensified López Portillo's conservative economic policies, with no apparent success; Mexico remained mired in a deep depression.

By the middle 1980s Mexico's policy makers were convinced that the import-substitution model of development institutionalized by Cárdenas and continued, with a strong shift to the right, by his successors, had exhausted its possibilities for growth. That model was based on state ownership of key industries, protection and subsidies for private industry, and such redistributive policies as the provision of social services, subsidized food prices, and land reform. The proofs of its failure included a chronic depression and a gigantic unpayable debt.

Confronted with that failure, Mexico's rulers chose to abandon the import-substitution model in favor of a new model, often called "neoliberal," that stressed the export of manufactured goods and integration with the world economy, especially with the United States. In line with neoliberal doctrine, tariff barriers would be lowered or eliminated, state industries and the communal *ejido* farming sector privatized, and price controls and subsidies lifted. The economic program of President de la Madrid marked a transition to the new economic model; its full implementation awaited the outcome of the election of 1988.

On the eve of that election, the rise of a pro-democracy faction opened a deep rift within the ruling party. Eventually this group broke away and organized the Democratic Revolutionary Party (PRD), with Cuauhtémoc Cárdenas, son of the former President Cárdenas, as its presidential candidate and a program calling for a mixed economy, greater social justice, and a return to the nationalistic ideals of the Mexican Revolution. Cárdenas led in the vote count by a wide margin when the computers "broke down." When the count was resumed the PRI candidate Carlos Salinas de Gortari had taken the lead and was ultimately proclaimed the winner. The flagrant computer fraud was later compounded by burning the ballots. Salinas continued de la Madrid's economic policy, stressing privatization, austerity, and the removal of barriers to foreign investment and imports.

One of the fruits of de la Madrid's administration was a large expansion of the program that permitted U.S. companies to establish plants (called *maquiladoras* or *maquilas*) for production of parts and their assembly on the

Mexican side of the border; U.S. customs regulations allowed the finished products to enter the United States with duty paid only on the value of the labor, not on that of the goods themselves. Critics charged that the combination of sweatshop wages and almost total disregard for the environment had created a "social and economic inferno" on the U.S.-Mexican border. These problems were multiplied by the North American Free Trade Agreement (NAFTA) ratified by the United States and Mexico in 1993. NAFTA eliminated tariffs between the United States and Mexico over the next fifteen years and permitted the free flow of investment capital across borders.

Despite deepening poverty and unemployment, there appeared little effective opposition to PRI's iron grip over Mexican politics as Mexico prepared for the presidential and congressional elections of 1994. Then two events shattered Mexico's surface calm and raised serious doubts about the ruling party's secure grip on power and its internal unity.

The first was a revolt on New Year's Day 1994 in the southern state of Chiapas, one of the poorest Mexican states, led by a self-styled "Zapatista Army of National Liberation." The rebels proclaimed NAFTA and its free trade program "a death certificate" for Mexico's native peoples and demanded sweeping social and political reforms. The government first responded with a savage counter-offensive, then called for a cease-fire and negotiations. In 1996 the government signed the San Andrés accords, halting troop movements in Chiapas and acknowledging Indian rights to create "autonomous communities." But in December 1997, in the village of Acteal, a paramilitary force linked to the ruling PRI massacred forty-five Tzotzil Maya Indians who supported the Zapatista cause. Zedillo's failure to carry out the San Andrés accords, continuing harassment of Zapatista communities by paramilitary bands, and provocative military movements that appeared designed to encircle the Zapatista communities and prepare the way for a full-scale invasion cast doubt on the government's sincerity and prompted Samuel Ruiz, the progressive bishop of Chiapas and the only public figure trusted by the Maya, to resign from the National Mediation Committee that had been negotiating a peaceful solution of the crisis. By the fall of 1999 a high state of tension prevailed in the area, and in the rest of the country fears were expressed that the governor of Chiapas, with or without Zedillo's consent, was in fact preparing a full-scale invasion that would achieve a "final solution" of the Zapatista problem.

In March 1994 Mexicans were again stunned when PRI's presidential candidate, Luis Donaldo Colosio, was assassinated while campaigning in the border city of Tijuana. Theories about the motives for the murder varied, but there was general agreement that it revealed deep splits within the ruling party. President Salinas quickly named Ernesto Zedillo Ponce de León as PRI's presidential candidate to face PRD's Cuauhtémoc Cárdenas and Diego Fernández de Cevallos of the right-wing National Action Party (PAN) in the August 1994 election. A new electoral code was supposed to ensure a clean, fair election, but massive fraud undoubtedly contributed to Zedillo's overwhelming victory. As he prepared to take office in December, Zedillo faced great economic problems, widespread resentment against the electoral process that brought him to power, and a broadening challenge from the Zapatistas of Chiapas, who convened a National Democratic Convention in August 1994 to enlist the aid of all Mexican progressive parties and groups in their struggle for social and political justice.

But the most immediate threat to the regime was the prospect of an economic collapse. NAFTA, which was supposed to bring prosperity to Mexico, had sharpened all its economic problems, including its debt problem. The removal of trade barriers caused an influx of U.S. agricultural and manufactured goods, threatening the destruction of Mexican farmers and manufacturers by competition from more technologically advanced U.S. producers. An overvalued peso, deliberately overvalued to inspire confidence in foreign investors and assure passage of NAFTA, contributed to the flood of imports. This led to a growing trade deficit, a decline in the value of the peso in relation to the dollar, and the flight of foreign and domestic capital out of the country. Meanwhile Mexico's foreign debt had risen from about $85 billion in 1982 to $140 billion in 1994. By December 1994, with $20 billion in short-term loans due in a few months, its foreign currency reserves almost exhausted, the peso in free fall, and capital flight accelerating, Mexico faced a replay of the 1982 debacle of inflation and looming default.

Once again foreign governments, led by the United States and international lending agencies, came to Mexico's rescue with a bailout package of loans and loan guarantees of almost $50 billion. But the price came high. In return for the $20 billion in loan guarantees from the United States, Mexico must put up $7 billion a year in oil export revenues as collateral to be deposited at the New York Federal Reserve; Mexico must also cut social spending, continue the privatization program, and keep wage increases low. Many Mexicans viewed the February 1995 deal not as a bailout but a sellout.

For ordinary Mexicans the cost of the crisis was more austerity, more hardships. Two million out of ten million Mexican workers earn only a minimum wage. The Mexican Confederation of Labor recently calculated that it took three minimum wages to buy a family's basic basket of food and domestic items. By 1996 55 percent of the population, 14.7 million more than in 1994, lived in extreme poverty.

The 1997 congressional elections offered convincing evidence of growing popular resistance to the PRI and its neoliberal agenda. Opposition parties gained a majority of seats in the Chamber of Deputies, dealing a severe blow to the president's nearly unlimited de facto power. Even more significant was the landslide victory of PRD's Cárdenas in the race for governor of metropolitan Mexico City, the home of a quarter of the nation's population. Like the Chiapas revolt, these events suggested that Mexicans were beginning to apply the lessons of their experience with the model of development that had collapsed so ingloriously in 1982 and again in 1994. But the PRI had not exhausted its bag of electoral tricks—fraud, vote buying, *caciquismo* (boss rule)—as was shown by its recent victories in a number of state elections, typically in states that were largely Indian, underdeveloped, and very poor.

Meanwhile confusion reigned within the PRI as battles broke out between the "dinosaurs," representing an old-line faction wedded to the traditional "hard ball" tactics of winning elections, and the modernizing Yale- or Harvard-trained technicians of the Zedillo stamp, who preferred the use of suaver tactics. When Zedillo, under immense pressure, announced that he had given up the traditional presidential role (*el dedazo*) of "fingering" his successor as PRI's presidential candidate in the looming 2000 elections, new and more bitter rifts broke out within the party. For the PRD, which perceived a solid possibility of gaining power in 2000, many questions remained unsolved. Could it overcome the personality conflicts and policy differences that still troubled the party? Could it forge a limited electoral alliance, as proposed by Cuauhtémoc Cárdenas, with PAN—a party that was to the right of PRI in some respects and gave support to unsavory PRI legislative projects that favored large corporate and banking interests?

The political fighting and infighting took place against the background of increasingly severe economic problems—though not as severe as those experienced by South American countries like Brazil—that reflected the impact of the Asian financial crisis of 1997–1999, itself part of a spreading cyclical world capitalist depression. The failure of the neoliberal agenda of successive PRI regimes to restore the Mexican economy to health challenged the PRD to offer new, innovative solutions that would enable Mexico to escape from dependency and the vicious debt trap that made genuine economic development impossible. Such solutions were certain to meet bitter opposition from Mexico's ruling elites and their foreign allies.

1. PORFIRIO DÍAZ, VICEROY OF MEXICO

The Age of Díaz (1867–1911) enriched a favored few at the expense of Mexico's millions. Shortly after the dictator's fall from power a cultured Mexican exile wrote the following appraisal of the Díaz regime.

A popular maxim said, "Mexico is the mother of foreigners and the stepmother of Mexicans." This saying, which passed from mouth to mouth and even appeared in books by foreigners,[1] summed up in a few words the financial, administrative, domestic, and foreign policies of General Díaz. And

---

Luis Para y Pardo, *De Porfirio Díaz a Francisco Madero*, New York, 1912, pp. 81–97. (Excerpt translated by the editor.)

nothing explains better why, while foreign countries showered decorations on Díaz and his sons, nephews, kinsmen, and lackeys and exalted him as the greatest statesman of Latin America, the Mexican people, outside the circle of his adoring favorites, heaped curses on him and waited impatiently for death to snatch him from the Presidency of the Republic or for some man to arise and topple him from his pinnacle of power. ...

The object of every national government is to improve the social and political condition of its people. A good government does not reject foreign aid, for that would be absurd and even impossible in the present state of civilization, but it insists that this cooperation always be subordinated to the national interest. Immigration is only desirable when the immigrant represents a civilizing force and joins his interests to those of the country in which he makes his residence.

Only colonial governments of the worst type have for their sole object the unrestrained, senseless, and disorderly exploitation of the national resources for the benefit of foreigners and the enslavement or extermination of the natives. The government of General Díaz belongs in this unhappy category. ...

The dazzling prosperity of the Díaz era was due in very large part to the exploitation of certain resources—of minerals, above all—on a greater scale than ever before. The export of these commodities, as well as that of certain tropical products in great demand abroad, increased in an astounding way. In only twenty years of Díaz' rule the export of minerals rose from a value of 36 million pesos (in 1890) to more than 111 million (in 1910). In the same period the export of henequen increased from a value of less than 6 million to more than 20 million pesos, and the export of other tropical products, such as fine woods, tobacco, coffee, etc., also rose sharply.

But aside from henequen, coffee, and some other products of particular regions, this prosperity was based on the exploitation of exhaustible resources owed by foreigners who did not even reside in Mexico. The lion's share of the 120 million pesos of exported minerals went into dividends for foreign stockholders; only the extremely low wages paid to the workers remained in the country. As in colonial times, ships sailed from Mexico with treasure drawn from the bowels of the earth by enslaved Indians, for the benefit of foreign masters who never set eyes on the places where those riches were produced.

As in colonial times, around these mines arose populous and hastily built centers. But again as in colonial times, the day had to come when the veins would be exhausted and the people would depart with empty purses, leaving only skeleton cities, vast cities of the dead like Zacatecas, Guanajuato, Taxco, that retain only the vestiges of their ancient splendor.

The same happened with our agricultural exports, except for henequen and coffee. ... As concerns the exploitation of the fine woods, it is well known that it was carried on in such a destructive way that whole forests were ravaged without seeding a single useful plant in the looted soil.

Meanwhile agricultural production for the internal market, the cultivation of the grains on which our people live, remained stationary or even declined in relation to the population; year after year it was necessary to import North American corn and wheat to fill the needs of the internal market.

Equally dismal are the statistics for industry: There were 123 textile factories in 1893; eighteen years later the number was 146. And only the fact that the textile industry, almost entirely monopolized by Spaniards and Frenchmen, enjoyed privileges that closed the door to similar foreign articles and compelled the people to buy high-priced articles of inferior quality, made this achievement possible. The tobacco and liquor industries, on the other hand, advanced by leaps and bounds. There were 41 factories manufacturing cigarettes and cigars in 1893; in 1909 their number had increased to 437—that is, ten times. The production of rum reached 43 million liters in 1909.

The panegyrists of General Díaz proclaim his greatness as an administrator. They base their claim above all on the construction of more than 20,000 kilometers of railroads. I have already explained the open-handed generosity of Díaz in granting concessions to American capitalists for the construction of railroads.[2] Each of these concessions was a gift, made directly to the capitalist involved or through the mediation of some favorite that he had bribed. All Mexico knows that many families owe their present wealth to concessions secured from General Díaz and sold to foreign capitalists. In the ministry of communications there were employees who defrauded the state of millions of pesos, taking bribes from individuals who obtained concessions and subventions for the construction of railways. It is no mystery that many of those roads were not constructed with the aim of favoring commerce or of meeting the needs of particular regions. ...

The official statistics maintain a profound silence concerning the nationality of the directors of the mining companies, the great agricultural enterprises, and of the manufacturing industries of Mexico. But everyone knows that more than 75 percent of them are foreign; as for the railroads, their foreign character is so marked that English has been the official language of the majority of lines.

In order to explain and justify this situation, which became so acute during the rule of General Díaz that it caused almost a crisis of "antiforeignism," some say that our lack of enterprise, our apathy, and our ignorance render us unfit to exploit our own resources, and that these must inevitably pass into the hands of foreigners.

I do not deny that from lack of education and on account of the social conditions in our country the Mexican people suffer from such defects. Nor do I make the mistake of attributing this state of affairs to General Díaz, or of demanding that he explain why the national character did not experience a radical change under his rule.

But this is not the only reason that Mexico is absolutely dominated by foreigners at present; furthermore, the government of General Díaz made not

the slightest effort to keep the foreign invasion within the limits of fair dealing and the national interest. The monopolization of business by foreigners
would have been legitimate and beneficial for the country if it had been the
result of free competition between the natives and the immigrants—if the
latter, through their capital and their spirit of enterprise, employed within
just and legal limits, had emerged victorious. ...

But for every property legitimately acquired, for every dollar, or franc, or
mark, or pound sterling invested in enterprises that yielded benefits to the
country, how many monopolies, servitudes, ruinous and truly iniquitous contracts did the government of General Díaz not leave behind it!

Not apathy and ignorance but tyranny deprived the Mexicans of the possession and exploitation of their own resources. If a Mexican sought the
grant of a waterfall, a forest, a piece of land, a mine, or a deposit of coal or
oil, his petition had to be supported and endorsed by some minion of the
President who secured at an exorbitant price the favor of having the matter
attended to with fair dispatch. Frequently the Mexican, having purchased in
this manner the services of public officials, would receive a round "No" for
an answer; and in a little while he would see in the Official Daily the an-
nouncement that the favor he was applying for had been graciously
granted—to none other than the person whose intercession he had sought!

And if this happened to Mexicans on a social level close to that of the privileged class, what must have been the condition of laborers, small farmers,
and artisans! Pity the unhappy peasant who, loving the soil he had inherited
from his forefathers and seized with a sudden passion for progress, undertook
to irrigate his inheritance, to buy machines and use fertilizers, and who by
means of patient and painful effort succeeded in obtaining the best yields and
in attracting the attention of the neighborhood to his land! From that moment was awakened the rapacity of the *jefe político*, of the military commander, of the secretary of the state government, or of the curate, canon, or
archbishop, who would not rest until they had despoiled him of his property;
and if he defended it with the admirable tenacity with which the Indian defends his land, he would land in the barracks, condemned to the slavery of
the soldier-convict, or a group of soldiers would take him out of jail and
shoot him in the back while on the march.

In the court archives of Mexico there are thousands of episodes of this
kind. I have seen many of them; I know in detail histories that would fill
books—stories of people dragged from their farms by soldiers in order to satisfy the greed of the governor, or the local commander, or the foreigner, supported by General Díaz.

In 1863 President Juarez, wishing to promote agriculture, issued the law of
vacant lands (*terrenos baldíos*), by which public lands were ceded to whoever
would locate, survey, and exploit them, paying for them at a fixed price and
receiving a part gratis in return for his engineering services. Basing itself on
this law, the government of General Díaz committed the greatest iniquities.

Documents published in Mexico show that time and time again certain magnates, seized by the fever of speculation in lands called "vacant," despoiled
not only individuals but entire towns that had worked and made their living
from those lands for centuries.

Among the many notions that certain sociological theories proclaim, and
that serve to justify robbery by conquest, there is a fine-sounding doctrine
that dazzles even educated and thoughtful persons. It affirms that if the
owner of a source of wealth does not exploit it he may rightly be despoiled
whenever there appears a claimant capable of making better use of it.

It would not have been so bad if this doctrine had really inspired and justified all these iniquities. One would have less cause for complaint if the natives
had changed from the class of owners to that of tenants, or even to that of
employees, peons, day laborers of the new owner, and if land once barely cultivated had begun to produce in abundance with the aid of irrigation, the
plow, fertilizer. If all the square kilometers of land seized from their legitimate owners during the reign of Don Porfirio were now in production, even
at the extremely low level of production typical of Mexican agriculture, all
the granaries of the Republic would now be filled, and from our ports would
depart ships loaded with wheat, flour, corn, and the many other products that
the benign climate of Mexico yields.

But that is not what happened; in the great majority of cases the inhabitants
were simply expelled and the lands closed to exploitation, awaiting the coming
of some Yankee prospector in search of vast tracts—to be used in bamboozling
his countrymen through the organization of one of many fraudulent agricultural companies. In official newspapers of the States I have seen the orders
given by the authorities to inhabitants of villages and towns to abandon their
homes and give up their lands to avaricious claimants. And those unhappy
Indians, whose only crime was that they lacked a written title to the lands on
which their forefathers had peacefully lived since long before the birth of
Columbus, frequently preferred to die hunted down like wild beasts, or to rot
in jail, to leaving voluntarily what for them was their only *patria*. ...

Governmental expenditures during the thirty-five years' reign of Don
Porfirio amounted to more, much more, than 2 billion pesos. This vast sum
was entirely at his disposal; it was tribute paid by the country that General
Díaz could have invested in bettering the social condition of Mexico. But of
this immense sum of money not a cent was ever invested in irrigating or fertilizing the land on which 12 million Indians passed their lives in struggle for
a handful of grain with which to sate their hunger. Nor was any part of it
used to bring to these people—the largest social class, the only class devoted
to the cultivation of the soil—some notion of justice or some education that
would enable them to take a step toward civilization. Not the least effort was
made to liberate the rural population from the slavery that made its life almost intolerable. Calling itself paternal, his government made not the slightest effort to rescue this enormous mass of people from the clutches of alco-

holism, which a rapacious master class injected into the veins of the people the better to ensure its domination.

That is why at the end of those thirty-five years the rural population of Mexico continues under a régime of true slavery, receiving a daily wage of a few cents, sunk in ignorance, without hope of redemption. And since the monopolies have greatly raised the cost of living, the situation of the people in general is much worse than when General Díaz rose to power. Above that great oppressed mass arose a wealthy, brutal, splendid caste—but when has the wealth of a master class served any other purpose than to oppress and degrade the serfs? Has it ever served to liberate them?

The influence of General Díaz was as disastrous and corrupting on the political as on the social life of Mexico. Arrived at the pinnacle of power, he could and should have modified his system without danger to himself in such a way that the people could gradually have been educated in the exercise of their rights. ...

But instead his policy of extermination, degradation, and prostitution was directed toward the concentration of power, and all the important changes that he made in the Mexican constitution were highly lethal to liberty and rendered the people increasingly incapable of governing itself. Thus, his most important reforms were designed to restrict the sphere of action of the town councils. Not even in the capital of the Republic—the center of culture, where the district action of the federal government was greatest—did he permit the existence of an elected council that would have charge of municipal taxation. On the contrary, he stripped the council of all its powers, converting it into an ornamental body, and put the municipal administration in the hands of the ministries. Another of his important reforms was to restrict trial by jury, and later he reformed the *ley de amparo* to the point where it was made inapplicable in civil cases. ...

These were the salient features of the political system of General Díaz, and they justify my affirmation that his government was a viceroyalty, bringing a peace of extermination and oppression; pompous, brilliant, and profitable to foreigners, but productive of ills to the *patria* that future generations may be unable to cure.

2. FOR LAND AND LIBERTY

In his Plan of San Luis Potosí, which was a call for revolution, Francisco Madero had emphasized political objectives, only lightly touching on the subject of land reform. But in the mountainous southern state of Morelos, where the Indian communities had long waged a losing struggle against the encroaching sugar haciendas, *the revolution, led by Emiliano Zapata, began under the slogan* Tierra y Libertad *(Land and Liberty). When Zapata became convinced that Madero did not intend to carry out his promise to restore land to the villages, he revolted and issued his own program, the Plan of Ayala, for which he continued to battle until the great guerrilla fighter was slain by treachery in 1919. Zapata's principled and tenacious struggle and the popularity of his ideas among the landless peasantry contributed to the adoption of a bold program of agrarian reform in the Constitution of 1917. Important provisions of the Plan of Ayala follow.*

The Liberating Plan of the sons of the State of Morelos, members of the insurgent army that demands the fulfillment of the Plan of San Luis Potosí, as well as other reforms that it judges convenient and necessary for the welfare of the Mexican nation.

We, the undersigned, constituted as a Revolutionary Junta, in order to maintain and obtain the fulfillment of the promises made by the revolution of November 20, 1910, solemnly proclaim in the face of the civilized world ... , so that it may judge us, the principles that we have formulated in order to destroy the tyranny that oppresses us. ...

1. ... Considering that the President of the Republic, Señor Don Francisco I. Madero, has made a bloody mockery of Effective Suffrage by ... entering into an infamous alliance with the *científicos*, the *hacendados*, the feudalists, and oppressive *caciques*, enemies of the Revolution that he proclaimed, in order to forge the chains of a new dictatorship more hateful and terrible than that of Porfirio Díaz ... : For these reasons we declare the said Francisco I. Madero unfit to carry out the promises of the Revolution of which he was the author. ...

4. The Revolutionary Junta of the State of Morelos formally proclaims to the Mexican people:

That it endorses the Plan of San Luis Potosí with the additions stated below for the benefit of the oppressed peoples, and that it will defend its principles until victory or death. ...

As an additional part of the plan we proclaim, be it known: that the lands, woods, and waters usurped by the *hacendados*, *científicos*, or *caciques* through tyranny and venal justice henceforth belong to the towns or citizens who have corresponding titles to these properties, of which they were despoiled by the bad faith of our oppressors. They shall retain possession of the said properties at all costs, arms in hand. The usurpers who think they have a right to the said lands may state their claims before special tribunals to be established upon the triumph of the Revolution.

7. Since the immense majority of Mexican towns and citizens own nothing but the ground on which they stand and endure a miserable existence, denied the opportunity to improve their social condition or to devote themselves to industry or agriculture because a few individuals monopolize the lands,

---

Gildardo Magaña, *Emiliano Zapata y el agrarismo en México*, Mexico, 1934–1937, 2 vols., I, pp. 126–130. (Excerpt translated by the editor.)

woods, and waters—for these reasons the great estates shall be expropriated, with indemnification to the owners of one third of such monopolies, in order that the towns and citizens of Mexico may obtain *ejidos*, colonies, town sites, and arable lands. Thus the welfare of the Mexican people shall be promoted in all respects.

8. The properties of those *hacendados, científicos*, or *caciques* who directly or indirectly oppose the present Plan shall be seized by the nation, and two thirds of their value shall be used for war indemnities and pensions for the widows and orphans of the soldiers who may perish in the struggle for this Plan.

9. In proceeding against the above properties there shall be applied the laws of disentail and nationalization, as may be convenient, using as our precept and example the laws enforced by the immortal Juárez against Church property—laws that taught a painful lesson to the despots and conservatives who at all times have sought to fasten upon the people the yoke of oppression and backwardness.

3. CARDENISMO:
IDEOLOGY AND SUBSTANCE

The need to defeat the armed peasant movements led by Emiliano Zapata and Pancho Villa and to secure the loyalty of Mexico's workers compelled the conservative Venustiano Carranza to promise land and labor reforms as spelled out in the Constitution of 1917. By the late 1920s, however, the ruling "revolutionary family," led by Plutarco Calles, had made a mockery of those promises. It required the Great Depression and the growing strength of a progressive wing of the ruling party to create the conditions for a new advance of the revolution, led by Lázaro Cárdenas. But what was the significance of Cardenismo, *the totality of policies and programs carried out during Cárdenas' six years in power? Was it really a sharp swing to the left and toward a collectivist society, as many Mexican and foreign observers at the time believed? Actually the major land and labor reforms, by increasing mass purchasing power, expanded the internal market for Mexican capitalism, and the concentration of political and economic power in the state was intended to create an infrastructure for industry and to mobilize capital and other resources for industry. A contemporary Mexican historian and specialist in the Cárdenas period discusses the essential meaning and content of* Cardenismo.

Cárdenas was most zealous in upholding what Jesús Silva Herzog has called with tongue-in-cheek "the most original originality of the Mexican Revolution"—an originality that was nothing more than a spurious social neutrality used to dress up an ideology of reconciling classes and the two

Arnaldo Córdova, *La política de masas de Cardenismo*, Mexico, Ediciones Era, 1973, pp. 73–76. (Excerpt translated by the editor.)

great opposed systems of the modern world, capitalism and socialism. In this Cárdenas was a true disciple of the Revolution, which had diffused among us the great fallacy of the spontaneous generation of our national system. "It would be contemptible and senseless," he once said,

> to attribute to the state and its leaders the suicidal intention of introducing in Mexico practices in conflict with the genuine and national elements of our Revolution. Social democracy is the ideal toward which our people has aspired and fought for in heroic struggles and finally achieved with the triumph of the Revolution. Mexican democracy identifies with the universal programs of advanced ideas, but its doctrine arises, with the characteristic proper to its historical past, from the specific problems of Mexico and the particular solutions that they require. The tactics, programs, and governmental policies of all those movements that have arisen as a result of situations existing in other countries—the situations completely different from ours—are equally alien to the Mexican Revolution.

And this man, who was about to transform the Mexican state into a monstrous Leviathan that would erase the last vestiges of democracy in our country, could also declare:

> In Mexico we struggle to destroy and are destroying, through revolutionary actions, the system of individualistic exploitation, but not in order to fall into the unhappy situation of exploitation by the state. Rather our intention is gradually to turn over to the organized proletarian collectives the sources and the means of production. Within this doctrine, the function of the Mexican state is not limited to that of a simple guardian of order, provided with tribunals that dispense justice in conformity with individual rights, nor is the state regarded as the owner of the economy, but rather as the regulator of the great economic phenomena that take place within our system of the production and distribution of wealth.

Now, Cárdenas must have known what the whole world knows, that when the state becomes "the owner of the economy" it is a result of the abolition of private ownership of the means of production, the source of that exploitation of man by man against which he claimed to struggle. But Cárdenas was a child of the Mexican Revolution. He was not fighting for the abolition of private property; he was fighting the private property interests—paradoxical as it may seem—*in order to preserve them*. In this he was only carrying forward the program of the Revolution. Every well-regulated capitalist state does this when it defends individual property against individual egotism. In Mexico, this was done by employing the convenient formula of class reconciliation, a formula that was given the bizarre name of "Mexican socialism." Thus Cárdenas proclaimed that

> the principal action of the new phase of the Revolution is Mexico's march toward socialism, a movement which is equidistant from the anachronistic norms

of classical liberalism and those of communism, which has Soviet Russia as its experimental laboratory. It distances itself from individualistic liberalism because it proved incapable of generating anything but the exploitation of man by man when it turned over to the unrestrained egotism of individuals the natural sources of wealth and the means of production. It distances itself equally from state communism because it is not in the nature of our people to accept a system that deprives it of the complete enjoyment of the fruits of its labor, nor does our people wish to replace the individual employer with the state-employer.

Now, given this policy of class conciliation, it is proper to ask: What did the system offer the working class that would compensate for the preservation of private ownership of the means of production, the source of exploitation? First, a program of cooperatives; second, acceptance of the struggle of the proletariat for its economic betterment on the institutional level, that is in terms of Article 123 of the Constitution. Nothing more. And the working class leaders, who never accepted the cooperative idea as a true solution, nonetheless decided that the second offer at least was just and in harmony with the conditions of the country.

4. CÁRDENAS SPEAKS

Mexico's struggle for economic sovereignty reached a high point under Lázaro Cárdenas. In 1937 a dispute between U.S. and British oil companies and Mexican unions erupted into a strike, followed by legal battles between the contending parties. When the oil companies refused to accept a Mexican Supreme Court verdict in favor of the unions, Cárdenas intervened. On March 18, 1938—celebrated by Mexicans as marking their declaration of economic independence—the president announced in a radio speech that the properties of the oil companies had been expropriated in the public interest. It should be noted, however, that the oil nationalization did not set a precedent; thus, Cárdenas allowed some 90 percent of the mining industry to remain in foreign hands. An excerpt from his message to the nation follows.

The history of this labor dispute, which culminates in this act of economic emancipation, is the following: In connection with the strike called in 1934 by the various workers' unions in the employ of the Compañía Mexicana de Petróleo "El Águila," the Federal Executive agreed to intervene as arbitrator to secure a conciliatory agreement between both parties.

In June 1934, the resultant Award was handed down and, in October of the same year, this was followed by an explanatory decision establishing adequate procedure for revising those resolutions which had not already been agreed to.

Mexico's Oil, Mexico, 1940, pp. 878–879.

At the end of 1934 and early in 1936, the Chief of the Labor Department, delegated by me for that purpose, handed down several decisions with respect to wage levels, contractual cases, and uniformity of wages, on the basis of the Constitutional principle of equal pay for equal work.

The same Department, for the purpose of eliminating certain anomalous conditions, called the representatives of the various trade-union groups into a conference at which an agreement was reached on numerous pending cases, others being reserved for subsequent investigation and analysis by commissions composed of labor and employer representatives.

The Union of Oil Workers then issued a call for a special assembly in which they laid down the terms of a collective contract which was rejected by the oil companies on its presentation.

Out of consideration for the wishes of the companies and in order to avert a strike, the Chief of the Labor Department was instructed to secure the acquiescence of both parties to the holding of a worker-employer convention to be entrusted with the task of establishing, by mutual agreement, the terms of the collective contract. The agreement to hold the convention was signed November 27, 1936, and in the meetings the companies presented their counter-proposals. Because of the slow progress being made, it was then decided to divide the clauses of the contract into economic, social, and administrative categories, so that an immediate examination of the first-named group might be undertaken.

The difficulties preventing an agreement between the workers and the companies were clearly revealed by the discussions; their respective points of view were found to be very far apart, the companies maintaining that the workers' demands were exaggerated and the workers, for their part, pointing to the companies' intransigence in refusing to understand their social necessities. As a result of the breakdown of the negotiations, the strike began in May 1937. In response to my appeals, the companies then offered an increase in wages and a betterment of certain other conditions, and the Union of Oil Workers decided to resume work on June 9th, at the same time bringing an economic action against the companies before the Board of Conciliation and Arbitration.

As a result of these events, the Board of Conciliation and Arbitration took jurisdiction in the case and, in accordance with the provisions of the law, a commission of experts, composed of persons of high moral standing and adequate preparation, was designated by the President of the Board.

The commission's report found that the companies could afford to meet the disbursements recommended in it, namely, an annual increase of 26,332,756 pesos, as against the offer made by the seventeen oil companies at the time of the strike in May 1937. The experts specifically stated that the conditions recommended in the report would be totally satisfied with the expenditure of the sum stipulated, but the companies argued that the amount recommended was excessive and might signify an even greater expenditure, which they estimated at a total of 41,000,000 pesos.

In view of these developments, the Executive then suggested the possibility of an agreement between representatives of the Union of Oil Workers and the companies, duly authorized to deal with the dispute, but this solution proved impossible because of the refusal of the companies.

Notwithstanding the failure of this effort, the Public Power, still desirous of securing an extrajudicial agreement between the parties at issue, instructed the Labor Authorities to inform the companies of its willingness to intervene with the purpose of persuading the Labor Unions to accept the interpretations necessary to clarify certain obscure points of the Award which might later lend themselves to misunderstandings, and to assure the companies that in no case would the disbursements ordered by the Award be allowed to exceed the above-mentioned sum of 26,332,756 pesos; but in spite of this direct intervention of the Executive, it was impossible to obtain the results sought.

In each and every one of the various attempts of the Executive to arrive at a final solution of the conflict within conciliatory limits, and which include the periods prior to and following the *amparo* action which has produced the present situation, the intransigence of the companies was clearly demonstrated.

Their attitude was therefore premeditated and their position deliberately taken, so that the Government, in defense of its own dignity, had to resort to application of the Expropriation Act, as there were no means less drastic or decision less severe that might bring about a solution of the problem.

For additional justification of the measure herein announced, let us trace briefly the history of the oil companies' growth in Mexico and of the resources with which they have developed their activities.

It has been repeated *ad nauseam* that the oil industry has brought additional capital for the development and progress of the country. This assertion is an exaggeration. For many years, throughout the major period of their existence, the oil companies have enjoyed great privileges for development and expansion, including customs and tax exemptions and innumerable prerogatives; it is these factors of special privilege, together with the prodigious productivity of the oil deposits granted them by the Nation often against public will and law, that represent almost the total amount of this so-called capital.

Potential wealth of the Nation; miserably underpaid native labor; tax exemptions; economic privileges; governmental tolerance—these are the factors of the boom of the Mexican oil industry.

Let us now examine the social contributions of the companies. In how many of the villages bordering on the oil fields is there a hospital, or school or social center, or a sanitary water supply, or an athletic field, or even an electric plant fed by the millions of cubic meters of natural gas allowed to go to waste?

What center of oil production, on the other hand, does not have its company police force for the protection of private, selfish, and often illegal interests? These organizations, whether authorized by the Government or not, are charged with innumerable outrages, abuses, and murders, always on behalf of the companies that employ them.

Who is not aware of the irritating discrimination governing construction of the company camps? Comfort for the foreign personnel; misery, drabness, and insalubrity for the Mexicans. Refrigeration and protection against tropical insects for the former; indifference and neglect, medical service and supplies always grudgingly provided, for the latter; lower wages and harder, more exhausting labor for our people.

The tolerance which the companies have abused was born, it is true, in the shadow of the ignorance, betrayals, and weakness of the country's rulers; but the mechanism was set in motion by investors lacking in the necessary moral resources to give something in exchange for the wealth they have been exploiting.

Another inevitable consequence of the presence of the oil companies, strongly characterized by their anti-social tendencies, and even more harmful than all those already mentioned, has been their persistent and improper intervention in national affairs.

The oil companies' support to strong rebel factions against the constituted government in the Huasteca region of Veracruz and in the Isthmus of Tehuantepec during the years 1917 to 1920 is no longer a matter for discussion by anyone. Nor is anyone ignorant of the fact that in later periods and even at the present time, the oil companies have almost openly encouraged the ambitions of elements discontented with the country's government, every time their interests were affected either by taxation or by the modification of their privileges or the withdrawal of the customary tolerance. They have had money, arms, and munitions for rebellion, money for the anti-patriotic press which defends them, money with which to enrich their unconditional defenders. But for the progress of the country, for establishing an economic equilibrium with their workers through a just compensation of labor, for maintaining hygienic conditions in the districts where they themselves operate, or for conserving the vast riches of the natural petroleum gases from destruction, they have neither money, nor financial possibilities, nor the desire to subtract the necessary funds from the volume of their profits.

Nor is there money with which to meet a responsibility imposed upon them by judicial verdict, for they rely on their pride and their economic power to shield them from the dignity and sovereignty of a Nation which has generously placed in their hands its vast natural resources and now finds itself unable to obtain the satisfaction of the most elementary obligations by ordinary legal means.

As a logical consequence of this brief analysis, it was therefore necessary to adopt a definite and legal measure to end this permanent state of affairs in which the country sees its industrial progress held back by those who hold in their hands the power to erect obstacles as well as the motive power of all activity and who, instead of using it to high and worthy purposes, abuse their economic strength to the point of jeopardizing the very life of a Nation endeavoring to bring about the elevation of its people through its own laws, its own resources, and the free management of its own destinies.

With the only solution to this problem thus placed before it, I ask the entire Nation for moral and material support sufficient to carry out so justified, important, and indispensable a decision.

The Government has already taken suitable steps to maintain the constructive activities now going forward throughout the Republic, and for that purpose it asks the people only for its full confidence and backing in whatever dispositions the Government may be obliged to adopt.

Nevertheless, we shall, if necessary, sacrifice all the constructive projects on which the Nation has embarked during the term of this Administration in order to cope with the financial obligations imposed upon us by the application of the Expropriation Act to such vast interests; and although the subsoil of the country will give us considerable economic resources with which to meet the obligation of indemnification which we have contracted, we must be prepared for the possibility of our individual economy also suffering the indispensable readjustments, even to the point, should the Bank of Mexico deem it necessary, of modifying the present exchange rate of our currency, so that the whole country may be able to count on sufficient currency and resources with which to consolidate this act of profound and essential economic liberation of Mexico.

It is necessary that all groups of the population be imbued with a full optimism and that each citizen, whether in agricultural, industrial, commercial, transportation, or other pursuits, develop a greater activity from this moment on, in order to create new resources which will reveal that the spirit of our people is capable of saving the nation's economy by the efforts of its own citizens.

And, finally, as the fear may arise among the interests now in bitter conflict in the field of international affairs that a deviation of raw materials fundamentally necessary to the struggle in which the most powerful nations are engaged might result from the consummation of this act of national sovereignty and dignity, we wish to state that our petroleum operations will not depart a single inch from the moral solidarity maintained by Mexico with the democratic nations, whom we wish to assure that the expropriation now decreed has as its only purpose the elimination of obstacles erected by groups who do not understand the evolutionary needs of all peoples and who would themselves have no compunction in selling Mexican oil to the highest bidder, without taking into account the consequences of such action to the popular masses and the nations in conflict.

5. THE NEW *LATIFUNDIO*

The Cárdenas land distribution dealt a crushing blow to the traditional semifeudal lati-fundio. From the first, however, the land reform suffered from structural defects. In many cases the peasants received parcels of land that were too small to be economically viable, while aid in the form of seeds, credit, and technical assistance was often inadequate.

*After Cárdenas left office, moreover, conservative Mexican governments increasingly
tended to favor large private farms and to neglect the communally owned landholdings,
called* ejidos. *The result was the rise of a new hacienda, or* latifundio, *with disastrous
social consequences. Today, by the government's own admission, 35 million Mexicans are
malnourished, while production of basic staple foods stagnates, imports of basic grains increase, and more and more acreage and resources are devoted to raising sorghum and
other crops used to feed animals in order to satisfy the taste of an affluent minority and to
producing fresh vegetables for the American market. Since Arturo Warman wrote the
essay from which this selection is taken, the very survival of Mexican small farmers has
been endangered by the signing of the North American Free Trade Agreement
(NAFTA) between the United States and Mexico (1993), which is expected to bring a
greatly increased importation of cheap corn from the United States, and by a recent reform of Article 27 of the Mexican Constitution that allows the lease or sale of* ejido
lands.

A history can be written in many ways. One possible way of narrating and
analyzing the agrarian history of Mexico during the last quarter-century is to
write the history of the new *latifundio*, an enterprise, legally nonexistent, that
has dominated the development of the country's agriculture. The history that
I tell here does not claim to be a formal economic analysis. ... This account
focuses on the qualitative social changes that have taken place in the Mexican
countryside and its effects on the country as a whole.

To define the new *latifundio*, even for the limited purposes of this essay, is not
easy. It is a kind of monster with a thousand heads and local forms that is protected by a legal fiction that hides or masks it. It does not exist for fiscal purposes and the registries of property titles meticulously deny its possibility. It de-
fies the registries of capitalism even as it enjoys its benefits. This "irregularity"
may serve to attempt a provisional and limited definition of the Mexican *latifundio*, conceived and implemented as a pillar of development of the industrial
capitalist type. Defined in the most general terms, the new *latifundio* is a capitalist enterprise devoted to the production of agricultural products for sale in a
large market with the aim of reproducing its capital and making a profit. Like
every other capitalist enterprise, it achieves its aim by its control and accumulation of the means of production and its control over the channels and mechanisms of exchange. What is peculiar about the new *latifundio* is that its control
of the means of production does not conform to the classic rules of the system
and is not necessarily connected with ownership. This is especially important
when the means of production is land, the material basis of agriculture, but it is
equally valid for labor, which is acquired through the system of peonage, and
for the capital involved, which in good measure is supplied by the state. This

---

Arturo Warman, "El neolatifundio mexicano: expansión y crisis de una forma de dominio," in
Ensayos sobre el campesinado en México, Mexico, Editorial Nueva Imagen, 1979, pp. 39–53.

"irregularity" of the new *latifundio*, and indeed of the social and institutional framework within which it operates, is the source of its dynamism and efficacy, but is also its Achilles' heel, its limitation, and the origin of its rapid decay and obsolescence, expressed in an agricultural crisis of enormous proportions.

The new *latifundio* began to make its appearance in the Mexican countryside during the Second World War. Its precursor, the great estate, had been liquidated by the revolutionary movement in some parts of the country and in many others by the world crisis of the thirties when foreign markets for its products had collapsed and the internal market could not absorb its output of raw materials. The Cárdenas land reform radically altered the agrarian structure and half of the cultivated area was turned over to the peasants under the *ejido* system. The distributed land was used principally for subsistence crops that were integrated into the national economy through the market. The system was modified to concentrate and transfer the surpluses of the peasant sector to the capitalist enclaves of the country. The great estate had appropriated peasant labor, converting that labor into commercial products, but allowed the peasants to grow the traditional crops for their own subsistence, obviously in order to lower wages, which only supplemented the food grown by peasants for their own use. After the land division it was the peasants' production that was appropriated, and the transfer of their surpluses became dependent on the mechanism of prices and its aids: usury, monopoly, and the ownership of the work animals that were rented to the peasants.

The Cárdenas land reform, in its aspect of a somewhat belated reaction to the international crisis, overlapped with the recovery of foreign markets. Those markets revived under the stimulus of a war economy (1939–1945). The nation, or rather its ruling groups, embarked on an industrialization program, once again found attractive the prospect of selling agricultural products in foreign markets that paid in foreign currency; that is, the prospect of returning to the system of expropriating peasant labor, separated from the means of production. But the land reform was a political fact that had unleashed powerful forces. To undo the land division was an impossibility; even its future suspension was inconceivable. The great estate could not be restored. From this contradiction arose the new *latifundio*.

Although the great estate could not be restored, it was possible to protect its remnants, which could be converted into territorial nuclei of a new type of enterprise. To this end the state took steps to protect and strengthen private landholdings capable of being used for commercial production. Some of these measures had a legal character. Under Cárdenas, for example, a law designed to stimulate cattle exports exempted from division cattle ranches with areas larger than permitted by the existing legislation.

The effects of the legal measures were multiplied by their institutional application. Despotism, bureaucratic inefficiency, and corruption, with results that always favored the large landowners, dominated the public agencies charged with administering agrarian policy. The grave consequences of the "reform" in the agrarian legislation were aggravated by political measures designed to benefit the large landowners. Physical repression of nonconformist peasants gradually revived after the Cárdenas era. One of the most serious steps in this direction was the permission given to the associations of cattle raisers to act as rural police on the pretext of pursuing cattle thieves; this permission was used to legalize the actions of the gunmen employed by the large landowners. Less dramatic, but perhaps more effective, was the creation of a single peasant organization that became a bureaucratic and political appendage of the government and was used for the performance of bureaucratic tasks and the distribution of various sinecures. The management of the organization was placed in the hands of officials named from above who assumed the representation of the peasants in order to control them. This was effectively achieved, thanks to a political measure of very great importance—the continuance of land division.

During the presidency of Ávila Camacho, distribution of land to the peasantry diminished; it reached its lowest point during the presidency of Ruiz Cortines. Under President López Mateos the quantity of distributed land tended to increase and it reached its peak under Díaz Ordaz, who distributed approximately as much land as Lázaro Cárdenas. But the quality of the distributed land steadily grew worse; the proportion of arable land was minuscule and it was almost totally useless for the planting of commercial crops; the rest was deserts, badlands, mountains, or even land under water. Land distribution became a political ritual devoid of any economic significance. Land was distributed to placate political demands, but with the intention of preserving rather than transforming the agrarian structure.

The result of the agrarian reform after Cárdenas has been to polarize the disparity of landholding. Landownership has steadily become more concentrated; this is shown by a comparison of census data for 1940, 1950, and 1960. It seems clear that when the figures for 1970 are in this tendency will be even more pronounced, and this does not take account of the frauds and shams practiced by the large landowners. But the tendency toward land concentration was not sufficiently intense to achieve the restoration of the great estate as the dominant form of exploitation. The great estate exists and never completely ceased to exist, but it is less important than the new *latifundio*. It is likely that the statistical concentration of ownership reflects the consolidation of the nuclei of the new *latifundio*, which extends its territorial sway through the mechanism of renting land—another legal impossibility.

The rental of *ejido* land is the most common means of increasing production by the new *latifundio*. It has taken different forms: direct rental, illegal and perhaps most frequent; "associations" between sharks and sardines, more subtle but equivalent to direct rent; various forms of credit, in which the lender makes the decisions with respect to crops, harvesting, and sale for the debtor. In the last instance the government plays the most active role as a new *latifundista* while private investors dominate in the others. The renting of land has become so general that there exists a large group of new *latifundistas* who possess no land whatever. With a few agricultural machines, some money, and a lot of connections, they cultivate enormous extents of land rented in lots. Some of them, like migratory peons, wander about according to the different agricultural seasons. Not only *ejidatarios* but many small landowners in the broad sense of the word, lacking the means to engage in commercial agriculture on their own, have been caught in the spider web of rent. Thus the new *latifundio* in its different forms has come to control almost all the land on which it is possible to obtain very high yields with very little risk. ...

Government policies in the fields of irrigation and road construction also furthered the expansion of the territorial area controlled by the agricultural entrepreneurs. Road construction made it possible for lands with the characteristic desired by the new *latifundistas*, but without access to markets, to join the march of progress. In a certain sense, the new roads were the vanguard of the new *latifundio*. Cotton was sowed in Chiapas, sesame in the hot lands of Guerrero, and rice in Sinaloa, and today a sugar mill is under construction in Chiapas. ...

The construction of irrigation works, the most sizeable item of public investment in the countryside, was perhaps the most valuable government gift to the new *latifundistas*. Since they did not own land, they were not about to invest to improve lands which did not belong to them. They were caught in a vicious circle; they were able and willing to invest, but outside of their own territorial nuclei they could not invest in land. The state assumed that task for them. The new irrigated lands, owned by *ejidatarios* or poor small landowners who lacked the resources to produce in the quantities demanded by the government in order to recover its investment, passed on their totality to the control of the entrepreneurs who possessed these resources. The advantage was immense, and the new *latifundio*, in return for the payment of a ridiculous rent that frequently did not amount to 5% of the value of the crop, acquired control of an enormous investment made by the state.

Frequently, even the resources used by the new private *latifundistas* to cultivate the lands opened up by the federal investment also came from the government. They obtained these resources through government credit facilities in their multiple forms. A good part of the government credit directed toward the countryside wound up in the hands of the new *latifundistas*, working through legal or illegal channels, again without leaving a statistical trace. They also captured the fruits of agricultural research. They were the beneficiaries of a "green revolution," conceived in entrepreneurial terms, whose techniques could only be applied in the conditions under which the new *latifundistas* operated. Many agricultural entrepreneurs took their capital out of agriculture and transferred it to more secure if less profitable fields, content to employ the government's resources for their own benefit.

The new *latifundio* obtained another enormous benefit from state intervention in control of the market through the establishment of guaranteed official prices for their products. These were fixed, in the 1950s, taking as base the costs and returns of the new *latifundistas*, figured with a juicy margin of profit; this allowed them to operate with complete security. When the prices of their products were frozen or increased much less than those of urban products, for the benefit of the urban sectors of the population, the new *latifundistas* could absorb the relative decline, thanks to the increased yields made possible by the "green revolution." Others, who operated in less favorable zones, could not stand the decline and gradually abandoned their crops, replacing them with others that required higher rates of investment. But all received another benefit in the fact that the price of corn, declining in real terms, remained fixed; since this price regulated wage levels in the countryside, the cost of labor to the new *latifundistas* went down.

All seemed to be going well, splendidly. The new *latifundio* grew and increased its production. Between 1942 and 1964 agricultural and cattle production grew by a healthy 4.6% a year, 1.5% more than the rate of population increase, and between 1945 and 1956, precisely when the most large-scale assistance was being given to the new *latifundio*, it grew at the spectacular rate of 5.9% a year. By the beginning of the 1960s, Mexico had achieved self-sufficiency in agricultural and meat production and adequately satisfied the national demand or underconsumption—whatever one wishes to call it. In 1965 great quantities of corn and wheat were exported. More important still, from the viewpoint of industrial development, the export of agricultural products grew at satisfactory rates. In 1960, 22% of agricultural production was exported and accounted for a little more than half of all the country's exports. The exported products were totally produced by the new *latifundio*: cotton (the most important), coffee, sugar, henequen, tomatoes, and meat. The agricultural sector was acquiring foreign exchange to compensate for the enormous deficit created by imports destined for the industrial sector. ...

From the state's point of view, things were going so well in the countryside that it decided there was no need to invest so much in agriculture when that money was badly needed for industry. Public investment in agriculture was never very great, especially if we consider that it was targeted at half of the population, at least. The highest figures for public investment in agriculture and cattle-raising correspond to the administration of Miguel Alemán, when almost 20% of total investments went to that sector. That was also the period when public investment in that sector was most clearly directed to benefit a small group of private new *latifundistas*. During the regime of Ruiz Cortines, public investment in the agricultural and pastoral industry sector declined to 13.6% of the total, and it fell below 11% under López Mateos and Díaz Ordaz. The abandonment of the countryside, covered up with rhetoric and symbolic distribution of land, had become clear by 1965. Its effects were mitigated by several years of good rainfall. Even so, the decline in agricultural and pastoral production as a proportion of the total national production was evident. In a suicidal manner, these facts were officially interpreted as clear proof of the triumph of industrialization and progress: Mexico was approaching the threshold of development.

Beginning in 1970 the decline accelerated and became clear to all. The crash was provoked by the international economic crisis, the greatest since the 1930s, but its deeper causes cannot be assigned solely to the erratic course of foreign markets or unfavorable meteorological conditions. The imports of corn and wheat, uninterrupted since 1972 and with no prospect of improvement in the short range, certainly the most troublesome aspect of the crisis, basically are caused by internal factors linked to the structure of production in the countryside and its articulation with industrial production and the service sector. The "peculiarity" of the new *latifundio*, its internal structure and its relations with other sectors, can serve as the point of departure for an inquiry into the nature and origin of the agricultural crisis.

For my guiding thread I shall take the results of that separation of the control of land from its possession that in good measure determines the composition of capital in Mexican agriculture and sets limits on its accumulation, though not its reproduction. The only land on which the new *latifundista* can make such improvements as irrigation, leveling, and conditioning of the soil is that which belongs to him. When such land exists, it forms a small portion in relation to the total area in which the entrepreneur operates and whose control he obtains by renting. He will not invest a cent in the rented area, and only in certain types of enterprises—dairies, for example—will he invest in his own land. Basically his profits depend on the extent of the area which he can cultivate, not on the yields that can be obtained. The new *latifundio* grows horizontally, above all, on land which does not belong to it. The disadvantages of investing in this land determine the fact that the major part of the invested capital goes into operating costs, for the purchase of machinery and to cover the costs of cultivation. Agricultural machinery has great importance for the new *latifundio*, not so much because of its technical or economic advantages but because it is the physical instrument by means of which the entrepreneur takes control of the land during critically short periods of time. Thus the production of the new *latifundio* is generally of the extensive type and cannot be transferred to more intensive types of cultivation that require treatment of the soil or other adaptations. On the other hand, the composition of capital explains, in part, the high rate of profit, sometimes amounting to 100% of the investment and normally exceeding the rate of profit achieved in other activities. ...

Its limitations as concerns investment in the countryside make the new *latifundio* the most effective instrument for achieving the greatest and most rapid transfer of resources from the countryside to other activities. This effectiveness may help to explain the unlimited assistance that the government has given to the most brutal and rapid agency for despoiling the countryside and its inhabitants. But the effectiveness of the new *latifundio* has a high price: the destruction of natural resources, often nonrenewable. Soils, forests, natural vegetation of economic importance to the peasants are annihilated; meanwhile pests increase, the immoderate use of chemical products becomes indispensable, and salinity and erosion grow. Obviously, this enormous price is not paid by the entrepreneurs, but by the peasants who regain the land after it has become a wasteland from which all good has been extracted, while the entrepreneurs search for or demand from the state new lands for their operations. ...

6. AFTER THE FALL:
MEXICO IN 1984

Even before the collapse of the oil boom and the ensuing economic crisis in 1981–1982, domestic and foreign critics had called attention to the structural weaknesses of the Mexican model of dependent development and its grave social consequences. The events of 1981–1982 dramatically exposed the fragility of the Mexican "economic miracle," based on foreign loans and investments and the export of a few staples. But Mexico's political leadership, headed by President Miguel de la Madrid, appeared to have learned little from that experience and was bitterly criticized for its adherence to traditional strategies in the pages of a much respected opposition journal, Proceso.

Hailed as a model country by the international economic community, Mexico aggressively pushes exports, carries out to the letter the demands of the International Monetary Fund, restructures and increases its foreign debt, weakens price controls, drives wages down, reduces import barriers, and opens its doors to foreign investments.

But the government's economic policy has another face: for each percentage point decline in inflation, it creates 55,555 new unemployed.

The reality is that the average per capita income in 1983, measured in dollars, was seven times less than in 1950.

In 1983 the Mexican economy lost three years of growth, paid approximately 1 billion, 500 million pesos in service on its foreign debt, reduced the purchasing power of wages by more than one-half and, for each temporary job that it created, created two new unemployed.

These are the worst socioeconomic results in fifty years. Since 1933, a year of sharp decline of the national economy, Mexico has not recorded a depression as deep as that in 1983.

Industrial production declined, foodstuffs traditionally produced in Mexico had to be imported, retail sales fell, and the internal market shrank. All this in order to reduce inflation.

And inflation was partly reduced. According to the official figures of the Banco de México, at the end of 1983 the national index of consumer prices stood at 80.7%, that is, 18 percentage points below 1982.

Juan Antonio Zúñiga, "Costo de la austeridad. Carestia, escasez, desempleo masivo," *Proceso*, no. 378, January 30, 1984, pp. 23–27.

But last year approximately 376,400 workers in manufacturing industry were discharged. Faced with a shrinking domestic market which made the large-scale manufacture of goods too costly, companies preferred to operate at lower levels and reduce their wage costs.

The economic policies of President de la Madrid's government gave a decisive impulse to the contraction of the domestic market. By opposing the increase in real wages demanded by the workers, and by relaxing price controls, he allowed the entrepreneurs to restore their profit levels by way of price increases.

Less production means less employment, less demand, and higher prices.

It seems that government policies are designed to establish a balance between the supply of and the demand for goods and services that would automatically eliminate the growth of prices. Since it was not possible to increase production—that is, supply—to match the needs of potential consumption, it was decided to contract the demand.

The credit and monetary strategies pursued by the government played their role in this process. The high rates of interest created an incentive for saving, and those who could saved instead of spending. The complement to this was a decline in the rate of growth of money in circulation; at the end of the year that rate stood at 41.5%, about 25 percentage points below the rate in December 1982.

The domestic market and production declined so sharply that the president of the National Confederation of Industrial Chambers (Concamin), Jacob Zaidenweber, declared that industry produced for only 20% of the population, with the remaining 80% having a very low capacity to consume.

...

The specialist Georgina Naufal Tuena, of the Instituto de Investigaciones Económicas of the National Autonomous University of Mexico (UNAM), sums up the unemployment picture in 1983 as follows:

"If we add to the 370,000 unemployed in manufacturing industry the 500,000—at least—in the construction industry and this year's new job seekers who have not found work (almost 200,000), we get the following results: at the end of 1983 the increase in unemployment was at least one million persons."

That is, for each decline of one percentage point from last year's inflation rate, 55,555 workers were made unemployed—and this does not take account of its impact in the rural areas.

The government was aware of the unemployment problem. To combat it, it created the Emergency Program for Employment. Up to August, it had managed to allocate 40% of the jobs it proposed to create in the rural areas and 150,000 in urban zones, according to the first report of President Miguel de la Madrid.

In sum, for each temporary job created under this program, two other persons were thrown out of work by the impact of the crisis and the government's economic policies.

Along with employment, production has declined. ...

Everything is down, except prices.

Meanwhile the secretary of the treasury, Jesús Silva Herzog, supported by the International Monetary Fund (IMF), managed to convince the international banks to extend the payment schedule on the foreign debt, but the country will have to pay more interest for this concession.

Thus the payment of $21 billion was restructured. In return for the extension of the schedule of payments, Mexico committed itself to pay $1 billion more each year. A great concession, indeed, for which we should be duly grateful!

For payment of the so-called service of the debt, which includes amortization plus interest, the country allocated $12 billion in 1983, one-fifth more than in 1982. But the debt was restructured!

In 1982, the Instituto de Investigaciones Económicas of UNAM estimates, of each hundred dollars that entered the country, thirty-two went exclusively to service the debt. In the first half of 1983 that share rose to forty-three dollars.

The outlook for 1984 appears to be no better. The Mexican public sector will allocate more than two-thirds of its revenues—36.7%—to the service of both the domestic and foreign debt.

Priority, in practice, has been placed on complying with the payment of service on the foreign debt. In social terms, this means that the Mexican workers toil in order to pay it. Their exploitation begins in the executive offices of Wall Street.

According to the Congress of Labor, if the resources used to service the foreign debt had been used to create new jobs, they would have sufficed to create 1.5 million jobs in manufacturing industry, almost 5 million in mining, and about 250,000 in the energy sector.

But this was not done. Instead the decision was made to orient the whole economic effort and to follow faithfully the line dictated by the IMF at the cost of the sacrifices of the Mexican people.

The constant increase of prices—for the only thing that went down was the rate of economic growth—combined with the rigid wage controls, reduced purchasing power to a level never before seen in our country.

The Institute of Economic Research of UNAM estimates that in 1982 the purchasing power of wage earners fell by 45.9%. This means that wage-earners secured only half the amount of goods and services they obtained in 1982.

The situation becomes even more serious if one considers that in 1982 purchasing power had already fallen 34.5%. This means that compared with 1981, in 1983 the wages of workers were virtually pulverized.

With a larger population to provide for, the production of needed goods has decreased.

In global terms, the gross domestic product, measured by the monetary value of the production of goods and services, declined 4% in 1983. Add to this the decline which took place in 1982, of at least 0.2%.

The Mexican economy moved backwards, losing three years of growth. Its present size, measured in 1970 pesos, is the same as that of 1979. But measured in dollars, the situation is different.

The gross domestic product of the national economy—measured in current dollars against current pesos—is the same as that of 1973. Ten years of decline.

If the value of the total production—in 1970 pesos—were equally distributed among all the country's inhabitants, each would receive 11,609 pesos, which, at the 1983 rate of exchange, would be equal to approximately $74.78.

In 1950, that is, thirty-three years ago, the gross domestic product was 4,588 pesos per capita, which, at the rate of exchange for that year—8.6 pesos to the dollar—equaled $526.90, according to data from the Banco de México.

This means that the average per capita income in 1983, in current dollars, was seven times less than that of 1950, when the country was preparing to "modernize."

Last year the economic policy of Miguel de la Madrid favored the financial and moneyed sector, giving rise to new social contradictions. Whoever had money to deposit in the bank enjoyed profits without any effort. Whoever did not have it, lost more of the little he had.

A person who deposited one and a half million pesos for three months, at an annual interest rate of 50% at the end of 90 days had gained more, without moving a finger, than a worker receiving the minimum wage gained in a year.

The price increases sharpened even more the unjust distribution of income. Unofficially, it is estimated that for each Mexican who lives well there are six who live poorly or very poorly.

The foreign debt continued to rise, though at a lesser tempo than in previous years. From $80 billion it rose to $85 billion. In 1984 it continues to rise.

The signs of indebtedness have been inverted. Instead of borrowing in order to grow and "modernize" the country, today we borrow in order to pay what we already owe—and the debt increases.

The crisis spills over into the streets. It dresses in rags, extends a hand to passersby, is translated into daily acts of violence, sets up a taco stand on the sidewalk, breathes fire through its mouth, emigrates to the United States and lands in its jails, wanders through the countryside in search of work and is paid with blood.

The workers, concludes the Instituto de Investigaciones Económicas, may be certain that at the end of 1983 their sacrifices have been absolutely futile as concerns containing inflation, high prices, and unemployment.

The goal for 1984 is to reduce the inflation rate 50% below that for last year. If in 1983, for each percentage point drop in inflation 55,555 workers lost their jobs, there is no reason to expect a decline in unemployment. On the contrary, everything points to a further rise.

This is the real face of the domestic economic policy followed by the de la Madrid government. Stripped of its makeup, that's how it is. A posture of submission abroad and inflexibility at home.

7. EXPLOSION IN CHIAPAS

The revolt that broke out in January 1994 in Chiapas, Mexico's poorest state, exposed how hollow was the Salinas regime's boast that Mexico was now fully a part of the First World. According to the Mexican economist José Luis Calva, the "time bomb" that exploded in Chiapas was the result of the government's neoliberal economic program, which included cutbacks in credits and subsidies for small farmers, and especially of its free trade policy, which is expected to lead to greatly increased importation of cheap corn from the United States. In Calva's view, the recent reform of Article 27 of the Mexican Constitution, ending land distribution and allowing lease or sale of communal ejido land, "detonated" the crisis. In the last analysis, the cause of the explosion in Chiapas was the extreme poverty of people in the Mexican countryside. This is a poverty of which Chiapas is only the most dramatic example and which the Salinas regime's policies have deepened. At the end of 1994 a tense, fragile truce continued between the Zapatista rebels and Mexican government troops who surrounded the area; there was no solution to the conflict in sight. A Mexican scholar discusses the background, significance, and lessons of the Chiapas revolt.

Not for twenty years has Mexico seen a revolt like that with which 1994 opened. I might add that the rural guerrillas of the 1970s in the state of Guerrero never had the capacity to wage a "war of positions" like that of the taking of San Cristóbal and five other towns. Within one month after the appearance of the Zapatista Army of National Liberation (EZLN) and the battles waged in the region known as "Los Altos," the Mexican political lexicon—unless there is a quick settlement of the conflict—had to become accustomed to using such terms as "prolonged popular war," "war of positions," "guerrilla war," "war of movement," and the like. Does this guerrilla force have the capacity to expand? What is its social base? How long has it existed? How will it impact the Mexican political system? In military terms, the EZLN showed its ability to use the factor of surprise—a key to success in all military actions—by occupying a city full of tourists in an operation that made the EZLN known throughout the country and the world.

The EZLN demonstrated its military capacity in the first ten days of the year (the military phase of the guerrilla offensive) with uniforms and a great quantity of armaments that included high-powered weapons. What was most significant is that it had a high military and political command. The now famous Subcomandante Marcos reminds some people of the Central American guerrilla commanders. Where did the EZLN get those arms? is a question

Raul Benítez Manaut, "El desafío de las guerrillas," *Nueva Sociedad*, Caracas, No. 130, marzo-abril 1994, pp. 24–31. (Excerpt translated by the editor.)

that should preoccupy all Mexicans and not just those of Chiapas. In that most impoverished of Mexican states—impoverished but full of natural resources—everyone knows that the arms traffic is a flourishing business. The arms came from Central America where the Guatemalan army reported nonexistent clashes with that country's guerrillas in order to sell them at free trade prices to cattle raisers, powerful landowners, and others. Some were sold by or came from the Nicaraguan contras or the Nicaraguan and Salvadoran armies. These arms helped to create a situation typical of Mexico's marginal rural zones, zones where there is no justice, where violence grows at an accelerating pace. In Chiapas the cattle raisers and great landowners mete out justice with their own resources, have their own arms and "white guards," in the best tradition of Porfirian Mexico or, for that matter, of Central America. These conditions recall those which gave birth to the guerrillas in Guatemala and El Salvador. The Nicaraguan counterrevolutionaries were also active arms traders, and now that the Central American wars have diminished in intensity—declining from "total wars" to "low-intensity wars"—the drug traffickers have become large-scale arms merchants.

In order for guerrillas to exist three conditions must be met: (1) a propitious social situation, known in revolutionary literature as "revolutionary preconditions," which certainly existed in Chiapas; (2) a receptive response from sectors of the population that have nothing to lose by taking up arms; and (3) a national political situation that denies participation and access to power to many people. These three conditions do not exist everywhere in Mexico but most definitely exist in regions like Los Altos of Chiapas and the Lacandon forests.[3]

The insurrection had three sets of causes, beginning with the way that the Mexican political system operates in the rural and indigenous areas of Mexico. I may say, by way of a hypothesis, that that system displays its most repulsive aspects in the countryside, and that Chiapas, as the most backward state of the country, is where its fissures and cracks are most apparent. The Mexican Revolution never came to Chiapas, there were no battles, and the great *latifundistas* opted not to resist the revolution, adapting their posture to the new revolutionary climate of the 1920s. They became unconditional allies of the new system in order to retain their properties. As a result the colonial and Porfirian structures remained intact: semislavery, company stores in the estates, illiteracy, "white guards" who dealt out their own private justice, and the silencing of peasant and indigenous movements that challenged the system by a permanent, violent repression. Another factor was the absence of an autonomous political power vis-à-vis the economic power. The great landowners, merchants, coffee barons, lumbermen, and cattle raisers of Chiapas were also its politicos. A handful of families virtually monopolized both economic and political power. Those peculiar conditions excluded Chiapas from the "benefits" of the Mexican political system, which here displayed only its negative aspects.

In addition, in the past twenty years there has taken place in Chiapas a process of political polarization, accompanied by a total rule of violence in the administration of justice. A large number of peasant movements, land occupations, and popular mobilizations organized by school teachers occurred. The ruling class responded to all this with direct repression. There was no attempt to use the Mexican political system's mechanisms for solving conflicts (negotiation and cooptation of protest movements and their leaders). That is why the leaders of the EZLN say that their organization was born in 1983, in propitious conditions that enabled them between 1983 and 1993 to develop what the theoreticians of guerrilla war call an "accumulation of forces," that is, to create a social support base.

Secondly, the social and economic conditions in Chiapas differed markedly from the rest of Mexico and closely resembled those in Central America. A quick glance at the available statistics provides the evidence. The Mexican government defines a condition known as "extreme marginality." Of Mexico's 90 million inhabitants, 25 million live in this state, meaning that their monthly income does not amount to two minimum monthly wages. (The minimum monthly wage in Mexico is 120 U.S. dollars.) In Chiapas 84.68 percent of the total population live in these conditions. Next comes Guerrero (78.67 percent), followed by Campeche, which also borders on Guatemala (77.78 percent), and Oaxaca (75.61 percent). In Chiapas 30.12 percent of the people are illiterate, 62 percent did not finish primary school, 74 percent live in crowded, "extremely unhealthy" housing conditions—dwellings without access to potable water or any other facilities. In Chiapas this population is concentrated in the townships of Las Margaritas, Ocosingo, Altamirano, Chamula, San Juan Cancuc, and San Cristóbal de Las Casas, the places where the revolt broke out. Chiapas is also the Mexican state with the highest percentage of activity devoted to agriculture (32 percent of production). In terms of gross domestic product, the national average is approximately 4,000 U.S. dollars, in the Federal District it rises to 8,000, and in Chiapas it is under 1,000. The figures for the three Central American countries that have experienced civil wars, Guatemala, El Salvador, and Nicaragua, respectively, are 924, 521, and 500 dollars. Thus the socioeconomic figures are almost the same, taking into account that for Chiapas the figure is raised by the production of petroleum and electricity, which does not benefit or influence the economic activity of the great majority of the state's population.

Thirdly, "modernity" does not exist in Chiapas, and the prospect that the Mexican economic recovery and the North American Free Trade Agreement between Mexico, the United States, and Canada will benefit the indigenes is quite remote. They are the victims of the system.

In the interviews during the occupation of San Cristóbal de Las Casas, Subcomandante Marcos declared that "the EZLN decided to take up arms in response to the ratification of the Free Trade Agreement, because it represents a death sentence for Mexico's native peoples, whom the government of

Carlos Salinas de Gortari regards as disposable." The process of "modernization" in Mexico, as in the rest of Latin America, has given rise to a great polarization in the social structure, to a new "dualism" that in Mexico divides the country, including its regions, in a very unequal way. Thus we observe an accelerated modernization of the northern part of the country and the Federal District, while the south (Guerrero, Oaxaca, Campeche, and Chiapas) remains on the margins. In this sense Chiapas is not only the doorway from Mexico into Central America; it is the Central American part of Mexico. ...

It seems that the Solidarity program to fight extreme poverty (PRONASOL[4]) came too late to Chiapas to contain an explosive situation, produced by social polarization and the application of neoliberal policies. Chiapas needs a political PRONASOL and a juridical PRONASOL. The government must bring justice to the imprisoned and dispossessed indigenes and, perhaps for the first time in the twentieth century, it must implement an agrarian reform in Chiapas, for everyone knows that the Tzetzales and Tzotziles have not benefited from the Mexican Revolution. ...

The events of Chiapas are a warning. It appears that Mexico needs more reform of its political and juridical system, for it has become clear that the gradual, slow, and uncertain transition to democracy implemented in Mexico since 1977—certainly the slowest in Latin America—is on the verge of failure. This reform must be accompanied by many economic transformations that will really improve the life of the poor if we are to achieve "modernity." If this is not done, Mexico will continue to be a mixture of a country belonging to the First World (thanks to NAFTA, Mexico is already part of North America) and a country of the Fourth World. No one wants Mexico to be another Peru, Colombia, Guatemala, El Salvador, or Nicaragua.

To conclude, let me quote from a surprising, self-critical reflection entitled "The Zapatista Triumphs," by an analyst who belongs to the PRI establishment: "The Zapatista army has shown that we cannot guarantee peace if we do not first guarantee democracy and social justice." What the Chiapas revolt has definitely exploded is the myth of a "social justice" supposedly guaranteed by the PRI, which in reality has used the resources of the corporatist state and the process of negotiation to stifle democracy.

8. DEATH OF THE "MEXICAN ECONOMIC MIRACLE"

The de la Madrid–Salinas neoliberal program of privatization and total trade liberalization, capped by ratification of the North American Free Trade Agreement, gave rise to a hectic financial boom as foreign investors rushed in to take advantage of the sale of virtually all of Mexico's state companies and the speculative opportunities it presented. But the boom, chiefly enriching foreign bankers, multinationals, and their native allies (by 1994 Mexico had 24 listed billionaires, just behind the United States, Japan, and Germany), did not promote sustainable economic development, was in fact detrimental to Mexican national industry, and failed to alleviate the plight of the 13 to 18 million Mexicans who live in what the United Nations calls "extreme poverty." The debt and monetary crisis of December 1994 plunged Mexico into a deep and probably prolonged depression. The Mexican collapse flashed a red light to other Latin American countries with immense foreign debts and economic programs largely based on volatile foreign investment. The following selection offers an analysis of the causes of the disaster and puts the blame squarely on the neoliberal, structural adjustment policies of the PRI leadership.

The Salinas government, of which Ernesto Zedillo formed a part, offered us "a happy and prosperous future" based on a neoliberal economic reform: complete freedom of foreign trade and NAFTA [North American Free Trade Agreement], privatization of state companies in the fields of infrastructure and services, unrestricted foreign investment, a struggle against inflation, strict control of wages and public spending, and the anti-poverty program of PRONASOL.[5] In his election campaign, Cuauhtémoc Cárdenas stressed the continuing crisis, the grave trade deficit, the destruction of our economic base, the speculative character of the foreign capital invested in the stock market and its volatility, the inexorable disappearance of our foreign exchange reserves, and the imminence of devaluation. During 1994, Salinas, PRI, and Zedillo denied these facts, hid from the Mexican people the grave economic reality, aggravated it by the multimillion squandering of their election campaign, and retained power by means of lies and fraud. It took only three weeks of Zedillo's government to prove that the neoliberal economic policy was not viable and for the promised "growth with stability" to fade away, making inevitable a massive (over fifty percent) devaluation of the peso.

Up to the last moment, the government and its party lied to the Mexican people. The Secretary of the Treasury (previously Secretary of Commerce and now the government's scapegoat) guaranteed to legislators a four percent economic growth rate, a four percent inflation rate, and exchange stability for 1995; when the "band" within which the peso could float was widened, the Pristas denied it was a devaluation. And when the Bank of Mexico withdrew from the exchange market and the collapse of the peso in relation to the dollar became evident, the Prista majority in Congress, deaf to the opposition's sound arguments, irresponsibly approved a budget that every first-year economics student knew would have to be completely restructured.

Emilio Pradilla Cobos, "Zedillo sabe cómo hacero" (Primera de dos partes), *La Jornada*, México, January 3, 9, 1995. (Excerpt translated by the editor.)

The PRI puts all the blame for the economic "instability" on the murders of Posadas, Colosio, and Ruiz Massieu—murders that the government cannot or does not want to explain;[6] and on the conflict in Chiapas, limited, according to the government, to four townships in the Southeast with an insignificant role in the national economy, whose people barely survive in extreme poverty and are excluded from the games of high finance. The government has prolonged and aggravated that conflict by its lack of proposals and effective negotiations, by electoral fraud, and by imposing Governor Robledo[7] in Chiapas (with President Salinas in attendance at his inauguration). Additionally, postelection conflicts show that elections managed by the PRI, that is by the Mexican state, are dishonest, dirty, and not credible to Mexican society.

The government has concealed the structural reasons for the permanent economic crisis because they form part of the neoliberal project that Prista governments have applied since 1983. The total, sudden, and uncontrolled opening up of the Mexican market has resulted in an accelerated growth of the trade deficit, due to an avalanche of imports much greater than the increase in exports. This deficit had to be covered at all costs by the indiscriminate entry of foreign capital and by contracting new foreign debts. The foreign debt has not ceased to grow, with the result that a large part of the available foreign exchange has to be devoted to the service of the debt. Today, with the peso's devaluation, a very substantial portion of the gross domestic product is committed to serving the debt. The uncontrolled influx of foreign capital has two objectives. One is speculation on the stock exchange. This speculative capital does not increase the productive base, is highly volatile, and flees at the least sign of a fall in the profit rate. The other objective is control of the industrial, commercial, financial, and service sectors, which send their profits abroad in dollars, without fertilizing the national economy. The destruction of the productive base of small and medium-sized agricultural, industrial, and commercial enterprises that cannot survive international competition or modernize leaves the Mexican consumer dependent on foreign goods. Mexico's almost total technological dependence, due to the absence of a local sector producing capital goods or engaged in research and development, is deepened by the drive to modernize at all cost.

We do not enjoy economic sovereignty; today the economy's direction is determined by a handful of great national and foreign capitalists and their speculative activities on the stock exchange and the money market. Their conservatism is such that they give unconditional support to the ruling party, demand more thorough application of the neoliberal model, and lament that the government does not have absolute control of the political and economic situation, but their own actions are harmful to the nation's economic and social stability. On December 29, Zedillo partially recognized these facts but not their causes or the responsible parties; consequently they remain without a solution.

Some PRI legislators who form part of the state apparatus and its high bureaucracy claim that the former government, not the present one, is responsible for the devaluation and its costs. Another smoke screen. The key figures in the present government were distinguished members of the Salinas camp and are committed to the neoliberal policy, whose continuity they proclaimed to the world. Salinas and Zedillo assured us that the macroeconomic adjustment had been successfully completed and it only remained to bring to fruition its "benefits" on the microeconomic level and achieve "wellbeing for the Mexican family." Today it is clear that the first assurance was a lie, and the second was campaign demagogy to win the elections. In the next six years we will have to pay the costs of their fiasco and bear the new lies with which they will try to cover up that fiasco, looking to the elections of 1997 and 2000. No doubt remains: Zedillo knows how to get things done.[8]

Who are the winners and losers by the fiasco of the neoliberal economic policy of Salinas and Zedillo, made evident by the recent massive devaluation?

The winners, if such there be, are the great national and foreign capitalists, the *money barons*—the international financial speculators, who consumed the Mexican foreign exchange reserves used to prop up the stock market and the money market and to guarantee the repatriation of their capital when the crisis was imminent, and who have now returned to buy up at bargain prices the shares of the remaining Mexican companies. The great Mexican-American commercial enterprises, which are hiding and marking up their imported and domestic goods. The moneychangers who speculate with foreign exchange. In a word, the handful of beneficiaries of the past and present neoliberal policy.

The losers are the losers of yesteryear. The small and medium-size agricultural, industrial, commercial, and service enterprises whose market has disappeared as a result of unequal competition with the monopolies and imported merchandise or as a result of the recurring and now aggravated collapse of the domestic market. The enterprises asphyxiated by debts in dollars or pesos—borrowed at high rates of interest, with high bank charges—that have come due, enterprises now menaced by the devaluation and the rise of interest rates. The entrepreneurs who lack liquidity, who cannot replace their equipment or modernize because of the high cost of imported machinery and equipment and who cannot obtain it in the domestic market because of the stagnation of the local capital goods industry.

Hardest hit are the wage earners on all levels, suffering from two decades of wage ceilings and the decline of their real income, and now obliged by a pact between government and employers to accept a ten percent wage increase that only hours later was nullified by a devaluation, decreed by the same government, whose inflationary impact cannot be foretold. Other losers are the new unemployed and the workers in the "informal" sector, who will have fewer clients for their subsistence activities. Will the workers silently accept this new and violent expropriation of their means of subsistence? Will they continue to submit to the iron control of a trade union bureaucracy fused with capital and its authoritarian state? Other losers will be the millions of debtors to banks and credit cards who believed the claims of stability, who went into debt and now must pay at exchange and interest rates much higher than when they contracted their debts. The spoliation of the majority of Mexicans in 1982 is being repeated; then they assured us that thanks to neoliberalism it could not happen again.

Ahead lie new threats. In the field of politics, the threat of a hardening of authoritarianism in Chiapas, Tabasco, Veracruz, Guerrero, Oaxaca, and the other impoverished and oppressed rural and urban areas whose just demands for justice, democracy, and development may be stifled with repressive violence: The bullyboys of the economic and political elite have tried to convince themselves and everybody else that the problems of the economy and the nation stem from "nonconformity." They will make a great mistake to think that all of Mexican society accepts this lie and that they have the support and justification they need to strike an exemplary blow. We must show them that they are wrong, that Mexicans yearn for peace with justice and dignity and will not accept this false solution.

In the field of economics, the PRI government's policy, delineated by Zedillo on December 29, will once again, in the name of "fighting inflation," tighten the screw of wage austerity and public spending in order to transfer all the costs of the crisis to the workers and taxpayers. He spoke of unspecified fiscal measures that will surely affect the welfare of the broad masses and expand the privatization of state companies (the state oil monopoly, Pemex, the state electricity company, and the state railroads may be among them, since very few are left), the infrastructures (roads, transport, communication), and services (Social Security, schools and universities, etc.) in order to cover the approaching fiscal deficit. These measures were foreshadowed in Zedillo's electoral campaign. The national patrimony, constructed with the taxes of all Mexicans, will continue to be auctioned off to the highest foreign or national bidders, transferred for their individual benefit, while we the taxpayers will continue to pay the enormous sumptuary expenses of the bureaucracy and the costs of the crisis of their policy. At the same time we will have to pay twice for public services, a just and lawful payment to the treasury and another to the private entrepreneurs. One more blow to the national sovereignty and the pockets of Mexicans.

Zedillo said nothing about modifying the neoliberal policy or about a new social policy, or about attacking the structural causes of this new crisis of Mexican capitalism; he spoke of deepening the policy, of purely conjunctural adjustments and more sacrifices for Mexicans. He fired the Secretary of the Treasury, made a scapegoat, but the nature of the government was unchanged. Zedillo's electoral promise of "wellbeing for the Mexican family" (whose family?) revealed its demagogic character only three weeks after he took office. "Zedillo knows how to get things done"; he learned from his neo-liberal teachers in the United States and got his practice in Salinas's government. Because of the characteristics of the Mexican government, we will have to stand six whole years of this political and economic drama. For us there does not exist the possibility, which exists in truly democratic countries, of a change of government.

18

༄

ARGENTINA:

THE STRUGGLE FOR

DEMOCRACY, 1890–1994

A FLOOD OF European immigrants and capital transformed the face of Argentina in the last decades of the nineteenth century. Cattle raising and agriculture made great progress, and a flourishing middle class, largely of immigrant origins, arose in Buenos Aires and other urban areas. In 1916 the long struggle of the middle class and its allies, organized in the Radical party, to win free elections and a share of political power succeeded when Hipólito Yrigoyen was elected president. But whether Radicals or Conservatives ruled, agrarian interests continued to dominate Argentine life; they were virtually unchallenged until 1930, when the Great Depression sharply reduced exports and imports and promoted a rapid growth of domestic industry.

The outbreak of World War II caused tension between pro-Allied groups and a nationalist military who held England and the United States responsible for Argentina's neocolonial status and wished to keep Argentina neutral in the great conflict. On the eve of the election of 1943 an army revolt, engineered by a powerful secret military lodge, brought to power a government dominated by ultranationalistic militarists.

A young army colonel, Juan Domingo Perón (elected president of Argentina in 1946, reelected in 1952), soon rose to leadership of the nationalist movement. His program, combining industrialization with a paternalistic effort to improve the condition of the working class, was expressed in the doctrine of *justicialismo*, which preached national unity and rejected class struggle. Despite his radical antioligarchical, anti-imperialist rhetoric, Perón made no serious effort to challenge the *latifundio*, a major cause of Argentine rural backwardness, or to restrict foreign investment in Argentine industry. In the postwar period declining demand and prices for Argentine exports

338

created difficulties for Perón's program. Economic distress and Perón's concessions to agrarian interests and foreign capital weakened his mass base, a coalition of industrialists and workers, and in 1955 a more conservative military ousted him and sent him into exile.

From 1955 to 1973 a hard-line military dominated Argentine political life, setting the rules for the game of electoral politics, ousting presidents whose policies displeased them and replacing them with governing military *juntas.* In 1966 the military ousted President Arturo Ilia, who had made conciliatory gestures toward the still powerful Peronist movement, and replaced him with a military *junta* headed by General Juan Carlos Onganía. His dictatorial regime, brutally and stupidly repressive, and strongly favorable to big business and foreign interests, created a wave of bankruptcies and strikes. The failure of Onganía's experiment in governing led to his dismissal and the rise of yet another military *junta* whose controlling figure was General Alejandro A. Lanusse. In March 1971 Lanusse promised to restore free political activity and allow the return of the Peronists to full electoral participation.

In March 1973 Hector J. Cámpora, a leader of the Peronist left wing, easily won the presidential election but resigned in July to pave the way for Juan Perón, just returned from exile in Spain. In September Perón, with his wife Isabel as his running mate, was overwhelmingly elected president. During his short tenure of office, Perón attempted to implement his old policies of economic nationalism, based on compacts between labor and industry. By July 1974, however, when Perón died, the Peronist movement had begun to disintegrate as a result of division between right and left wings. Under President Isabel Perón the right wing gained the upper hand, while the country slipped into economic chaos, accompanied by escalating violence on the part of rightist "death squads" against real or suspected leftist guerrillas and other dissidents.

In March 1976 the military again stepped in, ousting Isabel Perón and replacing her with a three-man military *junta.* The *junta* banned all political activity and waged a "dirty war" against so-called "subversives" that resulted in the disappearance of thousands of Argentines. In the economic field, it implemented a free market policy: Reduced tariffs on imported goods and reduced government economic activities led to a record number of bankruptcies and bank failures. In April 1982, with the economy in shambles, the president of the *junta,* General Leopoldo Galtieri, took a desperate gamble designed to divert attention from the economic crisis and rally Argentines behind the flag: He sent 9,000 troops to seize the Malvinas (Falklands) Islands in the South Atlantic, claimed by both Argentina and Great Britain for one hundred fifty years. Argentina's swift defeat in the ensuing war brought the downfall of the *junta.* In July 1982, Galtieri's successor, General Reynaldo Bignone, promised an end to military rule, with presidential and congressional elections to be held before the end of 1983.

In October 1983 the center-left Radical party candidate for president, Raúl Alfonsín, defeated the candidate of the badly divided Peronist party; his party also gained a majority in Congress. Taking office in December, Alfonsín offered a program of economic and social reform and promised to bring to trial members of the military *juntas* responsible for the crimes of the "dirty war." Several generals were in fact tried and convicted and awarded long prison sentences. Against overwhelming popular opposition, however, in 1987 Alfonsín ended prosecutions of most lower-rank military for human rights abuses on the grounds that they had simply carried out orders. Despite this lenient attitude, Alfonsín had to put down a series of mutinies by sections of the divided and disgruntled armed forces. His biggest problem, however, was an economic crisis of unprecedented proportions, complicated by a foreign debt that by 1989 had grown to $60 billion. Alfonsín's policies of austerity and faithful service of the foreign debt, demanded by the International Monetary Fund as a condition for new loans, devastated living standards and left no capital for development. By May 1989, as the country prepared to elect a new president, Argentina had the worst of all economic worlds: a profound recession with rising unemployment and an inflation rate of 12,000 percent.

Against this background of economic collapse, the election of the Peronist candidate, Carlos Saúl Menem, was a foregone conclusion. Contrary to all expectations, however, on taking office Menem did not repudiate the conservative, neoliberal policies that had led the country to an unprecedented crisis. Convinced that an even more powerful dose of those policies was needed, he announced a program of privatization of state-owned companies, the firing of thousands of state employees, and massive cuts in government spending. The privatizations of profitable state companies such as the national airline and the national telephone company were carried out with frenzied haste, both being sold for a fraction of their net worth. To combat inflation, in March 1991 Menem unveiled an economic plan making the Argentine currency convertible in relation to the dollar and ensuring wage and price stability by making massive cuts in government spending, largely at the expense of government services such as health, education, welfare, and pensions.

Menem's "shock therapy" succeeded in curbing inflation, and memories of the hyperinflation that raged under Alfonsín contributed powerfully to the Peronista (Justicialista) party's victories in the 1991 and 1993 congressional elections. But the program had an immense social cost: In Argentina, which until recently had the highest per capita beef consumption in Latin America, hunger, malnutrition, and diseases such as cholera, which is linked to extreme poverty, became endemic. A striking development was the appearance of a class of "new poor," including many members of Argentina's once substantial middle class. Growing concern over the social costs of Menem's neoliberal policy was accompanied by unease over the authoritarian temper of his regime, reflected in the bypassing of Congress through free use of executive decrees, the collection of intelligence on political opponents, and thinly veiled threats against dissidents and "subversives." Adding to the unease was a wave of corruption involving Menem's appointees and relatives. Many were also troubled by Menem's pardon of the generals who had been convicted and jailed for their crimes, part of his policy of cultivating warm relations with the military. Meanwhile there were ominous signs that all was not well with the economy. On the credit side, inflation was down to about 12 percent in 1993, foreign debt had been cut to 25 percent of the GDP, and the economy was growing at almost 9 percent a year. But Argentine agriculture suffered from low international prices, shrinking export markets, and the high cost of credit. The removal of tariff barriers brought a flood of cheap textiles and other imports, causing many factories to close. Even as the economy grew, so did unemployment, which rose to a combined unemployment and underemployment rate of 25 percent.

Despite widespread discontent, Menem, stressing the gains in reducing inflation, still playing the Peronista card, and supported by the corrupt leadership of the General Confederation of Labor and other Peronista mass organizations, won reelection in 1995 with almost 50 percent of the vote. One big surprise of the election, however, was the emergence of a new center-left coalition, the National Solidarity Front (FREPASO). Stressing the corruption of the Menem regime and the devastating social results of its neoliberal policies, FREPASO captured the majority of votes and the mayoralty in Buenos Aires. Another surprise was the total eclipse of the Radical Party. Drawing only 17 percent of the vote, it suffered its worst showing in the twentieth century.

What lies ahead for Argentina? The spread of the Asiatic crisis in 1997–1999 created turmoil in Argentina and neighboring Brazil. Given the expanding economic crisis in Latin America, it was no longer possible to claim that neoliberalism was the only game in town. Choosing her words carefully, Graciela Fernandez, a leader of FREPASO and a veteran of the 1970s human-rights crusade against the military tyranny that disappeared one of her children, made clear that a solution to her country's problems must include a redefinition of the "relationship between the powerful and the dispossessed." Such a solution required greater equity in relations between Argentina and the great core capitalist powers that have long dominated its economy and distorted its development. How Argentina will achieve these goals remains unclear at the moment.

1. THE BIRTH OF THE NEW ARGENTINA

Between 1880 and 1900 the immigrant, the railroad, the refrigerator ship, and other agencies of progress rapidly transformed the primitive Argentina pictured in Domingo

Faustine Sarmiento's Facundo. *Of all the factors making for change, none exceeded immigration in importance. An Argentine historian, José Luis Romero, surveys the economic and social consequences of this great movement.*

The Economic Transformation

In the half-century between 1810 and 1859 —the period which may be called "creole" in the strict sense —the population of the country rose from 405,000 to 1,300,000 inhabitants. This growth, due almost entirely to national increase, amounted to less than 900,000 in half a century—that is, to an average of 18,000 a year. For a territory of almost 3,000,000 square kilometers this rate of natural increase was insignificant. Clearly, the conquest of the desert could not be achieved by this means alone. A vigorous policy of stimulating immigration was needed, and that was the policy adopted by the Argentine government from the very beginning of the organized Republic.

The results were impressive. Thanks to active propaganda and generous official aid, a tidal wave of immigrants inundated the country. During the first administration of President Roca (1880–1886), 483,000 immigrants entered the country, and the average of 80,000 a year was exceeded several times, rising to 261,000 in 1889 and even more in 1906. Italians and Spaniards predominated, but there were smaller contingents of different national origins. This stream of immigration also stimulated natural increase. As a result of these developments, a rapid transformation of the Argentine population took place.

The first national census, taken in 1869, revealed a population of 1,830,214 inhabitants. Twenty-six years later, in 1895, the number had risen to 3,956,060—an increase of more than two millions, or an average gain of 81,500 inhabitants a year. Of that total, more than a million were foreigners and belonged almost entirely to the immigrant element. This will suffice to give an idea of the rapid transformation of Argentine society, especially if one considers that in 1869 the number of foreigners barely exceeded 300,000; their share in the population had thus risen from 16.6 percent to 25.4 percent. The passage of time strengthened this trend. The census of 1914 disclosed a population of 7,885,237; the increase of almost four millions in a space of nineteen years gave an average growth of 207,000 inhabitants a year, and the proportion of foreigners rose to more than 30 percent of the population. And in the sixteen years between 1914 and 1930 the population contin-

---

José Luis Romero, *Las ideas políticas en Argentina*, Mexico, Fondo de Cultura Económica, 1946, pp. 169–183. (Excerpt translated by the editor.) Reprinted by courtesy of the Fondo de Cultura Económica.

ued to increase at an annual rate of 223,000 until it reached the figure of 11,452,374.

This growing population tended to concentrate in the zone of the littoral, in the urban centers above all. Meanwhile the rural population, whose growth a sound policy would have encouraged, suffered a sharp decline. In 1869 the rural sector comprised 65.8 percent of the total population; in 1895, only 57.2 percent; in 1914, a bare 42.6 percent. And this process of decline has continued right down to the present, when the corresponding figure is 31.8 percent. The tendency toward urban concentration was most marked in Buenos Aires, which had only 85,400 inhabitants in 1852. After 1870 the city experienced an extremely rapid growth. By 1889 its population had passed a half-million mark, and the number doubled in less than twenty years, reaching 1,244,000 in 1909. In the next twenty years it doubled again, and, although it did not maintain that pace, it continued to grow at a rate that was always disproportionate to that of the rest of the country. Buenos Aires had the largest concentration of foreigners; it also had the greatest concentration of economic activity. Meanwhile the population of the interior regions—particularly of the Northwest—remained static as a result of their economic decay. Few immigrants settled in these zones, whose inhabitants retained the traditional creole traits. A marked contrast arose between the interior and the littoral, and this contrast soon became a distinctive characteristic of Argentine social life.

Population growth, added to other factors, gave an extraordinary stimulus to economic advance. Stock raising continued for some time to be the principal activity, but the crossing of breeds and other improvements changed its character. The new cattle industry opened wide vistas to our commerce, especially with the coming of refrigerator ships. But agriculture was the activity that benefited most from the new immigrant type of population. After the establishment of the colony of Esperanza in 1856, in the province of Santa Fe, important agricultural centers began to arise in the littoral. Fencing of the fields to protect them from the herds was begun, not without opposition, and cultivation was expanded and improved. The cultivated area increased from two million hectares in 1880 to five million in 1895, twelve million in 1905, twenty-six million in 1923, and thirty million hectares at present. This advance of agriculture, which contributed materially to the growth of wealth, was accompanied by a certain amount of division of the land. But over vast regions there existed—and still exist—extensive latifundia kept intact not so much by the needs of the cattle industry as by the stubborn monopolistic policy of the landowning classes. The development of mineral resources (especially of petroleum, after 1907) also made progress, but this expansion did not match the mighty advance of the agricultural industries, particularly in respect to exportable surpluses. Manufacturing and processing industry also grew after 1880. In 1895 there were 24,114 industrial establishments in the country, employing 175,000 workers. By 1913 the number of establishments had doubled, and the number of workers employed had risen to 410,000, with a five-fold increase in the capital invested. But industrial growth lagged far behind the expansion of foreign trade. From the time when the export of grain began—in the presidency of Avellaneda—exports and imports made equally rapid gains. The foreign trade figures reveal a massive economic activity, and in particular show the increasing volume of the capital involved. From 104 millions in 1880, the value of trade rose to 254 millions in 1889, and after a difficult period of political and financial crisis it reached 241 in 1898 and 724 in 1910. Aside from money in circulation, there was a sharp expansion of bank credits for both productive and speculative purposes, and large loans were contracted abroad, especially for public works.

In this field, extension of the railway network was the principal concern. "Whoever has attentively followed the progress of this country," said General Roca to the Congress on assuming the presidency in 1880, "must have noted the profound economic, social, and political revolution brought about by the railroad and the telegraph as they penetrate the interior. These powerful agents of civilization have made possible the achievement of national unity, the conquest and extermination of banditry, and the solution of problems that appear insoluble, at least at the present time. Rich and fertile provinces only await the coming of the railroad to increase their productive forces a hundredfold, thanks to the ease with which it brings to the markets and ports of the littoral all their varied and excellent productions. ..." This conviction guided Roca's economic policy. The 2,313 kilometers of track in existence when he came to power had increased to 5,964 when he left office in 1886. Four years later, on the outbreak of the revolution of 1890 during the administration of Juárez Celman, there were 9,254 kilometers of track; at the end of Roca's second administration, in 1904, the corresponding figure was 19,430. At the same time large sums were expended on other types of public works: the construction of bridges, dikes, and public buildings, and, above all, of the port of Buenos Aires, cost immense sums, which the State obtained by the use of its foreign and domestic credit, supported by the certainty that prosperity was a law of Argentine economic development. ...

Even a superficial consideration of the economic transformation that took place reveals its immense significance for Argentine social life. The rapid irruption of foreign elements, difficult to assimilate, changed the face of our population; the revolution in economic life produced an equally profound disturbance in the system of social relations. Of the old creole Argentina, ethnically and socially homogeneous, with its elementary economic system, there soon remained but a vague recollection, nostalgically preserved by certain groups that had lost their influence on the direction of our collective life. After 1880, approximately, the alluvial Argentina, the Argentina that arose from that upheaval, grew, evolved, and struggled to achieve a balance that only the slow processes of time could bring about.

Meanwhile the social and political history of Argentina developed to the rhythm of that process of stabilization, and the forms it assumed revealed their essential instability.

The Psychological Make-Up
of the New Society

The society formed by the incorporation of the immigrant mass in the creole element acquired the characteristics of a conglomerate, that is, of a formless mass, without definite relations between its parts or definite characteristics as a whole. The immigrant mass, considered by itself, had certain peculiar traits, but it soon entered into contact with the creole mass, and from this relation there arose reciprocal influences that modified the one as much as the other.

The psychology of the immigrant was determined by the impulse that had moved him to abandon his native land and seek his fortune in America. That impulse was fundamentally economic, and stemmed from the certainty that American life offered unlimited opportunities in return for intensive effort— effort that yielded only meager returns in zones of more advanced economy. Wealth, then, was the decisive motive, and everything that stood in its way appeared dispensable.

The conditions under which the immigrant mass began its search for wealth could not have been more favorable. In the atmosphere of our expanding economy a man of enterprising spirit, aided by the habits of hard work natural to the lands from which the immigrants came, had to triumph. And the immigrant triumphed in the majority of cases—which led to the rapid rise of a moneyed class psychologically characterized by an overvaluation of economic success. That, however, was not its only characteristic. The immigrant had broken his ties to his native land, and with them he abandoned the system of norms and principles that had regulated his conduct. As a citizen and as an ethical person the immigrant was an uprooted being to whom his adopted country could not offer—given its scanty population and the peculiar stage of development in which it found itself—a categorical, inevitable social and moral imperative in place of that which he had abandoned. The immigrant began to move between two worlds, and out of this situation arose a peculiar attitude which Sarmiento observed and defined as the early fruit of the policy of encouraging immigration. "The emigrant to South America," he wrote, "constantly dreams of returning to the homeland which he idealizes in his fantasy. His adopted land is a vale of tears that prepares him for a better life. The years go by, his business gradually attaches him to the soil, his family creates indissoluble bonds, gray hairs appear, and he continues to believe that some day he will return to that homeland of his golden dreams. Yet if one out of a thousand does finally return there, he discovers that it is no longer his homeland, that he is a stranger in it, and that he has left behind position, satisfactions, affections, whose place nothing can take. Thus, living two existences, he has not enjoyed the one and cannot enjoy the other; citizen of neither country, he is unfaithful to both, since he fails to perform the duties that both countries impose on those who are born and reside in them."

This attitude had no other basis than satisfaction with economic success; the immigrant preferred to feel that he was a foreigner, because in that status he could affirm his economic efficiency, his triumph, in contrast with the creole mass that lived in its own fashion, poor though not miserable, and enjoying its scanty spiritual pleasures. "In Buenos Aires," observed Sarmiento, "there takes place the transformation of the obscure immigrant who arrives with a stoop to his back, dressed as a peasant or worse, and dazed by the great city—first into a man conscious of his worth, next into a Frenchman, Italian, or Spaniard, according to his origin, then into a foreigner, with a title and dignity, and finally into a being superior to all about him."

This feeling of satisfaction was understandable. The immigrant was creating an economy which he dominated; with that economy he smashed the economic system that enabled the creole mass to preserve its humble dignity and the humble enjoyment of its spontaneous spiritual life. In the conflict between the two forms of economic life the rout of the traditional and the victory of the new were inevitable. As a result there arose a certain mutual hostility, expressed in the covert contempt with which the creole called the immigrant "gringo." In effect, the immigrant was displacing the creole and creating a standard of economic efficiency which made the latter his inferior economically, and, before long, socially as well.

Yet there soon began a rapid crossing between the immigrant mass and the creole mass. Frequent in the lower classes, it was no less so in the middle class that made its appearance at this time and was largely created by the upward movement of the successful immigrant. José S. Álvarez, in his *Tales of Fray Mocho*, documents with deft irony the social significance of this phenomenon, from which gradually emerged the typical Argentine middle class of the alluvial era, whose characteristics, not yet fixed, reveal the coexistence of creole ideals and the ideals of the immigrant mass, sometimes in struggle with each other, sometimes in process of fusion, and yet again juxtaposed without having made their definite adaptation.

The creole elite could hardly escape contact with the ascending immigrant wave, and within a few generations the descendants of immigrants began to merge with it; but the elite made an evident effort to preserve at least the institution of the creole landed estate, by means of a deliberate overvaluation of its characteristic mode of life. A leisurely manner, indifference to economic problems, country ways, and many other characteristics derived from the old rural and patriarchal view of life, now acquired a seal of elegance and became indispensable for whoever aspired to conquer the highest social positions. In the middle classes, on the other hand, immigrant social and economic ideals took firmer root, while among the humblest classes, even though immigrants and their descendants predominated, the creole spirit preserved a certain force that perhaps had its rhetorical aspects but nevertheless was the force of an elemental tradition, simple and rooted in the natural conditions of life. As concerns the folklore of the cities, at the opening of the century the popular song and dance began to assume hybrid forms that revealed the opposition between the new way of daily life and a design for living that seemed rooted in the earth; thus there arose the Argentine tango, saturated with creole spirit in its rhythmic, melodic, and literary elements, but also reminiscent of the more energetic attitude of the creole-immigrant conglomerate.

The principal stage for the activity of this conglomerate was Buenos Aires. "Who," asked Sarmiento shortly before his death, "are the citizens of this *El Dorado* foreseen by the ancient conquistadores, since of the four hundred thousand persons who inhabit it, the most industrious and modern part proclaims itself to be foreign, or at most acknowledges that it is the maker and builder of this transformation that is no transubstantiation, since each remains what he was: instrument, maker, builder ... ? And so there rises a great American city, all to let, with few householders, to be peopled by that world on the march which drops away from Europe like ripe fruit and is borne by the trade winds to our shores. Thus, growing by leaps and bounds, we shall have—if we do not already have—an American Tower of Babel, built by artisans of all tongues, who persist in retaining their separate languages and thus cannot understand each other. And so the great hope of the world of the future against a new cataclysm and deluge will be dissipated at the breath of any untoward event: a prolonged drouth, a foreign or civil war. For it is impossible to build a *patria* without patriotism, or a city without citizens, the soul and glory of nations." Thus did Sarmiento, a champion of immigration and unlimited economic progress, complain of the outcome of his program, of this serious impediment to the development of Argentine nationality. Another architect of progress, Roca, roundly affirmed that Buenos Aires was not a part of the nation, "because it is a foreign province." But neither Roca nor the other members of the oligarchy which dominated the country for so long a time could or would do anything to channel a larger volume of immigration toward the countryside. To do that it would have been necessary to modify the system of land use, create new centers of economic interest in the interior, assist new arrivals (who under existing conditions had no choice but to work as peons for low wages on the immense estates of the rich) to obtain homesteads. But nothing of this kind was done, and the immigrant took his revenge by remaining in Buenos Aires, where he sought his fortune not in productive tasks but in the business of distribution, thus augmenting the number of those who would enrich themselves by engaging in the secondary forms of economic life. "The city grew up in rivalry with the republic," Ezequiel Martínez Estrada points out—and that rivalry grows day by day, aggravated by the nature of the social content of the one and the other; because Buenos Aires is an amorphous conglomerate, still striving to take form; and the country is only in part that same conglomerate, in constant struggle with the forces of *criollismo*, tense and hostile in the zones beyond immigrant influence. And this duel obscures—and in large part explains—the indefiniteness of our social existence and the vicissitudes of our political life.

2. THE RADICAL TRIUMPH

In the period after 1880 the landed aristocracy—the principal beneficiary of the great economic movement created by the enterprise of the immigrant—grew increasingly indifferent to the interests and wishes of other segments of Argentine society. Middle-class resentment of oligarchical control of the political life resulted in the formation of the Radical party. From 1890 to 1912 the Radical party fought the oligarchy with agitation for electoral reform, revolts, and boycotts of elections. In 1916 the first truly free election in Argentine history raised the Radical leader Hipólito Yrigoyen (1852–1933) to the presidency. Yrigoyen's biographer and ardent admirer, Manuel Gálvez, interprets the meaning of the Radical triumph.

Before the advent of the Radicals, government was monopolized by the people of quality: the lawyers, the physicians, the *estancieros*, the intellectuals, the "well born." The middle class, like the common people, was kept away from power, save for an occasional youth who had distinguished himself by his merits and gained the entrance into society by means of an advantageous marriage. The lads of "good family," especially in the provinces, were members by birth of the National Party, whether they knew it or not. But the party only existed in name. There were no registers or members. On the eve of elections a handful of politicians formed committees financed by rich people—in exchange for future posts and other advantages—and sometimes by the unwilling contributions of officeholders. The local *caudillos* dragged their people to the committee meetings. At these affairs they did not discuss politics or enlighten the citizens concerning their civic duties. The meetings were Homeric feasts, built around barbecues in which whole steers were roasted and the people drank beer and rum and played at jackstones.

Manuel Gálvez, *Vida de Hipólito Yrigoyen*, Buenos Aires, n.d., pp. 190–193. (Excerpt translated by the editor.)

That was the extent of popular participation in political life. The *estancieros* forced their peons to vote for aristocrats whose ideas were opposed to the interests of the poor. The industrialists and all other employers of labor did the same. The government gave no thought to the oppressed classes. The lawyers who held the high government posts and received fancy salaries from great foreign firms let these enterprises exploit the Argentine worker without mercy.

With the triumph of Radicalism the middle class and the people entered on the scene. The colonial names went into eclipse. Henceforth government jobs would go to the sons of Spanish or Italian immigrants. In order not to scare the upper classes and create too many enmities at the start, Yrigoyen cleverly appointed persons of high social position to occupy certain important posts. But for each such appointment he made hundreds of the other kind. High society, the Old Guard, the opposition newspapers, waxed indignant or jeered at certain appointments. Even the neutrals joined in the laughter. There was a prevailing belief, of colonial origin, that only men of ancient lineage were qualified to govern or hold administrative positions. A minister without an illustrious name, or a fortune, or intellectual prestige, was unthinkable. The Radicals, never having governed, could not have held posts; and not only political power, but university education, and all activities in general, had been monopolized by the oligarchy.

The discharged dandies ridiculed the names of the new rulers—and their dress. They reported that the impossible cutaway of the Minister of the Interior—a provincial—had been presented to him by a certain large store on condition that he say that it was the product of a rival establishment. For the *porteño*, ill-fitting dress is proof of inferiority. A certain citizen of the Capital, seeing the celebrated writer Barrès at an affair in Paris, affirmed that a man who wore such "funny little pants" could not have talent. The Minister of Public Instruction, a primary-school teacher but also a lawyer, provoked a burst of hilarity. A detestably written "reflection" of his, in which he made malaprop use of a Latin sentence, won him an outpouring of burlesque Latin verses. The opposition exercised its wit—sometimes cruel—on the new government officials.

Only since the passage of the Sáenz Pena Law had the common people taken part in political life, not as a decorative element or as a gang grouped around its caudillo, but in its own name. Now the people ruled. The Radicals elected their candidates in direct primaries, and their opponents found it necessary to do the same; they too must organize themselves in committees, create a new political life. The picture of provincial politics drawn by Pellegrini, in which the governors were satraps, was no longer possible. A new day had come. It was the hour of democracy.

The Government House had changed its aspect. It was no longer the cold, almost abandoned place of yesterday. Formerly not a soul could be seen in the corridors, aside from employees. Now it was like a Moroccan mosque, smelling of the multitude, full of rumors, passions, hopes. The government of Yrigoyen, like the Radical Party, was very much alive. Its spirit, its coloration, was that of the people.

The Radical Party was idealistic and romantic. Leandro Alem, the John the Baptist of the new credo, infused it with his ideals: free elections, administrative honesty, the equality of men before the ballot box. The Radical Party was romantic because it was governed by sentiments, not by ideas. It believed that with its coming to power that program had been realized or was about to be realized. The Radical government had only to put into effect the perfect election law and carry out vigorously the promise of administrative honesty.

As a political party—that, and no more—the Radicals had no ideas. But all parties, sometimes without knowing or desiring it, follow some system of ideas. One of these ideas was the romantic spirit, which logically led the Radical Party to anti-intellectualism. Another was its democratic character. Yrigoyen gathered all authority to himself and in certain cases imposed his will, but he treated his adherents with simplicity and dominated in suave and indirect ways. For him there were no rich or poor; all were equal. The Radical committees led their own independent and sometimes excessively tumultuous life. They freely elected their own officers, and even their candidates for deputies, senators, and governors. As President, Yrigoyen only intervened to veto or recommend some nomination, but this by way of exception and always through his satellites, who would portentously affirm that they knew his preference.

The Radical Party, then, had come to power without a definite program. There was something utopian in Yrigoyen's dreams. Perfect governments do not exist anywhere. Caudillos and party chiefs promise what they cannot fulfill, and they promise because they know that they cannot fulfill. That was not the case with Yrigoyen. Introverted and fanatical, a man of very few ideas, he was convinced that the country only needed free elections to be absolutely transformed. ...

But if the Radical Party had no program of ideas, Yrigoyen did, although it was more a matter of intuition than of will and, naturally, not yet defined. That program had its origin in certain principles—half derived from the German philosopher Kraus and half Christian—in which he believed. We already know what they were: the equality of men and nations, human fraternity, peace, an austere life. His sense of human equality and fraternity was the source of his labor policy, which, in our milieu and in relation to the social policy of previous governments, was revolutionary. His love of peace and his concept of the "Nation" dictated his policy of neutrality during World War I. His belief in the equality of nations—a Krausian principle—guided his attitude in the League of Nations. But Yrigoyen did not formulate his program beforehand or have it clear in his mind. He was to formulate it and apply it according to the rhythm of events.

3. *PERONISMO*:
AN ECONOMIC INTERPRETATION

Popular hopes for a flowering of democracy under Radical leadership were not fulfilled. The Radicals proved incapable of giving a new direction to Argentine economic and social life. In 1930, following the first impact of the Great Depression, an army revolt ousted the Radicals from power without a fight. Their successors of the Conservative Restoration (1930–1943) proved equally lacking in solutions for Argentina's urgent problems. The Nationalist Revolution of June 1943, soon followed by the rise to power of Colonel Juan Domingo Perón, marked a turning point in Argentine history. An Argentine economist offers an analysis of Peronismo *and the reasons for its rise and fall.*

The process begun by the coup d'état of 1943 culminated three years later in the rise to power of Juan D. Perón, whose government hoisted the banners of economic independence and social justice (*Justicialismo*). Perón's economic program proposed to expand industrial development based on the internal market, which challenged the traditional linkage with foreign markets; and to promote a redistribution of income in favor of the wage-earning class, the major market for the simple manufactured goods that Argentine industry had to offer under existing conditions.

Peronismo's economic program had a defensive, nationalist character. It promised to protect native industry against foreign competition and proclaimed its enemies to be the oligarchy and imperialism. In practice, however, this program had a peculiar connotation that was closely linked to the nature of the industrial development under way and that accepted without questioning its dependent essence. *Peronismo* proposed to protect industrialization in general, opposing only efforts to restore the traditional domination of agricultural-importing interests, but it did not create the bases of a development independent of the great landowners and imperialism. Instead of promoting autonomous industrial development, it assumed a paternalistic attitude toward existing industrial development; instead of seeking to revolutionize social relations, it assumed a paternalistic stance toward the working class, seeking to promote its economic well-being within the existing framework of relations of production. This stance, a means of ensuring the survival of those relations at a time when large worldwide changes placed them in jeopardy, simultaneously served to create a market for the national capitalists. But *Peronismo* did not challenge the basis of rural backwardness (the *latifundio*),

Eugenio Gastiazoro, *Argentina hoy. Latifundio, dependencia, y estructura de clases*, Buenos Aires, Ediciones Pueblo, 1975, pp. 98–105.

nor did it question the dependent basis of the new industrial development, based on foreign monopoly investment in industry, or its failure to develop a capital goods industry or an intermediate goods industry of some complexity.

With the specific characteristics determined by our history, Peronismo retraced the road traveled by other national liberation movements directed by the national bourgeoisie, movements that have appeared in our time in many colonial and dependent countries. It attacked the superstructural manifestations of backwardness and dependency, and thereby promoted a relative internal democratization. It also challenged some elements of the old dependency, especially those linked to the traditional system of foreign trade and the foreign investments linked to that system. But it never attacked the pillars of dependency and backwardness, permitting the survival of the great landed estate and the entrenchment of foreign monopoly investment in industry. This formed part of a complex game of the industrial bourgeoisie, which simultaneously sought to achieve a dominant position in the structure of production and to associate itself with the most modern sector of the great landowners and with foreign monopoly capital, interested like itself in production for the domestic market.

The implementation of a nationalist doctrine, conceived as a program for breaking the hold of foreign dependence and developing an autonomous capitalism for the benefit of the industrial bourgeoisie, implies not only a confrontation with imperialism but with its domestic allies. The achievement of such a program is closely linked to the revolutionary potential of the industrial bourgeoisie, a potential determined by its origin and development within the complex of existing production relations and therefore by its relation to the landowners and imperialism.

In the particular case of the development of capitalism in our country—a development that left intact the bases of backwardness and dependency (the *latifundio*, of precapitalist origin, and imperialist oppression)—the individuals occupying the high peaks of industry arose, in large measure, from the ranks of the great landowners and in close association with foreign monopoly capital. The sectors of the big bourgeoisie not associated with foreign capital seek a place within the preexisting structure rather than to break with it. Moreover, their fear of a democratic mobilization of the working classes causes them to retreat from revolutionary changes and thereby limits their possibility of leading an alternative process of development, one that would require a confrontation not only with imperialism but with the great landowners and the big bourgeoisie associated with them. All this was reflected in the character of the nationalist *Peronista* doctrine, aggressive in words toward the oligarchy and imperialism, but reduced in practice to a generic protectionism of the domestic market and industrialization, with no effort to transform existing relations of production for the benefit of a relatively autonomous industrialization process. In fine, whatever may have been the intentions of the actors, this protectionism, granted that it made some corrections in the area of income distribution and favored the development of bourgeois sectors not associated with the dominant bourgeois groups, favored those groups above all.

Capitalist Development, 1945–1949

The period 1945–1949 in some ways marks the culmination of the process of Argentine capitalist development on an industrial base that began in the decade of the 1930s. The Great War had accentuated protective conditions for Argentine industry, even though it could not import needed machinery and other inputs (a situation that tended to sharpen the national spirit of inventiveness and promoted the use of hitherto neglected resources). In the immediate postwar period this development reached even higher levels thanks to a deliberate policy of protection that—though it did not attack the roots of the problems of backwardness and dependency—permitted a further expansion, especially in the so-called goods of "easy substitution" directly linked to mass consumption.

In this period, the accumulation of capital in industry was fundamentally based on the expansion of the labor force, an expansion that reduced the "reserve army of the unemployed" to a minimum. In global terms, the technical composition of capital remained unchanged and consequently productivity did not increase, and increases in production took place through the increase of the exploited labor force. The growing need for additional labor, felt most acutely in the industrial zone of the littoral and the Greater Buenos Aires area, was in large part satisfied by migrations from the interior of the country and above all from the countryside. ... This process of industrialization was also favored by the relative increase of industrial prices vis-à-vis agricultural prices; whereas the wholesale prices of industrial goods rose 94% in the period 1940–1945, wholesale prices of agricultural products rose only 44%. ...

Peronismo, as the expression of the needs of the Argentine industrial bourgeoisie, adopted economic policies and measures designed to favor it. These measures included the creation of the Industrial Bank, the channeling of credit toward industry through the nationalized Central Bank, the purchase of foreign supplies through the Institute for Trade Promotion (IAPI), the adoption of protective tariffs, and the grant of foreign currency at favorable rates of exchange for the external needs of industry. At the same time official policy encouraged the unionization of workers and promoted a redistribution of income that benefited the working class as a whole; wages were raised and price controls on goods of mass consumption served to prevent the inflationary process, in the prevailing oligopoly conditions of the marketplace, from causing excessive injury to wage earners.

The increase in the mass of wages increased the demand for goods of mass consumption, providing the import-substitution industries with a growing market. This was the case with the textile industry, whose share of the total output of manufacturing industry rose from 13% in 1935–1939 to 17% in 1945–1949. ... The participation of the state in investment acquired great importance, amounting to 34.3% of the total in the period 1945–1949, a figure much higher than that of previous or later periods, so that the state came to play a dominant role in the process of internal capital accumulation.

Despite all its stimuli to industrial development, *Peronismo* left intact the conditions that would lead to its own defeat, for it did not eliminate the bases of backwardness and dependency: the hegemony of the great landowners over capitalist development in the countryside and the hegemony of foreign monopoly capital over industrial development as a result of its continuing dependence on external sources for its basic needs.

Once the possibilities of expansion that the war had generated—notably by reducing imperialist pressure and allowing the formation of important reserves—had been exhausted, the limits of *Peronismo's* reformist industrial program became evident. The operations of industry increasingly depended on indispensable supplies from abroad, while the agricultural sector continued to be the principal provider of foreign exchange. Having failed to make a frontal attack on the agrarian problem and to change the essential character of the industrial development—its character of an appendage of the most developed capitalist countries—the Peronist big bourgeoisie gradually lost one position after another in its conflict with the great landowners and imperialism. The tendency toward conciliation with those forces gradually became a tendency toward integration; policies that favored the agricultural export sector and promoted foreign investment in industry and mining were adopted. Simultaneously a policy of "stabilization," freezing wages for two years, was put into effect. This, together with a growing emphasis on increasing productivity, implied a policy of supporting economic growth, not by removing the obstacles to its expansion, but by greater exploitation of the working class.

The objective of an autonomous capitalist development came ever more clearly into conflict with the actual road being traveled by Argentine capitalism, making evident the weakness of the national big bourgeoisie and its lack of the revolutionary initiative needed to take a truly independent path.

Economic Decline, 1950–1955

By the end of the 1940s, manufacturing industry needed ever more inputs from abroad to continue its expansion. These inputs consisted essentially of machinery and raw materials that were not produced at home. But as a result of stagnation and declining exports (the average annual value of exports in the period 1950–1954 was $1,056.5 million, compared with $1,172.6 million for the period 1945–1949), purchases abroad became increasingly restricted. Moreover, the bilateral trade agreements with foreign countries resulted in an increasingly unfavorable Argentine balance of trade. The Peronist government believed that the Korean War, by unleashing a third World War, would revive world demand for our products, permitting a new expansion of our economy. That is to say, the Peronist government continued to think in terms of a major advance of Argentine capitalism on the basis of favorable external conditions, instead of taking measures to break the economic domination of the great landowners and imperialism.

The conditions of the preceding period gradually gave way to new conditions. Increased productivity began to be the focus of governmental concern, and the capitalists began to press for a change in their favor in income distribution.

The real wages of industrial workers began to decline. For example, the real wages of skilled workers, which reached their maximum in 1948, had fallen 10% in the course of that year and fell another 26% in 1951, remaining at that level, with some fluctuations, until 1955. The wages of unskilled workers, which reached their maximum in 1950, fell 30% in that year, and remained at that level, with some fluctuations, until 1955. In order to resist this trend the working class resorted to strikes and even opposed the "Congress of Productivity." ...

The attitude of the Argentine government with regard to foreign capital gradually changed. The policy of nationalization of the foreign debt, transport, energy, and communications did not imply the nationalization of foreign capital invested in manufacturing industry (except the property of countries defeated in the war). On the contrary, the government promoted the influx of foreign capital into mining and industry, a tendency which found its juridical expression in Law 14.222 of 1953. But the law did not satisfy the demands of foreign monopoly capital. The results were the opposite of what was expected, for, with no increase in investments, the freeing of remittances abroad increased the outflow of profits and dividends, and there was actually a small repatriation of capital. The mass of foreign capital in the country, registered as such, basically in manufacturing industry, having risen from $1,740 million in 1949 to $1,870 million in 1955 (through reinvestment induced partly by restrictions on remittances abroad and above all because there existed an expanding internal market) fell to $1,860 million in 1955.

Thus Perón's paternalistic nationalism, in practice abandoning the reformist program which had generated a massive political support, sought instead to achieve an agreement with the great landowners and imperialism that would permit a new advance of Argentine capitalism, with the "collaboration" of foreign capital and intensified exploitation of the working class.

4. THE ARGENTINE MILITARY'S "DIRTY WAR"

The fall of Perón in 1955 ushered in an era of military rule that continued almost without interruption until 1983, when the military, completely discredited by its disastrous

*performance in peace and war, yielded to popular pressure for the restoration of demo-
cratic rule. The most sinister aspect of that unhappy period of Argentine history is the
"dirty war" waged between 1976 and 1983 by the military and by associated "death
squads" against the left and many other real or suspected dissidents. Calculations of the
number of people who were murdered or who "disappeared" range from 6,000 to
23,000. An actor in the "dirty war" relates some of its techniques.*

Thereby he sacrificed the most democratic features of *Peronismo*. But the oligarchy, emboldened by the impotence of bourgeois nationalism and
strengthened by the concessions that had been made to it, decided on the
overthrow of Perón, hoping thereby to remove the obstacles to a more active
participation of foreign capital in the Argentine economy.

The Argentine military repression did not even respect life in embryo.
"With pregnant women they introduced a small spoon or some other metal
instrument until it touched the fetus. Then they gave the woman an electric
shock of 220 volts. In a word, they electrocuted the fetus."

"What did you do when you witnessed such atrocities?"

"I vomited. What would you have had me do?"

Raúl David Vilarino, junior navy officer and a member of the so-called
Group of Tasks, actively participated in the military's "dirty war" against subversion, but now says that he feels nausea. He says that he still has some sense
of shame, but he is not going to weep or say that he repented too late.

He confesses, denounces, gives names, and describes atrocities in a very
long interview published in the Buenos Aires journal *La Semana* with the title, "I Kidnapped, Killed, and Saw Tortures in the Navy School of Mechanics."

"You never tortured anybody?"

"I never tortured anybody, thank God."

Vilarino defends himself. He insists that he is against torture, that torture
is never justified, under any conditions. He also tries to minimize the killings.
"If an assassin is one who kills another person, I am an assassin. If an assassin
is one who kills in cold blood, treacherously, in a cowardly way, I'm not an assassin. If I can sadly brag of anything, it's that I always would rather have
them shoot me than do such a thing."

He is disillusioned with his superiors. "I can't tell you how one feels when
he knows that the people who gave the orders, having decided they didn't
need us anymore, tried to get rid of us. Right now, as I give this account, I
feel persecuted, and I'm going to do something that will displease many colleagues who are still alive."

Lucia Luna, "Un actor de la 'guerra sucia' revela los crímenes de los militares," *Proceso*, no.
376, January 16, 1984, pp. 36–41.

He insists that his confession is spontaneous and that he is ready to pay for his offenses. But he warns, "I'm not going alone, we're all going together." And he begins to name names: Rear Admiral Rubén Jacinto Chamorro, director of the Navy School of Mechanics; Captain Arduino, head of studies at the school; Lieutenant Guerrello, his secretary; navy captain Vildoza, chief of the Group of Tasks; corvette captain Jorge Eduardo Acosta, chief of intelligence and torturer; Captain Francis Whamond, torturer; navy lieutenant García Velasco, alias Dante, torturer; the now famous Lieutenant Alfredo Astiz, torturer.

The list is endless. Vilarino puts special emphasis on the names of the doctors. "The principal one was Dr. Alberto, who liked to be called Mengele. He was in charge of all the tortures and displayed the greatest zeal of all in carrying them out. Sometimes he wore black gloves; he also ordered that a black eagle be painted on the walls of the officers' club. There was Dr. Magnasco, gynecologist, who together with Mengele had thought up the torture for pregnant women. José Luis, the odontologist, in charge of extracting molars from the dead—and from some who were not completely dead—in order to conceal their identities.

Vilarino also tells in some detail about Father Sosa, chaplain of the School of Mechanics. "He didn't wear a frock. He was a sort of cabaret priest. Once I asked him if he thought that what we were doing was right, and he said that one must think about these things like a surgeon. If you're going to amputate the evil you can't worry about the aesthetics of the patient."

But he assigns the greatest responsibility to Admiral José Emilio Massera, commander in chief of the navy. "Chamorro's only boss was Admiral Massera. It was Massera who signed the order to turn over a certain amount of money for the expenses of the Group of Tasks, which means that he approved of the methods it used."

Vilarino describes these methods, step by step. First the trailing of suspects, the break-ins, the arrests, the kidnappings. Then the jailings, the interrogations, the tortures. And, finally, the manner of disposing of the corpses.

In the beginning, he says, there were simple patrols, interceptions of mail and guerrilla missions, arrests of specific individuals. Later came the clean-up operations. A city block was cordoned off, traffic stopped, and a house-to-house search was made. Inside the houses they looked for subversive material. They also demanded documentary proof of ownership of everything of value—TV sets, radios, jewels, even money—and if a person could not prove ownership he was arrested. "You know, once the warranty has expired nobody feels obliged to keep a bill of sale. Then police would say those things were illegally acquired and would embargo them. I don't know where all those things went, but some turned up in the homes of officers or junior officers who needed a TV or a radio.

"When the operation was aimed at the arrest of some specific person or group, they would be more discreet. No more than four persons went along, in order not to arouse the whole ward. One man remained in the car and another on the street. Then they rang the door bell. If the door was not opened they would knock out the lock. They tried to work as discreetly as possible. In the case of farms or houses away from town, where they did not have to act with such propriety, they would enter shooting, having thrown a grenade to knock the door down. In the city they didn't do this, for why massacre people, especially if you've come to the wrong door."

"Were there many mistakes made?"

Vilarino admits that sometimes they came to the wrong address but did not stop to see if the occupant was really a guerrilla before killing or arresting him. In other cases, fear caused confusion. "A man would shut himself in or try to flee because he didn't know what it was all about. Then the commando decided that it was meeting resistance and killed or arrested him."

Other persons were shot down because they happened to be passing by at that moment or ran up in alarm to learn what was going on. "When bullets are flying they bear no name or address."

The ex–navy corporal tries to justify himself. They were psychologically conditioned to see an armed guerrilla behind each door and window. They were often received with fire. "There also were situations staged by the guerrillas to make us kill innocent people and prove that we were murderers." ...

Guilty or not, the worst off were the people they took alive. Vilarino tells what he saw in the Navy School of Mechanics. There was a door on which someone had written: "Road to Happiness." Behind it was the torture chamber: electric prods, the iron wirework of a bed connected to an outlet of 220 volts, an electrode of 0 to 70 volts, chairs, presses, pointed or cutting instruments, bicycle tires filled with sand that could be used to give blows without leaving a mark—and everything imaginable that could be used for torture.

He gives details of one of the tortures. "Did you ever receive an electric shock from a refrigerator, a bath faucet, or some electrical appliance? Multiply that by a hundred and then by a thousand. Add the cries of pain, and you will know what it feels like to be tortured. Then, conscious or unconscious, the prisoner was thrown into a cell and given a bucket of water with which to stuff himself, and the next day he suffered worse torments than when they left him."

With women especially, the corporal remembers, "they used techniques used by thugs in a gangster movie: burning with cigarette stubs, pulling or pinching the skin, beatings." Every kind of sexual abuse and torture, rapes, and the technique especially designed for pregnant women described above. Although he does not clearly say so, he suggests that many men were also sexually abused—more precisely, castrated.

Soon he recalls another very special torture that was inflicted in the submarine base of the naval station. "They made many prisoners dive without diving equipment or tube. They submerged them and then brought them up to see if they would talk. Below was a man in a diving suit or a frogman who struck and tortured them. When a prisoner came up he would lack a finger so that the others might see what would happen if they didn't talk. Or the prisoner might simply disappear. A launch with an outboard motor would be sent out to drag the corpse far enough away so that the public or people at the base could not see it." ...

Yet all this *danse macabre* managed to elicit very little true information. "After a torture session the majority of prisoners were ready to sign that they had killed President Kennedy or had taken part in the battle of Waterloo. That is why I say that the greater part of the data obtained by torture was unreliable; most often they were used to justify the arrest of the prisoners."

Vilarino continues trying to justify his own actions. He never kidnapped people. He just carried out the orders of higher-ups. "We believed in the policies we carried out because it had been charged that the Federal Police were involved both in guerrilla activity and law enforcement. Later I realized this was just an attempt to provide legal justification for the Group of Tasks."

The junior naval officer becomes confused and entangles himself. He accuses, denounces, and tries to shift responsibility to others. He admits mistakes and brutalities. He insists that he feels nausea and is ready to pay for his offenses. But in the end he is unrepentant and insists that he would do it all over again.

"You base your defense on the fact that you had no option, that you had to carry out your orders, because otherwise you would have suffered the same fate as the people you arrested. Are you aware that it was a matter of sacrificing many lives, many innocent lives, in exchange for your own?"

"Sure, but my life and the lives of my family come first. I had a wife and daughters, and would exchange many lives for the lives of those three. Even though I no longer live with my wife and daughters, their lives mean more to me than those of many 'disappeared' persons. You've never had people paint signs on the wall of your house; it's not a pretty thing. In a word, though I have left my wife and daughters, for the sake of their security I would do it all over again."

5. THE MENEM PHENOMENON: ARGENTINA, 1989–1994

The election of Carlos Saúl Menem as president of Argentina in 1989 ushered in one of the most thorough, brutal applications of the neoliberal economic program in any Latin American country with the wholesale privatization of state companies, the dismissal of thousands of state employees, and drastic cuts in social spending. Menem, who claimed to assume the mantle of Perón, formed alliances with his domestic and foreign enemies and dealt a death blow to what remained of Perón's nationalist project for economic independence. In addition to a sharp decline in Argentine living standards, his rule was marked by a strong authoritarian tendency and by corruption scandals that involved his appointees and relatives. Despite a string of electoral successes, by late 1994 his popularity had greatly declined and he faced growing opposition to his reelection. An Argentine scholar reflects on Menem's policies and their impact on Argentine life and politics.

We must insist that Menem's economic program, like the political and ideological programs to which he subscribes with such enthusiasm, clearly places his government in the universe of neoconservative regimes. These regimes have arisen as a result of the decomposition and crisis of "Keynesian" capitalism, that is, that whole swarm of agencies, regulations, and institutions that created the "welfare state." This redefinition of the complex relationship between market, state, and civil society has had two major consequences. In the first place, it has established "a regime of social accumulation" that has an increasingly exclusivist social-economic character and is marked by the ever larger role of institutional and decision-making mechanisms that erode and diminish popular sovereignty. The combined effect of these developments is to weaken the solidity of democratic institutions and undermine the foundations of a society that not so long ago based its legitimacy on the equal opportunities that it claimed to offer all its members. In the second place, it deepens the recessive tendencies of the economy and makes more difficult its successful insertion in the world market. In this respect, the declining trajectory of the United States and Great Britain, the "standard-bearers" of that new ideology, is quite illuminating. It is significant that the countries— Germany, Japan, and Italy—that showed less fervor in embracing the neoconservative creed obtained better economic results in the decade of the 1980s.

The application of this governing formula to a society such as the Argentine can only aggravate our economic troubles, deepen existing large social inequalities, and corrode even more the fragile ethical, social, and economic foundations of our democracy. It is unlikely that the construction of a "savage" capitalism like the one now in process of creation can be achieved in the framework of democratic stability: This, at least, has been the experience of countries where that tradition has been much older and more robust than in ours. To suppose, therefore, that one can impose with impunity cruel neoconservative policies without injury—perhaps irreparable—to Argentine democracy is a dangerous and irresponsible illusion. ...

The program makes no sense unless one accepts the old and tired argument that "God is Argentine." But the obduracy of the Menem government

---

Atilio A. Borón, "Los 'axiomas de Anillaco.' La visión de la política en el pensamiento y en la acción de Carlos Saúl Menem," *El Menemato. Radiografía de dos años de gobierno de Carlos Menem*, Buenos Aires, Ediciones Letra Buena, S.S., 1991, pp. 76–79. (Excerpt translated by the editor.)

is evident on all levels: pardons[1] that destroy the ethical foundations of the state and promote crime in a great variety of forms; political control of justice by the addition of members to the Supreme Court, which erodes the belief in equality under the law; the bypassing of Congress, which makes a sham of popular sovereignty; savage cuts in social spending that amount to the liquidation of any "social policy"; the strengthening of alliances with ruling classes; exclusive control of bureaucratic, nondemocratic mechanisms over the decision-making process; scandalous privatizations; reactionary changes in labor laws that supposedly make them "more flexible" and the destruction of public education and public health. These are the inevitable antidemocratic results of the imposition of the neoliberal paradise.

The question is very simple: Can such a program be carried out and maintained for a prolonged period in a democracy? It is very improbable: this model requires a profoundly authoritarian framework, because it carries out policies that expel and exclude the great national majorities, and this is very difficult to do in a democratic state. Moreover, such a neoconservative project, whose watchword calls for a massive transfer of the national patrimony to private hands and that assigns extremely profitable privileges—such as the collection of tolls, for example—to its friends, cannot be put in force without phenomenal doses of fraud and corruption unless the men involved are angels or innocent cherubim, which is not the case, at least in Argentina. A democracy, therefore, that reduces politics to a cold governmental exercise in the charge of "operators" and condemns the sovereign people to the role of mere spectators, a democracy that demonstrates by its deeds that it has no obligation or commitment to the poor and weak and has no concern for their fate, a democracy that manipulates justice to protect the powerful and its favorites while it imposes the law of the jungle on the shantytowns—can a democracy of this kind consolidate itself through successive endorsements at the polls? This has not been the case with the industrialized democracies.

What can happen and is happening right now is that a democracy of this kind begins to show severe signs of deterioration. It is already a commonplace to speak of a "crisis of legitimacy" in reference to the discredit that attaches to the political class. ... Without a decisive change of course the repudiation of the traditional political class will spread to the democratic system itself. In effect, it will be difficult to convince millions of Argentines that the disillusioning performance of democratically elected regimes does not necessarily refute the real possibilities that democracy offers for the exercise of popular sovereignty and the construction of a better society. The emptying of the democratic ideal of its libertarian and egalitarian content at the hands of successive governments may have corroded, perhaps irremediably, the beliefs and moral foundations on which the democratic system rests. If that were the case, its days would be numbered and Argentina would have to prepare to relive its old nightmares. The scenarios vary, from the chilling repetition of the "state terrorism" of the military dictatorship to the formation of a purely formal democracy sustained by the apathy of the masses, electoral abstention, and the rule of "everyone for himself" in civil society with its inevitable sequel: the destruction of state order, the re-privatization of violence, and the irrepressible rise of criminality in its multiple forms. ...

The painful experience of Colombia and Peru in recent years shows that this is not a merely hypothetical possibility, thought up by a melancholy spirit. My impression is that we have not yet reached that crossroad, but that we are approaching it with great velocity. Little time remains to correct the direction of government policy, to reorient it in a direction compatible with justice and equity. If this does not happen, we will have to recognize our failure and prepare for the worst.

19

❧

REPUBLICAN BRAZIL:

THE AWAKENING GIANT

THE BRAZILIAN REVOLUTION of 1889 moved the center of political gravity from the north to the south. The new republican Constitution of 1891 granted the states a larger measure of autonomy, but in practice the coffee planters and cattle raisers of São Paulo and Minas Gerais held the levers of power. A new economic and mental climate arose in the cities, where banks, stock exchanges, and corporations enjoyed a rapid growth, but the life of the countryside remained largely unchanged. The single-crop plantation system, under altered forms, continued to dominate economic activity, preventing balanced development and keeping the great majority of the people in poverty and ignorance.

Coffee was king under the Republic, while sugar, which had been seriously affected by the abolition of slavery, declined in importance. Cotton, cacao, and rubber were other leading export products in the twentieth century. The problem of overproduction and falling prices for coffee inspired schemes of "valorization"—official efforts to maintain prices at a high level by artificial means. After 1920 the chronic coffee crisis diverted some workers and capital to the manufacturing industry, which had a considerable growth in São Paulo, Rio de Janeiro, and other centers. But at the end of the 1960s Brazil remained a predominantly agrarian country.

The collapse of the coffee industry in 1929, combined with bitter interprovincial rivalries, enabled Getúlio Vargas, a shrewd *caudilho* from Rio Grande do Sul, to seize power through a coup d'état. The years of the Vargas dictatorship (1930–1945) saw sweeping centralization of power in the federal government, assistance to the new industrialists as well as to agriculture, and drastic curbs on labor and all opposition elements. Friendly to the United States—the largest market for Brazil's coffee—Vargas took his country into the war against the Axis in 1942. Although ousted by an army revolt in

October 1945, Vargas continued to be active in politics under the new Constitution of 1945, and in 1950 he was elected president of Brazil. A mounting inflation, an unfavorable balance of trade, and growing conservative opposition to his nationalistic economic and foreign policies were among the problems faced by his administration. The gravity of Brazil's economic and political crisis found dramatic expression when President Vargas took his own life on August 24, 1954, leaving a suicide note in which he laid the blame for Brazil's difficulties on predatory "international economic and financial groups."

Following a period of political turmoil, the election of 1955 raised to the presidency Juscelino Kubitschek, who basically continued the Vargas policies of forced-draft industrialization but with greater reliance on foreign investments. His successor, Jânio Quadros, elected in 1960, resigned after serving only seven months of his term, alleging that reactionary forces were preventing his reform measures from being adopted. He was succeeded by his vice president, Joâo Goulart, who continued the now institutionalized policies of pushing industrialization by large-scale issues of paper money; he simultaneously made concessions to the rising discontent of the masses by advancing a modest program of land and electoral reform. However, even this modest program frightened Brazil's large landowners, capitalists, and the military hierarchy, ever sensitive to the threat of social revolution. This union of vested interests responded by ousting Goulart in April 1964 and establishing a heavyhanded dictatorship. The new regime, headed by General Humberto Castello Branco, jailed or suspended the political rights of thousands of so-called extremists, including such world-famous scholars as the economist Celso Furtado and the sociologist Josue de Castro. The new regime held down workers' real wages, offered large incentives to foreign investors, and proclaimed its unswerving loyalty in foreign affairs to the United States, which responded with generous financial assistance.

A further shift to the right took place under General Arturo da Costa e Silva, who was chosen president by an obedient Congress in 1966. In December 1968 Congress was suspended, and a series of arbitrary decrees gave the military regime virtually unlimited powers. An ugly feature of the new order was widespread use of torture against real or suspected opponents. Resistance to the military dictatorship assumed various forms, including student demonstrations, protests by courageous church leaders such as Dom Helder Camara, archbishop of Recive, and some guerrilla activity that was gradually crushed.

During the first phase of the military dictatorship the Brazilian economy grew at an extremely rapid pace, thanks in large part to a flood of foreign loans and investments and the unprecedented exploitation of the working class. By the mid-1970s, however, the bloom was off Brazil's economic "miracle" and was replaced instead with growing deficits in the balance of payments, mounting inflation, and a foreign debt that was getting out of control. The recession of 1973–1974, after a weak recovery, gave way to an even more severe slump in 1980. The most direct cause of the crisis was an unmanageable balance of payments and a debt service problem; by 1982 the foreign debt stood at about $90 billion. A rescue operation by foreign banks and governments in the form of new loans gave Brazil some breathing space, but the problem remained as stubbornly intractable as ever. Meanwhile the austerity program adopted by the military government as the price of the rescue operation created new hardships for Brazil's masses, whose living standards had sharply declined since 1964.

Increasingly discredited and isolated, the military government sought a way out of its impasse by a policy of gradual retreat and concessions to the opposition. In 1982 the government permitted the holding of congressional elections, which inflicted a severe defeat on the government party. The process was capped by the presidential election of January 1985, in which Tancredo Neves, supported by a coalition ranging from the Communists to businessmen, defeated the government-backed candidate. Neves died in April after an illness that prevented his inauguration, and was succeeded by his vice president José Sarney, who pledged to carry out Neves's program, a program that stressed technical assistance and access to land for Brazil's impoverished peasantry and a larger role in government for trade unions and workers. But the promises of reform were not kept, and by 1988 a powerful Workers' party (PT) had arisen and scored major gains in state and local elections of that year. The presidential election of 1989, pitting the millionaire Fernando Collor de Mello against the trade-union leader Luiz Inácio da Silva (commonly known as "Lula"), was a frank confrontation between labor and capital. Collor narrowly won, but Brazilian politics would never be the same again.

On taking office, Collor attempted to implement a neoliberal program, featuring austerity and privatization of state enterprises, that had devastating effects on wages, employment, and living standards. The program encountered strong resistance from the militant Brazilian unions. Then, in a series of dramatic events in 1992, Collor's administration collapsed amid charges of personal corruption on a large scale. Collor, who had campaigned on an anticorruption platform, resigned just before Congress would have voted to subject him to an impeachment trial but still faced criminal prosecution on corruption charges. His vice-president, Itamar Franco, who had been left out of Collor's corruption scheme, was named acting president for the two remaining years of Collor's term. Franco, a somewhat eccentric centrist politician, announced that he would continue Collor's privatization program but would assign priority to a campaign against hunger and poverty.

To head his economic reform team, Franco appointed as finance minister the prominent political figure and sociologist Fernando Henrique Cardoso, whose program centered on deficit reduction through budget cuts and on securing the constitutional and fiscal changes needed to achieve tax reform; to privatize state companies in such sensitive areas as oil, mining, and telecommunications; and to promote foreign investment. But the program met strong resistance from left-wing parties and from members of Congress whose eyes were fixed on the upcoming general election in October 1994 and feared the impact of unpopular measures like tax reform on their own fortunes. That election would be the most sweeping in Brazilian history, with the president, two-thirds of the Senate, the Chamber of Deputies, the governors of all twenty-seven states, and deputies in the state assemblies, all coming up for election.

As 1993 drew to a close, it appeared certain that the Workers' party leader, Lula, who had a substantial lead in the polls over all other prospective candidates for president, would again be the standard-bearer of a united left, allied, as in 1989, with a variety of other reformist parties. As Lula campaigned tirelessly throughout the country, he repeated his pledge to implement an agrarian reform, increase agricultural production, and improve health and education. But in the course of the campaign the Workers' party substantially softened its position on issues like suspension of payment on the foreign debt and privatization. Some observers questioned whether this moderation would gain or lose it votes.

Lula's chief rival was finarce minister Fernando Henrique Cardoso, supported by almost all right-wing forces, who resigned his post to enter the presidential race. Cardoso's trump card was an economic stabilization plan, the "Real Plan," named after the new currency, that was introduced July 1. Under this tight-money plan, inflation fell from 46 percent in June to 6.9 percent in July 1994. Cardoso's strategy paid off, and on October 3 he won a sweeping victory, capturing 54 percent of the vote compared to Lula's 27 percent. The results illustrated the Brazilian elites' ability to manipulate economic policy to produce a "solution" whose success might be fleeting but that would work long enough to change the political balance of forces in their favor on the eve of a critical election.

Despite Lula's defeat, the left made large gains in the elections. In the Senate the PT increased its representation from one to five, including three women, two of them black, one a former rubber tapper, and another a shantytown dweller. With 60 of the 513 seats in the House of Representatives, the PT almost doubled its membership in the lower house and won three governorships. It remains the largest, most important left-wing party in Latin America.

Cardoso's honeymoon with the Brazilian public was short-lived. His program, consisting of a balanced budget and the Real Plan of maintaining parity with the U.S. dollar, temporarily tamed the monster of inflation, but it solved none of Brazil's structural economic and social problems. The high-priced Real actually created more difficulties for Brazil's exporters, while Cardoso's program of high interest rates to attract the foreign capital that was needed to finance the country's fiscal deficit tended to stifle domestic production.

Then the Asian financial crisis struck in 1997 and revealed again Brazil's vulnerability to external factors beyond its control. Panicky investors fled the Brazilian stock market, forcing Cardoso to double interest rates to 40 percent and seek IMF loans in return for a severe austerity package of budget cuts. At the same time, aware of the looming presidential election and seeking to defend his "leftist" credentials, Cardoso sought to protect social spending from these drastic cuts. Despite his efforts, the economic situation continued to worsen; by December 1997 official estimates put unemployment in Saõ Paulo, the country's industrial center, at 17 percent.

Nevertheless, the crafty Cardoso, who practiced neoliberalism while proclaiming his belief in the protective social function of the state, won reelection in his second race with Lula in the fall of 1998 with a little more than 50 percent of the vote. But the cascading socioeconomic problems of the country raised the question of how much longer the game of deception played by Cardoso and other politicians of the neoliberal cut could continue. In addition to the most inequitable income distribution in the world, Brazil has a grossly inequitable land distribution: 3 percent of the population owns 67 percent of the land. The Landless People's Movement (MST), supported by the Catholic Church, has pursued a militant program of invading uncultivated land, giving more than 140,000 families access to land. Cardoso's promise to give land to another 280,000 has not yet been kept. The accumulation of unkept promises, on the one hand, and poverty, on the other, has strengthened Brazilian suspicions that the politics of Cardoso, like those who preceded him, was another *engano* (deceit).

1. "THE OLD ORDER CHANGETH ... "

The abolition of slavery in 1888, followed the next year by the establishment of the Republic, consummated a long evolution in Brazil's economic and social life. Eminent Brazilian historian Pedro Calmon interprets these important developments.

In Brazil, the historical and chronological epochs do not coincide. Our sixteenth century began in 1532, with the founding of S. Vicente; the seventeenth, in 1625, with the restoration of Bahia; the eighteenth, in 1694, with the discovery of the mines; the nineteenth, in 1808, with the arrival of the Portuguese Court. Our twentieth century began in 1888–89, with the abolition of slavery, which transformed the economy, and the foundation of the Republic, which changed the political face of the country.

The Revolution of 1888–1889 was profound and general in its consequences.

More than a government fell before the advance of the new conditions of national life, before Federalism and revolutionary, Americanist liberalism. To

Pedro Calmon, *História social do Brasil*, Vol. 3, *A época republicana*, São Paulo, 1939, pp. 1–6. (Excerpt translated by the editor.)

the hierarchical and respectable society of the Empire succeeded a different society. The skillful, conciliatory formulas of Dom Pedro's parliamentary regime had long put off or concealed the collapse of the equilibrium between the old antagonisms of Brazilian society—the capital and the provinces, agriculture and industry, French and American models, order and idealism, the barons of the monarchy and the lawyers, traditional stability and rapid progress. But the machine went off its course amid the tumults of the eighties; there was the abolitionist campaign, the military question, the skepticism of the disgruntled parties (the Liberal Party, whose idealism had lost it the elections of 1881 and 1884, and the Conservative Party, which won empty victories in its exhausting struggle against erupting reforms), and the weight of years and illness pressing upon the Emperor.

A new generation demanded new laws.

The provinces of the South wanted tariff protection for industry; the North demanded protection for its decaying agriculture, credits, and free trade.

The sudden emancipation of the slaves inaugurated the epoch of immigration. High prices for coffee enabled São Paulo to bear the blow of abolition without disruption of its aristocratic plantation system. The *fazendeiros* could pay for labor and thus retain the workers they had acquired in recent years from the slave traders. Foreign colonists (beginning in 1888, 100,000 entered each year through the port of Santos!) swelled the ranks of the labor force.

But in the province of Rio de Janeiro and in the Recôncavo, agriculture languished and withered because of unfavorable conditions: an exhausted soil, ancient and divided estates of scanty yield, the patriarchal character of the economy, kept alive only by class spirit and the historic ties of the great families to the land on which they had lived for three centuries. The *usina*, the great sugar factory, destroyed the sugar mill of colonial type and swallowed up the properties of the old nobility. ...The axis of wealth, and with it the axis of power, shifted from the Recôncavo to the South. In 1887 the political poles were Cotegipe and Antonio Prado, or Paulino and Silveira Martins. The cycle of sugar against that of coffee and cattle. The binomial of the nineteenth century (sugar and coffee), perhaps the agricultural formula of the unity of the Empire in the epoch of the aristocratic latifundio and the baron-colonels, was shattered. Coffee could survive without the slave, and withstood the blow of abolition. But sugar, blockaded in Brazil by the terrific development of other sugar-producing centers, could not endure that shock. Sugar gave Brazil its independence in 1822. Coffee made the Republic in 1889.

Not that the conservative coffee planters were anti-monarchical by conviction and temperament. On the contrary, until 1888 they regarded the monarchy as their chief point of support. But they were tied to the mentality of a swift-moving civilization. They belonged to a time of audacious enterprises.

The divergence between the two economic zones was essentially a contrast in rhythms. Sugar moved slowly, coffee at a dizzy pace; one was a fixed, static culture, the other was extensive and expansive. The vertical line (sugar) combined with the horizontal (coffee) to define the "dynamism" of Brazil: solid and unstable, paralyzed in a conquest, the structural Brazil of the North, the polymorphic Brazil of the South. ...

The coffee planters and a climate of liberalism, well suited to the pursuit of individual and unlimited prosperity, arose together. They had no use for the maturity and serenity of that other agriculture, the slow-moving culture of the cane, which crystallized its social types in the shadow of the colonial sugar-mill, gaining in deep, sentiment-steeped roots what the coffee planter gained in new horizons. ...

If one word can sum up the political confusion of that phase of transition from one regime to another, that word is—impatience.

The effect of abolition was as great in the minds of men as in the material realm.

Three days had sufficed to bring crashing down the infamous system that had lasted three centuries. If total reforms were so easy, why hesitate to illuminate the land with the ardent new lights of the time? Federation in American style; a republic *à la française*; a strong government as taught by Auguste Comte; industries, factories, companies, banks, inflation, business, as in the United States—and away with senile caution!

The movement of ideas that brought the *coup d'état* of November 15 was freighted with that formless impatience as the summer wind is freighted with the tepidity of the earth, the fire of space. ... There arose a vague crusade against dogmas. A spiritual insurrection against the past, against consecrated values. A change of symbols, of principles, of ends. Instead of political continuity, the revolution; instead of monarchical ruralism, republican citizenship; no more national *unity*, but *union* of autonomous States; strong government, and not weak cabinet governments; speeches in the streets, not in Parliament; a "Jacobin" and lyrical nationalism, as in 1831, but with different models—democratic equality, a clamor of popular demands, and, in place of the ancient Emperor, a President-marshal. Let the giant learn to walk ... , urged the liberal propagandists. Let a democracy of labor replace patriarchal customs; let the States place no impediment in the way of prosperity; let the citizen not feel the restraining hand of government upon his new-found liberty, cut to the patterns of Gambetta and Castelar.

The army removed the barrier of the Empire from that road. ... The army precipitated the transformation; most important of all, it insured external peace, the appearance of transition without disorder. In the paralysis of the constitutional parties, of the old governing class, with its sense of organization it gave discipline and order to the nascent federation. An officer assumed the government of the province; supported by its garrison, he kept the officials at their posts, protected the magistrates in the performance of their duties. Anarchy was thus avoided.

Indeed, the least dramatic revolution was the political: the overthrow of the throne by the second brigade of Rio de Janeiro, commanded by Marshal

Manoel Deodoro da Fonseca. It was Brazilian society that experienced change from top to bottom. No superficial tempest, this; all social strata were affected by the upheaval. It was not so much a new régime as a new century that arose. Republic? Say, rather, the twentieth century.

Aristides Lobo, correspondent of the *Diario Popular* of São Paulo, wrote for his readers a letter that has the revealing quality of a portrait, on November 15, 1889:

"For the time being the aspect of the government is purely military, and so it should be. Theirs was the work, only theirs, because the action of civilian elements was practically nil. The people looked on, stupefied, astonished, dumbfounded without an inkling of what it all meant. Many honestly believed that they were watching a parade."

2. "... YIELDING PLACE TO NEW"

In the wake of the revolution came a flurry of modernization, of changes in manners, in values, and even in the physical appearance of some of Brazil's great urban centers. These changes were most marked in the federal capital, made into a beautiful and healthful city through the initiative and efforts of Prefect Pereira Passos and the distinguished scientist Oswaldo Cruz.

Eighteen-ninety was a year of rash gaiety, of a revolution in manners more intense and profound than the political revolution. Gone were the restraints of the hierarchy, of the polished and sober *bon ton* of the Empire. Rio de Janeiro was transformed from top to bottom. The new "republican equality" cut off its peaks; the new police force of Sampaio Ferraz cleansed its roots. The Great Boom, the *Encilhamento*, subverting economic values and making wealth a common and dominant ideal, suddenly destroyed the moderate and elegant conception of life that had long prevailed and that had been inherent and implicit in the monarchical system, with its lifetime Senate, the honors of the Court, the tradition that statesmen should grow poor in the public service instead of enriching themselves, the radiant, fastidious honesty of the Palace of São Cristovão. Barons with recently acquired titles jostled each other in the corridors of the Stock Exchange or in the Rua da Alfândega, buying and selling stocks; the tilburies that filled the length of São Francisco Street were taken by a multitude of millionaires of recent vintage—commercial agents, bustling lawyers, promoters of all kinds, politicians of the new

Pedro Calmon, *História social de Brasil*, Vol. 3, *A época republicana*, São Paulo, 1939, pp. 143–145, 164–169. (Excerpt translated by the editor.)

generation, the men of the day. They were shunned with dignity by the non-conformists, members of the old nobility, politicians of the Empire who held aloof; another year, and their number would be swollen by the disillusioned. But the Republic was not simply a movement against "Your Excellencies" in the name of plain "you." It took strong measures against hooliganism, against the disorders of the popular wards. In the very first days of the regime, Sampaio Ferraz cleaned out the vagabonds who had infested the city for a hundred years. ... The gangs and the "young gentlemen of quality" went out together. The symbol of the new governing class was the horse car—leaving from the corner of Gonçalves Dias Street—whose "bourgeois benches" united all the citizens in perfect equality.

Pleasure—easy, commercial, exotic—held sway. The coffee-houses were full, the Rua do Ouvidor thronged, the horse cars crowded. Roulette-wheels were installed in private houses; the club became a business center; the vicissitudes of the Great Boom were discussed at the tables of the confectionary-shops where literati, financiers, gamblers, and courtesans congregated and astounded, dazzled provincials looked on. "City of vice and pleasure" was how the annoyed Anselmo Coelho Neto described "the Federal Capital." ...

The Epidemic

That Federal Capital, refulgent in spirit and quivering with civic excitement, had its fashionable season and its season of gloom. The *carioca* unquestionably grew accustomed to yellow fever. He came to regard it as a cyclical scourge, his summer ailment, recurring each year between December and April and terrible at the start, especially for foreigners; but that soon ceased to disturb the routine life of the great city, which solved the problem as best it could. The people went to the mountains. They fled to the high spots of the surrounding countryside. They returned to nature, abandoning the city—and with it those who could not get away—to its periodic tragedy. There remained only the poor, the merchants, the officials. Petropolis offered its charms of a European city to the invaders of the upper class. It was even more imperial under the Republic, more opulent, more desired, but now without the examples of sobriety, the lessons in modesty, of Dom Pedro II.

In connection with the commemoration of the fiftieth anniversary of the arrival of the Sisters of Notre Dame de Sion in Brazil (they landed at Rio on October 9, 1888), their "diary" was published, with its disillusioned impressions of the plague-ridden Rio summer, of the horror inspired by the fever. ... One of the nuns, Mother Felix, soon died, and the others left for Petropolis. They were ordered to remain there, together with their school for girls, which, between 1889 and 1892, functioned part of the year in Rio and the rest of the time in the mountains. A teacher who kept his pupils in the city during the period of the epidemic, that is, during the summer, would have committed a crime. The capital became uninhabitable, particularly for foreigners. The obituary lists caused terror. Hundreds died each month.

The Renovation of Rio de Janeiro

Oswaldo Cruz and Prefect Passos were the powerful arms that awoke the sleeping city. It awoke with a start at the sight of the gangs of workmen that began to demolish the old Rio. ...

The monarchy fell in effigy in 1889.

The past really fell in 1904, with the passing of the narrow streets in the center of the city, with the widening of the city's heart, with the construction of modern avenues that would permit the free movement of a people fascinated by the civilization which thus made its triumphant entrance.

If the duel between sanitation and popular distrust had its trying aspects, from cold incredulity to armed resistance, the struggle of the city planner with the spirit of routine was no less dramatic and difficult. Both men could count on the absolute solidarity of the Federal Government; Cruz and Passos would not accept their dangerous missions on any other terms. The law of December 29, 1902, placed in the authoritarian hands of the Prefect almost dictatorial powers. Article 25, for example, authorized him to remove the occupants of condemned dwellings with the aid of the police and without judicial appeal. He got everything he asked for. Recalcitrants who beat at the doors of justice found themselves escorted away by armed soldiers. Passos was arbitrariness itself. It was a terribly lawless situation, in which a single man, absorbed in the mysteries of his plans, decided the fate of a city. But it was effective and necessary. A loan of six million pounds sterling that the Prefecture was empowered to float failed in Europe: Rio's business community covered it to the amount of four million pounds. Force and money—Passos' iron will would do the rest. That will did not weaken.

Cruz and Passos, working in concert, cultivated an ungrateful soil.

Hygiene depended on remodeling the city, on doing away with the cesspools and dissolving the ancient filth; and the old Rio could be made over only by conquering yellow fever. Each in his own field, the two dictators of public improvement encountered the same hostility. Oswaldo Cruz fought the battle of convictions—his struggle was the more abstract. Pereira Passos confronted a league of vested interests—his fight was more concrete. He faced the hostility of business, the property owners, the stubbornly, solidly conservative classes. The passivity of tenants, the force of habit, the new liberalism that taught the inviolability of the home, the old customs. ...

Had he attempted to realize partial reforms, like those carried out at the end of the Empire, like the opening of Gonçalves Dias (1854) and Senador Dantas streets or the ward of Vila Isabel, he would have met with universal applause. But his program, just like the hygienist's, was total and brusque.

Since 1871, as a member of the commission named by Minister João Alfredo, Passos had meditated on his grand project. He kept it to himself until 1902. In 1882, together with Teixeira Soares, he had obtained the franchise for the construction of the Corcovado Railroad. ... Now his plan consisted in tearing down the old buildings, in rectifying with rectilinear and tree-covered designs the tortuous colonial plan. No more unlighted hovels and big old houses falling into ruins, no more dirty streets and discolored façades, no more repellent odors of pestilent alleys, no more oppressive atmosphere of the colonial city. He used his engineering equipment like a broom. He had to sweep away the filth of a commercial city that had grown too fast within the small area that housed its asphyxiated prosperity and its slums, its plenty and its poverty, its warehouses and its congested society that gasped for breath within the narrow bounds of its historic walls. Passos attacked the problem as a whole. He dislodged without pity the merchants affected by the condemnations, and took for their basis the low declarations of value made for tax purposes. He gave the construction of the new arteries the appearance of a catastrophe. ... He worked with great haste. He knew that without drive and energy, without closing his eyes to cases of individual hardship, he could not carry his plan through. And the worst of all would be to leave the job half done, the houses torn down, the avenues still unopened, all buried in the rubble of the demolitions, with nothing to show for the destruction he had wrought. He had to be adamant in order to be efficient. On all sides he met with resistance. The newspapers hurled insults at him; the merchants whose interests were affected opposed him. He would be handed a court summons by day and by that night began levelling the walls. The controversy increased as endless points of law were invoked—but meanwhile the pickaxes did not stop. Without that useful and massive violence he would have failed at the very start—he and Oswaldo Cruz. His heroism consisted in making himself insensible to all protests. President Rodrigues Alves armed himself with the same stoicism. The tactic was a skillful one: first tear down, then be free to rebuild at will. ...

The first section of the new port at Rio de Janeiro was inaugurated November 8, 1906.

That year electric lights bathed the city in their luminous glow.

The Prefect wanted Rio to be the best illuminated city in the world.

It was the touch of magic needed to make the prodigy visible; from the deep ruins of the year of devastations emerged the modern outlines of the rejuvenated city.

"Rio is becoming civilized," sang the minstrels of the people. The patriarchal city that on other nights, dimly lit by gas lamps, had resounded with their languid serenades, was fleeing before their eyes. The hills of Rio, the Santo Antonio, the Castelo, the Conceição, the Favela, now ceased to be the refuges of poverty. Down below, swarms of workers advanced over the clouds of dust raised by the demolitions. And from the rubble emerged the shining tracks of the tilbury and the newly-arrived automobile. ...

3. THE VARGAS ERA

The collapse of Brazil's coffee industry in 1929–1930 had serious political and economic consequences. Widespread distress and discontent with Paulista domination of the national government brought to power a caudilho *from the cattle-raising state of Rio Grande do Sul—Getúlio Vargas. In the protective shadow of the Great Depression and with lavish assistance from the strongly nationalistic Vargas government, Brazil's infant industries made large progress. Meanwhile Vargas presided over an authoritarian regime that borrowed many of its trappings from the fascist states of Europe. Toppled by an army revolt in October 1945, he was returned to the presidency by a large popular majority in the election of 1950. His death by suicide in 1954 closed a formative epoch of Brazilian history. Brazilian Marxist historian Nelson Werneck Sodré offers a social and economic interpretation of the Vargas era.*

The principal problem posed by a crisis of such grave proportions and profound effects (the collapse of 1929–1930) was to find some way out for the Brazilian economy. The first reaction took the form of efforts to maintain export levels with products other than coffee, for the national economy depended on exports and one could not at once alter this long established fact. As a result of favorable external conditions and the use of production factors released by the decline of coffee, cotton began to assume importance as an agricultural product. The gold value of exports had been steadily declining since 1910; with the coming of the crisis the fall became catastrophic. The annual average value of exports in the period 1926–1930 had been £88,200,000 and in the five-year period 1931–1935 was barely £38,000,000 with a resulting sharp decline in the value of the national currency. Consequently Brazil began to import less, the volume of imports being reduced by two-thirds. Import capacity did not recover during the decade of the thirties; in 1937 it was even lower than in 1929. But if the reaction to the crisis were limited to substitution of cotton for coffee, former levels of development could not be attained. Events proved, however, that a more effective adjustment was possible. In 1933, when the United States still gave no signs of economic recovery, Brazil's national income had already begun to increase. This proved with absolute clarity that the Brazilian recovery did not depend, as

Nelson Werneck Sodré, *Evolución social y económica del Brasil*, Buenos Aires, 1964, pp. 83–88. (Excerpt translated by the editor.)

had traditionally been the case, on external factors, but rather on internal factors. This pointed to a new factor in national economic life.

The growth of the domestic supply of goods compensated for the decline in imports, and the domestic demand proved to be a dynamic element of the national economy. The process was marked by transfer of capital from one field to another, and not just from coffee to cotton, but from the agricultural sector to others, above all to the industrial sector. Henceforth every theory or plan that did not take into account the domestic market was condemned to failure or discredit. The textile industry, which did not regain the levels attained during the First World War until 1929, rose from a production of less than 500,000 meters in 1929 to 640,000,000 in 1933 and 915,000,000 meters in 1936. And the reaction was not limited to consumers' goods: in 1932 the production of capital goods rose by 60% over the figure for 1929, while imports fell to a fifth of the precrisis level. By 1935 liquid investments had surpassed 1929 levels. It was clear that the Brazilian economy had not only found within itself the stimuli needed to cope with a crisis of foreign origins, but had managed to produce the greater part of the goods needed to increase its productive capacity.

Between 1929 and 1937 industrial production increased by almost 50%, and primary production for the internal market almost 40%. Despite the depression, the national revenue increased in this period by 20%, with an annual per capita growth of 7%. Countries with similar economic structure which followed an orthodox economic policy, dictated from outside, had not emerged from the depression by 1937. The importance of this crisis for Brazil consists in the response given by the new factors to the difficulties it posed and in the dynamism it imparted to Brazilian development. Freed from imperialist pressure, these factors revealed an unprecedented capacity for national capital formation. In 1930 the annual service of the foreign debt required more than a million and a half *contos de reis*, while Brazil's net returns from foreign trade did not come to half a million *contos*. Consequently the suspension of this debt service represented a very great stimulus to the development of national productive forces, hitherto encased in the old production relations that were temporarily weakened by the crisis.

The economic recovery of Brazil, with the emergence and vigorous functioning of the new factors, threw into sharp relief the figure of Getúlio Vargas, who arrived on the crest of the revolution of 1930, the first Brazilian revolt that issued from the periphery of the country yet managed to triumph in the center, and the first such movement to display national characteristics, erupting in various regions of the country. While the victors prepared to give the country a new constitution, the Vargas government mirrored the struggle between the seigneurial class, entrenched in the *latifundio* but a participant in the revolution, and the middle class, which was one of its dynamic elements: the Constitution of 1934 reflected this collision. But the working class, which received the revolution with sympathy, although not a participant in it (despite the fact that since the strikes of 1917 it had already attained a relatively important political significance) began to play its own role on the political stage. The heterogeneous currents represented in the revolution were reflected with reasonable proximity in the variety of operating forces.

The general unrest, the clash of tendencies, the appearance of extreme factions, reflecting developments in the international plane led, first, to the *pronunciamento* of 1935, in which a national democratic front, accused of being communist, gave rise to an armed movement, and that of 1938, when a Fascist group attempted to seize power through a *coup d'état* in the capital of the Republic. The growing ascendancy of fascism on the international plane permitted Vargas to establish in 1937 the Estado Novo, a regime that, behind its facade of a police state and an apparatus of violence unheard-of in Brazil, nevertheless represented a way of achieving—or rather of attempting to achieve—some of the transformations characteristic of the bourgeois revolution, but without participation of the proletariat. For the rest, the Estado Novo attempted to mask and restrain the ever growing contradictions within the Revolution, seeking to reconcile the irreconcilable. The Estado Novo created a legislation with unequivocal nationalist tendencies, imposed a tutelage in the form of social legislation over the working classes, and pursued a foreign policy that sought above all the development of trade with foreign countries, notably with right-wing regimes; Germany became the second largest market for Brazilian products, achieving parity with the United States, which had held the first place.

When World War II broke out, Brazil was ruled by this regime, and Vargas as dictator pursued a policy of conciliation and compromise. But the change in the character of the war as the result of an alliance of countries with the most diverse systems against the totalitarian powers; and the aggression suffered by Brazil as a result of the torpedoing of its merchant ships while transporting troops in accordance with security agreements it had made with its traditional allies, profoundly influenced internal policy: Brazil was drawn into the war, and at its end constitutional norms again prevailed. The return to constitutionality took place under totally new conditions, for the military victory against Nazism gave ascendancy to the democratic forces, and the old contradictions grew even sharper. Vargas' sensitivity to the new conditions, the fact that he offered solutions that favored, to a certain point, the classes opposed to imperialism and the *latifundio*, led to his sacrifice: a military coup overthrew him in 1945. But the democratic interlude was of short duration: the government of President Dutra, resulting from the elections, carried out a policy advantageous to imperialism and the *latifundio*, and favored the traditional forces, which, uniting more firmly the weaker they became, sought desperately to halt the profound transformations through which Brazil was passing, and which even the Estado Novo could not halt.

Vargas returned to the helm as a result of an electoral victory (1951), after Dutra's disastrous policy had exhausted the foreign exchange reserves built up during the War by virtue of the fact that imports were practically suspended; the decline in imports was accompanied by large advances in the process of industrialization, which was about to culminate in the creation of a heavy industry as a result of the formation of the National Steel Company, a state enterprise of large proportions, and the opening of legislative debates concerning the state monopoly of oil exploitation, a monopoly (Petrobras) that was promptly established by law (1953). These changes led to a strengthening of the role of the state, and for this reason the reactionary forces directed their principal attacks against it. Shortly thereafter Vargas denounced the spoliation resulting from the export of the profits of foreign enterprises, and returned to his habitual policy of advance and retreat—a policy which only served to weaken him. This tactic clearly reflected the vacillations of the Brazilian bourgeoisie, simultaneously fearful of the strength of the working class and oppressed by imperialism, and therefore under pressure from both extremes. Getúlio Vargas, representative of the bourgeois revolution, sought to continue playing that role under ever more difficult conditions, but without the participation of the proletariat. This made enormously difficult the formation of a broad political base for the solution of the problems which he so effectively denounced and so timidly confronted. His uncertain destiny depended on the course of events. Alone, without the support of those who could have defended him, as a result of his systematic retreats and his political actions against the democratic and nationalist forces, he again failed to finish his term of office: on August 24, 1954, he found escape from his dilemma in suicide. But he left an enlightening denunciation, the most tremendous a man of his class had ever written of imperialism: a testamentary letter in which he indicated the true character of the internal conspiracy that caused his death. The instantaneous popular outcry provoked by his resignation and suicide prevented the reactionary forces from carrying out their plans to their logical conclusions. They could not prevent the holding of presidential elections or the assumption of power by the President-elect. The election and inauguration of Juscelino Kubitschek (1956), particularly after the military intervention of November 11 in favor of legality, undoubtedly represented a rout for imperialism.

The epoch of Vargas marks the beginning of a process to be known as the Brazilian Revolution: The structural transformations that the country needed demanded sweeping reforms and gave rise to events that showed the rapidity with which the Brazilian economy was being transformed. Vargas represented better than any other figure the first stage of that revolution by his false starts and conciliatory attitudes, by his tendency to put off solutions, by his correct vision and his weakness when it came to concrete acts, and above all by his fear that the Revolution might go beyond the limits of bourgeois interests.

4. The Conquest
of Brazilian Industry

The coup d'état of 1964 put an end to the populist political model and the nationalist model of economic development that were inaugurated under Getúlio Vargas and contin-ued more or less consistently by his successors after his death in 1954. The coup of 1964 brought to power a coalition of reactionary forces that feared that populist policies risked social revolution. The new regime accepted United States leadership in Brazil's economic development and foreign policy; the regime's dependence on the United States, coupled with its brutally repressive policies, led Brazilian educator Hólio Jaguaribe to call it "colonial fascism." The coup of 1964 gave a large impetus to foreign penetration and takeover of Brazilian industry, with resulting distortions of the economy. Brazilian eco-nomic development has a larger implication because similar processes are at work in other Latin American countries. Uruguayan journalist Eduardo Galeano describes the "denationalization" of Brazilian industry.

By 1964 Brazil's pharmaceutical industry was no longer Brazilian. Brazilian-owned laboratories accounted for only a third of total sales. Two years later, according to the Brazilian Association of the Pharmaceutical Industry, the situation had changed again: in 1966, Brazilian laboratories were reduced to a fifth of total sales. Wyeth, Bristol, Mead Johnson, and Lever had taken over Fontoura, Laborterapica, Endoquimica, and Gessy re-spectively, Brazilian factories producing drugs or perfumes, while a French firm had swallowed up the Silva-Araujo-Roussel laboratories.

The triumph of the military coup of April 1964 unleashed similar pro-cesses in almost every sector of Brazilian industry. By mid-1968 fifteen plants producing autos or auto parts had been absorbed by great North American or European enterprises. Among them was the state-owned Fabrica Nacional de Motores. In the electric and electronic sector, three important Brazilian en-terprises fell into Japanese hands. In plastics, North American firms took pos-session of four Brazilian-owned factories. Anaconda Copper threw itself on the production of non-ferrous metals. In mechanical and metallurgical indus-try, five North American corporations and a Japanese group gained control of six Brazilian enterprises of considerable size; the Companhia de Mineração Geral of the Jaffet group, one of Brazil's biggest metallurgical plants, was bought at a bargain price by a consortium composed of Bethlehem Steel, Chase Manhattan Bank, and Standard Oil. Two North American firms and a German firm invaded the chemical sector. Although the international corpo-

Eduardo Galeano, "¿Que bandera flamea sobre las máquinas? La desnacionalización de la in-dustria en el Brasil," *Cuadernos Americanos*, no. 6, November–December 1969, Vol. 167, pp. 7–25. (Excerpt translated by the editor.)

rations were interested in the dynamic industrial sectors above all, the traditional industries did not escape: factories producing cigarettes, inks, foodstuffs, textiles, glass, etc., also passed into foreign hands.

One of the few Brazilian industrialists who has resisted the invasion declared: "Experience shows that the product of the sale of a national enterprise often never even reaches Brazil, but remains to yield interest in the money market of the purchasing country." He adds: "Foreign groups make their deposits in foreign banks, prefer to buy in other foreign enterprises, obtain their insurance from foreign companies, and draw on investment funds that they themselves have created. In political terms, they exercise a growing influence. They do not need to own newspapers or television channels. They control enormous sums for publicity and thus, in one way or another, manage to influence the media for forming public opinion." These are the great multinational corporations in action, the "conglomerates" that in the era of monopoly capitalism combine industrial, commercial, and financial power. The testimony of this industrialist, among others, was taken by a commission especially formed by the Brazilian Congress before the military regime closed its doors. The commission investigated the subject and came to the conclusion that foreign capital controlled in 1968 40% of the capital market of Brazil, 62% of its foreign trade, 82% of its maritime transport, 77% of overseas air transport, 100% of the motor vehicle production, 100% of its tire production, more than 80% of the pharmaceutical industry, nearly 50% of the chemical industry, 59% of the machine production and 62% of the factories making auto parts, 48% of the aluminum industry, and 90% of the cement industry. According to the commission, half of the capital involved came from the United States; the North American firms were followed, in order of importance, by German, English, French, and Swiss enterprises. The report, which unfortunately is unknown in Brazil, contains extremely important data. It was about to be published when the government of Costa e Silva closed down the Congress. The Minister of Industry and Commerce, called upon to express his opinion by the Commission, declared his friendship for foreign investment and maintained that its penetration in Brazil was "greatly exaggerated," although he admitted foreign domination in the petrochemical industry, the steel and iron industry, the electrical industry, the chemical industry, the machine tools industry, naval construction, the automotive industry, glass, pharmaceuticals, perfumes, and caustic soda. The Minister of Labor denounced the transfer into North American hands of the traditional forest industries in the estuary of the Amazon. The Minister of Mines and Energy and the Minister of Foreign Affairs agreed that the measures adopted by the Castelo Branco government, permitting the free flow of foreign credit to enterprises, had placed Brazilian-owned enterprises in an unfavorable position. Both referred, especially, to the famous Instruction 289 of the beginning of 1965. Thanks to this instruction, some fifty important foreign enterprises gained direct access to outside sources of capital. While Brazilian enterprises paid up to 48% interest on the loans they obtained within the country, foreign enterprises obtained loans abroad at 7 or 8%.

This gave a decisive push to many Brazilian enterprises over the brink of bankruptcy. Internal credit was severely reduced in line with the prescriptions of the International Monetary Fund, and the level of consumption of the domestic market also fell as a result of the decline in the real value of wages. The Brazilian government protected the foreign enterprises to the extreme of guaranteeing a special type of exchange for the payment of external financing in case of devaluation. But in addition, as one gathers from the report of the parliamentary commission, nearly half the capital of the banks operating in Brazil belongs to foreign capital and 17 of the 27 investment banks in the country are foreign. Thus the foreign enterprises, taking advantage of their intimate links with international finance capital, were also able to obtain domestic credit denied to many Brazilian factories. As the tide rose, numerous Brazilian enterprises went under for lack of resources.

The architect of the policy of the International Monetary Fund in Brazil, the inventor of Instruction 289, Roberto Campos, explained the matter in these words, cited in the same report: "Obviously, men are not equal. Some are born intelligent, others fools. Some are born athletes, others paralyzed. The world is composed of large and small enterprises. Some die early, in the flower of life; others drag themselves criminally through a long useless life. There is a basic, fundamental inequality in human nature, in the nature of things. The mechanism of credit is not exempt from this condition. To ask that Brazilian enterprises should have the same access to foreign credit as foreign enterprises is simply not to know the basic realities of economic life. ..."

The author of these remarks, Roberto Campos, had been wisely dubbed Bobby Fields[1] by the Brazilian people. According to this brief but pithy "capitalist manifesto," the law of the jungle is the code that naturally rules human life and injustice does not exist, since what we call injustice is nothing more than an expression of the cruel harmony of the universe: the poor countries are poor because ... they are poor, our destiny is written in the stars and we are only born to fulfill it; some are condemned to obey, others to command. In the mouth of a Latin American, all this seems excessively close to treason. By no accident, shortly after, Roberto Campos made public a curious interpretation of the rising wave of nationalism in Peru. According to Campos, the expropriation of Standard Oil by the government of General Velasco Alvarado was only an "exhibition of masculinity," and nationalism served no other purpose than to satisfy the primitive human need to hate. But, he wrote, "pride does not generate investments, does not increase the volume of capital, does not create rational techniques of organization and, frequently, inhibits the growth of productivity." If these are the results of pride, what are the results of humiliation? Let us see.

The Figures and Methods

The military dictatorship born of the revolt of April, 1964, found in Roberto Campos the ideal Tsar for dealing with the national economy. The struggle against inflation, developed according to the prescription of the International Monetary Fund, served to cover up, like a deceitful banner, a policy of unrestrained surrender of the national riches. This handover may set a record in Latin American history, which certainly abounds in episodes of plunder: the government of Castelo Branco signed an agreement guaranteeing investments by the offer of "extraterritoriality" to foreign enterprises, permitted the free export of profits, reduced taxes on their income of foreign enterprises, and granted them extraordinary facilities to obtain credit; the richest iron deposit in the world was presented to the Hanna Mining Company, which also obtained authorization to construct a private port (in line with a plan worked out by Roberto Campos some years before, as "technical adviser" to Hanna); the Electric Bond and Share was paid an indemnity that exceeded several times the real value of their ancient "nationalized" installations; the state petroleum enterprise, Petrobras, was despoiled of its petrochemical monopoly, which passed into the hands of Philips Petroleum and Union Carbide; and of the production of bituminous shales; the level of real wages was reduced and the living standards of the workers were depressed; there was a sharp contraction of credit to national industry, whose denationalization was rapidly extended.

The "Program of economic action of the government," worked out by Campos, foresaw that as a result of this policy of stimulating and protecting foreign investment, foreign capital would flow in to give an impulse to the development of Brazil and contribute to its economic and financial stabilization. It foresaw new direct investments of foreign origin of 100 million dollars for 1965. Seventy million dollars arrived. For 1966, the plan foresaw 170 million dollars. Seventy-four arrived. And in 1967 new foreign investments amounted to 70 million dollars. In those same years, the enterprises remitted to their home offices, by way of profits and dividends, much greater amounts: in 1965, 102 million dollars; in 1966, 127 million dollars. In 1967 the flow of profits and dividends was almost double the new investment; 130 million dollars fled the country. To this must be added the fabulous quantity of dollars sent abroad in return for administration, technical assistance, patents, royalties, use of trademarks and commissions for imports; in 1967 the export of capital under those headings amounted to 170 million dollars.

Meanwhile the foreign debt grew until it reached the figure of four billion dollars, and with it grew the payment of interest and amortization, two categories which in 1968 involved the flight of 500 million dollars. The loans received with the framework of the Alliance for Progress imposed, as elsewhere in Latin America, the purchase of goods in the United States, whose machines are the most expensive in the world, and the transport of those goods in ships under the North American flag (which charge ten dollars more than other shippers for each ton of freight), in addition to the requirement that insurance be obtained from North American firms. For freight and insurance Brazil paid, in 1967, 110 million dollars. Add to all these bloodlettings clandestine remittances. In its report for 1968 the Central Bank admitted that aside from legal channels 180 million dollars left Brazil in 1966 and 120 million dollars in 1967.

The amount of dollars that departed was, we see, infinitely greater than that which entered. In sum, the figures for new direct investments in the "key" years of industrial denationalization, 1965, 1966, and 1967, were much below the level of 1961. How, then, without a massive avalanche of dollars, could foreign capital capture the major industrial base of Latin America?

In reality, the bases for this transfer of power had already been laid before, in the years of the industrial "boom" of Juscelino Kubitschek. When the military took power in 1964 the Brazilian investments were already in a very minority position in the private industrial sector. But denationalization accelerated at a vertiginous pace and the "last Mohicans" of the national bourgeoisie fell one by one into the asphyxiating embrace of foreign capital. The national entrepreneurs were gradually transformed into Brazilian directors of North American and European enterprises. The last redoubts of the enterprises of local capital remain in the sectors called "traditional" or "nondynamic," featured by very low indices of productivity. But the domination by foreign capital of the dynamic industries (chemical, metallurgy, heavy and light industry, electrical, communications, and automotive industry), which grow at an accelerated tempo, explains the fact that the share of foreign enterprises in the total production of Brazil is five times greater than the proportion of its capital in the total investment in industry.

Various factors facilitated the strangulation of national private industry. Among these, as we have seen, an important role was played by the contraction of domestic credit in a period during which, thanks to the fall in the real value of wages, the capacity to consume of the domestic market already very limited, in essence, by the rigid class division of Brazilian society, further declined. But other factors were at work. Celso Furtado says that "the critical point" is, in this respect, the passage to the second generation in the management of national enterprises that still have in Latin America a marked family character. "It is common," he says, "for the second generation to have the calling of coupon-clipper, which facilitates the transfer of the control of management." Thus the pioneering labor of the independent national entrepreneurs was reduced to a simple "clearing of the ground" for the expansion of North American corporations.

What were the methods of the foreign invaders? They are many. Enterprises have been conquered by a simple telephone call: a sharp fall in stock quotations, the recovery of a debt with the debtor's stock, systematic "dumping" or organized blackmail, the techniques of intimidation. Many of the denationalized Brazilian factories depended on the use of trademarks, patents, or technical assistance coming from the United States or Europe: all, as is known, must be paid for in dollars, and the long drought of circulating capital made it impossible to pay these debts, swollen by the devaluation of the cruzeiro. Technological dependence is paid for dearly; the "know how" of the monopolies also includes great skill in the art of devouring one's neighbor. There were also numerous cases in which foreign creditors converted the unpaid debts of Brazilian enterprises into investments: they collected those debts, in other words, by taking over the whole or a part of the installations and machines of their debtors. The figures of the Central Bank indicate that no less than 20% of the new direct investments of foreign origin during 1965, 1966, and 1967 in reality represented the conversion of previous loans into industrial investments.

On the "dumping" process, we have revealing testimony in the report of the above-mentioned parliamentary commission. Deputy Chaves Amarante told the story of the capture of a factory making adhesive tape, the Adesite, by a powerful North American enterprise, Union Carbide. The Adesite was a firm in Sao Paulo, "a firm organized by young, idealistic, enterprising, energetic men," says the deputy, "who organized a simple shop and transformed it into a factory of 30,000 square meters of construction space, with an output of nearly 500 million a month." The Scotch Tape Company, a well-known enterprise with its home office in Minnesota and universal tentacles, began to sell its own tape ever more cheaply in the Brazilian market. The sales of Adesite constantly diminished and the banks denied it credits. Scotch Tape continued to lower its prices: it reduced them by 30%, then by 40%. Now Union Carbide appeared on the scene. It purchased the Brazilian factory at a bargain price. Subsequently Union Carbide and Scotch Tape reached an understanding on division of the national market into two parts: they divided Brazil in half, each taking a half for itself. Then they agreed to raise the price of adhesive tape by 50%. This was the stage of digesting the prey.

5. BRAZIL'S "ECONOMIC MIRACLE":
AN ASSESSMENT

Thanks to a flood of foreign loans and investments and the superexploitation of Brazilian workers, under the military dictatorship imposed on the country in 1964 the Brazilian economy grew for a number of years at a rapid pace that aroused the admiration of some domestic and foreign observers. But developments since 1980 have shown that the "miracle" rested on very fragile foundations, while its social costs were immense. The bishops and other religious leaders of Brazil's northeast, the country's poorest, most abandoned region, describe those costs and other consequences of the military dictatorship's economic policies.

In the economic field, a great offensive, the greatest in Brazilian history, is being waged in favor of penetration by foreign capital. In order to ensure the rate of profit desired by the capital that invests here, the government willingly grants all the conditions and guarantees that it asks for. Not only does it lavish public funds to create an economic superstructure that will facilitate the conquest of resources and markets, but it even removes possible obstacles resulting from future political changes by offering guarantees to investors. Should those guarantees ever be overturned, Brazil could be charged with their violation before foreign tribunals.

The impetus with which the new economic policy was transformed from theory into practice made it possible to generate in a few years results that supposedly proved its inherent value. Beginning in 1968, Brazil's gross domestic product grew at an annual rate of about 10%. ...

The consequences of this "miracle" were the relative and absolute impoverishment of the Brazilian people. Concentration of income reached levels that explain better than anything else the true meaning of the government's economic policy. Between 1960 and 1970 the 20% of the population that constituted the sector with the highest income increased its share of the national income from 54.5% to 64.1%, while the remaining 80% saw its share reduced from 45.5% to 36.8%. The concentration of income appears even more alarming when one considers that in the same period the 1% of the population that represents the richest group increased its share of the national income from 11.7% to 17%, while half of the population, composing individuals with the lowest income, had its share reduced from 17.6% to 13.7%. The relative inversion of position meant that in 1970, 1% of all Brazilians received more than half of the national income.

The most serious aspect of the situation is that in order to bring the concentration of income to the indicated level, the purchasing power of the wage-earning masses was brutally reduced. Between 1961 and 1970 the fall in real wages, calculated on the basis of the official minimum wage, was 38%. In the same period the growth per capita of the national domestic product was 25.6%. ... To achieve the so-called "Brazilian miracle," the government, through regulation of the minimum wage, transferred to the classes who absorb the fruits of economic growth part of the income of the wage-earning classes.

Helder Camara y obispos de Brasil, *El grito del tercer mundo. Testimonios*, Buenos Aires, Meray Editor, 1974.

If economic growth impacts in this way on groups on the minimum wage level, it is reasonable to assume that its effects are much more severe on large sectors of the population who receive no income or whose income is below the minimum wage level.

The defenders of the system refute challenges to the income distribution by arguing that "the cake must grow so that it can be divided later on."

In fact, however, the concentration of income results, among other causes, from the need for a market that can absorb the goods produced by the foreign enterprises, which bring from their country of origin a technology that is unsuitable for the type of consumption that is most common in Brazil. This modern technology requires indexes of consumption that can be achieved only by the rich. Consequently we have a productive structure that inevitably conditions both the structure of production and consumption. Industrialization thus becomes an instrument increasingly devoted to the production of goods capable of satisfying the caprices of an ever more refined consumption, turning its back on the needs of the population. There are two other implications that should be mentioned. In order to provide the imported industrial equipment needed for the production of these goods, the country's foreign debt grows dangerously; it is now over $10 billion. At the same time the Brazilian economy wastes resources that could greatly benefit the development of society as a whole.

The concentration of income, meanwhile, tends to become ever greater, and this strengthens the class and power structure that made it possible. In the process of impoverishing the poor to increase the wealth of the rich, the concentration of income is the clearest proof of the oppression and injustice which the system of private ownership of the means of production, on which the Brazilian system is based, generates. The government not only tolerates it but promotes it by all possible means. The retrogressive nature of the Brazilian tax structure constitutes an indisputable example of this fact, for its three principal taxes contribute to this spiral of concentration. The tax for municipal services (between 6 and 10%) was established at a level that makes the tax on a meal at a luxurious restaurant less than that on a kilo of peas or manioc flour, which is subject to a sales tax of 17%. Since the tax is levied on the first commercial transaction, it favors the producing states like São Paulo to the detriment of the poorest states like those of the Northeast. Finally, the income tax, despite appearances, falls most heavily on low-income taxpayers, the wage earners. The employers always find loopholes in the legal provisions designed to stimulate reinvestment and capitalization that allow them to pay less taxes. ...

The government's massive use of propaganda, of soccer as a means of affirming patriotism and of mechanisms like the sport lottery as an illusory means of achieving economic success, has not succeeded in stupefying our people, who can properly assess the results of the "miracle."

The lack of freedom, the violent repression, the injustices, the impoverishment of the people and the sacrifice of national interests to foreign capital cannot be interpreted as signs that Brazil is achieving its historical mission. Brazil will find the road to greatness when, utilizing the vast material and human resources at our disposal, it constructs a society founded on our humanist and truly Christian traditions and values, a society that will enable it to play a role in the assembly of the peoples in creating a world from which the antagonisms of religion, race, class, and international aggression and exploitation will be banished. ...

The Agrarian Problem

Our peasants, as a general rule, continue to be bound to the plow and to various sharecropping systems which extract more value from their labor for the year than the value of the land that they work. The legal resources, like the Land Statute, to which they may appeal, in practice turn out to have little efficacy. In rental arrangements, for example, the peasants are made to pay a percentage of the value of the rented land that is much higher than the percentage fixed by the Land Statute. The landowner almost always demands a higher rate, and if the peasant does not agree, he will deny him use of the land in future years.

The situation of rural wage laborers is not very different. In theory, their working conditions are defined and protected by labor legislation. But observe what happens in the sugar zone, in a monoculture that employs the majority of rural wage-earners of the Northeast. We find that employers, in order to get around the provision of the labor laws and some provisions of the Land Statute, resort to mass expulsion of the peasants from their lands. ... The expelled workers then must live in congested conditions in shantytowns near the "evacuated" land, forming a reserve of cheap labor easily available to agricultural employers. Now, recruited as "clandestine workers"—a term derived from the fact that they accept employment without a formal labor agreement—they must accept a wage that is even below the legal minimum.

In this way the number of agricultural laborers with formal work agreements has in recent years undergone a sharp decline, so that the rural laborers of the sugar zone who work under such agreements regard it as a true privilege. ...

The trade unions, whose freedom has been destroyed, can do little in defense of their members, or obtain only such concessions as official policy is willing to grant. With the elimination of the genuine trade union leadership by repression, the number of puppets who occupy leading positions in the trade unions has grown. Meanwhile, the process of transforming what should be an instrument of struggle of the working class into a bureaucratic organism of official assistance is accelerating.

The structure of landownership, which gives rise to the iniquities of which the peasant is victim, and not the peasant's aspiration to possess land, generates the struggle for land reform. Supported by the landless peasantry who suffer most directly the consequences of that structure, the struggle grew in the Northeast, and as it grew it became a social objective of all the people of Brazil.

In fact, it was the demands for reform in that region that led to the adoption of the existing legislation regarding labor relations in the countryside and land use. That legislation contains some approaches that could lead to the progressive removal of the obstacles to land reform.

Condemned to marginality in the countryside, exploited, without access to land, the peasant must either continue his struggle for land or emigrate to the region's urban centers, to São Paulo or some other place where he continues to be exploited, whether in constructing Brasilia or the Trans-Amazonian Highway.

The city is only a continuation of his odyssey. Disqualified by his lack of skills to compete for the kind of jobs generated by industry, jobs whose number is inadequate to absorb the expansion of the urban labor force, he swells the unemployed in the service sector, trying to find some sort of activity that will enable him to satisfy his most elemental need: to kill his hunger.

His situation, however, does not distinguish him basically from those who are employed, because they, too, are victims of the process of marginalization inherent in the system. The surplus of labor, a structural fact, reduces their capacity to struggle for the conquest and preservation of their rights. On top of all this, wages are fixed at a level incompatible with the workers' most elementary needs.

In the city the signs of the human degradation produced by our capitalist system—prostitution, neglect of children and the elderly, premature death, the most refined forms of exploitation of labor—are more evident. ...

How can one call Christian a world whose normal functioning creates such iniquities?

6. BRAZIL ON THE EVE
OF THE ELECTIONS OF 1994

The elections of 1994 promised to be the most important in Brazil's history, with voters offered a choice between the neoliberal model of economic growth, based on exports and foreign investment, and a more autonomous model of development, oriented toward the internal market and the solution of the country's great social problems. As 1993 drew to a close, it appeared that the Workers' party leader, known as Lula, who had narrowly lost the presidency to the millionaire rightist Fernando Collor de Mello in 1989, had an insurmountable lead over all other prospective candidates for president. Brazil's elites now showed their great ability to maneuver. They launched the candidacy of Finance

Minister Fernando Henrique Cardoso, a prominent sociologist and leader of a small social democratic party. Cardoso claimed to represent "the viable left" as opposed to Lula's "utopian left"; in reality he was a champion of the new neoliberal orthodoxy. Cardoso's key to electoral success was a tight-money plan to attack Brazil's galloping inflation. Like similar plans elsewhere, it was based on reducing demand and was likely to produce a recession, but the hope was that it would work long enough to elect Cardoso president. The strategy was successful, and in October 1994 Cardoso gained a sweeping victory over Lula. But the new rightist government would have to deal with Brazil's gigantic economic and social problems, for which the neoliberal ideology offered few if any solutions. An Argentine journalist describes the background to the important election of 1994.

Despite the country's serious institutional shortcomings, today no one can seriously question the democratic conquests achieved by Brazil since 1985. The unveiling of innumerable corruption scandals, the almost unrestricted freedom of the press, the appearance on the political scene of new parties and nongovernmental organizations, and the rise of figures with a strong ethical message like that of the sociologist Herbert de Souza, with his campaign against hunger, confirm the stability of democracy in the largest country of Latin America. The hankering after a "Fujimori"[2] solution of some politicians and some elements of the armed forces encounters the solid resistance of a majority that rejects an authoritarian way out of the crisis.

Add to this optimistic panorama a macroeconomic situation that despite the concern caused by an annual inflation rate of 13,000 percent and a large budget deficit, is regarded as basically positive. A favorable trade balance of $13 billion, an annual 5 percent growth rate of the GDP, and a foreign exchange reserve of $35 billion are the statistical data that entitle Brazil to a place among the world's ten principal industrial powers.

The automotive industry, the locomotive of the Brazilian economy, sold 1,390,000 units in 1993, the best year in its history. The boom benefited above all the industrial triangle formed by São Paulo, Rio de Janeiro, and Minas Gerais, pockets of prosperity in a country that the Brazilian economist Edmar Bacha rebaptized as "Belindia," citing statistics that attest to the wealth of the industrial zones, similar to those of Belgium, and other data that reveal a misery comparable to that of the Indian subcontinent. This contrast finds its expression in an unequal distribution of national income, personified in 32 million hungry persons and 7 million street children. The transfer of income from the poor to the rich and the indifference of the state to social problems, an indifference that began under military rule and continued under Collor de Mello, have resulted in the virtual destruction of public

Esteban Engel, "Brasil: Las demandas acumuladas," *Nueva Sociedad*, Caracas, No. 130, marzo-abril 1994, pp. 10–14. (Excerpt translated by the editor.)

services, the collapse of the social security system, and neglect of public education and health. Add to this a state of insecurity whose most brutal expression is the death squads that still operate with impunity.

From Collor to Franco

The resignation of Collor de Mello at the end of 1992, after an unprecedented public mobilization that demanded his trial for corruption, closed the era of democratic consolidation. But although Itamar Franco, successor to the "maharaja of Alagoas," tried to imprint the seal of his taciturn character on the post-Collor era and complete his term without excessive shocks, he was unable to check the wave of change that began at the start of the decade.

In mid-1993, corruption scandals on the highest level, believed to have been purged with the departure of the Collor clan, spread to the Parliament, generating a new wave of demands for an institutional cleansing. Tens of deputies and regional politicians were accused and some were convicted. The "dwarfs of the budget," a coterie of some twenty legislators, had for years devoted themselves to plundering the public treasure, manipulating the transfer of public funds from the government to the federal states. These disclosures revealed a serious breach in the juridical organization of the Brazilian federation: A rigid administrative centralization, within a few blocks of the capital, Brasilia, was contradicted by the reality of the rule of provincial caciques and their unscrupulous parliamentary agents.

The discussion concerning the reform of the constitution of 1988, which the Parliament was supposed to complete during 1994, became the touchstone in the dispute between the "statist" sectors and the self-proclaimed "modernizers." The dispute made perfectly clear the loss of the consensus that the left and the right had maintained in recent decades with regard to the process of Brazilian development. The shared conviction that industrialization must go hand in hand with a policy to tariff protection and stress on the domestic market disappeared and gave way to a debate resembling those that went on in other Latin American countries that adopted "structural adjustment programs" in the early 1980s.

Although the opening of the economy had in fact begun in the Collor era, with the elimination of the barrier to the importation of computer information systems and the accelerated reduction of tariffs, the dispute over the framework within which economic development should take place heated up during the debate over revision of the Constitution. The National Confederation of Industries (CNI), supported by right-wing parties, became the spearhead of the revisionists, who regarded the elimination of the constitutional articles providing for labor's rights, restrictions on foreign investment, and defense of state enterprises as the master key to economic growth.

This pressure, exerted through a powerful and well-oiled lobby in Brasilia, received aid from foreign executives and analysts who raised the specter of disinvestment if the reform failed, demanding greater opening to foreign capital, the privatization of state enterprises, and more "flexibility" in labor relations. But the reform project remained stalled thanks to a government paralyzed by an avalanche of scandals and the firm opposition of the parliamentary left, headed by the Workers' party (PT).

The PT: From Insignificance to Leader of the Opposition

It was in fact the PT that ten years after its founding, with only 36 deputies and 1 senator in the Parliament, succeeded in uniting the opposition to the reform projects of a weak governmental coalition formed by the centrist Brazilian Democratic Movement party (PMDB) and the Social Democratic party (PSDB) of Fernando Henrique Cardoso. Created with the support of the metallurgical trade unions of São Paulo and the base communities of the Catholic church, the PT made a leap to the national scene by winning the mayoralty of São Paulo and gaining 44 percent of the vote for Lula in the second round of the elections of 1989.

These gains enabled the PT to break out of the obscurity to which the national media had condemned it and become one of the major political forces of Brazil and Latin America. A contributing factor was its capacity to articulate demands that transcended those of the working class of the great industrial centers and a section of the government employees, becoming the voice for the farm workers, people affected by droughts in the northeast, and the victims of human rights abuses.

Employing a strategy for reaching out to people never before used in Brazilian history, in mid-1993 Lula initiated the "citizens' caravans" in the interior of Brazil. These caravans, traveling a distance of 33,000 kilometers, visited small settlements and zones that hitherto had only known the visits of regional caciques. Crossing practically all of the states between Amazonas and Rio Grande do Sul, they succeeded in breaking the isolation imposed on Lula by the television networks and became a major news source in their own right. For thousands of people, Lula was the first politician of national stature whom they could see in person, and this alternative means of communication also enabled Lula to become familiar with the problems and concerns of the population.

The PT succeeded, moreover, in attracting to its ranks a portion of society eager to organize itself politically. Although the entry of remnants of the communist and noncommunist left led to a brief, bitter struggle of different factions, on the eve of the elections of 1994 the PT could claim that it was the only political group whose activity was directed by a program and not by personalities.

It was precisely its positions on polemical themes, its rejection of the constitutional reform, its criticism of the economic program, its resistance to privatization of telecommunications and petroleum, and its demands for legalization of abortion and marriage between homosexuals that drew the harshest criticism from the right. Because its factions ranged from the "Radical Democracy" of European-style social democrats to Trotskyite currents and independent groups linked to the Catholic church, the party formed an easy target in a highly personalized political struggle.

The undeniable differences within the PT came into the open in the course of the debate on the failed constitutional revision. In a confrontation similar to that experienced in the previous decade by the "realists" and "fundamentalists" of the German Greens, a majority of the PT's parliamentary group favored participating in the eventual reform. The national leadership of the party, however, dominated by the "Left Option" grouped around Secretary General Rui Falção, demanded that the deputies should not take part in the reform and should boycott sessions of the Parliament devoted to the subject and the special commissions created to work on the problem of constitutional revision. At the ninth National Meeting of the PT in early May 1994, Lula played the role of arbiter, skillfully juggling different options, and succeeded in filing away the sharp edges of the most controversial points of the party's platform (legalization of abortion, immediate moratorium on payment of the foreign debt) proposed by the "Shiite" wing, as the press chose to call the most radical factions.

From the Cardoso Plan to the Real Plan

The controversies about the Constitution did not wholly dominate the public's interest. Against the background of a galloping inflation, the need for putting the Brazilian fiscal house in order constituted the first point on the agenda of all the presidential candidates.

The move of Fernando Henrique Cardoso from the post of foreign minister to that of fourth finance minister in the Franco government inspired hopes of a change of course, especially in the urban sectors. Highly regarded because of his academic prestige, "FHC" assumed the finance ministry, reaffirming the support that his Brazilian Social Democratic party gave to Franco, who had watched his cabinet and parliamentary support dissolve month by month. The Brazilian Social Democratic party (PSDB), a splinter of the Brazilian Democratic Movement that united the opposition to the military in the 1970s, had managed to gain the support of middle sectors and important figures in the intellectual and artistic world. However, its lack of a solid organizational structure and of links to labor constituted its principal weakness and threatened to bring its rout at the polls.

In the last three months of 1993, Cardoso, supported by the technical experts who five years before had conceived the Plan Cruzado, put into effect a series of measures that the government claimed would attack the inflation problem at its roots. The frontal attack on inflation became the centerpiece of the official planning and Cardoso the "Wizard of Oz" in whom Franco, an acknowledged aficionado of Cardoso in economic questions, placed all his trust. Other decisions followed. In October, after an exhausting parliamentary negotiation that reinforced Cardoso's reputation as a skillful negotiator, he announced the creation of a Social Emergency Fund, designed to reduce the transfer of funds by the government to the federal states. The action amounted to a tacit accusation that the provinces were a "black hole" that was draining the treasury dry.

The Fund, with a life of two years and Parliament's support, attempted to break the straitjacket that the Constitution fastened on the central government's management of finances by compelling it to transfer 80 percent of tax revenues to the federal states. The second step was the creation of the Real Unit of Value (URV), a new index tied to the dollar and designed to make the evolution of wages and prices uniform with a single parameter. Although adoption of the URV was at first left to the economic actors, wages began to be indexed daily, partially reducing the inflationary losses caused by payment at the end of the month.

Conceived as the basis of a new money (the real), the URV went into force May 1, 1994, as the Brazilian version of Eastern Europe's fight against inflation. A currency board, attached to the Central Bank and the Finance Ministry, daily determines the value of the real on the basis of the evolution of prices, the quotation of the dollar, and the availability of foreign exchange. Although initial successes showed some check on the evolution of prices, inflation remained mired at indexes of 42 and 50 percent a month. Cardoso, with the advice of his Argentine colleague Domingo Cavallo, father of a convertibility plan that was one of the models of the Brazilian plan, then announced that the real would soon be put into circulation but gave no fixed date.

At the end of March, heartened by the positive responses to his plan and polls showing that he was a viable candidate for president and pressured by the deadline for making his candidacy official, Cardoso announced that he was resigning his ministry to enter the race for the presidential palace. The expectations aroused by his candidacy among sympathizers with the ex-minister and the PSDB gave way to disillusionment when he announced his decision to form an alliance with the Liberal Front party (PFL). The PFL was the principal heir of the Nationalist Republican Alliance (ARENA), the party created by the military during the dictatorship. Unlike the PSDB, the PFL had a solid party organization, 3 million members, and control of nine state governments. Cardoso's choice as running mate of a northeastern *caudillo* who had been the political godfather of Collor de Mello did nothing to silence his critics.

One of the motives of the alliance between Cardoso—who during the military dictatorship had passed his exile in Allende's Chile—and the heirs of the dictatorship was the regulation that allots television time for political propaganda according to the size of the parliamentary groups. This arrangement favored Cardoso's electoral coalition over Lula's PT. Cardoso's decision to launch the real on July 1, four months before the elections, also exposed him to criticism that his economic plan, conceived when he formed part of the government, had a political, cosmetic character. The criticism was especially pertinent because Cardoso linked his electoral success to the Real Plan.

A struggle over who should be the "anti-Lula" candidate also took place within the PMDB, the largest political group in Brazil, with 4.5 million members and an apparatus based on more than 1,600 mayoralties and 6 state governments. Weakened by the corruption scandals that involved some of its principal figures, the PMDB launched Orestes Quercia, the controversial ex-governor of São Paulo, as its candidate for president, dashing the hopes of former President José Sarney. The controversial ex-governor of Rio de Janeiro Leonel Brizola, who in 1989 had narrowly lost the second place in the presidential race to Lula, had no difficulty in winning the candidacy of the Democratic Labor party (PDT) but faced high levels of rejection both in his own state and in the south of the country.

Conclusion

Aside from the tasks that any new government must confront, the crucial question today is with whom it can align. The interim regime of Itamar Franco administered the country for two years almost exclusively with provisional measures that Parliament then watered down. The Cardoso government, ruling for four years, must base its activity on support by a parliamentary majority. However, the fractionalization of parties and regional caudillismo, compelling a permanent search for alliances, threatens a repetition of the continual state of uncertainty that Franco faced.

This circumstance is particularly tricky for Lula, since the PT today has only 36 of the 500 seats in Congress. The highly regionalist character of Brazilian voting and the absence of strong local political personalities among the PT's candidates make a significant increase in that number unlikely. This situation could lead to a repetition of the present impasse, in which the left cannot impose its will on the right, led by the PFL and the most conservative members of PMDB.

A conservative government, however, may succeed in excluding the new social forces from its planning. In that case an important part of civil society will remain on the margins of the political process and must wait another four years for an opportunity to satisfy its accumulated demands.

20

꩜

LATIN AMERICAN ROADS

TO SOCIALISM

THE CUBAN REVOLUTION of 1959 marks a dividing line in Latin American history. Before 1959, a capitalist model of development appeared to be the most viable means of escape for Latin America from its age-old backwardness and dependency, with a dynamic middle class leading a process of industrialization and social reform. But by the end of the 1950s these hopes for a capitalist solution for Latin America's problems had dimmed. The experience of such countries as Mexico, Brazil, and Argentina, in which capitalism had grown rapidly, suggested that as a rule the new industrial and financial bourgeoisie was as fearful of social change, as prone to encourage foreign economic interests and suppress dissent by violent means, as had been the traditional landed oligarchy. If Cuba's Marxist revolution could succeed where capitalist approaches had failed, sooner or later the revolution's success was bound to have great continental repercussions, particularly as the United States had long avowed that it would not allow a successful socialist, anti-imperialist revolution in its Caribbean backyard, a part of the world that for a century had been a secure U.S. preserve.

The Cuban Revolution did not begin as a socialist revolution. In his famous "History Will Absolve Me" speech, made at his trial after a failed attempt in 1953 to overthrow the dictatorship of Fulgencio Batista, Fidel Castro offered a program of social reform that was compatible with capitalism and capitalist democracy. But pressure from internal and external enemies—especially the implacable hostility of the United States—forced the revolution to move steadily to the left. Denied markets in the United States, Castro negotiated large trade agreements with the Soviet Union and other countries of the socialist community. By 1970 the Cuban Revolution had survived a grave economic crisis largely caused by the leadership's own mistakes, an invasion attempt by Cuban exiles in the United States organized by the

CIA, and a confrontation between the United States and the Soviet Union that brought a jittery world to the verge of a nuclear conflict. By 1985 the revolution was stabilized and institutionalized. A new constitution (1976) sought to depersonalize government and promote participatory democracy on all levels of Cuban life.

The upward movement of the Cuban economy, whose long-term growth rate was considerably higher than that of the rest of Latin America, was interrupted by periods of stagnation or decline that led to massive emigrations of Cubans to the United States in 1980 and again in 1994. The collapse of the Soviet Union and the socialist common market in 1989 deprived Cuba of its major trading partners and dealt a devastating blow to the Cuban economy. The crisis was aggravated by an intensified effort by the United States to strangle socialist Cuba through passage of the 1992 Torricelli Act, which extends the U.S. embargo against Cuba (in effect since 1960) to U.S. subsidiaries in third countries and bars any ship that docks in Cuba from entering any U.S. port for 180 days. The embargo has been condemned by overwhelming majorities of the U.N. General Assembly and by the leaders of all other Latin American countries. The collapse of the socialist economic community and the tightened U.S. embargo have reversed the trend of steadily improving social conditions and produced a decline in living standards. Despite the slippage in living standards, Cuba continues to lead all other Latin American countries in the quality of life it provides its children. Cuba's infant mortality rate in 1993, 9.4 per 1,000 live births, is among the lowest in the world and almost equal with that of the United States. Cuba's life expectancy rate, 76 years, compares to an average life expectancy of 58 years in the underdeveloped world. Cuba hoped to overcome its economic crisis by diversifying its trade links, vastly expanding tourism, discovering large offshore oil reserves, and developing new biotechnology and medical exports. And by 1999 Cuba seemed to have turned the corner. In 1998 it received more than 1.4 million tourists, mostly from Canada and Europe, and the number was expected to grow to 2 million. Cuba had more than 340 joint ventures with foreign companies, with a value of more than $2 billion. (U.S. corporate executives such as Dwayne Andreas of Archer Daniels Midland and Donald Fites of Caterpillar were eager to join the procession to Havana, but President Clinton, deferring to the Republican right and the anti-Castro Cuban-American National Foundation, still supports the embargo that bars trade with Cuba.) Cuba's biotech industry continues to make large strides in developing vaccines against AIDS, cancer, and other diseases. Cuba has also accomplished the largest conversion from conventional modern agriculture to large-scale organic farming in history.

Was it possible to achieve socialism in any Latin American country without some degree of armed struggle? The Chilean election of 1970, which brought to the presidency the socialist Salvador Allende, supported by a coalition of the Socialist, Communist, and Radical parties, put that question to a searching test. Allende assumed the presidency in November 1970 with a program for the nationalization of foreign-owned natural resources, key industries, and banks as well as a sweeping land reform. One year later the Allende government had strengthened its position by victory in municipal elections and had taken large strides toward achieving changes of such magnitude that they might prove irreversible. The United States, which had made frantic efforts to prevent the election and inauguration of Allende (including pressure on the Chilean military to intervene through a coup) now launched a campaign to destabilize the Allende regime and strangle the Chilean economy by denying credits and using other methods of economic warfare. This destabilization effort was synchronized with a parallel campaign mounted by Chile's capitalists and landed oligarchs to create political and economic chaos. The reactionary opposition profited by the discontent of large sections of the urban middle class, which resented the hardships of growing inflation and goods shortages and the decline in its standard of living vis-à-vis that of the working class. Meanwhile preparations for a right-wing military coup were under way. In September 1973 a military revolt led by General Augusto Pinochet broke out. Salvador Allende, refusing to surrender to the rebels, committed suicide after heroically defending the presidential palace with a few aides to the last. Scattered and poorly armed leftist resistance was speedily crushed.

The reign of terror that followed had no precedent in Chilean history. Thousands of Chileans were murdered, often after brutal torture; thousands of others fled into exile. The new ruling junta liquidated the radical changes and social reforms of the Allende regime and was guided in its economic policies by the free market theories of the Chicago school of Milton Friedman, with catastrophic effects on the Chilean economy and living standards. By 1985 the junta and its president, General Pinochet, had lost most of their original middle-class support. Pinochet's growing isolation reflected changes within Chile and the continent-wide movement in the 1980s away from authoritarian military rule. Even the United States, which had colluded with the 1973 military coup in Chile, now pressured the dictator to make a transition to democracy. Maneuvering to remain in power, Pinochet called for a plebiscite in which Chileans would vote on a proposal to grant him eight more years as president. In October 1988, Chilean voters, by a decisive margin, denied Pinochet a new term as president. In December 1989 the first democratic election since 1973 gave the presidency to the Christian Democrat Patricio Aylwin, favored by the United States. Aylwin, the candidate of a coalition of left and center parties, also had a clear majority in congress.

But the outlook for a genuine democratization of Chilean society remained clouded. To begin with, Aylwin (who had initially supported the fascist coup but later had a change of heart) operated within the limits imposed by the 1980 constitution crafted by Pinochet, which left him solidly entrenched in the Senate and the judiciary and gave the military an extraordinary degree of autonomy. Rather than challenge the legal and institutional heritage of the dictatorship, Aylwin adopted what has been called a policy of "gentle accommodation" with the military. This policy meant, among other things, that there was very little progress in bringing to justice the military who had tortured and killed thousands of Chileans. Secondly, Aylwin implemented even more energetically the export-led model of economic growth, based on foreign loans and investments, that the "Chicago Boys" had put in place, with a stress on such export products as seafood, fruit, and lumber at the expense of national industry and agriculture producing staples for the domestic market. Economists called attention to the vulnerability of the export-led model to changes in international prices and demand; environmentalists warned that the model was not sustainable over time because of soil erosion and excessive use of pesticides that endangered health. Again, Aylwin made virtually no change in the pattern of labor relations inherited from Pinochet, which subordinated the rights of labor to those of the employer. In democratic Chile, for example, farm workers are prohibited from striking during the harvest season, the time when a strike would be most effective. As a result, despite some improvement in living standards since 1989, Chilean society continues to be marked by great inequity and injustice. The vulnerable character of the current economic model and its failure to address the country's great economic and social problems contributes to keeping alive Allende's dream of a democratic socialism in the framework of a pluralistic political system.

In December 1993 Chileans elected the Christian Democrat Eduardo Frei, son of a reformist president of the same name, as president. He took office promising to continue the current economic course but vowed to end extreme poverty by the year 2000, reform the labor laws, and regain civilian control of the military.

But a series of events soon cast doubt on Chile's supposed economic and political stability. The onset of the Asian financial crisis in 1997, spreading to Russia and then to Latin America, exposed the fragility of Chile's export base, when the price of copper, Chile's principal export, plummeted. By 1999 the country was floundering in a recession with growing unemployment, an increasingly defiant and active labor movement, and spreading cracks in the ruling Christian Democrat–Socialist coalition. Those cracks were spotlighted following the 1998 arrest of the former dictator and current senator Augusto Pinochet in England when a Spanish judge investigating Pinochet's "alleged crimes against humanity" demanded that he be extradited to Spain. Socialist leaders generally supported Pinochet's extradition, but Christian Democratic President Frei protested that it would destabilize Chilean society. The Pinochet affair and the Spanish judge's request for pertinent documents from the United States also created uncomfortable moments for the Washington establishment in view of the leading role played by "elder statesman" Henry Kissinger and other U.S. officials in supporting the Pinochet putsch and fascist regime.

The revolution, led by the Sandinist Front of National Liberation (FSLN),[1] that toppled the Somoza dynasty of Nicaragua in July 1979 set the stage for an experiment in social and economic change unique in Latin American history. Most if not all of the Sandinist leadership accepted some form of socialism as their ultimate goal. But a striking feature of their socio-economic program was its moderate and gradualist approach. Even after the expropriation of the vast landholdings and other properties of the Somoza family and its collaborators, most of the economy remained in private hands. Large commercial farmers as well as peasant cooperatives and small independent farmers received aid from the government in the form of credits, guaranteed prices, and the like. At the same time the Sandinist state insisted that capitalists, whether large farmers or industrialists, display social responsibility by reinvesting part of their profits in their enterprises and complying with the reform legislation defining the rights of workers and tenants. Some capitalists accepted the new rules of the game with good grace; others sabotaged or abandoned their enterprises and left the country.

In 1985 the Sandinist revolution celebrated its sixth year in power. Those six years had seen some remarkable social gains: large progress toward the liquidation of illiteracy, the provision of free medical and dental care to the population accompanied by a sharp drop in infant mortality, and at least a modest overall rise in the standard of living of the masses. That progress would have been much greater had it not been for the fixed hostility of the United States under President Ronald Reagan toward the new Nicaragua. This hostility was reflected in a trade embargo that did great damage to the Nicaraguan economy, and above all in an undeclared "covert" war whose forms included the provision of financial and material aid to counterrevolutionary forces led by former commanders of Somoza's National Guard and the mining of Nicaraguan harbors by the CIA. The "covert" war clearly flouted U.S. laws, treaty obligations, and international law, a fact effectively conceded by the Reagan administration when it refused to accept the jurisdiction of the World Court in a complaint made by Nicaragua before that body against U.S. interventionist actions.

Following his election to the presidency in 1988, George Bush continued Reagan's policy of employing a mercenary puppet army to wear down the Nicaraguan government and economy, create war weariness, and eventually produce an internal collapse. The strategy scored a major success when a majority of Nicaraguan voters, voting, in effect, with a U.S. gun pointed at their heads, chose the conservative presidential candidate Violeta Chamorro over the Sandinista Daniel Ortega in the elections of February 25, 1990. But the FSLN remained the country's strongest political party. Supported by the powerful labor and peasant unions, it resisted with partial success efforts by the Chamorro government to dismantle the agrarian reform but could not prevent the new regime from implementing neoliberal economic policies that favored the old elites at the expense of the masses. As hunger, unemployment, and discontent grew, the coalition of parties that had supported Chamorro split into a moderate conservative wing loyal to her and an extreme conservative, even Somocista-like, wing that opposed her opening to the Sandinistas. Within the Sandinista camp a division also emerged between a social democratic faction that favored cooperation with Chamorro and a group that proposed firm opposition to her neoliberal program and return to the traditional Sandinista program of structural economic and social reform. With new elections scheduled for 1996, little time remained for the Sandinistas to reunite their leadership, rebuild their grassroots organization, and develop a coherent alternative program to the bankrupt neoliberal program of the Chamorro regime.

Arnold Alemán, a wealthy coffee planter of Somocista background, exploited these problems and with the support of U.S. backers went on to win the presidential election of 1996 with 51 percent of the vote. Once in office, Alemán forgot his promises of jobs and economic development and embarked on a neoliberal program of privatization, tariff reduction, and drastic cuts in social spending, advising Nicaraguans that "we have to take bitter medicine." By 1998 Nicaragua, which had made a promising start toward social reconstruction under Sandinista rule, was the second poorest country in Latin America after Haiti, with 70 percent of Nicaraguans unemployed or underemployed. The process was accompanied by a series of scandals and charges of illegal enrichment that provoked an investigation by the country's comptroller general. By his own admission—but without further explanation—Alemán's personal wealth increased by 900 percent between 1990 and 1996. Against this background of misrule and corruption, the ravages of Hurricane Mitch—itself a product of neoliberal misuse of land and resources—added to the miseries of the Nicaraguan people. But the Sandinista spirit of resistance to tyranny and injustice remained alive, reflected, among other ways, in massive demonstrations and blockage of roads against government officials who attempted to repossess 14,000 farms for failure to repay loans. And despite continuing factional disputes within the FSLN, there were signs that its leadership was moving toward unity and a coherent program of resistance and reform.

Revolutionary movements that asserted socialist ideals had also arisen in two other Central American countries dominated by corrupt and oppressive military establishments: El Salvador and Guatemala. In El Salvador the Farabundo Martí Front for National Liberation (FMLN), representing a broad coalition of social and political forces, waged a twelve-year struggle against a U.S.-supported government and army. Despite massive infusions of U.S. military and financial aid, by 1990 the FMLN controlled much of the country and showed an ability to launch powerful offensives at will. The changed balance of forces forced President Alfredo Cristiani (1989–1994) and his right-wing regime to accept proposals for U.N.-sponsored peace talks. Prolonged, difficult negotiations finally resulted in the January 1993 signing of peace accords that provided for the dissolution of the government's security forces; the creation of a new national police open to both members of the former national police and FMLN guerrillas; a reduction of the armed forces, to be cleansed of military personnel guilty of human rights abuses; and the holding of new elections in 1994 in which the left, for the first time in fifty years, could openly run. Those elections, marked by numerous irregularities due to fraud and incompetence, and by an abstention rate of about 50 percent that probably reflected fear and distrust of the government, gave victory to the ruling right-wing party and its presidential candidate, Armando Calderón Sol. But the FMLN secured 25 percent of the vote and established a substantial presence in the legislative assembly. Under new peace-time conditions, the FMLN began a political and social struggle that in time, many of its leaders believed, would lead to the achievement of a democratic socialist society.

In March 1997, fighting against odds that included shortages of campaign funds and the usual electoral frauds, the FMLN scored new gains, electing twenty-seven deputies, a third of whom were women, and winning control of fifty-three municipalities, including San Salvador; it could now claim to represent the majority of the population. This stunning reversal alarmed ARENA, which changed its tactics. In March 1999, it offered as its presidential candidate an obscure former professor, Francisco Flores, who promised social changes that would benefit the entire population and soft-pedaled the hard neoliberal content of the party's program. This shiny new image was also designed to erase memories of ARENA's bloody past. The FMLN candidate was Facundo Guadiano, a former guerrilla commander who with the advice of a team of U.S. advisers sought to present an image of moderation and conciliation. Voter apathy, reflecting the belief that neither candidate was addressing the country's major social and economic problems, made for a small turnout at the polls. Guadiano's defeat, despite the FMLN's excellent governing record on the local and national levels, may presage a return to power by the party's more socialist-oriented grouping. This string of gains and losses hints at the difficulties faced by a successful guerrilla organization in finding its bearings in a new time of peace and legality. Meanwhile the hard facts of Salvadoran life remained: 34 percent of the population lived in poverty, unemployment continued high, and debt service payments took one-third of all foreign-exchange earnings.

In Guatemala, where a CIA-organized coup had overthrown a democratic reformist government in 1954, a socialist-oriented guerrilla movement fought for decades against barbarous military regimes that employed scorched-earth tactics and massacres of Indian peasants to deprive the guerrillas of their support bases and drive them into remote jungles and mountains. Under international pressure, in 1985 the military permitted the election of a civilian president, Vinicio Cerezo Arévalo, but retained effective control of the country's life under Cerezo and his successors in the presidency. By the late 1980s the guerrilla military activities, led by the Guatemalan National Revolutionary Unity (URNG), were again increasing in scope and frequency. Under U.S. pressure, in 1993 the reluctant military accepted a proposal for U.N.-sponsored talks with the URNG, and by March 1994 a human rights accord that provided for international monitoring of army bases and guerrilla camps had been signed. But military hardliners, fearing the loss of their impunity, responded with a deadly wave of killings and disappearances, which the current president, Ramiro de León Carpio, appeared unable to stem. As 1994 drew to a close, the return of peace to Guatemala still appeared far off.

But the combined pressure of the international community, the armed insurgency, and a variety of local democratic movements led to new elections in November 1995. Álvaro Arzú Yrigoyen, who had campaigned for a negotiated peace with the insurgency, was elected. One surprise was the success of a new party, the New Guatemala Democratic Front (FDNG). Largely supported by the indigenous Maya element, it won about 8 percent of the vote, elected six congressional candidates, including three women, and won control of the important Maya center of Quetzaltenango. A left-wing coalition, the first such organization permitted in Guatemala since the CIA-organized coup overthrew the Arbenz regime in 1954, won eight seats in congress. Under the pressure of these events President Arzú signed peace accords with the UNRG that required UN verification of compliance with its provisions, including a series of social reforms: promotion of indigenous rights; legislative, judicial, and electoral reforms; and an overhaul of public security and national defense forces. One must not minimize the importance of the restoration of peace and other achievements of these accords. But many of the reforms will remain on paper as long as they are opposed by the military, the landed oligarchy, and its foreign financial allies. And to date little has changed in Guatemala. The socioeconomic system, one of the most inequitable in Latin America, remains in place. Even the military and paramilitary death squads, shielded by a 1996 amnesty law and a subservient judicial system, continue to operate with impunity. In April 1998 one such death squad assassinated Bishop Monsignor Juan Gerardi, a human-rights champion who had just published a report concluding that the army and its allies were responsible for 90 percent of the 200,000 civilians who were killed or disappeared during the civil war. The sad truth is that until the mass of ordinary Guatemalans—Maya, ladinos (non-Indians), former guerrillas, trade unions, peasant unions, the middle class—unite and form a countervailing power against the power of the landed and business elite and their foreign allies, Guatemala will remain a savage mix of the brutal society created by the sixteenth-century conquistador and the maquilized society created by modern neoliberalism.

A series of developments, including the collapse of the Soviet Union and other Stalinist-type governments in Eastern Europe, has led some observers to conclude that socialism had no future on this continent. This reaction may reflect a misreading of the situation. To begin with, the catastrophic economic and social results of the replacement of socialism by a "savage capitalism" in Eastern Europe suggests to many that capitalism may not be the wave of the future after all. Secondly, the adoption of neoliberal economic policies by such countries as Argentina, Brazil, Mexico, Venezuela, Peru, and Bolivia has not led to balanced development and rising living standards but has instead contributed to increased misery and social crisis. There is no evidence, in short, that stronger doses of capitalism can solve the problem created by Latin American dependent capitalism. Finally, contrary to a common assumption, left-wing or socialist-oriented movements are not dying on the vine in Latin America. Evidence to the contrary includes the survival, against all odds, of the Cuban experiment in socialism; the continued vitality of such movements in Central America; the rise of the powerful Workers' party in Brazil; the recent capture by left-wing parties of the mayoralty of Uruguay's capital, Montevideo, which has more than half the country's population, and the mayoralty of Venezuela's capital, Caracas; and, most recently, the revolt in the Mexican state of Chiapas led by the self-styled Zapatista Army of National Liberation (EZLN) in January 1994.

Among Marxist guerrilla movements, the most successful by far has been the Communist-led Revolutionary Armed Forces of Colombia (FARC). Created in response to the right-wing terrorist campaign waged against peasants and workers in the 1950s, the FARC has steadily expanded its power. Today its some 20,000 fighters control almost half of the national Colombian territory. Its popular base consists primarily of peasant communities that produce coca leaves and poppies as well as subsistence crops as the only alternative to the economic crisis. The guerrillas defend the peasantry against the government's herbicidal spraying of their fields and against the land-grabbing efforts of the new narco-bourgeoisie. They compel "fair" payment by the drug traffickers to coca growers for their products. In addition to providing protection, the guerrillas have assumed many functions of the state in the regions under their control. Although the current Washington line, in the words of drug czar General Barry McCaffrey, is that the guerrillas are "narco-corrupted cadres," the guerrillas are well aware of the devastating social and environmental effects of drug cultivation and have repeatedly proposed—without success—a program for the eradication of coca, poppy, and marihuana plantations by substitution of other crops, with government aid to farmers in land, seeds, and equipment. After suffering a series of military defeats, the Colombian government has resumed peace talks with the guerrillas, but the government's failure to move against the right-wing paramilitary forces, as demanded by FARC, and U.S. pressure on the government not to make excessive "concessions" to FARC, makes the success of the negotiations doubtful.

1. "HISTORY WILL ABSOLVE ME"

Fidel Castro made his entrance into history at dawn on July 26, 1953, when he led a tiny force of Cuban patriots, one hundred sixty-five men and two women, in an assault on the Moncada Barracks in Santiago de Cuba. The quixotic adventure ended in disaster. Nearly half the rebels were killed, many being tortured to death after capture. Those who survived were imprisoned. At his trial the twenty-seven-year-old Castro, a lawyer by profession and the son of a large landowner, made a five-hour defense speech in which he outlined the aims of the uprising. In a general way his speech offers a blueprint of the radical reform program that the Cuban Revolution was to implement, but the whole document bears the stamp of a democratic, romantic ideology that Castro would later abandon in favor of Marxism-Leninism. The title of this selection is taken from the final phrase of Castro's speech: "Condemn me. History will absolve me."

As soon as Santiago de Cuba was in our hands, we would immediately have readied the people for war. Bayamo was attacked precisely to situate our advance forces along the Cauto River. Never forget that this province, which has a million and a half inhabitants today, provides without a doubt the best resistance and the most patriotic men of Cuba. It was this province that continued the fight for independence for thirty years and paid the highest tribute in blood, sacrifice, and heroism. In Oriente, you can still breathe the air of that glorious epoch. At dawn, when the cocks crow as if they were bugles calling soldiers to reveille, and when the sun rises, radiant, over the rugged mountains, it seems that once again we will hear the cry of Yara or Baire.[2]

I stated that the second consideration on which we based our chances for success was one of social order because we were assured of the people's support. When we speak of the people we do not mean the comfortable ones, the conservative elements of the nation, who welcome any regime of oppression, any dictatorship, and despotism, prostrating themselves before the master of the moment until they grind their foreheads into the ground. When we speak of struggle, the *people* means the vast unredeemed masses, to whom all make promises and whom all deceive; we mean the people who yearn for a better, more dignified and more just nation; who are moved by ancestral aspi-

---

Fidel Castro's History Will Absolve Me, Havana, Impreso por Cooperativa Obrera de Publicidad, 1960, pp. 33–43.

rations of justice, for they have suffered injustice and mockery, generation after generation; who long for great and wise changes in all aspects of their life; people, who, to attain these changes, are ready to give even the very last breath of their lives—when they believe in something or in someone, especially when they believe in themselves. In stating a purpose, the first condition of sincerity and good faith, is to do precisely what nobody ever does, that is, to speak with absolute clarity, without fear. The demagogues and professional politicians who manage to perform the miracle of being right in everything and in pleasing everyone, are, of necessity, deceiving everyone about everything. The revolutionaries must proclaim their ideas courageously, define their principles and express their intentions so that no one is deceived, neither friend nor foe.

The people we counted on in our struggle were these:

Seven hundred thousand Cubans without work, who desire to earn their daily bread honestly without having to emigrate in search of livelihood.

Five hundred thousand farm laborers inhabiting miserable shacks, who work four months of the year and starve for the rest of the year, sharing their misery with their children, who have not an inch of land to cultivate, and whose existence inspires compassion in any heart not made of stone.

Four hundred thousand industrial laborers and stevedores whose retirement funds have been embezzled, whose benefits are being taken away, whose homes are wretched quarters, whose salaries pass from the hands of the boss to those of the usurer, whose future is a pay reduction and dismissal, whose life is eternal work and whose only rest is in the tomb.

One hundred thousand small farmers who live and die working on land that is not theirs, looking at it with sadness as Moses did the promised land, to die without possessing it; who, like feudal serfs, have to pay for the use of their parcel of land by giving up a portion of their products; who cannot love it, improve it, beautify it or plant a lemon or an orange tree on it, because they never know when a sheriff will come with the rural guard to evict them from it.

Thirty thousand small business men weighted down by debts, ruined by the crisis and harangued by a plague of filibusters and venal officials.

Ten thousand young professionals: doctors, engineers, lawyers, veterinarians, school teachers, dentists, pharmacists, newspapermen, painters, sculptors, etc., who come forth from school with their degrees, anxious to work and full of hope, only to find themselves at a dead end with all doors closed, and where no ear hears their clamor or supplication.

These are the people, the ones who know misfortune and, therefore, are capable of fighting with limitless courage!

To the people whose desperate roads through life have been paved with the brick of betrayals and false promises, we were not going to say: "we will eventually give you what you need, but rather—Here you have it, fight for it with all your might so that liberty and happiness may be yours!"

In the brief of this cause there must be recorded the five revolutionary laws that would have been proclaimed immediately after the capture of the Moncada barracks and would have been broadcast to the nation by radio. It is possible that Colonel Chaviano may deliberately have destroyed these documents, but even if he has done so, I conserve them in my memory.

The First Revolutionary Law would have returned power to the people and proclaimed the Constitution of 1940 the supreme Law of the land, until such time as the people should decide to modify or change it. And, in order to effect its implementation and punish those who had violated it—there being no organization for holding elections to accomplish this—the revolutionary movement, as the momentous incarnation of this sovereignty, the only source of legitimate power, would have assumed all the faculties inherent to it, except that of modeling the Constitution itself: In other words it would have assumed the legislative, executive and judicial powers.

This approach could not be more crystal clear nor more free of vacillation and sterile charlatanry. A government acclaimed by the mass of rebel people would be vested with every power, everything necessary in order to proceed with the effective implementation of the popular will and true justice. From that moment, the Judicial Power, which since March 10th has placed itself *against* the Constitution and *outside* the Constitution, would cease to exist and we would proceed to its immediate and total reform before it would again assume the power granted to it by the Supreme Law of the Republic. Without our first taking those previous measures, a return to legality by putting the custody of the courts back into the hands that have crippled the system so dishonorably would constitute a fraud, a deceit, and one more betrayal.

The Second Revolutionary Law would have granted property, not mortgageable and not transferable, to all planters, sub-planters, lessees, partners and squatters who hold parcels of five or less "caballerias" of land, and the state would indemnify the former owners on the basis of the rental which they would have received for these parcels over a period of ten years.

The Third Revolutionary Law would have granted workers and employees the right to share 30% of the profits of all the large industrial, mercantile and mining enterprises, including the sugar mills. The strictly agricultural enterprises would be exempt in consideration of other agrarian laws which would have been implemented.

The Fourth Revolutionary Law would have granted all planters the right to share 55% of the sugar production and a minimum quota of forty thousand "arrobas" for all small planters who have been established for three or more years.

The Fifth Revolutionary Law would have ordered the confiscation of all holdings and ill-gotten gains of those who had committed frauds during previous regimes, as well as the holdings and ill-gotten gains of all their legatees and heirs. To implement this, special courts with full powers would gain access to all records of all corporations registered or operating in this country (in order) to investigate concealed funds of illegal origin, and to request that foreign governments extradite persons and attach holdings (rightfully belonging to the Cuban people). Half of the property recovered would be used to subsidize retirement funds for workers and the other half would be used for hospitals, asylums and charitable organizations.

Furthermore, it was to be declared that the Cuban policy in the Americas would be one of close solidarity with the democratic people of this continent, and that those politically persecuted by bloody tyrants oppressing our sister nations would find generous asylum, brotherhood, and bread in the land of Martí. Not the persecution, hunger and treason that they find today. Cuba should be the bulwark of liberty and not a shameful link in the chain of despotism.

These laws would have been proclaimed immediately, as soon as the upheaval was ended and prior to a detailed and far-reaching study, they would have been followed by another series of laws and fundamental measures, such as, the Agrarian Reform, Integral Reform in Education, nationalization of the Utilities Trust and the Telephone Trust, refund to the people of the illegal excessive rates this company has charged, and payment to the Treasury of all taxes brazenly evaded in the past.

All these laws and others would be inspired in the exact fulfillment of two essential articles of our Constitution. One of these orders the outlawing of feudal estates by indicating the maximum area of land any person or entity can possess for each type of agricultural enterprise, by adopting measures which would tend to revert the land to the Cubans. The other categorically orders the State to use all means at its disposal to provide employment to all those who lack it and to insure a decent livelihood to each manual laborer or intellectual.

None of these articles may be called unconstitutional. The first popularly elected government would have to respect these laws, not only because of moral obligation to the nation, but because when people achieve something they have yearned for throughout generations, no force in the world is capable of taking it away again.

The problems concerning land, the problem of industrialization, the problem of housing, the problem of unemployment, the problem of education and the problem of the health of the people; these are the six problems we would take immediate steps to resolve, along with the restoration of public liberties and political democracy.

Perhaps this exposition appears cold and theoretical if one does not know the shocking and tragic conditions of the country with regard to these six problems, to say nothing of the most humiliating political oppression.

Eighty-five percent of the small farmers in Cuba pay rent and live under the constant threat of being dispossessed from the land that they cultivate. More than half the best cultivated land belongs to foreigners. In Oriente, the largest province, the lands of the United Fruit Company and West Indian Company join the north coast to the southern one. There are two hundred thousand peasant families who do not have a single acre of land to cultivate to provide food for their starving children. On the other hand, nearly three hundred thousand "caballerias" of productive land owned by powerful interests remain uncultivated.

Cuba is above all an agricultural state. Its population is largely rural. The city depends on these rural areas. The rural people won the Independence. The greatness and prosperity of our country depends on a healthy and vigorous rural population that loves the land and knows how to cultivate it, within the framework of a state that protects and guides them. Considering all this, how can the present state of affairs be tolerated any longer?

With the exception of a few food, lumber and textile industries, Cuba continues to be a producer of raw materials. We export sugar to import candy, we export hides to import shoes, we export iron to import plows. Everybody agrees that the need to industrialize the country is urgent, that we need steel industries, paper and chemical industries; that we must improve cattle and grain products, the technique and the processing in our food industry, in order to balance the ruinous competition of the Europeans in cheese products, condensed milk, liquors and oil, and that of the Americans in canned goods; that we need merchant ships; that tourism should be an enormous source of revenue. But the capitalists insist that the workers remain under a Claudian[3] yoke; the State folds its arms and industrialization can wait for the Greek calends.

Just as serious or even worse is the housing problem. There are two hundred thousand huts and hovels in Cuba; four hundred thousand families in the country and in the cities live cramped into barracks and tenements without even the minimum sanitary requirements; two million two hundred thousand of our urban population pay rents which absorb between one fifth and one third of their income; and two million eight hundred thousand of our rural and suburban population lack electricity. If the State proposes lowering rents, landlords threaten to freeze all construction; if the State does not interfere, construction goes on so long as the landlords get high rents, otherwise, they would not lay a single brick even though the rest of the population should have to live exposed to the elements. The utilities monopoly is no better; they extend lines as far as it is profitable and beyond that point, they don't care if the people have to live in darkness for the rest of their lives. The State folds its arms and the people have neither homes nor electricity.

Our educational system is perfectly compatible with the rest of our national situation. Where the *guajiro*[4] is not the owner of his land, what need is there for agricultural schools? Where there are no industries what need is there for technical or industrial schools? Everything falls within the same absurd logic: there is neither one thing nor the other. In any small European country there are more than 200 technical and industrial arts schools; in Cuba, there are only six such schools, and the boys graduate without having anywhere to use their skills. The little rural schools are attended by only half the school-age children—barefoot, half naked and undernourished—and frequently the teacher must buy necessary materials from his own salary. Is this the way to make a nation great?

Only death can liberate one from so much misery. In this, however—early death—the state is most helpful. Ninety percent of rural children are consumed by parasites which filter through their bare feet from the earth. Society is moved to compassion upon hearing of the kidnapping or murder of one child, but they are criminally indifferent to the mass murder of so many thousands of children who die every year from lack of facilities, agonizing with pain. Their innocent eyes—death already shining in them—seem to look into infinity as if entreating forgiveness for human selfishness, as if asking God to stay his wrath. When the head of a family works only four months a year, with what can he purchase clothing and medicine for his children? They will grow up with rickets, with not a single good tooth in their mouths by the time they reach thirty; they will have heard ten million speeches and will finally die of misery and deception. Public hospitals, which are always full, accept only patients recommended by some powerful politician, who, in turn, demands the electoral votes of the unfortunate one and his family so that Cuba may continue forever the same or worse.

With this background, is it not understandable that from May to December over a million persons lost their jobs, and that Cuba, with a population of five and a half million, has a greater percentage of unemployed than France or Italy with a population of forty million each?

When you judge a defendant for robbery, Your Honors, do you ask him how long he has been unemployed? Do you ask him how many children he has, which days of the week he ate and which he didn't, do you concern yourselves with his environment at all? You send him to jail without further thought. But those who burn warehouses and stores to collect insurance do not go to jail, even though a few human beings should have happened to (be cremated with the property insured). The insured have money to hire lawyers and bribe judges. You jail the poor wretch who steals because he is hungry; but none of the hundreds who steal from the Government have ever spent a night in jail; you dine with them at the end of the year in some elegant place and they enjoy your respect.

In Cuba when a bureaucrat becomes a millionaire overnight and enters the fraternity of the rich, he could very well be greeted with the words of that opulent Balzac character, Taillefer, who, in his toast to the young heir to an enormous fortune, said: "Gentlemen, let us drink to the power of gold! Mr. Valentine, a millionaire six times over, has just ascended the throne. He is king, can do everything, is above everything—like all the rich. Henceforward, equality before the law, before the Constitution, will be a myth for him; for he will not be subject to laws, the laws will be subject to him. There are no courts or sentences for millionaires."

The future of the country and the solution of its problems cannot continue to depend on the selfish interests of a dozen financiers, nor on the cold calculations of profits that ten or twelve magnates draw up in their air-conditioned offices. The country cannot continue begging on its knees for miracles from a few golden calves, similar to the Biblical one destroyed by the fury of a prophet. Golden calves cannot perform miracles of any kind. The problems of the Republic can be solved only if we dedicate ourselves to fight for that Republic with the same energy, honesty and patriotism our liberators had when they created it. ...

2. THE CUBAN EDUCATIONAL ACHIEVEMENT

In 1995 the Cuban Revolution was thirty-six years old, and Cubans could look back with pride on their accomplishments. Until their progress was recently halted by setbacks chiefly due to external events, it appeared that the great scourges of Latin America—hunger, unemployment, inadequate housing—had been liquidated or put in the way of disappearance. Cubans took special pride, however, in their educational achievement. A Great Campaign to wipe out illiteracy in the countryside, carried out with the aid of thousands of young volunteers from the cities, was launched in 1961 and soon achieved its goal. The Cuban educational system, specialists agree, was without equal in Latin America in its scope, modernity, and general quality. Jonathan Kozol, a North American educator who carefully observed the system and spent much time in discussion with students and teachers, reflects on what has been achieved and what yet remains to be done.

Whether we judge by technological progress, by classroom preparation in genetics, electronics, or statistics, or by the reverence which is shown for art, literature, and music in the Cuban schools, there seems no question but that quality has now almost caught up with quantity in Cuba's education scheme.

Effectiveness alone, however, does not measure up to the demands and expectations of a nation dedicated to the dreams of Che Guevara and Jose Marti. The patterns of reward for academic labor, as I have debated them at length with students at Martyrs of Kent, have to be considered also in a full appraisal of the ethical and economic consequences of the intellectual preparation offered to the Cuban population.

If the rewards for certain avenues of preparation far outstrip those of all the others, then we are forced to wonder whether this consideration will not be a primary factor in the choices pupils make as they progress from year to

Jonathan Kozol, *Children of the Revolution: A Yankee Teacher in the Cuban Schools*, New York: Delacorte Press, 1978, pp. 199–203. © 1978 Jonathan Kozol.

year and whether this will not subvert the model of the self-effacing man or woman Che Guevara held up as an ethical ideal.

It is apparent, for example, that the sheer material rewards for a career in medicine are very, very high in contrast to the earnings of a semi-skilled technician, and higher still in contrast to the earnings of an unskilled worker at a factory or on a farm. It is one thing to announce, as it was said to me so many times, that "individual achievement in this nation is respected always in an emulative sense," but it is another thing if certain groups of highly skilled professionals can win the privilege to eat in pleasant restaurants, spend weekends in delightful new hotels, and also find the funds to purchase air-conditioners, refrigerators, or TV—while others must accept a life of relatively unexciting and austere routine.

Compared to the United States, the range of salaries is very small indeed. It is also small in contrast to the gross extremes of misery and wealth that were the curse of Cuba for all its modern history prior to 1959. Furthermore, there is a large degree of equal privilege assured by virtue of the abolition or (as in Christina's case) drastic reduction of most housing rentals, as well as by provision of free health care for all people, free day-care, and free schooling costs—including the cost of meals and clothes, as well as books and travel and tuition for the pupils of the schools *en campo* and the other five-day boarding-schools such as Jose Marti. Admission, moreover, as we have seen, is strictly regulated to prevent the influence of parental power or prestige.

Even so, the persistent dangers of a potentially remorseless meritocracy remain. I see no means by which to balance out the efforts and the earnings, the delights and the extremes of physical effort in the swelter of intense humidity and heat, so long as salary differentials for the intellectual versus the manual labor of a Cuban citizen remain so great. Sandra said to me, in her heavy-throated voice: "I think you're right, the difference is too great. As history advances we'll reduce that disproportion. Someday, everyone who works as hard as possible should get the same."

It remains to be seen to what degree the socialist conscience of a child such as Sandra will find the means to bring the practical incentives into line with ethical ideals. It may well be that government leaders will, in time, no longer feel the obligation to conciliate or to reward, beyond a modest limit, those who already have their own reward in the ever-changing intellectual challenges and triumphs that cannot be separated from a certain number of sophisticated and complex careers. To add the economic bonus, too, and to do so four times over (as at present), does not seem in keeping with the words and goals of Cuba's revolutionary leaders.

There seems to me no question but that pupils such as Mario and Sandra are totally devoted to a process of increasingly egalitarian reward, but there is also Marisela, who made clear to everyone within that meeting room that she did not agree. Marisela was eloquent also—a lovely, generous, and persuasive human being. So it remains to be discovered in the years to come whether the children of the revolution are thinking more like Marisela or like Sandra, whatever their reverence for the words of Cuba's heroines and heroes and the views which they espouse.

Another ethical index of a social order and of its educational system is the visible degree of equal access it affords—for example, by the abolition of discrimination in regard to race and sex. In reference to the first it is astonishing to me to recognize, despite all prior doubts, that Cuba has, in fact as well as reputation, come to be a nation which is almost entirely color blind. My own best evidence proved to be my routine evening efforts at quick written recollections of the people I had met during the day. Often I would jot down ten or twenty characteristics of a child or a teacher or a principal whom I had met and chatted with that day—before it would occur to me to scribble down that he or she was white, black, or mulatto. Several times, I found that I could not recall.

To a large degree it has to be said that the emphasis of Abel Prieto on this point seems in retrospect to be disarmingly precise. Any social order that can help a well trained U.S. citizen to fail to recognize a detail of this kind clearly has managed to make a multitude of other factors both more memorable and more important than skin-color.

In regard to the rights of women it occurs to me that Sandra (and her older fellow citizens in the classes of the FOC [Federation of Cuban Workers]) said almost all there is to say. It is obvious that many years of self-deprecation on the part of women, as well as several centuries of absolute male domination, cannot be so rapidly erased as many Cuban men and women would like to be able to report. It's still unfair, as Sandra made quite clear; but, as she said, "I can tell you one thing: It won't be that way for long!"

Cuban women, without question, now have equal rights and equal status in the eyes of the law; they also shoulder equal burdens, such as late-hour duty (neighborhood patrol) within the vigilancia of the CDR [Committees for Defense of the Revolution]. More than once, both in Havana and in Santiago, a woman on guard duty for the CDR would ask me, in a gentle but insistent manner, to tell her why I happened to be looking with so much persistent curiosity into a dark store window in the early hours of the dawn.

For now, however, it is honest to say that women still are not afforded equal power and prestige with Cuban men, even in the face of the new, highly publicized and, in my own view, earnestly enacted Family Code and even despite the pleadings of Fidel.

One final criterion of the moral values of a new and revolutionary social order seems to me to be the way in which the government does, or does not, pay respect to older people. In Cuba old people are not easily relegated to the slag heap of retirement homes and welfare checks. I think of the vitality and optimism of Juan de la Cruz. I think, too, of the words of Rosario Garcia, herself moving now beyond the realm of middle age, who said to me: "There was a time when we were thinking mainly of the young. ... We sense today the very great untapped potential of the old, even the very, very old. ..."

Behind these words there is a dream, a principle, a powerful idea—one which has been voiced here also in the U.S. by Paul Goodman, who spoke often of the terrible wastage of the talents of old people. He argued in vain for the employment and the residence of older people in buildings where our infant children might be left in day care programs while their mothers and their fathers go to work. In many neighborhoods of Cuba this idea is now a viable reality: not an official government "plan" or "program" or the like but just a natural idea that grows in practice and in popularity with every passing year.

At stake here is not just the need "to keep old people happy" in an active and regenerative state of mind. It is the whole idea of work itself as a redeeming and rewarding need for every human being. Small kids, in third-grade classes I have had the chance to visit, work meticulously, though at a modest pace, in a forty-five minute period during which they take small amounts of tea from large imported barrels and then stitch that tea, by a well regulated process, into little tea bags for the use of Cuba's population. The children do not work unduly hard, nor do they injure their backs or strain their arms. They simply take a small, and seemingly enjoyable, role in helping to provide one of the basic needs of their society.

From young to old, the principle is the same. Those who can contribute to the common good do what they can. It is impressive to perceive how much the little kids can do. Older people work with these small children to assist them in their task. I think again, while in this class, of the slogan popular back in 1961, during the literacy work: "Those who know, teach. Those who don't, learn."

The heritage of the Great Campaign lives on.

3. Women's Liberation in Cuba

The struggle for women's rights is another area in which Cuba enjoys undisputed leadership in Latin America. Although Latin American women have made definite strides in the past half century toward emancipation from legal, economic, and political disabilities, throughout most of the continent the ideology of machismo (the cult of male virility and superiority), with its corollaries of patriarchal rule and the double sex standard, continues to reign. Cuba alone has taken decisive measures to end this rule. A milestone in this process was the Family Code of 1976, which gave the force of law to the division of household labor. The following excerpt describes the stages and strategies of the Cuban effort to achieve equality for women.

Isabel Larguía and John Dumoulin, "La mujer en el desarrollo: estrategía ye experiencias de la Revolución Cubana," *Casa de las Americas*, March–April 1985, Year 25, no. 149, pp. 37–53.

Cuba has made progress in the status of women without precedent in Latin America, and the strategy that made this possible is therefore worthy of study. To give some idea of the magnitude of this progress, let us first take as an example the index of women's economic activity. If we compare the Cuban index with that of the United States, we find that the change which there took half a century was achieved in Cuba in the nine years between 1970 and 1979. Another example is the incorporation of women in professional posts: in the five year period 1975–1979 they represented 80% of the professionals working in our country. To be sure, we are taking these examples out of context. To obtain a concrete idea of the strategy to achieve women's equality in Cuba, and its results, a complex analysis, beginning with the most general aspects, is necessary.

Today's socialist world, with its successes and perspectives, with all its problems, is still a young social organism in process of growth, in which everything has not yet settled, that still bears the imprint of past historical epochs. This is the case with the dynamic of the status of women under socialism today.

The struggle for women's equality in Cuba is conceived as inextricably linked to a general process of social transformation, part of the socialist revolution and the construction of a classless society. We do not consider it possible to make substantial advances through an isolated struggle of women and the activity of intellectual elites.

The profound inequality of the sexes created in conditions of backwardness and dependency is inseparable from the imbalances and antagonisms that governed all relations in our country, notably the relations between the different classes, regions, branches of activity, ethnic groups, and between the countryside and the city. The inequality of the sexes could only be overcome through a change that would correct the totality of these violent contrasts and imbalances. It was necessary to set in motion a process that, on the economic plane, would make possible a continuous expansion and democratization of employment and life outside the home, that would overcome the unequal levels of productivity, work skills, and earnings, and would simultaneously change the quality of ordinary people's lives and the services available to them. In order to achieve these goals, it was necessary to smash the structures that maintained underdevelopment, chronic unemployment, deformation of the productive structure, foreign dependency, and the corresponding educational system, the latifundist agrarian structure and, in its most general and essential characteristics, private ownership of the basic means of production. Thus, only as a result of the revolution could the special interests of women and the general interests of the entire country be harmonized. Both required the transformation of the fundamental structures and the conquest of underdevelopment in a way that corresponded to the interests of the great majority of the population. In their general aspects, these conditions are common to many underdeveloped countries. In order to understand the concrete problem of women in the

Cuban Revolution, we must take account of some specific traits that aggravated their economic exploitation and accentuated, in particular, the severity of the patriarchal structures to which they were subjected. Very briefly, we shall indicate these differentiating historical factors.

The majority of Cuban women lived in the interior of the country. But the characteristic deformation of the Cuban economy and the corresponding patriarchal tradition denied them access to direct agricultural labor, yet offered them no alternative source of income. The immense majority of women worked full-time in the direct reproduction of the labor force, in their homes. Women formed only 1% of the population that was recorded as occupied in agriculture. They were even forbidden to work on self-subsistence plots, and if a woman did such work because there were no males in the family she did so secretly, because women's labor was regarded by society as a whole as degrading to the head of the family. It dishonored him socially.

The fact that a peasant woman did not produce *visible* commodities with her own hands contributed to her lack of access to commercial activity. Since domestic industry did not exist in rural Cuba, women also lacked an artisan tradition. In contrast to rural areas in other parts of Latin America, the Cuban peasant woman did not make pottery, weave baskets, produce textiles or leather goods; as a rule she did not make any visible article of material culture that would establish her identity as a worker.

In contrast to other areas of Latin America, women did not participate together with men in direct agricultural labor. With rare exceptions, the cutting of sugar cane was exclusively male and seasonal labor. Underemployment and unemployment were chronic. It was unimaginable for women to work in a sugar mill, even as a cleaning woman.

The lack of sources of employment for women in the rural zones strengthened the sway of patriarchal standards of conduct. This situation, and hunger, spurred the migration of women toward urban areas, where the lack of opportunity to work in industry and services—due to the economic stagnation of the country—channeled them into domestic work or prostitution. According to the census of 1953, 13.7% of all the women in the country were economically active in that year; the figure includes seventy thousand domestics, that is, more than a fourth; there was a large number of official prostitutes; to these must be added those women who worked in services and stores and had to engage in a somewhat more veiled prostitution to supplement their miserable earnings.

The tobacco and clothing industries, which employed a certain number of women, as a rule were small, dispersed establishments that did not allow the creation of a class-conscious female proletariat that could influence the 86% of women who only did housework in their own homes.

There was no electricity in the countryside; 87% of all dwellings were lighted with oil lamps; 63% were huts with earth floors. Forty-two percent of the peasants were illiterate. Agricultural laborers suffered from a food defi-

cit of 1000 calories, with the result that 14% had tuberculosis, 13% had ty-
phoid, and 36% had parasitic diseases. In these conditions of general misery,
the home was school, hospital, old people's home, and haven for the unemployed.

The high level of male unemployment made the possible appearance of a
less skilled and cheaper labor force seem a threat. The taboos based on the
notion of the physical and mental inferiority of women attained their
supreme expression. The invisible labor of the housewife, her wifely and maternal *obligations*, were elevated to an almost religious level. The conception
of woman as an exclusively sexual being, as a biological being deprived of humanity was constantly renewed by the practice of prostitution. The combination of these adverse historical factors created in the daily consciousness a
structure of patriarchal values that was very difficult to break up and eliminate.

This was the situation in which the majority of the female population of
Cuba found itself on January 2, 1959.

The Strategy of Women's Liberation

In the struggle for national liberation a vanguard group of women had arisen
who together with the revolutionary leadership understood the necessity and
the interest of women in actively participating in the struggle that had begun
for the development of our country. They faced the difficult task of organizing a mass of women who lacked any idea of their fundamental rights.
However, women and the population as a whole possessed a lively and growing consciousness of the general problems of the country at that stage,
viewed in their totality as the problem of national liberation.

In August 1960 there was founded the Federation of Cuban Women
(FCW) as a mass women's organization in support of the revolutionary transformation of the country. The first nuclei arose throughout the breadth and
length of the country and grouped together the most progressive women of
each locality and a number of revolutionary ex-combatants and militants.

In focusing on the problem of women's equality, the revolutionary leadership took as its point of departure two basic historical regularities:

(a) It is impossible to achieve full and definitive liberation if it is not based
on the interests and awakened consciousness of all oppressed women. This
awakened consciousness should lead to a break with and subsequent elimination of the patriarchal ideology inherited from previous socioeconomic for-
mations.

(b) It is a historical regularity that the mass of women of the most exploited
sectors, in order to become active in the public sphere, must first pass
through the development of so-called traditional tasks before they can break
into fields that had previously been closed to them. This was the principal direction of the initial organizing effort, although from the first a number of

women of humble origin were placed in posts involving high skill and responsibility; both processes took place simultaneously.

In the beginning, the most modest efforts of activists to free women from their domestic confinement could provoke incidents of rejection and create a climate of confusion in the locality. The first leaders of the FCW in the most isolated zones had to face hostility and violent rejection by the traditional patriarchal ideology as well as attacks by counterrevolutionaries. The first successes in breaking with the traditions that kept women in a cloistered life were achieved through the most modest channels, based on values and activities traditionally regarded as "proper for women." The first step was to ensure that these activities should not be engaged in for the benefit of a tyrannical head of family but should instead serve the community. Cuban women accepted the slogans of the revolution as their own. They were ready to support and defend the decisive structural transformations of the first years without as yet questioning the traditional role of women in society.

Pursuing the goal that women's labor should be channeled toward the community and produce visible objects whereby women could establish their human identity, there arose the first gardens of the FCW, whose products were consumed by the local branches of the FCW. A stimulus was also given to the development of women's crafts and to women's participation in the construction and care of the first child care centers. The home began to open up toward social life, and women imperceptibly began to direct their activity toward the public sphere. Women's labor power ceased to be the private property of the husband, father, or pimp. By directing their efforts toward the service of the collective, women began to gain a sense of their own value and, fundamentally, of their ownership of the products of their labor. In the consciousness of the oppressed Cuban women began to arise two concepts that they regarded as inseparable, the concepts of collective and personal identity or, as they expressed it, revolution and women's liberation.

This initial period of the 1960s may be difficult to understand for those who champion women's rights without understanding revolutionary changes in their internal linkage. One of the most successful measures of that period was the creation of schools that taught girls to cut and sew, although Cuba did not then and does not now have an industry of dressmaking for export. These schools were given the name of Ana Betancourt, an illustrious nineteenth century patriot who at a very early date denounced women's inequality. They were designed for young women, living in the most remote areas, whose fathers not only opposed their learning to read and write and working for wages, but even their joining women's organizations. The nominal purpose of these schools was to teach young women to cut and sew, which required them to leave their isolated farms and come to the city. In fact, their training was complemented by a program of general political studies, and they became conscious agents of the profound transformations taking place in the country. When they returned to their homes they did so with the commitment to rescue other young women from their patriarchal isolation, becoming one of the channels through which the CWF continued its campaign to liberate the most oppressed Cuban women.

In 1961, the literacy campaign, which began a massive process of educational advance, above all in rural areas, brought out of their domestic isolation tens of thousands of young women in the towns and cities who worked for months as volunteer teachers, working shoulder to shoulder with their male comrades and for the first time exercising control over their own lives.

This voluntary work, a useful social activity that supported the gains of the revolution, attracted women because they could see their own progress reflected in those gains. It was a means of transition, enabling women to leave the hermetically closed home, lose their fear of the world outside the family, and gain confidence in themselves. It gradually prepared them to reinforce those gains by their subsequent incorporation in wage labor.

The struggle between the Revolution and its external and internal enemies, a struggle decisive for the destiny of the country, assigned an extraordinary importance to the defense of the homeland and was responsible for the first recruitment of a considerable number of women in the military forces. Women and society in general became aware of that need. Women began to enlist in the revolutionary militias and police, wore uniforms for the first time, and began to carry arms. Some entered military schools and obtained command ranks and responsibilities. Thus one of the most formidable barriers to the elimination of division of labor by sex was destroyed.

These initial measures, in themselves very modest, had the great value of mobilizing millions of women who began to destroy the very foundations of the patriarchal structure inherited from the colonial period and the slaveowners' hegemony, and reaffirmed by Cuban neocolonial society. In less than three years the prostitutes were reeducated and integrated with dignity in social life, production, and study. The same happened with the 70,000 domestic servants. By about 1970 the so-called "informal sector" had almost completely disappeared. ...

The Revolution struck a heavy blow at the anachronistic structures that impeded national development and opened the way for an expansion of employment without precedent in our history. By the mid-sixties the great mass of unemployed, whose number a few years before had risen to 16.4% of the labor force, had been absorbed. From that date the expansion of the labor force would basically be achieved by the incorporation of women in labor outside the home. Women understood that need, and in the course of the 1960s they joined the labor force from primarily patriotic motives. The FCW developed an intense activity to promote and facilitate the incorporation of women in production.

Beginning about 1960, the number of women who annually joined the labor force grew rapidly. But this was accompanied by considerable instability in women's labor, due to the lack of adequate means of support that would take account of the magnitude of the change with respect to traditional customs and usages. This led to the adoption of transitional measures designed to promote the permanence of women in the labor force and ensure that the growth of women's activity should not bring a breakdown of the traditional, still functioning mechanisms with respect to conduct, values, motives, self-images of men and women, and of the reality of the direct reproduction of the labor force—the domestic labor that in the decade of the 1960s was still carried on almost exclusively by women. ...

The Cuban Woman and the Private Reproduction of the Labor Force

The development and the level of equality achieved by Cuban women have been won in the context of a revolutionary transformation of the country, of a struggle against underdevelopment and the anachronistic capitalist society that supported it. Toward the end of the first decade of the revolutionary process, it became clear that the patriarchal family inherited from the old society was an obstacle to socioeconomic progress, and it joined a list of structures whose replacement was a very early strategic objective. We faced the task of transforming the relations between the sexes, with a view to establishing equality and greater freedom in the development of the human personality.

The gradual suppression of the home viewed as a private economic cell, as a work center devoted to the direct reproduction of the labor force, is an irreversible tendency of social development. But to replace the small domestic economy with a great socialized productive force not only requires a very high development of the productive forces but a concomitant technological redesigning of the human habitat, accompanied by the creation of a consciousness of a high social content. Such a development on a world scale can take place only after there is an end to the squandering of resources on armaments.

Despite the poverty of our country, the FCW fought from the first for the construction of services that could lighten the burdens of women's second, domestic work day. By 1981 the available services created by the revolutionary government included 92,000 places in child care centers and 200,000 places in part-time boarding schools *(semiinternados)*, exclusively for the children of working mothers. The number of scholarships to boarding schools *(internados)* rose to 589,000. The creation of workers' and students' dining rooms meant that the working woman did not have to return home during her work day. The tempo of integration of women in political and productive life attained very rapid rhythms. But the created services, although they represented very significant aid, could not replace the direct reproduction of the labor force in the home. These tasks continue to weigh on women.

The ideas of the past forbade men to perform the slightest domestic task or to participate actively in the care of their children. The division of labor within the family cast—and still casts—its shadow over public life. If a woman had to invest more than twelve hours a day in labor between her workplace and the home, she preferred employment where the work was lighter and involved less responsibility than would a man, who invested his working energies only in his workplace. How could this problem be overcome? Customs change slowly in a complex, contradictory process which requires a mix of vigorous state measures with ideological struggle and the erosion of old ways of life under the pressure of great material changes. ...

By the beginning of the 1970s there was already evident in Cuba a tendency toward the reorientation of social life, a tendency that had been gaining ground in the social psychology of the average Cuban, more especially in the homes of working women.

The motives and needs of the new life, the revolutionary activities and the ideals of social justice were little by little making their influence felt in the home and pushing for its reorganization. The process gained strength in 1975 with the adoption of two measures that both reflected this tendency and gave it new impetus. The First Congress of the Communist Party of Cuba held in that year approved Thesis III, "On the Full Exercise of Women's Equality," discussed and approved with amendments suggested by study circles on the grass-roots level in all workplaces and labor organizations. This thesis asserted that men should fully share with women all domestic tasks. This principle acquired the force of law in the Family Code which, renovating and systematizing family law, proclaimed shared responsibility in all domestic tasks. Its pertinent provisions constitute the new marriage vow and are explained and exemplified to the pair when they are asked if they are ready to assume this commitment. This code was subjected to the same process of mass discussion and approval as Thesis III.

A permanent ideological struggle is being waged in the bosom of society in order that men should share domestic tasks as a direct means of liberating women's creative capacities in a historic era of transition to a more developed society. ...

We believe that it was not pure chance that the years 1970–1971, when the great movement to incorporate women in the labor force began, were critical both for the growth and stability of women's employment and for the institution of marriage. The frequency of divorce increased very rapidly in that period, rising from 0.4% to 2.3%. Gradually, adequate solutions for the problems of that stage were found, however, and in the first five years of the 1970s the rate of divorce ceased to grow, declined a little to 1.7%, and then stabilized, while each year a large number of married women joined the labor force. These figures attest to the profound restructuring of values that took place in the social psychology of vast sections of the population. No revolutionary change can take place without upheavals of one or another kind, but in this case the transient instability had a positive effect. Whereas in 1960 a man felt dishonored if his wife worked, today he is ashamed if she does not work and tends to offer excuses such as: "She is sick"; "she has nervous problems" or "she has problems"; or "she is looking for work that suits her."

The Cuban woman, for her part, when she considers taking a man for her husband, today asks first of all, "Will he understand me?" meaning, will he understand her need and right to have an active and diversified social life and not expect to have a domestic slave, which requires that he share the housework.

The implementation of the Family Code is the hub of a direct and massive confrontation with the male-chauvinist standards and the basis of the division of labor between the sexes. Its objective is to liberate the energies of women so that they may direct those energies toward the various areas of social activity, thereby achieving the personal self-realization that formerly was forbidden to women.

Along with this there has taken place a transformation of customs in the realm of sexual relations and biological reproduction. Contraceptives and abortion are now freely available. The birth rate, like the infant mortality rate, has declined to levels that are generally found only in highly developed countries. The customs of today's young people are more permissive than those of their parents; they have definitively disposed of the myth of virginity. The double sex standard has also been banished. Such brusque changes cannot take place without producing tensions. They require adjustments in social consciousness. The FCW, the educational system, the press and television are promoting sex education in the interests of planned maternity, of avoiding hasty marriages, and of changing the image of the single mother in order that maternity should not interrupt education.

The full exercise of women's equality is not yet a perfect reality but an ideal for which a struggle is waged in all spheres and on all levels of Cuban life, as part of the Revolution and the national development, as a key goal toward which much progress has been made and toward which we continue to advance.

4. CUBA UNDER THE HAMMER

The collapse of the Soviet Union and the disappearance of the socialist common market in 1989 dealt a devastating blow to Cuba, halting the upward movement of the Cuban economy and producing a serious decline of Cuban living standards. Cuba's plight was aggravated by U.S. efforts to tighten the 30-year-old embargo against Cuba by penalizing third parties that wished to trade with the socialist nation. President Bill Clinton, who during his election campaign threatened to "drop the hammer" on Cuba, continued the U.S. posture of fixed hostility toward Cuba, a posture regarded as irrational by most other countries. Facing immense difficulties, Cuba displayed a remarkable resilience in its efforts to survive and overcome its economic crisis. An American academic offers his impressions of life in contemporary Cuba.

The following article represents the impressions about Cuban life and Cuban economic and political possibilities gained during a two month stay in February and March 1994.

The long-standing U.S. policy of encouraging highly visible "illegal" defections while refusing to grant significant numbers of visas to legal immigrants has led to an increased illegal immigration flow. Although not unprecedented (the early 1960s Mariel boat-lift) and on a much smaller scale than before, this flow has created new difficulties in U.S.-Cuban relations.

In the meantime, although the Clinton administration appears to have come down on the side of the hardline currents in the Cuban exile community, there is continuing evidence that the competition between the velvet glove and the iron fist approaches to destroying the current Cuban regime is proceeding; a debate between Pierre Salinger and Jose Mas Canosa on "Good Morning America" (ABC), recent public comments by elected officials (e.g., Rep. Lee Hamilton), and editorials in the *Wall Street Journal*, *The Economist*, and elsewhere urging an end to current hardline policies.

In any case, the latest spate of psychological warfare between Cuban and U.S. governments (which had by September 9 led to a negotiated settlement) does not provide sufficient new evidence for me to modify my analysis in any significant way.

∾   ∾   ∾

Since 1989, Cuba has lost 86 percent of its exports and thus, in a world where it is denied even normal trade credit, a comparable percentage of its imports. The 1993 sugar harvest was down 3 million tons from its level of around 7 million tons in 1991. Cuba currently has less than one half of the amount of combustibles once available to it (and on preferential terms) from the ex–Soviet Union. Shortages of food, transport, fuel, water, and electricity rule the day. The obvious consequences for production and consumption are immense and palpable.

Yet, by the way it has responded to the crisis it fell into and by using the reserves (in consensus, social solidarity, healthcare, and education) built up

Sinan Koont, "Cuba: An Island Against All Odds," *Monthly Review*, 46, no. 5, October 1994, pp. 1–18. (Reprinted with the permission of the author.) The notes that appeared in the original publication have been omitted here.

during thirty years of independence and social revolution, Cuba has managed to hang on to "normal" social life to a surprising degree, as I was able to observe during a recent two month stay (February–March 1994) at the FLACSO (Facultad Latinoamericana de Ciencias Sociales) branch at the University of Havana.

The extensive bus system of Havana, although reduced to a mere shadow, perhaps a quarter of its former self, continues to function haltingly with long lines at bus stops and mostly fictional timetables. Still, standing on Avenida 31 by the Puente Amandares on a balmy February afternoon, I counted eleven buses (different routes) going by in a ten minute period.

The modern, truck-fleet-and-dumpster-based garbage collection scheme has been hit hard by the shortage of gasoline. And it is not unusual to see overflowing dumpsters on city streets. Yet, incredibly and as a testament to the commitment of the municipal government to keep things going, at least a couple of times I saw functioning street-cleaning trucks with rotating brushes, water spraying, going about their business cleaning the Malecon (Havana's world famous waterfront) or Avenida 31.

The Cuban director Tomás Gutiérrez Alea's internationally acclaimed new film (a co-production with Spain and Mexico), *Fresa y Chocolate* [*Strawberry and Chocolate*], a sensitive treatment of homosexuality in Cuba, and critical of Cuban bureaucratic attitudes toward it, was showing to large crowds. I also attended a Sunday afternoon tango performance in downtown Havana by the visiting Argentine dancers and singers from the Universidad del Tango in Buenos Aires. It was quite a show, complete with fog generators for the appropriate lampposts-shrouded-in-fog effect needed for the soulful rendition of the Argentine blues. Even more impressive was a concert by Pablo Milanés before a capacity crowd of 5,000 at Teatro Karl Marx. The crowd was appreciative, good natured, enjoying the performance, showering Milanés with flowers (one or two at a time, presented by fans running onto the stage between songs), and making him deviate from the printed program with requests for old favorites.

On another front, the beaches of Havana (Playa del Este), about fifteen kilometers from the city and, in contrast to the tourist beaches at Varadero further away, "easily" accessible to Habaneros/as, were, on a Saturday visit I made there in February, full of people (mostly Cubans) enjoying themselves: horses and horseback riding, a couple of all-terrain vehicles, sailboats, wind-surfing, etc.

Also in February, the seven-game baseball championship, which the Cubans, somewhat more modestly than us, call their National Series, took place. Some of the games of the series, between the Industriales of Havana and Villa Clara, were played under the lights, televised on national television, and drew over 40,000 spectators (with free entry) to the stadium.

And finally, to bring life full circle, on a recent day in the huge, immaculately maintained Cementerio Colón (Columbus Cemetery), where

Columbus spent the nineteenth century, with its sculpted trees, wide avenues, tombs with English inscriptions (including a large black marble one belonging to the American Legion), Cubans buried with all the requisite somber ceremony the famous Cuban poet Eliseo Diego.

These are vignettes of normality, perhaps of unexpected normality. One obvious question that begs for an answer is: How do the Cubans do it? The magnitude of the economic shock they have had to endure in recent years would have surely put many a society into an uncontrollable tailspin. Can they continue doing it? What awaits them in the future as they try to integrate their socialist economy and society into a capitalist world and its markets?

But first it is worthwhile to consider how Cuba landed in this crisis to begin with. The immediate but only *partial* answer is the collapse in 1989 of the socialist bloc under whose political and economic wings Cuba had found earlier refuge from a hostile capitalist world, led by the United States, which had been blockading the island since 1960. But beginning in the mid-1980s Cuba found itself in increasing economic difficulties:

First, Cuba could not escape the debt crisis and its consequences, which affected all of Latin America (for which the 1980s were dubbed the Lost Decade by development economists). Its hard currency debt to the West went up from $2.8 billion in 1983 to $6.1 billion in 1987. In 1986 Cuba declared a debt repayment moratorium, and the Western creditors closed off all credit. Hard currency imports plummeted as a result.

Second, Cuba's response was to integrate itself more deeply into COMECON (the international economic organization of the socialist bloc) in its international trade. This integration was a mixed blessing at best. From its 1972 entry into COMECON, Cuba had gradually (but only partially) adopted Soviet-style economic institutions and practices—from "central" planning to style of local management. The resulting pattern of accumulation had by the second half of the 1980s, just as in the Soviet Union, led to a Brezhnev-era stagnation in Cuba. Although sizeable investment continued to occur (due to favorable pricing, credit, and technical aid policies of COMECON) and the capital stock increased by 31 percent between 1985 and 1989, the efficiency of this investment plummeted. Between 1981 and 1985, each peso invested had led to 53 centavos worth of additional product. The corresponding figure was only 2 centavos between 1985 and 1989.

Problems of efficiency, labor discipline, organization, and motivation, decentralization and scope for local participation—all these and their possible solutions were placed prominently on the Cuban agenda commencing with the 1986 Rectification Movement.

Although Cuban growth had slowed considerably prior to 1989, the collapse of COMECON caused even deeper dislocations in the Cuban economy, affecting exports, sugar, petroleum, and credits. In 1990, Cuba adopted a program called "Special Period in Peacetime," which remains in effect today. Its associated package of survival measures both ameliorated *and* exacerbated the consequences of the dislocations. Unlike the structural adjustments imposed by the International Monetary Fund on the rest of Latin America, which ignore distributional consequences, Cuba's initial measures sought to maintain and preserve the social gains of the revolution and the quality of life for all citizens: for example, the continuation of 70 percent of salary for workers whose workplaces had to close due to lack of inputs or energy; the extension of rationing to obtain a fairer distribution of a much smaller pie.

Among the negative consequences of these dislocations and the Cuban responses were the following:

(1) Large declines in production: The total social product registered falls off 24 percent and 15 percent in 1991 and 1992 respectively. Output of sugarcane fell from 7.1 million tons in 1989 to 4.2 million tons in 1992. Imports fell from $8 billion in 1989 to $1.7 billion in 1993.

(2) Macroeconomic imbalances: The policy of maintaining incomes (even when jobs are lost) and continuing price subsidies has given rise to enormous imbalances. Currently there are more than 11 billion pesos in circulation with little counterpart in available product, and only about one half of this 11 billion is in savings accounts in banks. The governmental budget deficit of 1993 was 4 billion pesos. To put these figures in perspective, the disposable national income of Cuba was 15.5 billion pesos in 1989, the last year for which official figures have been published.

(3) Labor discipline and efficiency: The problems above have been exacerbated as workers' earnings in pesos have increasingly lost their meaning as material incentives. The old "you pretend to pay us and we pretend to work" joke is more and more applicable in the Cuban context. Of course, the effects of energy and raw material shortages are also at work here, so the workers' withdrawal of effort due to falling real wages is not the only cause of lagging output.

(4) The black and gray markets: The "underground" economy, which, in any case, has an inherent tendency to appear in price control and/or rationing contexts, has enjoyed a spectacular growth, especially in tandem with the apparently inexorable dollarization of the economy through the burgeoning tourist sector and remittances from family members in Miami. We will return to a discussion of this phenomenon below.

The Special Period has meant not only a necessary, unavoidable adjustment to the new conditions and their adverse consequences listed above, but also a search beyond mere survival to find a way forward that preserves essential features of the Cuban model: the systems of education, health care, social welfare, and solidarity.

A successful re-insertion of Cuba into world markets (albeit for the third time since 1960 and under very adverse circumstances) is a sine qua non of any possible path of escape for the economy. Although sugar, nickel, and citrics continue to be the mainstays of export, the Cuban government's export strategy is an attempt to move away from the typical Third World pattern of agricultural and mineral exports. This strategy has concentrated the available resources in the promotion of tourism, biotechnology, and pharmaceuticals, basing itself on the wonderful Caribbean climate and Cuban beaches in the case of tourism, and a supply of highly educated scientists and well-prepared technicians for the others. Tourism promises rapid and continuing growth in hard currency earnings for Cuba. The others imply a shift in the mix of Cuban exports toward high value-added goods based on research and development, and also, at least temporarily, monopoly positions in certain niches of the global market.

Tourism is in fact booming, having gone from about 100,000 visitors annually at the beginning of the decade to a projected 650,000 in 1994. High-rise luxury hotels are going up (and have gone up) in Havana and Varadero, as well as other tourism centers on the island. Despite the absence of U.S. tourists (because of U.S.-imposed restrictions), visitors from Canada, Mexico, Germany, Spain, and elsewhere are enjoying Cuban waters in large numbers.

On the high-tech front, Cuba has been reaping the rewards of its comparatively large R&D efforts, and is marketing, among other products, vaccines against meningitis and hepatitis and an anticholesterol drug called PPG (for whose acronymic name I have heard two possible etymologies: Producto Para Ganar—product for profit—an early "joke" among the researchers that stuck, or Producto Para Ganado—product for cattle—harking back to possible origins in animal research).

One biotechnology firm I had a chance to visit, Imunoensayo, specialized in high-volume diagnostic testing of entire populations, using computer-aided essaying of samples. One of the firm's recent products is a mail-in AIDS test-kit. Imunoensayo already is in markets in Latin America and Europe (including the offspring of the ex–Soviet Union), and is trying to expand its market niches.

Sales of this and other high-tech firms are estimated to have earned in excess of $200 million in 1992.

Part of these gains in "non-traditional" exports (especially in tourism) have been obtained by attracting foreign investment (mostly in joint ventures), which is allowed under the 1992 constitution and operates under quite favorable terms. However, even assuming the best possible outcomes, Cuban export earnings will be lagging far behind the pre-1989 levels for a considerable length of time, in part because the favorable treatment Cuba received within COMECON is not likely to be duplicated in the future.

Consequently, a lot of the recent discussion within Cuba has focused on questions of efficiency, productivity, labor discipline, material and moral incentives for work, i.e., on how to get more output for less input. Also on the agenda is the need to reduce both social and individual consumption and budget deficits. There is a growing awareness (and consensus) that the distribution of free (or nearly free) goods and services has to be cut back and better targeted to just the "needy" segments of the population, even in the sacrosanct areas of health care and education. For example, a Cuban economist I interviewed could not see how, under the present circumstances, the Cuban state could continue providing free violin, swimming, and dance lessons for his seven-year-old grandson. Or, does it make sense to maintain cigarettes and rum, which are not basic necessities of life, on the ration book (*la libreta*), when the elimination of price and quantity restrictions of just these two goods could, it is estimated, bring in an additional 4 billion pesos, enough to cover the current budget deficit.

Part of the response of the Cuban government to the continually worsening economic circumstances were three measures put into effect in July 1993, the first two of which can be considered emergency measures which were more or less forced on the government by growing and unstoppable illegal market activities in U.S. dollars and small-scale private business (especially in the service sector).

The first measure was the decriminalization of the possession of U.S. dollars. Cuba had always had hard currency stores, the so-called *diplomercados*, for the foreign (diplomatic and tourist) community living in Cuba. Increasing quantities of dollars had, in recent years, been getting into private Cuban hands "illegally" through unilateral transfers from family members living in Miami and via tips from tourists in a sector enjoying explosive growth. Now Cubans can legally hold U.S. dollars and spend them in the dollar stores or in the streets as they see fit.

The second measure was the legalization of self-employment. Although some self-employment has been allowed in Cuba since the 1970s, its scope was greatly enhanced with this measure. Partly to legalize already occurring activity and expand the quantity of services being offered to the population, and partly to respond to increasing official unemployment, close to a hundred activities were opened up to self-employment. This *cuentapropista* sector has enjoyed rapid growth. More than 137,000 Cubans are now working for themselves: arts and crafts production, bicycle repair and parking, TV repair, etc. Here is one of my experiences with this sector as recorded in my journal of February 7:

> In the afternoon, I discovered that the back tire of my bicycle was losing air slowly. I asked Clarita (the housekeeper), whether she knew of a nearby repair place. She directed me to a service station about six blocks away. I walked the bike there only to find out the service station was not functioning any more. A man there directed me to a place a block away, but that place was closed. Another man there directed me to the corner of Third Avenue and Thirty Sixth. When I got there I saw a little sign stuck in a bush: "Ponches, No. 118." So I figured "ponches" must mean "flats," walked the bike to No. 118, and sure enough a very nice man fixed my flat (and oiled the chain and tightened the seat) for the princely sum of twelve pesos (= $.15 on the black market). An example of the effect of the new laws allowing for private work for oneself, i.e., self-employment.

Examples of this kind of activity abound: from a little storefront in Havana Vieja with an amateurishly hand-made sign announcing "Se parquean bicicletas" "bicycles parked," to a TV repairman who fixed the set in the apartment I rented for the last two weeks of my stay. There is also a flourishing Saturday market on the Avenida de los Presidentes, where vendors sell mostly their own arts and crafts work and where most of the shoppers are Cubans and not tourists. Here the dollar is king, but the peso is still used, some vendors willing to accept either currency at prices that imply wildly inconsistent exchange rates of the peso with the dollar.

Ironically, these two measures intended to regularize and bring under social control certain types of economic activity have been distorted in their effects by the generalized situation of scarcity (i.e., the insufficient supply of rationed goods and the non-availability of non-rationed goods for peso purchase). This has resulted in the exacerbation of certain difficulties, such as illegal dollar/peso exchanges and the illegal sale of goods (sometimes stolen) and services (e.g., prostitution) for dollars. There is now a more or less generalized hunt for dollars by the population through illegal, quasilegal, and legal markets. The official but not freely available exchange rate of the peso is around one peso per dollar. (There are a couple of different rates.) But the large quantity of pesos in the population's hands (with no counterpart in peso goods) had, by February 1994, brought the underground market exchange rate to about 100 to one. Given that the average salary is under 200 pesos per month (i.e., about $2 on the "free" market), most Cubans are essentially excluded from the dollar sector if they limit their "illegal" activities merely to the conversion of their salaries into dollars.

The Cuban government has understandably been slow or reluctant to make the dollars earned through the export sector available to the population for direct consumption (although tourism-sector workers have begun receiving 10 percent of their salaries in dollars). Also understandable, however, in the current circumstances of extreme material hardship, are the resulting illegal activities by Cubans trying to acquire dollars (if necessary, by undercutting the official prices while offering for sale goods pilfered from the state).

In the streets, visiting tourists can obtain PPG (the anticholesterol drug) for $2 (official price: $40), Cohiba cigars for $20 (price at airport: $240). They can buy meals in the (illegal) private restaurants called paladares for $2 to $3 rather than pay the $10 to $20 the tourist hotels charge. They can hire (illegal) taxis at half price or less compared with the official dollar-metered taxis.

In addition to general panhandling (not massive, but present), prostitution has reappeared (for the first time since the 1950s) at the interface of the Cuban and tourist populations, although it still only involves a very small, in fact tiny, minority of Cuban women. As to why this is happening, and given the tremendous gains of women in revolutionary Cuba (in education, jobs, equality with men, etc.), official Cuban interpretations tend to stress a loss of family values and moral degeneration. I heard Vilma Espin, a revolutionary leader and current head of the Cuban Women's Federation, presenting such an analysis on TV. Much more straightforward and economically convincing, however, is the argument that some Cuban women just cannot resist the temptation to earn 10, 20, or 100 times their monthly salary in *one* day, especially since a lot of necessities are available only with that kind of income.

Of the two measures discussed above, the dollar legalization is clearly an emergency measure, which will be reversed as soon as a viable Cuban currency, backed up by Cuban production, is re-established. The measure allowing for extensive self-employment may be more permanent, but can be seen as a correction to the excessive centralization after the 1968 abolition of all private retail trade. In any case, both of these measures were *forced* upon the Cuban government by the uncontrollable growth in *illegal* activities in these two areas prior to their legalization.

The third measure adopted in July 1993 was a major reform and reorganization of agriculture, which responded, at least in part, to problems that antedated the Special Period (the post-1985 decline in agricultural production and subsequent increase in state subsidies).

In this reform, perceived by some Cuban analysts as being important enough to be called the Third Agrarian Reform (referring to the first two in 1960 and 1963), new forms of rural production were established, dividing the gigantic state agricultural enterprises (which numbered fewer than 500) into smaller cooperatively "owned" and "administered" units, the Unidades Basicas de Produccion Cooperativa (UBPC). These new units are smaller but still quite large: about ten UBPCs per previous enterprise with 50 to 100 *co-operantes* each.

It should be noted that this reform involves substantial changes in the "ownership" of land and rural social relations, and would be much more difficult to reverse than the first two measures. The more permanent character of the third reform is apparent in the political bureau's characterization of its goals: to raise economic efficiency, to link incomes rigorously with the work contributed and production achieved, to strengthen the ties between the population and the land, to improve the conditions of life of the rural population, and to enhance the autonomy of local decision-making without the intervention of central authorities.

In order to achieve these aims, the cooperatives have been given indefinite usufruct rights on the land and are owners of all the means of production (except land), which they can buy or sell. They also own all they can produce, and have financial and considerable administrative autonomy.

A thorough discussion of the UBPCs would take us too far afield here; suffice it to say that Cuban hopes in agriculture are riding on them. And unfortunately, this, their first, season of operation will probably not yield enough hard data to assess the impact of this new form of organization adequately. Except for sugarcane, where the process is more or less complete, about one half of the UBPCs remain to be organized. In any case, the results are not yet in, amidst considerable confusion and uncertainty about prices, lines of authority, etc.

Another important and interesting process in the Cuban response to the collapse of the COMECON has been the attempt to involve all of the Cuban population in the discussion of possible solutions, partly as a way to find such solutions, but I think more importantly to build consensus around painful but necessary measures. On January 10, 1994, the CTC (Central de Trabajadores de Cuba) published an editorial in its organ *Trabajadores* in which it laid out what it thought to be the principal issues confronting Cuban workers, both at their workplaces and at the macro level. Workplace issues include, what actions to take to stimulate labor discipline and morale; how to produce more or produce better with less cost; where to "rationalize" personnel; what to do with unneeded workers; and how to reduce or eliminate subsidies. Macro-level issues are: how to deal with the excess of money in circulation; how to resolve the budget deficit; whether money accumulated in large quantities and by dubious means, by a small sector of the population, should be confiscated; what free goods and services should continue to be maintained; up to what point unprofitable enterprises should continue to be subsidized; what role prices should play; and whether there should be a tax on salaries.

In January, February, March, and April 1994, the CTC-organized discussions of these issues in each workplace in Cuba (including FLACSO, where I was resident) were in sessions of the so-called Parlamento Obrero (Workers' Parliament). The consensus built in these discussions was expected to lead to major decisions on free goods, prices, subsidies, and deficits, as well as on labor discipline and organization.

So where does Cuba find itself in mid-1994? It has in recent years suffered the cut-off of credits from the West, the collapse of the socialist bloc and the embargo/blockade by the United States (hardened in 1992 by the passage of the Torricelli Bill). Yet its system of governance and societal organization has not crumbled into dust. Despite the appearance of a few cracks in the edifice, and contrary to incessant predictions that the end is near, the basic consensus in Cuba continues to hold. Why? Two reasons stand out in my mind.

First: as we have seen, the Cuban government has attempted to confront the crisis with energetic measures, increased the scope of participatory democracy, tried to distribute the inevitable losses equitably, without allowing individual Cubans to face their problems in a dog-eat-dog world of unalloyed self-interest. The systems of education, healthcare, rationing, and social solidarity are still functioning. One crucial question is: how long, and at what level, can and will they continue doing so?

Second: Cuba's Third World socialism was home-bred and has significantly improved the lot of average Cubans, and differentially so of the Blacks (now in the majority) and women, in the sense that the sharp racial and gender-based discriminations of the pre-revolutionary era are no longer tolerated openly. Furthermore, unlike, say, East Europeans taking Western Europe as their model, the Cubans look to the rest of Latin America and seem to realize instinctively that their fate after the loss of independence, in a U.S.-dominated Caribbean, would be more like that of Nicaragua, Panama,

Grenada, and El Salvador. In any case, the Cubans' primary capitalist reference is in the "failed" periphery, and not the "successful" center (despite the allure of the nearby United States).

What does the future hold? If Cuba can weather its current crisis (by no means a certainty; I still remember a Cuban economist friend's genuinely uncertain question toward the end of my stay: "What do you think, Sinan? Will we make it?"), there is considerable potential inside the country for development and for an insertion into the capitalist world economy based on high value-added exports but consistent with the maintenance of an internal socialist order. This potential is grounded in an already in-hand and extensive physical and industrial infrastructure, a highly qualified, technically and scientifically trained workforce, and political stability based on consensus. Missing factors include: sufficient quantities of foreign capital, access to advanced technologies, and assured niches in international markets.

Of course, one serious historical and analytical question is whether such foreign investment, even if it were to occur on a sufficient scale, would translate into autonomous accumulation and development in Cuba, or merely lead to technological and financial dependency, profit repatriations, and surplus drain. After all, one can hardly claim that foreign investment has had beneficial effects everywhere it has been deployed over the centuries of imperialism. Will Cuba be able to master and use the foreign investment for its own ends, or will it succumb to its control in yet another example of "dependent" development?

In the United States, one potential source of markets, capital, and technology, meanwhile, there are moves to do away with the blockade. The usual left-wing support for normalization has been joined by an increasing chorus (mostly non-Cuban) of mainstream or right-wing commentary arguing that the Fidelista regime can best be undone by an opening of borders, normalization of relations and the consequent inundation of Cuba with things, people, investments, and ideas from the United States.

I don't think that Cuba has considered the implications of such a development with sufficient care. The cultural influence of the United States on Cuba remains immense: from the still-functioning 1950s vintage U.S. car fleet, to the readily available Miami radio stations (not just Radio Marti), to satellite-fed TV sets featuring CNN in otherwise very modest homes, to Cuban radio stations playing U.S. music, to the Disney Channel on TV Rebelde on Saturday mornings. A younger Cuban (thirty-something) I befriended thought Whitney Houston to be the ultimate in vocal artistry. The nostalgic reference set of a retired machinist whom I got to know fairly well consisted of people like Nat King Cole, Satchmo, and Frank Sinatra.

I am not sure what the implications of this cultural "hegemony" are for an independent Cuba in the Caribbean. There has not been enough public discussion of this in Cuba. The problem is not one of isolation. Cuba has diplomatic relations with over 140 nations, and substantial economic ties with scores of countries in Europe and Latin America. Still, any rapid and whole-sale opening up to the United States would, I think, have profound and pos-sibly traumatic consequences in the society and culture, as well as the politics and economics of Cuba.

In any case, Cuba, small but committed, appears to have been saddled with a historic burden well out of proportion to its size. It is one of the last surviv-ing potential transmitters of a hopeful legacy from humanity's initial twenti-eth-century experimentation with socialism, beginning with the 1917 revolu-tion in Russia. This situation may be a curse, it may be a challenge, but it is something Cuba cannot avoid—however much its people might wish to do so.

I would like to end with two stories based on experiences within one half hour of each other on the balmy last day of January 1994. They exemplify why, going beyond the usual references to education and healthcare, the pos-sible end of the Cuban attempt at socialism in a Third World context would be something for progressives to mourn.

My first visit to the Cuban History Institute (IHC), located in the Aldama building, a magnificent structure inherited from private wealth in Centro Habana, led to the following journal entry:

> I am home (of sorts) after an exhausting but rewarding afternoon at the Historical Institute of Cuba at the invitation of one of my "classmates," who is a researcher there. What a gem! They have an archive, a library, a technical sec-tion where they clean, restore and preserve documents, a film developing studio, a microfiche production facility and copiers from microfiche to paper, from pa-per to paper and from microfiche to microfiche. Even in this "special period," al-though they have eliminated air-conditioning from offices, they maintain strict temperature (+ or –2 degrees) and humidity controls in the library/archives. What is more impressive: they readily agreed to give me access to their materi-als. They have over fifty researchers working there, organized in six sections: (1) colonial history, (2) history of the republic, (3) history of revolutionary Cuba, (4) military history, (5) Fidel Castro's works, (6) professional help for amateur histo-rians in provincial areas.

I doubt I would have been able to make a similar journal entry in too many other Third World countries. Admittedly, perhaps this story has a particular resonance only for an academic like me. Still, observers of a different bent would have little difficulty in coming up with similar little gems: a child care center here, a sports facility there.

The second story is about an incident that happened in the park across from the Aldama, while I (accompanied by my bike) was sitting on a bench passing the time before my interview at the IHC. I struck up a conversation with two Cuban boys, David, seven, and Daer, ten. In the course of the con-versation, carried on in my halting Spanish, and in response to a question as to what I was doing there, I said: "Trabajo" "I work." Daer thought I had said "Trabaja?" "Are you working?" and looked at me with a total "I can't believe this" look and patiently explained, "Somos niños!" "We are kids!" Turns out they had a week's vacation from school. As they took off, David yelled over his shoulder: "Estamos jugando" "We are playing." Go tell that to the Nicaraguan kids in the streets of Managua, whom I also had an opportunity to observe within the last year, swarming around your car at each stoplight, trying to sell you gum, cigarettes, or newspapers for a few cordobas in order to survive.

Whether, normatively speaking, one should mourn it or not, is Cuban socialism's end inevitable? On this "positive" question one does not come away from Cuba, at least I did not, with a definite no or a definite yes. One thing that can be said is that Cuba is trying to adjust internally, both *economically* and *politically*, to the new realities in the world and at home. Whether these adjustments will succeed, or even be given sufficient time to mature, remains unanswered and unanswerable in the present, and we must await the "verdict" of history.

5. THE DEATH OF VICTOR JARA

The overthrow of the democratic Allende government by a military coup in September 1973 ushered in a reign of terror without precedent in Chilean history. Many thousands of Allende's followers were tortured and executed. As if aping the Nazis, the fascist junta showed a special hatred for the creators of culture and their works. The junta's soldiers attempted to purify Chilean culture by holding book-burning sprees. They devastated the home of Pablo Neruda, Chile's greatest poet and Nobel Prize winner, as he lay dying of cancer. And they tortured and killed Victor Jara, a beloved composer, folk singer, and theatre director, as described in the following account.

Victor Jara was brought to the Chile Stadium, together with the employees and students of the Technical University after the assault on that institution, on Wednesday, September 12. There an officer of the *carabineros* (national police) discovered him: "You're Victor Jara, you son-of-a-bitch." And so began the calvary of the distinguished composer, folk singer, and stage director. The officer threw himself furiously on Victor and struck him with the butt of his rifle on his stomach, head, everywhere. Victor fell down and another soldier joined in his punishment. They kicked him and hurled insults at him. One kicked him in the face, and an eye filled with blood. They yelled and beat him savagely. Victor curled up, but made no sound.

Centro de Estudios y Publicaciones, *Chile, una esperanza aplastada*, Estella (Spain), Editorial Verbo Divino, 1975, pp. 24–25.

The head of the "prisoner camp" arrived and said: "Let's cut off the hands of this son-of-a-bitch." He hit Victor with a stick. "Sing now, you bastard; get up!" he ordered. Then they bent him over, with his hands on a sawhorse, and began to beat his hands and wrists until they became a bloody mass. All this took place in a passage of the stadium. There were five thousand prisoners in the stadium and many were able to see the torture. Impotent tears streamed down the faces of all the witnesses. They had also received or were receiving their dose of punishment. Now Victor was down on the ground. They left him for a few minutes and then returned. They showed him off to the fascists who arrived as if he were a trophy of war. Three air force officers arrived and stopped in front of him, insulting and taking turns in kicking him. "Do you want a smoke, bastard?" they asked in a mocking tone. Victor did not respond. They put out a cigarette on one of his hands, a mass of wounds. The torture continued until very late in the afternoon of the twelfth. They left him unconscious all that night and the next day, the thirteenth, of course without food or water.

Then they seemed to forget him. They had other entertainments. Someone ordered that he should be taken away with the other prisoners. Signs of solidarity with Victor came from every corner of the stadium: pieces of bread, a biscuit, a jacket to keep him warm. Victor gradually came to himself. Now he was happy, though he suffered atrocious pain. He spoke of the future, of his wife and children. Meanwhile the stadium resounded with the groans of the victims of fascism. They killed and tortured in the presence of five thousand men. Some prisoners went mad and threw themselves down from the top of the stadium. Others cried and ran, and the lieutenants beat them till they died. From the underground rooms moans and cries rose day and night. Foreigners, "agents of international communism," suffered special agonies. Victor continued to recover, though his body was one large hematoma, his wounded eye continued to bleed, and his face showed the wounds he had received.

Saturday, the thirteenth, they announced a transfer of prisoners to the national stadium, and all thought that Victor would leave with the rest. It seemed they had finally forgotten him. That morning he began to dictate the verses that he entitled "Chile Stadium." He would never finish them. They took him, together with a group described as "Marxist specialists in explosives" out of the corridors. They took him into one of the rooms converted into torture chambers and the rain of blows began again. They stretched him out on the ground, spread his legs apart, and kicked him in the testicles. They attacked him with savage fury. They would leave and then return to the attack. A student who managed to come out of that inferno alive tells that at the end blood poured from his mouth, nostrils, ears, eyes. Thus died Victor Jara, who had sung of love, tenderness, and hope in the language of the humble. There he died, beaten to death by the irrational hatred of fascism. Afterwards, by way of an example to others, they left him lying in the foyer of the stadium.

6. Henry Kissinger
on Salvador Allende

The implacable hostility of the U.S. government to Salvador Allende and his socialist program contributed significantly to the destruction of Chilean democracy by the military coup of September 1973. The two principal North American actors in the tragedy of Chile were President Richard Nixon, who told our then ambassador to Chile that he would smash "that son-of-a-bitch Allende," and Henry Kissinger, who implemented Nixon's Chilean policy, first as national security adviser and then as secretary of state. CIA "covert" activities against Chile from 1969 to 1973, in the words of a former Chilean diplomat, "included everything from cloak-and-dagger operations, involving the murder of generals and civilians, to strangulation of the Chilean economy and subversion of its legally elected government." In the first volume of his autobiography, White House Years, *Kissinger offered a defense of the Nixon administration policy toward Chile. Juan Bosch, a prominent Dominican political figure, subjects that defense to a probing analysis.*

In the first volume ... of his book, *White House Years,* Henry Kissinger devotes thirty-one pages to relating the events, as he sees them, that culminated in the assassination[5] of President Salvador Allende. Those thirty-one pages make up a whole chapter that its author titles "The Autumn of Crises: Chile," and that begins by referring to the election of September 4, 1970. In those elections, writes Kissinger, "Salvador Allende achieved a plurality ... with a bare 36.2% of the popular vote."

Why did Kissinger begin the chapter in this way? With the obvious intent of impressing his readers, from the first, with the argument that the electoral victory of Popular Unity that brought Allende to power was not legitimate because he did not obtain more than half of the votes cast. This also makes perfectly clear from the first that with regard to Chile the former secretary of state of President Nixon was not really writing his memoirs but his defense, and that his account of what he did in the Chilean affair attempts to deform the truth so that his readers may absolve him of his responsibility for the years of suffering and humiliation, death, and misery that his actions and those of his government caused to the country of Pablo Neruda and Orlando Letelier.

In case the absurd argument of the number of votes obtained by Popular Unity should not suffice, Kissinger, acting as lawyer in his own defense, tries to justify his conduct with respect to Chile by alleging that the Chilean elections took place

---

Juan Bosch, "Salvador Allende en las memorias de Kissinger," *Casa de las Americas* (Havana), Year 22, September–October 1981, no. 128, pp. 100–103.

just as Moscow and Cairo were rejecting our protests of Middle East cease-fire violations; Jordan feared an imminent Iraqi move against the King; a Soviet naval force was steaming toward Cuba. On September 8, the day the Chilean developments were first discussed by an interagency committee, several airplanes had been hijacked in the Middle East and the Soviet flotilla was nearing the port of Cienfuegos. Six days later, on September 14, when Chile was next considered, the Jordan situation had deteriorated, and Cuban MiGs intercepted a U-2 flight seeking to photograph Cienfuegos and the mission had to be aborted. In the weeks that followed, our government pondered Chilean events not in isolation but against the backdrop of the Syrian invasion of Jordan and our effort to force the Soviet Union to dismantle its installation for servicing nuclear submarines in the Caribbean. The reaction must be seen in that context.

At whom was this long and unnecessary explanation, and its last words, in particular, directed? The reply to this question is found in the lines that follow immediately on the same page (p. 654):

> In any circumstances, Allende's election was a challenge to our national interest. We did not find it easy to reconcile ourselves to a second Communist state in the Western Hemisphere. We were persuaded that he would soon be inciting anti-American policies, attacking hemispheric solidarity, making common cause with Cuba, and sooner or later establishing close relations with the Soviet Union. And this was all the more painful because Allende represented a break with Chile's long democratic history and would become president not through an authentic expression of majority will but through a fluke of the Chilean political system. Thirty-six percent of the popular vote was hardly a mandate for the irreversible transformation of Chile's political and economic institutions that Allende was determined to effect.

The chief of foreign policy of the United States cannot conceive that any country in the world can accept as a democratic—and constitutional—principle that when there are three candidates for president the victory should go to the one who obtains more than 33.33% of the vote. This simply cannot be. In conformity with the rules of the only true, authentic democracy, the one invented by the authors of the Constitution of the United States, the only legitimate elections are those in which only two candidates vie for power. It was inconceivable and unpardonable, above all, that this violation of the principles that govern the functioning of capitalist democracy should be used to bring to power men who were not submissive subjects of Yankee interests. For this reason, that part of the chapter dedicated to Chile in *White House Years* ends with these words: "Two previous American administrations had come to the same conclusion. Two administrations had judged that an Allende government in Chile would be against fundamental American national interests. Our conclusion in 1970 was substantially the same."

Now, since those two previous administrations had been those of Kennedy and Johnson, and Johnson was no longer president at the beginning of 1970, it is plain that the Allende government, which began its mandate at the end of 1970, was born with a sentence of death that had been passed against it at least two years before, and this sentence of death was merely ratified by Kissinger and Nixon, designated by an overwhelming majority of mankind to judge the governments of this world, both the quick and the dead, and apply to them the sentences they deemed suitable.

Let me point out, however, that despite that previous sentence of death, if Salvador Allende had sent Kissinger and Nixon a message assuring them that Popular Unity would maintain a policy favorable to the national and world interests of the United States, Allende would have been kept in power, come what may, with the argument that in accordance with the Chilean constitution, Allende had obtained a legal plurality of votes over his rivals. For such is the arbitrary position of the high officials of the United States, who will even justify a crime on the grounds that it is their duty to defend the national interests of the United States—meaning thereby the interests of an oligarchy of multibillionaires.

To read, almost seven years after the murder of Salvador Allende, what Kissinger writes about the events that led to the murder of Salvador Allende fills one with bitterness and wrath, for a reading of those pages makes clear that the destiny of peoples like those of Latin America depends on astoundingly ignorant men, men who wield enormous power concentrated in engines of destruction which they set in motion without the least awareness of the forces they unleash. Kissinger was a poor devil, a sorcerer's apprentice who did not even know why he did what he did. He says (p. 656):

> What worried us about Allende was his proclaimed hostility to the United States and his patent intention to create another Cuba. It was his explicit program and indeed long-standing goal to establish an irreversible dictatorship and a permanent challenge to our position in the Western Hemisphere. And in the month of Cienfuegos it was not absurd to take seriously the implications of another Soviet ally in Latin America. Our concern with Allende was based on national security, not on economics.

What should we make of this paragraph? If what Kissinger calls his "concern" authorized the Nixon administration to dispose of Allende at any cost, including his physical elimination, by what right does the United States proclaim itself the world champion of democracy? Can a democracy resort to crime because it believes that its national security is in danger even before events prove the existence of a danger?

Kissinger affirms that between 1962 and 1964 the Kennedy and Johnson administrations contributed more than three million dollars to the political campaign of Eduardo Frei, who during those years was Allende's rival for the presidency of Chile; later he says that Johnson made available hundreds of thousands of dollars to Allende's enemies in order that the parties opposed to Popular Unity might win the legislative elections held in March 1969. He adds that North American aid to Chile during the Frei administration "totaled well over $1 billion, the largest per capita program by far in Latin

America," and explains that this was done "to strengthen the democratic forces against Allende."

The high point of this illuminating chapter of Kissinger's book appears on the last page (p. 683), in a paragraph that reads as follows: "The myth that Allende was a democrat has been as assiduously fostered as it is untrue. The fact is that various measures taken by Allende's government were declared to be unconstitutional and outside the law by the Chilean Supreme Court on May 26, 1973, by the Comptroller General on July 2, 1973, and by the Chamber of Deputies on August 22, 1973."

Naturally, after reading this paragraph, the ordinary reader must ask himself how Mr. Kissinger can call undemocratic a government in which the Supreme Court, the Comptroller General, and the Chamber of Deputies, which formed very important parts of the Chilean state apparatus, operated with complete freedom with respect to the executive branch of government. What emerges very clearly from the chapter on Chile in *White House Years* is that Allende's murderers dared to liquidate him because behind them stood the overwhelming power of the United States, and that in his eagerness to conceal the truth the serpent named Henry Kissinger ended up swallowing its own tail.

7. The Church
in the Nicaraguan Revolution

A distinctive feature of the Nicaraguan Revolution that overthrew the tyranny of the Somoza dynasty in 1979 was the role played by rank-and-file clergy in the revolutionary movement and their later involvement in implementing the goals of the revolution. On the other hand, the church hierarchy, headed by Archbishop Miguel Obando y Bravo, traditionally aligned with the wealthy class and late converts to anti-Somoza positions, grew increasingly hostile to the Sandinist government. Ernesto Cardenal, one of Latin America's great poets and minister of culture in the Sandinist government, describes the spiritual road traveled by a Jesuit priest who joined the revolutionary struggle.

Our people lived for four centuries in conditions of misery, malnutrition, illiteracy, and abandonment. They worked in unjust and inhuman conditions, lacking means of communication, schools, or culture. They had no part in determining the destiny of our country, no possibility of becoming the makers of their own history. Add to these evils the half century of Somoza dicta-

---

Ernesto Cardenal, "No crean las calumnias sobre la Nicaragua (carta a un amigo)," *Cuadernos Americanos* 44, March–April 1985, pp. 23–27.

torship, which inflicted on our country the greatest injustices, lack of freedom, and a constant and ferocious repression.

Our people have always fought, but only after the founding of the Sandinist Front of National Liberation (FSLN) in 1961 did they struggle in a truly organized and effective way. Thousands of Nicaraguans were assassinated in the course of those years. But new heroes always arose, heroes who fought, offering the last drop of their blood to free our people from slavery, without fear of Pharaoh.

Our Church lived in peace and tranquility with the oppressors. There are some significant facts. Nicaraguans will never forget that during the funeral of General Somoza García, founder of the dynasty, the then archbishop of Managua gave the dictator the title of Prince of the Church.

In 1967 several leaders of the FSLN were captured and later murdered; on that occasion the auxiliary bishop of Managua published an article in the government newspaper in which he practically justified the repression on the grounds that those young men, according to him, were Communists.

I shall never forget the day, on my return as an ordained priest to Nicaragua in 1968, when the popular struggle and the repression were growing daily, that I read the first pastoral letter of the bishops of Nicaragua. It offered no theological doctrine for a better understanding of God's will in those difficult times; it only required priests to wear black cassocks. Not a word about the black situation of our people. With some glorious exceptions, the Church maintained an alliance with the dictatorship.

I had to leave the country in 1969 for nine months in order to complete my religious training by taking the last course required of Jesuits, called the Last Probation. I asked to take it in the city of Medellín (Colombia), for there they had moved the site of the course from a lovely four-floor building set among gardens and sport grounds to a poor ward in the "misery belt" around Medellín. The previous year the Second General Conference of Latin American Bishops had been held there. I lived those months among people scourged by hunger, unemployment, illness, with no electric lighting or any other public service or convenience. I came to feel an enormous love for these people and my life with them marked me forever.

My Christian faith, my human feelings, and all that I daily saw and heard brought me to a conclusion that arose from the depths of my being: Things cannot go on in this way! It is not right that such misery should exist! God cannot be neutral toward this situation!

My spiritual experience among those poor people confirmed the conception that I drew from the Bible of a God who was not neutral, who heard the clamor of the oppressed and took their side. Never was the meaning of the Bible clearer to me than when I read it amid the quagmires and misery of that ward.

In mid-1970 I completed the course and returned to my country, but not before making a vow to the dwellers of that ward of Medellín: "I shall dedicate my life to the complete liberation of the poor of Latin America, in the place where I shall be most useful." I began to work in the Central American University (UCA) of Managua as co-director in charge of students. A long night continued to envelope our people: dictatorship, dependency, prison, torture, hunger, malnutrition, fear, death, and violation of all human and civil rights. The official Church continued to live peacefully side by side with that genocidal government. Only some half-dozen priests were attempting to teach the new pastoral that was born from the documents of Medellín.[6]

The Sandinist Front of National Liberation (FSLN) was already known to all and had gained the respect and sympathy of the people by its valiant and clean fight for the people and against the dictatorship. Inspired by the documents of Medellín and seeking the complete liberation of man, I and a few other priests began to participate in all the civic struggles of the people for liberation: demonstrations, occupations of churches, hunger strikes, speeches at meetings, articles in newspapers, etc.

We also began to take part in the struggle of the Christian student groups, which were to become so important later on.

The most significant moment in the Christian participation in the popular struggle was the occupation of the cathedral. Three of us, priests, accompanied by nearly a hundred students of the Catholic University, took part in a hunger strike in the Cathedral of Managua in 1970, demanding respect for the lives of all the university students who had been imprisoned in recent days, permission to speak to them and, in conformity with Nicaraguan law, that within two days they be freed or put on trial on specific charges.

The normal thing was for prisoners to be tortured for weeks in the offices of the National Security. The occupation of the cathedral created a nationwide commotion. The army surrounded the cathedral in a threatening manner. We rang the mourning bells every fifteen minutes, night and day, and announced that we would continue ringing them until justice was done and the law complied with. From the principal parishes of Managua came large groups of people who sat down in the plaza to show their support for us; thousands came, and other thousands passed by, greeting us from cars and buses. In three and a half days we made the dictator yield. For the first time a Christian group had taken part in a forceful political act. Messages of support were published by the Bible Study Classes (*Cursillos de Cristiandad*), the Christian Family Movement, the Christian grass-roots communities (*Comunidades de Base*), etc. In a few days the Bishops' Conference of Nicaragua published a letter condemning our protest. Thousands of Christians signed a respectful letter telling the bishops that the bodies of the students, who were being profaned and tortured in prisons, and not the temple of stone, were the temple of the Holy Spirit. But the most essential part of the letter was that in which the bishops were told that the people of Nicaragua had chosen the path of struggle for justice and that they, the pastors, instead of placing themselves at the head of that people, stood aside and condemned it. Henceforth Christians would be present in all the phases of the popular struggle.

In my talks before Christian groups I would say to them: Latin America is marching toward its transformation. Revolution would soon come to Nicaragua. It was important to be aware that the revolution would be made with the Christians, without the Christians, despite the Christians, or against the Christians. So many years later, people throughout the country have reminded me of that statement.

I knew how important it was that the Church should appear to have a role in this process, that our young people could see that the Church had a program of justice for the exploited; paradoxically, the problem of unity between Christians and revolutionaries did not arise from the latter, but from the Christians. I personally knew the founder of the FSLN, Commander Jose Carlos Fonseca Amador (assassinated in 1976), and knew his receptive attitude and desire for unity with the Christians. I studied the statutes of the FSLN, written by him in 1969, in which he speaks of religious liberty and support for the priests who work for the people. In 1970 I had an interview with Commander Jose Turcios, member of the national directorate of the FSLN (assassinated in 1973). He said to me on that occasion: "What matters is not that you believe there is another life after death and I don't; the basic question is whether we can work together for the construction of a new society."

The Christian grass-roots communities and the young Christians, above all, played an ever larger role in that slow and dangerous march toward liberation. Faith moved thousands of Nicaraguans who committed themselves to that struggle in a natural, spontaneous way. They understood that by fighting for justice and the poor they were following God's cause. Thanks to them, the Nicaraguan Revolution was made with the Christians.

When, in 1973, Commander Eduardo Contreras (assassinated in 1976) asked me to accept an official role in the work of the FSLN, I instantly accepted, remembering the parable of the Good Samaritan, for it seemed obvious that I should not act like that priest and that Levite who went around the injured man. The Samaritans of Nicaragua asked me to help cure our wounded people and, given my Christian faith, I could give only one answer: commitment. I continued to work with students, directing Bible Study Classes, conducting spiritual exercises, and retaining my chair of philosophy at the National Autonomous University of Nicaragua (UNAN), but at the same time collaborated secretly with the FSLN in the struggle for national liberation.

The cry of the oppressed and the realities of my country were forcing me to discover other aspects of my priestly ministry. There was no break with the priesthood; I merely accented more and more its prophetic aspect. It was an option fully compatible with the different aspects of the priesthood, an option based not so much on the elements of the ministry according to the Old Testament as on the prophetic aspects proclaimed by Jesus in the New.

My work was daily becoming more dangerous, since the greater part of my revolutionary activities were public. Somoza's authorities expelled me in 1970 from the National Autonomous University. In 1973 I participated actively in forming the Christian Revolutionary Movement (MCR), which formed so many cadres and leaders for the FSLN. The revolutionary leaders sent me to Washington in 1976 to denounce the crimes and violations of human rights by the dictator Somoza before the United States Congress. On my return to Nicaragua the president of the Nicaraguan Senate proposed that I be declared a traitor to my country. At that time we founded the Nicaraguan Commission on Human Rights.

A thousand details of the struggles, fears and hopes of the priests who participated in those years of struggle must remain untold for lack of space. Always inspired by our faith, but sometimes wandering in the dark, wishing to see and follow the Lord of History, when all we saw were crimes and the dictator's smiling face as he emerged victorious from every crisis. Sometimes our hopes faded. Often I was afraid, very much afraid, especially of being tortured. Despite the order of arrest issued against us, we entered Nicaragua July 4, 1978. Before two months had gone by, it became necessary to shift completely to underground work. Then came the September insurrection and the next year the final offensive which led to the triumph of July 19, 1979, won through the heroic sacrifices of 50,000 of my compatriots. We were not the only priests who contributed something to the struggle. Other priests aided the cause by preaching from their pulpits, while many religious men and women collaborated in the most varied ways with the guerrillas. Thousands of Christians fought from every trench and barricade in the fields and cities of Nicaragua. The bishops finally condemned in some of their writings the dictator's violations of human rights and on various occasions took firm positions against Somoza. But all this was accompanied by great contradictions; and right down to the day of victory the bishops wrote not a word in favor of the struggle of the FSLN. What was worse, they often condemned the struggle of the people when they condemned in their writings "violence no matter whence it comes," which placed on the same level the unjust violence of the oppressor and the just, legitimate violence of the oppressed people. Not until one week before the final offensive did the bishops justify the popular insurrection.

It is important for me to make clear that at no time were my decisions the result of a crisis of my priestly condition; they were the result of the spiritual journey of a priest who gradually discovered the prophetic dimension of his priesthood and the demands they imposed in a country like ours. Let me add that all the steps I took in those years were made in consultation with and had the approval of my spiritual superiors and had the approval of my order.

I am profoundly convinced that the Nicaraguan people were the motor that made possible my advance. My only merit was to place myself among them and let myself be pushed forward.

8. PRESIDENT REAGAN'S
"FREEDOM FIGHTERS"

*Even before President Ronald Reagan came to office in 1981, a "get-the-Sandinistas"
strategy was outlined in the Republican preelection Santa Fe Document. Following the
election, the Reagan administration authorized the formation of a military force composed chiefly of former Nicaraguan National Guardsmen with an initial acknowledged
budget of $19 million and Honduras as its staging area. This became the so-called
Fuerza Democrática Nicaragüense (FDN), usually known as the* contras. *Behind a
thin facade of civilian leadership, the FDN military strategy and tactics were dictated by
its commanders, almost all former National Guardsmen. Unable to defeat the Sandinist
armed forces in the field, the FDN engaged in hit-and-run raids from its Honduran
sanctuaries that took thousands of Nicaraguan lives and did great damage to the
Sandinist economy. Like Somoza's National Guard, the FDN became known for the
kidnapping and murder of civilians, rape, and other forms of savagery. Nancy Donovan,
a missionary of the Maryknoll Order who worked for twenty-nine years with
Nicaragua's poor, describes her encounter with the* contras, *whom President Reagan
called "freedom fighters."*

It is not easy to live in a war zone. The least of it was my being kidnapped
by *contras* early this year. The hard part is seeing people die and consoling
families. And it goes on and on in northern Nicaragua.

When I was kidnapped, I decided, "I am not going to think of these men as
killers. They are human beings and I am going to talk to them as much as I
can." In those eight hours I was held, as I walked in a column of 60 or so men
and a few women—all in uniform—I kept talking even though I could hear
shooting and realized that people I knew were being killed.

Earlier I had seen bodies brought back to town, some burned, some cut to
pieces. The *contras* don't just kill people; they dismember them.

We have had five bad incidents in the town of San Juan de Limay since
December 9 when our only bus was burned. That day *contras* kidnapped
many people and killed a Tel Cor (telephone company) crew of seven in-
stalling a line. The doctor tried to sew up the bodies for the wake, but the
young people helping him fled from the building. The doctor realized this
was too much for them to handle, so we just wrapped the bodies in sheets.
Now we're running out of sheets.

On January 8, I left Limay early in the morning for a meeting with Bishop
Rubén López Ardón in Estelí. Since there was no bus, I hitched a ride with a
family in a pickup truck. From Platanares, they had lost almost everything in a
December 27 attack on their small community. They gave a ride also to 18-

Nancy Donova, M.M., "Life in a War Zone," *Maryknoll* 79, no. 8, August 1985, pp. 24–27.

year-old Freddy. About six kilometers from Limay, we ran into a roadblock and five men in uniform ordered us into a gully with 25 men, women and children. Ten minutes later we were allowed to continue, but not the other 25.

At El Pedernal, four kilometers down the road, I left the truck to return to Limay and warn people of the ambushes. I hadn't walked far when two men stopped me and forced me to where 20 uniformed men had gathered a number of peasants they had picked up. We could hear gunshots and also heavy artillery fire. As we walked, other *contras* joined us. "You people complain that with the revolution there's a scarcity of certain things. So why did you burn our bus?" I asked. "Because it belonged to the state," they said. "Ask the people from Limay," I replied. "They will tell you it was their bus."

"Why do you kidnap and kill people?" I asked. "We only do that with Sandinistas and those in the army," they said. "But we weren't with the army," I countered. "You're all Sandinistas," they said.

The *contras* holding me wore good uniforms lettered FDN (Nicaraguan Democratic Force). One had "U.S. Army" emblazoned on his arm and another, "Soldier of Fortune, Second Convention."

Four FDN leaders interrogated me, wanting to know who my contacts were. They searched my bag, went through my address book and copied addresses of people in Limay. When they let me go, I made my way back to Limay. I must have walked 18 kilometers that day.

In Limay, I found out that 14 civilians had been killed in two ambushes. Two days later Freddy's badly tortured body was found. Similar atrocities take place all over the country. I have a list of 35 civilians killed in our area between December 9 and January 23. Many others have been wounded or kidnapped. The *contras* boast of 500 recruits a month—this is one way they get them. Kidnapping with its uncertainty may be worse than killing. Some mothers tell daughters, "If they want to take you, run. That way they will kill you."

This is life in a war zone and it isn't pretty. It isn't good. And when we hear that these things are being done by our own country, that is the hard part. We hear the U.S. government use the word "totalitarian" in regard to Nicaragua and it scares people. But we haven't seen it and we live there.

We see displaced people all over the zone and we can no longer reach many of the 33 villages in our parish of 14,000 people. It is dangerous even to go to Estelí on the main highway. Maryknoll and Church organizations in the United States and Europe are helping us build simple housing and now the government is contributing.

Our bishop calls Limay the Cinderella of the diocese because we have Mass only every six or eight weeks. But Sister Suzanne Deliee and I have been there more than four years. We have seen many improvements: a high school, preschool, a 700,000-tree reforestation project, two irrigation dams, the new road to Estelí, a town bus, telephone and telegraph lines, agricultural cooperatives, a tobacco project, new streetlights, encouragement of wood and stone crafts.

The *contra* record reads differently: nine road workers killed, as well as seven Tel Cor technicians, two tree planters and eight workers in an agricultural cooperative; Limay's only bus and four farm tractors burned. The list goes on and on—all destruction.

When I asked people in Limay if I should come to the United States, they said, "Tell the people, tell the President to stop the killing." Mothers wrote moving letters to U.S. mothers about how hard it is to live with this U.S. fueled war. Sara speaks of hearing her 16-year-old son's laughter even though it has been forever silenced.

9. THE NICARAGUAN
REVOLUTION UNDER FIRE

The Nicaraguan elections of February 25, 1990, resulted in a stunning upset by the opposition slate. Headed by Violeta Chamorro, the Union Opositora Nacional *(UNO), a coalition of 14 parties united only by their dislike for the ruling Sandinista Front (FSLN), received a decisive majority (55 percent) of the vote. Although Sandinista errors in policy contributed to that result, the most important single cause was the ten-year counterrevolutionary war organized and financed by the United States. This war left thousands dead, the economy in ruins, and nullified the promising beginnings made by the Sandinista regime in raising living standards through its agrarian, educational, and health reforms. The election and the winding down of the war was followed by an uneasy stalemate. Efforts by the regime of President Violeta Chamorro to dismantle the agrarian reform and other social conquests of the Sandinista revolution were partly beaten off by the resistance of the FSLN in alliance with militant labor and peasant organizations, but those efforts continued. Meanwhile the new government's "free market" economic policies, favoring big farmers and employers but ending the subsidies that had provided minimum protection for low-income groups, worsened an already calamitous economic situation. A journalist describes the aftermath of the election that ended ten years of Sandinista rule.*

Surreal sights can be seen in Acahualinca, Managua's largest garbage dump, on the shores of the lake. Human beings in a distressing state fight with vultures over the best of the rubbish's booty, in a country where almost nothing worth having is thrown away.

The headlines of Peru's major newspapers could be easily applied to Nicaragua: "European prices and African wages." The country is reverting to

---

Melba Jiménez, "The Seven Plagues Are on the Prowl," *Barricada Internacional* (Managua, Nicaragua), September 22, 1990, pp. 8–9.

the old pattern of a "banana republic," but facing the natural resistance of a 10-year revolutionary experience.

The government's misguided economic policies are leading the Nicaraguan people to unexpected degrees of hunger. Nicaragua is currently the most expensive country in Central America, but has the lowest per capita income.

Data compiled by the UN office in Nicaragua reveals that 80% of the population is "in a state of extreme poverty." "The situation is worrying," said Francesco Vincenti, local UN representative.

In just over four months almost 500 children have died of hunger, malnutrition, diarrhea and measles in Managua alone.

The drought—which affects 70% of the rural population—and the political situation are conspiring with fate to exacerbate the country's crisis.

Almost the entire harvest of corn, one of the mainstays of the Nicaraguan diet, was lost this year, while the cultivation of other basic crops is facing serious problems.

The gravity of the situation was also recognized by the Nicaraguan Bishops' Conference, presided over by Cardinal Miguel Obando. The bishops urged the government to find a solution to the economic crisis which, they admitted, hurts the poorest sectors of society.

Alarming

Unemployment, the drought and the constant devaluations (36 since April 25), as well as the increase in water, electricity, telephone and fuel rates, are factors of destabilization and tension.

The currency has been devalued 1,247%, while wages have increased only 541%. The official US dollar exchange rate rose 1,400% in real terms, from 51,200 córdobas to $1 in April, to 1.05 million at press time.

Wages have lost 59% of their buying power in only four months and prices increased 37%. In May a dozen eggs cost 180,000 córdobas, in September they cost over 1 million. A pound (.5 kg) of salt, which cost 5,000 córdobas then, now costs 30,000.

Economic analysts say that Nicaragua is transcending poverty and taking gigantic steps toward pauperism. "The government is applying monetary fund-style policies and 'shock' mechanisms to reduce inflation at the expense of the population's sacrifice," one expert commented.

The government has undertaken to pay the foreign debt even if it means unemployment, low wages and the elimination of social programs. The debt is $9.6 billion—the highest per capita in Central America.

Although the Sandinistas applied monetary fund-style measures, they continued subsidizing the main social services as well as a food package which somewhat cushioned the family economy.

More Surprises

Once the new government took office, subsidies disappeared, leaving most of the population unprotected.

Although the country's development is one of the government's strategic goals, its policies will lead to an increase in the rate of illiteracy, currently 20%, unemployment and a rise in infant mortality which has already claimed its first victims.

The only alternatives the government is offering oscillate between charity and a call for patience.

Faced with the urgent need for resources in the health care sector, the president called on the population to donate "sheets, pajamas and diapers" to the hospitals, even though many Nicaraguan homes lack these items.

The request was described as "absolute nerve" by Mercedes Tenorio, a trade union leader in the health sector. "The people can't hand over the little they have. That's the government's job because the Constitution says so; otherwise we'd be going back to charity."

"Solution"

It is never too late for masterful alternatives. Finance minister Emilio Pereira and his advisers suggested a reduction in health care and education spending, included in the country's general budget.

Should this proposal be approved by the National Assembly, two of the most sensitive social areas would be disrupted. Even more teachers would join the ranks of the unemployed, who now equal 40% of the economically active population. The education of at least 300,000 children, who would find themselves outside the school system, would also be affected.

The health sector would also be badly hit. Health minister Ernesto Salmerón revealed that at least 100 children die every month as a result of extreme poverty in rural areas. In recent weeks another 100 died in Managua of malnutrition and for lack of medicine.

Children under 15 and pregnant women, groups which in Nicaragua represent 56% and 24% of the population respectively, account for the highest percentage of deaths. Salmerón admitted that the incidence of endemic disease has increased and acknowledged the state's incapacity to resolve these problems.

Desperation

On the morning of September 3, war-wounded, mothers of soldiers killed in action, war widows and orphans went to draw their pensions and found to their surprise that they were to receive the ridiculous sum of 10 million córdobas (about $8 a month) with which they cannot even cover the most essential needs.

Their displeasure mounted when they were told that demobilized contras will be given the equivalent of $50 a month. Desperate, they decided to pressure the government publicly by occupying the National Television System's installations.

While the government continues to call for reconciliation, hunger and extreme poverty are wreaking havoc. "There can be no cooperation based on the sacrifice of campesinos and workers. If shoulders have to be put to the wheel, the bourgeoisie should put theirs too," former president Daniel Ortega said.

However, measures which could unleash greater social tensions, more opposition and new protests continue to be applied.

It cannot be ruled out that the discontent could reach levels similar to those in Venezuela, the Dominican Republic and Peru. In those countries, thousands of people made desperate by hunger violently looted businesses and farmlands in search of food.

"Will death squads emerge in Nicaragua to clear the streets of poverty, killing children and the homeless just as happens in Brazil?" a local priest wondered.

Every day the population becomes more convinced that the errors of the government's economic policy do not endanger the jobs of government ministers and officials. The price is much higher—the very lives of Nicaraguans are at stake.

10. DEADLOCK IN EL SALVADOR: A GUERRILLA LEADER SPEAKS

Civil war raged from 1980 until 1992 in El Salvador, a pseudodemocracy where real power had rested for decades with a corrupt and predatory military linked to a landed oligarchy traditionally known as "the Fourteen Families." Despite lavish U.S. assistance to the Salvadoran government and military (over $4 billion since 1980), they were unable to defeat the socialist-oriented Farabundo Martí Liberation Front (FMLN). In November 1989, responding to increased death squad and military terrorist activities, the FMLN launched a powerful offensive in the capital and on main highways of the country. The offensive proved the undiminished military and political strength of the FMLN and helped to produce an agreement to hold U.N.-sponsored negotiations between the belligerents. A key element of the FMLN agenda in these negotiations was a proposal for a gradual process of demilitarization that would ultimately dismantle both armies and replace them with a civilian police force. Although the guerrillas did not achieve all their demands, in January 1992 the two sides reached an agreement that provided for a reduction and cleansing of the armed forces and full integration of the insurgents into the country's political life. A guerrilla leader explains the FMLN position in the peace talks.

Carlos Fazio, "El arreglo en El Salvador, casi imposible; ambas partes exigen que el enemigo capitule," *Proceso* (Mexico), September 24, 1990, pp. 42–45. (Excerpt translated by the editor.)

Death has been her constant companion. Her nom de guerre is Rebeca Palacios. Her true name is Lorena Guadalupe Peña Palacios. A veteran commander of the Popular Forces of Liberation (FPL), she is also a member of the Diplomatic-Political Commission of the Farabundo Martí Front of National Liberation (FMLN).

She comes from a family of revolutionaries. Her father, Lieutenant José Belisario Peña, an old soldier and militant, has just died. "He was with us in the FMLN until we made him retire on account of his age." He was a born conspirator against dictatorships, taking part in coups against General Maximiliano Hernández Martínez in 1944; against Colonel José María Lemus in 1960; and against General Fidel Sánchez Hernández in 1972. "He was always organizing coups," says Rebeca Palacios, "and when the guerrilla movement appeared, he joined us. He was already old, but he insisted, so we took him along." During the 1981 offensive, he was chief of operations of the FMLN.

A long history, indeed, like the history of his children. All were members of the leadership of the FPL, and all, except Rebeca, are dead. Felipe Peña Mendoza, founder of the organization, died in combat in San Salvador in 1975, in a safe house; the war front of the central zone bears his name. Ana Margarita was a member of the central committee and disappeared in 1981. Virginia, in command of the Cerro de Guazapa, formed part of the military command of Chalatenango, and fell in combat July 12, 1986.

Interviewed during the negotiations between the Salvadoran government and the FMLN in San José, Costa Rica, Rebeca Palacios says, "We are not fanatics, eager for war. We want the war to end." But the condition for achieving a just and durable peace is the demilitarization of society. And the crux of the problem is that the army must disappear. For this reason, she adds, if the Armed Forces do not move at the bargaining table, "We will have to make them move in a different way." The statement alludes to the capacity of the FMLN to unleash new military offensives that will change the present correlation of forces.

In the previous meeting in San José, in August 1990, the FMLN presented a final proposal of 18 points. It proposed the dissolution of both armies. Clearly, the FMLN believed it was negotiating from a position of strength, and this led various analysts to conclude that the guerrillas wanted the negotiations to break down, or at least to get bogged down.

Commander Palacios does not agree. She replies, "The 18-point proposal in San José had a central objective: the demilitarization of society. But this was no novelty. Already at the meeting in Caracas the FMLN submitted a comprehensive document which argued that for our country to progress it is not enough to reform, purge, and restructure the Armed Forces; it is necessary to do away with the army. It is not a question of its size. The military dictatorship has existed for decades, and when it had only 12,000 men it was as cruel and criminal as it is now. It has always dominated the civil government."

She acknowledges that before the Caracas meeting the proposals of the FMLN with respect to demilitarization were more limited. For example, at Oaxtepec, at the beginning of 1990, the guerrillas proposed a purge and reduction of the army and trials and punishment for the individuals responsible for crimes like the murder of Archbishop Romero, but those proposals only caused the military to harden their stance and led them to "the mistaken belief that our limited proposals were due to our weakness, when in fact their purpose was to make possible a serious negotiation." The government and the military rejected those proposals outright. ... "It makes no sense, therefore, for them to say that we have radicalized our positions."

There is more. "Since we made those proposals we have become convinced that the problem goes far deeper. There was the murder of the Jesuits; the bombardment of urban as well as rural areas; the murder of the trade unionists of Fenestras; the continued activity of the death squads, without a single member of the military being put on trial or punished. The levels of corruption and criminality of the Armed Forces have convinced us that only a radical solution can solve the problem. Society must be totally demilitarized. That is the simple logic of our August proposal.

"At Oaxtepec we managed to get the subject of the Armed Forces put on the agenda. But they refused to accept any discussion of demilitarization. They said that the Armed Forces would purify and reform themselves, that a purge was not negotiable, that there was nothing to negotiate. But our interest was in negotiating, in bringing the two sides closer together. At San José, in August, the military commands presented a proposal of 33 points in which they defined the role of the Armed Forces in a democratic society. In sum, what they said was: 'The Armed Forces do not negotiate. The Armed Forces have their own mechanisms. We can transfer the National Police to one ministry, the National Guard to another. But no purges, no dissolution of any of the security services. The solution is for the FMLN to demobilize.'

"Or, putting it in another way, what they demanded was: 'Surrender. Give up your arms and we will make our own internal changes.' But this position does not correspond to reality or the prevailing balance of forces. A negotiation reflects a concrete balance of forces. If they have not been able to defeat us and make us give up our arms in the field, what is the basis for their posture? If they have not beaten us in the field they cannot demand at the bargaining table concessions that do not correspond to reality. ...

"What will happen? That depends on the attitude of the government and the North Americans. If the United States insists on giving the government unconditional aid, it will encourage the hard-liners in the Armed Forces. And the negotiations will bog down. If [President Alfredo] Cristiani and the military continue to demand that we demobilize and surrender, they will be responsible for intensifying the war. They have been intransigent. The FMLN has shown flexibility. We are receptive to all possible approaches. The ball is in their court."

11. NEOLIBERALISM AND CULTURE:
A VIEW FROM THE LEFT

The Brazilian Dominican Frei Betto, an advocate of liberation theology and ardent ad-
mirer of socialist Cuba, won Brazil's most prestigious literary award for a book of mem-
oirs, Baptism of Blood. *More recently he has published a fictional reconstruction of the*
life of Jesus that reveals a Christ "centered more on love than on guilt, more on justice
than the law, more on freedom than authority, more on joy than on the 'vale of tears.'"
In the brief following essay Frei Betto reflects on the impact that the dominant economic
model, neoliberalism, has exerted on culture. He sees it creating an "era of exclusion"
that accepts mass unemployment as natural and makes a fetish of commodities. It reduces
culture to simple entertainment, and life to a game in which, as in American movies,
"you get killed if you're not always alert and shamelessly cruel."

With the disappearance of socialism in the countries of Eastern Europe,
neoliberalism, which is the present form of capitalism, dominates the world
far beyond national frontiers. The economy has been globalized. Nation-
states, economically self-sufficient, tend to disappear. The president of City
Bank or Honda is more important—and powerful—than the president or
prime minister of many countries. Corporate executives wield more power
than members of Parliament or the president of a country.

In the first half of the twentieth century capitalism sought to strengthen
the state, from which the great enterprises "suckled" financial resources, exemption from fiscal burdens, and legal privileges. Now the multinationals
that control the economy of the planet insist on privatizing the state enterprises. That is, they want to weaken the state and strengthen the market—
fewer laws and more unrestrained competition. The mails, social security,
hospitals, schools, everything must be privatized, including beaches, streets,
police: One need only look around in our great cities to see the growing
number of closed streets with their walls and guard posts, and the multiplica-
tion of private security firms.

Under neoliberalism, the state tends to remain only as a regulator of juridical contracts and an organ for repression of discontented sectors—the excluded who pay with their lives for the security of those who live in islands of
opulence. Thus economic and political questions are decided less and less
within nations and more and more in the International Monetary Fund, the
World Bank, in the main offices of IBM or General Motors.

Frei Betto, "Neoliberalismo y cultura," *Casa de las Américas*, Habana, año xxxix, nos. 2–3,
Oct.-Dec. 1998, pp. 75–78. (Translated by the editor.)

The Era of Exclusion

Liberal capitalism used to speak of "national development" and became concerned when unemployment and poverty grew. Now, neoliberalism is concerned not with the inclusion of all, but with exclusion. In short, unemployment is not a problem for the system. It is a sign that more efficient organization of production and the technical advances that make machines more efficient than human labor—like the computer—are "liberating" workers. The system is interested not in a greater number of consumers in the market but more money in the hands of the present consumers.

Formerly, capitalism had the goal of producing for all the classes of society. There were much cheaper cars that members of the lower middle class could afford. Now, for example, neoliberalism produces only for the 40 million Brazilians who have access to the consumer's market, out of a total of 155 million. It should be added that half of those privileged persons concentrate in their hands more than 50 percent of the national income, which augments the production of superfluous goods, offered as if they were indispensable products.

The Fetish of Commodities

For neoliberalism, what matters is not progress but the market; not production, but speculation; not the quality of the product, but its promotional value; not the use value of a commodity, but the fetish with which it is invested. One buys a product for the aura that surrounds it and its supposed capacity to promote the user's status. Thus, it is not the human being who imprints value on a particular piece of cloth by using it as a shirt, but the shirt's brand that marks its user, just as a luxury car serves to exalt the social status of its owner. That is to say, he is esteemed on account of the goods that adorn his person.

Viewed through the neoliberal optic, a person in himself does not seem to have any value. Therefore one scorns and excludes a person who does not possess goods while one envies, courts, and celebrates a person who possesses them.

Work was formerly considered a factor of dignity and prosperity for human beings. Now the important thing is to gain money by speculation, live on rents, enjoy life without working. In the media, the happiest persons are the most idle ones. In the factories, the advance of computerization and automation is casting aside human labor, generating unemployment. One example: in 1980 the Volkswagen factory in Saõ Bernardo, Brazil, produced almost 1,000 vehicles daily and employed 44,000 workers. Today it produces almost 1,500 vehicles daily with only 25,000 workers.

Fragmentation and Privatization

Formerly a large enterprise processed the product from the raw material to the finished commodity. For example, a clothing factory sowed its own cotton. Now the production system is fragmented. One enterprise contracts with another to provide the raw material, and with another to install the equipment that it manufactures. This lowers the cost of labor and reduces demands about working conditions, destructures trade unionism, and paves the way for neoslavery.

The wave of privatization also reaches into hearts and minds. This is a time of prosperity for churches and sects that privatize the Christian faith, stripped (supposedly) of all social or political expression. Simple public concessions, like radio stations and television channels, are treated by their directors as if they were their private property, and they even complain when the state requests time to address the nation. Given the prevailing impunity, there are some who privatize law and justice after their own fashion, lynching suspicious persons, massacring prisoners, or exterminating children.

From the time Cain crushed his brother Abel, the history of humanity shows that the more wealth is privatized, the more misery is socialized. Death, by its nature, is a private experience. Love, on the contrary, always demands sharing and communion.

In Search of Utopia

Postmodernism, inspired by the neoliberal wave that is destroying the planet, is fashionable in esthetics and lifestyle. It is the culture of evading reality. In fact, we are not happy with inflation or with our daughter who spends more on pills to lose weight than on books; and we are profoundly troubled to know that in this country impunity is more powerful than the law. Even so, we are not hopeful of change. We retreat from the social to the private. We have torn up the old banners of our ideals and transformed them into dotted neckties. There are no more utopias of a distant future. Nowadays, it is considered politically incorrect to propound the thesis that we may attain a society in which all will have equal rights and opportunities.

Nevertheless, melancholy weighs on our spirits. We smile skeptically and we can't stand to listen to speeches. Though they may please the eye, we do not believe the ads we look at. All that interests us is improving our interpersonal relations and the comfortable nests we live in. We lead lives of simulation even when we appear to enjoy ourselves, entertain, or love. The television series is an illusion, a lie, yet is more real and consistent than our lives, corroded as they are by disenchantment; disillusionment pervades the essence of the few values we hold.

Today the ephemeral, the individual, the subjective, and the esthetic predominate. What analysis of reality foresaw the return of Russia to a class-based society? We are content to capture fragments of the real (and to accept that knowledge is a collective construct). Our knowing process is characterized by indeterminacy, discontinuity, and pluralism. Our distrust of reason throws us into the realm of the esoteric, into the spiritualism of immediate consumption, consumer hedonism, a progressive *Miamization* of habits and customs. We are in a state of shipwreck or, as Heidegger foresaw, journeying down lost paths.

This time of shadows and impasses leaves a vacuum that is immediately occupied by adverse forces in social life as well. There would be no drug traffickers if there were not addicts with hearts broken by lack of affection and lack of a future, with no prospect of securing a professional training, with minds atrophied by a poor education and a lack of affordable books and art. But when the government of a country refuses to fund education adequately, pays teachers badly, and does not require that television—a public concession—contribute to raising the cultural level of a nation, then we must not be surprised when for this disinherited generation the lines separating bandits and police, corruption and professional activity, and the right to life and the risk of death have become blurred.

Without the recovery of ethics, citizenship, and liberating hopes, and of a state that is willing to defend the interests of the majority, there will be no other justice than the justice that the strongest obtains by snatching it.

Culture Reduced to Simple Entertainment

Under the electronic avalanche that reduces happiness to consumption, we enter two blind alleys. The first is mimicry. What is good for the United States is good for Brazil and the other Latin American countries, with the exception of Cuba. Our culture has been reduced to simple entertainment for people who surround themselves with the paraphernalia displayed in the windows of our shopping centers. Swiftly we cover the trajectory that leads from physical beauty to the public display of cellular phones, from the summer house to the imported car, never considering that we owe a debt to society. We enter the second blind alley that leads to ethnic tension, religious fanaticism, vociferous chauvinism, and an intolerance that insists on ignoring pluralism and democracy, viewed not only as equality of rights and opportunity but as the right to be different.

Exposed to the electronic media that offer us happiness in flasks of perfume and soft drinks, joy in boxes of cigars and tin cans, we have no need for Santa Claus nor time to enjoy infancy. We have lost the capacity to dream, and in return we have only gained emptiness, perplexity, and the loss of identity. Happiness, we find, taken in chemical doses is more accessible than taking the difficult road of educating the personality. We commercialize the marriage relation, kinship ties, and friendship. In this game, as in American movies, you get killed if you're not always alert and shamelessly cruel.

There is hope only for those who believe that this deluge cannot drown all dreams; for those who dare navigate—no matter how weak the winds—on the wings of solidarity with the excluded in the struggle for justice, the cultivation of ethical sense, the defense of human rights, and the tireless search for a world without frontiers between the rich and the oppressed. But that is another story that demands much faith and a certain dose of courage.

21

~

LATIN AMERICAN WOMEN,
PAST AND PRESENT:
THE STRUGGLE FOR EQUALITY
AND SOCIAL JUSTICE

THE STRUGGLE OF Latin American women against the Hispanic tradition of the patriarchal family and its ideology of machismo—the cult of male superiority—and its corollary of a sexual double standard is acquiring new relevance and importance in a time of profound transformation of the Latin American economy and society. Before the European conquest, most Indian societies were marked by a high degree of gender equality, with women's activities viewed as complementing those of men. In Inca society, for example, weaving and spinning were regarded as peculiarly women's work, and plowing and bearing arms as the special tasks of men. But these activities were viewed as having equal importance. The growth of militarism and the state in advanced societies like the Aztec and the Inca, however, led to a decline in women's status. The Aztec "speeches of the elders" warn the wife that "your obligation is to obey your husband. You are to make the beverage, the food for him, and his shirt, his cape, his breeches." Aztec women also worked as doctors, artisans, merchants, and priests.

The Hispanic conquerors introduced their own system of male domination, expressed in the customary right of fathers to arrange marriages for their daughters and in a double standard of sexual morality that demanded strict chastity or fidelity from wives and daughters but not husbands and sons. But we know that many colonial Hispanic women disregarded conventional morality and church laws by engaging in premarital and extramarital sex. The economic, social, and physical subordination of colonial women to

455

men was to some extent limited by the Hispanic property law, which required equal division of estates among heirs and gave women the right to control their dowries and inheritances during and beyond marriage. Some Hispanic women operated as entrepreneurs independently of their husbands and many managed a husband's business after his death. However, Indian women (with the exception of a favored elite group) suffered severe loss of status as a result of the Hispanic hierarchical system, which viewed the Indians as an inferior race (*gente sin razón*); during and after the Conquest Indian women were frequently subjected to rape and other forms of abuse. Despite the damaging impact of Hispanic patriarchal and hierarchical relations, Indian women were not passive victims. They had economic importance as producers and traders of goods, owned property in their own right, litigated, countered male abuse with a variety of strategies, and played leading roles in organizing resistance to Spanish measures that threatened their communities. Thus Indian and mestizo women played important military roles in the great 1780–1781 revolt of Tupac Amaru against Spanish rule in Peru.

The coming of Latin American independence in the 1820s did not better the status of women. Indeed, their civil status probably worsened as a result of new bourgeois-style law codes that strengthened a husband's control over his wife's property. The democratic, liberal movements of the first half century after independence did stimulate some developments in favor of women. In Argentina, Sarmiento wrote that "the level of civilization of a people can be judged by the social position of its women," and in both Argentina and Mexico there arose normal schools for the training of women primary school teachers. In a number of countries after 1870 there arose small feminist movements, largely composed of schoolteachers, that formed societies, edited journals, and worked for the cultural, economic, and social improvement of women. In the last decades of the century, with the development of industry, women in increasing numbers entered factories and sweatshops, where they were often paid half of what male workers earned and became a source of superprofits for capitalist employers.

In the first half of the twentieth century the struggle for women's rights gained a new momentum, in part as a result of the Mexican Revolution of 1910 and such modernizing reformist movements of the 1930s and 1940s as those led by Lázaro Cárdenas in Mexico, Juan Perón in Argentina, and Getúlio Vargas in Brazil. Women actively participated in these movements and sought the inclusion of women's rights in their reform programs. More recently, ever growing numbers of women have entered the labor force, driven by the frequent unemployment of male partners or the difficulty of supporting a family on one wage. This development has introduced new strains into Latin American family life and has sharpened demands for social legislation to protect working women and their children. The participation of many women, sometimes in leading roles, in armed struggles like the Nicaraguan and Salvadoran Revolutions, has also given new impetus to the growth of Latin American feminism. Its program has broadened far beyond the initial stress on voting rights and education to include sexual rights and a variety of other demands. The expansion of women's activities has enlarged their world, given them a new self-confidence, and hardened their determination to never again be relegated to their traditional domains—kitchen, children, and the church. In response to the negative impact of economic neoliberalism and globalization on the lives of most Latin American women and their families, the feminist movement is increasingly allying itself with leftist parties and trade unions to struggle against those economic policies. In turn, it is asking them to include feminist issues like women's reproductive health and sexual rights in their programs.

As the year 2000 approached, Latin American feminism could point to some gains, most obviously, achieving the right to vote in all Latin American states and obtaining passage of protective social legislation for women (not always enforced). But the goal of ending the old unequal relations between the sexes is far from being realized. Machismo still flourishes in most Latin American countries, and great income disparities between the sexes remain, with most women employed in unskilled, low-income jobs. Socialist Cuba has made the greatest progress in these and other areas (see selection 3 in Chapter 20) and is still the only Latin American country that provides abortion on demand.

1. AN AZTEC MOTHER ADVISES HER DAUGHTER

On the eve of the Spanish Conquest the simpler Indian societies (tribes and bands) were typically characterized by gender equality and male–female complementarity, which recognized the equal importance of the special tasks performed by men and women. The situation with respect to the more complex, class-structured societies like the Aztec, Inca, and Maya is another matter. In these societies the rise of militarism and a warrior class to which women had no access had eroded women's status to a significant degree. Some historians argue that Aztec male–female complementarity was maintained by symbolic means that equated giving birth with capturing a prisoner, dying in childbirth with being captured or killed in battle. A man's success in battle corresponded to the care that a woman took of his household. Aztec women were active in a wide variety of professions ranging from priest and doctor to sorcerer and prostitute. But Aztec sources and Spanish accounts based on them make clear that patriarchal family relations existed in Aztec society. This is evident from the "speeches of the ancients," passed on by memory from generation to generation, in which Aztec elders counseled the young. The following excerpt reveals some tampering by pious hands that substituted the Christian God for the Aztec supreme divinity, but it provides a sense of the coloring of Aztec speech and offers insight into Aztec social and family relations. It also points up an apparent contradiction in Aztec civilization: The "Assyrians of America," whose plunder empire rested on the foundations of war and human sacrifice, advised their children in speeches that are full of tender affection and precepts of charity and fair dealing.

My daughter: I bore you and have taught you good breeding and good order, and your father has honored you. If you are not what you should be, you may not live with good and virtuous women; nor will any man take you for wife.

Hardship and suffering are our lot in this world, and our powers daily waste away. We must serve God, that He may aid us and give us health; we must live with diligence and care to obtain our needs.

See to it, then, beloved daughter, that you are not careless or lazy. Be cleanly and diligent, and look after the house and keep all in order as it should be, each thing in its place. Thus will you learn what you must do in your house when you marry.

Wherever you go, go with great modesty. Do not hurry or laugh as you walk, and do not glance about, either at those coming toward you or at any other, but go your way; and thus will you gain honor and good name.

See that you are well behaved and speak soberly; reply civilly to any who question you.

Perform your household duties, weave and embroider; and so you will be well beloved and will merit the food and clothing you receive. In this labor you will find comfort and will thank God that he fitted you for it.

Give yourself not to sleeping, to the bed, to laziness. Do not be used to sitting in the fresh cool shade; for this teaches sloth and vice, and with such a habit one does not live well or decorously. Women who give themselves over to it are not loved.

Whether seated or standing, walking or working, my daughter, always think good thoughts and work well; and do what you must do to serve God and your parents.

If you are called, do not wait to be called a second time, but go promptly to do what you are ordered to do, to avoid giving offense or making it necessary to punish you for your sloth and disobedience. Listen well to what you are ordered to do, and do not give a rude reply. If you cannot do what is asked of you, make your excuses civilly, but do not lie or deceive anyone; for God sees you.

If another is called and she does not promptly respond, do you go diligently and hear and do what that one had to do; and thus will you be loved.

If someone offers you good counsel, take it; do not reject it, lest that person grow angry with you and hold you in scorn.

Alonso de Zorita, *Life and Labor in Ancient Mexico,* translated and edited by Benjamin Keen, Rutgers University Press, 1963, pp. 148–151.

Walk modestly and quietly, not in such a way that men will think you giddy.

Be charitable; do not scorn or hate others; and be not avaricious.

Do not assign a bad sense to the words of others; do not envy the good that God was pleased to do to others.

Do not cause others hardship or suffering; for thereby you will bring the same on yourself.

Do not do evil; and do not follow the promptings of your heart; for thereby you will make yourself evil and will ensnare yourself to your own hurt.

Do not keep company with women who lie, or are lazy, or gad about, not with low women, lest you harm yourself. Attend to your housework, and do not frivolously leave your house. Do not frequent the market place, or the public squares or baths; for this is very bad and leads to perdition and harm. And one who follows evil courses finds it difficult to give them up; for evil inspires evil desires.

If a man speaks to you, do not believe him and do not look at him; be quiet and pay no attention to him. If he follows you, do not reply to him, lest your speech trouble his heart; and if you take no heed of him, he will stop following you.

Do not enter a stranger's house without cause, lest he bring some charge against you.

If you enter the house of relatives, show respect to them and be not lazy; do what you see is fitting for you to do, and do not simply look at the women who are working.

When your parents give you a husband, do not be disrespectful to him; listen to him and obey him, and do cheerfully what you are told. Do not turn your face from him; and if he did you some hurt, do not keep recalling it. And if he supports himself by your industry, do not on that account scorn him, or be peevish or ungracious; for you will offend God, and your husband will be angry with you. Tell him meekly what you think should be done. Do not insult him or say offensive words to him in front of strangers or even to him alone; for you will harm yourself thereby, and yours will be the fault.

If someone visits your husband, thank him for coming, and do him some service. If your husband is disabled, you must show him how he is to live; and you must take care of the household, and secure persons to work your fields and store the harvest; and you must not be negligent in anything.

Do not waste your estate, but aid your husband; and you will obtain what you need for yourselves and your children.

My daughter, if you do what I have told you, all will love and esteem you. I have complied with my duty as a mother. If you take my advice, you will live happily; if you do not, the fault will be yours, and the future will show you the results of not heeding this advice. It shall never be said that I failed to advise you as a mother.

2. A HEROINE OF
THE TUPAC AMARU REVOLT

Indian and mestizo women played distinguished military roles in the 1780–1781 Tupac Amaru uprising in Peru, the greatest in the wave of native revolts that shook the Spanish empire in the last decades of the eighteenth century. The rebel leader's wife, Micaela, served as his principal adviser from the beginning, and in his absence assumed full direction of the movement. After an initial victory over a small Spanish force sent from Cuzco, she strongly advised an immediate advance on the city, taking advantage of the chaos and panic that reigned there. The capture of Cuzco, ancient capital of the Inca empire and center of Spanish power in the Andean highlands, would have been a stroke of the greatest moral and military significance. Tupac Amaru decided instead to invade the provinces to the south, promising to return immediately and advance on Cuzco—a promise he failed to keep. By the time he returned, Spanish reinforcements had reached Cuzco from Lima and the golden opportunity had vanished. The bitterness of Micaela's letter to Tupac Amaru reflects her appreciation of the immensity of his blunder. Despite her harsh approaches, her letters to Tupac Amaru "contain notes of profound and laconic tenderness" ("Chepe" was an affectionate nickname for her husband).

Dear Chepe:

You are causing me mortal concern. While you saunter through the villages, wasting two days in Yauri, showing no sense of urgency, our soldiers are rightly becoming bored, and are leaving for their homes.

I simply cannot endure all this any longer, and I am ready to give myself up to the Spaniards and let them take my life when I see how lightly you regard this serious matter that threatens the lives of all of us. We are surrounded by enemies and constantly insecure; and on your account the lives of all my sons, and of all our people, are in danger.

I have warned you again and again not to dally in those villages, where there is nothing to do—but you continue to saunter, ignoring the fact that the soldiers are running short of food. They are receiving their pay, but the money will not last forever. Then they will all depart, leaving us to pay with our lives, because you must have learned by this time that they came only for reasons of self-interest, and to get all they could out of us. They are already beginning to desert; they are frightened by the rumor spread by Vargas and Oré that the Spaniards of Lampa, united with those of other provinces and Arequipa, are going to surround you, and so they want to get away, fearing the punishment that might befall them. Thus we will lose all the people that I have gotten to-

Micaela Bastidas to José Gabriel Tupac Amaru, December 6, 1780, in Francisco A. Loayza, ed., *Martires y heroinas*, Lima, 1945, pp. 48–51. Cited in Benjamin Keen, ed., *Readings in Latin American Civilization, 1492 to the Present*, Houghton Mifflin, Boston, 1955, p. 175. (Translated by the editor.)

gether for the descent on Cuzco, and the forces at Cuzco will unite with the soldiers from Lima, who have been on the march for many days.

I must tell you all this, though it pains me. If you want to ruin us, continue to sleep and commit such follies as that of passing along through the streets of Yauri, and even climbing to the church tower—actions certainly out of place at this time, and that only dishonor you and gain you disrespect.

I believed that you were occupied day and night with arranging these affairs, instead of showing an unconcern that robs me of my life. I am already a shadow of myself and beside myself with anxiety, and so I beg you to get on with this business.

You made me a promise, but henceforth I shall not heed your promises, for you did not keep your word.

I do not care for my life, but for the lives of my poor children, who need all my help. If the enemy comes from Paruro, as I suggested in my last letter, I am prepared to march to meet them, leaving Fernando in a secure place, for the Indians are not capable of acting by themselves in these perilous times.

I gave you plenty of warnings to march immediately on Cuzco, but you took them all lightly, giving the Spaniards time to prepare as they have done, placing cannon on Picchu Mountain, and devising other measures so dangerous that you are no longer in a position to attack them. God keep you many years. Tungasuca, December 6, 1780.

I must also tell you that the Indians of Quispicanchi are tired of serving as guards so long a time. In fine, God must want me to suffer for my sins. Your wife.

After I had finished this letter, a messenger arrived with the definite news that the enemy from Paruro is in Acos; I am going forward to attack them, even if it costs me my life.

3. A Colombian Aristocrat Advises His Daughter

Independence did not bring freedom from male domination for Latin American women; indeed, their dependency on fathers and husbands probably increased. Church and parents taught women to be sweetly submissive, having no will of their own. Typical of the patriarchal attitudes that prevailed in the mid-nineteenth century with regard to relations between husband and wife is the advice that Mariano Ospina Rodríguez gave in a letter (October 21, 1864) to his daughter María on the eve of her marriage to José Mariano Roma y Batres.

Cited in Alberto Saladino García, "La función social de las mujeres entre los liberales latinoamericanos," *Siglo XIX*, Año 1, numero 2, julio-diciembre 1986, pp. 181–183. (Excerpt translated by the editor.)

Dear Daughter:

Tomorrow you will enter on a new stage of your life, one that must continue until death. In this new existence to which God calls you, your happiness will depend principally on your conduct, even in the most insignificant acts. Your happiness depends ... on the sincere and constant practice of these modest virtues: humility, patience, resignation, abnegation, and ... the proper conduct of the domestic relations that depend on those same Christian virtues.

From now on the most important and interesting person in your life, the primary object of all your attentions, cares, and concerns is your husband.... Your husband is your lover, your best friend, your protector, your companion on the voyage of life, and these conditions produce relations and obligations that will occupy every moment of your life. One of your first concerns will be to study your husband's inclinations, habits, and tastes, so that you may never contradict them. Never try to impose your will or ask him to sacrifice his habits or tastes, no matter how insignificant; on the contrary, act in such a way that he may continue them without interruption.

Frequently it may happen that you and he have different habits and tastes; never hesitate for a moment to sacrifice your own.... Do not say a word if you feel offended; retire from the scene, if at all possible, and in a few minutes you will feel the satisfaction of knowing that you have mastered yourself and avoided a dispute that could cause a long resentment.... Never argue with your husband, whatever the reason.... If you feel that your anger is about to burst out, remember your father, imagine that he stands before you, his heart full of painful reflections ... and that with his finger on his lips he is saying to you: "Silence."

4. FLORA TRISTAN:
PIONEER FEMINIST AND SOCIALIST

Not all upper- or middle-class Latin American women in the nineteenth century obeyed the conventions or rules of conduct propounded by the conservative father in the last selection. One rebel against such rules was Flora Tristan (1803–1844), daughter of a Peruvian aristocratic landowner and officer and a French mother. Her short, stormy life has recently drawn increasing attention from students of the early history of feminism and socialism. Although she spent most of her life in France, she is regarded by Peruvian feminists and leftists as one of their own. A woman of striking beauty, she separated early on from her husband and became active in French feminist and socialist circles about 1835. In 1835 she published a novel, Méphis, *which proposed the transformation of society according to feminist and socialist principles, and in 1840* Promenades in London, *a description of the monstrous contrasts between wealth and poverty in the English metropolis. In her last book,* The Workers' Union *(1844), she called for "the working men and women of the world"* to unite, anticipating by four years Marx's appeal in The Communist Manifesto. *Her writings are dotted with other striking statements: "The most oppressed male can oppress another human being who is his own wife. Woman is the proletariat of the proletariat." And "the liberation of women is the necessary condition for the liberation of men." In her* Promenades in London *she describes the vast extent of prostitution in the city and reflects on its causes.*

Prostitution is the most horrible plague produced by the unequal distribution of goods in this world. This infamy withers mankind and is a greater assault on society than crime.

Prejudice, misery, and slavery combine their disastrous effects to produce this appalling degradation. If women were not persuaded that chastity is a virtue—a virtue that is not obligatory for men—society would not reject them for having yielded to the feelings of their hearts, and women who are seduced, deceived, and abandoned would not be reduced to prostitution. If women were permitted to have the same education and engage in the same employments and professions as men, they would not be more prone than men to live in misery. If women were not exposed to all the abuses of power by the despotism of *patria potestas* [the father's complete control over his family] and the indissoluble nature of marriage, they would not always have to choose between the alternative of suffering oppression or infamy.

Virtue or vice assume the freedom to do good or evil, but what can be the morality of a woman who is not mistress of herself, has no means of her own, and whose whole life has prepared her to either escape from a man's arbitrary conduct by use of her wits or be coerced by seduction? And when she is tortured by misery, when she sees that men enjoy all the good things of life, will not the art of pleasing in which she has been educated lead her inevitably to prostitution?

It follows that society is to blame for this monstrosity and that women must be absolved of it. As long as women are subject to the yoke of men or prejudice, as long as they do not receive the most minimum professional education and are deprived of their civil rights, no moral law can exist for them. As long as they can only have access to possessions by appealing to the passions of men, as long as they cannot have title to anything and can be despoiled by their husbands of the property they acquired by their labor or by inheritance from their fathers, as long as they can only be secure in their possessions or liberty by being celibate, no moral law exists for them. It can be said that until women are emancipated, prostitution will continue to grow.

Flora Tristan, *Ensayos escogidos. Prólogo y selicción: Eduardo Nuñez*, Ediciones Persa, Lima, 1974, pp. 157–159. (Excerpt translated by the editor.)

5. OF MAN, WOMAN, AND TIME

In the first half of the twentieth century Latin American women made some strides to-ward emancipation from political, economic, and legal disabilities. Their struggle to gain the vote began around 1914 and ended successfully when Paraguay finally granted women suffrage in 1961. A pioneer in that struggle was the Chilean Amanda Labarca. In 1922 she became the first woman professor at the University of Chile and in 1931 was named director of secondary education, the highest post ever attained by a woman at that time. In a book published in 1934 she reflected on the gains and the losses in the struggle for women's liberation.

Progress is as tortuous as the advance of the tide. An inviting beach beck-ons it inland; a rocky shore detains it. So it has been with the wave of femi-nism. Great Britain, Scandinavia, the Soviet Republics, North America, have incorporated its theses—once regarded as so daring—in their daily life. France and many of the Latin countries only tolerate it in their mental diet, without having fully digested it; and doubtless in more than one secluded val-ley of the Cauca or the Amur one can still live pleasantly under the omnipo-tent rod of the patriarchal master. What is true of the horizontal of geogra-phy is also true of the vertical of social classes. Conduct that the aristocracy regards as scandalously emancipated is an imperative not even discussed in the classes that live under the lash of poverty. And for the Latin girl of the middle class it is often a tragicomedy.

The first theorists of feminism paid dearly for their apostolate. They con-soled themselves, in part, by reflecting that the sorrows they endured would help to fill the cup of happiness of the future. Has their hope been realized? Or, after the solution of certain problems, have not other, unforeseen prob-lems arisen, perhaps more difficult than the old ones? Has not that cup of happiness been dearly paid for? Has feminism brought gains or losses to the Latin-American middle-class girl of today?

Gains. First of all, the consciousness of her own worth in the totality of hu-man progress. Today's girl knows that there are no insurmountable obstacles to the flight of her intelligence; that the question of whether her entire sex is intelligent will not be raised before she is permitted to engage in any intellec-tual activity; that in the eyes of the majority her womanhood does not mark her with the stigma of irremediable inferiority, and that if she has talent she will be allowed to display it.

Amanda Labarca Hubertson. ¿A dónde va la mujer? Santiago de Chile. 1934, pp. 241–247. (Excerpt translated by the editor.)

The law codes have returned to her, in large part, control over her life and property. She has well-founded hopes of seeing abolished within her lifetime the laws that still relegate her, in certain aspects, to the position of a second-class citizen, and that accord her unequal legal treatment.

She has made progress in economic liberty, basis of all independence, whether it be a question of a simple individual or one of nations. Today she is gaining admission into fields of labor forbidden to her mother.

Before her extends an unbounded horizon of opportunities. Hopes! She can live her years of illusions imagining—like every adolescent male—that the whole world awaits her, and that only her own limitations can prevent her from ascending the highest peaks of this world.

She has won liberty, including—it may seem ridiculous to mention it—the liberty of going about without papa or the classic brother at her side. To be sure, I do not speak of a nineteen-year-old Amy Johnson, who cleaves the air in a fantastic flight, without other pilot or mechanic than her youth, her skill, and valor, from England to remote Australia, in a secondhand plane that any established ace would have scorned as useless.

She has lost, in the first place, the respect of the male majority. One might say that formerly consideration for women formed part of good breeding, and it was denied only to one who by her conduct showed that she did not merit it. Today it is the other way around. In general, woman receives no tribute, and she must prove convincingly that she is a distinguished personage before receiving the homage that once was common.

Which has diminished—the respect or the quality of respectability?

It is worth one's while to analyze the point.

Men used to expect of women a stainless virtue, perfect submission—after God, thy husband, orders the epistle of St. Paul—and a life-long devotion to the orbit in which her man revolved. A saint in the vaulted niche of her home, saint to the world, mistress of her four walls, and slave to her man. In exchange for this—respect and devotion. True, the father or husband sometimes played the role of sacristan to the saint. They allowed no one to fail to reverence her, but they themselves took liberties and even mistreated her— conduct that the saint had to bear with resignation … she had no recourse. It is also true that there are personalities that break all shackles, and that, with or without laws, ever since the world began there have been women who with the rosy point of a little finger, or armed with a gossamer web, have governed husband, children, home, and estate as they willed. But we are not concerned with male or female exceptions.

It is unnecessary to refer again to the upheavals that the invention of machinery brought to the world, the sharp rise in the cost of living and the pauperization of the household, which from producer was reduced to being a simple consumer. It became impossible for a man of average means to satisfy the needs of all his womenfolk, and women had to enter offices, the professions, and other remunerative employment that had been men's traditional source of income. Woman has gone out into the world, and although this fact in itself is an economic imperative and does not essentially imply the abandonment of any virtue, the ordinary man has denied her his respect. As if it were not much more difficult, and consequently more meritorious, to preserve one's purity, sweetness, and delicacy amid the turmoil of the world than in the secluded garden of the old-time home!

On entering the economic struggle she rubs shoulders with misery. Yesterday she only knew of it by hearsay. Today it bespatters her. The rawness of life surrounds her. Often she must solve the problem of staying in the path of rectitude without the help of, or even defending herself from, the man who is ready to exploit any of her weaknesses. For the ordinary man, woman's freedom is license: her equality, the right to treat her without courtesy.

She has lost in opportunities for marriage, for establishing a household, and for satisfying that yearning for maternity that is her fundamental instinct. The more cultured a woman, the more difficult for her to find a husband, because it is normal for her to seek refuge, understanding, and guidance in a person superior to herself. And the latter do not always prefer cultured women. They imagine that knowledge makes them unfeeling—an absurd notion—that it makes them domineering—which concerns not acquired knowledge but character—or that it makes them insufferably pedantic. I regret to say that here they have a little justice on their side. Knowledge is such a recent attainment of women that the majority make an excessive show of it. We play the role of the *nouveaux-riches* of the world of culture. For their wives men prefer the "old-fashioned" girl.

That is the pathos of the tragedy of middle-class women in the Latin countries. Evolution has taken place in opposition to the fundamental convictions of men, who only tolerate it—in the case of their daughters, for example— because imperious necessity dictates it, and only with profound chagrin. Men—I repeat that I speak of the majority—continue to judge women from the viewpoint of fifty years ago, and if they retain some respect and esteem in their inner beings, they tender it to the woman who remained faithful to the classic type—the woman who has progressed they place very close to those for whom they have no respect.

Men cannot understand that external conditions—culture, profession, liberty—have not radically transformed the classic femininity, the maternal instincts, the impulses of the sweet Samaritan, the yearnings of a noble spirituality. The cases of this kind that he knows about do not convince him; he imagines that they constitute exceptions.

Nor are men of more advanced ideas free from this attitude. And it would be amusing—if it did not have tragic implications—to observe what a socialist, a radical, a communist, proclaims on the public platform and what he praises in the intimacy of his home.

Man and woman. Feared and beloved master; slave, sweetly or tyrannically subjugated; wall and ivy. Today divergent and almost hostile, but not comrades. Woman and man cannot yet be comrades, save in an infinitely small number of cases. The relationship of comrades implies equality, confidence, and the same criteria for judging each other.

"But if she acknowledges her bitter lot, why not turn back?" more than one naive soul asks. Impossible. Time does not turn back. The sharp point of its whirling lance moves on, heedless of shattered lives. New social theories will solve these problems and create new ones on the way to an inscrutable future that human faith—a flame that wavers but that only death can extinguish—imagines must be a better one.

Meanwhile, sisters, let us not preach feminism to women; let us win over the men, in the hope that our daughters may pay less dearly for their cup of happiness.

6. A NEW FEMINISM

Globalization and neoliberalism have had a devastating effect on the living standard of Latin American working people and middle-class people. Consequently, many feminist activists have drawn closer to the trade union movement, the first line of defense against the assaults of foreign and domestic capital on popular interests. Brazilian Mary García Castro, professor of sociology at the Federal University of Bahia, describes the rise of a "working class feminism" that unites women within feminist organizations and labor unions in the forging of a feminist politics that incorporates class and gender perspectives.

In recent years a political practice that is embedded firmly in both class politics and the feminist movement has emerged in Brazil. It has links to some feminist organizations, labor unions and parties on the left, and insists on the importance of the feminist transformation of leftist political parties and labor unions from the inside. It is critical of the free market, and does not reject the use of multiple forms of struggle. There is no doubt that this class-based feminism has benefited greatly from the ideas and the gains of the larger feminist movement. It has incorporated feminist understandings of the public and private spheres into its discourses about working women, demanded the inclusion of issues such as reproductive health and sexual rights in discussions about women in the workplace, instituted training courses on gender issues for both men and women within labor unions and political par-

Mary García Castro, "The Rise of Working Class Feminism in Brazil," *NACLA Report on the Americas*, vol. 32, no. 4, January-February 1999, pp. 28–32. Translated from the Spanish by Marcial Godoy-Anativia. Reprinted by permission of *NACLA Report on the Americas*. The notes that appeared in the original publication have been omitted here.

ties, and fought to make leadership positions as well as political education accessible to women activists.

The engagement of labor-movement and community-based feminists in these activities suggests that they have not abandoned the class-based perspectives embedded in the revolutionary politics of years past. Not only are they constructing a feminist politics which actively draws from perspectives of class, gender and increasingly of race, but they are exerting a powerful influence on the broader feminist movement. Autonomous transnational feminist networks now address many of the issues of concern to the labor-based feminists, though without any concern for working-class organization. It is urgent that Brazilian women workers themselves begin to participate in class-based transnational feminist networks.

The rate of unionization among Brazilian women has notably increased in recent years, and the growth in the rate of women's labor-force participation has been dramatic. In the 1970s, the percentage of adult women in the labor force was 20%, but by 1990, the figure surpassed 40%. Many women workers have gained employment in service-sector jobs, often in major multinational corporations. They are also employed in large numbers as household workers. The employment of women in many highly modernized industries like banks and packing plants, as well as the increase in the number of women working in the informal sector, suggests the existence of a combination of traditional and modern forms of work. But despite the growing incorporation of women workers into the institutions of paid employment, there seems to be little change in male-female income inequality, in the sexual division of labor within the household, or in the power relations of gender hierarchies.

Beyond this, the positive trends have developed alongside rising unemployment rates, growing job insecurity within increasingly flexible labor markets, attacks on the gains of the labor movement and a dramatic rise in job-related illness. In other words, while there have been substantial political gains, this has not mitigated the adverse effects of a neoliberal and increasingly globalized economy on the lives of working-class Brazilian women.

All this suggests that the "issue" of women is not just about granting "citizenship" or "human rights" to women, but also about the need to rethink leftist ideologies and practices. The experience of recent years suggests that the left must incorporate the unemployed and the informal sector as well as those groups organizing around issues like local, ethnic or sexual identity into the classic frameworks of class analysis.

The case of Brazil is particularly significant to this project because in addition to its firm insertion into the neoliberal process of globalization, it is one of the few countries in Latin America where women's issues are accorded a prominent place in political life and official discourse. Through its rhetoric and a series of less-than-effective social programs, the government of Fernando Henrique Cardoso has situated itself as the champion of women and blacks. It has supported antidiscrimination legislation and affirmative action policies at the same time that it has cut funding for public education and eliminated public-sector jobs in social services and local public administration—both major sources of employment for women.

Clearly, the increasing labor-force participation of women cannot be seen only as a gain. The trend is in large part the result of the impoverishment of working families. Low-income married women with children are entering the labor force at a time when services, child care and schools are suffering cutbacks. Older girls within these families are then forced to bear the brunt of child care in the absence of their mothers.

There remain great income disparities between men and women as well as between social groups in Brazil, much of which is accounted for by the distribution of occupations. Women are still concentrated in unskilled, low-wage jobs. Paid housework remains one of the major source of jobs for poor women, particularly black women. In addition, women's employment is highly susceptible to national and international economic fluctuations. The traditional sources of women's jobs such as retail commerce and the service sector were disproportionately affected by the high levels of unemployment between 1990 and 1997. On the other hand, women have increasingly been able to find industrial and manufacturing jobs that in the past were almost exclusively reserved for men. The hiring of women in manufacturing is intensified during economic downturns, when companies try to save on labor costs.

In rural areas, the numbers of women engaged in unpaid labor remains disproportionately high. In 1995, 41% of working women in rural areas were not being paid wages for their labor, in contrast to 21% of men. According to a report published by the National Commission of Rural Working Women of the Confederation of Agricultural Workers (CONTAG) in 1997, women account for 40% of rural labor, working for an average of 15 hours per day.

Many companies have an explicit preference for women workers, particularly in the service sectors of the economy. Close to 50% of bank employees, for example, are women. They tend to be assigned simple and repetitive administrative duties, and despite the fact that they average more years of schooling than their male counterparts, close to 70% of them have low-level filing jobs, are much more closely supervised than the predominantly male tellers, and have fewer opportunities of career advancement. In recent years, however, there has been a growing presence of women in the sale of financial services, a field allowing for somewhat greater autonomy and remuneration. These women are generally expected to work longer hours, which has led to an increase in stress-related illnesses.

Recent investigation has documented a dramatic rise in repetitive stress disorder (RSD) among women in many fields of both paid and unpaid labor. RSD is most prevalent in jobs that involve word processing, data entry and cash-register operation. It is provoked and aggravated by work-related stress and anxiety, and is associated with muscular stress, long work days and the lack of regular rest periods. Close to 80% of workers who suffer from RSD in

Brazil are women, and it is clearly associated with the double burden of a long working day and domestic responsibilities. Public health advocates have warned that RSD is assuming epidemic proportions in Brazil, accounting for almost 70% of disabilities due to occupational illness.

Women who work in stressful service jobs, however, are not always critical of their working conditions. The combination of a socialized sense of responsibility and the desperation for employment seems, in fact, to have bonded many women workers with their employers. Research in São Paulo's largest banks has found a high degree of company identification and an acceptance of gender-based roles within the workplace. A woman branch manager told an interviewer that "women are better at sales because people often repress their emotions, and women are more sensitive. They know if the client is sad or anxious. One can't treat all customers in the same way. Women are better able to communicate; to convince customers; to reel them in."

New models of workplace organization implemented by business elites are meant to appeal to this sensibility by emphasizing participation, "moral satisfaction," the analogy between the factory and the family, communication, cooperation and leadership based on professional authority rather than hierarchical control. Far from instilling any sort of worker solidarity, however, this new language of production is intended to encourage competition among employees in order to increase productivity, and to discourage anything which might disrupt the relationship with management. Within this model, union organization and collective bargaining are replaced by direct and individual negotiation.

In an essay about industrial development in Brazil, sociologist Magda Neves documents the implementation of Japanese models of workplace organization through which "a controlled and coercive form of participation is imposed which seeks to achieve the maximum level of consensus through a complete partnership between management and the workers." Jobs in this sector are relatively stable and offer benefits which are attractive to many workers. Neves points out that this "new rationality" appeals to workers on two levels. "The first is the emphasis on quality production, which through quality control or discourses of 'total quality,' seeks to invest the worker with a sense of responsibility, creativity and decision-making powers. The second seeks to shape the attitudes of workers by appealing to values of cooperation, integration and self-esteem." The bitter irony is that these values, now at the service of profit-making firms, have historically been part of the emancipatory discourse of movements like socialism and feminism.

Over the past decade, women activists have successfully placed gender issues on the agendas of the most powerful labor organizations in Brazil. Women's departments have been created in many locals, and in 1986 the National Women Workers' Commission (CNMT) was created within the Unified Workers' Federation (CUT). This commission has approved measures to force employers to recognize maternity rights, and has implemented campaigns against gender-based discrimination, violence and sexual harassment in the workplace. In addition, the CUT has approved a quota system to assure women leadership positions within union structures and has recognized domestic workers' organizations. The federation has also worked to change the male-oriented nature of traditional labor organizing.

Feminist labor organizers have made gender relations among their male comrades a focal point of their efforts. The goal is to change the traditional union attitudes which reward standard male behavior, such as speaking loudly at meetings, and which fail to recognize how women's domestic obligations limit the extent of their union participation. CONTAG, one of the biggest union confederations of Latin America, made a significant symbolic gesture by referring to its big March 1998 policy meeting as the "Seventh National Congress of Men and Women Rural Workers," formally recognizing that labor is not only the domain of men.

But these are small, initial steps. "It is not enough to be revolutionary during elections and to call on women to come out and participate in events," says Patricia, a member of the directorate of the Department of Women of the Union of Bank Employees in Bahia, who is also a member of the Communist Party of Brazil and the Union of Brazilian Women. "It is also not enough to include a paragraph about women's rights in all political speeches as is currently in vogue. We have opened up a discussion about gender among men and women, and we are sponsoring several debates about sexual harassment, even within labor unions."

At CUT events, child care is always provided. In the Union of Bank Employees in Bahia, as a result of a 1993 initiative of its Women's Department, members have openly debated a number of controversial issues such as homophobia among workers. Issues like women's double workday, sexuality and affection are actively debated in the union. In the 1990s, women's organizations within unions even spread to other political arenas, including some which have long been considered difficult to organize. There are domestic workers' unions throughout Brazil. In many states, as is the case in Bahia, domestic-worker organizers are also active militants in black social movements. According to CONTAG, women now compose 22% of the nine million union members in rural areas, more than half of whom became involved after 1985. And women's centers have sprouted within the organizations of landless workers in various states, particularly in the context of leadership training.

"We are like society," says Valdirene de Oliveira, a 24-year-old Landless Movement (MST) leader in Matto Grosso, "and society is comprised of all kinds of people. Male dominance is strong, something that begins by educating boys to be macho. We will achieve equality by educating men and women within the Movement. Before, women stayed in the kitchen, but we are becoming more involved in everything, in land invasions, in meetings, and we also want to discuss health, rights and our relationships with men."

Valdirene, who followed her parents into the movement at age 15, sees the struggle for women's rights as "part of the class struggle," and this is a growing sentiment within the MST. "The issue of the ownership of land," she says, "attracts women's attention within the Movement, and we are fighting to recognize women's land ownership rights, along with legal rights to benefit from land. On the other hand, we have to work harder to equalize relationships within the family, because many times a woman signs a land deed because her husband insists. This kind of pressure often exists within the family. By beginning with issues like land, we can address others, like domestic violence, AIDS prevention, and the relationships between men and women."

Not all feminists, of course, even class-based feminists, agree completely with Valdirene's perspective. Women in CONTAG and in the Rural Women's Movement (MMTR), for example, while strongly supporting the struggle for land, consider that not all issues are class issues, and that there are conflicts between women and men that go beyond class-based identities. Nonetheless, the implementation of quotas for women's leadership is a real achievement, and all feminists agree that the fight for affirmative action laws and policies that guarantee the rights of women workers must continue.

In spite of the gains made by feminists within labor organizations and the increase of women's labor organizing, however, union members recognize that a daunting problem still faced by women workers is the lack of job stability in an increasingly insecure and flexible labor market. Trade unionists and leftist activists have recognized that strategies to confront gender- and race-based inequalities must not be limited to the institutions of the labor movement itself. Labor organizations must confront the reorganization of work, including the implementation of technologies which make workers redundant. Feminists and political parties linked to unions must also begin to forcefully counter the neoliberal attacks on workers in the name of productivity and modernization.

Meanwhile, Brazil's class-based feminism can be found in unions, in leftist political groups and in struggles that are armed when necessary, such as the landless movement. This women's movement challenges the contention that women should abandon the revolutionary project of creating a classless society. Instead, it advances a radical feminist project to eliminate a multitude of oppressions.

22

◆

THE TWO AMERICAS

A FEELING of great admiration dominated the attitude of Latin American leaders toward the United States from the era of independence to the closing years of the nineteenth century. That feeling, explains the Mexican philosopher Leopoldo Zea, "derived from the negative attitude of the Latin American toward his own historical and cultural heritage." But in the case of some, notably among the Mexicans, the sentiment of admiration was tempered by resentment and misgivings about past and prospective territorial losses to the young colossus of the north. Others, like the Chilean Francisco Bilbao, already questioned the North American scale of values, setting Latin love of beauty and the spiritual values against alleged Yankee materialism and egotism.

After 1890 the increasingly aggressive foreign policy of the United States toward some of its southern neighbors rapidly depleted the Latin American reservoir of good will toward the republic of the north. The Yankeemania of Domingo Faustine Sarmiento turned into the Yankeephobia of Manuel Ugarte, Eduardo Prado, and Rufino Blanco Fombona. The transition in attitude was strikingly revealed in the writings of José Marti, epic chronicler of the United States from 1880 to 1895, whose reportage, long favorable to the United States, grew increasingly hostile toward the end of his journalistic career.

Latin American ill will toward the United States, stimulated by many North American acts of intervention, reached a climax in the 1920s. Official awareness of the adverse economic and political effects of this hostility, and pressure from an aroused public in the United States, brought a gradual revision of policy toward Latin America and flowered into the Good Neighbor Policy under the second Roosevelt. Between 1933 and 1945 the old one-sided treaties were abrogated, the right of intervention was completely abandoned, and economic and cultural relations were greatly expanded. The Good Neighbor Policy proved its value during the critical years of World War II.

However, in the years that followed the war, rifts began to appear in the New World Alliance. Dissatisfaction with U.S. foreign economic policy was one source of friction between the erstwhile good neighbors. Latin American leaders resented the position taken by both the Truman and Eisenhower administrations that Latin American developmental loans must be financed for the most part by private capital rather than by intergovernmental loans. A rising wave of nationalism opposed to all foreign-owned enterprises in the area added to the difficulties of the United States in Latin America.

Moreover, many Latin Americans accused the United States of supporting right-wing dictatorial regimes, like those of Trujillo in the Dominican Republic and Batista in Cuba, that oppressed their own peoples but protected the interests of foreign investors. The same critics charged that the U.S. government and North American business interests sometimes connived with reactionary local groups to destroy Latin American governments seeking to carry out necessary reforms. Widespread accusations of "intervention" and "Yankee imperialism" were raised in Latin America when the Arbenz regime in Guatemala, having launched a sweeping agrarian reform, was overthrown in 1954 by a revolt that had encouragement and assistance from the United States; and U.S. assurances that the Arbenz regime had been "Communist-dominated" failed to quiet the protests.

The hostile demonstrations against Vice President Nixon on the occasion of his visit to Latin America in 1958, the riotous outbreaks in the Panama Canal Zone in 1959, and the break in diplomatic relations between Cuba and the United States early in 1961 as a result of sharp charges and counter-charges between the two countries were so many indications of the low point to which relations between the two Americas had fallen. In April 1961 the disastrous defeat of an invasion of Cuba by a force of counterrevolutionary exiles—an invasion organized and prepared with the aid of the Central Intelligence Agency of the U.S. government—plunged American prestige in Latin America to new depths. In apparent response to the threat of yet another and more powerful invasion from the United States, Castro invited the placement of Soviet ballistic missiles in Cuba. World peace hung by a thread in October 1962 when President Kennedy imposed a blockade of Cuba in order to end the build-up of Soviet missile bases on the island. The crisis ended with a compromise by which the Soviets agreed to remove their missiles in return for a pledge by the United States not to invade Cuba.

Meanwhile the Kennedy administration had responded to the challenge of Castroism by launching the Alliance for Progress, a program combining large-scale outside aid for Latin America with massive projects of internal reform. But a decade later the program was almost universally pronounced a failure. The coming to the presidency of Vice President Lyndon B. Johnson, following the assassination of President Kennedy in November 1963, appeared to signal a shift toward a tougher Latin American policy, stressing cooperation with conservative and militarist elements in Latin America for the maintenance of the status quo. In April 1965 President Johnson dispatched a force of marines to the Dominican Republic, allegedly to assist in the safe evacuation of U.S. and other foreign nationals; critics pointed out that the U.S. intervention effectively served to frustrate the efforts of rebels to overthrow a ruling military *junta* and return the reform-minded former president Juan Bosch to power. The result was a new wave of anger and bitterness toward the United States in the Dominican Republic and throughout Latin America. That the election of Richard Nixon to the presidency portended no basic change in the Latin American policy of the United States became evident from the Rockefeller Report (1969), with its stress on giving support to Latin American police and military forces in their struggle against "subversion."

Under President Jimmy Carter (1977–1981) there was a softening of the "hard" Republican line toward Latin America reflected in his stress on human rights issues in dealing with Chile, Argentina, and Brazil, countries whose governments were among the worst violators of human rights; this softening also was reflected in Carter's tentative efforts to reach an accommodation with the new Sandinist government of Nicaragua. In both areas, however, Carter's posture was fluctuating, uncertain. Under his successor, Ronald Reagan (1981–1989), the "hard" line in dealing with Latin America regained full ascendancy. The undeclared "covert" war against Sandinist Nicaragua, the invasion of the tiny Caribbean island of Grenada in 1983 on security grounds that were clearly specious, and the decision to support a NATO ally, Great Britain, against Argentina in the 1982 Malvinas-Falklands War were among the major Latin American policy decisions of the Reagan administration. The same "hard" line was pursued by President George Bush (1989–1993) against Sandinist Nicaragua and against the Panamanian ruler Manuel Noriega when he displayed an inconvenient independence and ceased to be "our man in Panama." The invasion of Panama in December 1989, resulting in the loss of thousands of Panamanian lives and the capture of Noriega, appeared to mark a return to the discredited policies of "gunboat diplomacy."

The Latin American policy of President Bill Clinton could be appropriately summed up as "more of the same." Clinton's stand on a series of issues reflected the essential continuity of the Reagan-Bush Latin American policy. The Reagan and Bush administrations, using the massive Latin American foreign debt as a weapon of coercion, had imposed on the area, with the cooperation of local elites, a neoliberal economic system based on free trade, austerity, and privatization of state enterprises that nullified the area's past advances toward economic independence and caused large increases in poverty. The logical next step was incorporation of the area into a Western Hemisphere common market that would aid the United States in its competition with Japan and the European Community. This was the meaning of the North American Free Trade Agreement (NAFTA) with Canada and Mexico, negotiated by Bush and pushed through Congress by Clinton over the virtually unanimous opposition of the labor movement, which feared a heavy loss of domestic jobs. The same essential continuity was reflected in Clinton's hard-line stand toward Cuba and his pressure on President Jean-Bertrand Aristide of Haiti, ousted by military plotters in 1991, to accept a return to power in 1994 under the control of U.S. intervention forces.

Meanwhile, due to various circumstances, much new light has recently been thrown on the darker side of U.S. policy in Latin America. We now know, for example, that the CIA cooperated with contra drug traffickers during the "secret" war conducted by the United States against the Sandinistas. After the overthrow and flight of the dictator Alfredo Stroessner, a vast cache of documents—known to Paraguayans as "the archives of terror"—was unearthed in Asunción, Paraguay. The documents illuminate the role played by the United States in "Operation Condor," a secret plan among the security forces of six military dictatorships, initiated in 1975 by General Manuel Contreras of Chile, to destroy left-wing dissent in their countries. The plan allowed security forces of the six nations to pursue their targets across borders. The *New York Times* (August 11, 1999) commented that the archives, although already "sanitized," suggest "that United States officials backed Condor nations not only with military aid but with information" concerning the individuals they pursued. A State Department spokesman shrugged off inquiries on the subject, claiming it was "ancient history." But much the same pattern is evident in present U.S. policy toward Colombia, the third largest recipient of U.S. military and financial aid, a country whose military and security forces are notorious for their violations of human rights.

1. THE UNITED STATES
AS MODEL

Latin American leaders in the nineteenth century, seeking to orient their countries in new and progressive directions, regarded the United States and England as their models. None expressed such passionate attachment for the United States and its institutions as did the Argentine Sarmiento, who visited this country in 1847 and again (as Argentine minister) in 1865–1868. The following selection is from his Travels in France, Africa, and America.

Europeans and even South Americans find fault with the Yankees for many defects of character. For my part, I respect these very defects, which I at-

---

Allison W. Bunkley, ed., *A Sarmiento Anthology*, Princeton, N.J., Princeton University Press, 1948, pp. 220–226. Reprinted by permission of Princeton University Press.

tribute to the whole human race, to our times, to hereditary preoccupations, and to the imperfection of our minds. A people composed of every nationality on earth, as free as the air, and with no tutors, armies, or bastilles, is the product of all their human predecessors, European and Christian. Their defects, therefore, must be those of the human race at any given period of its development. But as a nation, the United States is the final result of human logic. They have no kings, nobles, privileged classes, men born to command, or human machines born to obey. Is not this result consonant with the ideas of justice and equality which Christianity accepts in theory? Well-being is more widely distributed among them than among any other people. Their population is increasing at an unparalleled rate. Production is making astounding progress. Do freedom of action and lack of government enter into this, as Europeans assert? They say that this prosperity is all due to the ease of taking up new land. But why, in South America, where it is even easier to take up new land, are neither population nor wealth on the increase, and cities and even capitals so static that not a hundred new houses have been built in them during the past ten years? No census has yet been taken on the mental capacity of the people of any nation. Population is counted by noses, and, from such figures, the strength and position of a nation are computed. Perhaps for war—looking at a man as an engine of destruction—such statistical data may be significant, but one peculiarity of the American invalidates even this calculation. One Yankee is worth many of other nationalities for killing men, and therefore the destructive capacity of the United States might be estimated at two hundred million people. The rifle is the national weapon, target shooting is the sport of children in the forest states, and the practice of knocking squirrels out of trees by shooting their feet off, in order not to injure the pelt, produces an astonishing skill which is universally acquired.

United States statistics show that the number of adult males corresponds to a population of twenty million inhabitants—well educated, able to read and write, and enjoying political rights, with exceptions which do not vitiate the essential correctness of the deduction. The American male is a man with a home or with the certainty of owning one, beyond the reach of hunger and despair, able to hope for any future that his imagination is capable of conjuring up, and endowed with political feelings and needs. In short, he is a man who is his own master, and possessed of a mind elevated by education and a sense of his own dignity. ...

2. THE TWO AMERICAS

The Chilean writer Francisco Bilbao, though not unmindful of the achievements of North American democracy, called attention to certain defects in the North American character and sounded the alarm against the expansionist designs of the United States against Latin America. It should be noted that he wrote the following lines at a time (1856) of aggressive North American diplomacy and filibustering expeditions designed to secure Cuba, Central America, and portions of Mexico for the United States.

Today we behold empires reviving the ancient idea of world domination. The Russian Empire and the United States, two powers situated at the geographical as well as political extremes, aspire, the one to extend Russian slavery under the mask of Pan-Slavism, the other to secure the sway of Yankee individualism. Russia is very far away, the United States is near. Russia sheathes its claws, trusting in its crafty snares; but the United States daily extends its claws in the hunting expedition that it has begun against the South. Already we see fragments of America falling into the jaws of the Saxon boa that hypnotizes its foes as it unfolds its tortuous coils. First it was Texas, then it was Northern Mexico and the Pacific that hailed a new master.

Today the skirmishers of the North are awakening the Isthmus with their shots,[1] and we see Panama, that future Constantinople of America, doubtfully suspended over the abyss and asking itself: Shall I belong to the South or to the North?

There is the danger. Whoever fails to see it, renounces the future. Is there so little self-awareness among us, so little confidence in the intelligence of the Latin American race, that we must wait for an alien will and an alien intellect to organize us and decide our fate? Are we so poorly endowed with the gifts of personality that we must surrender our own initiative and believe only in the foreign, hostile, and even overbearing initiative of individualism?

I do not believe it, but the hour for action has arrived.

This is the historic moment of South American unity; the second campaign, that will add the association of our peoples to the winning of independence, has begun. Its motive is the danger to our independence and the threat of the disappearance of the initiative of our race. ...

The United States of South America has sighted the smoke of the campfires of the United States. Already we hear the tread of the young colossus that with its diplomacy, with that swarm of adventurers that it casts about like seed, with its growing power and influence that hypnotize its neighbors, with its intrigues among our peoples, with its treaties, mediations, and protectorates, with its industry, its merchant marine, its enterprises—quick to note our weaknesses and our weariness, quick to take advantage of the divisions among our republics, ever more impetuous and audacious, having the same faith in its imperial destiny as did Rome, infatuated with its unbroken string of successes—that youthful colossus advances like a rising tide that rears up its waters to fall like a cataract upon the South.

Francisco Bilbao, *América en peligro*, Santiago de Chile, 1941, pp. 144–154. (Excerpt translated by the editor.)

The name of the United States—our contemporary, but one that has left us so far behind—already resounds throughout the world. The sons of Penn and Washington opened a new historical epoch when, assembled in Congress, they proclaimed the greatest and most beautiful of all existing Constitutions, even before the French Revolution.

Then they caused rejoicing on the part of sorrowing humanity, which from its torture-bed hailed the Atlantic Republic as an augury of Europe's regeneration. Free thought, self-government, moral freedom, and land open to the immigrant, were the causes of its growth and its glory. It was the refuge of those who sought an end to their misery, of all who fled the theocratic and feudal slavery of Europe; it provided a field for utopias, for all experiments; in short, it was a temple for all who sought free lands for free souls.

That was the heroic moment of its annals. All grew: wealth, population, power, and liberty. They leveled the forests, peopled the deserts, sailed all the seas. Scorning tradition and systems, and creating a spirit that devours space and time, they formed a nation, a particular genius. And turning upon themselves and beholding themselves so great, they fell into the temptation of the Titans. They believed they were the arbiters of the earth, and even rivals of Olympus.

Personality infatuated with itself degenerates into individualism; exaggeration of personality turns into egotism; and from there to injustice and callousness is but a step. They would concentrate the universe in themselves. The Yankee replaces the American; Roman patriotism, philosophy; industry, charity; wealth, morality; and self-interest, justice. They have not abolished slavery in their States; they have not preserved the heroic Indian races—nor have they made themselves champions of the universal cause, but only of the American interest, of Saxon individualism. They hurl themselves upon the South, and the nation that should have been our star, our model, our strength, daily becomes a greater threat to the independence of South America.

Here is a providential fact that spurs us to enter upon the stage of history, and this we cannot do if we are not united.

What shall be our arms, our tactics? We who seek unity shall incorporate in our education the vital elements contained in the civilization of the North. Let us strive to form as complete a human entity as possible, developing all the qualities that constitute the beauty or strength of other peoples. They are different but not antagonistic manifestations of human activity. To unite them, associate them, to give them unity, is our obligation.

Science and industry, art and politics, philosophy and Nature should march in a common front, just as all the elements that compose sovereignty should live inseparable and indivisible in a people: labor, association, obedience, and sovereignty.

For that reason let us not scorn, let us rather incorporate in ourselves all that shines in the genius and life of North America. Let us not despise under the pretext of individualism all that forms the strength of the race.

When the Romans wished to form a navy, they took a Carthaginian ship for their model; they replaced their sword with that of Spain; they made their own the science, the philosophy, and the art of the Greeks without surrendering their own genius; they raised a temple to the gods of the very peoples that they fought, as if in order to assimilate the genius of all races and the power of all ideas. In the same way should we grasp the Yankee axe in order to clear the earth; we should curb our anarchy with liberty, the only Hercules capable of overcoming that hydra; we should destroy despotism with liberty, the only Brutus capable of extinguishing all tyrants. And the North possesses all this because it is free, because it governs itself, because above all sects and religions there is a single common and dominant principle: freedom of thought and the government of the people.

Among them there is no State religion because the religion of the State is the State: the sovereignty of the people. That spirit, those elements, we should add to our own characteristics. ...

Let us not fear movement. Let us breathe in the powerful aura that emanates from the resplendent star-spangled banner, let us feel our blood seething with the germination of new enterprises; let us hear our silent regions resounding with the din of rising cities, of immigrants attracted by liberty; and in the squares and woods, the schools and congresses, let the cry be repeated with all the force of hope: forward, forward! ...

We know the glories and even the superiority of the North, but we too have something to place in the scales of justice.

We can say to the North:

Everything has favored you. You are the sons of the first men of modern Europe, of those heroes of the Reformation who crossed the great waters, bringing the Old Testament, to raise an altar to the God of conscience. A knightly though savage race received you with primitive hospitality. A fruitful nature and an infinite expanse of virgin lands multiplied your efforts. You were born and reared in the wooded fields, fired with the enthusiasm of a new faith, enlightened through the press, through freedom of speech—and your efforts were rewarded with abundance.

You received a matchless education in the theory and practice of sovereignty, far from kings, being yourselves all kings, far from the sickly castes of Europe, from their habits of servility and their domesticated manners; you grew with all the vigor of a new creation. You were free; you wished to be independent and you made yourselves independent. Albion fell back before the Plutarchian heroes that made of you the greatest federation in history. It was not so with us.

Isolated from the universe, without other light than that which the cemetery of the Escorial permitted, without other human voice than that of blind obedience, pronounced by the militia of the Pope, the friars, and by the militia of the kings, the soldiers—thus were we educated. We grew in silence, and regarded each other with terror.

A gravestone was placed over the continent, and upon it they laid the weight of eighteen centuries of slavery and decadence. And withal there was word, there was light in those gloomy depths; and we shattered the sepulchral stone, and cast those centuries into the grave that had been destined for us. Such was the power of the impulse, the inspiration or revelation, of the Republic.

With such antecedents, this result merits being placed in the balance with North America.

We immediately had to organize everything. We have had to consecrate the sovereignty of the people in the bosom of theocratic education.

We have had to struggle against the sterile sword that, infatuated with its triumphs, believed that its tangent of steel gave it a claim to the title of legislator. We have had to awaken the masses, at the risk of being suffocated by their blind weight, in order to initiate them in a new life by giving them the sovereignty of the suffrage.

We who are poor have abolished slavery in all the republics of the South, while you who are rich and fortunate have not done so; we have incorporated and are incorporating the primitive races, which in Peru form almost the totality of the nation, because we regard them as our flesh and blood, while you hypocritically exterminate them.

In our lands there survives something of that ancient and divine hospitality, in our breasts there is room for the love of mankind. We have not lost the tradition of the spiritual destiny of man. We believe and love all that unites; we prefer the social to the individual, beauty to wealth, justice to power, art to commerce, poetry to industry, philosophy to textbooks, pure spirit to calculation, duty to self-interest. We side with those who see in art, in enthusiasm for the beautiful (independently of its results), and in philosophy, the splendors of the highest good. We do not see in the earth, or in the pleasures of the earth, the definitive end of man; the Negro, the Indian, the disinherited, the unhappy, the weak, find among us the respect that is due to the name and dignity of man!

That is what the republicans of South America dare to place in the balance opposite the pride, the wealth, and the power of North America.

But our superiority is latent. We must develop it. That of the North is present and is growing.

Just as Cato the Censor ended all his speeches with the destructive phrase *Delenda est Carthago* [Carthage must be destroyed], thus at the end of all argument only one creative idea presents itself: the necessity of an American Union.

What nation shone more brilliantly in history than Greece? Possessing in the highest degree all the elements and qualities that man can display in the plenitude of his powers, united for the full development of personality, she succumbed through internal division, and division quenched the light that her heroism had maintained. We are barely born, and in our cradle serpents assault us. Like Hercules, we must strangle them. Those serpents are anarchy, division, national pettiness. The battle summons us to perform the twelve symbolic labors of the hero. In the forest of our prejudices monsters lurk, spying upon the hour and the duration of our lethargy. Today the columns of Hercules are in Panama. And Panama symbolizes the frontier, the citadel, and the destiny of both Americas.

United, Panama shall be the symbol of our strength, the sentinel of our future. Disunited, it will be the Gordian knot cut by the Yankee axe, and will give the possession of empire, the dominion of the second focus of the ellipses described by Russia and the United States in the geography of the globe.

3. OPERATION GUATEMALA

In the years that followed World War II, rifts began to appear in the New World Alliance. Latin America's "revolution of rising expectations" and its demand for drastic social reforms inevitably threatened vested interests at home and abroad, particularly in the United States. A major crisis soon arose in Guatemala. In 1944, following the overthrow of the tyrant Jorge Ubico by a revolutionary movement led by the distinguished educator Juan José Arévalo, the new government launched a sweeping land reform in a country where twenty-two families owned about 1,250,000 acres of land. Native and foreign interests affected by this and other reforms, including the powerful United Fruit Company, hurled charges of communist control at the Guatemalan government, then headed by President Jacobo Arbenz Guzmán. A major U.S. diplomatic campaign to isolate Guatemala, together with large-scale financial and military assistance to an invasion force of right-wing dissidents and mercenaries, brought the collapse of the Arbenz regime in 1954. Guillermo Toriello, Guatemalan ambassador to the United States at the time, describes the preparation of Operation Guatemala and his futile efforts to prevent its success.

In 1947 the United States Ambassador to Guatemala was Richard C. Patterson, a friend of President Truman, to whose election campaign he had contributed. A man of imperious, arbitrary temper, he soon identified himself with the United Fruit Company and with the domestic opposition because of his dislike for the Guatemalan Revolutionary Movement. On one occasion he actually had the nerve to say to President Arbenz: "I don't like Zotano and Mangano, and I would like you to remove these officials." Another time he said to a government minister: "Fifteen million dollars could settle all our problems with you." Let me say in his behalf that he did not always show antagonism toward our government; he sometimes tried in a friendly, though crude way to gain the goodwill of high officials by bribery. In a single day he

Guillermo Toriello, *La batalla de Guatemala*, Santiago de Chile, 1955, pp. 45–57. (Excerpt translated by the editor.)

destroyed the splendid work of rapprochement, of broad and cordial under-standing, achieved by his predecessor, Ambassador Edwin Kyle. In 1950 his fraternization with the domestic opposition and his interference in our inter-nal affairs reached such a point that the Guatemalan government had to de-clare him *persona non grata*.

Under Dean Acheson, the State Department fell under the influence of the hostile propaganda directed against Guatemala by the United Fruit Company, but relations were maintained on a correct if somewhat tepid level. As early as 1949, the United States refused to permit the export of military equipment to Guatemala, the Department of State alleging that this restric-tion conformed to the law concerning reciprocal assistance for defense (Public Law 621), which provided that before authorizing the sale or trans-fer of war materiel to another country the United States government must satisfy itself that that country participates with the United States in a regional agreement on collective defense. Guatemala did not adhere to the Rio Pact of Reciprocal Assistance, nor did it have—at least until June 29, 1954—a bilateral defense agreement with the United States. However, in other re-spects the relations between the two countries continued cordial, and there was satisfactory cooperation in matters of common interest.

The Republican Party Comes to Power

In January 1953, there was a change of administration in the United States; a new party took over the reins of government. An anticipation of catastrophe ran throughout Latin America. Our peoples feared the rise of the Republican Party, symbol of the "Bad Neighbor," whose policies of the "Big Stick" and "Dollar Diplomacy" the Latin American republics had learned at painful cost under previous Republican administrations. What new mask would the Republican wolf now assume? Could the recent honeyed proposal that we be "good neighbors" represent a new technique of the same old Republican in-terventionist policy?

Changes in the State Department

With the Republicans in power, the official attitude toward Guatemala also changed sharply. To the State Department came John Foster Dulles, member of the law firm Sullivan and Cromwell of New York, which had represented the United Fruit Company for many years past. Dulles himself drew up the draft of the contract made by the United Fruit Company with the Guatemalan government in 1930 and 1936.

John Moore Cabot, of the Boston Cabots, became Under Secretary of Inter-American Affairs. Boston was the seat of the Banana Empire, and the Cabot family has been intimately linked to the United Fruit Company for a long time. The same can be said of the Lodge family; and a Henry Cabot

Lodge was head of the permanent delegation of the United States to the United Nations. There is a popular saying in Boston concerning these families: "The Lodges speak only to Cabots, and the Cabots speak only to God." But the Cabot Lodges present something of a puzzle. To whom do they speak? To God alone, it seems.

A Coalition of Forces and Interests

From the point of view of the traditional Latin American policy of the Republican Party, a policy that was aggressive, interventionist, and favorable to great monopolistic interests, the Guatemalan October Revolution represented a serious danger because of its nationalist, popular, and democratic character. Guatemala was a bad example for the other peoples of Latin America. This example must not be permitted to prevail.

The traditional Republican policy fused in a very natural way with the desires of other forces of reactionary and authoritarian tendency. One was the feudal oligarchy of Guatemala, which formerly had enjoyed a monopoly of political power. Another was the secret organization created some years back by the Franco government of Spain for the undermining of Latin American democracies. Its aim was to create in America regimes that would resemble the Spanish Falangist regime and that would lend the latter some of the international support that it badly needed. This organization, with abundant means and agents, was supported by some American dictators like Trujillo. It operated actively in Guatemala, had recruited some Guatemalans into its service, and had invited some officers of the national army to join its ranks. In addition to its preeminently conspiratorial activity, this secret organization carried on some activities of a visible character: the appeal to *Hispanidad*; the malicious exploitation of the Catholic sentiments of our people; the intensive diffusion of Falangist propaganda by Catholic clergy in its service.

As for the United Fruit Company, the fiasco of more than thirty conspiracies of the traditional Latin American type had evidently convinced it that that method would no longer serve to liquidate a revolutionary government like that of Guatemala, firmly rooted in the people. Something else had to be done, on a much vaster scale.

The new complexion of the Republican Administration in the United States, particularly that of the Department of State, and the traditionally aggressive Latin American policy of the Republican Party, lent itself marvellously to a union of forces that sought to employ the old procedure, dressed in a new garb, *intervention*.

The fact that leading figures in the United Fruit Company held key positions in the United States government made it easy for the company to achieve such a union of forces and to transform its private fight with the Guatemalan government into a formal conflict between the two countries.

This is precisely what the President of the United Fruit Company, Kenneth Redmond, had earlier announced in a confidential interview.

"Henceforth it will not be a question of the people of Guatemala against the United Fruit Company; the question will become one of communism against the right to life, property, and the security of the Western Hemisphere." The interviewer added that Mr. Redmond was convinced that there would be a change of administration in Guatemala; he could not give the exact date, but it was not very distant.

Thus was formed the portentous triangle—United Fruit Company, Department of State, CIA—which was to carry out "Operation Guatemala" with the assistance of Franco's agents and the local oligarchy. In some *sanctum sanctorum* of the great Yankee Chancellery it was decreed: "*Delenda est Guatemala* (Guatemala must be destroyed)" and the lot was thrown that decided the tragic destiny of our country. ...

The Master Plan Is Born

Very soon it became widely known that this coalition of forces was active and delineaments of the "Master Plan," the logical result of the subservience of the State Department to the United Fruit Company, became visible. "Operation Guatemala," a consequence of that plan, also counted on the collaboration of the CIA, whose head, conveniently enough, was Allen Dulles, brother of the Secretary of State.

The plan, combining the resources of that triangle, had the following general characteristics. Two different lines of action would be pursued simultaneously. The first would carry the case of "the red menace in Guatemala" by pseudo-correct diplomatic channels to the ministries of America and inter-American conferences; the second would clandestinely prepare armed aggression against Guatemala, but giving it the name of an "internal revolt" that seemingly involved not at all the correct, "very fair" attitude of the State Department.

To support these actions, pressure should be maintained on Guatemala in all its official diplomatic and commercial relations with the United States; the Guatemalan government would suffer boycott in its relations with other countries in the United States sphere of influence; and an enormous propaganda campaign, using the Communist scarecrow, would create throughout America a state of mind that, whether from genuine alarm, cowardice, or servility, would give the United States a free hand in Guatemala.

In sum, a gigantic project, on a scale sufficient to battle a first class enemy power, was organized with the sole aim of restoring the unjust privileges of the Banana Empire and other monopolistic enterprises, but was disguised by dressing it in the evangelical cloak of a "noble struggle against communism."

Preparations

The "Master Plan" was soon put into effect. The Department of State had already presented its claims in connection with the expropriation (already indemnified) of idle lands of the United Fruit Company in the Pacific zone of Guatemala. A defamatory propaganda was intensified, using the press, radio, and television in the United States and the rest of America.

To replace Ambassador Schoenfeld, an honest and thoughtful career diplomat, Washington sent to Guatemala a rascally type by the name of John E. Peurifoy.

Contact was made with the principal elements of the Guatemalan opposition and, finally, Carlos Castillo Armas, a former soldier who had rebelled against the Guatemalan government (1950) and was currently in Honduras, was selected as an ideal instrument of the United Fruit Company–State Department–CIA plan. A lawyer in New Orleans served as the go-between who paid the monthly expenses of the conspiracy and for the purchase of war materiel. Castillo Armas in turn maintained a confidential agent at the State Department whom he paid with funds that he received from the United Fruit Company.

Through an arms dealer of Dallas, Texas, Castillo Armas was provided with the military supplies he needed: machine guns, submachine guns, rifles, 100- and 200-pound bombs for aerial bombardment, hand grenades, ammunition, explosives, radio transmission equipment, uniforms, tents. He also obtained within United States territory and at nominal prices P-47 planes and transport planes that belonged to the United States government. (Note that such equipment, being property of the United States government, cannot be exported without its express authorization; even when sold to a friendly government, such government cannot transfer or otherwise dispose of it without the previous consent of the United States.)

At the end of 1953, ten pilots and ten airplane mechanics enlisted with Castillo Armas, without loss of United States citizenship. They were to receive $500 a month until summoned to their work of destruction and murder; thereafter they would receive $1000 a month plus bonuses. Recruitment of mercenaries at $300 a month, not clandestinely but publicly, even through printed fliers, began in Honduras and Nicaragua.

All this war materiel was transported from the United States to Nicaragua and Honduras without any effort at concealment. Later the base of operations and the supplies were moved to Honduras. Castillo Armas' uniformed soldiers loaded truckloads of armaments in plain view of passersby at the United States embassy in Tegucigalpa, Honduras. Castillo Armas' mercenary troops freely circulated throughout Honduras, making conspicuous show of their abundance of United States dollars. These troops were moved to Copan, campaign headquarters near the Guatemalan frontier, in full daylight, wearing their uniforms and carrying their arms, using both their own airplanes and Honduran public services of land and air transport.

Arms, munitions, United States government planes, war materiel of every kind, North American pilots and mechanics, Castillo Armas, millions of dollars changing hands, an unheard of tolerance on the part of Honduras and

Nicaragua, ships equipped for commando operations, and the like. Who could believe that all this happened without the complicity of the United States government?

The State Department Drops Its Mask

As long as the conspiratorial activities of the United Fruit Company and allied interests had the character of a private struggle against the Guatemalan revolutionary movement, the State Department maintained a discreet attitude and abstained from public statements about the Guatemalan situation. This does not mean that there was an absence of attacks, echoing the defamatory propaganda of the United Fruit Company, by other official figures. In the United States Congress, especially, various senators and representatives linked to the Banana Empire or allied interests made continuous capricious attacks on the Guatemalan government.

On October 14, 1953, the State Department first spoke out publicly against Guatemala. John Moore Cabot, in a speech before the Federation of Women's Clubs in the State Department auditorium in Washington, referred extensively to Guatemala, to "gratuitous attacks against the United States and its citizens from official Guatemalan sources," concluding with the warning that "no regime that openly plays the Communist game can expect from us the positive cooperation that we normally extend to all our sister republics."

Doubtless that conclusion was geared to "Operation Guatemala," now in full movement, and did not reflect a sincere ideological stand on the part of the State Department, for in the same speech the United Fruit Stockholder, referring to Argentina, noted the good relations that were being established with that country and observed: "Frankly, its different philosophy and economy are none of our business." One standard for Guatemala, another for Argentina.

This first official statement against Guatemala was systematically followed by other, increasingly aggressive statements by Cabot and Dulles himself, in line with the Master Plan.

Diplomatic Maneuvers

At the end of 1953 the Council of the Organization of American States met to prepare the agenda for the Tenth Inter-American Conference.

This presented an excellent opportunity. The Master Plan called for the State Department to operate on the Inter-American diplomatic front, generally, in order to create the proper atmosphere for the armed aggression; and, especially, in order to give the United Fruit Company's struggle against Guatemala the character of a grave inter-American problem that required the collective action of the members of the continental community.

But the State Department could not find an appropriate formula that would exonerate its actions from having a clearly interventionist character. Whatever the form employed, the common action of the other American republics in the Guatemalan case had to appear for what it really was: an intervention in the internal affairs of a member of that community, in gross violation of the principles of the inter-American system.

Fortunately for the State Department, Mr. Dulles' talent, evidenced by his numerous diplomatic triumphs in Europe and Asia, found the solution for the problem of squaring the circle. In order that some may not accuse us of intervention, let us say that foreign intervention is already in progress in an American country and that we are merely going to its aid. Let us call the hateful nationalist, democratic movement in Guatemala a "Communist intervention," and then it will become clear that, inspired by the great democratic tradition of the United States, in order to save "Christian civilization," we must liberate Guatemala from that foreign aggression.

The time for action had come. The proposed agenda of the Conference had been circulated among governments and had been returned with their observations. At the last hour the State Department requested inclusion in the agenda of the point, "Intervention of International Communism in the American Republics."

None could mistake the significance of this point. By that date the shape of the conspiratorial diplomatic plan against the [Guatemalan] October Revolution was too clear for anyone not to see that the United States proposal was an integral part of that plan. ...

And the United States policy of boycott and encirclement of Guatemala bore its fruit at the Conference: nineteen delegates folded under Mr. Dulles' pressure and voted in favor of the United States proposal, leaving Guatemala alone in defense of a fundamental principle of the international system: nonintervention.

A Fleeting Hope

In January 1954, I was finishing my assignment as ambassador of Guatemala to the United States. Together with my government, I felt the most profound concern over the sombre perspectives that the political aggression of the United States projected for my country. We had exhausted all the possibilities of reaching a decorous understanding; all our overtures had fruitlessly broken against the intransigence of the State Department. We knew it would give us no truce or quarter.

Given this situation, we concluded that the only hope for preventing the realization of the sinister plan being prepared against Guatemala was to take the question directly to the President of the United States and discuss it with him, amply and freely.

But in the United States it is very difficult for a Latin American ambassador to obtain an interview with the President or even with the Secretary of State, by contrast with the situation in our own countries, where any chief of mission finds an easy access to the offices of those high officials.

The persons Latin American ambassadors can easily see in Washington are officials of the sixth class (in charge of the desks of the respective countries), and, by appointment, officials of the third and fourth classes, such as the Assistant Secretary and the Vice Assistant Secretary for Inter-American Affairs.

Although I had on various occasions intimated to the State Department my desire to speak with President Eisenhower, unfortunately it always turned out, so I was told, that he was very busy, "too busy, you know."

Convinced that I would never obtain an interview through conventional channels, at a banquet that President Eisenhower gave for the Diplomatic Corps in the White House (December 15, 1953), I utilized the opportunity to ask him directly for an audience. He granted it immediately, asking me to make the necessary arrangement with the Under Secretary of State, General Walter Bedell Smith, to whom he would speak about the matter. Next morning I spoke with that official who, having been informed by the President, indicated to me that he would arrange an interview for the following January, since Mr. Eisenhower continued to be "too busy" with his vacation and other important matters.

In the second week of January I reminded Smith of his commitment and he said the President continued "very busy," but he would try to get me an audience, on condition that I had a previous talk with him (Smith) to explain the purpose of my interview with Eisenhower. Although it seemed an extraordinary demand, I restrained my natural impulse to reject it in view of the interests at stake.

On January 14 I had a talk with General Smith. I was introduced by John M. Cabot, Assistant Secretary for Inter-American Affairs, and had to request him to leave so that I could speak alone with the Under-Secretary of State. My reason was the desire to spare Cabot embarrassment when I alluded (as I had to allude) to his connections with the United Fruit Company, a point I had discussed directly with him on various occasions.

I found Smith forewarned and badly informed about the Guatemalan reality. He had with him the file of State Department reports on Guatemala, and I could see that his view of the situation was a direct consequence of having leafed through that one-sided and tendentious material. After an interview of an hour and a half during which I gave him a detailed account of events, corroborated by the documentation and maps which I had brought with me, General Smith's attitude changed completely. He now shared my sense of the gravity of the situation and agreed that a change in the conditions under which the United Fruit Company and other North American monopolies operated in my country was necessary. He could not have been better disposed toward an amicable understanding and working out of all our problems. He displayed greater optimism concerning such a perspective when he learned that in a few days I would assume charge of the Guatemalan ministry of foreign affairs, although he remarked, to be sure, that in that position I would be in a better position to hamper "the subversive activities of international communism." Assuredly impressed by the gravity with which I regarded the situation and the policy of the State Department, he showed a lively interest in arranging an interview for me with President Eisenhower at the earliest possible date.

Two days later, January 16, the President received me. He was accompanied by John C. Moore, who this time remained during the interview. If Smith was poorly informed about the Guatemalan situation, the President was even more so. All he knew was "the Communist danger to the Continent," the "Red menace" that was Guatemala. He was greatly surprised when I described the economic subjection in which the foreign monopolies held us and the conspiratorial activities in which they engaged in order to destroy the democratic movement in Guatemala. I pointed out that one of the phases of that conspiracy was precisely the gigantic campaign of defamatory propaganda which made us appear to be Communists.

He was deeply disturbed when he learned of the extraordinary privileges those enterprises enjoyed and the connections between the United Fruit Company and the State Department. He found it difficult to believe that these companies paid no customs duties and that some of their contracts would not run out until the next century. With a terrifying naiveté, he suggested that on my arrival in Guatemala I should discuss ways of reaching a settlement with Ambassador Peurifoy. Naturally—at least that was my impression—the President knew nothing of "Operation Guatemala" in which his own State Department and his own embassy in my country were involved.

I had to express my deep skepticism concerning his suggestion, discreetly noting that Mr. Dulles was a member of the law firm of the United Fruit Company and that Mr. Cabot (who was present) and his family were stockholders in the same company. The President must have found my arguments reasonable, for then he proposed formation of an impartial mixed commission of Guatemalan and United States citizens that should discuss on the highest level the problem of the monopolistic enterprises in Guatemala and all other matters causing friction between the two countries. I indicated that I was in entire agreement with him, in principle, and that I was confident my government would receive his proposal with enthusiasm.

For a few days I had the illusory hope that through President Eisenhower's intervention and the realization of his project—the mixed commission—the progress of the State Department's sinister plans could be brought to a halt. Unfortunately, very soon I had to admit that the President's good intentions were that and nothing more. They proved totally incapable of preventing the advance of the aggression that was already under way. All had been a vain hope.

4. THE INVASION OF PANAMA:
A LATIN AMERICAN VIEWPOINT

George Bush, elected president in 1988, continued Reagan's Latin American policy of reinforcing U.S. control over the region by means that included military, political, and economic subversion of left-leaning regimes; propping up unpopular right-wing governments with military and economic aid; and the use of "gunboat diplomacy" as a last resort. The end of the Cold War deprived the United States of its stock-in-trade, the bogeyman of "international communism"; but a new villain, the Latin American drug trafficker, provided a convenient pretext for armed intervention. The need to seize the Panamanian dictator Manuel Noriega and bring him to trial on drug charges was one reason cited by Bush for the invasion of Panama in December 1989. Although the U.S. media accepted the official explanations almost without dissent, the great majority of Latin American states denounced the invasion as a violation of international law and inter-American treaties; and Latin American observers, like the one quoted below, subjected the official U.S. reasons for the action to sharp criticism.

While Gorbachev offers peace to the powerful, Reagan makes war on the weak, using a new ideological dodge as a pretext. Take the case of Panama.

The United States gave four reasons and objectives for invading Panama. Of these, three are irrelevant as always and the fourth establishes an unacceptably terrifying precedent. The four reasons must be rejected. Historically, the United States has used "gunboat diplomacy" in Latin America and the Caribbean more than fifty times.

The first official reason for the invasion of Panama was "to protect American lives" there. This pretext had diminished credibility, for the cry of "wolf! wolf!" has been used before in Latin America. It loses all credibility when the United States conveniently fails to intervene to protect its citizens when they are assassinated in El Salvador and other foreign countries. For the rest, the danger to American lives is a hundred times greater every day and night in Washington, D.C., "the murder capital of the United States," and in other American cities to which Bush has hardly applied his policy of protecting North American lives and waging war against drugs (he prefers to wage that war on foreign battlefields). Moreover, the homeless in the cities of the United States were more likely to die as a result of the wave of Arctic cold in December 1989 than was any American citizen as a result of the political heat wave in Panama—that is, before the U.S. invasion that took the lives of twenty-six of its own citizens.

The second official reason was the restoration of democracy in Panama. The credibility of this pretext has also been reduced by the fact that the

"4 pobres razones," *Nueva Sociedad,* no. 106, marzo–abril, 1990, p. 16.

United States conveniently failed to intervene to restore democracy in Chile or in Guatemala, where democracy had been destroyed by military supported by the United States. It would be difficult to count all the undemocratic and anti-democratic regimes that the United States has supported; undoubtedly there have been more than fifty. The installation of the Endara government at the point of North American bayonets in a U.S. military base diminishes the credibility of the U.S. esteem for democracy in Panama and that of the Endara government itself. Endara's subsequent admission of his inability to govern in the face of the all-powerful North American occupation has the same effect. The gratuitous destruction of Panamanian lives and barrios, of that country's laws and economy, the indiscriminate and irresponsible manner in which the U.S. military bombarded, burned, shot, and terrorized, together with the total disregard for Panamanian human and individual rights, hardly augurs well for the credibility of the U.S. esteem for democracy in Panama or for humanity there or anywhere else.

The third official reason and justification for the invasion of Panama was "to ensure the functioning of the Panama Canal" in accord with the obligations established in the Torrijos-Carter Treaty. However, it was the United States itself that, after the invasion, for the first time in the Canal's history, suspended and later restricted its functioning for reasons that had nothing to do with natural causes. Moreover, although the treaty clearly distinguishes between intervention in the Canal and in Panama itself, the U.S. armed forces violated this distinction and the treaty itself. What was worse, the chief of the U.S. armed forces in the Canal Zone threw salt on Panamanian wounds by trying to justify these actions with the supposed reason that "according to the treaty we have a full right to be here" in Panama itself. Consequently, this reason also lacks justification.

The last and most credible official reason was "to seize and later bring Noriega to trial" in Miami. However, no matter how much Noriega justly and indisputably deserves to answer for the crimes and other evils with which he is charged, the much greater evils of the military invasion of a country and its people cannot be called good—for two evils do not make a right. This supposed reason and unjustified action first conceal and ultimately reveal another interconnected series of very disturbing reasons for the U.S. invasion of Panama—reasons that little by little are coming to public light.

5. THE UNITED STATES AND LATIN AMERICA'S FOREIGN DEBT

Latin America's staggering foreign debt, projected by the World Bank to reach $547 billion in 1994, is commonly regarded as the greatest obstacle to the region's economic development and political stability. In February 1989, after newly elected President Carlos

Andrés Pérez of Venezuela imposed a severe austerity program in response to the conditions set by the International Monetary Fund (IMF) for new loans, a popular explosion rocked the capital city of Caracas, with tens of thousands taking to the streets, rioting and looting shops. This outbreak quickly spread to other cities and towns and was savagely repressed, with perhaps a thousand killed and thousands of others wounded. An event of this kind taking place in oil-rich, democratic Venezuela was an alarm, warning that the patience of the Latin American masses had reached its limits. In response, U.S. Treasury Secretary Nicholas Brady hastily announced a debt relief program for Latin America that encouraged U.S. banks to make new loans or accept reductions in the principal or interest of existing loans. However, there is growing acceptance in Latin America of Fidel Castro's view, argued here by a high Cuban official, that the debt is unpayable under existing conditions.

In Latin America the foreign debt is no longer a subject of scientific debate; it has become a source of social crisis. Venezuela is there to prove it. ... The imposition of measures based on the policies of the International Monetary Fund (IMF)—policies that cause the decline of living standards and negatively influence development—provoked not a political debate or an organized protest but the "social explosion" that Fidel Castro years ago predicted would be the result of such policies. President Perez put his finger on the problem when, in a press interview, he explained the cause of what had happened in his country. That cause, he said, was "the policy of the great industrial powers to compel us to pay our debts when we cannot rationally do so." For that reason, he rightly concluded, "we have no alternative but to pose before the creditor countries their responsibility for the certain destabilization of democratic processes in Latin America."

Viewing the problem of the foreign debt from a political perspective, we must note in the first place the fact, emphasized by Fidel Castro, that it is unpayable. No one has been able to challenge scientifically this assertion. It is interesting that the two organizations that concern themselves with the economy of our Latin American and Caribbean continent, the Economic System of Latin America (SELA) and the Economic Commission for Latin America (CEPAL), have recognized that the debt is unpayable, although they qualify this statement by noting that the debt is unpayable in the present *international economic conditions*. The data that support this conclusion are well known. In the period 1973–1981 the foreign debt represented 38 percent of the value of Latin America's gross industrial product; in the period 1982–1987 that figure grew to 56 percent. As regards individual countries, the corresponding figures for that period are 110 percent for

---

Carlos Rafael Rodriguez, "Sobre la deuda externa," *Casa de las Americas*, 1990, Volume 30, no. 175, pp. 126–132. (Excerpt translated by the editor.)

Costa Rica, 90 percent for Chile, 65 percent for Mexico, 88 percent for Uruguay, 61 percent for Peru, 58 percent for Venezuela. ...

This ruinous relationship appears more tragic if we recall that in order to grow and above all to develop, the Latin American and Caribbean economies for a long time to come will need to obtain international financing and foreign technology; that is, they will continue to be net importers of capital. The fact that in recent years the region has been transformed into a net exporter of resources, transferring $180 billion to the international financial centers in the last seven years alone, is sufficiently revealing of the critical state of affairs. ...

It is necessary to change the existing approach to the debt problem. The "case-by-case" approach, which until now has been favored by the North American creditors, places the debtors in a defenseless position. The unity of the creditors must be confronted with the unity of the debtors. Disunited, divided, and dispersed, we lose all capacity for confronting the creditors. We know that the cases differ and the creditors we face are not always the same. ... But the question is not one of collective negotiation—although this would be preferable and I believe that eventually life will impose that solution—but of achieving a common point of view that would unify our positions in the face of the very united, firm, and negative position of the lenders. The Southern Commission, whose chair is Julius Nyerere, and of which I am a member, has proposed that such a Forum of Debtors be created in the shortest possible time.

If, as we hope, that Forum becomes a reality, it will not only considerably strengthen the position of the debtors—giving it solidity and cohesion—but will also modify their attitude, which until now has been uncertain and wavering.

How can we solve simultaneously the problem of a debt that cannot be paid and the problem of an international financial system that recognizes the political nature of the problem but refuses to admit that the debt is producing the collapse of the economy of the debtors?

Let me be frank. None of the solutions attempted to date satisfies the interests of Latin America and the Caribbean. All fall far short of meeting their needs. The "swaps" designed to convert the debt into investment have one clear purpose: to increase the power of the banks and the transnationals in the Latin American economy. That is, they serve to consolidate the economic dependency of Latin America without even providing the region with the immediate financial resources that it needs. That solution can only satisfy those who proclaim that dependency is the only way out for our economies. ...

All other solutions, however, have been overshadowed by the formula presented by U.S. Secretary of the Treasury Nicholas Brady at the Bretton Woods meeting. ...

The Brady Plan has aroused hopes in some, suspicions in others, but in view of its significance we cannot disregard it. The North American banks are the principal creditors of Latin America and together with the international financial institutions, represent a decisive portion of the Latin American foreign debt. Thus the United States must play a key role in any discussion of our continent's foreign debt. Let us consider some facts.

The United States has influenced the debt question in a variety of ways, all of them negative.

1. It has maintained high interest rates, due in the first place to the North American trade and financial deficit and to its aim of securing, by means of high interest rates, the flow of capital to the United States. The fear of inflation also stimulates high interest rates.

2. It has sought for domestic reasons to achieve self-sufficiency in products that could be exported from Latin America to the United States.

3. For the same reasons, and despite official professions of economic liberalism, it has maintained a protectionist attitude toward Latin American products.

4. There has been a drastic decline in the flow of North American financing to Latin America, both in the form of bank loans and in direct investments.

5. The system of unequal exchange has continued, with a continuing rise in the price of U.S. industrial goods, while the value of the primary products that Latin America exports continues to fall or stagnates. The fall of the dollar has also contributed to a real devaluation in the price of these products in the European and Japanese markets.

6. In its discussions with Latin America, the United States has imposed isolation on the Latin American debtors, demanding a "case-by-case" discussion of the debt problem.

7. Finally, the refusal of the U.S. government to assume any of the losses that the banking system may incur as a result of the debt crisis constitutes an almost insuperable obstacle to a possible solution.

The Brady Plan does not offer an answer to any of the grave problems that the United States has created for the economies of the region.

The first point made by the Brady Plan is the need to reform the Latin American economies if we want them to grow. But the reforms that Mr. Brady proposes—like those proposed by Dr. Henry Kissinger in an article for popular consumption—do not correspond to the Latin American and Caribbean interests; they reflect a striving for North American domination. Let me begin with the affirmations of Kissinger, who is more precise on this point than Secretary Brady. According to Kissinger, debt relief must be linked to certain conditions. It is important to note exactly what these conditions are. For Dr. Kissinger, debt relief—and let me stress here that "relief" is an inadequate word—requires privatization of the Latin American economy and liberalization as regards the flow of capital to our countries, as well as a reduction of state intervention. In a word, the elimination of all the defenses that in past years limited the freedom of foreign investment and of the policies that assigned an increased role to the state in the Latin American economy. Kissinger's proposals are in keeping with the economic liberalism that currently prevails in international circles. But if we review the history of Latin America in the period prior to the recent past, we see that the conditions whose return Dr. Kissinger regards as desirable are precisely the conditions that existed here for long decades and that gave rise to our backwardness. Conditions, in a word, whose return would restore the absolute domination of imperialism.

The limited economic progress made in Latin America before the crisis of the 1980s had its origin in protection for domestic industrial production and the assumption of a directing function by the state, with a resulting growth of the public sector. To be sure, in many countries this was mixed with concessions to the transnationals and a resulting transnationalization of the economies. The process was also attended by many errors and not a little corruption in the sphere of the state. It is these errors and this corruption that must be eliminated, but without a return to the period in which our economies were at the mercy of foreign decisions. The move to economic liberalism that is now demanded would lead to a greater transnationalization, to a loss by the Latin American economies of their national character and, as experience has already begun to show, to an intolerable economic situation for the workers, the middle sectors, and for the broad sectors that occupy a marginal position in society—that is, for the majority of the population. Moreover, the experience of various countries shows that policies of economic liberalism strike a heavy blow at the native industrial sector.

For these reasons, we cannot accept the conditions that the United States seeks to impose on Latin America—conditions whose point of departure is the wrongly understood interests of the United States.

Just as we reject the idea, repeatedly voiced by Brady, that solutions of the debt problem must be based on a "case-by-case treatment," so we accept his other two premises—namely, that growth is essential for the resolution of the debt problem and that the debtor nations continue to need external resources.

Brady's formula, however, operates not on the basis of those premises but on a very different one.

The only novelty of the North American position represented by the Brady Plan consists in its acceptance of the thesis that the debt must be reduced; but the Plan does not even dare to suggest how much it should be reduced. Morover, Brady proposes a voluntary reduction, and one must ask what is the maximum reduction that the banks will accept without a state guarantee of compensation to the banks. It is true that the principal banks (Chase, Citicorp, Manufacturers Hanover) have accumulated reserves that put them in a stronger position; but it is equally certain that a collapse of the debt structure through default would create extremely grave financial problems.

For the rest, Brady has found a heavenly name for the adjustments imposed by the IMF; he calls them "sound policies." Is a policy that creates more unemployment, larger cuts in workers' wages, and more economic stagnation "sound"? Can one consider "sound" a policy that is associated with hunger and backwardness and that generates explosions like that which took place in Venezuela?

Brady calls for a reversal of the flight of capital from Latin America, but he omits mention of the fact that that capital, the capital of associates of the North American banks, fled because its owners placed profits above patriotism and sought the high interest paid in the United States, whose economy was more solid and secure than that of Latin America. Can we hope that patriotism alone will induce that capital to return to our lands, with economies in recession and devalued money?

The experience of Mexico has shown that the repurchase of the debt in secondary markets raises the cost of the depreciated debt in those markets and that the reserves of the Latin American states are insufficient to repurchase more than a small part of the debt.

Brady proposes that the IMF and the World Bank make loans to those countries to replenish their exhausted reserves, but this will only serve to raise the debt to even higher levels.

In fine, the Brady Plan may achieve a moderate reduction of the debt of one or another country, but will only prolong the existing critical situation.

His so-called voluntary reductions based on the market, combined with what he calls "sound policies," are essentially more of the same.

It is necessary, therefore, to begin with a different vision of the problem. Since there are no short-term solutions that can reconcile the immediate interests of debtors and creditors, we must gain time for the maturing of conditions that will permit discussion of the debt problem in the necessary depth and detail.

The events in Venezuela are an alarm, calling for immediate attention to the problem. ... The changing international climate is creating new possibilities for world peace and the end of the armaments race, or at least a drastic slowing of that race. This leads me to recall the linkage between peace, disarmament, and development, on which Bush, the Pope, Gorbachev, and Fidel Castro appear to agree.

I may recall that Fidel Castro was the first to propose the large-scale use of the funds saved by disarmament to find a solution for the debt problem that would avoid creating a crisis for the international financial system. But his proposal is making slow headway, although it is gaining ever greater approval.

I repeat: It is necessary to gain time. And since we speak of gaining time, it is again necessary to mention a word that arouses horror or aversion in many people: *moratorium*. I am not speaking now of a unilateral moratorium declared by the debtors but of a moratorium accepted and discussed by both parties. ... A long-term moratorium of twenty or thirty years, with interest terms sufficiently low to allow the debtors to receive some benefit from the postponement, while affording the creditors some compensation for the extension given by the moratorium. ...

The moratorium would also make possible the reconstruction of the economic flow from North to South, but on different terms than those of the 1970s. On this point we must be realists; it is necessary to change "the rules of the game." The bankers have learned the lessons of recent years, of their irresponsibility, and weigh each loan with scrupulous care. The Latin American peoples, who in the last analysis are the ones that must pay the debts, must take measures through their democratic institutions to prevent the loans from becoming sources of improper profit through administrative corruption and the wasteful investments that such corruption breeds. The Latin American democracies must put an end to those negative factors and to the flight of capital from our countries to the international financial centers. Both the savings achieved by liquidating the debt and the financing obtained on new terms must be devoted to investments for development.

What Latin America asks, what the underdeveloped countries are demanding, is not that the United States and other powerful international economic centers like the European Community simply subsidize their economies as an act of international generosity. That is not what is at issue. If we inhabit a single world, that world must not be permanently subdivided between the haves and the have-nots. That opposition is not only morally indefensible but practically dangerous and, above all, irrational. Any economic calculation will show that if the underdeveloped world, with its four billion persons, is transformed into a developed world, and the disinherited of today become tomorrow's consumers, the positive economic effects of this change will not only benefit the South but will yield high returns to the North. We are not asking the North's leaders for an act of charity, therefore, but for actions that would demonstrate their capacity for intelligent decisions.

The North American leaders should understand, *must* understand, that just as the time has passed when the marines could land in Haiti, Santo Domingo, or Central America in order to collect debts, so the time has passed when the peoples could be condemned to hunger without provoking a popular reaction of anger and fury.

Each day that passes without a solution of the problem of the foreign debt implies not only further decline for the economies of the continent and the Third World in general, but the risk of uncontrollable outbreaks like those in Venezuela. And those outbreaks affect not only the governments involved but the United States. Not a few North American leaders are aware of that fact.

That is why it is reasonable that the money of North American taxpayers be used to pay off the debt, even though it temporarily benefits a few powerful banks. Those banks could in their turn be compelled to return their gains through taxation. This, however, would require a change in the policy established by Reagan and followed by Bush of exempting the most influential economic groups in the United States from tax burdens.

We believe that the application of an important part of the funds saved by cutting military budgets to liquidating the debt and lowering the rate of interest would be the most effective way of establishing the linkage between disarmament and development that U.S. government officials have verbally accepted.

We are suggesting something never done before, but we confront many situations never seen before. Venezuela is there to remind us of that fact.

Notes

(Those notes followed by "B.K." are by the editor; others are part of the original sources.)

Notes to Chapter 2

1. Gonzalo Fernández de Cordoba (1453–1515), Spanish general whose brilliant victories in the Italian wars won him the sobriquet of *El Gran Capitán* (The Great Captain).

Notes to Chapter 3

1. Motto translated by the editor. —B.K.

2. Oviedo refers here to the custom of meeting at the cathedral of Seville to arrange all manner of contracts. This gave rise to the practice of hiring and negotiating with soldiers bound for the Indies. The soldiers awaited outside the church the results of the conferences that the merchants and captains held within; from these conferences often developed many of the great American conquests and expeditions. —B.K.

Notes to Chapter 6

1. William Shakespeare, *Measure for Measure*, Act V, Scene 1. —B.K.

Notes to Chapter 7

1. Tribe here may be understood to mean clan or kinship group. —B.K.

Notes to Chapter 8

1. This tax was designed to strengthen the Armada de Barlovento, the Spanish squadron guarding the Windward Islands.—B.K.

Notes to Chapter 12

1. When Brazil was in its infancy, the clergy could not subsist on their tithes, and therefore petitioned the government of Portugal to pay them a certain stipend, and receive the tenths for its own account: this was accepted: but now the tenths have increased in value twenty-fold, the government still pays to the vicars the same stipends. The clergy of the present day bitterly complain of the agreement made by those to whom they have succeeded.

Notes to Chapter 13

1. The majority of the clergy of Pernambuco, both regular and secular, are of Brazilian parentage. The governor is an European, and so are the major part of the chief officers, civil, military, and ecclesiastical but the bishop is a Brazilian, and so is the *ouvidor*.

2. The term of *Senhor* or *Senhora* is made use of to all free persons, whites, mulattos, and blacks: and in speaking to a freeman of whatever class or colour the manner of address is the same.

3. To this statement some explanation is necessary, owing to the regulations of the Portuguese military service. Privates are sometimes raised to commissions by the intermediate steps of corporals, quartermasters, and sergeants. These men gain their ensigncies without any relation to their birth: and though a decidedly dark-coloured mulatto might not be so raised, a European of low birth would. It is to enable a man to become a cadet, and then an officer without serving in the ranks, that requires nobility of birth.

Notes to Chapter 14

1. Hence the well-known proverb: "The father a merchant, the son a gentleman, the grandson a beggar," which characterized in a few words this transition from wealth gained by labor to idleness and prodigality, and from that to misery. This prodigality had a long history. Balbuena, in his *Grandeza mejicana*, a poem written in 1603, includes among the circumstances that made life in Mexico City pleasanter than anywhere else in the world,

> *"That prodigal giving of every ilk,*
> *Without a care how great the cost,*
> *Of pearls, of gold, of silver, and of silk. ..."*

2. Of the one hundred and seventy viceroys who governed in America until 1813, only four had been born there—and that by chance, as the sons of officeholders. Three of them were viceroys of Mexico: Don Luis de Velasco, son of the Luis de Velasco who also held that office and died in Mexico in 1564; Don Juan de Acuna, Marquis of Casafuerte, born in Lima, who governed the viceroyalty between 1722 and 1734 and died there, being buried in the church of San Cosme de Mexico; and the Count of Revilla Gigedo, who was born in Havana while his father was captain-general of the island of Cuba, whence he was transferred to the viceroyalty of Mexico. The three were models of probity, capacity, and zeal. Of the six hundred and two captains-general and presidents, fourteen had been creoles. ...

3. Of the seven hundred and six bishops who held office in Spanish America until 1812, one hundred and five were creoles, although few held miters of the first class. ...

4. Hidalgo was actually fifty-eight years old in 1810. —B.K.

5. Historians are not in agreement concerning the time of the first meeting between Iturbide and Guerrero. For a discussion of the controversy, see William S. Robertson, *Iturbide of Mexico*, Durham, N.C., Duke University Press, 1952, pp. 64–65. —B.K.

Notes to Chapter 15

1. The reference is to the Chilean Liberal revolt of 1851, crushed by the administration of President Montt with a heavy loss of life. —B.K.

2. An ironic reference to D. F. Sarmiento's book, *Civilization and Barbarism, The Life of Juan Facundo Quiroga*. —B.K.

3. Literally, "bigwigs," nickname given to Chilean conservatives by their liberal opponents in the period after the winning of independence. —B.K.

4. The author afterwards learned that Facundo related this story to a company of ladies, and one of his own early acquaintances testified to his having given his father a blow on one occasion.

5. The radical (as opposed to the moderate) wing of the Liberal Party. —B.K.

Notes to Chapter 16

1. "For if the victor had the gods on his side, the vanquished had Cato." Lucan, *Pharsalia*, Book I, verse 128. —B.K.

2. A bill that empowered the British government to take unilateral measures to suppress the Brazilian slave trade. The act aroused great resentment in Brazil. —B.K.

Notes to Chapter 17

1. See Terry's *Mexico*.

2. In an earlier chapter Pardo explained Díaz' rise to power by U.S. assistance, allegedly given in exchange for future economic concessions. —B.K.

3. The region of Los Altos is inhabited by Tzotziles, Tzetzales, Tojolabales, and other indigenous groups. It is one of the Mexican zones with the highest rate of demographic growth and has the highest incidence of poverty in the country. In the nineteenth century the Lacandon forest had an area of 1.3 million hectares and was totally unpopulated. At present it covers only 390,000 hectares as a result of the destruction of the forest through colonization. In 1960 there were only 5,000 Lacandones; at present, as a result of uncontrolled colonization by indigenes from Los Altos, the population is 300,000. This the social base of the EZLN, according to the best available evidence. The zone of Los Altos has a population of 500,000, almost all of indigenous origin. The state of Chiapas had 3,210,496 inhabitants in 1990, according to the National Population Council.

4. The official name of Solidarity is Programa Nacional de Solidaridad (PRONASOL).

5. The National Solidarity Program (PRONASOL), initiated by the Salinas administration, accounted by 1991 for 35 percent of the government's nondebt spending. Ostensibly designed to assist Mexico's poorest classes, it also served PRI's electoral ends by targeting selected communities to receive supplies and equipment for local development projects. —B.K.

6. A reference to three highly publicized and still unexplained murders. The 1993 murder of Cardinal Juan José Posadas has been charged to drug traffickers; the 1994 assassinations of PRI presidential candidate Luis Donaldo Colosio and PRI General Secretary José Francisco Ruiz Massieu have been variously attributed to drug traffickers, warring factions within PRI, or a mix of both. The latest act in this continuing

drama of crime and intrigue is the arrest in early 1995 of former President Salinas de Gortari's brother, Raúl, charged with masterminding Ruiz Massieu's murder. —B.K.

7. The PRI governor-elect of Chiapas, Eduardo Robledo, was inaugurated in December 1994 with Salinas's approval despite charges that the August 21 election had been tainted by widespread fraud. —B.K.

8. A sarcastic reference to a slogan of Zedillo's 1994 presidential campaign. —B.K.

Notes to Chapter 18

1. This is an allusion to Menem's pardon of top military commanders and two presidents who had been convicted and imprisoned for their human rights abuses during the military dictatorship. —B.K.

Notes to Chapter 19

1. A play on *campos*, meaning "fields." —B.K.

2. A reference to the seizure of power by Peruvian President Alberto Fujimori in 1992. —B.K.

Notes to Chapter 20

1. Named for Augusto César Sandino, leader of a prolonged guerrilla struggle against U.S. interventionist forces in Nicaragua, 1927–1933.

2. *Yara and Baire.* "Yara" on October 10, 1868, was the first battlecry for independence. The cry of "Baire" on February 24, 1895, announced the final drive to liberate Cuba from Spanish rule.

3. *Claudius Caecus.* Refers to Roman Emperor who so oppressed the plebeians that they left Rome.

4. *Guajiro.* Term usually refers to modest and underprivileged farmers in Oriente province.

5. The available evidence now suggests that Allende, like another Chilean anti-imperialist president, José Balmaceda, chose to commit suicide rather than surrender to military rebels. —B.K.

6. A reference to the second conference of Latin American bishops, held at Medellín, Colombia, in 1968, whose conclusions resembled those of the so-called "theology of liberation." —B.K.

Notes to Chapter 22

1. The reference is to the filibustering expedition of the U.S. adventurer William Walker, who established a short-lived dictatorship in Nicaragua. He was executed by the Hondurans in 1860. —B.K.

Glossary of Spanish, Portuguese, and Indian Terms

ADELANTADO. Commander of a conquering expedition; governor of a frontier or recently conquered province.

ALCABALA. Sales tax.

ALCALDE. Magistrate of a Spanish or Indian town who, in addition to administrative duties, possessed certain judicial powers as a judge of first instance.

ALCALDE MAYOR. Governor of a district or province.

ALFAQUÍ. Moslem spiritual leader and teacher of the Koran.

AMIN. A Jewish broth.

ANDÉN. Agricultural terrace, widely used in Incan agriculture.

ARROBA. Measure of weight (about 25 pounds).

AUDIENCIA. The highest royal court of appeals within a jurisdiction, serving at the same time as a council of state to the viceroy or captain-general.

AYLLU. Indian village community and kinship group in the Andean highlands.

CABALLERIA. Tract of land, about 33⅓ acres.

CABILDO. Municipal council.

CACIQUE. 1. Indian chieftain. 2. A local political boss.

CAPATAZ. Overseer or foreman.

CAPITÃO-MÔR. Commander in chief of the military forces of a province in colonial Brazil.

CARGA. A measure of six and one-half bushels.

CAUDILLO (CAUDILHO). Military or political leader or strongman.

CHAPETÓN. A disparaging name applied to European-born Spaniards in the South American colonies.

COLEGIO. School or college.

COMUNERO. A member of a popular revolt movement against Bourbon tax and fiscal policies in New Granada (Colombia) in 1781.

CONQUISTADOR. Conqueror.

CONSULADO. Colonial merchant guild and tribunal of commerce.

CORREGIDOR. Governor of a district.

CORREGIMIENTO. Territory governed by a corregidor.

CORTÉS. Spanish parliament or legislature.

CROWN FIFTH. The *quinto*, or royal share of the spoils of war.

CRUZADO. Ancient Portuguese gold coin.

DONATARIO. Proprietor of an original land grant in colonial Brazil.

EJIDATARIO. Member of an *ejido*.

EJIDO. An agricultural community that has received land in accordance with Mexican agrarian law.

ENCILHAMENTO. Great movement of financial speculation in the first years of the Brazilian republic.

ENCOMENDERO. Holder of an *encomienda*.

ENCOMIENDA. Grant of allotment of Indians who were to serve the holder with tribute and labor.

ESTADO. Measure of length (1.85 yards).

ESTANCIA. Ranch (Argentina and Uruguay).

FANEGA. A measure of grain (about 1.60 bushels).

FINCA. Farm or ranch.

FISCAL. Crown attorney.

FUERO. Privilege or exemption.

GACHÚPIN. A disparaging name applied to European-born Spaniards in New Spain.

GAUCHO. Cowboy of the Plata region.

GUAIPIL (HUIPIL). Square, sleeveless blouse worn by Indian women in some parts of Mexico and Central America.

GUAJIRO. A small, underprivileged farmer in Cuba, especially in Oriente province.

HACENDADO. Owner of a hacienda.

HACIENDA. Estate or landed property.

HIDALGO. Nobleman.

HUACA (GUACA). Incan shrine or sacred object.

INTERNADO. Boarding school (Cuba).

JEFE POLÍTICO. Governor of a district.

JUICIO DE AMPARO. Protective writ; writ of injunction (Mexico).

JUNTA. Council.

LATIFUNDIO. Large landed estate.

LATIFUNDISTA. Owner of a latifundio.

MAMELUCO (MAMALUCO). Mixture of white and Indian (Brazil).

MAYORDOMO. Steward of an estate.

MESTIZO. Mixture of Indian and white.

MILPA. Plot of Indian maize land (Mexico).

MITA. Periodic conscription of Indian labor in the Spanish colonies.

OBRAJE. Factory or workshop in the Spanish colonies.

OIDOR. Spanish colonial judge; member of *audiencia*.

PÁRAMO. High and cold region.

PATIO. Yard or courtyard.

PATRÓN. Master, landlord.

PATRONATO REAL. Right of the Spanish crown to dispose of all ecclesiastical benefices.

PESO. Spanish coin and monetary unit.

REGIDOR. Councilman.

REPARTIMIENTO. 1. An assignment of Indians or land to a Spanish settler during the first years of the Conquest. 2. The periodic conscription of Indians for labor useful to the Spanish community. 3. The mandatory purchase of merchandise by Indians from colonial officials.

REPARTO DE MERCANCÍAS. See REPARTIMIENTO 3.

RESIDENCIA. Judicial review of a Spanish colonial official's conduct at the end of his term of office.